MAGNIFICAT

The Life and Times of Timothy Cardinal Manning

by Msgr. Francis J. Weber

Saint Francis Historical Society
Mission Hills, California 1999

The author wishes to gratefully acknowledge the William R. and Virginia Hayden Foundation and the Dan Murphy Foundation for their generous financial support in the publication of this book.

Kimberly Press, Inc.
Santa Barbara, California
1,500 copies

Library of Congress Cataloging-in-Publication Data

Weber, Francis, J.
MAGNIFICAT - The Life and Times of Timothy Cardinal Manning / by Francis J. Weber.
p. cm.
Includes bibliographical references and index.
ISBN 0-87461-914-9
1. Manning, Timothy. 2. Catholic Church -- United States -- Bishops -- Biography. 3. Cardinals -- United states -- Biography.
I. Title.
BX4705.M313W43 1999
282' .092--dc21
[B] 99-8179
CIP

Acknowledgements

Charles Bransom - Episcopal linealogist for the American hierarchy.
Mrs. Joan Cronin - Sister of Timothy Cardinal Manning.
Sir Daniel Donohue - Gentleman-in-waiting to the Holy Father.
Sir Stanley Hayden, K.S.G.
Msgr. Peter Healy - Former director of the Diaconate ministry.
Sister Miriam Joseph Larkin, C.S.J. - Former secretary for the archdiocesan Liturgy Commission.
Mrs. Hermine Lees - Editor of the Los Angeles Catholic Directory.
Mrs. Breda Lucey - niece of Timothy Cardinal Manning.
Roger Cardinal Mahony - Archbishop of Los Angeles.
Msgr. Jeremiah Murphy - Former superintendent of Catholic high schools and colleges.
Doyce B. Nunis, Jr. - Editor of the *Southern California Quarterly*.
Dorothy O'Donald - Long-time friend of Timothy Cardinal Manning.
Msgr. Lawrence O' Leary - Former director, Propagation of the Faith.
Rev. Timothy O'Sullivan - Secretary for the Diocese of Cork and Ross.

In addition, the author is grateful to Gladys Posakony who read the manuscript and corrected the galleys and Catherine Campbell-Towell who typed the manuscript.

Table of Contents

Appendices

Preface

Someone once wrote, and wisely so, that Timothy Manning "would be longer remembered for what he said and wrote than for what he did." For that reason, this book favors Manning's utterances and writings over his factual accomplishments. Throughout this book, Timothy Manning occupies center stage and, as one might expect, his performance in that magisterial role was sterling. He surely needs no apologist.

Since this biography deals chiefly and primarily with the person of Timothy Manning, it shouldn't be regarded as a definitive or exhaustive history of the apostolates, commissions, agencies and departments over which he presided, except insofar as he related directly to them and their functions. Manning was a permissive leader rather than an innovative administrator. He rarely initiated programs, but allowed them to happen and he encouraged others to present and implement their ideas. Only infrequently did he interfere at the administrative level and, when he did, it was generally in the form of an encouraging word, a congratulatory letter or a laudatory affirmation.

Manning was never threatened or compromised by the successes of subordinates nor was he resentful of seeing others praised. Nothing so pleased him as watching honors and plaudits conferred upon his sacerdotal co-workers or the curial staff. Probably no other member of the American hierarchy wore the mitre and carried the crozier more gracefully or humbly as did Timothy Manning, Archbishop of Los Angeles.

Though this writer assiduously recorded the accomplishments of Timothy Manning in the archives,[1] he never expected or aspired to be the cardinal's biographer. When *His Eminence of Los Angeles*[2] appeared at the bookstalls, I suggested to Cardinal Mahony that it might be wise to visit Manning's birthplace, interview his sister, relatives and close friends and otherwise prepare the way for an eventual biography. Mahony graciously and enthusiastically concurred and even obtained a grant from the Dan Murphy Foundation for the project.

When I wrote Manning's niece, Breda Lucey at Gougane Barra, and told her of my imminent journey, she wrote back to say that "the cardinal had told us that one day you would make a visit."[3] I interpreted that as Manning's endorsement for taking on the burden of writing his life, surely an ambitious undertaking for a sixty-four year old priest of mediocre health. Since then, the Lord has provided the strength and means for completing this work. Hopefully, from his place in heaven, Timothy Cardinal Manning will be pleased.

There are those who have contended, sometimes vociferously, that "nothing happened during the Manning years." Not so, as this book amply demonstrates. Fasten your seatbelts and we will put that minority contention to rest for all time.

Msgr. Francis J. Weber

Notes to the Text

1 The writer denies the allegation made by Cardinal Manning to 14,000 parish representatives at the Sports Arena on November 30 that "Msgr. Weber, our archivist, has a secret intent to put me in a glass case in a corner of his museum when I die." See *The Tidings*, December 5, 1986.

2 This biography of James Francis Cardinal McIntyre was published by the Saint Francis Historical Society.

3 AALA, Breda Lucy to Francis J. Weber, Gougane Barra, April 10, 1997.

1. The Early Years

In one of his many reflections on his Irish birthplace, Timothy Manning noted in 1975, that "the history of our nation is the long, sad story of a people bent beneath the weight of a cross. Even at this hour the fair head of our land is crowned with thorned wire. Facing westward to the sea, she has suffered from every wayward wind and weather. Orphaned from the continent of Europe, she has clung to an ancient faith when dungeon, fire, famine and the sword were readied to retrieve it from her."[1]

It was into that ancient faith that Timothy Manning was born. Though the Manning name can be traced far back in Irish annals, it is also fairly common in England. Some of the Mannings of Dublin and Cork were known to be of English descent.[2] Timothy Manning, the second of the cardinals to bear that family name, often identified himself with Henry Edward Manning who served as Archbishop of Westminster, 1865-1892.

Early this century, the village of Ballingeary in Ireland's County Cork was a small community of about 250 people, located forty miles from Cork City. An isolated town, the closest railway line was seventeen miles away. Life there was rustic and the people quite ordinary. Their work included such occupations as cobbler, weaver and schoolmaster.

The Mannings of Ballingeary, married in the chapel of Saints Finbarr and Ronin, were a typical Irish family solid in their faith and expressive in its practice. Cornelius (1878-1954), like his ancestors before him, was a blacksmith. Tall, masculine and strong, as befitted his trade, he was the only smith for many miles. He spent most of his time fabricating wrought iron works and shoeing horses. A native of Ballingeary, he attended the village school which would be equivalent to today's high school. Though his sympathies were with the nationalist movement, he never took any active part in local politics. As was customary in the Ireland of those days, he was a strong force in the family.

Also born in Ballingeary, Margaret Cronin (1872-1964) was a small woman with silken hair. Highly religious, she "always lived in the presence of God."[3] She attended daily Mass and recited one or more

Ballingeary

Except for transportation and communications, Ballingeary is little changed from the way Timothy Manning first knew it just after the turn of the century. One of Ireland's most charming villages, it has two churches, both of which are filled for Sunday Masses. Youngsters appear mostly untouched by the vices of the modern world. A local writer once observed that "when a person dies, he goes to heaven, or is it Ballingeary."

The house in which Timothy Manning was born is still in the family and is presently occupied by a great-grandchild of Cornelius and Margaret, Joan. A marker on the front reads: "Timothy Cardinal Manning, Archbishop of Los Angeles was born in this house on November 14, 1909."

Immediately across the street from Manning's birthplace is the forge where Cornelius worked as a blacksmith. Abandoned now for some years, it was a favorite hide-out from British troops by local partisans.

It was in this islandic chapel that Timothy Cardinal Manning offered daily Mass whenever he visited Gougane Barra.

This statue of Saint Joseph was a gift of Cardinal Manning, as were the colorful Stations of the Cross from Mexico.

The plaque erected in the chapel honoring the cardinal, with its incorrect birthdate, was put in place by Breda Lucey, his niece.

Chapel of Saint Finbarr

Gougane Barra (Saint Finbarr's Hollow), situated on a small island in the lake, was the site on which Finbarr, the patron saint of Cork, founded a monastery. The tiny chapel was built around 1900 on the island which is now linked to the mainland by a short causeway.

rosaries every day of her life. Margaret spent her evenings sewing and knitting. In Manning's later years, her last born acknowledged that it was his mother who "was the provider and it was her effort that made it possible for us to get an education. In those times, education was the only escape from peasantry and she gave us that opportunity by her management of the family finances." Her faith "was tremendously strong. She never suffered illness and, quite appropriately, she died at the kitchen table, working to the last."[4]

The family home for the Mannings and their four children[5] had been built for Margaret on a half acre of land as a place where she could care for her invalid mother. After her marriage, she and Cornelius took up residence in the two story bungalow which was located on the main road. Ballingeary was in the midst of a Gaelic stronghold, and the Manning youngsters were all fluent in the Gaelic language.

Like all his siblings, Timothy was born at Ballingeary. He was baptized on the day of his birth, November 14, 1909 at the local Catholic church by Father C.O. Leary.[6] The atmosphere in which Timothy was raised was totally religious. The youngster's earliest memories "were those of my mother shaping the sign of the cross on my forehead." Daily recitation of the rosary was a family ritual and Timothy recalled that "even in later years when I took my mother for a ride around the countryside, the first order of business was the rosary."[7]

Reflecting on those early years at home, Manning characterized his parents as being "strict and rigid in their interpretation of propriety, much like all Irish families of that time. We all had a native respect for parental authority." The family setting, lacking the distractions that plagued later generations, allowed him to grow up in "a beautiful, rustic, Nazareth-type of life, full of dignity and respect."

Home training was crude but highly effective. "We gathered around a little coal oil lamp in the kitchen to do our homework, read aloud and converse. It was a real familial living." There was time for play, chores and learning. "Ours was a primitive cultural background. We played the usual games" and the youngsters "were allowed to associate freely around the immediate vicinity of the home."

Being in a rural setting, the Manning home had a variety of domesticated animals. In addition to chickens, there were sheep, pigs and a cow. Wool from the sheep was clipped, combed, washed and carted into black and white cords and then strung into a grayish thread. Manning recalled often wearing clothes "taken from our own sheep."[8]

When he was four and a half years old, Timothy was enrolled in the local National School for boys. It was a two room schoolhouse, with the initial two grades in a single room and the rest of the grades in the other

Like many of his village contemporaries, Cornelius Manning suffered intermittently from the "Irish disease." This practice bothered Timothy immensely and he rarely mentioned his father. Indeed, most of the family nurturing seems to have come from his mother.

In addition to the traditions of piety and good example handed on to her family, Margaret Manning was able to provide her children with certain luxuries by sewing for neighbors and operating a small boutique in her home which offered baked goods and assorted sweets.

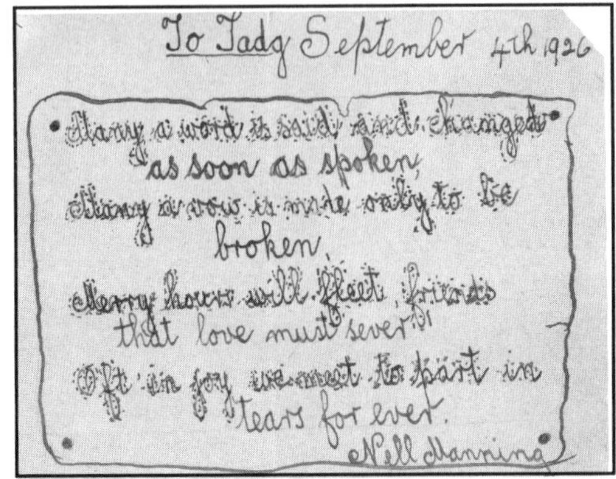
To Tady September 4th 1926

Many a word is said and changed as soon as spoken,
Many a vow is made only to be broken,
Merry hours will fleet, friends that love must sever,
Oft in joy we meet to part in tears for ever.

Nell Manning

This verse was written to Timothy Manning by is sister in 1926. Nell later died of tuberculosis.

Timothy is shown here with a relative, Annie Scott and the family dog. On the back he wrote "clothes were all home-spun from the sheep's back to mine."

one. There were probably about a hundred boys altogether. The schoolmaster, Padraig MacSweeney, was an important figure in village life, and his influence on the youngsters was extensive. Before leaving there, Timothy had memorized two of Shakespeare's plays, "Julius Caesar" and "Macbeth," a remarkable feat of mental endurance even in those days. The first book he read was *Alice in Wonderland*. He also read extensively from the works of Dickens. Timothy recalled bicycling to the local library several times a month.

In 1922, Timothy moved on to the Irish Christian Brothers School in Cork City. He disliked that experience intensely, claiming that "learning was beaten in." However he acquired it, Timothy's diligence was rewarded by scrolls of literary excellence each year there.[9]

From his earliest days, Timothy served daily Mass and participated in all the liturgical and devotional activities of the local parish. He was enamored of a number of priests, including Father Seamus O'Flynn and Father James O'Callaghan, the latter of whom was executed by the English.[10] When later asked when he first considered studying for the priesthood, Timothy responded that he had "never had any other thought" in all his life.[11] His parents encouraged but never unduly influenced that decision.

Among the reading matter that found its way to the Manning home was *Far East*, a publication about missionary activities in the Orient. "The marvelous accomplishments of the Columban Fathers were widely-discussed among young people" of that time and early on, after seeking the advice of the local priest, Timothy asked to be considered as a clerical aspirant for a missionary diocese at one of Ireland's Apostolic Colleges.[12]

Mungret was founded in 1881, under the auspices of the Society of Jesus, as a residential college in Limerick City. Its apostolic school, opened a year earlier, was moved to Mungret in 1882 and located in a house adjoining the Jesuit presbytery. In the early years, about half the college students were "seminarists" and others were lay students.

The prospectus for the Apostolic School of the Sacred Heart stated that the "object was to train boys for the priesthood, in order to increase the number of English-speaking missionaries throughout the world." Applicants were expected to be "very promising boys with a decided vocation." Qualities required of candidates were "good health, good appearance, mental abilities above the average, sincere piety, a solid vocation to the priesthood and an earnest desire for missionary life." The courses extended over six or seven years, beginning with Grammar and concluding with Philosophy. Students completing the courses at Mungret were "ready to enter upon the higher ecclesiastical studies."

This first school which Timothy Manning attended had two classrooms, grades one to seven. In addition to Gaelic, youngsters studied religion, mathematics, elementary science, history, lingual arts and literature.

Though all the evidence points to November 14, 1909 as the day Timothy Manning was born and later baptized in this font at Saint Finbarr's Church in Ballingeary, he always insisted on using October 14th as his "official" natal day. Even his mother said that he was a "Sunday's baby" which would favor November 14th in 1909, a Sunday.

CERTIFICATE OF BAPTISM

I Hereby Certify that it appears by the BAPTISMAL REGISTRY of the Parish of IVELEARY, in the COUNTY OF CORK, that Timothy Manning (sometimes written as Mangan) was born November 14th 1909 and was BAPTISED according to the Rites of the ROMAN CATHOLIC CHURCH by the Rev. C. O'Leary P.P. on the 14th day of November in the year of our Lord, 1909.

Names of Parents, Cornelius Manning (Mangan) & Margaret Cronin

Names of Sponsors, James Cronin & Kate McCarthy

Signature of Clergyman, Robert J. Burts PP

Dated this 27th day of [illegible] 1929

HICKEY & BYRNE, CORK.

Students were free to join either the secular priesthood in the foreign missions or to enter a Religious Order of their choosing. No student was asked or even allowed to apply for missionary work involving exceptional difficulty, except at his own earnest and persevering wish. Seminarians were encouraged to pay as much as they could of their tuition; the remainder was raised from other sources. The "pension" at that time was sixty guineas a year. There were burses available which allowed a limited number of students to pay only fourteen guineas each half year. Parents and guardians were expected to provide clothes and traveling expenses.

A period of six months was set aside as a sort of postulancy during which a boy was to think and pray over his vocation and "to understand its nature and the duties of the college." If at the end of that time, he decided to continue and, if the superior considered that he had sufficient promise of an apostolic vocation, he would become a regular pupil of the Apostolic School. Parents were alerted "not to interfere with their son's vocation, nor to make any difficulty in taking him back immediately to his family, if he should be judged unfit for apostolic life."[13] Parental relations were carefully nurtured, and students were sent home on vacation during the summer and at Christmas time.[14]

In September 1923, Margaret and Cornelius Manning journeyed to Limerick City where they presented their son as a candidate for the ministry. In the college annual for that year, young Manning was numbered among the ten "apostolics" in the "first junior" class. He took an active role in the Sodality of the Blessed Virgin which was described as upholding "its pre-eminent position in the house." He also had part in a play entitled "The Sign of the Cross" wherein he played a page to Nero. His studies went exceedingly well that first year, and his name was included on the "Christmas Honor List" for both English and Irish.[15]

A half century later, Manning recalled his days at Mungret: "We had a six-day week, each day filled with chores, manual duties, study and prayer. Occasionally we were allowed to take supervised walks away from the institution. Mass was obligatory. The whole life was based on that practiced in the Jesuit novitiate. A number of my peers eventually did enter the Society in later years." In a further elaboration, he noted that "we lived in a huge dormitory. It was really like something out of Dickens. Discipline was strict, but most of us were exceedingly grateful for the chance of getting an education and making the acquaintance of new friends. The food was terrible and the building badly heated. But complaints were few."[16]

In those days and even into fairly modern times, the Irish clergy considered many areas of the United States as "missionary territory."

Timothy Manning played the role of Jolland in the play "Vice Versa" in this feature photo from the Mungret Annual.

Timothy Manning is featured here in the Mungret Annual for 1927 as a gold medal winner for Irish story-telling.

This interior view of the chapel at Mungret College, Limerick, was taken during Timothy Manning's years there as a student.

Mungret College has been closed and is now operated by the Baptists.

Earlier, Father James Cronin, a cousin recently ordained for the Archdiocese of San Francisco, suggested that Manning apply for the service of the Church in California.[17] The rector at Mungret pointed out that of the three California dioceses, Los Angeles-San Diego, then under the direction of another Munsterman, Bishop John J. Cantwell, was the most needy. When Cantwell later visited Mungret looking for clerical candidates, the rector presented Manning's name for consideration.

Shortly before Timothy's graduation from Mungret, Nell Manning, one of his sisters, died from tuberculosis, not an uncommon disease in Ireland of the 1920s. As a precautionary measure, Margaret Manning applied for a grant whereby Timothy could go to Davos, in Southeast Switzerland, for medical observation. He spent the winter there in a village reserved for tubercular victims. Though he never actually contracted the dread disease, Manning found the dry climate highly conducive to the betterment of his overall physical health.

Upon Timothy's return to Ballingeary, Margaret insisted that the two of them go on pilgrimage to Saint Patrick's Purgatory at Lough Derg in County Donegal. Saint Patrick's Purgatory was the principal landmark on the medieval maps of Ireland and was, for example, the only Irish site named on a world map of 1492. In 1928, over 9,000 people, mostly from Ireland, visited the lonely rock island which was and remains the scene for one of the Church's most arduous religious encounters. The experience of that three-day sojourn left an indelible impression on Timothy Manning and a whole section in this treatise is devoted to the program of prayer and penance which he repeated no fewer than twenty-six times in his lifetime.

In 1928, Timothy took passage on the *SS. Cleveland* which sailed from Cobh (formerly Queenstown), a seaport in Cork Harbor, on October 18. His ticket for the steerage section of the ship was paid for by his family. The exceedingly rough trip lasted eight days. Fortunately, Manning was spared from the seasickness that plagued most of the passengers as the vessel plowed through the choppy waters of the North Atlantic. Passengers were forced to move about the ship by ropes, and one elderly lady disappeared on the voyage, presumably lost at sea.

Manning carried with him few earthly possessions. He acquired his first black suit from a former seminarian who met the ship in New York and provided the youthful Irishman with hospitality for four or five days in Yonkers. While in New York, Manning and his friend visited Saint Patrick's Cathedral. Noticing that a priest was celebrating Mass at the altar of Saint Therese without a server, the two knelt down outside the marble railing and answered the prayers in flawless Latin. Afterwards, the priest invited the two young men to breakfast in the rectory. That

The parish of Iveleary (territory of the O'Learys) has two churches. The altar and two of the colorful windows in this one dedicated to Saint Finbarr were the gift of Timothy Manning in memory of his parents, Cornelius and Margaret.

A last picture of Timothy Manning taken outside the local church before his departure to America.

Gougane Barra Hotel

This hotel is picturesquely situated on a slight rise overlooking Gougane Barra Lake, source of the River Lee. Owned and operated for several generations by the Cronin family, it is a celebrated home-away-from-home to discerning travellers wishing to tour the beauty spots of West Cork and Kerry. It is about a mile and a half from Ballingeary and it was here Timothy Cardinal Manning stayed during his trips to Ireland.

encounter was historically significant for it was the first time Manning met the man he would one day succeed in Los Angeles - Father J. Francis A. McIntyre, then Vice Chancellor for the Archdiocese of New York.

In addition to visiting the Statue of Liberty, numerous museums and other local attractions, Manning also saw his first "talkie" motion picture at an old Broadway theatre. His experiences provided a wonderful account for his first letter home. Later he purchased a ticket to San Francisco on the Santa Fe railroad. He fondly recalled arriving at Barstow where he first stepped onto what was then the Diocese of Los Angeles-San Diego which would be his home for the next fifty-seven years.

A seminarian who was already at Saint Patrick's when Manning arrived provided the following anecdote:

> The story goes that two young men, from different parts of Ireland, travelled by ocean liner to New York and from there by train to Oakland, then by ferry to San Francisco, and finally by train to Palo Alto.
>
> They had each spotted the other at various times en route – a single man, dressed in a conservative black suit, keeping somewhat to himself while on shipboard, as a good seminarian should – but each had been too shy, or too unconcerned, to approach and speak.
>
> However, by the time they realized that each was going by train to the West Coast, they had struck up a polite conversation, and one had admitted that he was going for "further education" at a "private institution" in California, while the other implied that his firm was sending him for "research" on the West Coast.
>
> Each detrained at Palo Alto without noticing that the other did also. Each hailed a taxi, bundled his luggage into it, and gave the driver his destination.
>
> The two taxis arrived at the front door of the Seminary at the same moment, and the two men stepped out, to greet each other and shake hands for the first time. One said, "I'm Sheamus Nash," and the other said, "My name is Timothy Manning."[18]

Then regarded as the "cadillac" of American seminaries, Saint Patrick's had opened its doors to the first students on September 20, 1898. It served as the provincial seminary for several jurisdictions, including

Like 2.5 million Irish between 1845 and 1960, young Timothy Manning left Ireland from Cobh (Queenstown) on October 20, 1928. He took transit on the S.S. Cleveland which is shown here in the midst of a violent storm at sea.

Seminarian Timothy Manning is shown here with his classmates at Saint Patrick's in Menlo Park.

the Diocese of Los Angeles-San Diego. The institution was staffed by the Sulpician Fathers, a congregation of priests devoted exclusively to the education of clerical aspirants. Most of the faculty members in the late 1920s were Frenchmen who were recognized scholars in their respective disciplines. Father Henry Ayrinac, the rector, had been at his post since 1904 and was a legendary figure on the American ecclesial scene.

Though he found the faculty somewhat aloof, Timothy Manning, like most of his peers, had great veneration for the teaching skills of the faculty. He found the academic atmosphere far superior to what he had known at Mungret. Manning was equally edified by the domestic department at Menlo Park which was entrusted to the Little Sisters of the Holy Family from Canada. The food was superb, at least by his standards, certainly better than he had known at home or at school.

The nineteen-year-old Irishman had no problem adjusting to the work pattern at Saint Patrick's. Students arose at 5:25 every day of the year, except on Good Friday. There was meditation, Mass, breakfast and then classes until noon. A short recreation period after luncheon was followed by more classes and study which concluded with a spiritual conference. After supper, there was a two hour study period. Thursdays were "free" and students were encouraged to "take walks" or ride their bicycles through the charming environs of Menlo Park.

Tobacco was allowed, and it was in his early years along California's Pacific Slope that Manning took up cigarettes. Student recreation consisted mostly of athletics of various sorts. Manning did not participate much in those activities except for tennis and croquet which he enjoyed immensely. Manning liked swimming and could frequently be found in the pool provided through the kindness of the Flood family, San Francisco scions. "Smokers" were common events on Thursday evenings and generally lasted from supper until bedtime. Manning frequently took part in the skits, plays and musicals staged for the student body. Though prohibited, many of the students had battery-operated radios which could pick up stations in San Francisco. After the cold and rainy days in Ireland, Manning found California climate refreshing and only rarely did he experience a mild cold while at Menlo Park.

Studies came easily to Manning who possessed a near photographic memory. Even though he didn't study overly much, he read voraciously from the extensive tomes in the student library. His grades were quite good, though several of his professors felt that he could have done better.

Aerial view of Saint Patrick's Seminary in Menlo Park.

Deacons John Flack, James Nash, Bernard Gannon, Harry Mitchell and Timothy Manning at Saint Patrick's Seminary, Menlo Park.

Shortly after becoming Auxiliary Bishop of Los Angeles, Timothy Manning had this statue erected outside the parish church of Saint Finbarr in Ballingreary "in memory of the exiles of Iveleary."

Cross Point of Manning's Academic Record[19]

1930-1931

Dogma	8
Moral	9
Scripture	8
Church	7.7
Homiletics	8
Language	7
Liturgy	7.7

Dogmatic theology was especially appealing to Manning. He retained the copy books made in his daily classes through his lifetime. He avidly devoured such journals as the *Homiletic* and *Pastoral Review* and the *American Ecclesiastical Review* and took copious notes as he read through back issues. Secular publications were "off limits," but most of the students kept up with the "funnies"and sports in the Sunday newspapers. Feeling that the homiletic program was seriously deficient, Manning and several companions worked diligently at improving their techniques in public speaking. Archbishop John J. Mitty of San Francisco strongly advised students to listen to and then discuss topics presented on the "Catholic Hour" which aired on radio every Sunday afternoon. Manning also developed his writing abilities and was a frequent contributor to the seminary journal, *The Patrician*.

The daily attire for seminarians was the cassock or soutain which was worn for classes, religious functions and other formal occasions. A black suit, with vest and Roman collar, was the street dress, and that practice was one that Manning observed assiduously during all the years of his ministry.

As was the case with his contemporaries, Manning engaged in several apostolic work assignments. He taught catechism at Saint Peter's in San Francisco and Saint Thomas Aquinas in Palo Alto. He was quite proficient as a teacher, and the youngsters in his classes responded well to his presentations, noting that they were never dull nor boring. Even then, Manning was a spellbinding speaker.

Though he professed no strong political leanings, Manning and most of his confreres felt a kinship with Herbert Hoover who resided in nearby Palo Alto. Most of the students reflected the "insular" viewpoints of San Francisco's local citizenry. When it came to elections, Manning had to content himself with being an observer, since he was not yet a citizen. Active in choral groups at the seminary, Manning was enamored with and became the house authority on rubrics. He served often as "Master of Ceremonies" for grand celebrations, executing gracefully the most complicated liturgical movements in the seminary chapel.

Manning's years at Menlo Park coincided with the "great" depression in the United States and the deprivations caused by that calamitous era were keenly felt at the seminary. Coming as he did from a relatively poor and rural area of Ireland, Manning was perhaps better suited for these economically lean days than many of his contemporaries. Somehow authorities managed, even in those trying times, to improve the seminary heating system and provide water for each of the student rooms. Seminarians were expected to pay at least part of their tuition, though officials were willing to relax that policy in the case of more promising students. Manning, unable to pay, signed a promissory note for $3,000 which was due within fifteen years after ordination.

Father Lyman A. Flynn, a member of the faculty at Menlo Park, described the seminarian, Timothy Manning, in those days: "He was a moderate lad, slight of build, quiet, a very gentle man. He was a topflight student. He could have chosen any one of half a dozen fields to specialize in and he would have excelled. In class, he gave evidence that he was going to be an outstanding preacher."[20]

Among the more historically significant events at Menlo Park in Manning's time occurred on October 20, 1930, when New York's Patrick Cardinal Hayes and Archbishop John J. Mitty hosted a group of bishops and clergy for the installation of Father James Lardner as rector. Subsequently, the youthful clerical candidate for the Diocese of Los Angeles-San Diego was pleased when Thomas K. Gorman and Robert E. Lucey, both fellow Southern Californians, were consecrated bishops in 1931 and 1934. He would later know and work closely with both of those prelates.

From his earliest moments in California, Manning felt attracted to the rich ecclesial history and folklore associated with *El Camino Real*. In an unsigned editorial for the very first issue of *The Patrician*, he wrote that:

> There was never a road more glamorous with romance or more eloquent with service than *El Camino Real* on which still linger the gray ruins of once stately Mission structures that reared their high towers against the sky sometimes on a plateau and again in the heart of a deep valley. Looking back through the vistas and perspective of the years one recalls how within a period of fifty-four years from the first foundation at San Diego in 1769 to the rearing of the last

> tower at Sonoma in 1823, the grey-robed, sandaled sons of St. Francis carved out of the sheer desolation of a wilderness not only a spiritual empire, but an agricultural and industrial empire as well. The result of the achievement was that California in the days of the glory of the missions was the happiest land the world has ever known. There was the joy of work, the voice of prayer, peace and plenty.

Manning concluded his first published essay with references to the contemporary missions, a theme that would later figure prominently in his interest and writings:

> Even though the missionaries labor zealously; though they work and toil, and even lay down their lives in leading the non-believers to the Catholic religion; though they employ all industry and diligence and all human means, still all this will be of no avail, all their efforts will go to naught, unless God touches the hearts of the non-believers to soften them and to draw them to Him. It is easy to see that everyone has the opportunity to pray, and so this help, the very nourishment of the missions, is within the power of all to supply.[21]

Manning's first meeting with Bishop John J. Cantwell took place when the prelate visited Menlo Park accompanied by his secretary, Father Joseph T. McGucken. The students "gathered in military fashion at the entrance and he spoke briefly to us."[22] He would not see the bishop again until the day of his ordination in 1934.

That Manning highly esteemed the seminary faculty is evident in many ways. An example would be his description of Father John M. Redon whom he portrayed as:

> Silently moving along corridors, other-worldly in his speech and bearing, graciously minimizing our scholastic blunders, directing our footsteps across the sanctuary, in conferences unfolding to us the lives of the Saints, gently pronouncing words of absolution over our troubled souls, standing always as a symbol of everything we hold most dear in seminary life, linking us with the ancient traditions of his Community and the land from which he came, his room became the first place of pilgrimage when we returned.[23]

Mungret Alumni In The Archdiocese Of Los Angeles

NAME	YEARS AT MUNGRET
Reverend Patrick Casey	1918 - 1923
Rev. Michael Casey	1927 - 1934
Rev. Daniel Collins	1927 - 1931
Rev. Patrick Collins	1919 - 1923
Rev. John Devlin	1912 - approx.
Rev. John V. Fitzgerald	1916 1919
Rev. James J. Flanagan	1924 - 1929
Rev. Richard Hennessy	1914 - 1918
Rev. Michael A. Hunt	1930 - 1932
Rev. Andrew McGrath	1930 - 1932
Rev. Timothy Manning	1922 - 1927
Rev. Michael P. O'Sullivan	1919 - 1923
Rev. Maurice Ryan	1913 - 1919
Rev. Michael Sheehan	1910 - 1914

Timothy Manning, as layman, priest, bishop and cardinal visited Saint Patrick's Purgatory at Lough Derg no fewer than twenty-six times.

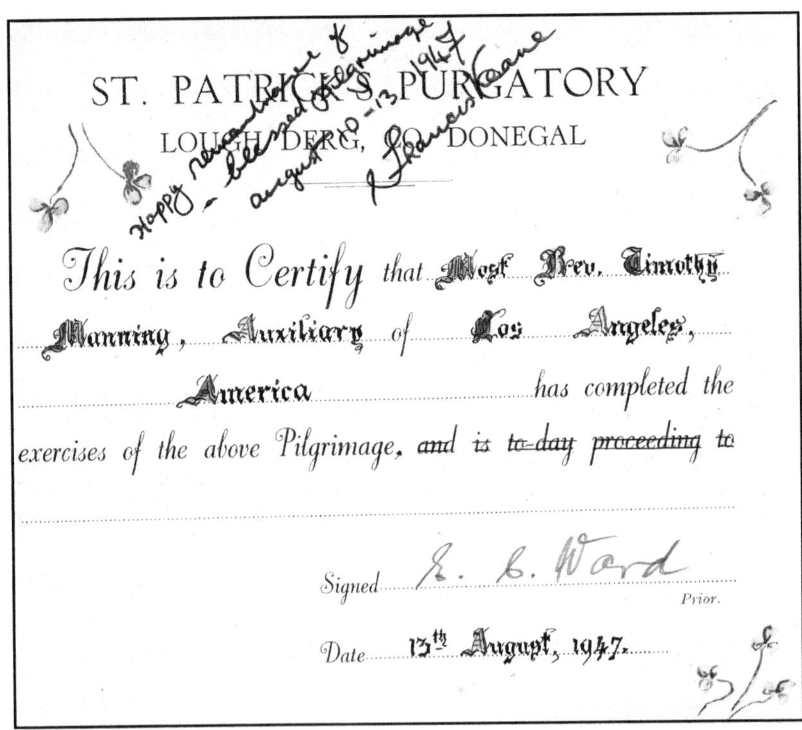

ST. PATRICK'S PURGATORY

LOUGH DERG, CO. DONEGAL

This is to Certify that Most Rev. Timothy Manning, Auxiliary of Los Angeles, America has completed the exercises of the above Pilgrimage, ~~and is to-day proceeding to~~

Signed E. C. Ward
Prior.

Date 13th August, 1947.

A commentator about these years at Saint Patrick's Seminary has observed that the 600 graduates who served in the dioceses of the west and across the Pacific held their spiritual lives in the highest priority. "They read their breviaries, fingered their beads and fostered Eucharistic devotion." And in addition, "all possessed a sense of competence to perform well in parochial work."[24]

Notes to the Text

1. *The Tidings*, October 10, 1975.
2. Edward Mac Lysaght. *Irish Families. Their Names and Origin* (Dublin, 1957), p. 221.
3. Archives for Archdiocese of Los Angeles (hereafter referred to as AALA), Biographical Interview with Timothy Cardinal Manning, Los Angeles (July 1, 1975).
4. AALA, Biographical Interview with Timothy Cardinal Manning, Los Angeles (October 1, 1970).
5. Viz., Joan (b.1905), Nell (1907-1927), James (1911-1980) and Timothy (1909-1989).
6. AALA, Certificate of Baptism, Parish of Iveleary in the County of Cork, transcript dated April 27, 1929.
7. AALA, Biographical Interview, (October 1, 1970).
8. *Ibid.*
9. *Ibid.*
10. A native of Castletown-Kinneigh, O'Callaghan was ordained at Maynooth in 1908. At the time he was a guest in the home of Liam de Roiste, a well-known volunteer "on the run" from the British. A group of soldiers broke in and one shot the priest at point-blank range. Father O'Callaghan died in the North Infirmary. Manning later recalled the incident, saying that "the first priest I knew as a boy was murdered in his bed by English occupation troops." (*The Tidings*, March 29, 1985). Father Christy O'Flynn (1881-1961), a colorful and nationally-known cleric, was a masterful speaker who developed a unique method for helping those suffering from speech impediments. For the story of his life, see Raymond Smith, *Father O'Flynn - The Well of Love* (Dublin, 1961).
11. AALA, Biographical Interview, (October 1, 1970).
12. AALA, Biographical Interview, (July 1, 1975).
13. *Mungret Annual* (July, 1924), pp. iv-v.
14. The boarding school at Mungret College was closed in 1974. Up to that time, the number of apostolic students ordained was 701. Three

others became professed religious and forty-four died before completing their studies. Priests from Mungret worked in all five continents. Timothy Manning was the only one ever to be a cardinal.

15. *Mungret Annual* (July, 1924), 206.
16. AALA, Biographical Interview, (October 1, 1970).
17. Father Cronin, a brilliant student, was ordained for the Archdiocese of San Francisco on March 12, 1927. After studying for six years in Rome, he returned to the Bay Area as curate in Berkeley. He later went on the inactive personnel list.
18. This anecdote was attached to a letter sent to this writer by Raymund Wood, April 11, 1997. Wood wrote about his years at Saint Patrick's Seminary in his autobiography, *No Candidate for Sainthood* (Encino, 1994), pp.80-90.
19. The scale for the grades was: 10-perfect, 8-9 very good and 7-6 good. See AALA. Report of Examination, Saint Patrick's Seminary, Menlo Park, 1929-1934.
20. Quoted by Will Lissner in the New York *Times*, January 22, 1970.
21. *The Patrician I* (November, 1930), 3.
22. AALA, Biographical Interview (October 1, 1970).
23. *The Patrician* (June, 1947), 24.
24. See James P. Gaffey's highly interpretative treatise, *Men of Menlo. Transformation of an American Seminary* (Lanham, 1992), p. 14.

2. *Priestly Ministry*

Timothy Manning was ordained by Bishop John J. Cantwell on June 16, 1934 at Saint Vibiana's Cathedral in Los Angeles. His aged aunt and Father James Cronin were the only two family members in attendance at the ceremony during which six diocesan deacons and one religious were advanced to the priesthood.[1] For some strange reason, there was no account of the ordination ceremony in that week's Catholic newspaper. However, thirty-nine years later, Mary Lanigan Healy recalled the first ordination she had attended in her weekly column for *The Tidings*:

> Once the impressive ceremonies began, those within the sanctuary rail lost identity, other than their status as priestly candidates. It was a new and wonderful experience to come so close to such an important event.
>
> Somehow there was an air of timelessness about it all as the figures, with the then Bishop Cantwell in the center, became part of an ancient drama from which they were to emerge as ministers of the Gospel. The splendor of form and voice filled the cathedral, and for that matter filled the world.
>
> This all had something to do with that rock upon which the Church was built and those gates of hell which had no chance against it. And then as those white-clad figures lay prostrate upon the floor, and the magnificent Latin phrases of the Litany of the Saints swept back and forth across them, it made me want to cry but I couldn't tell you why.

The writer recalled that after the ceremony, as "the newly ordained priests came to the altar rail to bestow their first priestly blessings upon the hundreds who waited in long lines to receive them, they all became quite human and individual again, with tired faces showing physical and emotional strain, and locks of hair falling boyishly across their

Ordination Certificate made for Timothy Manning in 1934.

A Remembrance
of our
Ordination

Archdiocese of San Francisco

Reginald V. Brennan	Peter A. Kelly
Vincent I. Carroll	John P. Quinn
Nicholas P. Connolly	Aloysius B. Sullivan
Thomas P. Gilbert	John J. Wagner

Diocese of Helena
Edward F. Moran

Diocese of Monterey-Fresno
Fred P. Crowley

Diocese of Port-of-Spain
Max E. Murphy

Diocese of Sacramento
John K. Connelly

Diocese of Spokane
Joseph W. Brunner

Diocese of Tucson
Arthur F. Gramer

Diocese of Los Angeles
John G. Flack

Bernard J. Gannon	Harry E. Mitchell
Timothy F. Manning	James F. Nash

Pray for us.
CLASS OF 1934
St. Patrick's Seminary

I gCUIMHNE DILIS

an lae úd
n-ar ghlacas

NAOMH ORD NA SAGARTACHTA

agus fós i gCuimhne mo

CHEUD AIFRINN NAOMHTHA

an 16adh agus an 17adh lá June,
1934.

✠

Taḋg Ó Mongáin.

foreheads and smiling at kinfolk and friends and strangers and grasping hands and looking a trifle surprised each time their own fingers were kissed by those they blessed.[2]

It is easy enough to reconstruct Manning's sentiments from his later writings.

> In this priesthood there is no *quid pro quo*. There is no time schedule. There is no given number of years that we must work. There is no commensurate reward for what we do. That is totally alien, secular and offensive to our concept of priesthood.
>
> We are totally at the service of God in His people. Without limitation, without expectation of reward, without looking for applause or esteem. We are doing only what we have committed ourselves to do. Otherwise we are simply hirelings and counterfeits.[3]

The Vicar General for the diocese, Msgr. John J. Cawley, had invited Manning to offer his first Solemn Mass the following day in the cathedral at 10:30 a.m. Cawley saw to it that the music provided by the choir was even more dramatic than usual. Seminarians from Los Angeles College, the preparatory seminary, assisted at the liturgy, and Father Ray Tepe served as deacon.

In his homily, Father Martin McNicholas reviewed the theological and scriptural notion of priesthood as it had unfolded through the centuries. McNicholas exhorted the newly ordained priest "to go forth today as the champion of truth and morality . . . unafraid but secure and confident in the knowledge that the God of Abraham, Isaac and Jacob is with you." He told Manning that as he began his priestly trek along *El Camino Real*, he should know that the eyes of his noble "predecessors are upon you, a Peter, a Paul, an Xavier, a Patrick and our own Junípero Serra who, like you, left their father's house in a distant country to preach the Gospel." He reminded Manning that when "your day has come, yours too will be the reward that is theirs, an eternal and glorious participation in the priesthood of Jesus Christ."[4] Like most of McNicholas' panegyrics, this one took on its own life and was used by others in later times for similar occasions.

Many of the same sentiments were voiced a week later when Father Timothy Manning offered a second Solemn Mass at San Bruno. The preacher said that the real sermon would be:

Father Manning's only pastoral experience was obtained in the parish of the Immaculate Conception.

During his eight years as Archbishop's Cantwell secretary, Manning lived in the former King Gillette mansion here in Fermont Place.

Pope Pius XI was in the twilight of his pontificate when Father Manning was studying in Rome.

Aerial view of the Istituto di Cura Quisisana in Rome where Father Manning had his operation in 1937.

> Preached from the altar steps this morning, when the Sacred Host and the Consecrated Cup are raised before your eyes, that seeing, you may adore. I can but voice the prayer that is in all our hearts, that the ministry of this new priest, this new leader, this new teacher, this new physician of souls – above all, this new minister of the Undying Sacrifice, may be a holy and a blessed one. If there be happiness this side of paradise, may it be his in fullest measures. If there be sorrow, may it be borne with the spirit of Christ's priesthood. Throughout his days, and for eternity, may he stand at the altar of God, repeating the words which generations before him have murmured: "I shall go to the altar of God, unto God Who giveth joy to my youth."[5]

In mid 1934, just a few days after ordination, Father Timothy Manning was appointed curate at Immaculate Conception parish at Ninth and Green streets in central Los Angeles. The youthful priest was indeed fortunate in being apprenticed to Msgr. Francis Conaty who had served as pastor since 1911. A nephew of Bishop Thomas Conaty, for whom he acted as chancellor, the monsignor had built the church, rectory and school and was, by that time, one of the diocesan patriarchs.

The remnants of the earlier, more affluent neighborhood were still visible. Though social flight to the suburbs had begun, the parish was still vitally functional. The episcopal residence on Burlington Avenue was one of the many fine homes in the area. The Scotts, Bayers, Cahills, Youngs, Desmonds, Martins, Schneiders, McGarrys and Firestones were among families active in parochial affairs.

It was a busy parish and every hour of the day was consumed in looking after the nearly 1,500 Catholics listed on Conaty's carefully-kept register books. In addition to several large rest-homes, Good Samaritan Hospital, perched at the top of Ingraham Street, consumed much of the duty schedule. There was no parish car and the rickety old streetcar that plied its way up and down ninth Street was the chief mode of transportation to and from the rectory.

The Immaculate Heart Sisters staffed the school which had two grades in each classroom. On the upper story was the parish hall. Father Manning and Sister Eileen MacDonald traded off teaching religion. Manning was also charged with training the altar servers, a task he performed with utmost efficiency. A portion of each day was devoted to taking census, and Conaty boasted that every doorbell in the parish was rung at least once a year. Evenings were occupied with convert

Father Manning as a Roman student in 1935.

Maning and a friend visit the Leaning Tower of Pisa in 1935.

PONTIFICIA UNIVERSITAS GREGORIANA

R. D. Timotheus Manning

e Dioecesi Angelorum

studiorum curriculo in Facultate Juris Canonici Pontificiae Universitatis Gregorianae rite peracto, experimenta praebuit iis qui ad Lauream contendunt praescripta, atque in primis dissertationem scriptam a censoribus approbatam palam defendit.

Quare cum Professorum suffragiis magna cum laude probatus exstiterit, professione fidei ad normam art. 38 Const. Apost. «Deus Scientiarum Dominus» emissa, renuntiari poterit *Doctor in* Jure Canonico, ubiprimum dissertationem, secundum revisorum animadversiones emendatam, ad normam Statutorum Universitatis typis ediderit eiusque exemplaria Moderatoribus Universitatis exhibuerit.

Romae, die 12 Julii 1938

RECTOR PONT. UNIVERSITATIS GREGORIANAE

Vincentius A. McCormick, S.J.

PRAEFECTUS STUDIORUM UNIVERSITATIS

[illegible signature]

SECRETARIUS UNIVERSITATIS

Ferd. Bauer S.J.

classes, baptismal catecheses, marriage preparation and family counseling. Bishop John Cantwell often referred to Conaty as a "model" pastor, and indeed he was.

The monsignor was a gracious and kind man who insisted that each priest attached to the parish have a regular day off every week. Though he and the others often had little financial resources, no beggar ever left the rectory hungry. Recovery from the 1929 depression was slow and there was a parochial indebtedness of $200,000, a huge amount in those days. Manning recalled that "we laboriously counted pennies after Sunday Masses to live on the following week."[6] Priests earned $33.33 a month and, more often than not, the parish was unable to satisfy that claim. Manning had nothing but fond memories of his tenure at Immaculate Conception parish. Indeed the experiences there served him well for the years ahead. Soon it was time to move on, and that he did with understandable natural reluctance.

In March, 1934, in his first letter to Bishop Cantwell, Manning said that his aunt would be "traveling to Ireland" that summer and had invited him to accompany her "to visit my home and parents."[7] The chancellor intercepted the request and fired back a curt reply saying that "the bishop is rather surprised that, in view of the fact that the diocese has been taking care of your tuition at Menlo Park, you are able to spend this amount of money on a vacation, having made no effort to defray any of your expenses while in the seminary."[8]

A year later, Manning again asked for permission to visit Ireland and, during his interview with Cantwell, the bishop "expressed his intention of permitting" Manning "to do further studies,"[9] ostensibly as a preparation for teaching Canon Law at the seminary then being planned for the diocese. In September, Msgr. Bernard Dolan, the Chancellor, dispatched a letter to the rector of the North American College asking him to find a place of residence for Father Manning "whom the bishop is sending to Rome to take courses in Canon Law."[10]

After a sojourn in Ireland, Manning arrived in Rome on October 26, 1935. At that time, the Eternal City presented a host of conflicting and complicated scenarios. For the most part, Manning was more observer than participant in the intrigues that had engulfed the Church since Peter first brought Christianity to Rome. Mussolini was still popular throughout most of Italy, not only because he was clever at manipulating crowds, but because he was still achieving beneficent reforms. There was mixed reaction to the Fascisti among the mostly Catholic inhabitants of Rome. Mussolini was lauded for his tasteful reconstruction of the city, especially the clearing away of the cluttered Borghi in

Pontificia Universitas Gregoriana

Clerical Education in Major Seminaries

ITS NATURE AND APPLICATION

EXTRACT
FROM A THESIS PRESENTED TO THE FACULTY OF CANON LAW
OF THE PONTIFICAL GREGORIAN UNIVERSITY, ROME

BY
TIMOTHY MANNING
PRIEST OF THE ARCHDIOCESE OF LOS ANGELES

1946

John J. Cantwell (1874-1947) was Bishop of Los Angeles-San Diego when Father Timothy Manning first came to the southland jurisdiction.

order to open up a broad approach in front of Saint Peter's Basilica. Few could have predicted the excesses that would surface in later years.

By the time of Manning's arrival, the rector of the American College had found lodging for him at the Casa Pensione San Carlo. He had also been registered for classes in Canon Law at the Pontifical Gregorian University, an ancient school that had its origin in the *Collegium Romanum* founded by Ignatius Loyola. The Jesuits, who had taught at the "Greg" since 1824, had established the Faculty of Canon Law in 1876. Since 1930, the university had been housed in a large building designed by G. Barluzzi on the Piazza della Oilotta.

Msgr. Dolan wasn't pleased with the cost of Manning's lodgings which ran to about $60 a month. He suggested that the young priest look around "to see if you can get something more in line with the ability of the diocese to pay."[11] In mid-December, Manning moved to the *Colegio Teutonico* in Camposanto, which he described as "one of the cheapest institutions in Rome."[12] It was nominally a German college with an excellent library. Unhappily, few people there spoke English. Several weeks later, Father Frederick C. Dietz, rector of the Maryknoll College, told Manning that there was a vacancy in his house and invited Manning to take up residence at 83 Via Sardegna. So anxious was Manning to accept the offer, that he even offered to ask his parents to pay the difference in cost there from the German college.[13]

Manning was a facile student and his grades at the "Greg" were outstanding, even by Roman standards. Like most graduate students, he spent at least an hour each day and more on weekends walking the streets and alleyways of Rome, trying to absorb the rich history and abounding culture. Not infrequently, he would be asked to accompany visitors from the United States around the sites of the city and, invariably, they were impressed by his knowledge of the city's environs.

The shortage of funds was a constant problem for Manning during his years in Rome. Msgr. Dolan was notoriously penurious and would send only enough money to pay for tuition, room and board. There was never anything left for laundry, books, transportation or personal needs. Much of his correspondence from Rome was absorbed in asking for funds, something that Manning found intensely distasteful. His mother sent him a monthly check and others of his relatives from Ireland were also generous.

Among the more memorable historic events occurring during the years was the conclusion of the Italo-Abyssinian War on May 5, 1936. Manning was among the Romans who congregated in the Piazza Venezia to hear Mussolini boast of his nation's military supremacy.

Father Manning inspects progress of work at Saint John's Seminary, Camarillo.

Father Manning was Master of Ceremonies for the celebrations marking the centenary of the Catholic hierarchy in California.

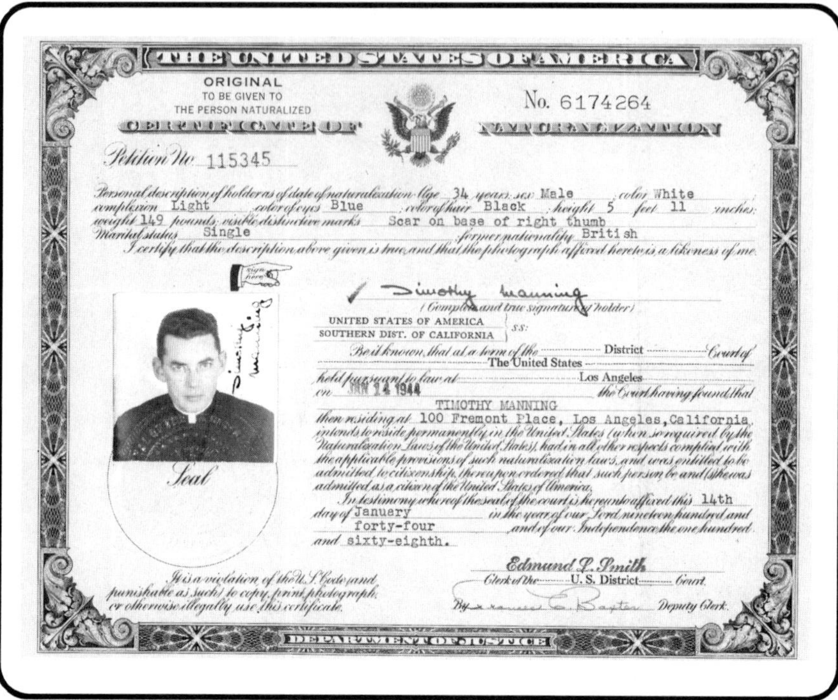

THE UNITED STATES OF AMERICA

ORIGINAL
TO BE GIVEN TO
THE PERSON NATURALIZED

No. 6174264

CERTIFICATE OF NATURALIZATION

Petition No. 115345

Personal description of holder as of date of naturalization Age 34 years; sex Male color White complexion Light color of eyes Blue color of hair Black height 5 feet 11 inches; weight 149 pounds; visible distinctive marks Scar on base of right thumb
Marital status Single former nationality British
I certify that the description above given is true, and that the photograph affixed hereto is a likeness of me.

Timothy Manning
(Complete and true signature of holder)

UNITED STATES OF AMERICA
SOUTHERN DIST. OF CALIFORNIA } ss:

Be it known, that at a term of the District Court of The United States held pursuant to law at Los Angeles on JAN 14 1944 the Court having found that TIMOTHY MANNING then residing at 100 Fremont Place, Los Angeles, California intends to reside permanently in the United States (when so required by the Naturalization Laws of the United States), had in all other respects complied with the applicable provisions of such naturalization laws, and was entitled to be admitted to citizenship, thereupon ordered that such person be and (s)he was admitted as a citizen of the United States of America.

In testimony whereof the seal of the court is hereunto affixed this 14th day of January in the year of our Lord nineteen hundred and forty-four, and of our Independence the one hundred and sixty-eighth.

Seal

Edmund L. Smith
Clerk of the U.S. District Court.
By [illegible] E. Baxter Deputy Clerk.

It is a violation of the U.S. Code (and punishable as such) to copy, print, photograph, or otherwise illegally use this certificate.

DEPARTMENT OF JUSTICE

Several days later, Il Duce announced the establishment of the Italian Empire, proclaiming Victor Emmanuel as King-Emperor.

In May, 1936, Manning was included in a special audience given by Pope Pius XI to the students of the North American College. The Holy Father gave an informal and fatherly talk which lasted about fifteen minutes. Afterward, Manning was among those personally greeted by the pontiff. Though he attended numerous liturgical events at Saint Peter's Basilica presided over by the Holy Father, this was the only time that he personally spoke with the pontiff once characterized by Mussolini as "that obstinate old man."

As a seminarian, Manning had gotten to know San Francisco's Archbishop Edward J. Hanna during the prelate's monthly visits to Menlo Park. Because of what would now be diagnosed as Alzheimer's Disease, the archbishop had agreed to retire in 1935 and take up residence in Rome. At Cantwell's behest, Manning frequently visited the archbishop who was living at the Villa San Francisco on the Via de Monte Parioli. In one of his letters, Manning reported that Hanna retained his unpretentious and winsome manner and looked to be "in very good health."[14] Indeed the archbishop lived on for almost another decade during which time he was cared for by the Franciscan Tertiaries. Students and priests in the Rome of those times were recognizable by the color of the sashes on their cassocks. On one occasion, Manning and a friend used the color code to their advantage. They outfitted Hanna in all his purple finery and led him into three choice seats at a papal ceremony in Saint Peter's Basilica.

In July, 1936, Manning received the pleasant news about the establishment of a second metropolitan province in California, a move which resulted in the creation of the Archdiocese of Los Angeles. He wrote to Cantwell, now archbishop, that "the news of the recent honor conferred upon Your Grace has re-echoed here in joyful hearts."[15] In a subsequent letter, Manning said that "it has increased the happiness of our Christmas here in Rome to know of the crowning honor conferred upon you and upon our diocese." He further noted that he was "in Los Angeles in spirit during the celebration and followed with much interest the various news reports" of the events on that occasion.[16]

As Manning neared completion of the work for his licentiate, Cantwell was informed by officials at the "Greg" that the young priest would be an ideal candidate for the doctorate. Accordingly, the archbishop wrote suggesting that "the addition of a doctorate will mean a great deal to you and also to me."

Before leaving Ireland for Menlo Park, Manning had written to Bishop James E. Walsh of Maryknoll about the possibility of doing missionary work in China. Walsh, then Prefect Apostolic of Kong Moon, responded and thus began a life-long relationship between the two men. In May, 1937, Bishop Walsh, by then the Superior General of the Maryknoll Fathers, was in Rome for an official visitation. Walsh invited Manning to accompany him to the North American College for a reception honoring Msgr. Fulton J. Sheen and former Democratic presidential contender, Alfred E. Smith. Just two days earlier, Smith had been received by Pope Pius XI. In his brief talk to the seminarians on that occasion, Smith was impressed by the Holy Father's alertness and grasp of world events.

Surely Manning's greatest crisis ordeal in Rome was health-related. Though he had reported to Cantwell, as late as December, 1936, that he "had been blessed with good health," he had long suffered from ulcers.[17] On March 7, 1937, he suffered a severe hemorrhage in his room at Maryknoll. Happily, Father Robert Brennan a fellow Californian also living at Maryknoll, discovered the unconscious priest and had him taken to the Istituto di Cura "Quisisana" on the Via Gran Giacomo Porro.

The next morning, Dr. Mario Margottini performed emergency surgery, removing two-thirds of Manning's stomach. For several days, his condition was critical. In subsequent weeks, Bishop Walsh arranged that Manning recuperate at Maryknoll under the watchful supervision of several medical missionaries. By May, tremendously improved, he wrote to Cantwell that God "had been very good to bring me through a dangerous operation," noting his hope that "what I have lost in the school of Canon Law, I have gained in the school of suffering."[18] Back home, Msgr. Dolan, in a rare burst of generosity, sent Manning a check for $265 from the Priests Relief Society to help offset the medical costs.

During that summer, Manning hired himself out as a guide for a group of American tourists who were visiting Germany and several other European countries. The archbishop approved and told him that he was "very wise to take advantage of free fares to get to see some of the world." He went on to say that "a knowledge of the world at the present time will be a decided asset to you in the future." [19] In December, Manning reported that he was taking five hours of classes each week, devoting all the rest of his time to reading and gleaning for the writing of his dissertation.[20]

Obsessed as he had become with plans to inaugurate a major seminary for the Archdiocese of Los Angeles, Cantwell suggested that Manning's dissertation be devoted to some aspect of priestly formation, a proposal approved by the faculty of Canon Law at the Gregorian. There were four chapters in the 176 page typed treatise, one each for Historical

Development, Fundamentals of Clerical Education, Nature and Instruments of Clerical Education and the Elements of Clerical Education.

His exhaustive treatment, published under the title *Clerical Education in Major Seminaries. Its Nature and Application*, was written under the careful direction and scrutiny of Father Adam Ellis, a distinguished Jesuit Canon Lawyer,[21] Manning pointed out how ecclesial legislation "covers the qualities of the professor, the course of studies, the text books, the time to be devoted to the various stages of formation, in all, the succession of events that shall lead a young man on until he has attained that priestly quality that will make him both salt and light of the world into which he goes." Though the contention cannot be verified, it is likely that Ellis leaned heavily on Manning's researches as part of the *Enchridion Clericorum* which was issued at Rome in 1938 by the Sacred Congregation of Seminaries and Universities for which he was one of the compilers.[22]

In June, 1938, Cantwell arrived in Rome for his quinquennial visit with the Holy Father, his first as a metropolitan archbishop. Because of the curtailment in the pontiff's availability, due to his failing health, Manning was unable to accompany Cantwell to the Vatican. Cantwell told a reporter that he was struck by the "Pope's continued interest in books - his preservation of the instincts of the born librarian." He enthusiastically drew the archbishop's attention to some rare volumes from the Ambrosian library.[23] From that interview one can sense that Cantwell would have been happier had more notice been given to his *relatio* which painstakenly outlined ecclesial activities in Southern California since 1934, his last visit to Rome.

A few days later, Manning left Rome with the archbishop and Msgr. Joseph McGucken for Ireland where they participated in the silver jubilee ceremonies for Mother Regis Cantwell at the Ursuline Convent in Blackrock, County Cork, on August 11. From there Manning journeyed to Ballingeary where he visited his homestead. While at Gougane Barra, he delivered the homily for the annual observance of the Feast of Saint Finbarr. He set out for the United States on October 2.[24]

When Manning eventually arrived in Los Angeles, early November, he told a friend, "I found myself welcomed as the new secretary to the archbishop, to my great surprise and no little trepidation." He explained how the position "carries with it regular office work at the chancery and also Master of Ceremonies at all pontifical functions, so that it is a complete monopoly of time." With his new appointment, he resided at the rectory of Cathedral Chapel parish so that he was "always within close call."[25]

Father Manning congratulates his friend, Joseph T. McGucken, upon his appointment as Auxiliary Bishop of Los Angeles.

Father Manning acted as Master of Ceremonies for Archbishop Cantwell during the official visitation to Mexico City's Shrine of Our Lady of Guadalupe in 1941.

Throughout Manning's tenure as Cantwell's *aide de camp*, the Chancery Office was located on the seventh floor of Edward Doheny's Petroleum Building on Olympic Boulevard between Figueroa and Flower streets. Those were the years before the street was widened and the frontage of the building had a wide expanse of green lawn.

Manning rarely spoke about his father and, though he lived on until 1954, there are no references to Cornelius in any of his son's letters. Whatever was lacking in their relationship was compensated for by Archbishop Cantwell. In a note to a friend, Manning noted that "in all the years I have been with him, he has been a father to me." When he was made a monsignor, he said that "while I have been promoted to the Household of Pius, I am glad that I am still a part of the Household of Cantwell."[26]

In the preface to Cantwell's biography, Manning recalled that the archbishop "endowed those who were trained under him with unreserved trust. He gave a man a task to do, accepted his competence to do it, and did not question the decision in which the task terminated. For this we valued his confidence in us." Manning concluded by saying that Cantwell "was a worthy successor to the prelates who preceded him. He piloted the Church of Los Angeles from a frontier rim of the Christian world to the edge of greatness in the family of American jurisdictions."[27]

After Manning's move into the episcopal residence at 100 Fremont Place, he became subject to the house rules observed by the archbishop and his ever-present sister, Nellie, even to the extent of dutifully reciting Night Prayers in common at 10:00 p.m. Though there was a housekeeper and driver, Nellie Cantwell was the dominant authority, and she insisted that all her regulations be minutely observed. There was even a curfew which no one dared to violate without prior notification. Regulated as his lifestyle was in the years, 1938-1946, Manning enjoyed and prospered in those surroundings. Commenting on his years as secretary for Cantwell, Manning confided to an acquaintance that "the last seven years have not seemed nearly as long as the first seven I spent here and as the entire did not seem as long as any of the periods I spent in Rome. I am very happy in my surroundings and well taken care of."[28]

Throughout his life, Manning was most at home in the pulpit, on the podium or speaking over the airways. His greatest endowment was that of speaking and he will be remembered far longer by what he said than by what he did. Manning began his long career on the lecture circuit early in his ministry. In February and March 1940, he delivered a series of fascinating lectures at Cathedral Chapel parish on the virtues of penance and hope.

He was a favorite speaker at receptions and professions of religious. At Nazareth House in Orange, on July 2, 1942, Manning spoke about obedience, noting that "the whole life of Christ was one of obedience. His food and drink was to do the will of His heavenly Father. For thirty years, He was obedient to Mary and Joseph."[29] In an address at Holy Souls Convent, he anticipated the words later used at Vatican Council II by pointing out that "the Mass in everything. All our prayers and good works get their worth only from the Mass. It is like a great mountain peak capped with eternal snows, with its head piercing the heavenly clouds, and from its summit running down rivers of water, north, south, east and west giving fertility to the hillsides and watering the widening plants, filling the world with abundant life."[30]

Manning always related well to seminarians. He gave the five day retreat at Los Angeles College in 1945 during which he presented a classical portrayal of the students' state of life, Holy Eucharist, the Blessed Mother, death and heaven. To this day his listeners recall Manning's carefully crafted words.

Shortly after returning to the United States in 1938, Manning began the process of becoming an American citizen. After submitting the usual paperwork, he was informed that his absence from the country for three years broke the continuity of his residence, thus requiring him to re-apply and wait another five years. An appeal to a local lawyer had no effect. Eventually on January 14, 1944, he achieved full citizenship status.[31]

The appointment of Father Manning as a papal chamberlain by Pope Pius XII, on April 15, 1943, occasioned a host of congratulatory letters from all strata and areas of the archdiocese. In his response to old friends in Ireland, the monsignor said that he felt "very unworthy of it" and acknowledged that the honor was "entirely due to the great-heartedness of our beloved archbishop who is close to the hearts of all his priests."[32] To another he said that "there is only one feature of this promotion that I relish, and that was the happiness I knew it would give my mother."[33]

When Manning was raised to the domestic prelacy, November 24, 1945, Archbishop Cantwell took the occasion to write Margaret Manning at her home in Ballingeary:

> You will be glad to know that never was there given in this diocese an honor to anyone, which received such general commendation. You will be glad to know that your son is

Msgr. Manning and Bishop McGucken greet the Archbishop and Nellie upon their return from Ireland.

Msgr. Manning is shown here with Archbishop Cantwell, his sister, Nellie, Msgr. Michael O'Connor and Father Robert Brennan.

Msgr. Manning stands before the altar in the Archbishop's chapel at 100 Fremont Place.

> keeping in good health, and when it is at all possible, we shall send him to see the mother whom he loves so well.
>
> He is in every sense a great help to me and a consolation. It is not often that a bishop finds a young man so helpful as I have found the young man whom you cherished for so many years. I am grateful to you for your own prayers, and pray Almighty God to give you length of years and happy days.
>
> When this letter reaches you Christmas will have passed, but it will be the dawn of the New Year. I pray that the New Year may be full of consolation and spiritual strength to you and yours, my dear Mrs. Manning.[34]

During the rest of his days as secretary, Manning kept a rather low profile.[35] The quality of Cantwell's talks and writings improved markedly in those years. Manning later admitted his role in that aspect of the archbishop's ministry by saying that "we who wrote for him jested that, by the time a comma was altered here and there by him, or a sentence rearranged, he proceeded as though the entire composition was of his making."[36]

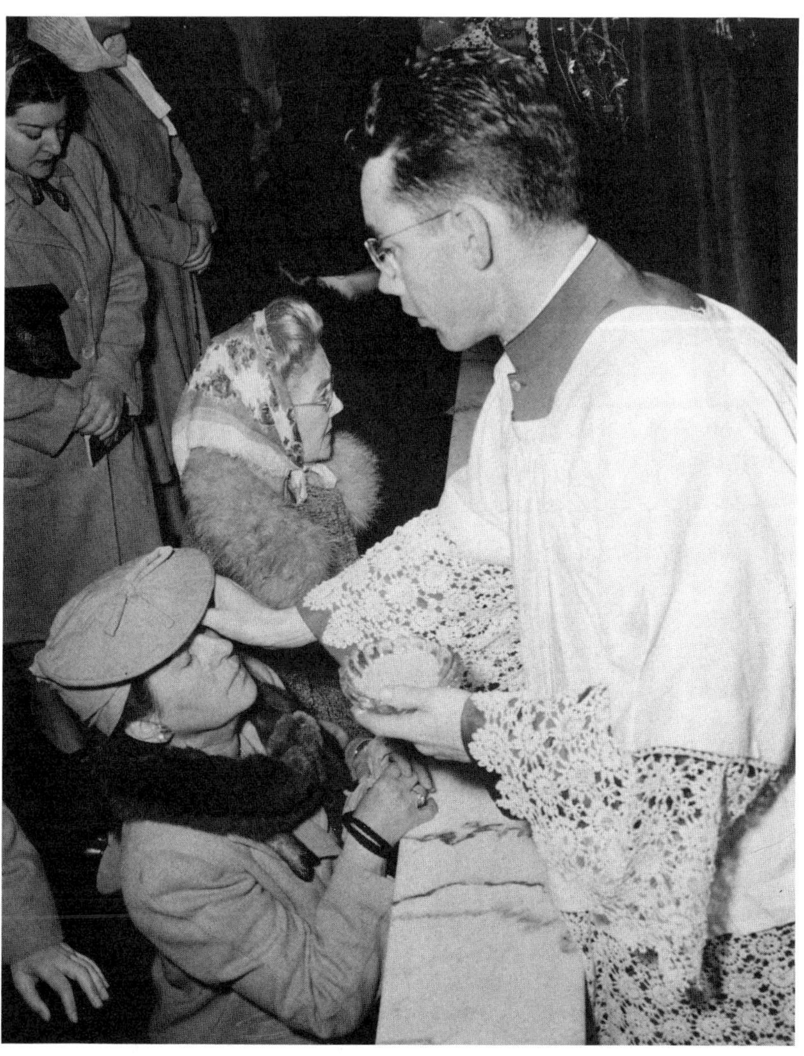

Msgr. Manning distributing ashes at Saint Vibiana's Cathedral.

Msgr. Timothy Manning.

Notes to the Text

1. There were six other priests ordained that morning, namely Patrick Crowley, John Flack, Bernard Gannon, Harry Mitchell, James Nash and Francis Watterson, C.M. Thirteen others were ordained elsewhere for the Archdiocese of San Francisco and the Dioceses of Helena, Port-of-Spain, Sacramento, Spokane and Tucson.
2. *The Tidings*, February 9, 1973.
3. *Ibid.*, June 2, 1978.
4. AALA, "Sermon Preached at First Solemn Mass of Father Timothy Manning," Los Angeles, June 17, 1934.
5. AALA, "Sermon Preached by Rev. Robert Dwyer," San Bruno, June 24, 1934.
6. Francis J. Weber (comp.), *Times of Tension. Moments of Grace. The Homilies, Addresses and Talks of Cardinal Timothy Manning* (Los Angeles, 1990), p. 435.
7. AALA, Timothy Manning to John J. Cantwell, Menlo Park, March 1, 1934.
8. AALA, Bernard Dolan to Timothy Manning, Los Angeles, March 8, 1934.
9. AALA, Timothy Manning to Bernard Dolan, Ballingeary, July 24, 1935.
10. AALA, Bernard Dolan to Joseph Breslin, Los Angeles, September 26, 1935.
11. AALA, Bernard Dolan to Timothy Manning, Los Angeles, December 3, 1935.
12. AALA, Timothy Manning to Bernard Dolan, Rome, December 27, 1935.
13. AALA, Timothy Manning to John J. Cantwell, Rome, May 25,1936.
14. AALA, Timothy Manning to John J. Cantwell, Rome, December 27, 1936.
15. AALA, Timothy Manning to John J. Cantwell, Rome, October 18, 1936.

16. AALA, Timothy Manning to John J. Cantwell, Rome, December 27, 1936.
17. AALA, *Ibid.*
18. AALA, Timothy Manning to John J. Cantwell, Rome, May 4, 1937.
19. AALA, Timothy Manning to John J. Cantwell, Rome, December 7, 1937.
20. AALA, Timothy Manning to John J. Cantwell, Rome, December 7, 1937.
21. Manning successfully defended his dissertation in July, 1938.
22. The dissertation was subsequently published by St. Anthony Guild Press in 1946.
23. *The Tidings*, August 29, 1938.
24. *Ibid.*, September 9, 1938.
25. AALA, Timothy Manning to William Leonard, Los Angeles, April 19, 1939.
26. AALA, Timothy Manning to Maureen McGuinness, Los Angeles, March 5, 1943.
27. Francis J. Weber, *John Joseph Cantwell, His Excellency of Los Angeles* (Los Angeles, 1971), p. ix.
28. AALA, Timothy Manning to M. Ahern, Los Angeles, November 27, 1945.
29. Francis J. Weber (comp), *Times of Tension. Moments of Grace. The Homilies, Addresses and Talks of Cardinal Timothy Manning*, p. 15.
30. *Ibid.*, p. 20
31. AALA, Certificate of Naturalization, Washington, D.C., No. 6174264.
32. AALA, Timothy Manning to Mr. and Mrs. Martin Cleary, Los Angeles, August 5, 1943.
33. AALA, Timothy Manning to Maureen McGuinness, Los Angeles, March 5, 1943.
34. AALA, John J. Cantwell to Margaret Manning, Los Angeles, December 20, 1945.
35. Among the few "perks" of serving as secretary to the archbishop, was that of looking after the cemeteries. By a long tradition, the "director" would go by streetcar for a visitation of Calvary Cemetery every other Thursday afternoon, thus providing the only "time away" from the office allowed in those heavily-structured days.

Like his two predecessors, John J. Devlin and Joseph T. McGucken, Manning would frequently take in a matinee performance at the Philharmonic Auditorium on the way home. Manning recalled how, one morning at breakfast, Cantwell, after reading the newspaper, announced to Manning: "The Philharmonic is closed today. I presume you won't be going to Calvary."

36. Francis J. Weber, *John Joseph Cantwell, op. cit*, p. ix.

3. *The Bishopric*

For most of his life Archbishop Cantwell enjoyed remarkably good health. However, late in 1941 Auxiliary Bishop Joseph T. McGucken noted that for "the first occasion in the years I have been with him," he had not been feeling well. "He realizes it is necessary for him to relax a bit in his tremendous activities."[1]

Never one to tolerate illness in himself or others, Cantwell carried on through the hectic war years with his usual energetic pace. Early in 1946, he confided to his sister that he had "met with a little accident that kept me in bed for a week, and still has me under-the-weather."[2] That "little accident," probably a minor stroke, happened at the Ambassador Hotel where he fell and cut his shin bone. Later that year, one of Cantwell's close friends was advised that the archbishop had "not been well. These past weeks he has been in bed, but, thank God, he seems to be improving wonderfully, and is beginning to think about getting up. His varicose veins became inflamed and phlebitis set in one leg but the swelling is now going down and with it the danger of a blood clot in his system."[3]

In any event, as early as January 1946, Cantwell noticed that even with the help of Bishop McGucken, he felt "unable to do necessary things." He wrote Francis Cardinal-designate Spellman, a long-time friend, asking the Archbishop of New York, to "use your good offices to get me a second auxiliary bishop" for the archdiocese. Hoping to short-circuit the normal selection process, he didn't want to write to the Apostolic Delegate "unless you advise the contrary."

Cantwell then presented "the name of the Right Reverend Timothy Manning, who recently received from the Holy Father the distinction" of a domestic prelacy. The archbishop further noted that Manning was "an eminent man, and has received his degrees in Rome." He went on to say that "he is very popular with the priests, and no man in the diocese would be more acceptable to the clergy, if the Holy Father saw well of commending him to me as a second auxiliary." Cantwell concluded by observing that "if the Holy Father could see his way to appoint Dr.

The Most Reverend Timothy Manning, D.D., J.C.D.
Titular Bishop-elect of Lesvi
and
Auxiliary Bishop-elect of Los Angeles
requests the honor of your presence at his
Episcopal Consecration
The Most Reverend John J. Cantwell, D.D.
Archbishop of Los Angeles
presiding
The Most Reverend Joseph T. McGucken, D.D.
Auxiliary Bishop of Los Angeles
Consecrator
The Most Reverend James E. Walsh, M.M., D.D.
Titular Bishop of Sata
and
The Most Reverend Thomas A. Connolly, D.D., J.C.D.
Auxiliary Bishop of San Francisco
Co-Consecrators
The Cathedral of Saint Vibiana
Los Angeles
Tuesday, the fifteenth of October
Nineteen hundred and forty-six
at ten o'clock
Sermon by
The Very Reverend Thomas C. Mulligan, S.S., S.T.D.
Rector of Saint Patrick's Seminary, Menlo Park

First "official" photograph of newly-consecrated Timothy Manning, Auxiliary Bishop of Los Angeles.

Manning, at your request, a great deal would be done to relieve me of the many tasks that are involved in the administration of a diocese like Los Angeles."[4]

Spellman replied promptly and said that he would present the Holy Father with the request "on the occasion of my first audience with him." But he pointed out that Cantwell "would do well to present this petition to the Apostolic Delegate as of necessity he will be queried, and therefore I think it is better to have your formal request go through the ordinary channels." He then reminded Cantwell about the necessity of presenting "the name of three eligible candidates while at the same time indicating your own preference and the reasons for this preference."[5]

So the day after receiving Spellman's recommendation, Cantwell wrote to the Apostolic Delegate, Archbishop Amleto Giovanni Cicognani, noting that the Archdiocese of Los Angeles was "rapidly becoming one of the major metropolitan areas of the country" and observing that with "this growth there is corresponding growth of the spiritual care of the growing Catholic population." In order to "lighten our burden," he was petitioning for a "second auxiliary bishop." In accordance with the mind of the Holy See, he was submitting "herewith the names of three of the priests of this archdiocese who, are, to my mind, worthy candidates, and would comply with the canonical requirements for such an office." They were Msgr. Martin McNicholas, Father Alden J. Bell and Msgr. Timothy Manning. Cantwell concluded by saying that his "personal preference and desire would be the appointment of the Right Reverend Timothy Manning. For many years he has lived in my home, and been active in my curia. I believe also, that he would be very acceptable to the priests and people of the archdiocese. He is familiar with the nature of diocesan work and is a graduate of the Gregorian University in Rome."[6] The salient parts of the official petition are here reproduced:

Most Holy Father

> Prostrate at the feet of Your Holiness, the under-signed, John Joseph Cantwell, Archbishop of Los Angeles, humbly presents for your august consideration the following petition.
>
> It is not unknown to Your Holiness, especially since you have honored this archdiocese in person by a memorable visit, that the metropolis of Los Angeles is rapidly becoming one of the major centers of population and industry in the

Timothy Manning received episcopal ordination on October 15, 1946 from the hands of Auxiliary Bishop Joseph T. McGucken in Saint Vibiana's Cathedral. Shown in the background is one of the co-consecrators, Bishop James E. Walsh of Maryknoll, who was later to spend twelve years in a communist prison in China.

***TITULAR SEE** – The above map by Tidings Staff Artist Dennis McCarthy shows the location of the Titular See of Lesvi to which Msgr. Manning has been named as well as to the rank of Auxiliary Bishop of Los Angeles.*

AUG 23 1946

Former See of Lesvi, Algeria Had Last Ordinary, 484 A. D.

The Titular See of Lesvi, which can't be located on present day maps of North Africa, was in Algeria near Setif.

During World War II thousands of Allied troops landed in Algeria under British General Montgomery to chase General Rommel and the Nazis from Africa in May, 1943.

However, Lesvi itself hasn't been active as a Catholic diocese since Bishop Vadius was exiled by King Huneric in 484, according to the Catholic Encyclopedia.

When it existed in the fifth century Lesvi was stationed 25 miles from Tupusuctu or Tiklat, and about 18 miles from Horrea Aninici, now Rin-Roua, south of Bougie.

The town of Lesvi was on the River Savav, but there are no remains to be seen. Previous to Bishop Vadius there was a Bishop Romanus, a Donatist, who was present at the Convention of Carthage in 411.

> United States. Already during our episcopate, the diocese has been twice divided and there is every indication that this phenomenal growth will continue.
>
> The burdens of the spiritual administration are correspondingly increasing. Each year many new churches, schools, hospitals and the like are being erected, and the prestige of the Church must be maintained as the representative of God in the community at large. We deem it not inopportune, however, to petition Your Holiness graciously to give to us another auxiliary bishop, so that the ever increasing labors may not be too heavy upon us and our auxiliary bishop, and that the Church of God may keep pace with the growth in the civic life.
>
> We humbly petition for this exalted position the name of Right Reverend Timothy Manning. For many years he has been a member of our household, and our curia, and has been made familiar with our needs. We are confident that he has the canonical requirements to render him acceptable for such promotion. He has completed a post graduate course in Canon Law at the Gregorian University in Rome, and gives evidence of his devotion and loyalty to the Holy See. Recently he has been elevated by Your Holiness to the rank of Domestic Prelate.
>
> With profound humility, therefore, we respectfully petition that the Right Reverend Timothy Manning may be elevated to the episcopate, as auxiliary to the Archbishop of Los Angeles. We are soliciting the kind help of His Eminence, Cardinal Spellman, Archbishop of New York, both as an old friend to us, and one acquainted with our circumstances, to place this petition at the feet of Your Holiness.[7]

The Apostolic Delegate, while promising to make known Cantwell's "desire to have the burden of administering the great metropolitan see of Los Angeles lightened by the granting to you of a second auxiliary," called Cantwell's attention to the fact that "it has been the unvarying practice of the Holy See for many years now to nominate to the episcopal office in this country only those priests who have been born here."[8] Being "foreign" himself, Cantwell bristled at the suggestion that preference would be given to native-born candidates. He pointed out to Cicognani that "during my episcopate the diocese has had to depend largely on a supply of outside priests, coming for the greater part from Ireland. How zealously they have worked is evident from the condition of the Church in California today. A new generation of priests is coming from our own seminary. These young men are mostly native to this country, but are as yet too young to be seriously considered for this particular purpose of which I write."

Cantwell didn't feel that "an eligible candidate should be disqualified simply because, "by an accident of birth." he was not native to the area. The archbishop was so incensed that he considered "it advisable to communicate with Our Most Holy Father directly, to beg his consideration of my preference when it comes to him through the normal channels of the Sacred Consistorial Congregation."[9]

On the same day, Cantwell complained bitterly to Spellman "about the current policy of the Holy See to nominate to the American hierarchy only those who have been born in this country." He said he felt obliged to "supplement my preference with a direct appeal to Our Most Holy Father for a dispensation in this regard."[10] Spellman phoned Cicognani and, a few days later, the Apostolic Delegate thanked the Archbishop of Los Angeles "for making known to me the extraordinary circumstances which prevail there and which impelled" him to speak out so forcibly. Since Cantwell felt that his *terna* of candidates, two of them foreign-born, were the best qualified, he would "submit the matter to the judgment of the Holy Father."[11]

In subsequent months, Cicognani added two verbal stipulations to the appointment; the new auxiliary was to understand that the nationality issue would impede his ever being an "ordinary" or residential bishop and Cantwell was to "loan" the services of Bishop McGucken as Apostolic Administrator to the Diocese of Monterey-Fresno whose bishop had suffered an irreversible cerebral hemorrhage.[12]

The complicated and time-consuming process of sending out scrutinial letters to representative clergy and laity took several additional months. After voluntarily agreeing to observe a permanent and absolute secrecy, each respondent was directed to answer questions about the candidate's spiritual and pastoral qualifications. The responses, together with any further correspondence, were returned to the Apostolic Delegation.[13] When Archbishop Cicognani was assured of Manning's worthiness, he set in motion the finely-tuned wheels of ecclesial machinery by sending the nomination to the Sacred Consistorial Congregation. After one of its plenary sessions, the Cardinal Prefect was authorized to present Manning's nomination directly to the Holy Father for final approval. At that juncture, it is likely that the Pope was reminded of Cardinal Spellman's earlier intervention, as well as Cantwell's request

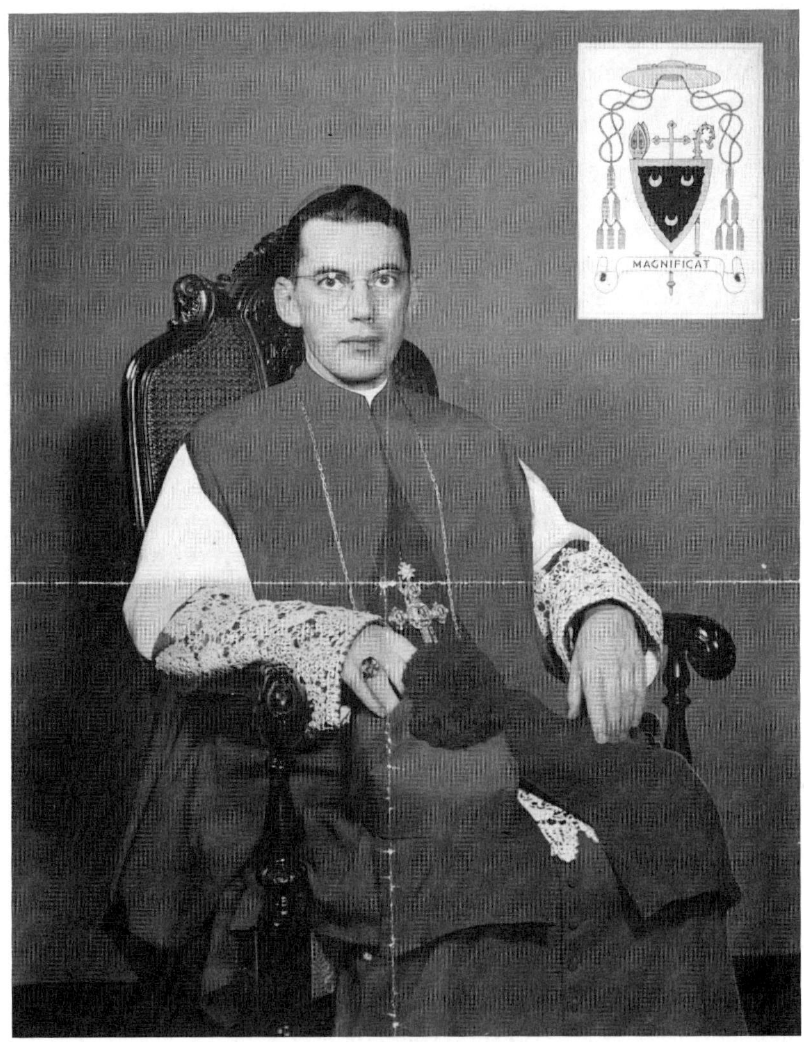

Special issue of The Tidings.

LUNCHEON

IN HONOR OF

THE MOST REVEREND

TIMOTHY MANNING, J. C. D.

TITULAR BISHOP OF LESVI

AND

AUXILIARY TO THE ARCHBISHOP OF LOS ANGELES

AMBASSADOR HOTEL

Cocoanut Grove

LOS ANGELES, CALIFORNIA

OCTOBER THE FIFTEENTH

NINETEEN HUNDRED AND FORTY-SIX

that an exception be made to the nationality requirement. Once the pontiff signified approbation, the papal bull was drawn up on parchment and transmitted by diplomatic pouch to the Apostolic Delegation in Washington.

Finally, on August 3, Cicognani informed Cantwell that "the Holy Father graciously granted your petition for a second auxiliary bishop, and it is his intention to nominate for that post your secretary, Monsignor Timothy Manning."[14] On the same day, the Apostolic Delegate informed Manning that "it is my gratifying duty to inform you that His Holiness Pope Pius has in mind to promote you to the titular episcopal see of Lesvi and to designate you as a second auxiliary bishop to His Excellency, Archbishop Cantwell."[15] In his response to the Apostolic Delegate, Cantwell expressed his "profound gratification" that the Holy Father had acceded to his request and he thanked Cicognani for "your own kind intervention in this matter."[16]

The public announcement of Msgr. Timothy Manning's assignment to the titular See of Lesvi and his simultaneous appointment as Auxiliary Bishop of Los Angeles was made on August 17, 1946.[17] It was a total surprise. Every generation seems to have its "bishop-watchers" who predict and second guess appointments to the hierarchy. In Manning's case, even the most astute clerical gossips were caught entirely off guard. Though Cantwell's ill health was widely known, few knew how bad it was and fewer still imagined that he would go the route of another auxiliary, of which only New York and Baltimore in the United States then had more than one.

The first to be notified of the appointment was Margaret Manning. Cantwell sent a telegram which read: "This morning we received from the Apostolic Delegate the announcement of your devoted son to the dignity of an auxiliary bishop of Los Angeles. May his joy be yours. Congratulations and blessings."[18]

The appointment was well received in official and public circles. Father Thomas J. McCarthy, editor of *The Tidings*, said that "he richly deserves the signal honor" noting that "his priestliness, charm, quiet courtesy, all these are marks which have endeared him to priest and laymen alike." McCarthy also saluted Manning's parents noting that it was "under their roof that his vocation first was fostered. It was because of their unselfish giving that he left hearth and home to come as a student for the priesthood in America."[19]

Mary Lanigan Healy, once referred to as the "voice of the laity" for the Church in Southern California, expressed the sentiments of many in her weekly column, "Among Us."

> We were busy with Saturday morning chores when a friend phoned to say he had just heard over the radio the good news that Msgr. Timothy Manning had become a bishop. And we heard our voice answering him as pleased and excited and proud as though this were a personal matter, as though it were an affair of intimate concern to us that the Holy Father had given the Archdiocese of Los Angeles another bishop.
>
> And straightaway we knew it was just that. And we knew that it was quite fitting that we should stand there on the edge of the half mopped floor, with the washing machine muttering in the distance and children shouting in the yard; and sense identification with a bishop. And everywhere in the city the selfsame thing was happening. People were standing right in the midst of their workaday world, yet moving along in a fine procession headed by a figure robed in red.
>
> One woman recalled how young Fr. Manning had given her mother Extreme Unction some years ago when he was stationed at Immaculate Conception; another spoke of the beautiful three hour service at St. Michael's Church last year. A nun mentioned a gracious courtesy. And a little boy said he would always remember that the monsignor had given him a present on his First Communion Day. It was just as though we were comparing souvenirs before we placed them away to be cherished even more than before. So we reached down in memory and considered the most splendid of them all.[20]

Manning's closeness to the seminary community is reflected in an essay that appeared in the quarterly publication for Los Angeles College. Written by John Vaughn, who later would become Minister General of the Order of Friars Minor, it said that "as seminarians, we thank God and our Holy Father for giving our archbishop such an able auxiliary, and we fervently pray that the Lord will bless this, his newly-anointed one, with all the graces necessary for his new state in life."[21]

Scarcely any copies of the manifold letters received and sent by Manning to well-wishers or those involved in the liturgical services or civic tributes have been retained in the archdiocesan archives at Mission Hills.[22] One of the exceptions which probably speaks for the others, was sent to a Jesuit friend whom he had known at Limerick:

The coat-of-arms for the Manning family dates from 1578. Described as "Gules three crescents gold with bordure gold," the arms are surmounted by the symbols of the hierarchy, mitre, cross and crozier. Above these symbols is a bishop's hat with six tassels hanging on each side of the shield. The hat and tassels are green, the heraldic color for a bishop. Below the coat-of-arms is the motto, "Magnificat," chosen because of Timothy Manning's devotion to the Blessed Mother.

Bishop's Crozier

The crozier presented to Bishop Timothy Manning by a friend is of hand-carved ivory and silver mixed with gold. It was made by Hindu craftsmen on Malabar coast of south India from a design by Eric Sauter, a Los Angeles artist. The figure of Our Lady, under the title of the Immaculate Conception, and Bishop Manning's coat of arms were carved from solid ivory. Arrangements in India for making of the unique crozier were directed by Malabar Rite Archbishop Mar Gregorios of Trivandrum. Malabar craftsmen are reputed to be the world's finest artists in ivory carving. The crozier was subsequently given to Bishop Thaddeus Shubsda of Monterey. It was later dropped, but then restored through the efforts of Richard Menn. It is now on exhibit in the Historical Museum attached to the Archival Center, Archdiocese of Los Angeles.

> The providence of God works in strange patterns, and it is no small wonder to me that I should be called to walk among the prophets of Israel. One of the very pleasant results of this appointment has been the reception of letters from Mungret men all over the world and to share in their joy. The *Alma Mater* was of course very proud, but I feel I carry its honor in a fragile vessel.[20]

Another letter, found in the papers of James Francis Cardinal McIntyre, was sent to Manning by the newly-appointed Coadjutor Archbishop of New York: "Please accept my prayerful wishes on your selection as bishop." Then, prophetically, he said that "I trust we can work together for God's kingdom in the years ahead."[24]

In those days after Manning's appointment became public, Cantwell rallied somewhat from his illness. An elevator was installed in the episcopal residence and McGucken thought that "his good, strong constitution will stand him in good stead and that he will be quite well if he doesn't try to rush around too much."[25] Earlier, Cantwell had told Cardinal Spellman that "I feel very well, but [am] getting like an old house that needs to be put in repair - the shingles need to be fixed and the plumbing put in order."[26] Despite his own optimistic health appraisal, Cantwell's memory began to fail noticeably, and he became amenable to curtailing drastically his public appearances. When Cardinal Spellman ever-so-diplomatically suggested that Bishop McGucken be designated as principal consecrator for Manning's episcopal ordination, Cantwell went along with the idea and agreed to "preside" at the ceremony.

Because of Manning's long time devotion to Saint Teresa of Avila, the sixteenth century mystical writer canonized in 1622 by Pope Gregory XV, it was decided to schedule the consecration ceremony for October 15 at 10:00 a.m. Due to the seating limitations at Saint Vibiana's Cathedral, only 2,000 invitations were issued to the clergy and laity active in one or another archdiocesan activity. Manning asked his close friends, Bishops James E. Walsh of Maryknoll and Thomas A. Connolly of San Francisco to assist Bishop McGucken as co-consecrators. Two other archbishops and seven bishops also attended the event which was broadcast, for the first time, on radio.[27] This marked only the sixth time that an episcopal ordination had taken place in the Los Angeles cathedral.

A colorful special insertion was provided by *The Tidings* in its issue for October 11th. A writer for the archdiocesan newspaper told how "in the rich splendor of the Catholic Church and with symbolism dating back to the early centuries of the Faith," the bishop-elect would be invested with symbols of his new office. He also recalled that "it was before this same high altar of Saint Vibiana that Msgr. Manning's priestly hands were first anointed on June 16, 1934." According to the newspaper account, the actual ceremony would be divided into four parts; the reading of the papal mandate; the preliminary examination of the candidate; the consecration proper and the investure. The oath of office and the blessing of the mitre, crozier and ring were to take place on the preceding evening by the Vicar General.

In its issue for the following week,[28] *The Tidings* recorded how "in the brilliant ceremonies repeated periodically over a span of 20 centuries in the Catholic Church, another bishop was added to the long line of successors to the first apostles."[29]

In his masterful homily Father Thomas Mulligan, rector of Saint Patrick's Seminary in Menlo Park, outlined the role of a bishop and the virtues expected of one invested with that noble calling. He observed that "the rich pageantry and cloth of gold that we have seen today are but the outer vesture that adorns wholly spiritual things. Beneath those signs and symbols are great invisible realities. Indeed, there is a great unseen Presence here, for through human instruments Christ is here working the inner transformation of a man." He portrayed Manning as taking an "equal place with the three bishops who consecrated him, and with the purple-clad bishops and archbishops who throng the sanctuary of this venerable cathedral church. Now he belongs beside the bishops of every race and tongue who rule God's world-wide Church today, and he even shares the episcopal dignity with the Twelfth Pius, now gloriously reigning."

Mulligan concluded by addressing the newly anointed prelate in these words:

> Most Reverend Bishop Manning, you belong to a sacred dynasty with magnificent traditions. Garcia Diego, first Bishop in this California region, and John Carroll, first Bishop in the United States, those great men are your kindred. So too are Francis de Sales and Charles Borromeo, Bonaventure and Albert, Patrick and Finbar, Augustine and Chrysostom, Timothy and Titus, Peter and James and John. Christ has given to you, as He gave to those of that illustrious line, the fullness of the priesthood. With jubilant hearts, we offer thanks to God.[30]

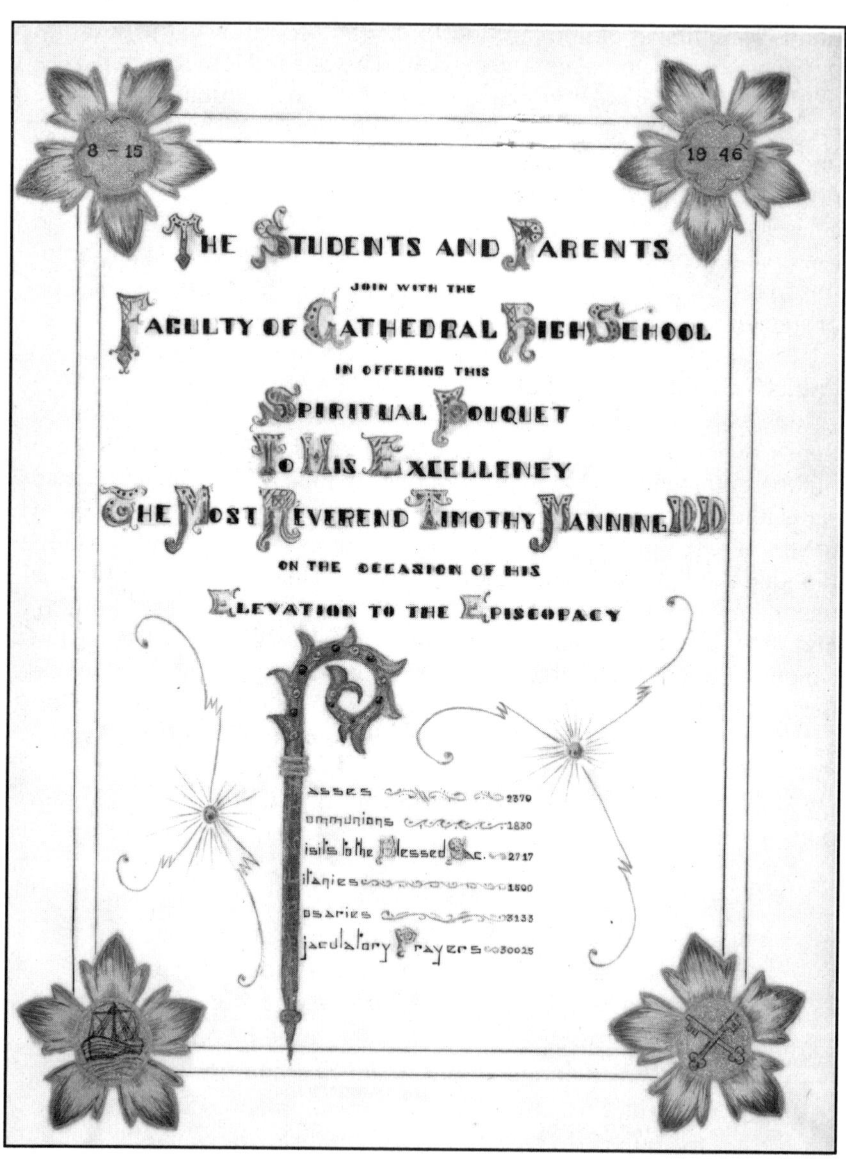

8 - 15 1946

THE STUDENTS AND PARENTS
JOIN WITH THE
FACULTY OF CATHEDRAL HIGH SCHOOL
IN OFFERING THIS
SPIRITUAL BOUQUET
TO HIS EXCELLENCY
THE MOST REVEREND TIMOTHY MANNING D.D.
ON THE OCCASION OF HIS
ELEVATION TO THE EPISCOPACY

Masses 2370
Communions 1830
Visits to the Blessed Sac. 2717
Litanies 1590
Rosaries 3133
Ejaculatory Prayers 30025

A

REMEMBRANCE

OF MY

CONSECRATION

OCTOBER 15th, 1946

+ *TIMOTHY MANNING*

Auxiliary Bishop of Los Angeles

Manning's personal thoughts and aspirations on that day went unrecorded. However, in a homily prepared for a similar ceremony a few years later, he interpreted the occasion in terms of the charge given to the new bishop to preach the Gospel:

> First of all the Church, through her bishops, is charged with a royal mandate to propagate to the ends of the earth that faith which is the solitary substance of our hope in a hapless world. She must hold high the light which will shine across the encircling gloom. Darkness covers the souls of men in sin as surely as it shrouded primeval creation. It is the mission of the gospel to shine through that darkness, not to dispel it, for it will last until the morning star rises again in the eternal heavens.
>
> Secondly, the Church must preserve that faith intact so that as from a fountain, men may drink at its pure flow until the end of time. Heaven and earth will pass away, but not the Word of God. Cultures will be swept down in the great currents of history, princes of this world will fall like stars from the heavens above. Heresies like hurricanes will leave the wisdom of the world windswept of all that is not founded and rooted in the belief in God. But the gates of hell itself shall not prevail against the Word of God.
>
> Thirdly, this pearl of incomparable price must be shielded from the enemies who would rob or destroy it. The amphitheatres of the Roman Empire, the barbaric diabolisms of primitive tribes, the scaffolds of the northern reformers, the firing squads and concentration camps of modern enlightenments, all these have failed to destroy. The mass-rocks of Ireland, the crosses of Japan, the gibbets of Tyburn, and the iron curtains of middle-Europe will bear testimony on the day of judgement to the Master's prophecy "Have confidence for I have overcome the world."[31]

Following the ceremonies at the cathedral, 400 clergymen joined in felicitating Bishop Manning at a luncheon in the Coconut Grove of the Ambassador Hotel. The bishop told his confreres that his heart was "impatient to express every debt of gratitude, every pledge of loyalty, every protestation of fidelity. But my tongue can only lisp the language of the heart." He had "no illusions of merit and no pretension to honor" and made that protestation "on the very lintel of the life which I enter this day." Manning dutifully thanked the Holy Father, the archbishop, his ordaining bishops, the clergy, religious and seminarians for their prayers and good example over the years. He was especially grateful "for the friends who sustained me on the way. They have all been stamped by the divine trademark of their brotherly love." Noting that "in my going and coming out among my priestly acquaintances, I have never known but only the most Christlike spirit, warmest hospitality and enduring friendship." He concluded by saying that "being only a child, unschooled in the persuasive ways of human wisdom and confident only in the providential guidance of our heavenly Father, I step into the future with my mother's song on my lips - *Magnificat anima mea Dominum.*"[32]

Two days later, Bishop Manning began dispensing the Sacrament of Confirmation, a ministry which would stretch over the ensuing forty-three years. During that time, Manning would administer that sacrament more widely to an estimated 650,000, more than any other bishop in California's history. In his first episcopal homily, delivered at Our Lady of Lourdes Church in Los Angeles, he said that "The Church is speaking with the wisdom of centuries behind her, and she has ordained that Confirmation be given to the young people at a turning point in their lives when they will either follow the road that leads to good or the one which leads to evil." He believed that "there is one saving quality of childhood which they should never lose and which, if they follow it, will invariably lead them into the right road. That is the respect for authority." He felt that authority was eminently characteristic of a child. A child never questions authority and is always on sure ground. Our Divine Lord Himself had this in mind when He said that 'unless you become as little children, you shall not enter the Kingdom of Heaven.' "[33]

It was another eight months before Manning was able to return to Ireland. He left Los Angeles on June 29, 1947 and then sailed from New York on the *SS. America*. He arrived "to be greeted by a typical Ballingeary reception. Flags were spangled on archways, flowers and confetti were strewn on the cobblestone streets. Irish hearts were happy as His Excellency enthusiastically greeted the villagers, but none so happy as that of a frail woman who leaned on the Bishop's arm. She was Margaret Manning, his mother."[34]

It was during this pleasant interlude in Ireland that a silver chalice, a replica of the famous Timoleague chalice, was presented to Bishop Manning on behalf of the Gaels of Cork. The function took place in the Imperial Hotel, in Cork City. According to a newspaper article, the people of his homeland "were especially proud of him as he was a son

This first photograph of the newly consecrated Timothy Manning as titular Bishop of Lesvi was taken immediately after the ceremony in the sacristy of Saint Vibiana Cathedral. He is holding the crozier belonging to Archbishop John J. Cantwell.

Bishop Manning in attendance at a Boy Scout Jamboree.

of Ballingeary, the place which held such a large part in the hearts of all those present. He had come back from his many years in America unchanged in his love of everything Irish and in his conviction of the importance of the Irish language." Manning replied that "after the coldness of exile," he was heartened "to come to warm himself at the heartstones of the Faith of the Irish people."[35]

Notes to the Text

1. AALA, Joseph T. McGucken to Joseph Byrne, Los Angeles, October 29, 1941.
2. AALA, John J. Cantwell to Mother Regis Cantwell, Los Angeles, February 25, 1946.
3. AALA, Joseph T. McGucken to Joseph Byrne, Los Angeles, September 29, 1941.
4. AALA, John J. Cantwell to Francis Cardinal Spellman, Los Angeles, January 15, 1946.
5. AALA, Francis Cardinal Spellman to John J. Cantwell, New York, January 19, 1946.
6. AALA, John J. Cantwell to Amleto Giovanni Cicognani, Los Angeles, January 23, 1946.
7. AALA, John J. Cantwell to Pope Pius XII, Los Angeles, n.d.
8. AALA, Amleto Giovanni Cicognani to John J. Cantwell, Washington, D.C., January 30, 1946.
9. AALA, John J. Cantwell to Amleto Giovanni Cicognani, Los Angeles, February 7, 1946.
10. AALA, John J. Cantwell to Francis Cardinal Spellman, Los Angeles, February 7, 1946.
11. AALA, Amleto Giovanni Cicognani to John J. Cantwell, Washington, D.C., February 13, 1946.
12. Interestingly, another of three candidates, Alden J. Bell, was also foreign born and years later, he was named to the bishopric without any restrictions.
13. For an explanation of the normal process for selecting bishops, see Francis J. Weber, "Episcopal Appointments in the U.S.A.," *American Ecclesiastical Review* CLV (September, 1966), 178-191. One item that was apparently never discussed, at least in the extant correspondence, was Manning's age. At thirty-seven years he was the youngest priest in the world named to the bishopric. This fact alone attests to the influence exercised in the process by Francis Cardinal Spellman.

14. AALA, Amleto Giovanni Cicognani to John J. Cantwell, Washington, D.C., August 3, 1946.
15. AALA, Amleto Giovanni Cicognani to Timothy Manning, Washington, D. C., August 3, 1946.
16. AALA, John J. Cantwell to Amleto Giovanni Cicognani, Los Angeles, August 8, 1946.
17. See Los Angeles *Times*, August 18, 1946.
18. Tipperary *Star*, August 24, 1946.
19. The Tidings, August 23, 1946.
20. *Ibid.*
21. *The Prep* II (Fall, 1946), 6.
22. Clare Berger, Manning's long-time secretary, remembered seeing a scrapbook in which all the congratulatory letters were mounted.
23. AALA, Timothy Manning to C.P.Finn, S.J., Los Angeles, September 23, 1946.
24. AALA, J. Francis A. McIntyre to Timothy Manning, New York, September 10, 1946.
25. AALA, Joseph T. McGucken to Joseph Byrne, Los Angeles, September 12, 1946.
26. AALA, John J. Cantwell to Francis Cardinal Spellman, Los Angeles, April 30, 1946.
27. Those attending were Archbishops Edward D. Howard (Portland) and Edwin V. Byrne (Santa Fe) and Bishops Robert J. Armstrong (Sacramento), Thomas K. Gorman (Reno), Charles F. Buddy (San Diego), James P. Davis (Puerto Rico), Joseph C. Willging (Pueblo), Gerald Shaughnessy (Seattle) and Joseph M. Preciado Nieva (Darien, Panama).
28. Historical parallels are always interesting. In the same issue that reports Manning's consecration is a picture of young Roger M. Mahony who, with his brother, was one of eight sets of twins attending Saint Charles parochial school.
29. October 18, 1946.
30. *The Tidings*, October 18, 1946.
31. AALA, Text of a sermon prepared for the episcopal ordination of John J. Scanlan of Honolulu, September 21, 1954.

32. Francis J. Weber (comp.), *Times of Tension. Moments of Grace* (Los Angeles, 1990), pp. 53-54.
33. *Ibid.*, p. 55.
34. *The Tidings*, July 18, 1947.
35. AALA, unidentified newspaper article, n.d. (July, 1947).

4. Auxiliary Bishop

Because of its relative rareness in the United States, the role of an "auxiliary" bishop was ill defined in the 1940s. Having no canonical duties and exercising no administrative obligations, he functioned as a "stand-in" for the archbishop at confirmations, graduations, dedications and other assorted liturgical and civic occasions. During the final months of the Cantwell regime in Southern California, Bishop McGucken and the archdiocesan consulters made most of the decisions, even when McGucken was serving as apostolic administrator in Monterey-Fresno. That left Manning as "point man" for the four county archdiocese, a role in which he endeared himself to clergy and laity alike.

Bishop Manning and others thought that a vacation in Ireland might restore the health of Archbishop Cantwell. He and his sister, Nellie, left for the Emerald Isle in the spring of 1947, but upon his return to Los Angeles, Cantwell's memory had deteriorated, and he required almost constant medical care which was provided by the Brothers of Saint John of God. So rapidly did his condition decline that Bishop McGucken was summoned home from Buenos Aires where he was representing the American Hierarchy at Latin America's Marian Congress. Cantwell died in his sleep on October 30.

Bishop Manning was devastated. Though he didn't preach at any of the formal ceremonies, he did provide a written tribute which appeared in *The Tidings* under the masthead: *L'Envoi.*

> The eyes are closed now. The staff is laid by. The tributes have all been paid – rich, wonderful tributes; – and the living have taken final leave of him who is dead. Los Angeles will not soon again witness, in the passing of any public servant, so warm, whole-souled, and moving a demonstration of affection as that tendered this week to the memory of Archbishop John J. Cantwell.
>
> Some people forgot to come but not the poor. Far into the night on the eve of his burial they stood five and six abreast

far down on Second Street waiting for one last glimpse of him who had served them so well.

All along the line of his funeral route they took their places where they would not be noticed, where their names could not be taken down. There were no distinguishing marks to single them out. They were the good, faithful sheep who knew a shepherd when they saw him and who knew that the hills which he tended could never be the same for his going. They came out to pay him their affectionate tribute and of all the tributes paid him in the press, radio and by the Church, there was none to compare with theirs in simplicity and genuineness.

They had penetrated the secret of Archbishop Cantwell's power. It was a secret wrapped in the folds of prayer and because they understood he was a man of prayer – whose prayer was unceasing in their behalf – they thought it only fitting to pray for him every step along the way to his final burying place. No one who saw their faces along the funeral route can soon forget how genuinely they mourned their archbishop. It was a rare and wonderful acknowledgment of the place he had won in their hearts during the thirty years he had ministered to their spiritual and material needs.

The surest test of greatness is determined by the response which a man evokes from the hearts of his people. Great men need no press agents. They need no one to interpret them to the people. By last Wednesday's demonstration it was clear that Archbishop Cantwell's greatness was touchingly acknowledged. The sheepfold is turned in now and the shepherd is gone. Another will come and take his place on the hillsides of California. And he will lay claim to the hands and hearts of all in his charge. He will not mind if some small part of his people's affection is reserved, not for him, but for the shepherd who has now laid aside his staff and is gone home to God.[1]

Chancery officials at Los Angeles were not surprised by the appointment of New York's coadjutor archbishop, J. Francis A. McIntyre, especially after a clandestine visit to Los Angeles of Francis Cardinal Spellman some weeks after Cantwell's funeral. While locals had hoped that Bishop McGucken would be named to the vacancy, those ac-

Bishop Manning's first ordination took place in the sanctuary of Santa Barbara Mission.

During the annual Christmas party held at the Ambassador Hotel, December 18, 1955, the Auxiliary Bishop of Los Angeles presented rabbits to the excited youngsters.

quainted with contemporary procedures for such appointments were not surprised that a senior prelate and a total outsider was given the position.

Manning sent a telegram to the new archbishop pledging his allegiance and good wishes. In his response, McIntyre said that he was "deeply grateful for your kind expression of felicitations and good wishes."[2] McIntyre journeyed west by rail and Manning travelled to San Bernardino, where he boarded the train and accompanied the archbishop on the last leg of his trip. At the east Los Angeles station, several hundred children from neighboring schools gathered for a formal greeting.

In his talk following the installation ceremony at Saint Vibiana's Cathedral on March 19, 1948, Manning said that "our new archbishop comes to us mounted on the wings of the incessant prayers with which we petitioned an occupant for the vacant see." He pointed out that there was no "wall surrounding our metropolis for it is a city of legendary limits. There are no gates except in the hearts of its people, and they will open one by one to welcome him as he walks among them"

> This is a wonder-city to which our new archbishop comes. It is yet the adolescent progeny of the new age, still seeking to find its ultimate strength, awkward in its growth, yet inching its way upward to tower above its contemporaries in the American family of towns. Over the hills and into the adjacent valleys it spills like something poured out, waiting to assume its permanent form, to congeal and settle. It knows only the restless Pacific and the rock-rimmed desert for its boundaries.
>
> Our roots are altogether Catholic and the blood of the *conquistadores* flows in our veins. The little Plaza Church is hidden under the shadows of the great municipal buildings, but hidden only as a pearl of great price. Its origin is coeval with the *pueblo*, they bear a common name, they share a common patronage. It was a place of worship (1781) five years before the first Catholic structure was erected in the City of State of New York.
>
> The lintel and the latch of every door are symbols of our welcome. When sorrow comes no one carries it alone. Always there is a song to gladden the lonely hours. Even our dead, those brethren of ours, priests and bishops, who have gone before us, they too are intimate to all our gatherings;

> their names are spoken in the long nights, their deeds are told with scriptural solemnity. "*Congregavit nos in unum Christi Amor.*"[3]

On the very day of McIntyre's installation, Manning was named chancellor, a position which gave him an official and canonical role in the administration of the archdiocese. Basically, in the old Code of Canon Law, the chancellor was to take care of the curial records, oversee daily chancery operations and perform other duties entrusted to him by the archbishop. In Los Angeles that role also entailed overseeing the management of the seminaries and their students.

In the final months of 1950 Holy Year, Manning made plans to visit the Eternal City for the first time since he completed his studies in 1938. Enroute he stopped in Ireland where his mother and sister joined him and Fathers Bernard Gannon and James Hourihan for the trip to Rome. While in Eire, Manning sent a letter to *The Tidings* in which he explained how his native land was a "prelude to the threshold of the Apostles in the Eternal City." He drew attention to the "unmistakable link between Ireland and Rome in this year of jubilee."

> Ireland's heart rests in Rome. We love and understand Rome more when we have Irish loyalty in our souls. Rome is no longer the Rome of the Caesars not even of the sawdust Caesar. It is uniquely now, more than ever during the period of papal sovereignty, the City of the Pope. What is inscribed in marble on her thoroughfares is verified in fact. Pius, by the Grace of God, is the "*Defensor Civitatis.*" In him Rome rises above the ruins of the surrounding barbarism and faces the world in all the splendor of her ancient majesty.
>
> Here at the ultimate Thule of the world's habitations, our hearts rejoice that we have passed on our way across the green fields of Ireland to the Italy-blue of Mary's protection, sure in the solidity of the Faith of Peter and of Patrick and of Pius.[4]

In Rome, Manning showed his fellow travellers the historic sites, especially Santa Croce which had always occupied a special place in his heart. It was a most rewarding experience to present his mother and sister to Pope Pius XII who received them cordially, with words of affection for both Ireland and Los Angeles.

In addition to his many other duties, Archbishop McIntyre expected his auxiliary to speak at all major liturgical events at the cathedral. An

As Auxiliary Bishop, Archbishop and Cardinal, Timothy Manning was probably the most travelled member of the American hierarchy. He is shown here leaving August 19, 1950 aboard the Cunard White Star Liner, Mauretania.

Bishop Manning here participates in a rally for The Tidings *in Santa Barbara.*

example would be an assembly of nearly 3,000 boys who filled Saint Vibiana's on February 11, 1951 to honor a teenager "who was man enough to achieve holiness," Blessed Dominic Savio. Together the boys sang the psalms, canticles and hymns of Vespers in honor of Our Lady. Through the historic cathedral and into the gray afternoon outside carried the voices of the thousands of boys who filled the pews and crowded the standing areas.

Just before the chanting of the *Magnificat*, the boys heard Bishop Manning tell them about Dominic Savio who had been a schoolboy like themselves. The bishop described the three characteristics of a growing boy – Dominic Savio, any boy. 1 – An impatience to be grown up, to be a man. 2 – A regard for womanhood. 3 – An instinct for authority, for leadership. "Now," continued Bishop Manning, "there are two forces in the world trying to get control over those three instincts":

> The first force is the devil, acting not manifestly, not so that you can see his hand, but acting through agents, through organizations, through un-Christian groups, through bad leadership so that he may in time corral all those instincts to himself and bring that boy to destruction. We are witnesses to this in our own day. Where a boy anticipates being a man, the forces of evil try to make him less a man. All that ruggedness, the discipline, the control over our senses that is the essence of manhood – all is gradually being emasculated, weakened. The result is a teenage group soft, spineless and selfish, lacking discipline and respect for the presence and authority of their elders.
>
> You don't have to go beyond the front page of last week's *Tidings* to see what that softness has done on the battlefields, where a chaplain and a general are quoted as lamenting and bemoaning the absence of discipline and sometimes the cowardice of those who have not trained their manhood in their growing years.
>
> The forces of evil are attempting to capture a boy's second instinct by undermining his sense of purity, by destroying his respect and reverence for womanhood through certain fashions, amusements and songs. The attempt to capture a boy's instinct for authority is exemplified in the inroads in education by Communism. The result of the revolt against the teaching of authority of the land has caused gang warfare, gang destruction.[5]

At the conclusion of the services, Archbishop McIntyre conferred Benediction and the thousands of boys recited the Divine Praises. A reporter said that "each returned to his own school, carrying with him a vivid sense of the spirit of a saintly boy who could have been a student at any school here - and who because of that is a model for all Catholic boys everywhere."[6]

That Bishop Manning was a keen observer of things historical is nowhere more obvious than in a sermon he preached on October 26, 1951 to 2,000 members of the Holy Childhood Association:

> The San Fernando Valley is honored in song and in story. You may look down upon it on a clear wind-swept day from a vantage point on Mulholland Drive, and you are speechless at its majesty and beauty. One hundred thousand acres of verdure, interlaced ribbonwise with thoroughfares, arrayed with homes like whitecaps on the sea, and ringed around with sentinel mountains like faithful watchdogs guarding a slumbering beauty. This miracle of loveliness had but one explanation, water.
>
> Once, not so long ago, well within the memories of the older citizens of our community, the San Fernando Valley was a barren desert. It was hinterland to the real city on the other side of the Cahuenga Pass, alien as Mojave, forbidding as Death Valley. In what is perhaps the most dramatic moment in the history of Los Angeles, in September, 1913, a great engineer, William Mulholland, officiated at a ceremony held in Owensmouth, which we now call Chatsworth.
>
> The flood gates of a great water system were opened up, and in unforgettable words he spoke his speech to the citizens of Los Angeles, saying, "Here it is, take it." The story of the channeling of water to Los Angeles is a brutal story, leaving in its wake, like flood waters on a rampage, a record of sacrifice and desolation and debris that is unequalled in our western history.
>
> The waters have their origin in the melting snows that eternally crown the great giant of all American mountain peaks, rising 14,474 feet above the sawtooth spinal column of the High Sierras. These waters flow down the eastern slopes of the mountains into the Owens Valley, and then, through the genius of engineering, are corralled and decoyed

Father James W. Richardson, C.M. and Msgr. Raymond O'Flaherty assist Bishop Manning in the distribution of certificates to graduates of Saint Vincent Hospital's School of Nursing in 1947.

Auxiliary Bishop Manning spoke often from the pulpit of Saint Vibiana's Cathedral.

> through mountain pass and valley, over a distance of 240 miles to empty into the thirsting belly of the San Fernando Valley.
>
> To some depths, averaging perhaps a thousand feet, the water sinks till it meets rock, so that the whole area below the earth of the valley is like a water reserve that through wells and pumping can be brought to the surface to give greenness and beauty and fruitfulness to every growing thing out of the joyful earth.
>
> My dear children, I can think of no happier illustration than this to give you a concept of the great missionary movement of the Church, to show you how necessary is the cooperation of the least one among you and to inspire you to a ceaseless program of prayer and education for this vital extension of the kingdom of Christ on earth.[7]

There was something of the journalist in Bishop Manning. In early 1952, for example, he complied with a request from the editor of *The Tidings* to keep a journal on his journey to the International Eucharist Congress in Barcelona, Spain from May 17 to June 1. He was especially impressed with what he called "the corporate surrender of Spain to the Providence of Almighty God" when Generalissimo Francisco Franco consecrated his nation to the Blessed Sacrament. Following is a portion of his log which appeared in the archdiocesan paper over several weeks:

> About thirty of our number come from California. Everyone else on board, has either been to California, wished they were from California or hope to see it before they die. All the New Yorkers think of Los Angeles in terms of our archbishop. They are hard to convince that he is so much part of California that he can use an expression such as "the easterners."
>
> We write these lines on Ascension Thursday. Tomorrow we dock for two days at Lisbon, during which time we shall visit Fatima. Yesterday we called at Ponta Delgada, the port-town of the island of San Miguel in the Azores. Were we to go no further, the trip would have been rewarding. This island is wayward from the regular ocean routes. Ours was the first major ship to call here. The last passenger ship called six months ago. If the tourist world ever discovers it for what

> it is, there will be found an emerald jewel long lost in the Atlantic. It is reminiscent of Santa Catalina and slightly longer. It rivals the green of Ireland. Every inch of it even to the top-most hills is cultivated. Long lines of men bead the fields, horizontal with the brown earth, tilling as they slowly move.
>
> At the far reaches of the land there is a lake of volcanic origin, a crater-lake, unspoiled by commercialism, rivalling Killarney. Azaleas and rhododendrons line every inch of the roadway, ready to burst in bloom. The women and children lined the roadways as we passed, their faces telling the simplicity of their faith, close to the gospel ideal of child-like Christianity, spreading blossoms before the cardinal as he passed among them. They are of the stock among whom Our Lady might walk and be at home. They sting the conscience in recollection of their sophisticated contemporaries who might traffic in the shops of Fifth Avenue or Wilshire Boulevard.
>
> On second thought perhaps we should not wish for them a window to the western world, nor a doorway to our way of life. Let them alone with the soil, and with God; let the dream pass, let them sink back from our memories into that older century of faith and simplicity which they have kept untarnished from the world's way. Tomorrow then to Fatima and the gentle air where angels walk with children and children still know wonder.[8]

In 1952, Bishop Manning went to Salt Lake City where, on January 13, he delivered the sermon for the dedication of the magnificent new pipe organ for the Cathedral of the Madeleine. He portrayed the organ as the natural agent wherewith the "bewitching charm of music" is made to come alive. As he often did, he then expressed the message of his words in a meaningful analogy.

> Each human life is likened to an organ pipe. It is singular and alone. Of itself, it may appear the essence of drabness and monotony, as uninspiring as inert wood or metal. Yet, expose that life to the listing of the Spirit which indwells in sanctified man and that soul becomes alive and vibrant.

Bishop Manning blesses new mausoleum at Holy Cross Cemetery.

Father Frederick Kass and Bishop Timothy Manning put the cornerstone in place at Saint Pius V Church in Buena Park.

Bishop Manning presents Ad Altare Dei medal to a member of the Boy Scouts of America.

> Combine such a force with thousands of other like lives each responsible for an individual contribution to the score of life. Place all those lives at the disposal of our creator and then what harmony and beauty will rise up from this guilty globe to rival angelic choirs beyond the limits of the stars.[9]

Among the many roles occupied by Manning over the years was that of serving on the Bishop's Committee on Motion Pictures, replacing Bishop McGucken who had served out a full term in that capacity. The statistics at the time were rather alarming, with only 44% of the films issued the previous year being judged fit for family viewing. Over 35% were found to be morally objectionable. Manning took his role seriously and, quite often spoke out about the low moral tone of films. On February 1, 1953, he gave the homily at a Mass at Saint Vibiana's Cathedral for representatives of the Motion Picture Industry.

> The actor shall totally submerge himself into the character of the one he portrays. His mind and mannerisms shall be so convincing to the mind of his audience that they forget the one and remember only the other. Running through the entire thought of St. Paul, as expressed in his epistles, this portrayal is predominant. He speaks of "putting on Christ, " "having the mind of Christ," "loving one another in Christ, " eating and drinking for His glory until the individual portrays Christ to the world. A woman when she is loved decks herself with beauty. A soul that is loved by Christ will wear all the garments of virtue that will please Him.
>
> Sin is rebellion against such a doctrine, an assertion of one's own personality breaking through the Christ that surrounds us. Scandal is its ultimate abomination because if we, by word or deed shall defile the image of Christ in the mind of a child whose angels see the face of God in heaven, then it were better for us had we never been born.
>
> Men and women whose names are household words the world over, and those others whose talents are steps on the ladder by which they rise, have a tremendous responsibility for the good edification of all who look up to them as heroes for admiration.
>
> May the good God ordain that through a gathering such as this, our vision of the things of Christ shall be renewed and

> the awesome quality of our responsibility realized. May the ultimate applause be yours when you shall step from the stage of life and the curtain of time is quietly lowered. May you qualify for the heartrending challenge, which under circumstances altogether otherwise, was flung across the fires in the courtyard of the High Priest by the servant-maid to Peter: "You also were with Jesus of Nazareth, even your very speech betrays you."[10]

The bestowal of the "red hat" or cardinalate on the Archbishop of Los Angeles was as unprecedented as it was unexpected. Manning's reaction to that singular distinction took the form of a release dated December 2, 1952.

> When two celestial bodies coincide with our line of vision the heavens are illumined with a new brightness. Something of this kind has occurred in the designation of the Metropolitan of Los Angeles in the person of Archbishop McIntyre to the Sacred College of Cardinals. Of himself, our archbishop had the ingredients of greatness. They would have come full round in any walk of life he entered. The City and See of Los Angeles, too, had itself the stuff of princeliness among its American contemporaries. We like to think that what Los Angeles needed to crown its glory was the person of Archbishop McIntyre, and what the archbishop yet required was the scope and the challenge of Los Angeles to cap his native genius with red for his crowning. We are jealous of his new honors and will boast that they must spill over onto all the children of his jurisdiction and the citizens of our community like red sunset tinting our hills and valleys.[11]

In January of the following year, in an address to the Newman Club of Los Angeles, Manning noted that the "cardinal was fashioned from his youth for honor. Nature gifted him with a noble mind and heart and a physical bearing that would be princely beneath Rome's Purple. Providence has mated him to a great archdiocese of destiny. The man, and the hour and the place articulate glory." He went on to say:

> In adolescence and early manhood, at the century's beginning, his young world was no wider than Manhattan. The air

Fathers James Hourihan, Bernard Gannon and Bishop Manning as they departed from Cobh to Rome for the 1950 Holy Year.

Bishop Manning's preaching at Saint Patrick's Cathedral in New York.

Bishop Manning's greets General Douglas MacArthur.

> of early New York was clean then, its climate fair for the making of men. It was the composite of all the things men loved and lived by. It was the New York he knew and passionately loved and would have never left behind. Only the vision of a fairer town would elicit him away from the counting houses of men. Once in the long ago another man would likewise leave his tables of exchange in some nameless town of Galilee and never again look back.[12]

Cardinal McIntyre was pastoral minded long before that characteristic was included by the Holy See as a requirement for episcopal candidates. He was anxious that his auxiliary bishops serve as active pastors of busy parishes. Feeling that no bishop could know or understand the real world without regularly hearing confessions, McIntyre himself spent many hours in the "confessional" every month, often at Cathedral Chapel parish or Our Lady's Chapel in downtown Los Angeles.

On several occasions during the early years of the McIntyre regime, Manning was offered a pastoral assignment, but each time circumstances militated against his acceptance. Finally, with the demise of Msgr. Victor Follen, one of the archdiocesan patriarchs on September 20, 1953, Manning was named pastor of Saint Gregory's, a parish four miles from central Los Angeles, just adjacent to the archiepiscopal residence in Fremont Place.

Canonically erected in 1923, Saint Gregory's was one of the square mile enclaves established by Cantwell in the Wilshire District. Temporary facilities were utilized until a temporary church could be erected at 907 South Norton Avenue. A school was opened in 1925 under the direction of the Sisters of the Holy Names. The permanent church was dedicated in 1938. By the time of Manning's arrival, he found a community of loving and giving Catholic people worshipping together and educating their children in the modest but attractive environment of their "parochial plant."[13]

Though Manning initially found the challenge of adjusting to parochial life somewhat difficult, he managed with tact and sensitivity to ingratiate himself into the atmosphere of a very typical parish. Though ably assisted by a series of administrators, Manning was anything but an absentee pastor.[14] He officiated at baptisms, weddings and funerals, took a regular turn in the confessional, joined in social gatherings, visited the school and engaged in all the other tasks associated with the parochial ministry. He found the parish a refreshing place after a long day at the chancery.

In February, 1954, Manning organized the Legion of Mary and he made it a point to be present at their weekly meetings, supervising personally their work of visiting the ill and shut-ins, making hospital visitations, taking parish census, teaching CCD and promoting the Enthronement of the Sacred Heart. He also inaugurated a Junior Legion of teenage boys which met on Sunday mornings after the 9:30 Mass. He later observed that "the biggest indication of the generosity of youth is the Boys' Legion of Mary I've had in my fourteen years at Saint Gregory's. They're heroes. They go to communion every Sunday. Each one puts in four hours a week of personal sacrifices."[15]

There were numerous physical additions introduced at Saint Gregory's during Manning's tenure, including a new rectory, convent and school addition. The bishop was especially proud of the new bell which he had cast by John Taylor and Company of Loughborough, England. Manning enjoyed parish life. In the commodious new rectory, with its common room leading to the living quarters, he and the other priests gathered every evening for night prayer. Weekly meetings were held with curates and lay leaders in the parish which was also served by a highly efficient guild system.

Looking back on his fourteen years at Saint Gregory's, Manning could validate McIntyre's insistence that he take a parish. He wrote that "being a parish priest is the perfect school for the pastoral office of bishop, better than any degrees, administrative experience or higher education. It gives him an understanding of all the problems of priests and people, their lives, their trials, their patterns of communication and, above all, it gives him a degree of knowledge which is one characteristic Our Lord gave for the true apostle: 'I know mine and mine know me.' "[16]

With the transferral of Bishop McGucken to Sacramento in 1955, Manning's role in the archdiocese was expanded with his appointment as Vicar General on November 29.[17] Manning was now the second ranking official in the archdiocese and, in that capacity, he shared canonical jurisdiction with the cardinal.

Among the most memorable incidents that befell the Church in Southern California during those years was a tragic bus accident on September 30, 1957 in which three youngsters from All Saints parochial school in El Sereno were killed. The homily preached at the funeral Mass was "vintage" Manning, insofar as it touched all the bases of human suffering. He began by saying that "we who are of the household of the faith must, on certain occasions, make profession of that faith for it is the substance of the things we hope for and the evidence of the things we see not:"

Auxiliary Bishop Timothy Manning in his curial office.

Bishop Manning served for several years as a member of The Los Angeles City Library Commision.

Auxiliary Bishop Manning served as Pastor of Saint Gregory's Parish from 1953 to 1967.

Coadjutor Archbishop Manning served as Pastor at Saint Brendan Parish in 1969-1970.

> Here we stand on the edge of a chasm of sorrow and tragedy. To human eyes and to the mind of the world there is no comfort or consolation. Our faith gives us a bridge to carry us safely over that grief and to understand the mystery of God's way with us.
>
> Only the stark tragedy of it can send a shudder of reality through the veins of our community. We will not enter within that closed cloister of grief which is the sanctity of the families who mourn their passing. It is too sacred a ground for us to venture into and it has already been violated by a sensational loving public.
>
> At this moment more truly than at any other passing from death to life can we truly say – May the choirs of angels and the martyred innocents meet them at their coming and take them to the altar of the Lamb where there is no longer mourning or crying, but only a new name and a holy song upon their lips, and the brief waiting until we come to be one with them again in the family and home of our Heavenly Father.[18]

For some time, Cardinal McIntyre had sensed a lack of conformity between his views on liturgy and those of his auxiliary bishop. For his part, Manning had always been open to and supportive of the new liturgical awareness that was sweeping the United States in the mid 1950s. As early as 1958, the cardinal mentioned what he considered to be this "disharmony" suggesting that the Apostolic Delegate might wish to intervene. As sympathetic as he may have been, Archbishop Cicognani wrote to say that "Your Eminence will understand that I myself cannot write to advise the auxiliary bishop for the conclusion might be that he should be given another post - and this does not depend on me."[19]

In the meantime, preparations were underway for celebrating Manning's silver jubilee of priestly ordination at Saint Vibiana's Cathedral on June 15, 1959, a celebration that proved to be a bittersweet experience for Manning, possibly the most troublesome in his life. The celebration itself went quite well. "In an unspoken manifestation of the unity of the priesthood, nearly every priest of the archdiocese was present" for the event. The cardinal presided and there were great numbers of Sisters and lay persons who had come to know the bishop over the years.

Msgr. Martin McNicholas, who had preached at Manning's first Mass a quarter century earlier, again stepped into the pulpit for a memorable address. After pointing our that "honors, dignities and titles are his in goodly numbers," the homilist did not want to use the occasion for listing accomplishments. Instead he said that:

> Learning, leadership and accomplishment are qualities we priests rightly expect in a bishop, but our devotion and love and loyalty, our praise and commendation are begotten only by his priestliness, his comradeship, his sympathy and his oneness with us. The greatest title any man can aspire to, the greatest blessing any man can attain to, the greatest commendation he can receive from God, is to be a good priest. 'You shall be holy unto Me because I the Lord am holy' is a command, not an exhortation or a wish."[20]

What appeared outwardly as a lovely celebration and a fitting tribute was anything but that for McIntyre who took offense at the manner in which the chants were directed from the pulpit. He interpreted that as a radical and unauthorized departure from the normal procedure of having the choir in the loft, apart from the congregation. The cardinal drafted a pencilled letter to the jubilarian, who was already on his way for a visit to Ireland.

> I must confess that I was startled this morning when I observed the complete organization of the sisters and priests of the archdiocese and which was expressly at your insistence. Even admitting a possible validity of interpretation of the recent instructions that might have put the circumstances under the guise of a seminary or monastery, the procedure was undoubtedly an innovation and the ordinary should have been consulted when such was planned and executed. Further, his presence gave an approval which he has made clear was not his intention. Thus it was a deliberately planned defiance of the will of the ordinary.[21]

Further, McIntyre had learned "from some of the participants" that Manning was fully aware that he would not approve of the actions. Hence he was faced with the specter of his Vicar General acting in defiance of his policies. He told Manning that if he could not find it within his convictions "to desist from your promotion of a schism in the archdiocese, I shall be forced to ask your resignation as Vicar General." He said that already it was "a scandal amongst the clergy and I am

Bishop Manning leads procession into Saint Vibiana's Cathedral for the funeral of Archbishop John J. Cantwell.

Bishop Timothy Manning incenses the newly-returned coffin bearing the restos of the Right Reverend Francis Mora, one-time Bishop of Monterey-Los Angeles.

Bishop Manning rides the final miles with Archbishop McIntyre to Los Angeles in 1948.

Francis Cardinal Spellman visited Los Angeles many times during his years as Military Vicar for the Armed Forces.

convinced immediate action is necessary."[22] At the conclusion of his hand-written draft, McIntyre appended the observation that "It pains me very much to pen this letter but there has been created a circumstance that demands positive and definite action." The next day, McIntyre wrote a second letter:

> For some time I have observed a non conformity and sometimes opposition to the principles and policy that I have followed since coming to Los Angeles. I have been reluctant and unwilling to accept that attitude as deliberate. However, after witnessing yesterday the highly organized and defiant exhibition with a complete absence of conference, I can only assume that you have been willing to take the responsibility of the ensuing scandal to the clergy and religious.
>
> Frankly, I am not willing that this scandal perdure. When non conformity exists between the cardinal and his Vicar General, the people suffer. I am willing to be a patient sufferer but am unwilling that the good of the people suffer. You have seen fit to force the issue and the decision is now yours. I shall expect your answer in ten days. Asking the Lord to guide your common sense, I am...[23]

It is not clear whether McIntyre sent both letters to Manning or just a single one. But the message was clear enough: he was peeved at what he interpreted as a departure from what he expected of his Vicar General. During his address to the priests gathered the following week for their annual retreat at Saint John's Seminary, the cardinal went public with his displeasure, making it quite clear that he alone was the policy maker for the archdiocese.

Manning, who left for Ireland shortly after the celebration, did not receive McIntyre's letter or the several cables sent by sympathetic priests for several days. Devastated, he wrote immediately to the cardinal:

> This is in reply to your letter handed to me this morning. The reproaches hurt deeply. I hope that the silent bearing of them will be some reparation for all my faults. With all my heart, I apologize for all the distress I have caused you.
>
> If it pleases you to accept it, I am herewith tendering my resignation from the office of Vicar General and its related responsibilities. I will abide by your further instruction. Please be assured of my prayers always.[24]

Interestingly, Manning did not deny the allegations nor try to explain them. Clearly he had not realized that his actions and those of others would unleash such a firestorm.

McIntyre responded that it wasn't his wish to accept the resignation, though he did admit that "I am equally hurt by the entire incident." He felt the "circumstances were of grave import" and demanded that he speak out. With that exchange of letters, McIntyre was satisfied and considered the matter closed. Unquestionably, McIntyre had overreacted to a presumed challenge to his authority. By the time that Manning returned to Los Angeles, the cardinal had put aside the incident and never again mentioned it. Sensitive man that he was, Manning brooded over the incident for years and was never able to put it totally out of his mind.

VATICAN COUNCIL II

The role and function of non-residential bishops at ecumenical councils is ambiguous at best. Since they are not shepherds of a flock in the fullest sense, they have a lesser role to fulfill in the college of bishops. Until fairly recent times, there were relatively few auxiliary bishops even in the United States and it was only in the 1960s that their number began proliferating.

At the opening of Vatican Council II, on October 11, 1962, Timothy Manning was among the senior auxiliary bishops in all the world, having served in that capacity for some sixteen years. Cardinal McIntyre invited Manning to accompany him to the inaugural session of the council, but made it clear that he was expected to return home shortly thereafter. McIntyre wanted an episcopal "presence" in Los Angeles at all times and he reasoned that allowing his auxiliary bishop to tarry in Rome would be productive to neither the Church at large nor the Archdiocese of Los Angeles in particular. Though he never voiced his personal views to the cardinal, Manning was clearly disappointed at not being able to remain in Rome. When later asked what he would have done differently in his life, he responded that "I would have attended all the sessions (of the Vatican Council) and every one of its explanatory classes."[25]

While he was among those who felt that the conciliar gatherings should have devoted more of their deliberations to the role of Mary in the Church, Manning went out of his way to note that "there should be no cause for anxiety among our people that the position or prerogatives of Our Lady are in any way being minimized." As to whether to include the discussions on the theology of Mary with the schema on the Church or to reserve that for separate treatment in a treatise of its own, he

Cardinal McIntyre, Bishop Manning, Msgrs. John Rawden and Lawrence Gibson and Sir Daniel Donohue greet Pope John XXIII.

Fathers Lawrence Donnelly and Patrick Languille look on as the Bishop Manning greets contest winner in the Holy Childhood Campaign.

Msgrs. Patrick Dignan and Fidencio Esparza escort Bishop Manning in the procession for Mary's Hour in the Los Angeles Memorial Coliseum.

quoted Peter Gregory Cardinal Agagianian that "no vote on either side can be construed as constituting any lessening of the dignity of the Blessed Virgin or any diminution of her preeminent role in the Church." Manning went on to say that:

> The schema or treatise on the nature of the Church is a formulation in human terms of a great mystery. The Church is portrayed as God's family, founded on the Apostles, fed by His Body and His holy Word, reaching for forgiveness, charity and holiness through humility and suffering. Seeing the Church through this image of a family, it is natural that God would provide a mother for it. Viewed in this context, the council Fathers who voted this decision considered it as appropriate to include the treatment of Mary as part of the schema or treatise dealing with the nature of the Church.
>
> His Mother, radiant with all the privileges and graces bestowed upon her by Him, is now held before the world as the mother of His family, the almoner of His mercy, the sanctuary of our sighs, our mother, our life our sweetness and our hope. Certainly, any interpretation of the council's action which would tend to cast a shadow on the luminous love and honor with which we venerate her would be a distortion of Catholic truth.[26]

Though he attended only a few of its sessions, Manning was greatly influenced by the teachings of the council, as well as by the tone and spirit of its pronouncements. That he studied and carefully digested the conciliar teachings is evident in all his post Vatican II writings, talks and actions. An acquaintance in Rome provided Manning with copies of the various conciliar documents as they progressed from one draft to another. His letters and conversations during those three years abound in references to the deliberations being conducted half a world away in the Eternal City. He told a friend that Vatican Council II provided a welcome and unique opportunity of returning to his studies of earlier years at Menlo Park.

Cardinal McIntyre asked Manning to represent him at the closing of the council in December of 1965. A document by Manning among papers at the Archival Center states:

> For the official record of the archives, I wish to record that, on the occasion of my attending the concluding sessions of the Second Vatican Council, December 7 and December 8,

Auxiliary Bishop Manning enters the chambers of Vatican Council II.

Bishop Timothy Manning, extreme left in sixth row, attends final public plenary session of Vatican Council II in St. Peter's Basilica. At left Council official reads one of the documents terminating the session.

I likewise acted in the capacity of procurator for His Eminence, James Francis Cardinal McIntyre, Archbishop of Los Angeles. His absence was dictated by a recuperation from surgery.

His Eminence had previously written to the Secretary of State, His Eminence, Cardinal Cicognani, advising him of my coming. I was received in audience by Cardinal Cicognani at 1:30 p.m., December 6. He, in turn, advised the office of the Secretary General of the council, Archbishop Felici. The archbishop's office telephoned me at the hotel advising me how to proceed in this matter. On the day of the final balloting, I cast he votes in my own name, and signed the single document as procurator for His Eminence.[27]

At the suggestion of Msgr. Patrick Roche, Manning wrote a personal memoir of the council for the readers of *The Tidings*.

It was my privilege to have been present at the opening of the Vatican Council on October 11, 1962, and again at its closing December 8, 1965. Between these two events, as between the pillars of Hercules which guard the passage of the Mediterranean waters at Gibraltar into the Atlantic ocean, the Church passed out of this Mediterranean cradle and into the ocean sea.

Until now she has been Mediterranean in the sense that she was in the middle of the world but, with the changing of the center, of necessity she too must find her pivotal place in the modern world. She steps from the shelter of European things into the heart of the world of today. Like the householder of the gospel, she brings from her treasures new things and old, the restatement of the ancient truths and the message for modern mankind, its intellectuals and artists, its rich and poor, its distaff and its young.

Three years ago she was venerable with age; today she walks rejuvenated as a queen. Perhaps the single byproduct of the sessions of the Vatican Council which meant most to its participants was the discovery of the fraternity that binds the bishops of the world. We did not always know one another's names, but we had affinity with those who sat with us, those who were across the aula from us, those we met

Bishop Manning and members of the Los Angeles curia bid adieu to Cardinal McIntyre on his trip to become a member of the Sacred College of Cardinals.

Bishop Manning and Msgr. Anthony Brouwers return home from their first airflight to Europe in 1952.

> in the coffee shops, on the streets, and in the diversified meetings that were held here and there throughout the Holy City.
>
> Surely it was this fraternity that was immortalized in the inspiration of the Holy Father to give to each of us the gold ring that was to become, in his words, the bond of charity that linked us all together, and together with our common Father. It is not likely to occur again in our lifetime, but it has made this interval of our pilgrimage something for which there is no definition or description this side of our uniting in heaven.
>
> Somewhere in the footnotes to this council will be mentioned that extraordinary shaft of sunlight that came wayward from an uncovered window in the transept of St. Peter's and, at the moment of the consecration of the concelebrated Mass on December 7, rested directly on the Holy Father. It was not so much that he was bathed in it as that the altar table seemed on fire with it as reflected back upward in his face. Neither thunder and lightning nor such a shaft of sunlight are abnormal on the Roman December scenes, but to have sat there and witnessed the coincidence, conveyed a sensible communication of tranquility and radiance and joy descending over the assembled council. Rome and Istanbul embraced beneath the baldachin of Bernini. Emotion ran through the hearts of everyone as the Holy Father gave the embrace of peace to the representative of Archbishop Athenagoras of Istanbul.
>
> The Council concluded with the resounding *"Christus Vincit"* as if the very obelisk in the center of the square spoke the words that are inscribed at its base and that root the Church so deeply in the heart of Rome; the Church that embraced the world like the Bernini colonnades, and that yet, like the obelisk, pointed ever heavenward. And so it ended with the universal shout: "That Tiber trembled underneath her banks – to hear the replication of our sounds made in her concave shores–"[28]

Whenever Cardinal McIntyre was absent from Los Angeles, Manning was in charge. Often he acted in the name of the cardinal, as happened when President John F. Kennedy was assassinated in 1963. Manning

Cardinal McIntyre and his Auxiliary Bishop with Pope Paul VI.

Msgr. James Hourihan and companion examine Greek ruins.

offered a memorial Mass at Saint Vibiana's Cathedral after which he issued a statement which was circulated nationally by the press:

> A lamentation springs from every heart all over the world with the assassination of President Kennedy. His death has been a holocaust in the exalted service of his nation. May the mercy of the great God preserve us all in this sad hour and give full measure of comfort to the family which is weighted with this burden of awful sorrow.
>
> We call upon our people to attend the requiem Masses which shall be offered in every parish for the eternal repose of his noble soul, according to the schedule which each pastor will arrange and announce to his people.[29]

The Manning imprint was evident in many areas of the archdiocese over those years. It was he who laid out the floor plans for the Chancery Office and it was he who designed the modern brick education building across the street from the chancery. He had a hand, one way or another, in the construction of hundreds of other facilities throughout the four county jurisdiction.

Manning continued some existing customs and inaugurated other new ones as he moved around the archdiocese. Among his favorite visitations was the one he and seminarians made each December 27 to Saint Ann's Home for the Aged on East First Street. That tradition, begun by Archbishop Cantwell on his name day, entailed greeting the patients, distributing gifts, administering Confirmation and presiding at a buffet hosted by the Little Sisters of the Poor. His last visit in 1966 marked the twenty-ninth time he had been there.[30]

He also went on the Feast of the Holy Innocents to celebrate Mass for the novices of the Sisters of Saint Joseph of Carondelet at Mount Saint Mary's College. On the feast of Saint John Bosco, Manning travelled to east Los Angeles to offer Mass for the 1,100 boys at Bishop Mora Salesian High School. At least once a year, he would confirm and visit with gifted children whom he considered as "one of the unmeasured blessings that had come my way. I count it as the tenderest experience of any I have ever had in the archdiocese. They're assured saints, assured of eternal beatitude."[31]

During his twenty-one years as auxiliary bishop, Manning participated in many civic projects, including serving as a member of the Los Angeles City Library Commission and *El Pueblo de los Angeles* State Park Commission. One of his long-standing positions was that of chairing of the annual procession honoring Our Lady of Guadalupe. At different times he was president of the archdiocesan Building Commission, archdiocesan consulter and member of the Seminary Committee.

Timothy Manning served the Lord for over two decades as an auxiliary bishop. He fulfilled that role with effectiveness and dignity. Now it was time to move on.

Bishop Manning and Father Anthony Brouwers welcome visitors to the new Chancery Office facilities at 1531 West Ninth Street.

In this photograph are almost all the living California bishops at the time - viz., John J. Ward, Leo T. Maher, Hugh Donohue, Francis Furey, Joseph T. McGucken, Merlin Guilfoyle, Timothy Manning, Floyd Begin and Aloysius Willinger at Fremont Place, the home of James Francis Cardinal McIntyre.

Notes to the Text

1. *The Tidings*, November 7, 1947.
2. AALA, J. Francis A. McIntyre to Timothy Manning, New York, February 16, 1948.
3. Francis J. Weber (comp.) *Days of Change, Years of Challenge* (Los Angeles, 1987) pp. 28-30.
4. *The Tidings*, October 27, 1950.
5. *Ibid.*, February 16, 1951.
6. Hollywood *Citizen News*, February 12, 1951.
7. *The Tidings*, October 26, 1951.
8. *Ibid.*, May 30, 1952.
9. *Ibid.*, January 18, 1952.
10. *Ibid.*, February 6, 1953.
11. Francis J. Weber (comp.), *Days of Change, Years of Challenge*, p. 64.
12. *Ibid.*, p. 66.
13. See John Freeman, *St. Gregory Nazianzen Parish Golden Jubilee* (Los Angeles, 1973).
14. *V.g.* Fathers Michael Collins, Melville Young and Patrick Reilly.
15. *The Tidings*, December 15, 1967.
16. *Ibid.*
17. *Ibid.*, December 2, 1955.
18. *Ibid.*, October 4, 1957.
19. AALA, Amleto Giovanni Cicognani to James Francis Cardinal McIntyre, Washington, D.C., March 10, 1958.
20. *The Tidings*, June 19, 1959.
21. AALA, James Francis Cardinal McIntyre to Timothy Manning, Los Angeles, June 15, 1959.
22. *Ibid.*

23. AALA, James Francis Cardinal McIntyre to Timothy Manning, Los Angeles, June 16, 1959.
24. AALA, Timothy Manning to James Francis Cardinal McIntyre, Ballingeary, June 18, 1959.
25. AALA, Biographical Interview with Timothy Cardinal Manning, Los Angeles, (August 24, 1981).
26. *The Tidings*, November 1, 1963.
27. AALA, Statement of Timothy Manning, Los Angeles, December 16, 1965.
28. *The Tidings*, December 17, 1965.
29. *Ibid.,* November 29, 1963.
30. *Ibid.,* December 30, 1966.
31. *Ibid.,* December 15, 1967.

5. *Bishop of Fresno*

On October 25, 1967, Archbishop Luigi Raimondi, the Apostolic Delegate, announced that, with the retirement of Bishop Aloysius J. Willinger, the Diocese of Monterey-Fresno had been divided into two separate jurisdictions. Thereafter, the area comprising the newly re-aligned Diocese of Fresno would embrace an area of 35,239 square miles in Fresno, Inyo, Kern, Kings, Madera, Merced, Maricopa and Tulare counties. Statistically there would be seventy-six parishes, forty-five mission churches, twenty-one stational chapels, 161 priests, 330 sisters, sixty-six seminarians, four Catholic hospitals for a Catholic population of 297,979 souls.[1] At the same time, Raimondi informed the press that Pope Paul VI had appointed Timothy Manning to be the residential bishop of Fresno.[2] From Los Angeles, Manning committed himself "to the charity of the prayers of all those who hold me in their hearts." He acknowledged that it would "be no small matter to leave Los Angeles" where he had worked for the first thirty-three years of his ministry. He spoke of parting as a "death rehearsal," noting that "the affection of priests and people here, especially my parishioners at Saint Gregory's, is rooted around my heart."[3]

In his statement, James Francis Cardinal McIntyre said that "our grief of loss experienced in the cessation of the long years of exemplary service to the Archdiocese of Los Angeles by Bishop Manning is only exceeded by the joy we experience in the prospect of his taking on a responsibility of greater magnitude and accepting a larger scope for his highly cultivated qualities." McIntyre spoke of Manning as still being "in the prime of intellectual dynamism and strong in physical stature. We may look to his leadership in broader fields with expected joy and anticipation as he will foster and cultivate a greater realization of God's presence amongst us and amplify the growth of God's friendship within us. We are assured that the bountiful blessings of Our Lady, the Mother of God, will ever prevail over him as he will minister to a glorious people of God in our neighboring diocese."[4]

The sentiments voiced by McIntyre were echoed by others, both in Los Angeles and Fresno. Msgr. Patrick Roche, editor of *The Tidings*, wrote one of his classical editorials in which he spoke for the Catholic populace of Southern California in expressing both joy and sorrow:

> This week's announcement of Bishop Manning's appointment to the See of Fresno renews this pattern in the lives of all of those who have known him and have come to revere and love him with the passage of years. And these are many. Though this is his adopted city, he has long since made it his own. In the broad and varied scope of his experience as priest and prelate among us, Bishop Manning has left the impress of his character upon this archdiocese, its people and its institutions. We part with him reluctantly and somewhat selfishly.
>
> There is no plot of earth in these four counties which has not felt the tread of his feet, no parish, school or hospital which has not felt the guiding genius of his hand. It can be safely estimated that a half-million of our people have been signed with chrism by his fingers in the Sacrament of Confirmation, as he raised them to the dignity and strength of mature Christian life. And there are the countless thousands of others who have been lifted to new insights in their faith through the persuasive eloquence of his tongue.
>
> These are the reasons why this parting is a sad one. Yet the sorrow is solaced by the knowledge that the separation is no distant one. The dioceses of our state are bound together by the heritage of their missionary origins. We are a common stock, and the blood of our spiritual ancestors warms our veins and gives sinew to our allegiance and friendship. The Diocese of Fresno is sister to our own; a few years ago we were as one. The appointment of Bishop Manning continues a precious family relationship, and in that is all the Church enriched. In the fertile heartland of our state, a spiritual harvest awaits him, and we rejoice that he has been chosen as its husbandman.[5]

On November 11, the priests of the archdiocese tendered a farewell luncheon for Manning. On that occasion, the bishop described the course of a priest's life as a series of deaths and resurrections. And although today "there is a rending asunder of the roots of my heart," he said, "there is the new birth of my life in the Diocese of Fresno." Manning expressed his appreciation of the years he had spent under the guidance of the late Archbishop Cantwell and Cardinal McIntyre, thanking the cardinal for "the example of his total dedication to the Church and the people of Los Angeles." In closing his brief remarks, he exhorted his brother priests to preserve their spirit of unity. That spirit, he said, "has been achieved and purchased at the cost of sacrifice, and sometimes heartache and pain, but it is the most precious thing we possess."[6]

Later that week Manning was feted by several civic bodies. His service on the *El Pueblo de Los Angeles* State Historical Monument Commission was featured in an illuminated resolution presented to him by the commission at a luncheon hosted by Hernando Courtright. The Los Angeles City Council and Mayor Sam Yorty also presented him with resolutions of gratitude for his contributions to many civic enterprises and for his sixteen years of service as a member of the Library Commission.

In an interview for *The Tidings*, Manning reflected on the episcopal office, enumerating three qualities for a bishop:

> First, I think that the bishop is totally expendable for his people. Secondly, there is a bond of unity between bishop and priests, which the Vatican Council calls presbyterium. The bishop is localized to the people by every priest. Third, there must be absolutely patent sincerity in bishop and priest if they are to serve the people of God, for the cry now is against all forms of shallowness and masquerade.

Ultimately, in any age, he said, the inner qualities of a bishop must reside in a profound holiness and faith. What would a bishop expect of his people?

The response to a bishop from his people would come from the creation of a local community through which all the great challenges of Christianity would be accomplished: 1-praise of God; 2-association with one another; 3-dialogue with non-Catholics. This is where the secret strength of the Church lies. A rural diocese has a great opportunity for the flowering of such a community.[7]

December 15, a clear, wintry day, full of the crisp reality of life in Central California, was a perfect setting for the installation of a new shepherd for what was known as the "valley of grain and wine." The ceremony itself began at 4 o'clock. As the Mass continued, it grew dark and bitingly cold outside. Inside the sixty-four year old cathedral there was a warmth that came not from the crowd of 600 persons, but from

HIS EXCELLENCY

THE MOST REVEREND TIMOTHY MANNING, D.D., J.C.D.

REQUESTS THE HONOR OF YOUR PRESENCE

AT THE

CEREMONY OF HIS INSTALLATION

AS

BISHOP OF FRESNO

FRIDAY AFTERNOON, THE FIFTEENTH OF DECEMBER

ONE THOUSAND NINE HUNDRED AND SIXTY-SEVEN

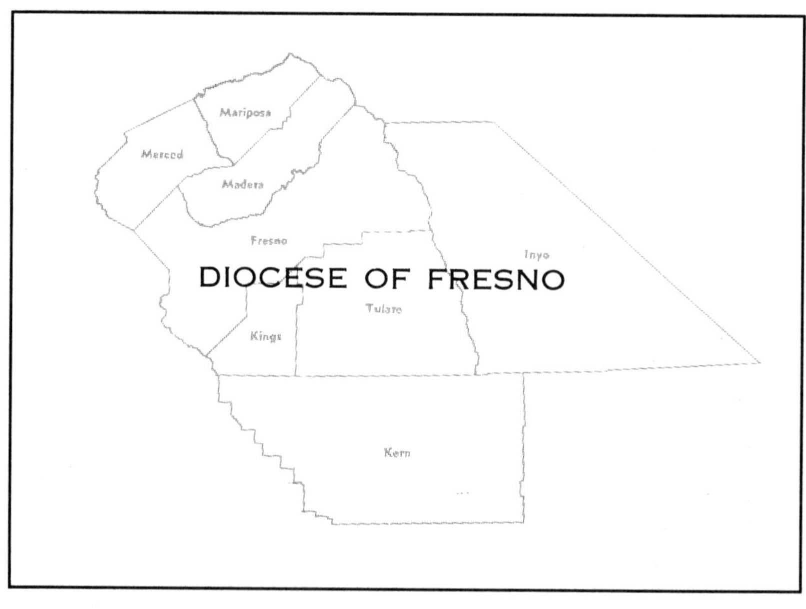

the strength of their responses to the prayers and the resonance of their full-hearted singing.

Concelebrating the Mass of installation were six Fresno priests representing various decades of age groups among the local clergy. Thirty four archbishops and bishops, several hundred priests and friends from Los Angeles had traveled over the snowy pass of the Tehachapis for the historic event.[8] Presiding was James Francis Cardinal McIntyre who had journeyed from Monterey where he was present for the inauguration of the newly-proclaimed Diocese of Monterey. The local newspaper described how "monsignors in their reddish-purple cassocks, priests in black and white, nuns in traditional 'long gowns' and veils or fashionable 'new look outfits' and a sprinkling of lay people joined in the hymns and prayers."[9]

After escorting Manning to his *cathedra* or episcopal seat, Archbishop Luigi Raimondi said that "The primacy of Peter is a gift to the Church because in him Our Lord wanted to establish the stone of unity and of firmness. The role of the Holy Father is to be the cornerstone of the visible Church and so to give firmness and unity to the construction. He continued:

> A bishop comes to you conscious of his responsibility to the Christian community. He knows he is the servant of all. He knows that he will have to render an account of his work for souls. Bishop Manning stands before you with the grace of the Holy Spirit he has received in its fullness. He has received an immense divine treasure and has the corresponding duty to share this treasure with all. He will live now more fully than ever to serve you, to exercise the ministry of Jesus Christ among you.[10]

Manning's homily was a moving act of allegiance to the Diocese of Fresno:

> As a lover to his bride, I now vow my life, my talents and my honor, to the service of this diocese. For it shall I spend myself, and be spent. Its joys and hopes, its griefs and anxieties, shall be my very own. Its people shall be my people, and its God shall be my God.
>
> By mandate the best part of my heart must be consecrated to its priests and seminarians. They are set apart for the Gospel of God and are forbidden to be conformed to the

> world. Together with their bishop they share in the one and same priesthood. Together shall they assemble the people of God into a sacrifice, living, holy and pleasing to God until the Lord returns. As brothers and friends we shall exchange mutual help and counsel, and share in charity and obedience.
>
> We recognize among us especially, and we pledge our service to that wonderful variety of religious life in which the members imitate Christ, the virgin and the poor man, and who follow Him in obedience for the enrichment of the Church. They are at the service of the Church and we shall strive together with them toward that holiness and service for which we are anointed and consecrated.
>
> The laity, by their very vocation, shall seek to build up the Church, to sanctify the world and give it life in Christ. They shall seek the kingdom of God by ordering all temporal affairs according to the plan of God. As individuals, all lay people are obliged to engage in this apostolate. They must reach men and contribute to the salvation of the world by public worship, by penance and the voluntary acceptance of the hardships of life.[11]

At Manning's behest, there was much about the day that was historic. In a poignant reminder of the apostolic continuity represented by the hierarchy, he wore the episcopal ring used fifty years earlier by John J. Cantwell when he was installed as Bishop of Monterey-Los Angeles. Manning had received the ring from Cantwell at his own consecration in 1946.

In an article appearing in the *Central California Register*, one writer reflected further on Manning's mentor and how the "unmistakable figure of that tall, erect churchman could almost be seen lurking in the shadows during the ceremony."

> Though long since departed from the scenes of his earthly endeavors, the imprint of John Joseph Cantwell remains indelibly attached to the Church in Central California. It was he who brought about its juridical formation; it was he who governed it in the earliest years of its existence; it was he who proposed its initial Ordinary; it was he who guided it as part of his metropolitan province, and it was he who arranged for its administration in days of tribulation.

> That the hand of the southland prelate still influences the destinies of the Church in Central California can hardly be disputed, for the archbishop's long-time friend will soon arrive in Fresno, there to gather the harvest first sown by another Irish-born pioneer almost half a century ago.[12]

The Diocese of Fresno had been managed well during the stewardship of Bishop Aloysius Willinger. Even with the dismemberment of the Monterey jurisdiction, the physical assets were sound if not abundant. A delegation had approached Manning before his arrival, suggesting that the management of the curia desperately needed reorganization. There were complaints that the chancellor, Msgr. James Culleton, who had held that office for over thirty years, was unresponsive and totally out-of-touch with the post Vatican needs of the local Church.

After listening, consulting and praying over the matter, Manning came up with an ingenious way of solving the administrative logjam. He promoted the chancellor to the position of Vicar General and named an energetic and talented young priest, Father Denis J. Doherty, as chancellor. At the same time, Manning entrusted the day-to-day operation of the diocese to Doherty, while restricting the duties of Vicar General to mostly perfunctory activities. In that gentle manner, Manning rewarded but defanged Culleton and opened up a direct channel of communication with his priests. It was a win-win solution to a difficult problem. Later he requested the title of Protonotary Apostolic for Culleton.

Inasmuch as the retired bishop had decided to remain in his residence, Manning acquired a modest home at 1113 West Celeste Avenue where he was able to live comfortably. While occupying his predecessor's office in the chancery on North Fresno Street, Manning began an ambitious visitation program whereby he would visit every parish in the far-flung, eight county diocese at least once a year. Within a few weeks, he was calling all the priests by their given name. Manning's onc verbalized complaint was that the Holy See had not left a single one of the California missions in his jurisdiction. He once proposed to the Bishop of Monterey, Harry Clinch, that Fresno be given "a window to the sea that would contain at least one of Serra's missionary foundations." Had he remained in Fresno, he probably would have pursued that request.

Each week, Manning visited retired Bishop Willinger, seeking his advice and counsel. Always charming and open to suggestion, Manning was known for being approachable by the priests and he made it clear that his availability was to have no restrictions. Each priest carried the bishop's personal phone number in his wallet. Most of the clergy and laity appeared to like Manning, even though he didn't remain long enough to inaugurate any significant changes other than cosmetic ones.

In the first of his major appearances, Manning exhorted thousands of children and young people "to give to the Church the heroism, nobility and sacrifice it needs at this time." He also warned them "not to be deluded by some in the Church who minimize the idea of sacrifice and are making concessions to the comforts of the world." Manning reminded the children that the name of Abraham occurs in the Canon of the Mass and in the *Magnificat*:

> He is called a father of faith and in this Year of Faith he is a great model for us. The reason is this: he was called by God to leave home and family, go into a strange land and wait for the fulfillment of a promise. This, to this day, is the missionary's formula – to leave home and family and go into a strange land to wait for God's word to be fulfilled.

The bishop told how "this was exemplified in California itself by the journey of a young man, Junípero Serra, of Mallorca who left home and family to bring the faith to this land."[13]

The bishop's Christmas message to the people of Fresno was issued in Mid-December:

> For the first time the new shepherd of the Church in Fresno summons his people to the crib of Bethlehem. The things that have come to pass are for our mercy and for our peace. Let us proclaim once more the tenet of our ancient faith. Jesus is the Lord. We adore Him. He is the only way, the everlasting truth and the eternal life. We hope in Him. He has come within the dimensions of our human heart so that we can embrace and love Him.
>
> We will find Him in the midst of the congregation, in the text of the inspired Word, in the sick and poor and homeless and above all in the reception of the Eucharist. Only as we are humble shall we find Him. For a surety of our finding He will be with Mary His mother. May His peace descend upon us, into our hearts and homes and across the weary war-torn barricades which divide us from our brothers and sisters. May His special benedictions be with all of us in the wonderful Diocese of Fresno.[14]

Archbishop Luigi Raimondi, Apostolic Delegate, presents crozier to newly-installed Bishop of Fresno.

Bishop Aloysius Willinger, C.Ss.R., leads his successor to the cathedra or bishop's chair in Saint John's Cathedral.

Bishop of Fresno con-celebrates Mass with priests of his new diocese.

James Francis Cardinal McIntyre presides at the installation of the suffragan Bishop of Fresno.

Early in 1968, Manning prepared a series of commentaries on the pastoral letter on the Church which had been issued by the bishops of the United States. The commentaries, which were recommended as study guides at the parochial level, revealed Manning's acute pastoral grasp of the Church's role in the post Vatican era: He noted that "there is an urgency compelling the attention of all, especially her own children and demanding their involvement." Manning felt that compelled to express two "cautions" to his people:

> We must not demean the religious past of the Church. Certainly some oppressive patterns of the past have been eliminated or are in the process of being phased out. We must be in continuous relation with this past. We must admire its faithfulness to God and have the courage to do things that can be done better than in the past.
>
> The Church is always that of the present moment, served by the insights of theologians and the dedication of people of prayer. However, we must beware of those who invoke the label of the contemporary for the destructive criticisms and attitudes which diminish the Church and faith. They give prayer and the pursuit of holiness second place. Their attack on the so-called structure of the Church takes a primacy and the apt phrase or formula gets the publicity. We must not forget that we are dealing with the Church of the Living God and we approach its renewal in humility, patience and love.[15]

Manning always worked and related well with young people. That facility is obvious in an address which he gave at the 65th annual Convention of the National Catholic Educational Association held at San Francisco in April of 1968. Therein he pointed out that "the final voice and word of the council was reserved for and directed to youth." He said, "the Church, now adorned with the beginnings of new beauty, would turn toward the rising generation. To it would she transmit the treasury of her teaching, and to it would she entrust the great updating which would be her response to the modern world and its claims in the post-atomic age:

> From her rich treasure the Church selects four virtues to commend to the young, so that, in their enthusiasm, they would build a better world than their elders had. These

> virtues are generosity, purity, sincerity and respect. Each of them merits at another time a pause for deeper awareness to realize why they are so necessary and applicable within this context of change.
>
> It is the ultimate and central mission of the Church, through education, to put Christ at this center, and through Him and in Him to give cohesion and depth and meaning and beauty and dignity to the mystery of life, to answer the question each generation must of necessity ask.[16]

Throughout his ministry, Bishop Manning was faithful to the Magisterium of the Church. When Pope Paul VI issued his pastoral letter, *Humanae Vitae*, Manning summoned the faithful "to attend and consent" to the pontiff's pronouncement on birth control:

> The letter contains the traditional teaching of the Church. We must first pay tribute to the courage of His Holiness. For his alone was the decision after consultation with eminent authorities, both lay and clerical. Conscious of his unique position as supreme teacher, after hours of prayerful thought, he issued his decree. This authentic teaching of the Pope must, in the words of Vatican II's "Dogmatic Constitution of the Church, be acknowledged with reverence and the judgements sincerely adhered to."
>
> Our bearing with it is not easy for it is a hard saying. Yet it comes from him who has compassion on the multitudes. The Christian life is no easy one. We enter by a narrow and a lowly gate. We take up a cross that we might enter into life. The kingdom of heaven suffers violence.
>
> Priests will be united with their bishop, and bishops with the Holy Father in the strong defense of the Church's teaching on the control of the appetite through which life and love are dispensed, and by which the race is preserved. May God grant to our beloved faithful the wisdom to see the dignified truth and holiness of this position. May He give strength to accept and fulfill the discipline and the joys of love with no denial or diminishing of its purity. May those who voice dissent and contradiction be preserved from the odium of scandal, and may we all be attentive to the words of eternal love and life.[17]

The most critical challenge that faced Manning in Fresno was the "grape controversy" which had divided the growers of Central California from their workers. It was a problem which caused the bishop, ever a bridge-builder, many sleepless nights. In August 1968, Manning directed that a Mass in honor of Saint Joseph the Worker be celebrated in every parish on the following Labor Day. The intention of the Mass was to be "a return to agricultural peace and gratitude to God for an abundant harvest." Alluding to the Delano grower-worker dispute, the bishop emphasized the role of the church in reconciliation:

> Before God, we have tried to give an impartial statement of the teachings of the Church on the rights to organization, whether on the part of labor or management. Again and again, the bishops of California have urged the intervention of the civil authority for legislation or mediation in this anguished problem.
>
> To do less, or to remain silent, would be to forfeit the responsibility of teacher which is inherent in the mission of the Church. In fulfilling these duties there is a sharing in the misunderstandings and reprisals that have plagued all labor problems from the beginning. In God's name, let us meet at the altar and beg for the charity of reconciliation, remove all bitterness and as brothers, begin once more to cooperate, to forgive and understand.[18]

In March of 1969, Manning commended President Richard M. Nixon's decision to order a cabinet-level study of the nation's farm labor problems. In his letter to Nixon, the bishop said that "we in California have felt the bitter anguish of the grape strike in Delano, and have realized the necessity for national legislation to protect the rights of both farm workers and farmers."

> The National Conference of Catholic Bishops issued a statement of Farm Labor last November in which the bishops of the United States stressed the important need for national action to find just and lasting solutions to the complex labor problems in agriculture. This one dispute has created sharp divisions among the people of the San Joaquin Valley, an area so richly blessed by God. It is my prayer that your secretaries of Labor and Agriculture will make positive rec-

> ommendations that will aid in promoting justice, peace and harmony to the entire agriculture community.[19]

Late in June 1969, Manning hailed the offer of the growers in the Coachella Valley and Arvin areas of California to negotiate with the United Farm Workers Organization Committee, AFL-CIO. He issued a statement on the matter which said:

> This dispute has been accompanied by ever-increasing tensions and has created unspeakable anguish and division throughout the agricultural community. We are heartened to know that serious dialogue will now replace emotion-filled charges. It would be unwise and even incorrect to assess that one side is right or the other wrong. Better, let it be said that a moment always comes in a man's relationship with other men when reason and understanding must triumph over attitudes founded on emotions.
>
> Difficult hours and days lie ahead in which to reach a just and equitable solution. It would be folly to suggest that such a complex issue will give way to simple solutions. But the first step must inevitably be taken. I commend the leaders of the table grape growers in the Coachella Valley and in the Arvin area for their courage to respond to the farm workers' repeated calls for discussions. While we welcome such serious discussions, it is with renewed hope that we await national legislation which will protect and guarantee the collective bargaining rights of all farm workers, as well as afford protection for our farmers.[20]

In a resume of Manning's work among the growers and workers, Msgr. Roger Mahony said that "he shared the bitter anguish of those involved in the Delano farm labor dispute far more than human hearts are capable of revealing. He longed for justice and peace among our rich Valley's agricultural community. He studied the issues well, and was unmoved by emotional facets of the problem. His was a servanthood of justice and reconciliation. While he leaves before a final and lasting peace prevails, we are assured of his willingness to bear this burden with us and to pray that God will lead us all to a sure and peaceable solution."[21]

Manning was ever attentive to the natural beauty of his diocese. In December 1968, for example, he joined some 400 persons at the

General Grant Sequoia, the nation's Christmas Tree, asking them "to seek the same humility which the 267 feet high tree seems to manifest:"

> Today we are pilgrims at the foot of this historic tree. It ruled here in isolated splendor even when the tree flourished on Golgotha, It is a symbol of God's abiding love, giving growth and fruitfulness, newness and sap of life, enduring, eternal, clapping its leafy hands in joy for the coming of the Lord. May we learn humility here, may we rest in the shadow of the Divine Providence, may we hunger here for a sharing too in the new name, the hidden manna, and "the right to eat from the tree of life that stands in the garden of God." May this Christmas Tree of the Nation be mirrored in our hearts with memories of all the Christmases we have loved long ago, and may its fair fruit be peace – peace for our land, for our fellow-man, and for our restless hearts.[22]

There were strains of disappointment in Fresno when Manning returned to Los Angeles. But, overall, the people there recognized that Manning was moving to an expanded role of shepherdhood. In an editorial entitled "Farewell to the Archbishop, " the editor of the *Central California Register* said "at such a time as this we do not intend a continuous lament on the loss of our bishop and our friend. This because we will still be of concern to him inasmuch as we are part of the Metropolitan Province of Los Angeles – an ecclesiastical structure which one day he will govern and direct:"

> We know we speak for all our readers, and for all God-fearing people in the valley, when we express to Archbishop Manning prayerful best wishes for a most fruitful period of service to the Church in the City of the Angels. We hope Archbishop Manning will always consider Fresno as his second home. In wishing him farewell, we declare that we will always have a place set at the table . . . where he will always be welcome to break bread.[23]

Not to be overlooked was a tribute to Manning written by Msgr. Roger Mahony who would one day succeed Manning in Los Angeles:

> As our beloved Archbishop Timothy Manning answers God's call for fuller service in Southern California, his mem-

Bishop Manning greets his faithful of Fresno for the first time.

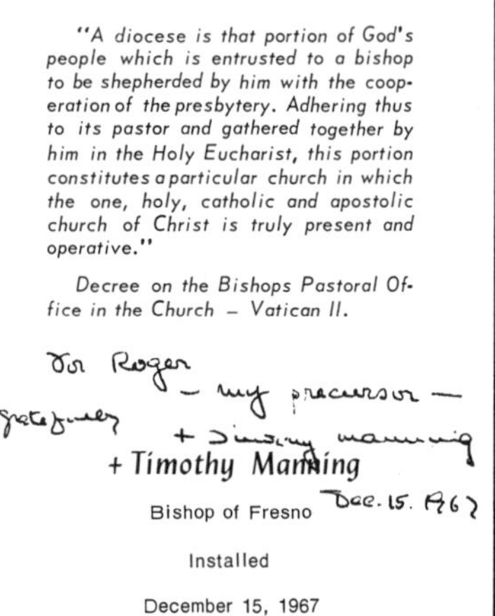

"A diocese is that portion of God's people which is entrusted to a bishop to be shepherded by him with the cooperation of the presbytery. Adhering thus to its pastor and gathered together by him in the Holy Eucharist, this portion constitutes a particular church in which the one, holy, catholic and apostolic church of Christ is truly present and operative."

Decree on the Bishops Pastoral Office in the Church — Vatican II.

For Roger — my precursor — gratefully + Timothy Manning

+ Timothy Manning

Bishop of Fresno Dec. 15. 1967

Installed

December 15, 1967

Memorial card signed by Bishop Manning to his friend, Msgr. Roger Mahony.

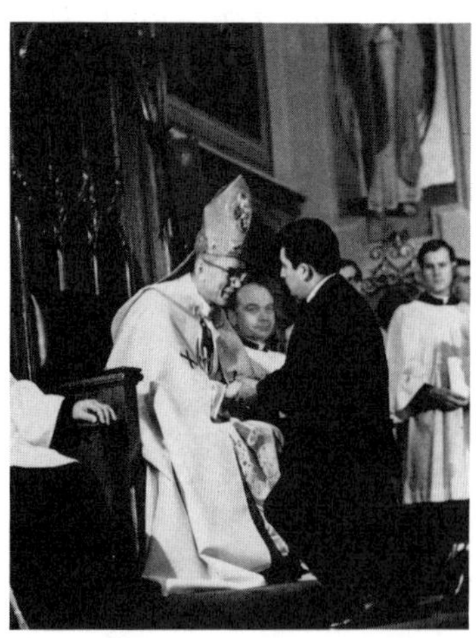

New Bishop of Fresno greets civic officials.

Saint John's Cathedral was crammed to overflowing, with many priests from Los Angeles in attendance.

Bishop Manning and Msgr. James Culleton who was named Vicar General.

Cesar Chavez signs grape strike agreement as Manning and other ecclesial figures observe. Shown in the upper left is Father Roger Mahony who played a key role in the settlement.

ory here will be indelibly emblazoned as a man – a bishop of compassion. Those of us who were privileged to serve with him in carrying out Christ's social mission in the Diocese of Fresno will long remember his attitude and example of compassion.

He approached the problems of our diocese's poor and distressed with an insight that brought him to share their sorrows, sufferings and disappointments personally. Archbishop Manning's deep compassion was revealed most singularly when he presided at the monthly meeting of the Diocesan Urban and Rural Task Force. These meetings sapped his heart's compassion, because although he saw how much was being done through the many diocesan offices, he was also aware of the many pressing human needs. His feeling for the people was sincere and without limit.

Through Archbishop Manning's urging and direction, the Diocesan Housing Committee was established to answer the desperate need for adequate housing for so many of our families. The walls of those new homes will reach skyward to serve as a witness to our bishop's concern and compassion.

Two special groups of young people captured the attention of Archbishop Manning's compassionate concern. Children and youth occupied a special place in his priestly heart, after the example of Christ in the Gospels. Teenage boys without a home of their own were offered the solace and guidance of San Felipe Boys Home in Bakersfield. Unwed mothers would now be assured of a home where understanding and acceptance of their special problems were evident. Villa Carmel surely meets the test of a compassionate atmosphere.

The rural, poor families of the San Joaquin Valley created an immediate challenge to Archbishop Manning. He was instrumental in bringing the Daughters of Charity into the Diocese to begin the Sisters' Rural Services Program. These apostles of St. Vincent de Paul walk the paths of the families with whom they are working and share their daily concerns with them. The Sisters have brought Christian hope to these families – a hope founded on the pleas of personal compassion.

Two special groups of laymen became endeared to him. The St. Vincent de Paul Societies and the Catholic Women's Sunshine Club captured a renewed dedication from the charitable compassionate heart of their Shepherd. While his

> departure is a painful loss, his memory rings loudly above any sound of despair.

Mahony concluded his remarks by noting that "only God knows the number of people he helped. Christ's counsel that unpublished charity is the finest charity prompted him to assist many people directly. Just recognition and reward await him in God's kingdom."[24]

In addition to establishing his own diocesan "task force" patterned after the National Urban Task Force, Manning erected four parishes and five missions in his eighteen months in Fresno. He also authorized formation of a priestly senate, the outlines of which would be utilized later in Los Angeles. Though Manning's Fresno interlude may not be remembered for its quantitative achievements, it was indeed a qualitative performance. While Central California provided Manning with many happy memories and associations, it hadn't as yet become his "home." He was later heard to say that the single happiest memory of his life was seeing the city-limits sign of Fresno in his rear vision mirror.

Notes to the Text

1. Los Angeles *Times*, October 26, 1967.
2. *Central California Register*, October 22, 1967.
3. *The Tidings*, October 27, 1967.
4. *Ibid.*
5. Ibid.
6. *Ibid.*, November 18, 1967.
7. Ibid., December 15, 1967.
8. Los Angeles *Times*, December 16, 1967.
9. Fresno *Bee*, December 16, 1967.
10. *Central California Register*, December 21, 1967.
11. *The Tidings*, December 22, 1967.
12. *Central California Register*, December 14, 1967.
13. *The Tidings*, November 3, 1967.
14. *Central California Register*, December 21, 1967.
15. Francis J. Weber, (Ed), *Times of Tension. Moments of Grace* (Los Angeles, 1990) p. 240.
16. See NCEA *Bulletin* for August, 1968.
17. *The Tidings*, August 30, 1968.
18. *Ibid.*
19. *Ibid.*, March 14, 1969.
20. *Ibid.*, June 20, 1969.
21. *Central California Register*, August 1, 1969.
22. *The Tidings*, December 27, 1968.
23. August 1, 1969.
24. *Central California Register*, August 1, 1969.

6. Archbishop of Los Angeles

Manning fully intended to live out his life in Fresno, expecting and hoping for nothing more than looking after the spiritual needs of the Catholic Church in Central California. While he had become sincerely attached to the clergy and laity of Fresno, his heart remained behind in the southland. His happiest days were those when a visitor from Los Angeles stopped for a chat. The bishop had not been told that his appointment to Fresno was part of a larger scenario which related to the eventual retirement of James Francis Cardinal McIntyre.

In mid-1967, McIntyre had been asked by Pope Paul VI to consider the appointment of a coadjutor who would eventually succeed him as Archbishop of Los Angeles, with the understanding that the cardinal could exercise a veto over any candidate proposed by the Holy See. During the succeeding months, several (probably as many as three) names were discussed and each time, McIntyre expressed reservations. Early on, McIntyre wanted the nominee to be an experienced ordinary, as opposed to an auxiliary bishop or a senior priest. Ultimately an agreement was reached whereby Auxiliary Bishop Timothy Manning would be named to the then vacant Diocese of Fresno, with the understanding that he would eventually return to Los Angeles as coadjutor if he did well in Central California[1]. McIntyre, who had never been close to Manning, harbored some doubts as to his administrative abilities. At the same time, the cardinal clearly appreciated the fact that no one knew more about the Archdiocese of Los Angeles, its clerical and religious personnel, its internal working and its ecclesial history than Manning. It was further stipulated that Manning would not be privy to his possible return to Los Angeles. If any problems surfaced in Fresno during Manning's tenure there, another candidate would be proposed. That this arrangement was never disclosed publicly is obvious from such spurious comments as the one by Kenneth Lamott that Manning had been "exiled to Fresno" because "his views on social issues were too liberal for the cardinal."[2]

It was during a banquet at the Elk's Hall, on the day of Manning's installation at Fresno, that McIntyre gave the first hint of his own future.

In a tribute to Bishop Aloysius J. Willinger, the cardinal jokingly said he would monitor the activities of the retiring prelate over the years ahead as a possible pattern for the final chapter of his own service to the Church.

Cardinal McIntyre was pleased with what he observed during the months of Manning's episcopate in Fresno. He was especially happy with the way the prelate handled the delicate negotiations over the grape dispute involving Cesar Chavez and the growers, much of which was engineered by a priest of the area who would himself eventually become Archbishop of Los Angeles, Msgr. Roger M. Mahony.

Manning liked to recall that when the Apostolic Delegate inquired as to whether he would be willing to return to Los Angeles as coadjutor, it took him all of twenty seconds to respond in the affirmative. The next morning, at 6 o'clock, he telephoned Clare Berger, his secretary who had accompanied him to Fresno, with these words: "Start packing, Clare, we're going home."

On June 11, 1969, during breakfast with an assemblage of priests at Saint John's Seminary, Camarillo, McIntyre announced that the Holy Father, "acting on our advice and encouragement," had named a new coadjutor archbishop for Los Angeles, "a man known and loved by everyone in this room and in the whole archdiocese, Timothy Manning." Judging from the enthusiastic and sustained applause, Manning was indeed a welcome choice. Concluding his remarks with a wink in his eye, McIntyre reminded his listeners that he was still the residential ordinary and would remain as such for the foreseeable future.

The next morning's papers had the news. Dan Thrapp told readers that "Bishop Manning, a hard-working Roman Catholic prelate who for twenty-one years was auxiliary bishop here, has been named coadjutor archbishop with the right of succession of the Los Angeles archdiocese."[3] Cardinal McIntyre also issued a formal statement saying that "the now mature and progressive Archdiocese of Los Angeles has been favored with a coadjutor archbishop through the graciousness of our beloved Holy Father is a welcome recognition of a devoted people and a source of joy to them."

> We are particularly grateful that the new coadjutor will be our known and sincerely revered Archbishop Timothy Manning. He has served the Archdiocese of Los Angeles for many years and endeared himself to the hearts of clergy and people. We welcome joyfully his return to our midst.
>
> My personal and official association with Archbishop Manning has been a very rewarding experience during these

> twenty years. We are now assured of a continuance of cooperative administration on a well established basis of concordance.
>
> The archdiocese rejoices in the coming of Archbishop Manning and the security of his continuance in succession. We are confident that his welcome will be most gracious and elicit fervent prayers from the faithful that will be productive of mutual blessings upon all.[4]

Manning's formal statement which first appeared in the *Central California Register*, reads as follows:

> By God's grace this appointment returns me to Los Angeles, where once more I will be at the service of its wonderful people. For this I was ordained, both priest and bishop. It is a time for loyalties, and mine are unreservedly pledged to Our Holy Father, Pope Paul. It is only with him, as a body with its head, that unity, truth and service are assured within the Church.
>
> My assignment is as helper to Cardinal McIntyre. I shall try to be just that, with renewed affection and gratitude, quietly and generously. His achievements and dedication are a precious legacy for the Church in Los Angeles. A little longer in Fresno, and my heart would have been irrevocably trapped here. Its people are precious in the sight of the Lord. Particularly do I wish to pay tribute to its grand priests. They are holy and humble servants, each in his own place. Bishop Willinger has been a friend, a confidant, and a comfort to me during my stay here. I would have him know publicly of my esteem and gratitude.[5]

Predictably, the clergy, religious and laity of Los Angeles were delighted at the prospect of Manning's return. In a editorial for *The Tidings*, Msgr. Patrick Roche greeted the "joyous news" by saying that it was "a marvelous and kindly disposition of Divine Providence that has arranged for his return:"

> In the broad and varied scope of his experience as priest and prelate among us, Bishop Manning left the impress of his character upon this archdiocese, its people and its institutions. He was our auxiliary bishop for twenty-one years, and those years can never be torn from the fabric which he

> helped to weave. He was an auxiliary in the truest sense of that word, zealous, faithful, loyal and patient, the strong right arm of the Ordinaries whom he served during the tumultuous expansion of this archdiocese.
>
> There is no plot of earth in these four counties which has not felt the tread of his feet, no parish, school or hospital which has not been touched by the guiding genius of his hand. It can be safely estimated that a half-million of our people have been signed with chrism by his fingers in the Sacrament of Confirmation, as he raised them to the dignity and strength of mature Christian life. And there are the countless thousands of others who have been lifted to new insights in their faith through the persuasive eloquence of his tongue.
>
> His months in Fresno, though brief, were intense and fruitful ones. There he has left something of himself, part of that same legacy with which we have been enriched. And in this are the priests and people of Fresno strengthened and consoled in this hour of parting from him. The Diocese of Fresno is sister to our own; a few years ago we were one. The appointment of Bishop Manning as our new coadjutor archbishop continues a precious family relationship, and in that is all the Church enriched. We are a common stock, and the blood of our spiritual ancestors warms our veins and gives sinew to our allegiance and friendship.[6]

Father Michael Collins spoke for others in the priestly ranks when he told a reporter that "it fills the hearts of everyone with happiness and joy and a feeling of 'welcome home where you belong.' And that's the mind of the archdiocese, 100 percent."[7] A "spot check of persons who worked with him showed they found him to be fairly open to changes while at the same time being a strong believer in Church authority. They also said he kept up on his reading and was a good speaker."[8]

Early in June, the recently-appointed coadjutor of Los Angeles preached at the dedication of a new church for Saint Basil's parish in the mid-Wilshire District. He used that occasion to caution that the Church "is facing an effort to unseat ancient truths by seeming to give the People of God a freedom of choice about them."

> The Church stands irrevocable and unmoving, and will not yield the smallest meaning of these words. For them men have died. Here there are no two churches. There is no

In Joyful Remembrance
of the
Liturgical Reception
at Saint Vibiana's Cathedral
of
† TIMOTHY MANNING
Coadjutor Archbishop of Los Angeles
and
† JOSEPH P. DOUGHERTY
Auxiliary Bishop of Los Angeles
on the Feast of
Our Lady of the Angels
in
California's Bi-Centennial Year
1969

— • —

"In California is my life and there,
God willing, I hope to die."
Junipero Serra

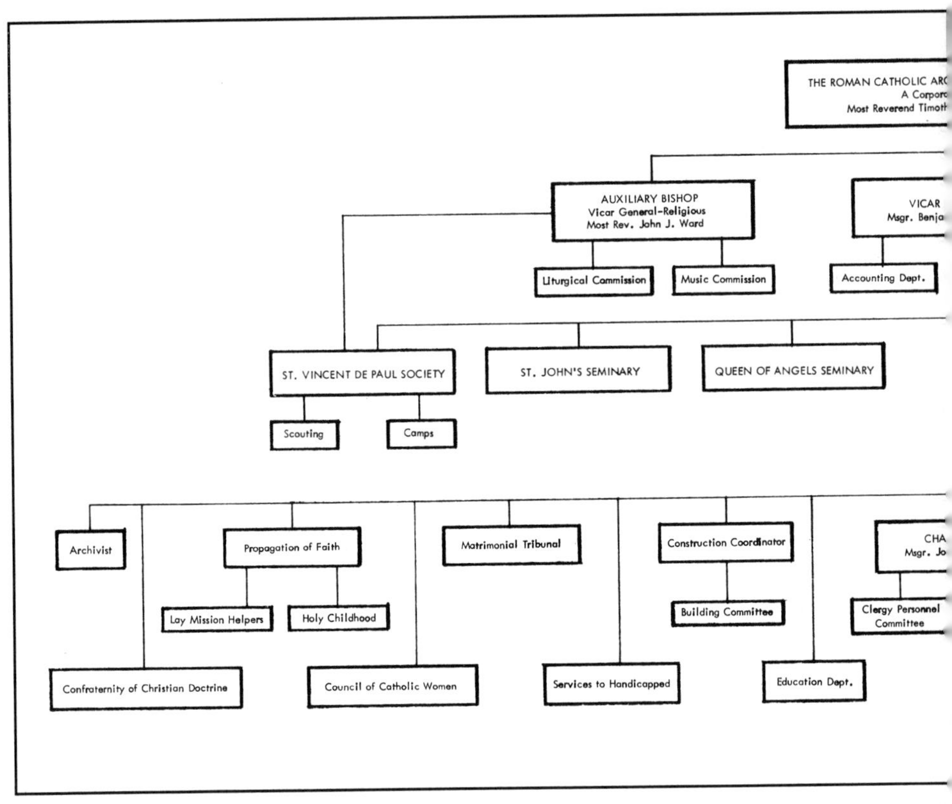
THE ROMAN CATHOLIC ARC
A Corpora
Most Reverend Timoth
AUXILIARY BISHOP
Vicar General-Religious
Most Rev. John J. Ward
VICAR
Msgr. Benja
Liturgical Commission
Music Commission
Accounting Dept.
ST. VINCENT DE PAUL SOCIETY
ST. JOHN'S SEMINARY
QUEEN OF ANGELS SEMINARY
Scouting
Camps
Archivist
Propagation of Faith
Matrimonial Tribunal
Construction Coordinator
CHA
Msgr. Jo
Lay Mission Helpers
Holy Childhood
Building Committee
Clergy Personnel Committee
Confraternity of Christian Doctrine
Council of Catholic Women
Services to Handicapped
Education Dept.

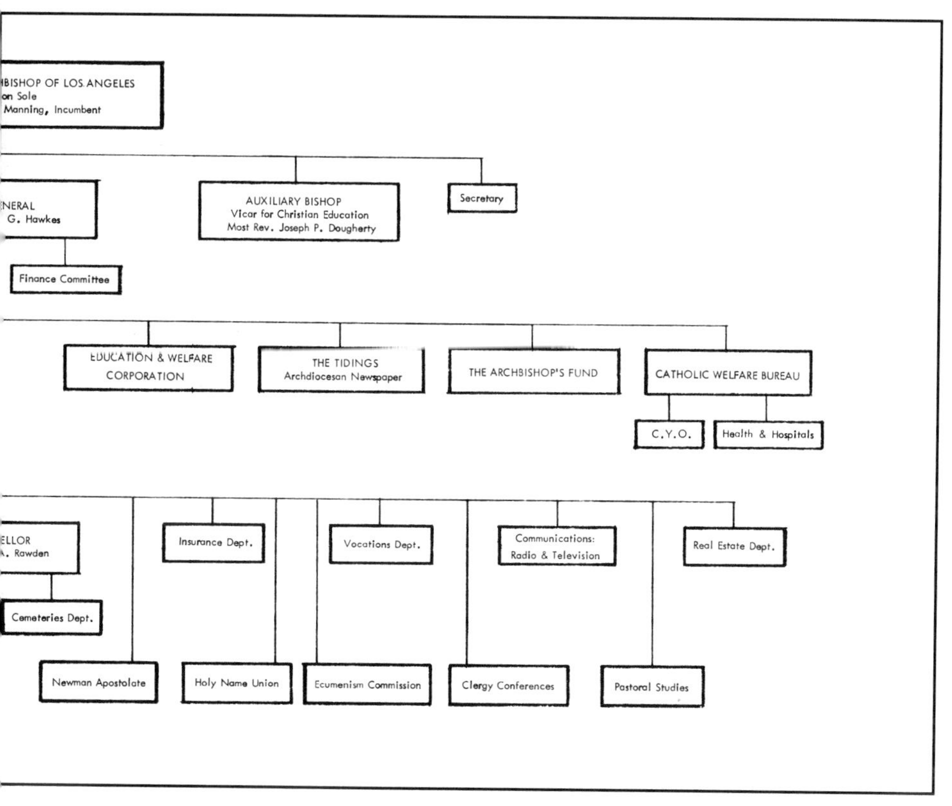

BISHOP OF LOS ANGELES
on Sole
Manning, Incumbent
NERAL
G. Hawkes
AUXILIARY BISHOP
Vicar for Christian Education
Most Rev. Joseph P. Dougherty
Secretary
Finance Committee
EDUCATION & WELFARE CORPORATION
THE TIDINGS
Archdiocesan Newspaper
THE ARCHBISHOP'S FUND
CATHOLIC WELFARE BUREAU
C.Y.O.
Health & Hospitals
ELLOR
. Rawden
Insurance Dept.
Vocations Dept.
Communications:
Radio & Television
Real Estate Dept.
Cemeteries Dept.
Newman Apostolate
Holy Name Union
Ecumenism Commission
Clergy Conferences
Pastoral Studies

Coadjutor Archbishop Timothy Manning was welcomed to Los Angeles at Saint Vibiana's Cathedral on the Feast of Our Lady of Angels, 1969.

> underground church and an overground church. There is no charismatic church and a hierarchical church. There is no mystical body and a human society. There is only one Christ, human and divine, walking across the centuries. "I am with you all days, even to the consummation of the world... Thou art Peter and upon this rock I shall build my church and the gates of hell shall not prevail against it."

"These things are being challenged," the archbishop said, "by men who have pushed God back and have made him unrelated to the circumstances of daily life and have raised a banner that says God is dead. Against this," the archbishop said, "stand the opening words of Genesis in which God commands man to have dominion over the earth. Man, in doing so, evidences God better than any secondary arguments."[9]

Manning's installation was scheduled for August 2 at St. Vibiana's Cathedral. The papal bull, signed at the Vatican on May 26, 1969 and countersigned by Aloysius Cardinal Traglia, read as follows:

> Such has been the growth of population in the illustrious Archdiocese of Los Angeles in California, and so many have been its projects designed for the development of the Christian religion that it has become necessary to give to its present archbishop (a personage, who by his prudence, solicitude and concern has most devotedly cared for his flock) a helper who will give him not only the assistance desired but also one who will be prepared, should the see become vacant, to bring to fruition the plans of his jurisdiction. And so, venerable brother, we have decided to call you to the burden of this office. Your virtue and renown are already well known to Us. Since you already have the dignity of the episcopate and are experienced in matters involving men and their affairs, we feel that you will, in a special way, fill the office with great fruitfulness.
>
> Accordingly, having consulted our venerable brother, the cardinal prefect of the Sacred Congregation of Bishops, We, by our supreme and apostolic authority, release you from all responsibilities for the See of Fresno and nominate you to the See of Capri, now vacant and for this instance raised to archiepiscopal dignity. At the same time We appoint you as coadjutor, with the right of succession, to our venerable brother, the Archbishop of Los Angeles in California, with all the rights and obligations assigned to that office.

> For the rest, We pray that the gifts that God has given you will be exercised with the greatest care so that our venerable brother, the archbishop, may rejoice in your appointment and that the people whose pastor you will be, will be drawn to holiness by your example.[10]

Over 1,400 priests jammed the cathedral for the historic ceremony. Most of the bishops in the west also attended the event. Cardinal McIntyre introduced and welcomed Manning, noting that:

> On this day in the City of Los Angeles in California in the year 1969, it falls to our happy privilege to acclaim the return to our beloved and much appreciated city of one who, while not a native of our city or our land, has spent the largest share of his life in its confines and in the service of our devoted people of California, and this during a time of great expansion.
>
> Archbishop Manning, in the graciousness of Our Holy Father, comes back to Los Angeles embellished with the right of succession as Archbishop of Los Angeles. Hence, his resumption of the responsibilities heretofore exercised with the Ordinary of Los Angeles as vicar general will be reunited in the inevitable prospect of continuity.
>
> Archbishop Manning, we welcome you most heartily in the name of the clergy and the religious, as well as the laity of Los Angeles. In this welcome we include the gratitude of the civil authorities for the part you have played in years past in services rendered in so many instances, and particularly in retaining the traditions of the Franciscan Fathers in dedicating our *pueblo* to Our Lady of the Angels.
>
> It is appropriate, indeed, that this day is the feast of the Portiuncula. This is a well known and prominent feast and devotion of the Franciscan Fathers. They were responsible for the planting of the Catholic faith in all of California. Their footprints and traditions and blessings have remained with us for the many intervening years, and we relish the coincidence of Your Excellency's return on this cherished feastday of the Plaza Church.
>
> My dearly beloved of the clergy, my deeply respected Sisters in religion, my cherished friends of the laity, I take great delight in presenting to you formally this morning in the name

> of Our Holy Father, His Excellency, Archbishop Timothy Manning, as our new archbishop with right of succession.[11]

Archbishop Manning's talk was carefully crafted to cover all the bases. It was among his finest and most relevant addresses:

> As a prelude to this moment, we have been on spiritual pilgrimage. In this month of Apollo our journey paused at the tomb of Fray Junípero Serra at Carmel, to celebrate Mass at the threshold of the tombs of the apostles Peter and Paul, to receive the meaningful benediction of our Holy Father, and at Lourdes to invoke Our Lady who, under the title of Our Lady of the Angels of the Portiuncula, is venerated in Franciscan liturgy this fine day. We are sensitive to the shadow of the cross that must be associated with our mission. The time has come for the Church in America to enrich the treasury of suffering that is the mysterious source of benediction. Its bishops must lead the way.
>
> Anyone called to follow the Lord must take up the cross. This is impossible without the strength of love. May these words be a protestation of our love for this See and its people; a love that seeks to endure whatever cross the future fashions so that Christ and His glory may increase, and that His flock may be fed with the example and the wisdom which comes only through the cross.As we are led by the Lord of history into a new age, it is inevitable that there will be some change. Social entities, forms of cultures, traditions and ways of life will be altered modified or discarded. In instances where the concept of the Church was attached to such life patterns or propagated through them, there will be profound alternatives.
>
> More and more, membership in the Church will be found to be asserted with intense personal conviction, by contrast with the brilliance of a world of science which does not consciously need the fact of God. For this reason some authorities predict that the number of believers will diminish and the community of the faithful will again be a "little flock." Yet it will be an abiding witness within the larger community, speaking with a clear and respected voice the message of the Gospel, and staking its hope and love in the remembrance of the Lord.

> The bishop aspires to no position of power or wealth or social prominence. He stands in relation to the flock entrusted to his care. More than this, however, there is unfolding in our time the great mystery of co-responsibility with the pope over the universal Church. This is the doctrine of collegiality. The bishop is ordained a member of the College of Bishops, and then given a particular See for the exercise of his ministry. This function of the bishop is exercised in terms of authority. We must believe that there is a sacred order provided by Christ for the governing of His Church. This authority must not be mistaken for its counterfeits of authoritarianism, triumphalism or legalism.
>
> Where Peter is, there is the Church. So our obedience is a loyalty, a love, a devotion. Accepting the person, we accept the truth. This then is the only authority we profess, the only obedience we claim. It brings the mind a captive to the truth of Christ, and the heart a slave to His love.
>
> Here in this sanctuary and in this holy sacrifice we are exemplifying this fundamental truth. The dissent and the shouting will magnify awhile, then die. Only within the shelter of legitimate authority which strives to remain within its own limitations, will we find the serenity and peace which is our birth-right, and through which alone we are secure in our journey with Him and toward Him, who is the way, the truth and the life.[12]

Though Manning had expressed a desire not to serve as a pastor during his coadjutorship, the cardinal felt that it would be appropriate for him to take up once again the pastoral office, this time at Saint Brendan's parish in Hancock Park. On August 2, the day of his installation, Manning also assumed his former position as Vicar General for the Archdiocese of Los Angeles.

Manning had barely arrived in the southland, when he was approached by a noisy demonstration at Saint Brendan's. One hundred "concerned Catholics" demanded that he set aside $10 million for "black and brown grassroots community organizations for development of programs conducive to communities to take control of their own institutions, to be followed by a yearly allocation of the same amount."[13] In his typically gracious style, Manning listened attentively and assured leaders that he would take the matter under consideration.

Even most liberal pundits considered the demands as "institutional blackmail" which would "open the gates to complete anarchy with regard to *who* can demand *what* of public institutions." The editor of *Ave Maria* said that "our disagreement with some of the policies of the archdiocesan administration (in Los Angeles) will not prevent us from recognizing the boorishness of their demands:

> They are apparently unaware that Bishop Manning is not going to be in a position to allocate any of the resources of the archdiocese until he becomes administrator of the archdiocese. He has the right to succeed; but he has no special authority as long as Cardinal McIntyre remains in office. The authors demand that Bishop Manning repudiate all wars (not too difficult, unless you include wars against racism, authoritarianism, injustice, etc.), that he publicly support the grape boycott and the boycott of all Safeway stores, that he sell some church property on Wilshire Boulevard, stop all building, investigate the hiring practices of all businesses patronized by the archdiocese, pay better wages to nonclergy employees of the archdiocese, *etc.*
>
> They demand that he take up residence in a poor ghetto, hand over the financial and administrative details of the Church to competent laymen (presumably after he had handled all the above financial details) and repudiate all clergymen who drive high-priced cars and live in plush rectories. These L.A. Catholics, undoubtedly concerned with worthy values, make the pursuit of such values – by themselves and others – look like jungle warfare. And this is just one more way in which we can lose the whole blamed effort.[14]

The transferral of authority began on January 22, 1970, when the Los Angeles *Times* announced that "James Francis Cardinal McIntyre, for half a century bulwark of conservatism in the Roman Catholic Church, retired Wednesday as head of the Archdiocese of Los Angeles."[15] By virtue of his earlier designation as coadjutor with the right of succession, Manning immediately became residential archbishop and metropolitan for the province of Los Angeles. In his statement to the press, Archbishop Manning said:

> My first word on this eventful day is to proclaim that I am one in mind and one in heart with our Holy Father Pope Paul, the Supreme head of the Church in the body of Christ. I am

> deeply grateful to His Eminence Cardinal McIntyre for his gracious action in allowing that the destinies of the archdiocese of Los Angeles be entrusted to me at this moment. Perhaps he might say, as Paul did to the Philippians: "Timothy's record is known to you; you know that he has been at my side in the service of Gospel like a son working under his father."
>
> By and large the archdiocese is today what he has made it, giving it princely dimensions and knowing the agony and the anxiety of its shepherding. While he deeply merits a surcease from his labors we beg that we shall be close enough to be guided always by his service and example. God grant that we shall not fail.

Then Manning spelled-out his priorities:

> The prime charge given to a bishop is to proclaim the Gospel of the Lord, and to provide the means of sanctity and salvation to the people of God. To fulfill this awesome responsibility he is given the fraternity of a priestly brotherhood. This is called the presbytery. The priests and those preparing for the priesthood must, therefore, be the first subject of his solicitude. They shall be so to me.
>
> Secondly, the people of God who form the Church receive the word of God and bring it to fruition in their lives. This is done through all forms of religious education and to this continuous task do we set our hands. With rich and authentic liturgy and with a reason for the faith we profess, we shall bear witness to the redeeming love of Christ.
>
> Thirdly, we are deeply concerned that the Church must make her own the social needs of the world of men and women, their griefs and anxieties. She must engage in conversation about these problems, apply the light of the Gospel to their healing, give witness to the truth, rescue rather than sit in judgment, serve rather than come to be served.
>
> We have nursed no ambitions toward this position as an honor to be pursued. It is accepted as an expression of the will of Our Heavenly Father. We pledge to spend ourselves and be spent in the fulfillment of that will, of loving those we serve even though we ourselves be loved less. We place

CHURCHES DEDICATED DURING THE ARCHIEPISCOPATE OF TIMOTHY CARDINAL MANNING

DATE	CHURCH	PLACE
April 5, 1970	Santa Barbara	Santa Ana
April 12, 1970	Assumption of the Blessed Virgin Mary	Pasadena
April 12, 1970	St. John the Baptist	Baldwin Park
May 3, 1970	Our Lady of Lourdes	Tujunga
September 12, 1970	Our Lady of Guadalupe	Oxnard
October 25, 1970	Saint John of God	Norwalk
December 19, 1970	Our Lady of the Valley	Canoga Park
December 20, 1970	Saint Cyprian	Lakewood
May 2, 1971	Our Lady of Guadalupe	La Habra
January 16, 1972	St. Mary	Fullerton
January 30, 1972	St. Sebastian	Los Angeles
March 5, 1972	St. Edward	Capistrano Beach
March 26, 1972	St. Lucy	Los Angeles
November 19, 1972	St. Martin	Yorba Linda
March 19, 1973	St. Bernardine Chapel	Los Angeles
May 6, 1973	Our Lady of Perpetual Help	Los Nietos
December 16, 1973	St. Jude	Westlake Village
February 25, 1974	St. Simon & Jude	Huntington Beach
November 4, 1974	San Fernando, Rey de España (church replaced ruined one)	Mission Hills
December 29, 1974	Saint Mary Magdalen	Camarillo
April 27, 1975	Saint Louise de Marillac	Covina
November 9, 1975	Saint Peter	San Pedro
February 1, 1976	Saint Francis of Assisi	Fillmore
June 6, 1976	Sacred Heart	San Buenaventura
June 20, 1976	Saint Peter Claver	Simi Valley
December 19, 1976	Our Lady of Victory	Los Angeles
February 26, 1978	San Buenaventura Mission (consecration of church)	San Buenaventura
November 8, 1981	Saint Jude	Westlake Village
June 24, 1984	Saint Basil (consecration of church)	Los Angeles
September 29, 1982	Holy Cross	Moorpark

HEALTH CARE EXPANSION DURING THE ARCHIEPISCOPATE OF TIMOTHY CARDINAL MANNING

FACILITY	PLACE	YEAR	CATEGORY
Saint Mary's Bauer Hospital	Long Beach	1970	New Hospital
Saint Jude Hospital	Fullerton	1971	North Wing
Santa Marta Hospital	East Los Angeles	1972	New Hospital
Holy Cross Hospital	Mission Hills	1972	Replaced earlier facility
Saint Mary Hospital	Long Beach	1972	Chest Clinic
Saint Joseph Hospital	Burbank	1973	New Wing
Saint Mary Hospital	Long Beach	1974	Saint Mary-Bauer Medical
Saint John Hospital	Santa Monica	1974	Kennedy Regional Center
Santa Marta Hospital	East Los Angeles	1974	Emergency Unit
Daniel Freeman Hospital	Inglewood	1975	Rehabilitation Unit
Saint Vincent Hospital	Los Angeles	1975	Replaced earlier facility
Saint John Hospital	Santa Monica	1976	Mental Health Center
Little Company of Mary Hospital	Torrance	1976	New Unit
Saint Francis Hospital	Santa Barbara	1977	New Unit
Daniel Freeman Hospital	Inglewood	1977	Rehabilitation Center
Saint John Hospital	Santa Monica	1978	Ambulatory Center
Marian Hospital	Santa Maria	1981	Major Expansion
Marina Mercy Hospital	Marina del Rey	1981	Recently Purchased
Santa Teresita Hospital	Duarte	1984	Surgical Wing
Doheny Eye Hospital	Los Angeles	1985	Relocated

> ourselves as mendicants to beg the charity of the prayers of those for whom we are called and commissioned, so that God's name will be hallowed, His kingdom advanced and His will be done, on earth as it is in heaven.[16]

In a lengthy interview with reporters from the Los Angeles *Times*, Manning indicated that he would "bring a new look to the Archdiocese of Los Angeles" by emphasizing a willingness "to listen to militants seeking social change." He wanted "to bring young people more closely into the Church." He agreed that the Church "must engage in conversation about the world's problems" by giving "witness to the truth," serving rather than trying to be served. He considered himself a "moderate" in churchmanship, preferring that description to either "liberal" or "conservative." Manning considered narcotics "the major problem facing youth today." He was "deeply concerned that the Church must make her own the special needs of the world" populace.[17]

Manning was also interviewed by other newspapers. He told the Los Angeles *Herald-Examiner* how, in Fresno, he had founded a clerical urban task force that met each month with him and with local government officials. "Many good solutions have come out of those meetings," he said. He also doubted whether any schools would be built in the near future "because of the increasing cost of education and a shortage of teaching nuns, brothers and priests." He said that "religious education will have to be diversified, " explaining that more emphasis would be placed on catechetical classes and adult education. The reporter predicted that "communication will probably come to distinguish Archbishop Manning's style of office, just as organization best described Cardinal McIntyre's style."[18]

Don Jardin, a writer for the *National Catholic Reporter* predicted that "Manning will be his own man." After interviewing the archbishop in his office, he said that Manning gave "the impression of being self confident and ready to put his own ideas to work." He agreed with those who felt that Manning "will take the nation's fourth largest Catholic diocese in the direction he sees fit." While admitting that the archbishop "is a theological conservative" and that "he employs pious language frequently," he said that "this is expected to help in relations with Catholic conservatives." As if to warn the archbishop about the pitfalls of not "moving ahead," Jardin said that "he undoubtedly will not enjoy the same immunity that has been shown to the octogenarian cardinal in the post-Vatican Council days."[19]

In her weekly column for *The Tidings*, Mary Lanigan Healy praised the archbishop for his willingness to listen:

> It is a different, difficult and demanding era in which we find ourselves. Everywhere there are anguished questions. What are the answers? Not simple, not easy. Perhaps the strong, calm voice of the new archbishop indicates a place to begin: "We will listen to anybody." This is a prologue to solutions. It leads toward a united effort of all the people of God and their Shepherd. If there is need for a listening post here on earth, it goes without saying that there is, and always has been, a need for one higher up. It is there.
>
> As individuals and as a nation, it is essential that the truth be kept in mind. Each man in his time does what he sees to do, according to his own heart and conscience. And although the names change upon whom we ask God's blessing from our altars, the Church remains the same. We can only ask God to "bless us everyone" and to help us to know and to love one another in a truly Christian way.[20]

The archbishop's new curial staff was announced on January 30. Auxiliary Bishop John J. Ward and Msgr. Benjamin G. Hawkes were named Vicars General; Msgr. John A. Rawden was appointed chancellor and Father Clement Connolly secretary.[21] Several weeks later, Manning named six new consulters to augment those inherited from the previous administration. They were Msgr. John Hughes, Fathers Kieran Marum, John Sammon, Edward Sexton, Ramon Soriano and Francis J. Weber. Also instituted was a "term basis" whereby each new appointee would serve for only five years.[22] It was also announced that the new archbishop would live at Saint Vibiana's Cathedral, in the heart of the inner city. Msgr. Patrick Roche, rector of the Cathedral, took Manning's place at Saint Brendan's.[23]

His first weeks in office were busy ones. One of his long-time friends wrote a "diary" of those days which was published in *The Tidings*:

> In his first month as spiritual shepherd of the flock of Los Angeles, Archbishop Timothy Manning has touched all the main dimensions of pastoral life. In the first month already there has been joy and sadness, care and concern, all the elements that weather the life of a pastor.[24]

Manning rarely lost his sense of humor, even when things went poorly. On January 25, he dropped in unannounced at the 34th Annual Breakfast for the archdiocesan Union of Holy Name Societies. It was one of the last commitments that McIntyre wanted to personally fulfill. When asked to speak, Manning said that "after four days as Archbishop of Los Angeles, I wonder if His Eminence would like to have the job back?"[25] The comment brought down the house. As he was leaving, he remarked to the chairman of the event: "I wasn't kidding."

The final phase of Manning's installation ceremonials occurred on June 17 when he received the sacred pallium, a circular band of white wool worn by metropolitan archbishops. In the presence of 262 priests, McIntyre invested him with "the fullness of the episcopal office," the distinctive garment blessed by Pope Paul VI in a consistory at Rome on May 18. One clerical wag observed, upon leaving the chapel, that "it was the last time McIntyre would be pulling the wool over Manning's eyes."

Notes to the Text

1. For the interesting background of this arrangement, see Francis J. Weber, *His Eminence of Los Angeles, James Francis Cardinal McIntyre*, (Mission Hills, 1997), II, 640-646.
2. "A Quiet Revolt," *Horizon* XII (Winter, 1970), 71.
3. Los Angeles *Times*, June 12, 1969.
4. *The Tidings*, June 13, 1969.
5. June 13, 1969.
6. *The Tidings*, June 13, 1969.
7. *National Catholic Register*, June 22, 1969.
8. *National Catholic Reporter*, June 18, 1969.
9. *Ibid.*, July 9, 1969.
10. *The Tidings*, August 8, 1969.
11. *Ibid.*
12. *Ibid.*
13. Los Angeles *Herald-Examiner*, July 5, 1969.
14. *Ave Maria* CX (July 26, 1969), 2.
15. Los Angeles *Times*, January 22, 1970.
16. Los Angeles *Herald-Examiner*, January 22, 1969.
17. January 22, 1970.
18. January 25, 1970.
19. *National Catholic Reporter*, January 28, 1970.
20. January 30, 1970.
21. *The Tidings*, January 30, 1970.
22. *Ibid.*, March 20, 1970.
23. *Ibid.*, February 20, 1970.
24. *Ibid.*
25. Los Angeles *Times*, January 26, 1970.

7. *Province of Los Angeles*

Organizationally, the Metropolitan Province of Los Angeles, over which Timothy Manning presided as archbishop from 1970 to 1985, was one of thirty districts into which the Catholic Church in the United States was divided. When Manning took office, the province included the Archdiocese of Los Angeles and the suffragan Dioceses of Monterey, Fresno and San Diego. In his role as metropolitan, symbolized by the sacred pallium, Manning was expected to see that the faith and ecclesial discipline were carefully observed in his three suffragan dioceses.

FRESNO

Manning's close association with the Diocese of Monterey-Fresno stretched back to the administration of Bishop Philip G. Scher. When Scher died, Manning was asked to represent Archbishop J. Francis A. McIntyre who was enroute to Rome for his cardinalatial investiture. In his homily for the funeral, Manning said that Scher's life was a "veritable commentary" on the Gospel of Saint Luke where the Lord draws a comparison between His apostles and the hired worker who spends the day ploughing in the field and tending the cattle.

> There was no divided interest in his life; it was dedicated in its totality to the things of Almighty God. There was no looking back, no hungering after other avocations. Always his passion was that the direction of men's minds and hearts should forever be polarized to eternity. Full well he knew that any man putting his hand to the plough and looking back is not worthy of discipleship with Christ.
>
> Now he is dead and we shall reverently lay away his body as a seed in the earth, beneath the upturned soil. He would seem to have said to us that he was indeed the unprofitable servant, surrendering in humility and self-abandon all claim

> to thanks or glory, serving his Master to the utmost of his being and then stepping aside into the evening of silence.[1]

Roman officials occasionally sought Manning's advice about appointments outside his own archdiocese, especially within the Metropolitan Province of Los Angeles. Interestingly, he was not asked nor did he even know who would be his successor at Fresno until it had been decided and announced by the Apostolic Delegate. Some years later, however, when candidates were being considered for the position of coadjutor to Bishop Hugh A. Donohoe, Manning took the opportunity of proposing the name of Father Jose de Jesus Madera who had served successfully as pastor of Our Lady of Guadalupe in Oxnard. When the appointment was made, the cardinal issued the following statement:

> It is most important that what is found in his person be reflected in all of the Catholics of the Diocese of Fresno – a faith that knows no boundaries or barriers, but in Christ creates one family of love and of service to the whole Church. We are personally well aware of the fabric of this diocese, its riches and its struggles, its plurality of peoples and its agonies. It is our firm belief that the new Bishop Madera will be the point at which all these concerns will meet. He will be the "suffering servant" among you who will carry in his person all your travail. We who are of the Archdiocese of Los Angeles are particularly grateful for his appointment. For fifteen years he served as a priest in pastoral work in Oxnard. We know personally of his sincerity and of his holiness and of his zeal. Take him to your heart and create for us in the Diocese of Fresno a model of harmony and peace and pastoral activity that will bring joy to the whole Church of God.[2]

ORANGE AUXILIARY

During the early 1980s, Manning expressed himself several times as being much impressed by Father John T. Steinbock who had served as parochial vicar at Saint Vibiana's Cathedral, since 1981. The two were much alike, insofar as they were non-directional in their demeanor. When Bishop William Johnson was seeking names on his *terna* for an auxiliary in Orange, the cardinal enthusiastically recommended Steinbock as his favorite of the three candidates submitted to the Apostolic Delegate.

In his homily at the Mass during which Steinbock was advanced to the bishopric, the cardinal reflected upon the nature of the episcopacy, noting that "the purpose of the bishop is twofold: to proclaim the Gospel and to bring together in unity the dispersed members of the human family." He stressed that the bishop acting "through the outpouring of the Holy Spirit is the authentic authority of the Church" in a given area. Manning asked the congregation "to respect the bishop. He's the target today of much criticism that's helpful to him because it makes him aware of how he must work better to be with Christ. The bishop is a human being who speaks haltingly, faultily, but listen to him." Calling for obedience, Cardinal Manning warned the congregation about the danger of being "take it or leave it, marginal Catholics." He praised the new bishop. "For eleven years and more I have lived under the same roof with him, seen him night and day and can testify before God to that extraordinary sacrificial love that he has for the marginal people of the world, knowing them by name, being generous with them, loving them, bringing out with his humor the hidden depths of their own reserves, the elderly, the derelicts."[3]

MONTEREY

A close relationship between Bishop Harry Clinch and Manning had developed during the eighteen months the latter served in Fresno. The two prelates agreed from the outset to discuss openly and forthrightly any problems that might be occasioned because of the division and redistribution of the common assets and debts shared by the two jurisdictions. Clinch was an ideal team player and Manning cherished his collaboration during the ensuing years. He remained at his post until 1982 and often invited the cardinal to his home for golfing tournaments.

As the time for his retirement approached, Clinch described to Manning the qualities he wanted to see in his successor. All the indicators pointed to Auxiliary Bishop Thaddeus Shubsda of Los Angeles, and after further negotiation with the Apostolic Delegate, Shubsda was assigned to Monterey where he succeeded the "gentle rock on which the Diocese of Monterey was built and who hands over a diocese and community of faith abundantly blessed by our Heavenly Father." Manning publicly thanked Shubsda "for his priestly service to his native city and diocese. May he now widen his tent to enclose all of God's people in the Diocese of Monterey. Our diocese was once called Monterey-Los Angeles. May the residue of that affinity remain in our hearts through the good Bishop Thaddeus Shubsda."[4]

The cardinal journeyed to Carmel where he presided at Shubsda's installation. In his homily Manning said:

> The dust in the ground beneath our feet here is unquestionably the holiest in all of California because here lie the mortal remains of Fray Junípero Serra, and, side by side with him, his dearest companion, Father Juan Crespi. All of the sanctities, all of the history, all of the glory of our California church and state are interred here in this holy soil. It is fitting that we should begin this ceremony, this episcopal installation in this place. Equally important is the fact that on this very day in the year 1769 Junípero Serra first set foot on California soil in San Diego. Two hundred years ago Crespi was buried here in this church. Two years later Junípero Serra himself was buried here.
>
> We now verify for you from the depth of our own knowledge that the shepherd whom God has given you today is a man who is intimately in love with Christ. His whole life has been a serving of Christ. There are no two Bishop Shubsdas, only one. He is totally transparent. The love of Christ shines out through him. We swear to that because this we know. We know that he will expend himself night and day going from parish to parish proclaiming the Gospel and being witness to the love of Christ.
>
> Monterey is the mountain of the king. The second chapter of Isaiah says let us go up to the mountain of the house of the Lord. There He will show us His ways and we will walk in His Paths. When you walk in His paths you are walking the Camino Real. Today, people of Monterey safely follow on the Camino Real the royal way that will lead to the holy mountain of the king. Cherish your bishop. May he have many, many years.[5]

SAN DIEGO

Manning's interest and concern for the Diocese of San Diego predated his days as metropolitan archbishop. When Charles Francis Buddy, the founding bishop of San Diego, died, Manning journeyed to San Diego and there delivered a homily that outlined the many accomplishments of his episcopal confrere.

> It is too facile entirely to catalogue the items of achievement in the pontificate of this bishop. We would venture to hint at the shape of that history. These four counties comprised the last frontier of the Church in the United States. To the south, another nation with a climate then unfavorable to religion, westward the limitless ocean, easterly the desert, and to the north the new metropolitan community, jealous of rivals until she would become the mistress of the west. Into this pocket, like a pilgrim, came the Missouri prelate, rich in a Roman tradition and in Roman friends, youthful as the prairie, handsome and noble in bearing. To the desert and the river and the sea he would give challenge. For him the faith knew no frontiers. His episcopate stands as a proof of his courage and his zeal. Higher education, seminary training, convert crusades, immigrant solicitude, literary ventures – all these were assembled to put the Church in the Diocese of San Diego prominently and progressively outdistancing most other sees in the network of jurisdictions that cover the United States. The first bishop of a diocese is eternally a foundation rock to its progress, a founder of a dynasty to his successors and the prelude and cradle of its subsequent greatness. Charles Francis Buddy was all this, and his name now stands linked with Garcia Diego, Joseph Alemany and Eugene O'Connell, founders of the hierarchical church in California. Yes, we may safely predict that the memory of Bishop Buddy will live as a great churchman and as a champion in a chapter of salvation history here in California.[6]

After Manning became archbishop, he and his neighbor to the south, Bishop Leo T. Maher, became kindred souls in many ways and their relationship over the years was pleasant and productive. Manning attended the episcopal ordination of Gilbert Chavez as auxiliary of San Diego in 1974 and, five years later, Manning was the principal celebrant for the funeral obsequies of Msgr. John Purcell. In 1982, the cardinal sent a gracious letter which the *Southern Cross* used in its issue marking Maher's silver episcopal jubilee. In his acknowledgement Maher thanked the cardinal for his "supportive letter" and noted that these "twenty years have seen the office of the bishop take on a more dynamic role in every phase of the Church."[7]

SAN BERNARDINO

Cardinal Manning was aware of and approved of the plans submitted by Bishop Leo Maher to the Holy See for division of the Diocese of San Diego. The proposal, calling for erection of a separate ecclesial jurisdiction for San Bernardino and Riverside counties, allowed for eighty-five parishes to accommodate the 236,048 Catholics residing in that 27,047 square mile area.[8] Maher was adamant that his auxiliary, Bishop Gilbert Chavez, who already lived in San Bernardino, was not administratively qualified to head the new diocese.

On July 18, 1978, the Apostolic Delegation released word that Pope Paul VI had approved Maher's plan and created a new Diocese of San Bernardino, with Father Phillip F. Straling as the residential bishop.[9] As Manning had predicted, the appointment of an Anglo to head the eleventh of California's dioceses, in an area where the population was predominantly Hispanic, unleashed a brief firestorm by those who considered it "an insult to the Hispanic community of California and the country." Letters of protest were dispatched to the Holy See. According to a source, "everyone had expected, or at least it was rumored, that it would be Bishop (Juan) Arzube." Other prominent candidates mentioned were Bishops Chavez and Manuel Moreno, as well as Father Peter Luque.

Straling, who had the support of his close childhood friend, Archbishop John R. Quinn of San Francisco, in addition to that of Maher, sidestepped the criticism cleverly by pointing out that "it was not my choice to be made bishop. Those who make these decisions surely must know the needs of the Church. They also know that San Bernardino is an area of many cultures and many peoples."[10] Happily, the discontent dissipated rather quickly when the bishop-elect pledged to provide an episcopal vicar for Hispanics in the organizational structure of the new diocese. Cardinal Manning was asked to consecrate Straling at ceremonies held at Raincross Square in Riverside on November 6, 1978.

SAN FRANCISCO

Manning's longest acquaintance in the hierarchy was Joseph T. McGucken who had served as Archbishop of San Francisco since 1962. Close friends for almost half a century, they spoke at least weekly by telephone, sharing their aspirations for God's people in California. The cardinal thought that the retired Archbishop of San Francisco was treated poorly in his declining years. Especially was he peeved that Roman authorities appointed his successor prior to formally acknowledging McGucken's mandatory retirement letter in 1977. Always a stickler for protocol, Manning felt that his lifelong friend "deserved better treatment by virtue of his many accomplishments as priest, bishop and archbishop." Nor was the cardinal pleased with the "shabby manner" in which McGucken was ignored during his final years, "relegated to his tomb as if he had never existed." Incidentally, this matter was never voiced by McGucken, but by clerical friends in San Francisco whom the cardinal had known from seminary days.

A measure of Manning's affection for his counterpart to the north is evident in his eulogy for McGucken delivered in Saint Mary's Cathedral on October 31, 1983. It had been written on a piece of cardboard as Manning made his way back to California from Rome by airplane.

> Others of us were privy to his friendship. For me, myself, our lives were entwined for over fifty years. We lived together in the same house. We served the same Archbishop Cantwell and fulfilled in succession the same duties. We were accorded the same episcopal lineage when he, together with the then Auxiliary Bishop of San Francisco, Thomas A. Connolly, and the holy martyr Bishop James E. Walsh of Maryknoll ordained me a bishop in 1946. As much as any man I shared his sorrows and his joys, and mourn his passing as none other. Others who served with him in the Los Angeles, Sacramento and San Francisco chanceries hold him in holy remembrance, many of them in tears.
>
> He was a dear friend, in fraternity, in his great sense of conversation, his humor, his unfailing sympathies and, in a strange, inexplicable acceptance of God's will. Once in our young years of togetherness, he told me he had vowed never to complain; I firmly believe he kept that vow to the end. Through all the changes he had to undergo, through the difficulties of administration, in all of this there was never an expression of dissent. He was totally submissive and subservient to God's holy will as it came to him, and never more so than in the vesture in which he now lies.
>
> In 1941 in the cathedral church of Los Angeles he lay prostrate on the floor with the book of the gospels over his shoulders and his head. And now, at the end of the long years, he lies once more in a total submission and subjection prostrate before his God, subservient only to the book of the

> gospels which is open over his head. Archbishop McGucken was first and foremost eminently a churchman. He had no other vocation, no other diversion, no other ambition except the Church. In his episcopal career he touched all of California. He was ordained a priest for the Diocese of Los Angeles – San Diego, which today has generated the Archdiocese of Los Angeles, and the Dioceses of San Diego, Orange and San Bernardino.
>
> He was for a time the administrator of the Diocese of Monterey-Fresno, today divided into two separate dioceses. As Bishop of Sacramento and as Archbishop of San Francisco his servanthood touched the present day dioceses of Santa Rosa, Stockton, San Jose and Oakland which were within his metropolitan jurisdiction. The entire state of California had become his field of labor. It will never happen again.
>
> He had an extraordinary love for the Mexican people, long before it was the imperative it is today. He foresaw the claim of that ethnic group to our attention, to our respect, to our care. In the beginning of the Archdiocese of Los Angeles he pursued relentlessly the learning of the language and the building of schools.
>
> Here inside this stunning cathedral church which he built we are living in a parable. The great architect of St. Paul's in London, Christopher Wren, is buried within that cathedral, there is, however, no monument erected to him there. There is only an inscription on the slab over his resting place. It reads: "*Si monumentum quaeras, respice*." "If you seek his monument, look around you." The very building in which he lay buried was his monument. So let it be with Archbishop McGucken. Let this white dove of a holy place tell "The City" and the world that Joseph Thomas McGucken was here.[11]

Manning had known McGucken's successor, Archbishop John J. Quinn, for many years in San Diego and Oklahoma City. Quinn and his mother accompanied the cardinal-designate to Rome for Manning's investiture in the Sacred College in 1973. Four years later, Manning accepted the invitation to preside at Quinn's installation in San Francisco. While retaining an outward cordiality during the years after 1977,[12] Manning and Quinn were never close. Especially was that obvious during the time when Quinn served as President of the National Conference of Catholic Bishops, when Manning was rarely if ever

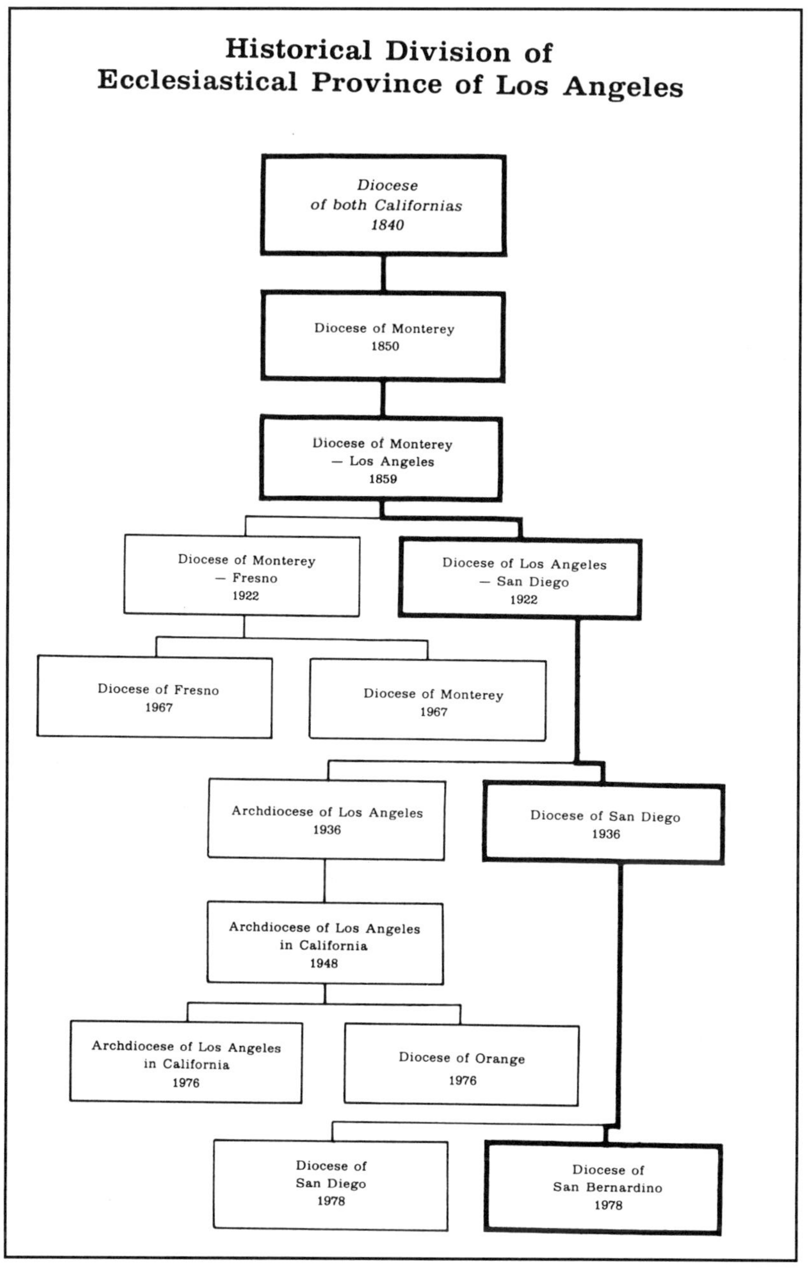
Historical Division of
Ecclesiastical Province of Los Angeles
Diocese of both Californias 1840
Diocese of Monterey 1850
Diocese of Monterey — Los Angeles 1859
Diocese of Monterey — Fresno 1922
Diocese of Los Angeles — San Diego 1922
Diocese of Fresno 1967
Diocese of Monterey 1967
Archdiocese of Los Angeles 1936
Diocese of San Diego 1936
Archdiocese of Los Angeles in California 1948
Archdiocese of Los Angeles in California 1976
Diocese of Orange 1976
Diocese of San Diego 1978
Diocese of San Bernardino 1978

Archbishop Joseph T. McGucken
San Francisco

Archbishop John R. Quinn
San Francisco

Bishop Phillip Straling
San Bernardino

Bishop John Steinbock
Santa Rosa and Fresno

consulted about matters affecting the Church in the United States or worldwide.

When Quinn delivered his widely-heralded address about the Church's ban on birth control, at the Sixth Synod of Bishops in Rome, Manning observed: "There goes San Francisco's chance for a red hat." Though Quinn may have thought otherwise, the Holy See never seriously considered him as a replacement for Manning in 1985. When Quinn announced his unprecedented "leave" from San Francisco, in November of 1987, Manning was heard to observe that "a shepherd, even if wounded, never leaves his sheep untended." The only episcopal presence in San Francisco during that five month hiatus was a retired and physically impaired auxiliary bishop. Manning, by then retired, accepted an invitation to be principal celebrant and homilist for the Christmas midnight Mass at Saint Mary's Cathedral that year and again the next morning at 10:30.

TUCSON

The long tradition of harmony and mutual cooperation between the Archdiocese of Los Angeles and the Diocese of Tucson can be traced back to 1936 and the establishment of the Metropolitan Province of Los Angeles. At the time, Tucson was attached to the new district as a suffragan see. Heading the Arizona jurisdiction since 1923 was Daniel J. Gercke who was even then acknowledged among the patriarchs of the American Church. When Gercke died in March of 1964, the then Auxiliary Bishop Timothy Manning delivered a truly memorably panegyric which he entitled, after Willa Cather's great work, "Death Comes to the Archbishop."

> Death has come for the archbishop. In the eighty-ninth year of his age; in the sixty-third year of his priesthood and in the forty-first year of his episcopate, on March 19, 1964, at fifteen minutes past five in the morning, Daniel J. Gercke, recent Bishop of Tucson, then Titular Archbishop of Cotyaeum, passed out of this world and entered into eternity.
>
> In fancy we like to think of the dear archbishop met at the entrance to Paradise and companioned to the Most High Priest by those "Soldiers of the Faith" whose seeding he watered and harvested in this recovered wilderness. Archbishop Lamy will be there, who, one hundred years ago, on

> March 19, 1864, entered Tucson for the first time to claim it for the jurisdiction of Santa Fe; Archbishop Salpointe, first Vicar Apostolic of the Arizona territory, who resigned from Santa Fe to return here to Tucson and to lie buried in its Cathedral.
>
> In that company surely would be found Fray Francisco de Porras, first Franciscan missionary among the Hopi Indians; Fathers Kino and Salvatierra, intrepid Jesuits pioneering north from Sonora, sanctifying with their foot-falls the rich earth of Arizona; Fray Francisco Hermenegildo Garces, apostle of San Xavier del Bac, lovely cradle of the faith in the desert.
>
> Daniel Gercke was of their company and their kindred. Somehow, he was the termination of the apostolic age of the faith which they began and, at the same time, the architect of the new Church of Arizona wedded to the twentieth and nuclear century.[13]

The cordial relationship between Los Angeles and Tucson continued even after 1967, when the Holy See transferred the Arizona jurisdiction to the Metropolitan Province of Santa Fe. Bishop Francis Green was a friend of Manning from their days together at Saint Patrick's Seminary in Menlo Park and it was their mutual recommendation that Los Angeles auxiliary, Manuel Moreno, be named fifth Bishop of Tucson in 1982. At that time, the cardinal told a gathering of priests at Mission Hills that in Moreno's crest "there were two intimations of his quiet, unassuming servanthood. One is a cross taken from the brooch of Our Lady of Guadalupe. It tells priests the Blessed Mother figures in their priesthood." The second element is the legend on the crest taken from the motto of the Cursillo movement, God counts on me, I count on God: "*Cuento con Dios*."[14]

BOLSENA

Since the mid-1960s, one of the most visible American clerics serving at the Vatican was Msgr. Justin Rigali, a priest of the Archdiocese of Los Angeles. Understandably, Rigali was among those prominently mentioned as possible successors to Manning as he approached the mandatory retirement age of seventy-five.

Born in Los Angeles, on April 19, 1935, the son of Henry and Frances (White), Rigali studied at Holy Cross School prior to entering, in 1949, the archdiocesan preparatory seminary, then located at 241 South Detroit Street, in the Hancock Park area of the city. He was ordained to the priesthood by James Francis Cardinal McIntyre, on April 25, 1961, at Saint Vibiana's Cathedral. Following a brief tenure as curate at Ascension Church in Los Angeles and Saint Raymond's Church in Downey, Father Rigali was selected for graduate studies at Rome's Pontifical Gregorian University. In 1964, shortly after completing his thesis on *The Law of Tutela-An Historical and Juridical Study*, Father Rigali was awarded a doctorate in Canon Law.

In response to a request for a priest from Los Angeles to work in the papal diplomatic corps, Cardinal McIntyre asked Father Rigali if he would care to attach himself to the Vatican Secretariat of State. There he took further courses at the Piazza Minerva's Pontifical Ecclesiastical Academy prior to his formal induction into the Holy See's far-flung diplomatic mission. Father Rigali's initial appointment came, in 1966, when he was named secretary of the Apostolic Nunciature in the island-nation of Madagascar. He served at Tananarive for four years. On July 11, 1967, he was given the rank of monsignor and named a chaplain of His Holiness, Paul VI.

Manning liked and confided in Rigali. When the fifty year old priest was named a titular archbishop and head of the Pontifical Ecclesiastical Academy in 1985, the cardinal hastened to pledge "our prayers."

> A wave of joy followed on the announcement of the honors accorded to Monsignor Justin Rigali. He has been our boast as he stood by the side of three successive Popes and mediated for us their benediction and their caring. He must surely be unequaled in his fidelity to the See of Peter and his timeless service to the successors of Peter. In speaking with him from Rome, he asked particularly to extend his greetings to the Church of Los Angeles and to speak his gratitude for his belonging to it. We pledge him our prayers for now, and in the high destiny to which he is called.[15]

AUXILIARY BISHOPS

Having served for almost a quarter century as an auxiliary bishop, Manning had a great appreciation of that position and how its usefulness could be further extended in the work of the modern Church. He had come to share in his predecessor's view that auxiliary bishops should be functioning pastors of busy parishes. In those days, an auxiliary was appointed to the "person" of the residential bishop, a role that ceased with the latter's death, removal or retirement.

When Manning became archbishop, he "inherited" Bishop John J. Ward as auxiliary. Born September 28, 1920, the son of Hugh J. and Mary (McHugh) Ward, John attended Holy Cross School and Los Angeles College, before entering Saint John's Seminary in 1940. The last of the priests ordained by Archbishop John J. Cantwell, young Father Ward served as assistant or lived in residence at Saint Vibiana's Cathedral, Saint Hilary (Pico Rivera), Transfiguration, Holy Spirit, Saint Thomas and Saint Ambrose. He also served a brief stint as procurator for Saint John's Seminary and during his time at Camarillo was instrumental in building the rectory for Saint Mary Magdalen's parish.

In 1950, he was sent to study Canon Law at The Catholic University of America and afterwards was assigned to the archdiocesan matrimonial tribunal. For the next decade, he acted as notary, secretary and vice *officialis*. He was made a Papal Chamberlain in 1960 by Pope John XXIII. In October of 1963, Msgr. Ward was informed by the Apostolic Delegate that he had been named Auxiliary Bishop of Los Angeles. Ward, the first graduate of Saint John's Seminary raised to the episcopacy, was the fifteenth Californian and the fourth native Angelino to wear the mitre. His was the eighth consecration to take place in Saint Vibiana's Cathedral.

Manning had preached at Ward's episcopal ordination in 1963. In part, he said:

> The intellectual background of the new bishop will derive from another maternal source, the "Alma Mater," in which he was schooled. We pay tribute, therefore, to the Sisters of St. Joseph of Carondelet who taught him at the historic school of Holy Cross, happily commemorated on his episcopal shield; to the Vincentian Fathers who guided him in our minor and major seminaries, of which he is the proto-prelate; to the Catholic University of America which skilled him in the science of Canon Law to fulfill his wearying duties at Chancery.
>
> Toward the end of this ceremony, the young bishop will walk, clothed in the full garments of his office, down the center aisle of this venerable church. Meanwhile, the choir captures all our pent-up gladness and releases them to the joyous strains of the *Te Deum*. May this journey be symbolic

> of his walking down the road of the life that lies ahead, secure in the affection of his friends and in the goodwill of all to whom he turns his face, and always in his own heart, the ceaseless thanks of unending *Te Deum*.[16]

JOSEPH P. DOUGHERTY

The other auxiliary, Bishop Joseph P. Dougherty (1905-1970), had been installed in that position on the very day that Manning took up his duties as coadjutor. Dougherty had earlier served as Bishop of Yakima, Washington. In 1969, he retired after a series of unfortunate financial reverses had driven his diocese to the brink of bankruptcy. Later, with the approbation and encouragement of Pope Paul VI, Cardinal McIntyre welcomed Dougherty to Los Angeles as auxiliary and pastor at Saint Alphonsus Parish.[17]

During his short tenure, Dougherty captured the hearts of everyone. "Those fortunate enough to have known Bishop Dougherty during his brief sojourn in Southern California were deeply impressed by the very unusual spirituality and charm of a man steeped in the priestly traditions of piety and sanctity. His sudden death, almost exactly nineteen years after his appointment to the bishopric, deprived the Church of a dedicated apostle, a devoted pastor, an exemplary priest and a holy man."[18]

Archbishop Manning issued the following statement on that sad occasion:

> For one brief year his presence in our midst was a benediction. Death, like a lover, was his constant companion. He bore on his frail body the indefinable claim which she had on him and he cautioned his associates not to wonder should they find him, unawares, in the embrace of death. He came to us as one from a far country with the remembrance of rugged journeys and holy tasks etched into his features. One could sense a haunting of other times and values in his relation with the present. A gentle spirit, tried in a sacrificial furnace, illuminated his whole frame. Everywhere he had been, while here, he had left behind a gracious and hallowed blessing that delighted children and adults when their paths would cross again.[19]

OTHER AUXILIARY BISHOPS

One ecclesial chronicler thought it quite appropriate that the first "dual" episcopal appointments in California's ecclesial annals was announced at the very moment when most of the southland was rocked and shattered by one of the most devastating earthquakes on record, February 10, 1971. Msgr. William R. Johnson was named to the titular See of Blera and Father Juan Arzube to the titular See of Civitate and both assigned as auxiliaries to the Archbishop of Los Angeles. Several usually reliable local pundits suggested that at least one part of the *terna* was a holdover from the McIntyre era, something that must remain in the realm of speculation for the immediate future.

The appointment brought to the episcopal ministry two prelates richly gifted with pastoral experience, administrative ability and balanced thought – men abundantly endowed to share the burdens of caring for the spiritual destinies of 44% of the state's total Catholic population. Though comprising only one of California's nine ecclesiastical jurisdictions, the 1,707,605 People of God living in Santa Barbara, Ventura, Los Angeles and Orange Counties had a proud heritage upon which to build the area's future.

The priestly life of Bishop William R. Johnson mirrored the growth and development of Catholic charities in the United States in the post World War II era. He was born in Tonopah, Nevada, on November 19, 1918, the son of Jorgen and Marie (O'Connell) Johnson. The family moved to Los Angeles in the early 1920s in the hopes that the milder climate would restore Jorgen's failing health. Young William enrolled at Saint Ignatius School, where he received his elementary education from the Dominican Sisters of Mission San Jose. He entered Los Angeles College in 1932, as a clerical aspirant for the Diocese of Los Angeles-San Diego. Upon completion of his theological courses at Saint John's Seminary, Camarillo, Johnson was ordained to the priesthood by Archbishop John J. Cantwell, on May 28, 1944. After serving several years in the parochial ministry, Father Johnson was sent to the Catholic University of America, where he obtained a Master's degree in Social Work. He was named Assistant Director of the Catholic Welfare Bureau in 1948. With the appointment of Msgr. Alden J. Bell to the bishopric, in 1956, Johnson advanced to the directorship of the bureau. Four years later, he was elected to the Board of Directors for the National Conference of Catholic Charities and, in 1964, president of that body.

On January 25, 1960, Pope John XXIII bestowed the title of papal chamberlain on Father Johnson. Five years later, he was promoted to the domestic prelacy. During his years as director, Monsignor Johnson inaugurated separate divisions of Catholic Social Service and Catholic Community Service. The new charities building at 1400 West Ninth Street was erected under Johnson's guidance in the early 1960s. Between 1962 and 1968, Msgr. Johnson also served as Pastor of the inner-city parish of Holy Name. He was transferred to American Martyrs in 1968 and, in 1970, he became Parochial Vicar for Saint Vibiana's Cathedral.[20]

Juan Arzube was born in the picturesque seaport city of Guayaquil, on June 1, 1918. His earliest education was acquired at the Christian Brothers foundation in those Ecuadorian surroundings. In 1927, Juan was taken to England where he studied at Saint George's in Weybridge, and Saint Joseph's in Beulah Hills, completing his first two years of secondary education at Cardinal Vaughan School in London. Following the family's return to Ecuador, in 1932, Juan enrolled at Quito's Colegio San Gabriel. He completed his preparatory courses at the Colegio Vicente Rocafuerte, in Guayaquil, where he received his Bachelor of Arts degree in philosophy.

In 1937, wishing to round out his Latin sensitivity and English sternness, Juan applied to and was accepted as a graduate student at Rensselaer Polytechnic Institute, at Troy, New York. After four years of intensive work, he returned to Guayaquil with a highly-coveted degree in civil engineering. Hoping to launch out into some other phase of engineering, Juan returned to New York, where he planned to further augment his study. When employment opportunities beckoned to California, in 1944, he came to Los Angeles, to take up work at a correspondence school, monitoring English lessons and translating materials into his native tongue.

Juan's lifestyle was radically altered by a retreat he made at Malibu, in 1945. Having strayed from the sacraments, he made his reconciliation with great diligence and fervor. From that time onward, he began to feel a lack of fulfillment. God had entrusted him with special gifts, which he wanted to utilize in the most effective manner possible. Those sentiments became more pronounced after his religious experience at Malibu.

In the fall of 1947, Juan entered the preparatory seminary for the Archdiocese of Los Angeles and took accelerated courses in Latin and Greek. The following September, he enrolled at Saint John's Seminary, Camarillo. Ordained on May 4, 1954, by James Francis Cardinal McIntyre, the young priest's initial assignment was the curacy of Saint Agnes Church, in downtown Los Angeles. After three years of feverish activity, Father Arzube was transferred to the predominantly Mexican American community comprising Resurrection Parish. In late 1960, Father Arzube moved to the south central part of Los Angeles as assistant pastor of Ascension Parish. His apostolic endeavors in that busy metropolitan area lasted until October, 1963, when McIntyre named him to El Monte's Nativity Parish. There he supervised erection of the handsome shrine of Our Lady of Guadalupe, a mission church of which he was the canonical administrator, in 1968.[21]

Upon receiving word of the appointment, Archbishop Manning issued a formal "welcome" to the new auxiliary bishops:

> This is a splendid moment in our history. The appointment of Monsignor Johnson serves to cast the spotlight on the whole sweep of the activities of the Church in its witnessing and mission in the field of social service. He has eminently served as the director of our charitable apostolate and, in doing so as a bishop, will give added grace to his dedication. Father Juan Arzube has quietly fulfilled his mission of service these many years. He is rich in the commendation of his fellow-priests and cherishes the total approval of all whom he has served. For the Spanish-speaking people of our flock he will be the pledge and fulfillment of our concern for their spiritual and temporal welfare. Both men are particularly dear to us. We are much comforted in their designation. We solicit the prayers of all our people that God will bless and sustain them in the difficult apostolate for which they are now set apart.[22]

With creation of the Diocese of Orange and the appointment of Bishop William R. Johnson as its first residential ordinary, Manning inaugurated the long and tedious process of having two additional priests named to the bishopric. On December 20, 1976, at a special consistory called by Pope Paul VI to proclaim the impending beatification of another American prelate, Bishop John N. Neumann,, it was announced that Msgrs. Thaddeus Shubsda, pastor of Saint Paul's Parish and Manuel Moreno, Vicar for Saint Vibiana's Cathedral, had been assigned to the titular see of Trau and Tanagra as auxiliaries to Timothy Cardinal Manning. Those two prelates were the twenty-third and twenty-fourth native Californians named to the episcopate and the eighth and ninth to serve as auxiliaries or episcopal assistants in the Archdiocese of Los Angeles.

Thaddeus Anthony Shubsda was born in Los Angeles, on April 2, 1925, the son of Julius and Mary (Jelski) Shubsda. He attended public school until 1936, when he enrolled at Our Lady of Lourdes, then under the direction of the Presentation Sisters. Upon graduation from Verdugo Hills High School in Tujunga, in 1939, "Ted" entered Los Angeles College, the preparatory seminary for the Archdiocese of Los Angeles. Ordained on April 26, 1950, by James Francis Cardinal McIntyre, Father Shubsda offered his first Mass at Our Lady of Bright Mount Parish. After serving as curate at San Antonio de Padua and Saint Vibiana's Cathedral, he was appointed to the Matrimonial Tribunal, where he worked from 1964 to 1968. He was made a monsignor in 1965 by Pope Paul VI. In 1968, Msgr. Shubsda was named Associate Director of the Propagation of the Faith and, in that capacity, he worked closely with the Holy Childhood Association and the Lay Mission Helpers. For thirty years, Shubsda served as Spiritual director for the Catholic Labor Institute, a group of Laymen dedicated to promulgating and teaching the social doctrine of the Church.

Manuel Moreno, born in November 27, 1930, in Placentia, attended Saint Mary's parochial school in Fullerton, Fullerton High School and the University of California at Los Angeles where he received a degree in business administration. Ordained April 25, 1961, he did graduate studies in Rome and later occupied several pastoral posts while serving as notary in the matrimonial tribunal. In addition to serving as Rector for Saint Vibiana's cathedral, Msgr. Moreno was the founding director of the Cursillo movement and director for the *Movimiento Familiar Cristiano.*

In his announcement to the news media, Cardinal Manning noted that "the bishops-elect had a rich pastoral background; both are fluent Spanish-speakers, both are native to our southland and both are held dearly in the hearts of priests and people. With their assistance the burdens of my office will be lightened and the various parts of the archdiocese" enjoy the frequent presence of the new bishops. Manning concluded by praying the "fullness of apostolic blessings upon them that Our Lady of Angels will look upon them as her special sons."[23] As an aside, the cardinal related that on that very morning, Bishop-elect Shubsda had been held-up at gunpoint and robbed in his rectory by two gunmen.

Bishop Moreno was subsequently sent to San Buenaventura where he served as Episcopal Vicar for Ventura county until 1982. Though retaining his residence and pastorate in Los Angeles, Bishop Shubsda served as Episcopal Vicar for Santa Barbara county for the next five years. In mid 1982, he was transferred to the residential bishopric of Monterey.

The announcement of Manning's third and final selection of auxiliary bishops was dramatically disclosed during the Chrism Mass for Holy Week at Saint Vibiana's Cathedral in 1983. A great burst of applause surged from the congregation in the century old cathedral as the bishops-designates Msgrs. Donald Montrose and William Levada rose from the clerical ranks and made their way to the altar.[24]

Donald Montrose, who had served as archdiocesan Superintendent of High Schools and Colleges from 1964 to 1977 and pastor of Resurrection parish since 1970, was born on May 13, 1923 at Denver, Colorado. A graduate of Cathedral High School and Los Angeles College, he was ordained on May 7, 1949. Most of his years were spent as teacher and later principal of Mater Dei High School.

William Levada, a native of Long Beach, California, was a former professor at Saint John's Seminary and President of the Priests' Senate. He served on the staff of the Sacred Congregation of the Doctrine of the Faith in Rome. Later, he was executive director of the California Catholic Conference. Born on June 15, 1936, he studied at Saint Anthony's Elementary School and Saint Mary's in Houston, Texas. Ordained in Rome on December 20, 1961, he subsequently received a doctorate in theology at the Pontifical Gregorian University.

The two appointees were popular choices. Likely Montrose's name had been on earlier *ternas*. In his account of Levada's appointment, John Dart told readers in the Los Angeles *Times* that his credentials "might augur well for an influential career in the Roman Catholic hierarchy."[25] Though Manning would never discuss the matter, many of the local clergy interpreted Levada's appointment as instigated by unidentified "Roman officials," possibly as an attempt at influencing the choice of Manning's eventual successor.

Like his predecessor, Manning occasionally sought the advice of the presbyterium for candidates to the bishopric. In March of 1975, for example, he wrote a "confidential" letter in which he said:

> I solicit your counsel in a matter of unique importance. As Ordinary of the Diocese, I have the obligation to submit to the Holy See a list of priests who are judged worthy and qualified to exercise the episcopal office. Each year the bishops of the Province meet to consider prudently the men who should be promoted to the episcopate.
>
> I invite your assistance in helping me to prepare for this meeting. Would you kindly send me, personally, the name or names of those priests whom you, in your wisdom and experience, believe should be considered as candidates. You are free to suggest priests from either the secular clergy or religious clergy.

LOS ANGELES AUXILIARY BISHOPS

Auxiliary Bishop
Juan Arzube

Auxiliary Bishop
Joseph Dougherty

Auxiliary Bishop
William Johnson

Auxiliary Bishop
William Levada

LOS ANGELES AUXILIARY BISHOPS

Auxiliary Bishop
Donald Montrose

Auxiliary Bishop
Manuel Moreno

Auxiliary Bishop
Thaddeus Shubsda

Auxiliary Bishop
John Ward

> While I shall treasure your contribution in this regard, I must bring to your attention a provision in the "Norms for the Selection of Bishops." My consultation with you in this regard must be a "secret and individual consultation." You are not free in conscience to discuss with anyone the fact that you have been consulted, or the names you have submitted. I am confident that you realize that the very nature of the subject, the good of the Church and the individual welfare of the priests you have recommended demand such confidentiality.[26]

Among the names that consistently surfaced from this and subsequent appeals were Monsignors Clifford Parker, Thomas Kiefer, John Rawden and Fathers Luis Valbuena, Royale Vadakin, John Cosgrove and Joseph Pollard.

CALIFORNIA CATHOLIC CONFERENCE

Possibly because he dreaded making decisions, Manning found it easy to endorse the notion of collegiality that emanated from Vatican Council II. In the late 1970s, Manning and several other California bishops established an ecclesial "umbrella" for the fifty-eight counties in the Golden State. Its objectives and goals would parallel and localize those used by the United States Catholic Conference.

The California Catholic Conference was formally established in February, 1971. It was an outgrowth of the California Conference of Catholic Health Facilities and the Catholic Schools of California, organized two years earlier. The functions of the Conference fell into three general categories: (a) providing liaison with state departments and with the legislature, (b) disseminating information to Catholic associations and organizations, to other state conferences and to the United States Catholic Conference and (c) coordinating interdiocesan activities in the areas of education, welfare and related items.

An informational newsletter was to be published monthly and a large amount of correspondence maintained with the archbishops and bishops attached to the jurisdictions of California. Organized as a direct result of Vatican Council II and the 1971 Synod of Bishops, the California Catholic Conference would be actively involved in a myriad of public affairs integral to the preaching of the Gospel and the betterment of justice, peace and general welfare.

The conference was to be a mouthpiece for the California bishops. An executive director would coordinate the day-to-day activities of the Conference, assisted by office personnel who would serve as staff to the bishops. Associated with the CCC were the diocesan directors of welfare and social service agencies, the superintendents of schools and coordinators of religious education, campus ministries and Catholic cemeteries. Among the arms of the California Catholic Conference established in ensuing months were divisions of Education, Hispanic Affairs and Social Welfare. Another satellite group closely affiliated with the California Catholic Conference was the California Association of Catholic Hospitals. The existence of the CCC confirmed the conciliar belief and ideal that "when the insights of prudence and experience have been shared and views exchanged, there will emerge a holy union of energies in the service of the common good of the churches."[27]

According to a report in *The Tidings*, the Conference was intended to provide the Church with a vehicle for speaking with a united voice and for acting with joint effort and resources in promoting the welfare of the Church, as well as for the common good of all the state's residents. A central office was located in Sacramento where Msgr. John S. Cummins, the first executive director, would assist the planning and coordinating activities falling under the auspices of the Catholic Church. Manning was elected proto President of the Conference.[28]

ON RETREAT

One of the benefits attached to membership in the California Catholic Conference is an annual retreat for members and, later, all the hierarchy in region XI of the NCCB, which included California, Utah, Nevada and Hawaii. The eight day retreat, begun the first week of the year, was held at *El Retiro* in Los Altos. Total silence was observed during those days when the Spiritual Exercises of Saint Ignatius were presented to retreatants.

In 1980, Cardinal Manning kept a log for the retreat which was subsequently published in the archdiocesan newspaper:

> There are no group conferences. Each bishop has a spiritual director. For one hour each day the director programs for his candidate the sequence of exercises to be followed. These are reflected upon in four separate hours of meditation. The Liturgy of the Hours for morning and evening is recited in common. Each mid-day there is a half-hour of

shared prayer based on the reading of a Gospel extract. Mass is celebrated in common before the evening meal and a homily is given by one of the directors. The meals are conducted in silence, a silence sustained by soft background music from a tape collection.

A by-product of this time of seclusion is the bonding together of the member bishops who are involved. A non-verbal intimacy is established which increases the charity of our fraternity and links us together in our sorrows and our joys as we serve God's holy people. This time the newly designated Coadjutor Bishop of Fresno, Joseph Madera, was present. It was such an appropriate induction for him into the mini-college of bishops that makes up our Region XI.

Why do the bishops make such a retreat? All of them at other times in the year are engaged in a retreat with the priests of their dioceses. Why this exclusive one? The reasons are many. There is the prime call to give to the Divine Majesty an affirmation of our praise, reverence and service. There is the sure need, accentuated by his high responsibilities, for the bishop to pursue the salvation and sanctification of his own soul. It is likewise a testimony, whence we write these lines, to our people that for them also do we sanctify ourselves, so that together we may grow in love and become a more fitting gift which Jesus will present to His heavenly Father.

We are grateful for the prayers and sacrifices of the many who remembered us. All the cloistered communities of women were specifically engaged in sacrificing for us. Some who are terminally ill with cancer offered their sufferings for us. May God reward them all. We pray too that the call to the Spiritual Exercises, or to a retreat experience will be answered by many priests and people, especially by our youth, all for the greater glory of God.[29]

N.C.W.C. AND N.C.C.B.

Though he dutifully attended the annual meetings of the National Catholic Welfare Conference and its successor, the National Conference of Catholic Bishops from 1946 onward, Manning rarely expressed his views on the floor except in cases where he had been designated to give a committee report. Yet, he diligently studied the reams of weekly briefs that came across his desk from the conference headquarters and he was always ready to cast an informed vote on the manifold issues before that assembly. Manning was mostly a silent observer who felt ill-at-ease participating with his episcopal confreres in their often heated and spirited exchanges. John Tracy Ellis once asked one of the cardinals how Manning stood on some crucial issues, only to be told that "the gentle-mannered Irishman prays while the rest of us quarrel. This body needs more Mannings and fewer Deardens." Manning was appalled when a newly-consecrated California bishop asked for and was given permission to address the assembly at his very first meeting. He later observed that "it was as if the man were running for public office."

Once again, it was in preaching that Manning "came alive" on the national scene. On numerous occasions he was asked to deliver the homily for some outstanding anniversary or ecclesial commemoration. A prime example occurred in 1974, when he agreed to speak at a Mass concelebrated by the bishops for the observance of the Holy Year at the National Shrine of the Immaculate Conception in Washington, D.C.

After referring to the presence of a nearby foreign embassy, he told how in that embassy the language of their homeland was spoken, the interests of that nation were pursued. "It is a little island of a foreign country in the midst of our own." Then he noted that "we are the representatives of heaven in this world. Its language must be our own. Its interest must be pursued by us and on its behalf we have to challenge or rebuke the world when it contradicts what we stand for. The sign and language and food of our embassy is the Eucharist. It is entrusted to bishops first and then to every priest insofar as he localizes the bishops to each congregation. It is our badge of unity and love." The cardinal then referred to the gospel of St. Luke announcing the proclamation of a year of favor from the Lord in which glad tidings are to be brought to the poor, liberty is to be proclaimed to captives, sight is to be restored to the blind and prisoners are to be released:

> The Church through her ministers claims to be the protector of Christ in the world, asserts that the Spirit of the Lord is upon her. However, we are here up against an insurmountable obstacle. How can the Church relate to the poor, to the outcast, to the lowly to the suffering except in terms of condescension, patronizing, letting crumbs fall from a sumptuous table. The poor will accept but they are wounded by condescension and patronizing. They are diminished in their personhood by receiving.

> There well may be but one way in which they will receive without this wound and that is when the giver is no longer bending down, but is equally lowly and poor and suffering. And when there is a bond of love. Then the illegal alien, the rejects of skidrow, the dropouts of society, the forgotten in prison cells, the reaching hands of the elderly in the sanitariums – these will recognize us if we walk among them as one of them, like Damien at Molokai – "We lepers" – and our credibility is stabilized. The kingdom of God is surely here. Then only can we turn to the modern world and ask: Who do you say that I am? We are the workers of peace, the guardians of unity and the messengers of love.[30]

Manning's last and probably best presentation to the American hierarchy was a two-part conference he gave at Collegeville on June 27, 1988. In part he said:

> In the hill-towns of Mediterranean countries you may see a piazza or plaza in front of the cathedral church. In the middle of that open space there will be a fountain of sparkling water, Narrow streets open into the square. Each morning women will come through these corridors with containers to draw water from the fountain to provide for their daily household needs. The bishop of the local Church is like that fountain for his priests and people. He is the center of their worship, the source of their holiness and the nourishment of their daily thirstings.

Manning told how, on September 16, 1987, the Holy Father, John Paul II, met with the bishops of the United States at the historic San Fernando Mission and in the adjoining facilities of Our Lady Queen of Angels Seminary in Los Angeles. He then quoted the Pope's homily at morning prayer in the Old Mission chapel:

> Our task as Bishops in the Church today is still centered in the person of Jesus Christ. We are witnesses to his cross and resurrection. Each of us has been consecrated by the Holy Spirit to be for our people a living sign of Jesus Christ,

> a living sign of the praying Christ who himself took time during his public ministry to be alone with his Father in prayer;
>
> a living sign of the compassionate redeemer who healed the sick, forgave sinners and comforted the sorrowful;
>
> a living sign of the love of our Savior, a love which is stronger than sin and death;
>
> a living sign of the fidelity of the Lord, and therefore, like Christ, a sign of contradiction.
>
> In the midst of our priests and among ourselves as bishops, each of us is meant to be a sign of Jesus' fraternal love.

Manning concluded by saying that "Here at St. John's in Collegeville, we absent ourselves for a few hours from the concerns of our agenda to reflect on these words of the Holy Father and on our own spirituality as bishops. The level of holiness of priest and people is conditioned and measured by that of the bishop. The old adage like priest, like people is more pertinent when applied to the bishop: like bishop, like priest. Therefore, the bishop must be able to say to people and priest, with St. Paul be followers of me, as I am of Christ."[31]

Notes to the Text

1. Francis J. Weber (comp.), *Times of Tension, Moments of Grace* (Los Angeles, 1990), Pp. 117-118.
2. *The Tidings*, March 7, 1980. Madera's years in Fresno were tumultuous and he later was appointed auxiliary for the Military Ordinariate. For a brief sketch of his pre-Fresno days, see Francis J. Weber, *California: The Catholic Experience* (Los Angeles, 1981), Pp. 193-194.
3. *The Tidings*, July 20, 1984.
4. *Ibid*, June 4, 1982.
5. *Ibid*, July 4, 1982.
6. *Ibid*, March 11, 1966
7. AALA, Leo T. Maher to Timothy Cardinal Manning, San Diego, April 15, 1982.
8. *Southern Cross*, July 20, 1978.
9. Los Angeles *Times*, July 19, 1978.
10. *Ibid*, August 24, 1978.
11. *The Tidings*, November 4, 1983.
12. *Vg*. 1977 to 1980.
13. *The Tidings*, March 20, 1964.
14. *Ibid*, February 26, 1982.
15. *Ibid*, June 14, 1985.
16. *Ibid*, December 13, 1963.
17. See Francis J. Weber, *His Eminence of Los Angeles. James Francis Cardinal McIntyre* (Los Angeles, 1997), Pp. 563-565.
18. Francis J. Weber, *The Pilgrim Church in California* (Los Angeles, 1973), p. 103.
19. *The Tidings*, July 17, 1970.
20. Francis J. Weber, *California Catholicity* (Los Angeles, 1979), Pp. 119-120.

21. *Ibid*, Pp. 121-122.
22. *The Tidings*, February 12, 1971.
23. Ibid, December 24, 1977.
24. *Ibid*, April 1, 1983.
25. Los Angeles *Times*, April 2, 1983.
26. ALA, Timothy Cardinal Manning to Clergy, Los Angeles, March 14, 1975.
27. Francis J. Weber, *California. The Catholic Experience* (Los Angeles, 1981), Pp. 231-232.
28. *The Tidings*, January 22, 1971.
29. *Ibid*, January 18, 1980.
30. *Ibid*, November 29, 1974.
31. *Times of Tension. Moments of Grace*, Pp. 426-428.

8. Diocese of Orange

Orange County was established on March 11, 1889, when the loosely-knit cluster of *ranchos* then comprising the area were severed from the southeastern part of Los Angeles County. On May 16, 1975, the archivist for the Archdiocese of Los Angeles was asked to give "a description of the area" for a study that was being made "about the desirability of" creating a diocese in Orange County.[1]

> Though it is generally assumed that the county's full name was chosen to accentuate the citrus industry, there is a greater likelihood that the appellation was imported by Andrew Glasswell, a native of a Virginia County named to honor the son-in-law of George II. Catholic penetration, on a permanent basis, can be traced to All Saints Day, in the year of American Independence, when Fray Junípero Serra founded the seventh of California's missions at San Juan Capistrano.
>
> In 1860, Bernardo Yorba built the chapel of San Antonio de Santa Ana on his extensive lands. Priests from San Gabriel attended the distant outpost in the years immediately following. When Saint Boniface Parish was created at Anaheim in 1889, its boundaries were co-extensive with those of the newly-formed county. Regular mission stations were cared for at Santa Ana (Saint Joseph's) and Yorba (San Antonio). That year also saw the inauguration of Catholic education with the establishment of Saint Catherine's Academy at Anaheim.
>
> The area is rich in Indian-Spanish traditions. There are 160,168 people in the county with Hispanic surnames and 108,167 of them speak Spanish as their mother tongue. (That's roughly 13% of the total population)

> STATISTICS: Probably no other of the nation's 3,049 counties can match the temperate climate, geographical attractions and scope of religious, education and recreational facilities adorning the 782 square mile area known as Orange County. It is bounded geographically by the counties of Los Angeles, San Bernardino, Riverside, San Diego and forty-two miles of Pacific coastline.
>
> The county seat is located at Santa Ana, which is thirty-one road-miles southeast of Los Angeles. Of the twenty-six incorporated cities in the county, Anaheim has the largest population (185,105), followed by Santa Ana (168,205). The latest figures place the count for the City of Orange at 82,795.
>
> Orange County has been one of the nation's most spectacular growth areas. During the 1960s, its advance in population exceeded that recorded in forty-one of the United States. Presently, there are 1,605,700 recorded inhabitants in the county. Orange has evolved from an abundantly-rich agricultural region into a progressive, industrially-oriented metropolitan area. Inasmuch as three -fourths of the county's 500,480 acres are subject to urbanization, there is every reason to believe that Orange is destined to be an even more dominant force in the industrial and financial life of California.
>
> Indeed, its average rainfall (15 inches), rate of sunshine (from 60 to 80% of the year) and mean temperature (from 48 to 76 degrees) all portend a future of unlimited proportions, to say nothing of the recreational facilities and potentials.2

Promotional literature aside, Orange County was and remains a most attractive area of the Lord's vineyard. In his memoirs, Captain T. Anson Smith recounted a serious illness and hospital confinement he underwent in 1932 at Saint Joseph's Hospital in Orange. One day, the chaplain approached the patient to talk "about heaven, hell and all that Catholic stuff." The priest seemed perplexed when Smith proclaimed: "Good Father, neither you nor your pope could promise me anything better than I have experienced here. This beautiful city and county of Orange is heaven enough for anyone. With it I have no more to desire."[3]

Speculation about the erection of a diocese in Orange County had been "table talk" for many years at clerical gatherings. Among the already existing jurisdictions in the United States, the size, Catholic population, geographical location and mild climate of Orange gave the area a unique prominence in the American Church, something long recognized by Vatican bureaucrats. Nor were those factors lost at the local scene. As early as 1922, when the Sisters of Saint Joseph of Orange moved their headquarters from Northern California to Orange, the then Bishop John J. Cantwell told his secretary, Father John J. Devlin, that "those nuns know what they're doing. You will live to see a diocese in Orange County." And he did.

In the mid 1950s, Archbishop Amleto Giovanni Cicognani, the Apostolic Delegate to the United States, a widely-read man, perhaps knowing of T. Anson Smith's memoir, suggested that James Francis Cardinal McIntyre investigate the possibility of establishing one or more new dioceses within his jurisdiction. The cardinal admitted, in his reply, that "he would welcome a diminution of his responsibilities, but pointed out that any division should proceed along county lines." He observed that "where that had not been done in the United States, all kinds of legal problems had later developed."[4]

As for the northern area of the archdiocese, McIntyre noted that "were Ventura and Santa Barbara larger in population, they would make a splendid diocese," but at that time, such a jurisdiction would have only twenty-six parishes. That area constituted about 4.5% of the total Catholic population or about 259,000 people. The cardinal observed that 89.7% of the Catholics in the archdiocese lived in Los Angeles County.

Regarding Orange County, the cardinal pointed out that "its development in recent years has been rapid and we would rather expect that it will require a total of forty or fifty parishes within the next three or four years." He already had property for nine or ten contemplated parishes which would be commenced as soon as priests were available. McIntyre thought that "Orange County would be self-supporting and is already in itself a well established unit."[5]

Included with his observations were some charts that gave statistical data about the question:

Los Angeles County	5,250,000	or	89.7 percent
Ventura County	148,200	or	2.5 percent
Santa Barbara County	111,000	or	1.9 percent
Orange County	340,000	or	5.9 percent

These four counties are divided into parishes, as follows:

Los Angeles County	215 Parishes
Ventura County	13 Parishes
Santa Barbara County	12 Parishes
Orange County	29 Parishes

McIntyre noted that the gross income of Orange County was less than 6% of that in Los Angeles. School expenses were relatively higher in Los Angeles County. Orange County, because of its recent development, had a little higher debt, about 8% of that of Los Angeles, as against a population of 6%. Ventura and Santa Barbara were relatively low in debt, each being less than 2% of Los Angeles County. The percentages of their assets followed closely the population proportions. The financial income for the entire archdiocese was broken down in the following chart:

Counties	Los Angeles	Orange	Santa Barbara	Ventura	Total
Ordinary Income	12,364,052.18	737,199.48	301,400.95	238,832.38	13,641,484.99
Ordinary Expenses	5,009,747.00	348,460.47	173,505.21	125,195.96	5,656,908.64
School Income	3,421,665.10	150,493.28	60,732.08	62,732.08	3,695,199.78
School Expenses	4,363,511.75	209,101.09	68,592.84	74,058.19	4,715,200.87
Advance from Parish for School	1,018,550.18	64,567.45	12,513.05	11,995.81	1,107,626.49
Total Amt. of Debt	12,269,374.91	1,087,100.63	207,474.43	218,991.97	13,782,941.94
Paid on Debt during Year	2,557,678.83	188,189.00	15,000.00		2,760,867.83
Parish Money Invested	7,707,969.99	901,212.10	274,615.73	90,000.00	8,973,797.82
Cash on Hand, End of Year	22,970,329.19	214,617.41	93,374.29	128,834.39	23,407,155.28

Archbishop Cicognani thanked McIntyre for his lengthy and extensive report and noted that "as things stand, I can see that there are great difficulties involved." He concluded by assuring the cardinal that I have deep appreciation for your evaluation of the situation and your conclusions will be mine.[6] Except for a statistical update in May of 1961, no further official discussion was made about splitting the archdiocese in McIntyre's time.[7]

Archbishop Jean Jadot, one of Cicognani's successors as Apostolic Delegate to the United States, approached Timothy Cardinal Manning with the request that the bishops in the Province of Los Angeles undertake a study of possible new dioceses in Southern California. He said that it "would be natural for their attention to be directed to Orange County as one possibility and to Riverside-San Bernardino as another."[8]

Responding from Ballingeary, where he was on vacation, Manning suggested that his Vicar for Finance, Msgr. Benjamin G. Hawkes, be delegated to prepare statistical study on the subject which the bishops could use as a guideline in their next meeting.[9] Jadot agreed, but specified that Hawkes "would not attend the meeting at which the bishops would discuss the matter."[10]

In his exhaustive report, Msgr. Hawkes first presented a series of charts as follows:

Comparative Statistics	
Total Population	
1974	1,646,300
1970	1,460,000
1965	1,110,211
1960	688,922
1955	329,081
1950	212,364
1940	130,760
Projected Population	
1980	2,275,000
1990	2,850,000
2000	3,250,000
Catholic Population	
1974 (18.11%)	298,205
1970 (18.36%)	268,233
Area	
Total county	782 square miles

Orange County Statistics		
CHURCHES		43
MISSIONS		8
PRIESTS (Active & Inactive)		
Secular		96
Religious		56
Externs		11
SEMINARIANS		
High School		15
College		40
Theology		12
SISTERS		462
SCHOOLS		
Elementary		Students
Parochial	33	14,332
Private	2	570
Secondary		
Diocesan	2	2,231
Private	4	1,462
TOTAL	**41**	**18,595**
MINOR SEMINARIES (Religious)		1
BROTHER'S JUNIORATE AND NOVITIATE		1
COLLEGE (Religious Women)		1
HOSPITALS		2
SPEECH AND HEARING CLINIC		1
CATHOLIC SOCIAL SERVICE OFFICES		2
FACILITIES WITH INSTITUTIONAL CARE FOR CHILDREN		2
ADOPTION SERVICE		1
HOME FOR THE AGED		1
SUMMER CAMP		1

Commemorating
the Establishment of
the
Diocese of Orange
in California
and
the Installation of
The Most Reverend
William R. Johnson, D.D.
Bishop of Orange
June 18, 1976
Holy Family Cathedral
Orange, California

Memorial Card

Holy Family Cathedral on June 18, 1976.

Financial Considerations	
ASSETS:	
Value of Properties:	
Assessed Value	9,892,780
Market Value(1)	39,491,120
Savings (Parish Deposits)(2)	1,275,125
Checking (In Banks) - (1-1-74)	712,421
Real Estate:	
Future Sites (10) - cost	1,185,945
Income Properties	————
Used by Religious	187,467
Cathedraticum (1% of Ordinary Income)	54,878
Seminary Fund (Burses)	————
Stocks & Bonds (Market Value)	————
Cemetery Care Fund(3)	634,249
DEBTS:	
Loans to Parishes(4)	2,918,610
Balance due on Construction Contracts	575,905
INCOME: (Year ending 1-1-74)	
Ordinary	5,487,790
Other Income (Building Fund Drives)	1,857,644
Special Collections	299,464
EXPENSES: (Year ending 1-1-74)	
Ordinary	3,277,491
Extraordinary (Property & Building)	1,431,552
Subsidy for Parochial Schools	1,228,601

(1) This Market Value represents an accepted formula of four times the County Assessor's assessed valuation. However, we must remember these are all single purpose buildings and in most instances would not realize anywhere near Market Value on a sale.
(2) These deposits are with the Chancery on which 5.5% interest is received by the parish.
(3) These funds are on deposit with the Chancery, for which 4% interest is paid.
(4) These loans are with the Chancery Office on which 6.5% interest is paid.

Hawkes reported that the country had increased 400% in the preceding twenty years. Since 1960, there had been a population growth of nearly 1,000,000 persons. Projections then available indicated that another 629,000 would be added in the next six years. He noted that less than 50% of the county had been developed, pointing our that two large ranches accounted for a very large portion of this underdeveloped area. He predicted that "when those holdings open up, the expansion will explode."

The vicar then analyzed the implications of dividing the diocese, from a strictly financial point-of-view.

> It has been possible for the Church to keep pace with the population growth only because of the financial credit of Los Angeles. By itself, this county could never have borrowed sufficient funds to finance the churches and schools needed and constructed. By itself, there would be no diocesan high schools. One of the private high schools was paid for by Los Angeles at a cost of $2,000,000 and given to the Servite Fathers. To another private high school the diocese contributed $500,000.
>
> The present debt on the parishes is $2,918,610. However, Los Angeles just paid off $425,000 of Orange County parish debts as of August 31, 1974. In the preceding five years, a total of $2,653,000 was given by Los Angeles to these same parishes. If these donations were not made, the present debt would be $5,571,610. There are presently four CCD buildings and two auditoriums under construction or on the planning board. The balance due on these contracts is $575,905, which will increase the county's debt.
>
> Los Angeles' credit is based in a considerable degree on the value of the future parish sites and income properties. If Orange County is separated, the new diocese would have to finance, in addition to the parish debts, the nearly $1,200,000 in future parish sites. Excluding Orange County, the parishes of Los Angeles, Ventura and Santa Barbara Counties are borrowing five and one-quarter million dollars.
>
> A recapitulation of the county's finance requirements, if these were independent of Los Angeles, are as follows:

Present Debts on Parishes	$2,918,610
Balance Due on Contracts	575,905
Future Parish Sites and Properties used by Religious (cost)	1,373,412
Total:	**$4,867,927**

> The above total excludes any additional financing which will definitely be required if the needs of the Catholic population are to continue to be provided for by the Church.
>
> Orange County with its 782 square miles is 8.3% of the present area in the Los Angeles Archdiocese. The Catholic population of 298,205 is 15% of the present Catholic population in the Los Angeles Archdiocese. However, 35.6% of the present parish debt in the archdiocese is on Orange County parishes. Last year's Ordinary Income in Orange County was only 18% of the total Ordinary Income of the archdiocese. Orange County parish deposits total only 11% of the present parochial deposits in the archdiocese.

Hawkes saw two positive advantages in making Orange County a diocese, namely the reduction in the size of the archdiocese which would render the Ordinary of Los Angeles "more available to expend his energies on Los Angeles and the other two counties" and that "the people of Orange County would more easily know their bishop." He felt that "Orange County could operate independently," but he felt that "the price it would pay for this canonical independence" would far outweigh the advantages. "The price would be a severe restriction in their credit and ability to meet loan commitments - loans which should be available if they are to meet the expansion demands in this area. When these demands are met, debt reduction is also reduced considerably." He concluded by suggesting that appointment of an episcopal vicar for Orange County would avoid the pitfalls of division while reaping many of the advantages.[11]

When the bishops assembled in early November, the report prepared by Hawkes was discussed and debated. Auxiliary Bishop William Johnson, whose antipathy for the vicar and his policies had been manifested publicly on many occasions, argued that the pastoral advantages for a new diocese in Orange far outweighed and even negated the financial considerations. Finally, the bishops unanimously voted to endorse the Apostolic Delegate's call for dividing the Archdiocese of Los Angeles along the lines proposed by Jadot. Cardinal Manning sent the minutes of the meeting to the delegation, along with the offer of speaking personally with Jadot on his coming visit to the east.[12]

On November 18, Manning met with Jadot at the Apostolic Delegation offices in Washington, D.C. The delegate noted that Hawkes had expressed "certain misgivings about the financial ramifications of such a move" and asked Manning to give him the names of others"who might be able to give informed comments on this plan." Jadot also wanted "the names of likely candidates" for the position of bishop "with an indication of the reason for your choice." He also recalled Manning's verbal suggestion about "the desirability of the title of San Juan Capistrano even though the See might be located in Anaheim."[13]

Because of the Holy See's inordinate obsession with secrecy, even by such "liberal" churchmen as Jadot, there are numerous gaps in the correspondence on this and related issues. However, it is not unreasonable to conjecture that Cardinal Manning placed Johnson at the head of his list for Orange. And, all things considered, even Hawkes would later observe that Johnson was the logical and probably best person for that position.

One of the reasons that the Roman Curia makes so few mistakes is that it acts so deliberately. Almost a year and a half later, on March 1, 1976, Jadot wrote Manning saying that he was "very happy to tell you that the Holy Father intends to establish a new diocese consisting of Orange County and has in mind the appointment of the Most Reverend William Johnson as its first Ordinary." In that same letter, he had been directed "to inquire whether you find the title of *Santa Ana* acceptable or whether there would be any serious objections to that name." If that were acceptable, could Manning let him know which church in that city could serve as cathedral.[14]

In one of his rare outbursts of irritation, Manning responded, in his own hand, and, "with emphasis," that "the title of Santa Ana would *not* be acceptable." The city lacked "significant identity." It had no church that was fitting for a cathedral and "the title would be at odds with the name of a Diocese of Orange." Then, erroneously, he said that "the city is called after the last Mexican governor of California, not after Saint Anne." (Actually, Manning was wrong. The last Mexican governor was Pio Pico.) Manning reminded Jadot that the question of title had already been agreed upon, *viz.*, that it would be "the Diocese of Orange, that the See city be that of Orange and that the cathedral be the church of the Holy Family." He pointed out that the church was "modern and modest" and that it was located near "the compound of the Sisters of Saint Joseph of Orange which encompasses a college and hospital and house of studies." The cardinal emphasized that Orange is "the natural center of all Catholic activity in the county." He concluded by insisting that his views, shared by Bishop Johnson, be forwarded to the Holy See.[15]

On March 30, 1976, the Vatican announced the creation of a new diocese for Orange County and named the Most Reverend William R. Johnson of Los Angeles as its bishop. In a feature story, John Dart wrote in the Los Angeles *Times* that "Johnson and Orange Catholics will have the chance to shape their own approaches to Catholic issues and innovations." The bishop said "he did not foresee any major changes in policy or operation for the new diocese, the formation of which was the subject of rumors for many years." The story credited James Francis Cardinal McIntyre with pushing "parish and school expansion in Orange County in anticipation of the new diocese." Manning was quoted as saying that "there was no conscious delay in forming the new diocese. The Church works very slowly in those matters. There was a normal maturing of the idea."[16]

The updated statistics for the new diocese indicated a total population of 1,646,000 persons, of whom 334,000 were Catholic. There were forty-four parishes, eight missions, six Catholic high schools and two Catholic hospitals in the new See. The area was served by 108 diocesan priests, fifty-seven religious priests, 484 Sisters and sixty-six seminarians.

Bishop Johnson, speaking at a press conference said he accepted the new appointment "with gratitude to God and the Holy Father. It is a real joy and a challenge." The very name, Orange, he said, "suggests a golden treasure and the new diocese is all of that in its physical characteristics, its people and its traditions.

> The area is small enough to be unified as a true community and large enough to encompass a substantial number of generous hearted people. These, along with the dedicated priests and religious who serve them are the richest endowment one could hope for.[17]

Cardinal Manning also issued a statement in which he said that:

> Today the Church in Southern California takes a great step forward. The first church and the first community of faith was established in what is now Orange County two hundred years ago at San Juan Capistrano. Today is the fulfillment of that early deeding. The new diocese gives promise of being all that the Second Vatican Council envisioned for a diocese with its bishop very much present to his people and, together with him, forming one People of God.
>
> We must have special gratitude to His Eminence, Cardinal McIntyre. It was his foresight and husbandry that made possible at this time the realization of an independent juris-

diction in Orange County. For many years he had envisioned it and we are glad he has seen its dawning.

The new bishop is taken from our side. His priestly years, in God's providence, were a splendid preparation for the task now given him.. It will not be easy to part with him, but there will be great joy in seeing his shepherding of his own people. Our prayers go with him and surround all the new diocese. A county line does not sever our love or our traditions. It is enough that God be praised and served.[18]

On May 18, the Apostolic Delegate released a statement from Washington, D.C. which read:

The erection of the Diocese of Orange in California and the appointment of His Excellency, the Most Reverend William R. Johnson, as the first Bishop of Orange in California was announced by His Holiness, Pope Paul VI, on Tuesday, March 30, 1976. The implementation of this decision of Pope Paul will occur with the execution of the Papal Bull issued by the Holy See at 4:00 p.m. on June 18, 1976.

At this time, the Diocese of Orange in California will acquire its own identity as a juridical entity. At this time, also, it will factually and definitively be an independent jurisdiction of the Roman Catholic Church wholly separated from the Archdiocese of Los Angeles which jurisdiction prior to that date will have included the California counties of Los Angeles, Orange, Santa Barbara and Ventura. As of June 18, 1976, at 4:00 p.m. all Catholic parishes, institutions, schools and whatever was formerly within the jurisdiction of the Archdiocese of Los Angeles in the county of Orange will come under the total direction of the newly established Diocese of Orange in California.. The above facts are presently certain. In no manner can they be considered to be speculative.[19]

In anticipation of the actual erection of the new diocese and the installation of its first bishop, Cardinal Manning issued a "greeting and a farewell" to the press:

On June 18, 1976 a new people will be gathered together. In solemn ritual and by proclamation of Papal documents

Archbishop Jean Jadot installs new Bishop of Orange.

Holy Family Cathedral for installation of Bishop William Johnson.

Marywood Center - Diocese of Orange.

Bishop William Johnson, a.k.a. "William of Orange".

> this body will be claimed for Christ under the title of the Diocese of Orange in California. To serve its members a shepherd will come among them, a high priest to sacrifice in their name and a teacher to show them and lead them on the holy way. Like Eve, drawn from the side of Adam in his slumber, like the Church drawn from the side of the second Adam in the slumber of the cross, this new organism of faith is drawn from the side of the parent Archdiocese of Los Angeles.
>
> It is a time for joy and a time for sorrow. The joy is a mother's joy, in giving birth. The sorrow is the severance that is caused by that joy, birth-pangs. It is for us who remain to rejoice in this new creation, to felicitate its Pastor and to stand watching southward as this people shall increase in numbers and in grace. Personal ties more close than brotherhood will be touched but not broken because our priestly fraternity is not confined within the limits of county lines.[20]

The actual inauguration ceremonies were scheduled for June 18 at Holy Family Cathedral in Orange. Archbishop Jean Jadot, twenty-five archbishops and bishops and more than 200 priests from the Archdiocese of Los Angeles and the Diocese of Orange crowded into the church. The local press covered the event, noting that:

> With the pomp and circumstances of ancient ceremony, Orange County's 322,000 Catholics received their own bishop and a parish church became a cathedral Friday. The Most Reverend William R. Johnson became the Bishop of the Orange Diocese among an assemblage of robed and gloved clergy carrying glinting swords and wearing plumed helmets. His religious jurisdiction in the newly formed Catholic governing seat extends to one-fifth the county's population and Holy Family Catholic Church, 566 S. Glassell Street, where he was installed, became the Orange diocesan cathedral.
>
> As bells tolled outside the cathedral and trumpets flourished throughout the ceremonies, the new bishop assumed his seat of authority over Catholics in the county, resting in the "*cathedra*," the cathedral chair. He took a silver and wooden shepherd's staff representing his role as shepherd

over the flock of God here while parishioners responded with thundering applause.[21]

The official decree erecting the new juridical unit of Orange was proclaimed at the ceremony. It reads as follows:

The Roman pontiffs have always given special care in establishing churches and adjusting their hierarchical order whenever the care of souls and the circumstances of place and time seem to require it for the Lord.

To this end, His Holiness, Pope Paul VI, by Divine Providence, has maturely studied the facts and heard those concerned, supplying insofar as needed the advice and consent of those who have legitimate concern, including those who may even have presumed that they had such a concern, wishing to provide for the needs of the Province of Los Angeles in California and the spiritual good of the faithful living there, established a new diocese.

WE, therefore, John Jadot, Apostolic Delegate, selected by His Holiness Paul and given all necessary and opportune faculties to accomplish His desires, fulfilling His mandate, by virtue of these Apostolic Faculties, now DECREE AND ORDER the following:

From the Archdiocese of Los Angeles in California WE hereby separate that part embracing the civil county of Orange and from it WE establish and declare established a new and distinct diocese which WE direct shall be called "Orange in California." The seat of the new diocese shall be in the City of Orange with the Church of the Holy Family as its cathedral.

WE grant the same rights and privileges to the City of Orange which other episcopal cities enjoy and WE grant to its cathedral and bishop the same rights, privileges, honors, insignia, benefits and prerogatives which other Cathedral Churches and their bishops possess and enjoy under the common law, holding them, however, to the same correlative duties and obligations. As to the clergy specifically, WE decree that they shall be deemed aggregated to the Church in whose territory they now legitimately dwell.

All documents and legal papers which affect the new diocese shall be transferred as soon as possible from the curia of the Archdiocese of Los Angeles in California to the

> curia of Orange in California where they shall be carefully kept in the archives. WE desire and order that this our DECREE shall have its full legal effect and juridical force as of the eighteenth day of June in the year one thousand nine hundred seventy six.[22]

It was almost dark when the historic ceremony drew to a close. As he proceeded down the aisle, Cardinal Manning was heard to say that "nothing is quite so fragrant as the blossoming of an orange."

Notes to the Text

1. AALA, Renzo Frana to Francis J. Weber, Washington, D.C., May 16, 1975.
2. "California's Catholic Heritage" in *The Tidings*, June 18, 1976.
3. Unpublished manuscript of T. Anson Smith (Los Angeles, 1961), p. 47.
4. Francis J. Weber, *His Eminence of Los Angeles. James Francis Cardinal McIntyre*, (Mission Hills, 1997), p. 374.s
5. AALA, James Francis Cardinal McIntyre to Amleto Cicognani, Los Angeles, February 27, 1957.
6. AALA, Amleto Cicognani to James Francis Cardinal McIntyre, Washington, D.C., March 2, 1957.
7. AALA, "Orange County Statistics", May 20, 1961.
8. AALA, Jean Jadot to Timothy Cardinal Manning, Washington, D.C., August 10, 1974.
9. AALA, Timothy Cardinal Manning to Jean Jadot, Ballingeary, August 22, 1974.
10. AALA, Jean Jadot to Timothy Cardinal Manning, Washington, D.C., August 27, 1974.
11. AALA, "Report on Orange County," Los Angeles, September 1, 1974.
12. AALA, Timothy Cardinal Manning to Jean Jadot, Los Angeles, November 7, 1974.
13. AALA, Jean Jadot to Timothy Cardinal Manning, Washington, D.C., November 19, 1974.
14. AALA, Jean Jadot to Timothy Cardinal Manning, Washington, D.C., March 1, 1976.
15. AALA, Timothy Cardinal Manning to Jean Jadot, Los Angeles, March 8, 1976.
16. Los Angeles *Times*, March 31, 1976.
17. *The Tidings*, April 2, 1976.
18. *Ibid.*

19. AALA, Jean Jadot to Timothy Cardinal Manning, Washington, D.C., March 18, 1976.
20. *The Tidings*, June 11, 1976.
21. Orange *Register,* June 19, 1976.
22. AALA, *Delegatio Apostolica - Decretum*, Washington, D.C., June 4, 1976.

Dilecte Fili,
salutem et Apostolicam Benedictionem

Timotheo Manning

Archiepiscopo Angelorum in California

Tibi per has litteras significamus in proximo Consistorio Nos esse te cooptaturos in Sacrum S.R.E. Cardinalium Collegium, ut peculiarem benevolentiam Nostram tibi pandamus, utque tua erga Ecclesiam promerita huius insignis dignitatis praemio decoremus.

Scias interea quae tibi per has litteras significavimus, omnino sub secreto servanda esse, usque dum publici iuris fiant.

Apostolicam Benedictionem tibi ex animo in Domino impertimus.

Ex Aedibus Vaticanis, die XVIII mensis Ianuarii, anno MCMLXXIII, Pontificatus Nostri decimo.

Paulus P.P. VI

COLLEGE OF CARDINALS — UNITED STATES OF AMERICA

	Name	*Birth Date*	*Birth Place*	*Sacer. Ord.*	*Episc. Ord.*	*Procl. Card.*	*Archdiocese or Curia*	*Died*
1	John McCloskey	1810	Brooklyn	1834	1844	1875	New York	1885
2	James Gibbons	1834	Baltimore	1861	1868	1886	Baltimore	1921
3	John Farley	1842	Ireland	1870	1895	1911	New York	1918
4	William O'Connell	1859	Lowell, Ma	1884	1901	1911	Boston	1944
5	Dennis Dougherty	1865	Homesville, Pa	1890	1903	1921	Philadelphia	1951
6	George Mundelein	1872	New York	1895	1909	1924	Chicago	1939
7	Patrick Hayes	1867	New York	1892	1914	1924	New York	1938
8	John Glennon	1862	Ireland	1884	1896	1946	St. Louis	1946
9	Samuel Stritch	1887	Nashville	1910	1921	1946	Chicago	1958
10	Edward Mooney	1882	Mt. Savage, Md	1909	1926	1946	Detroit	1958
11	Francis Spellman	1889	Whitman, Ma	1916	1932	1946	New York	1967
12	James Francis McIntyre	1886	New York	1921	1941	1953	Los Angeles	1979
13	Richard Cushing	1895	Boston	1921	1939	1958	Boston	1970
14	John O'Hara, C.S.C.	1888	Ann Arbor	1916	1940	1958	Philadelphia	1960
15	Aloisius Muench	1889	Milwaukee	1913	1935	1959	Curia	1962
16	Albert Meyer	1903	Milwaukee	1926	1946	1959	Chicago	1965
17	Joseph Ritter	1892	New Albany	1917	1933	1961	St. Louis	1967
18	Lawrence Shahan	1898	Baltimore	1922	1945	1965	Baltimore	1984
19	Patrick O'Boyle	1896	Scranton	1921	1948	1967	Washington	1987
20	John Krol	1910	Cleveland	1937	1953	1967	Philadelphia	1998
21	John Cody	1907	St. Louis	1931	1947	1967	Chicago	1982
22	Francis Brennan	1894	Shenandoah, Pa	1920	1967	1967	Curia	1968
23	John Dearden	1907	Valley Falls, RI	1932	1948	1969	Detroit	1988
24	John Carberry	1904	Brooklyn	1929	1956	1969	St. Louis	
25	Terence Cooke	1921	New York	1945	1965	1969	New York	1983
26	John Wright	1909	Dorchester, Ma	1935	1947	1969	Curia	1979
27	Luis Aponte Martinez	1922	Puerto Rico	1950	1960	1973	San Juan	
28	Timothy Manning	1909	Ireland	1934	1946	1973	Los Angeles	1989
29	Humberto Medeiros	1915	Azores	1946	1966	1973	Boston	1983

This chronological enumeration lists appointees within the same year in order of their accession to the archbishopric.

9. *The Cardinalate*

Though it was known that the Holy See would not appoint a cardinal to any place where a retired but voting elector resided, there was a precedent for naming a cardinal to an area where the retired incumbent was past eighty years of age and thereby ineligible to vote in a papal election.[1] Yet few ecclesial prognosticators were expecting Manning to be made a cardinal quite yet.

During the early weeks of 1973, Pope Paul VI finalized plans to fill the vacancies that had occurred in the Sacred College of Cardinals since 1969 by naming thirty new members from around the world. The new appointees would bring the college to a record-breaking 145 members, 103 of whom would be eligible to vote in the next papal consistory. The announcement that Los Angeles would be the first archdiocese in the United States to have two resident cardinals was disclosed to the press on February 2, 1973. One local newspaper said that the appointment was indeed significant because it indicated that Rome was aware that "the country needs greater representation in the ruling body of the Church."[2]

Manning was enroute to a visitation of Lay-Mission Helpers in New Guinea, after having attended the International Eucharistic Congress in Melbourne. Contacted at the apostolic nunciature in Tokyo, Manning said he "was delighted" but really hadn't had time to react with a formal statement. He did say that it was "a terrific honor, especially for Los Angeles, and particularly for my archdiocese."[3] A few days later, the cardinal-designate sent the following message to the people in the Archdiocese of Los Angeles by telephone:

> This appointment by our Holy Father opens in my heart three flowing streams of gratitude which converge full-tide into one. My gratitude is extended first to Almighty God for all His blessings of the past, crowned now by the blessing which He bestows on His people of Los Angeles in recognition of their generous faith.

> That gratitude pours out next to Our Holy Father, Pope Paul, for his expression, through my person, of his paternal love and esteem for a flock devoted to him. And finally, and most close to home, my gratitude embraces my brother bishops and priests, and the Religious and laity of the archdiocese, with whom I have been associated and sustained in warm and holy friendship and fraternity for nearly forty years. I am a suppliant for their continued prayerful intercession in the new office to which Our Holy Father has called me.[4]

Editorial reaction to the appointment was universally positive. The Los Angeles *Times* led the nation's newspapers in its accolades:

> The elevation of Archbishop Timothy Manning to the College of Cardinals was as welcome as it was expected. In his three years as leader of the Los Angeles archdiocese, he has shown himself to be as resolute in action as he is modest in spirit. His approach to the needs of those in his charge, so numerous and so diverse, is well expressed in his own words: "The Church must engage in conversations about the world's problems. We must have dialog about it. We must apply the healing message of the Gospel to those issues."
>
> His own healing message has already been made evident in Los Angeles, within his own church, and to those many outside to whom he has extended the hand of friendship. Now the action of Pope Paul VI has honored the man and the archdiocese, and given the Roman Catholic Church a broader opportunity to have the benefit of his special gifts.

In his weekly column, Dan Thrapp credited "the slender, youthful appearing prelate" with doing much to still the unrest, even the tumult of the last decade which sometimes disturbed the surface of the archdiocese which includes 1.8 million Catholics.[5] *Time* magazine told its readers that Manning was a "traditionalist who insists on the need for ecclesiastical authority. But he wields it much more gently than his predecessor, James Francis Cardinal McIntyre. Manning has cooled off the disputatious Los Angeles archdiocese by visiting widely among its parishes, supporting its large Mexican-American community and listening patiently to suggestions from his priests.[6]

From the White House, President Richard M. Nixon sent a message which said that: "It was particularly heartwarming to see that you have recently been nominated to the Sacred College of Cardinals, and Mrs.

Nixon and I want to send our warmest congratulations at this happy time for you. We know the boundless human spirit that marks your devotion to God. The spiritual leadership you have provided in your community has served to strengthen the moral fiber of our nation at a time when this strength is more needed than ever. As Californians, we feel a special pride in this recognition of your efforts."[7]

Approached at Saint Basil's rectory, James Francis Cardinal McIntyre issued the following statement to the press:

> The announcement of the designation of Archbishop Timothy Manning as a cardinal of the Roman Catholic Church, and thus as a member of the cabinet of His Holiness, is another distinct honor and recognition for the city and people of Los Angeles. Their loyalty and devotion to religion and to the American spirit of God and country warrants this recognition and insures to the future an abundance of God's bountiful blessings. In my capacity of retirement, I welcome this recognition of Archbishop Manning and his service to the Church and I assure him of my constant and loyal support.[8]

Several thousand letters and telegrams were received over the following week. Mayor Tom Bradley wrote to say that "those of us in government who have had the honor of knowing and working with you on various mutual causes, share the joy of this occasion;"[9] Chief of Police Ed M. Davis viewed the appointment as "a tremendous personal tribute to your dedication and service over the long years;"[10] District Attorney Joseph Busch said he had "long been aware of your total dedication to the spiritual and physical welfare of the people of your see and recognize the benefits that Los Angeles has received from your episcopacy"[11] and, legendary member of the county Board of Supervisors, Kenneth Hahn, wrote that "your gracious personality always radiates a civic gathering or a program and I just wanted to offer my personal congratulations."[12] Members of the ecumenical community were extremely gracious. Dr. Martin I. Douglas of Temple Beth Torah, for example, said he had been "deeply impressed by the warmth and friendship you displayed and your deep concern for the burning issues of our day." He told the cardinal that "my congregation joins me in the hope and prayer that with this great honor and title bestowed upon you, that you will have the opportunity to develop even further the spirit of brotherly love and compassion which have characterized your calling."[13] On and on the list could go. But, without exception, the messages were gracious, cordial and congratulatory.

"Accept this ring from the hand of Peter as a sign of love for the Prince of the Apostles and concern for the Church committed to his care."

Vatican's Audience Hall of Paul VI.

"In praise of Almighty God and the favor of the Apostolic See, receive this biretta as a sign of the cardinalatial office. Show yourself intrepid for the Christian faith, the peace and tranquility of God's People and the spreading of the Holy Roman Church. This you must do even to the extent of shedding your blood."

Msgr. Patrick Roche expressed the local Church's reaction to Manning's elevation in his weekly column, "*El Rodeo.*"

> Last Friday brought the news that our archbishop had been elevated by Pope Paul to the College of Cardinals. To that happy and unexpected announcement our people and our archdiocese have responded with a burst of joy and gratitude. And this, not only because of the honor which has been bestowed upon one we love so well, but also because the Holy Father has again given evidence of his paternal affection for the people whom the new cardinal shepherds.
>
> For we are his sheep, the flock he tends, and our hearts are lifted at this recognition of the wisdom and prudence and care with which he has guided us. What we are, what we will grow to be, in the unfolding drama of each person's salvation, must be assessed in large part to the pastoral solicitude of those who have carried the shepherd's staff before us, pointing the way beyond the distant hills.
>
> For the flock inevitably takes on the character of the shepherd, bending the steps of its journey to the path which he treads before it, shaping its attitude and its vision to the nuances of his gentle voice and the benevolent touch of his guiding hand. And while the archbishop, reached this week in a pilgrimage to mission lands, characteristically assesses this present honor as a tribute to his people, the fact remains that his people are himself.
>
> In the broad and varied scope of his work as priest and prelate among us, Archbishop Manning has left the impress of his character upon this archdiocese, its people and its institutions. He was our Auxiliary Bishop for twenty-one years, has been our archbishop for three, and those years can never be torn from the fabric which he helped to weave.
>
> There is another way, and, a more subtle one, in which he has formed and shaped our people. The Church depends upon the character of her priesthood for her continued vitality, purity and growth. And through all his years with us, the archbishop has quietly held before his brother priests in the archdiocese an image of the priesthood which shines in brilliant contrast to the dull distemper of our times.
>
> When, early in 1970, he was appointed as the ordinary of the archdiocese on the retirement of our beloved and heroic Cardinal McIntyre, he held a conference in which he listed

> the three primary areas of his concern. First, and typically, he described the nourishing of the fraternity of the priesthood. As the second object of his solicitude, he listed all forms of religious education, "that the people of God who form the Church receive the word of God and bring it to fruition in their lives." Thirdly, he stated the concern with which the Church must embrace the social needs of the world's people, their griefs and their anxieties, and enter into conversation on these problems, striving towards their healing. In this dimension of his shepherd's work, he echoed one of the great clarion calls of Vatican II, a call needing fresh and new response in each era of the Church's life, building upon the structures of what has gone before.
>
> To these concerns, etching the horizons of all his hours, are now added the new responsibilities of the rank and office of a cardinal of the Church. In his message to us on news of his appointment to that high place, he asked for our continued prayers. These we all pledge to him with wholehearted will.[14]

The cardinal-designate returned to Los Angeles on February 12 and, in his first interview with the press, repeated that "this honor was bestowed more on the Los Angeles archdiocese than on himself." He commented "that he would not have gone on his missions-visiting trip to the Far East had he known of the Vatican announcement was to come on February 2." He said he was only informed of his elevation two days earlier. He begged off several questions relating to amnesty for draft evaders, saying that "he had not thought enough about the issue." But he did respond, when asked about the possibility of an American becoming pope: "It's not impossible, but unlikely."[15]

At a subsequent press conference, Manning said he "would rather be a priest today than at any time in the past thirty-nine years because the Church is promising, vigorous and vibrant." He said that the Church was facing three great challenges: the defense of life, the war on pornography and the giving of whole witness to truth and the Gospels under all circumstances."[16]

On February 26, 1973, the cardinal-designate went back to his one-time parish of Saint Gregory where he greeted the people, offered Mass and participated in a grand fiesta. In part he had this to say:

> As we came into church today, we came through the ranks of the young children – little boys and little girls from the

> school – from the tiny tots up to the officers of the school. Again you say thanks be to God that although we've made a mess of things, in many ways, we older people, yet you look at them and here is the second Spring. They're not just a new patch in an old garment, they're a totally new garment. Christ is weaving that garment with new priests and new sisters and new parents and out of them will come the fathers and mothers, the priests and sisters, the cardinals of tomorrow, and you walk with hope and with great joy.[17]

Manning delayed his departure for Rome so he could be present at Youth Day, the annual Congress of the Los Angeles Confraternity of Christian Doctrine at Anaheim. Speaking to 7,000 high school students, the cardinal-designate said:

> Only love, the love of God, can satisfy the longings of the human spirit. Technologically we've perfected the computer. We've decided we can satisfy every human need through machinery and technology. Dachau, Nagasaki and Vietnam are the climax of what technology has done to us. Technology has culminated in death from the sky that leaves a dark mushroom cloud of fear and destruction.
>
> The counterculture created by your generation is a revolt against the insincerity and phoniness of many of the things presented to you. It has tried to satisfy man's hungers in psychedelic drugs, in protests, in freedom marches, but it has failed to quiet the hungers. We have desecrated the earth as at Nagasaki. And what is God doing? He's sending new and brighter flowers upon it. So God renews His Church.
>
> You are God's answer to all the ages gone by. We thank God we have lived to see this day. We are here to make an act of faith in you. You are the Church. We place ourselves at your service. You are the bride of God, Who loves you so much. Love Him. You have the words of eternal life.[18]

The cardinal-designate and his companions left for the Eternal City at noon on March 2. Accompanying him were Archbishop Joseph McGucken (San Francisco), Bishops John J. Ward, Juan Arzube, Leo Maher (San Diego), Harry Clinch (Monterey), John Quinn (Oklahoma City), a small group of classmates, and associates in various apostolates of the archdiocese, including Msgrs. Benjamin Hawkes, vicar general, James Hourihan, Patrick Roche, Fathers Clement Connolly, August Moretti, Royale Vadakin, Francis Weber and Sir Daniel Donohue.[19] In addition to the official delegation accompanying California's Cardinal-designate to the Eternal City, several hundred other priests and laity arranged to reconnoiter in Rome for the occasion.

ROMAN CHRONICLE

Even the shortest chronicle of events associated with the subsequent trip to Rome indicates how the bestowal of the "sacred purple," even in its abbreviated form, remains one of the most symbolic and historical of the Church's many ceremonials. The first official function was a con-celebrated Mass, on Sunday morning, March 4, at the North American College. Archbishop Timothy Manning, assisted by thirty-six representatives of the Golden State's presbyterate, offered the Eucharistic liturgy for those who had gathered on the Janiculum Hill to honor the People of God at Los Angeles in the person of their Chief Shepherd.

Following that colorful event, which was televised for CBS-TV by KNXT News, the California delegation walked the short distance to the Piazza di San Pietro for the weekly blessing by Pope Paul VI. Cardinal-designate Manning devoted the rest of the day to a personally-conducted tour of Rome for his family and personal guests.

On Monday morning, those members of the Sacred College residing in or visiting the Eternal City gathered in the Vatican Consistorial Hall, at 9:30, to hear the pope formally announce his appointees to their collegial body. The pontiff reaffirmed the role of cardinals as his "principal counsellors and collaborators," supporting his "apostolic office of governing the Church." Pointing out that the composition of the Church had greatly increased in recent years, the Holy Father noted how the augmented membership of the Sacred College would "lend dignity and assistance not only to the entire college of bishops but also to our own person."

At the conclusion of the secret consistory, the cardinals adjourned to the Vatican Audience Hall, where their newly proclaimed confreres and their parties were waiting. Jean Cardinal Villot, the papal Secretary of State, publicly announced the names of the new cardinals, handing to each the *biglietto* or formal letter of appointment. The Holy Father then joined the assemblage for the ceremonial bestowal of the zucchetto and biretta. Upon completion of the scriptural readings, the pontiff delivered a short homily welcoming his new "brothers" and scoring the additional duties incumbent upon members of the Sacred College. The profession of Faith was made, followed by an oath of fidelity and obedience to the pope and his successors. The prayer for the conferral of the zucchetto and biretta recalled the dignity of human life as symbolized by the blood-red color of the cardinalatial vesture. After receiving the instruments of their new office, the cardinals exchanged the kiss of peace with the Holy Father and their senior confreres in the Sacred College. The ceremony concluded with a prayer for the faithful and the Apostolic Blessing.

The Eucharistic liturgy concelebrated by Pope Paul and the twenty-nine new cardinals took place in the evening, at 5:30, in the Vatican Patriarchal Basilica. Following a short homily, wherein the pontiff dwelt upon the double charism of stability and progress, the prelates were given specially-cast rings to symbolize the oneness of mind existing between the Sacred College and the See of Peter. As a further sign of personal affection for the Archbishop of Los Angeles, the Holy Father personally distributed Holy Communion to Cardinal Manning's brother and sister. An informal reception was held that evening on the Janiculum Hill, at which Cardinals Luigi Raimondi, Luis Aponte Martinez, Humberto Medeiros and Timothy Manning greeted the American community of Rome and the numerous friends and well-wishers who had gathered for the investiture ceremonies.

Most of Tuesday was devoted to curial duties and visitations of the various dignitaries in the ecclesial and civil administration of the Vatican. A dinner that evening was hosted by Cardinal Manning for the 122 clergymen attached to or connected with the Church at Los Angeles. In a moving tribute to his longtime friend and collaborator, Cardinal Manning attributed "primatial status" of the California Church to Archbishop Joseph T. McGucken of San Francisco.

At 5:00 in the afternoon of Ash Wednesday, the cardinal arrived at Circonvallazione Clodia 135, to take canonical possession of his titular Church of Santa Lucia di Piazza d'Armi, a reinforced brick structure built in 1938 for the growing number of Catholics clustered at the foot of the Montemario section of Rome. His Eminence was greeted by Don Alessandro Plotti, the pastor of the 18,000 inhabitants in that mid-city parish.

On Thursday morning, as a further indication of esteem for the People of God in California, the Holy Father received the priests and a representative group of laity from the Golden State in the Clementine Hall of the Vatican Palace. Expressing his regrets that the demands on his time and the circumstances of the season did not allow for a larger delegation, the pontiff recalled his long association with James Francis Cardinal McIntyre, "a grand and wise churchman," and the deep re-

The reinforced brick structure of Santa Lucia di Piazza d'Armi is a architecturally non-distinctive edifice built in the early days of the Mussolini regime in Rome.

La Chiesa di S. Lucia - titular church of Timothy Cardinal Manning.

New cardinals proclaimed in 1973, greeted by Karol Cardinal Wojytla, Archbishop of Krakow, the future Pope John Paul II.

Newly proclaimed Timothy Cardinal Manning is greeted by an old friend, John Cardinal Wright of the Roman curia.

spect he had for his successor in the archiepiscopate of Los Angeles. Pope Paul hoped that the honor bestowed upon God's People in Southern California would be an added incentive for their growth in personal sanctity and service to neighbor.

The event-packed days in the Eternal City concluded at the Altar of the Chair, in Saint Peter's Basilica, much the same as they had begun on the Janiculum, with a Eucharistic liturgy offered by Timothy Cardinal Manning with his sacerdotal co-workers in the vineyard of California.[20]

On March 9, Cardinal Manning left Rome and flew to Dublin where he received a memorable reception by President Eamon de Valera, the Primate of All Ireland, the Apostolic Nuncio and other Irish dignitaries. From the capital, Manning and his party journeyed by train to Cork City where the first Corkonian ever elevated to the cardinalate was greeted with a gigantic civic procession. The principal address for that occasion was given by Archbishop McGucken who said that "California owed a deep debt of gratitude to Ireland for having given it Cardinal Manning and all the other Irish priests who had served in that state in the past hundred years, watering and bringing to fruition the seeds of faith which had been planted so many years earlier by Spanish missionaries. He paraphrased an old Spanish toast in wishing the new cardinal health, wealth and the loving cooperation of his faithful people for many years to come."[21]

Then it was on to Ballingeary for a reception "the likes of which had never been seen in the village." Bonfires blazed on the hilltops above the valley, flags flew from housetops and there was bunting across the roadways.[22] At the Mass, Manning said that "with gratitude we come back to thank our forefathers, our teachers, our priests and all who were instrumental in nourishing his vocation." He noted there "could be no survival of the faith unless it were rooted in sacrifice and penance. Today, with affluence, people were becoming spiritually impoverished and sinking into despair, because material things do not satisfy." He prayed "that affluence will never rob us of our heritage."[23]

A reporter for an Irish newspaper told the moving story of how "a little boy knelt between his parents at the altar rail" of the parish church and, when Communion time came, "the priest bent low to place the Sacred Host on his tongue, then bent down lower still to kiss the seven year old gently on his forehead."[24] Finbarr Lucey of Gougane Barra had received his first Holy Communion from the cardinalatial hands of his great uncle Tim.

Before Mass ended, Bishop William Johnson, who had joined the group in Rome, said that he felt compelled to speak on behalf of the priests of California.

> The cardinal is yours by birth; he is ours by service and our minds and hearts are one with you. We are grateful to you and assure you we will love and cherish him for all the days that God will give him to the people of God of the archdiocese. We are grateful for all the service that he and all the Irish priests have given to California. I thank Ballingeary and Ireland which watered and brought to fruition the seed first planted by the Spanish missionaries.[25]

Msgr. Patrick Roche, editor of *The Tidings*, described the activities at Ballingeary from another perspective:

> He never left us. He was with us all the time. And he is here with us tonight. The schoolmaster of Ballingeary, addressing the crowd which had gathered in the night in the village square, voiced the theme of a cardinal's homecoming. And he was there indeed. One of their own, born and raised in this village, now returned to them again as a Prince of the Church they all loved so well. They knew that he had come home, as he had come home so faithfully in all the passage of the years, as simple priest, then as bishop, and now as cardinal, to the haven of the Faith in which he had been conceived and born and nurtured in the long ago.
>
> There is nothing of triumphalism in his homecoming. In the dusk of the Irish evening, on the gentle winding road between Cork and Ballingeary, the hills were lighted with the bonfires of welcome and joy, the torches of peat and paraffin flung their flames aloft into the night sky, the high thin swirl of the pipers stirred the blood and set one's memory dancing. But it was all wrapped up in the simplicity of a people who welcomed him, not as a victorious conqueror, but as one of their own. And as the bells of the village church pealed forth the message of his coming, a hush fell over the crowd, gathered from every cot and village tucked in the encircling hills, and trudging up the long road to Ballingeary, as they waited for him once more to enter his native church and bless and consecrate it anew with the blessing of Peter, by a new title now so close to them.
>
> It was a grand night in Ballingeary, but a night which only the people of Ballingeary could understand. As the cardinal

THE METROPOLITAN DISTRICT OF LOS ANGELES - 1973

(the onetime Diocese of Monterey-Los Angeles)

		Archdiocese of Los Angeles	Diocese of San Diego	Diocese of Fresno	Diocese of Monterey	TOTALS
Population	Total	9,216,669	2,629,405	1,172,808	484,363	13,503,245
	Catholic	1,791,932	512,412	268,145	95,000	2,667,489
Clergy	Diocesan	676	390	120	79	1,265
	Religious	728	112	47	38	925
Religious	Sisters	3,168	829	251	220	4,468
	Brothers	334	22	21	33	410
	Baptisms	64,327	14,350	8,737	2,819	90,233
Sacraments	Marriages	14,936	3,341	2,151	957	21,385
	Deaths	13,161	2,341	1,761	916	18,179
	Parishes	324	164	84	43	615
Jurisdictions	Missions	37	29	47	15	128
	Stations	17	11	13	3	44

Cardinal Manning is flanked by Carabinieri (National Police of Italy) as he enters his titular church of Santa Lucia in Rome.

Cardinals McIntyre and Manning meet at LAX following the consistory in Rome.

Jerry Dunphy of KNXT greets Cardinal Manning in Los Angeles after the consistory.

> stood before them on the platform erected outside his home, his words comprised only a few simple sentences. The torches which had lighted his path to home, he said, "were torches which contained the flame of human hearts, his and their own."
>
> And he thanked them then, for a welcome which no other new cardinal could hope to encounter on his return to his native land and people, a welcome wholehearted in its warmth, all-embracing in its fullness, utterly simple with the simplicity of the Faith which wrapped him in the mantle of Peter, who was their chief shepherd and the guide of their souls. The old men wept that night in Ballingeary; the wide-eyed children caught a vision which will be forever bright in the tales of their children and the children yet to come. For this was the night that their cardinal, blood of their blood, bone of their bone, had come home to Ballingeary, and Ballingeary had once more opened its heart to him.[26]

For some inexplicable reason, which he would never discuss, the cardinal vetoed overtures by the civic community of Los Angeles for a public reception upon his return from Rome and this he did over the unanimous objections of his own curial staff. In retrospect, it was a most unwise decision and thereafter Manning's relationship with the "city fathers" was cordial but never close. They rightly felt left out of a most important event in the history of Southern California.

Television station KNXT filmed the entire ceremonies in Rome. Commentator Jerry Dunphy provided the narrative which traced Manning's life from his days as a young priest to his investiture in the Sacred College. The program aired in prime time on March 9 and then was rebroadcast several times.[27]

President Eamon de Valera escorts Cardinal Manning into Arus An Uachtarian, Dublin, upon his return from the papal consistory.

In happy remembrance of the Elevation to the Sacred College of Cardinal Manning 1973 With congratulations, prayers and good wishes from Sister Margaret Mary (Mackey) and Sister M. Colette (Mackey)

Notes to the Text

1. Namely Paris.
2. Los Angeles *Herald-Examiner*, February 2, 1973.
3. *Ibid.*
4. *The Tidings*, February 9, 1973.
5. Los Angeles *Times*, February 4, 1973.
6. 101 (February 12, 1973).
7. AALA, Richard M. Nixon to Timothy Cardinal Manning, Washington, D.C., February 6, 1973.
8. *The Tidings*, February 9, 1973.
9. AALA, Thomas Bradley to Timothy Cardinal Manning, Los Angeles, February 6, 1973.
10. AALA, E. M. Davis to Timothy Cardinal Manning, Los Angeles, February 13, 1973.
11. AALA, Joseph P. Busch to Timothy Cardinal Manning, Los Angeles, March 5, 1973.
12. AALA, Kenneth Hahn to Timothy Cardinal Manning, Los Angeles, February 9, 1974.
13. Martin I. Douglas to Timothy Cardinal Manning, Los Angeles, February 27, 1973.
14. *The Tidings*, February 9, 1973.
15. Los Angeles *Times*, February 14, 1973.
16. Monterey *Observer*, February 28, 1973.
17. *The Tidings*, March 2, 1973.
18. *Ibid.*, March 9, 1973.
19. *Ibid.*, March 2, 1973.
20. This account was written by the author as one of the eleven chapters in *An Historical Perspective* which was issued as a forty-two page booklet commemorating Manning's elevation to the cardinalate. It also appeared in the *Observer* (Monterey), March 21 and *The Tidings*, March 30, 1973.

21. Cork *Examiner*, March 12, 1973.
22. *Irish Press*, March 12, 1973.
23. Irish *Independent*, March 12, 1973.
24. Cork *Examiner*, March 12, 1973.
25. Irish *Times*, March 12, 1973.
26. *The Tidings*, March 30, 1973.
27. *Ibid.*, March 2, 1973.

10. Pope Pourri

Timothy Manning was a "churchman" in the traditional sense of that term. He viewed the Catholic Church, with all its human frailties, as the bark of Peter, the vessel of promise and the ordinary channel of salvation. For him, the Holy Father was, as his many titles suggest, the Bishop of Rome, the Prince of the Apostles, the Supreme Pontiff of the Universal Church and the Patriarch of the West.

In March of 1976, Manning issued a declaration of his faith in the papacy and the pope. So pivotal was that statement to understanding the cardinal that we have included it as an appendix of this book. He warned that the "faithful must shun" interpretations and teachings claiming that "dogmatic formulas cannot signify truth in a determinate way, but can offer only changeable approximation to it." For his part Manning clearly and unequivocally asserted his unchanging "belief in the supreme, full, immediate and universal power of the pope in the care of souls."

> Since he is the pastor of souls, and of my soul in particular, I for my part have certain responsibilities toward the Supreme Pontiff. These are three: reverence, obedience and prayer. He is not simply a figure-head of a great world-wide organization to receive the adulation Christ, the "stand-in" for Christ and my reverence must be accordingly. My obedience is two-fold; to his disciplinary provisions for my spiritual guidance; and to his teaching in matters of faith and morals. My prayers for him are liturgical in every Mass I attend where his name is mentioned in the Eucharistic Prayers; it is also a part of my private prayer life, praying for his intentions each day and for the guidance of the Spirit in all his activity.[1]

It was Pope Pius XII who appointed Manning a titular bishop in 1946.

Here Manning is shown with his mother, Fathers James Hourihan and Bernard Gannon shortly after being received at the Vatican by Pope Pius XII.

Pope John XXIII
(1958-1963)

Pope Paul VI
(1963-1978)

Pope John Paul I
(1978)

Pope John Paul II
(1978)

AD LIMINA VISITS

Residential bishops are obliged to visit the Holy Father every five years. During these ad *limina Apostolorum* visitations, "ordinaries" or residential bishops are expected to deposit detailed reports (called quinquennials) of activities in their respective jurisdictions with the Holy Father and other concerned Roman authorities. They are also expected to visit and pray at the tomb of Saint Peter in the Vatican basilica.

Manning's first *ad limina* visitation took place in late October of 1974. The forty-nine page quinquennial[2] followed the usual formula regarding chapters and answers. There was an addendum indicating certain of the offices and special projects initiated since the 1969 report. In his cover letter, Manning noted that this "survey of activities in the Archdiocese of Los Angeles bears evidence of magnificent pastoral leadership and the husbanding of the resources" belonging to the Church. He pledged that "insofar as our human frailty allows us to know, we are confident that the report indicates a Church as alive to the faith and to its obligations toward its fellow-man; this, despite the prevailing trend of secular humanism and materialism."[3]

Upon his return to Los Angeles Manning, recalling his meeting with Pope Paul VI on October 23, said that "the Holy Father spoke touchingly of Cardinal McIntyre and signified his affection for him by giving me a rosary to bring to him." He also told readers of *The Tidings* that "the Holy Father sent his blessings to all people of the archdiocese" and he "singled out for more lengthy concern and greetings to the seminarians and the Sisters."[4]

When the cardinal went for his next *ad limina*, in 1978, he was elected spokesman for all the bishops of Region XI, an area which included all of California, Nevada, Utah, Hawaii and the Pacific Islands. His meeting with the Holy Father was scheduled for October 5. In more recent times, the format of the papal visit had changed from a private audience to one with all the bishops of a given region. Such group meetings allowed the Holy Father an opportunity for giving a substantial address on problems in the areas represented. This time the quinquennial report had grown to 118 pages, containing thirteen chapters, one each for administrative organization, religious atmosphere, economic condition, sacred liturgy, clergy, religious and secular institutes, Propagation of the Faith, seminaries, Catholic educational institutions, laity, ecumenism, Catholic welfare and pastoral questions. At the end were statistics of personnel and resources.[5]

Manning left on April 10, 1983 for his final ad limina visit, conveying a 136 page quinquennial report covering the spectrum of the Church's life and work in the archdiocese from 1978 to 1982. The report detailed pastoral, administrative, economic, liturgical, educational, catechetical, ecumenical and other religious and pastoral matters, as well as apostolic action by the laity. Among the facts indicated in the report was the influx of Latin Americans, Asian and Pacific people into the archdiocese.[6]

In his "reflections" on returning from that visit, Cardinal Manning recalled that "all roads lead to Rome." He felt that was especially true in modern times"for Rome provides a recurring center of gravity for a world that has otherwise lost its meaning and direction." Then he pulled aside the veil that normally covered such visits by relating how his time in Rome was spent:

> The overseeing of the Catholic Church throughout the world is delegated by the Pope to certain offices that are designated as the Roman Curia. This consists of the Secretariat of State which coordinates the various activities, nine congregations and an additional complex of offices and tribunals. Part of the Roman journey is to visit some, not all, of these bases, insofar as they are concerned with the local Church from which the bishop comes.
>
> With that in mind we visited the offices that deal with the Doctrine of the Faith, the Congregation for Bishops, that of the Sacraments and Divine Worship; the unit for the Clergy, for Religious and Secular Institutes, and for Justice and Peace. Each of these has relevance to the progress of the faith in our local Church of Los Angeles. The official call upon the Congregation for Catholic Education was enriched by the social association with one of our own American cardinals who presides over it, William Wakefield Baum.[7]

1975 HOLY YEAR

For the sixth time in the twentieth century, a Holy Year was proclaimed for Catholics by Pope Paul VI in May of 1973. The theme for the 1975 jubilee was "a reconciliation born of true conversion and repentance, a reconciliation of God with man and of man with his fellow man, a reconciliation bearing authentically human, ecclesial and ecumenical dimensions." In former times, the local observance of the Holy Year took place throughout the Christian world during the twelve months following the celebration at Rome. That process was reversed for the twenty-sixth of the jubilee years. The innovation was explained by the Holy

Father as a means of honoring "the local churches, active members as they are of the one and universal Church of Christ."

In mid 1973, Manning was named "by the National Conference of Catholic Bishops to supervise Roman Catholic participations in the United States for the forthcoming Holy Year."[8] Manning addressed a pastoral letter to the faithful of the archdiocese in which he noted that there would be two aspects of the jubilee year. "It will be celebrated in Rome and in the local churches, extending from Christmas Eve, 1974 to Christmas Eve, 1975, marked by the opening and closing of the Holy Doors in the four major Roman basilicas." He said that the celebration locally would begin on the first Sunday of Advent:

> The theme of the Holy Year as selected by the pope is that of "Reconciliation and Renewal." This theme will affect man in his relationship with his own self, with his fellow-man, individually and in society and in humility and love with his Creator. The observance in the local Church will consist of liturgical services and pilgrimages to designated churches; the use of the theme of the Holy Year in all diocesan and parochial gatherings, and an increase in charitable activities.[9]

In an interview with Wally Burke, Manning described the upcoming Holy Year as "a great renewal of faith in the person and teachings of Christ, in His Church and the complete reordering of our own lives in conformity with the Word of God. It is the reconciliation of ourselves with our individual brothers and the reconciliation of group with group," the cardinal counselled. "And above all the humble bowing down before our providential Father who cares for us. These thoughts," Manning told Burke, "will transcend the boundaries of our Church and should have a call to all men."[10]

Near the end of summer, 1974, Manning sent a pastoral letter to the clergy:

> The Holy Year as it applies to the local Church will end with December. The celebration in Rome begins with the opening of the Holy Door on Christmas Eve. In the interval between now and then, we again invite our people to enter into the holy task of renewal and reconciliation, which is the purpose of this time of grace. Renewal is an interior change, a deeper awareness of what it means to be a Christian. A powerful instrument in that change of heart is the frequent

> use of the Sacrament of Penance. The Church invites us to share deeply in its richness.
>
> Reconciliation is fourfold: with our Heavenly Father, with our brothers and sisters, within ourselves and with nature itself. The story of man is the long, sad history of this fourfold rift. We ask for an intensification of all our striving for holiness during this seasonal time. Particularly do we suggest the practice of pilgrimages to the missions and to the churches selected as places of pilgrimage and indulgence during the year.[11]

The forty-third annual procession in honor of Our Lady of Guadalupe, staged on December 15, was proclaimed "a major Holy Year event."[12] Families from all parts of the archdiocese were invited to march the mile long route in East Los Angeles. Manning designated the procession as a pilgrimage that would enable participants to gain the plenary indulgence for the Holy Year.

An official Holy Year pilgrimage of over 300 persons left Los Angeles for Rome in early October. They were welcomed upon their arrival at Fiumicino Airport by Cardinal Manning who made arrangements for them to be present for the canonization of Blessed Oliver Plunkett, on October 12. After the usual visitations of the four major Roman basilicas, the group gathered at the cardinal's patronal church, Santa Lucia, where special services were held in honor of the newly canonized Irish martyr. From Rome, the cardinal led the pilgrims to Lourdes and the grotto where Our Lady appeared to Saint Bernadette.[13] Newspapers reported that the Holy Year accounted for the greatest number of pilgrims to Lourdes of any year in its history. Back in the southland, Manning said he sensed "a grass roots demonstration of faith" during the Holy Year. He thought it was probable "that the surge of the pilgrimages comes from the rank and file of the Church."

> The people came in far greater numbers than apparently had been anticipated. This illustrates the essential Roman quality of our faith. There is a tendency today to individualize the local church. The danger is that it will go off into its own orbit. This is especially true of indigenization, which is valid but which can be over-done. The pilgrimages are an affirmation that the Church is still Petrine and Roman, despite the attributes of indigenization.[14]

PAPAL CONCLAVES

When word reached Los Angeles that Pope Paul VI had died, Cardinal Manning was as deeply touched as would be the son of his natural father. The pontiff had appointed him to Fresno, then to Los Angeles and finally to the Sacred College of Cardinals. But, more than that, Manning loved and respected Pope Paul as the one who courageously and fearlessly breathed new life into the post conciliar Church. It would have been a far different world without the soft-spoken Montini. Manning released a statement to the press which pretty much summed up his personal sentiments:

> We feel a deep sense of grief for the Church and personal loss on the death of our Holy Father, Pope Paul VI. Our admiration has been constant for the caliber and the achievements of this saintly man. His has been the mammoth task of completing and implementing the directives and the spirit of the Second Vatican Council. His statements and his work for world peace, for justice on all levels, and for human life and dignity are monuments to his great heart. He has addressed every major issue of Church and international life in this complex age. We ask our people and the entire community of Los Angeles for prayers for his soul, and we ask also their prayers for the guidance of the Holy Spirit in the later task of choosing his successor.[15]

From Gougane Barra, where he was on vacation, Manning told a local reporter, that he regarded Pope Paul as the greatest pontiff of the century. Although he didn't have the outgoing charm of John, he had John's heart. "His job was to pilot the Church from pre-Vatican II to post-Vatican II and I believe he did this with great vision. He has left the Church a very solid base on which the new pope will be able to build and further the work."

Although there were great achievements during his pontificate, Cardinal Manning said that he believed the late Holy Father regretted the dissenting voices in the Church since Vatican II and the fact that so many priests had left the Church. "His rule was firm, though his ruling hand was light. Many another pope would have dealt more harshly with dissenters," Cardinal Manning said. He added that the thrust of the next papal mission will be to continue Pope Paul's work for social justice and peace.[16]

From Ireland, Manning went to Rome, there to engage in the primary role of a cardinal, that of electing a successor to the papacy. In the Eternal City, during an interview with Louis B. Fleming, Manning said that he was confident that the conclave of cardinals would reach agreement on a new pope with about a week of work. "It seems to me that a trend will definitely be established by the fifth or sixth day." But Manning also acknowledged the inexperience of the conclave. "We're all like new boys in school," he said. "Most of us are doing this for the first time." Meanwhile, Manning found the days before the conclave useful. "There is no consultation about individuals," he said. Manning favored choosing an Italian for three reasons:

> For the finesse in Church government that they have traditionally demonstrated, because of the intimate geographic relationship between the Vatican and Italy and because the pope is bishop of Rome.

Manning said he wanted a pope who, in the area of doctrine, will resist the "rise of liberalism that would throw overboard all of the inherited sanctions, especially in the area of sexual morality." He wanted a pope with firm "heart" who, like John XXIII, is "the incarnation of the spark of divine love." Manning saw little differences among the leading candidates in the area of doctrine and discipline but he acknowledged that in the area of "heart," or charisma, the judgment is more difficult. Charisma in this sense would be defined as an extraordinary power given by God to a Christian for the benefit of the church. The cardinal admitted that he still was not sure what priority should be attached to this area.[17]

The cardinal found this trip to Rome different from all the many others he had made. Only ten of the 115 eligible voters were cardinals at the time of the previous conclave. He was the only native-born Irishman in the conclave, since the primatial see of Armagh was vacant. He knew personally about half the electors from his participation in two synods. A few days after his arrival, Manning was interviewed at Villa Stritch by John Maher. Once again he said that he didn't want a "liberal churchman" elected because he who becomes pope"is the servant of the Gospel. The Gospel is not liberal, it's very demanding. You can't tamper with the Gospel. Again, it's the narrow gate." He also thought that the new pope should have a good television image. "That is the basic medium today through which people are informed. People can't read anymore. If a man has a good TV image, that's a very strong plus in his favor." Cardinal Manning also stressed the importance of pastoral orientation in a pope. "From my own experience as a bishop, pastoral experience is of paramount importance. I don't say the new pope must have had pastoral experience, but his pastoral orientation is of prime importance. He should be one in whom people can sense immediately warmth of heart."

The cardinal pointed out that the formula Jesus used in directing Peter to take care of the followers of Jesus involved love. "The feeding of the flock is a matter of love," the cardinal said. "He should not so much be less theological as one whose words are more readily understood." The next pope should be someone who can "identify with the deep concerns of humanity today. He should be tender, sensitive. He can't be a cloistered man." Discussing the situation the new pope will face, the cardinal said: "The trend in the modern world is a liberal trend, to the easy way in everything. The demands of the Gospel have not changed and they're calling for the hard way."

> Applying this to areas where the church is in conflict with the modern world, such as sexuality, there has been a break with the traditional sanctions that surrounded sexuality. The Church has withstood that. That is one reason for a certain falling away.[18]

The cardinal participated in the richly symbolic funeral of Pope Paul VI. He was especially moved at how the pontiff's casket was placed on the cobblestones in front of Saint Peter's Basilica. After the final services, Manning was among the small number of cardinals who accompanied the cortege to the catacomb area of the basilica where most of the recent popes were interred. Paul VI had insisted that he be buried in the ground, with only a simple marker placed atop his grave. Manning remarked to a companion that "there's a democracy about death that truly affects those of us who are bystanders. May we be worthy when our time comes."

Several accounts of the conclave have been published, but Manning once observed that none he had seen was totally accurate. Interpreting seriously the oath of secrecy taken by all the participants, he never disclosed anything about the proceedings that wasn't available from other sources. But he was exceedingly pleased with the selection of Albino Cardinal Luciani as Pope John Paul I and the odds are that Manning was an enthusiastic supporter of the Patriarch of Venice. Luciani possessed all the qualities that Manning had associated with the new pontiff. Manning said in Rome that "the key to the selection of Cardinal Albino Luciani as the new pope lay in the qualities represented

Pope John XXIII at the beginning of Vatican Council II.

The cardinal's friendship with Pope Paul VI dated from the 1950s.

To our Venerable Brother Cardinal Timothy Manning, Archbishop of Los Angeles. We cordially impart our Apostolic Blessing, invoking upon him strength and joy in the Lord Jesus, and commending his pastoral ministry to the intercession of Our Lady of the Angels.

From the Vatican, May 29, 1978.

Peramanter in Domino

Paulus P. P. VI

by his choice of names. John and Paul. Everything John XXIII and Paul VI stood for is sanctified in this man," Manning said after emerging from the Vatican conclave.

> It was the first time any pope has chosen a double name, but it was also revealing because of those two previous popes' names he chose. Whether the new pope will be more like John or Paul – well, we'll just have to wait and see.

Manning said he had met Luciani and "found him to be a man of intellect, simplicity and charm." He agreed with others that Luciani was "rich in pastoral experience - as opposed to experience in the curia, the Vatican bureaucracy, and thus could give to the Church the benefit of his experience in dealing with the problems of priests and the laity."[19] William Tuohy told readers of his column that "Cardinal Timothy Manning believed that Pope John Paul will adhere closely to traditionalist policy lines in this new role as pontiff." Manning felt the new pope would not be swayed by calls for more progressive leadership and doctrines – made by some senior Church prelates in Northern Europe, the United States and Latin America.

The interviewer said that "while Manning has no private pipeline into the Apostolic Palace, he nevertheless knows the new pope and has a good deal in common with him since their careers have been quite similar. Both men have spent long years in bishoprics; both were created cardinals in the same consistory – March 5, 1973 – and both have had to deal with the practical problems of a large archdiocese.

> Neither prelate has spent any time in the curia, that central body of church leadership that sometimes produces cardinals and even popes who seem little acquainted with the bread-and-butter problems of priests working in the field. And both men, despite their ready smiles and easygoing manner, hold rather austere views of what it means to be Christian – and of the policies the Church should pursue in the coming years. For these reasons, Vatican observers believe the doctrinal views of the sixty-eight year-old Manning may closely reflect those of the new pope, who is sixty-five. Manning forecast little change in church policy toward such controversial matters as birth control, abortion, women priests and the relaxation of celibacy rules for clerics.[20]

In his first pastoral letter after returning to Los Angeles, Manning appealed to the faithful of the archdiocese for an added devotion to the Blessed Virgin Mary:

> In his opening address to the Catholics of the world our Holy Father, Pope John Paul, invoked Our Lady, the Mother of the Church. Through this also he touched our hearts. What better way could we be aligned with him in placing ourselves under her protection than through her most holy rosary. For this reason, we make this urgent appeal to all of the faithful of the archdiocese to make special efforts during the month of October to pray the rosary. If it is not already a family practice, we urge that it might become so. Where such a devotion exists, may it continue to be a source of benediction on the household. For a special intention during the month, we would ask that the rosaries be offered for vocations to the priesthood and religious life. This is in response to our most pressing needs.[21]

The sudden death of the "September pope" was totally unexpected. That the Holy Father's precarious health may have been known to his electors was reflected in a comment made by Manning to an acquaintance that "hereafter I am sure the electors will demand some sort of assurances about any future candidate's health." In any event, the cardinal issued the following announcement:

> The death of Pope John Paul has stunned and saddened the Church and the world. His brief pontificate was like a meteor passing through a dark sky. For a moment the earth was illuminated by it. Warmth and pastoral love possessed the land.
>
> It is a time to bow before the unsearchable ways of Divine Providence. Perhaps this hour is a reminder to all of us that our life here is brief and tenuous, and that we should not be anxious for the things that will pass.
>
> The Church will go on. Another pope will succeed to the Chair and responsibilities of Peter. In the interval we shall pray for the deceased pope, recall his momentary radiance, and then busy ourselves for another election. May the gracious God who gave us John Paul give us another of his kind and spirit.[22]

Bishop John J. Ward was the principal concelebrant for a Mass offered at Saint Vibiana's Cathedral on October 7. Manning immediately left for Rome and there participated in the funeral ceremonies for the Holy Father. In Rome, Cardinal Manning said that "everyone wants a pastoral pope like the one that has just passed on, a pope speaking the language that everyone will understand. I think there are many with such qualities. We are here with much pain but in the awareness that Pope John Paul brightened the whole world with his smile and goodness. In thirty-four days he probably said what he had to say, that is, that this world has need for humility and simplicity. He gave people that joy and warmth that it needed so much.[23]

When asked the details of the second conclave, Manning smiled and replied: "oh, it was much like the earlier one." Again, the various accounts are as interesting as they are improbable. Manning would never indicate whether he supported the candidacy of Karol Wojtyla but likely he did. Except for not being Italian, the Archbishop of Krakow, personified all the qualities Manning wanted to see in the next pontiff. Manning had an effective way of skirting delicate issues. In an interview given to *The Tidings* shortly after coming back to Los Angeles, he concentrated on the person of Pope John Paul II and never once tipped his hand about any of the details of the conclave:

> The pontiff's whole life has been based on a clear, beautiful profession of faith in Christ. In his act of faith in the Church there is a sense of the imminence and reality of the Church to which he is totally committed; there are no half measures in this commitment. It was only faith in these two basics that would make him accept the papacy. Given these two basics, everything he does will refer to that integral loyalty and consistency to Christ with which he'll pursue and allow to grow the unfolding of Vatican II.
>
> I'm thoroughly convinced that he'll take no nonsense in the process. He went out of his way, for example, to mention the liturgy and caution against extremes in it. The two John Pauls averted to the fact that liberties taken with Vatican II were not justified. I think also, and this is a conjecture, that court ceremonial has hemmed in the papacy for hundreds of years. This is not going to inhibit John Paul. He'll be a pope among the people. He has not merely sensed the hunger of the people, but he comes from a place where it's either the whole integrity of faith – or nothing, a place where faith comes through live.[24]

Addressing the Ladies of Charity at their 15th annual luncheon, Manning described conclave procedures – the voting routines, living and dining quarters, and the assisting personnel from elevator boys to doctors to confessors. During the first conclave, he was quartered in a small office where one desk was placed atop another to make room for a bed, and at the second, he shared a Vatican roof-top apartment with five other cardinals. A small dining room was his bedroom. The general congregations held daily between the funeral for one pope and the conclave for election of another gave the electors a good opportunity to get to know one another. "Here was the universal Church, cardinals from all over the world," Manning observed. After the election, and acceptance of the new pope, each cardinal went up to pledge his obedience.

> When Cardinal Wyszynski, the older Polish Cardinal and primate, went up to kneel before Pope John Paul II, there wasn't a dry eye. It was one of the most emotional things I have ever seen.[25]

ATTEMPTED PAPAL ASSASSINATION

On May 13, 1981, Pope John Paul II was shot at close range as the vehicle in which he was riding moved slowly through a gathering of 20,000 people assembled for a general audience in Saint Peter's Square. Rushed immediately to Gemelli Polyclinic Hospital, the Holy Father underwent surgery for the repair of intestinal damage and less serious wounds to his right forearm and left forefinger.[23]

Cardinal Manning was shocked at the news and wrote his reflections which were published in their entirely by several newspapers.

> Concentric waves of grief and shock spread out across the entire world from the Piazza of Saint Peter's in Rome on Wednesday, May 13. There, the spiritual leader of millions of Catholics and the man of God recognized as such even by the secular world, fell wounded from a would-be assassin's bullet. Somehow, in his affliction, all humanity is stricken. No matter the motive of the issue, violence against other men is always a tragedy. It is significantly more so when that violence is directed against a religious leader.
>
> It is true, nonetheless, that good can come even from so great a tragedy. There has been a great solidarity of righteous-

> ness and prayer, a knitting of the human family into one texture of loving care. We are thrust into a realization that human planning alone does not bring peace or progress to our planet: Peace comes as a gift from the Prince of Peace and in answer to prayer. The message of peace and reconciliation he has enunciated to the world, is now punctuated with bullets in his body.
>
> The Holy Father was aware of his vulnerability in his desire to reach out to all people and to touch as many as possible. He is the "good shepherd" who is willing to lay down his life if need be for the people. Such exposure on his part will always involve risk, but we conjecture that he will not surrender his gift of communication and intimacy with his people to the gunsight of some negative mind. The world, and above all the Church, cannot allow itself to be lessened by those whose minds or motives are marginal. The Gospel is to be proclaimed to all, and the vicar of our Lord must be available to all.
>
> The pope teaches even through his personal tragedy. Perhaps he is calling us now to a renewal of faith in the way of peace and non-violence, to reverence for the God-given dignity and value of each person on this planet. We must reverse the latter-day proposition that life is cheap and that the gun rules. Our faith is contrary: Life is God's gift and the rule we live by is that of the Prince of Peace.[26]

1983 HOLY YEAR

In 1983, Pope John Paul II called an extraordinary Holy Year to commemorate the 1,950th anniversary of Redemption. Manning inaugurated the jubilee in Los Angeles with a Mass at Saint Vibiana's Cathedral on Easter Sunday. While designating other churches, including the California missions, for gaining the traditional indulgences, he invited "in sequence and in pilgrimage, all the organizations of faith in the archdiocese" to the cathedral for community celebrations. In a pastoral letter, the cardinal said:

> Tenderly, as is his want, the Holy Father places all this venture under the protection of the Blessed Mother that she, who first opened for us the doors to our Redeemer, may "intercede for us and obtain for us the grace of a fruitful

> celebration for the Jubilee Year . . . and show again to the whole Church, indeed to all humanity, the blessed fruit of her womb, Jesus, who is the Redeemer of each and every one." So, in God's name and under the protection of Our Lady of Angels, we inaugurate in the local Church the Year of Jubilee of 1983-1984. May God be merciful to us all.[27]

Some time later, during a gathering of 10,000 persons at the Religious Education Congress in Anaheim, Manning outlined a proposal for the ensuing months:

> First, the reconciling with one another and with our heavenly father. Secondly, that we may grow in the love and the knowledge of Jesus Christ Our Lord. Already on Thursday 10,000 teenagers filled this room to the rafters. They were a credit to the places they came from, to the homes from which they sprang, a wonderful reassurance that all is well with their generation as long as young people like them are among us. We asked them also to put reconciliation as one of the high points of their year especially the reconciliation, if needed, with their parents. There should be a renewal of their bond. To you, their parents, elders, we ask likewise for the same grace, the grace of reconciliation, of renewal, backing up the love that is already there.

Referring to the Gospel about the woman taken in adultery and forgiven by Christ, the cardinal said the coming year offered opportunity for return from infidelity. "Those of our kindred, of our blood, of our homes who have drifted away, wandered from the mercy of Christ might also be brought back to his loving forgiveness to hear Him say 'Neither will I condemn you.'" The cardinal asked that there be a prayer "that we become grasped by Christ as we penetrate more and more into the knowledge of Christ, the historical Christ, the Risen Christ, the glorified Christ, the Christ of the Eucharist, the Christ in the Church.

> Christ of the Virgin's womb, Christ of the Upper Room, Christ of the empty tomb, Christ of the day of doom, Christ in this white host.[28]

On another occasion, the cardinal suggested the reality of sin and the need for reconciliation during the Holy Year. He noted that "God makes overtures to us asking us if we are in a habitual state of sin to change our lives, if we are unconsciously living in a sinful mentality, to turn around and change our lives. God makes overtures to us asking us to come back to Him." Scripture, he said, is filled with instances of God offering His mercy to men. Probably the most beautiful of all lessons regarding this invitation to return is that of the Prodigal Son where love and mercy are offered rather than recrimination and condemnation.

> What more can God do to let us know of His welcome and His mercy than the image He gives in that parable? Make an act of faith in God's mercy. God's love is for us.[29]

During a visit to Rome, during which Manning joined throngs of pilgrims passing through the holy doors of the four major basilicas, he told a reporter that:

> Above all, the visit to Rome is crowned with an audience with the Holy Father. Any incumbent in that high office has an awesome presence and in fidelity to the mandate of the Lord, confirms his brethren of the hierarchy in faith and love. This is true in exceptional dimension with John Paul II. Despite the incomprehensible demands on his time and presence for peoples of all the world, high and low, in public and private, he yet gives the undivided attention to each one admitted to his presence as though no one else were waiting in the sidelines.[30]

At the conclusion of the jubilee year, Manning wrote to the clergy, pointing out that the papal crest of John Paul II was embellished with a cross, and in the lower right-hand corner a large letter "M."

> The Supreme Pontiff has reflected long on the truth of Christ as the Redeemer, and of Mary, the Mediatrix of All Grace. We think that these two motives are articulated in the crest. It is not surprising, therefore, that at the conclusion of the Holy Year the Holy Father would wish to dedicate the world to the Immaculate Heart of Our Blessed Lady. For this "Act of Entrusting to Our Lady" the Holy Father has composed a special prayer. The words of it are from the Act of Consecration he made at Fatima on May 13, 1982. In accord with his wishes we ask, therefore, that at the Masses on Saturday, March 24, in which the Annunciation of the Lord is

anticipated, or at the Masses the following day, the third Sunday of Lent, the people of God in our parishes be requested to recite together this holy prayer. In this way we will be responding to the expectations of many human hearts and to the devotion of those who hold their gifts of salvation and peace through the mediation of Our Lady. May she, who is Queen of Angels, bring you all her peace.[31]

JOURNEYING WITH HOLY FATHER

It was announced in late April of 1984, that "because of the links between the Church of Los Angeles and the Churches of Asia and the Pacific," Pope John Paul II had invited Cardinal Manning to share his pastoral journey to those regions in May. Manning loved to travel and the prospect of being part of the papal entourage surely must have pleased him. He left Los Angeles and journeyed to Fairbanks. The Holy Father's plane had flown the great circle polar route from Rome to where he met briefly with President Ronald Reagan who was returning from China.

The cardinal noted that the presence in Los Angeles of 250,000 Korean immigrants did indeed give the Church in Los Angeles a great affinity to its counterpart in Korea, a Church, he noted, that had the distinction " of being founded by lay-persons."[32] The Holy Father's journey to Korea would celebrate 200 Columban years of Christianity in that nation. Manning anticipated visiting the grave of Bishop Thomas Quinlan, a Columban missionary who was captured by the Japanese in World War II and was later taken captive by the North Korean communists.

In his diary of the journey, Manning remarked how admirable it was "to see in our time, under the guidance of the Holy Spirit, a new Pentecost, a new spring vibrating in the lands of the distant East. The signs of the times were there for the Church to read. One by one the countries severed their ties from their colonial origins. Local governments took over. The wisdom of the Church worked apace. Native hierarchies were established – local vocations were fostered, indigenous religious communities adorned the local churches. Art and architecture and music reflected the cultural richness of primitive peoples. All the while the essential collegial connections with the See of Peter were fostered and strengthened. National colleges flowered in Rome. Representatives of the distant churches were summoned to the service of the dicasteries of the Holy See."

Cardinal electors processing into the Sistine Chapel for the election of a new Roman pontiff.

Ballot used in conclave to elect Pope John Paul I.

Eligo in Summum Pontificem

....

The "September Pope" meets one of his electors immediately after the conclave.

Manning felt that "one thing alone remained to integrate the mission churches to the mother and teaching mistress of all the churches. That was the visible presence of the successor of Peter, the Bishop of Rome. An apostolate begun by Pope Paul VI took him to lands outside of Europe with astounding results. This spirit has been eminently pursued by Pope John Paul II." This was the twenty-first of the pontiff's missionary journeys. Manning observed that the pattern of the visits was constant:

> There is the gracious exchange of greetings with the civil authorities, the open-air Masses to accommodate the crowds no building could contain, the intimate dialogue with the local hierarchy, the expressed concerns for native vocations, the affectionate exposure to seminarians and religious communities, the gracious ecumenical meeting, the "suffering of the little children to come unto him," the compassionate contacts with the sick, the empathy with the youth, always the peak of his enthusiasm, the seeking of Christ in the prison yards.[33]

POPE JOHN PAUL II IN LOS ANGELES

Manning was retired when Pope John Paul II came to Los Angeles in 1987. Karol Cardinal Wojtyla had visited the archdiocese in August of 1976, as an extension of his pilgrimage to the International Eucharistic Congress in Philadelphia. That Southern California made a deep impression on Cardinal Wojtyla is obvious from a letter which Pope John Paul II sent to Cardinal Timothy Manning on November 20, 1980, wherein he stated that "it is always a joy to recall my own visit to Los Angeles. How impressed I was by the many monuments to the faith that were planted there and elsewhere along *El Camino Real* by Fray Junípero Serra and his Franciscan collaborators."

The Holy Father went on to say that "it is my hope that this religious tradition of Los Angeles will remain a source of pride and challenge for all the sons and daughters of your city, for all who live within her hospitable boundaries and for all who are chosen to serve her common good." In concluding his personally-signed letter, sent on the occasion of the city's bicentennial, the pontiff said that "in manifesting my deep interest in the destiny of the entire people whom you serve, I commend your city to the protection of Our Lady of the Angels, and I ask for all its inhabitants the bountiful blessings of God our Father."[34]

From the outset, officials from the National Conference of Catholic Bishops in charge of orchestrating the Holy Father's activities in Los Angeles made it abundantly clear that Cardinal Manning would occupy only an ancillary role during the papal visitation. There was only one residential archbishop and, by that time, it was not Timothy Manning. As one might have expected, the cardinal graciously abided by that decision and kept a low profile. When the pontiff left, Manning wrote a memoir for the local Catholic paper:

> He has come and he has gone. For forty-eight hours the September air was filled with the blessing of his presence. A tranquility of peace descended upon our cities. Men and women, whether present at papal events or through the splendid exposures of television, basked in the radiance of his personality. His name was on everybody's lips. His uplifted hands were metaphors of peace and love. His limitless energies caused wonder and admiration. His smile brought tears of responding emotion to unashamed eyes. What a moment to remember in our distressful lives.
>
> And his message and his voice! Clear and definitive words that carried the gospel of truth and compassion to all levels of our life and culture. The poor and lonely, the indigent and refugee, the young and old, the media of communication, the assemblies of bishops and priests, religious and laity, these and countless more, were drawn captive to his healing presence, were enlightened by his uncompromising pastoral statements, were called to the mission of the gospel, were prodded to holiness, were alerted to the cross as the concomitant to the hope of salvation. May we be worthy of his presence, attentive to his words, genuine in our surrender of reconciliation, faithful in our prayers for him, and with him join the great chorus of praise and adoration of the Triune God.[35]

SYNODS OF BISHOPS

The gathering of bishops on an international, national, territorial, or provincial basis to discuss and determine in a collegial manner the procedures most beneficial for the Church is called a Synod of Bishops. The term has been applied most specifically to the international Synod of Bishops held in Rome and opened by the reigning pontiff. Here bishops from all over the world, some representing national conferences of bishops, others present because of their leadership in a specific missionary territory, come to discuss matters pertaining to the Church universal.

In response to an inquiry about the nature of the Synod of Bishops, Cardinal Manning said that after every ecumenical council, "there is a progression of Spirit over the Church. This has been especially so since Vatican II." Postconciliar development had been directed largely by synods which the cardinal called "the eye of the rejuvenation of the Church."[36] Manning was personally involved in three of those synods. In 1977, he was one of the nineteen participants appointed by the Holy Father for the synod that would deal with "catechetics in our time with special reference to the catechesis of children and youth."[37] The rest of the 185 delegates were major religious superiors or delegates of their respective national conferences of bishops. The month long meeting began at Rome on September 30.

Thc cardinal predicted that "the American delegation would make significant contributions to the world Synod of Bishops" insofar as catechetics in the United States is "superbly alive." Americans, "with their experience and expertise, will have much to give the synod." He noted that "the history of the Confraternity of Christian Doctrine and the present activities on religious education here in Los Angeles are indicative of that sense of life." Manning singled out three tasks facing the synod fathers:

> One will be to evaluate the receptivity of the present culture, its capacity for absorbing the faith. Second will be to study new means of communication best adapted to that receptivity – modern means to reach people. Third will be to accommodate the transcendent truths of our faith to both the means of communication and to the capacity of the modern mind."[38]

In an interview given in the Eternal City, Manning said that much of what was being discussed at the Synod of Bishops about catechetics was already in operation in the United States. The burden of the discussion in the small language-groups in which synod participants had been meeting, Cardinal Manning said, "is to clarify in our own minds the nature of the commitment which is the focal point of catechesis and how to relate it to the lives of men, women and children," and, secondly, how to build a community. One view repeatedly expressed, the cardinal noted, holds that "the group is the normal means through which

Cardinal welcomes Pope John Paul II to the United Nations.

Cardinal Manning at the Synod of Bishops in October, 1977.

catechesis occurs." The cardinal also cited as examples some groupings emerging in the United States, such as the *cursillos*, or short courses in Christianity. Participants in *cursillos* in the Los Angeles archdiocese, the cardinal said, continue to associate in small groups after the *cursillos* are completed. He also cited marriage encounter and charismatic prayer groups as other forms of small communities or groups that are developing. As a consequence of the synod, the cardinal said he would stress in Los Angeles small groups and person-to-person relationships with the young.[39]

A Roman reporter told his readers that Cardinal Manning appealed to the Synod of Bishops to heed the cries of today's young people. "The alienation of youth from the institutional Church, their frustrations, hurts, their insecurity, their longing for person - to - person recognition, their desires for some answers to the mystery of life, of their roots and their identity – all these are crying out to us for recognition, response and healing." The signs of the times, the cardinal said, show that young people are concerned about relationships and want a return to emphasis on the two great commandments of love of God and love of neighbor "rather than duty or observance only out of discipline." Catechesis of youth "can take place adequately only with the wider concept of ministry to youth. The ministry begins with the adult who must be trained to deal with youth and to transmit authentic values. Adults must live the Gospel message so that young people not only understand it, but see it exemplified."

Calling for recognition of the place of youth-to-youth ministry, the cardinal suggested that a ceremony of commitment could be used. This youth-to-youth ministry, he said, includes: proclaiming the message through doctrine and discussion suitable to youth's intellectual needs and questions: establishing community with the characteristics of smallness, participation and being known by name through such programs as weekend prayer, search, encounter or retreat experiences: opportunities for mission and service that are "substantive and adult in their challenges." Cardinal Manning appealed to the synod delegates to "show further awareness that these youths are a substantive part of the Church" and to address the youth of the world "through a vehicle of communication which is accommodated to their lifestyle."[40] Upon his return to Los Angeles, the cardinal told how the fifth world Synod of Bishops had affirmed that "catechesis is the number one priority in the Church today:

> The goal of catechesis is to bring about personal commitment to Christ. The primary focus of catechesis is the family

> and particularly its adult members, for unless they are formed the chances of success in catechizing children are seriously hampered.

"Catechesis," said the cardinal, "is a service of the Word, a service that brings to fulfillment that Word and integrates it into the life of the Christian. The central core of the whole synod operation was that the essence of catechesis must be the person and the mystery of Christ. That must be at the heart of everything you do. All of the activities of catechesis flow from that. It's not just a matter of teaching children. Catechesis covers a whole gamut of concerns.

> The model for all catechesis and the core of all catechetical understanding is the rite of initiation for adults to baptism. The home must be involved, the parish, the communications media so that there will be a commitment to the life of Christ.

Having attended all the synodal sessions, Manning gave an intriguing insight into the working of the synod. The bishops carpooled to the synod hall. Working hours were 9 to 12:30, then 5 to 7. After supper there would be informal study from 9 to 11. The process of discussing and synthesizing the substance of the synod's recommendations was practical and democratic. "In the first three days," Manning recalled, "there were 126 eight-minute interventions by synod participants." At the end, thirty-four wide-ranging propositions were submitted to the Holy Father. "It was the will of the synod that the Pope be asked for an encyclical on catechesis. The synod sent delegates to convey this to the Holy Father."[41]

In preparation for the 1980 Synod of Bishops, Manning circulated a questionnaire among the Catholics of the Archdiocese of Los Angeles on family life and spirituality. The responses were fascinating. Two clear cut conclusions emerged from the tabulation; families seek mutual support in the Church through such means as group discussions for various age groups and they seek to develop a community of faith and support of values. There was also a desire for support and encouragement of persons leading a single life. The chief problem expressed in families was lack of communication.

Six specific questions were asked in the survey:

1. **What types of programs would you like to see the Church provide to assist you in family life education?**

By far the greatest assistance sought was with intrafamily communications problems (110 respondents). Help in understanding children was asked by eighty-eight persons; counseling for school age and teens was asked by eighty respondents and help with discipline was asked by seventy-three.

These suggestions came in letters:

"We should have something like the Mormon's family home evening."

"Give us help in teaching children and young adults to withstand tremendous outside pressure from peers and, as stressed by Pope John Paul, to stop escaping through drugs, sex and violence."

"Programs are needed for the eighteen to thirty year old singles. Our four boys completed college. They never caused us trouble, but they drifted away from the Church."

"Definite education on alcoholism is needed for all family members. Teachers should be educated to understand pupils affected by alcoholism in the family."

2. What are some of the strengths in today's families and marriages?

The survey indicated respondents believed there was better communication, more family programs and education and greater love and respect. Letters said there was greater candor in marriage today, more openness and awareness of individuality, greater understanding by the church, more awareness of a need for closeness.

3. What are some values that need greater emphasis?

Respect and reverence for others (48). Morals and basic education (35). Family unit (26). Education for marriage (22). Spirituality (15). Communication (15).

Letters offered the following additional opinions:

Archdiocese of Los Angeles in California

United States of America

Quinquennial Report

January 1, 1978 to December 31, 1982

Ad Limina Visit

Every five years, each juridic unit in the Catholic Church must submit a quinquiennial report of activities to the Holy See. In more recent times, the bishops of an area meet with the Roman pontiff after submitting their reports.

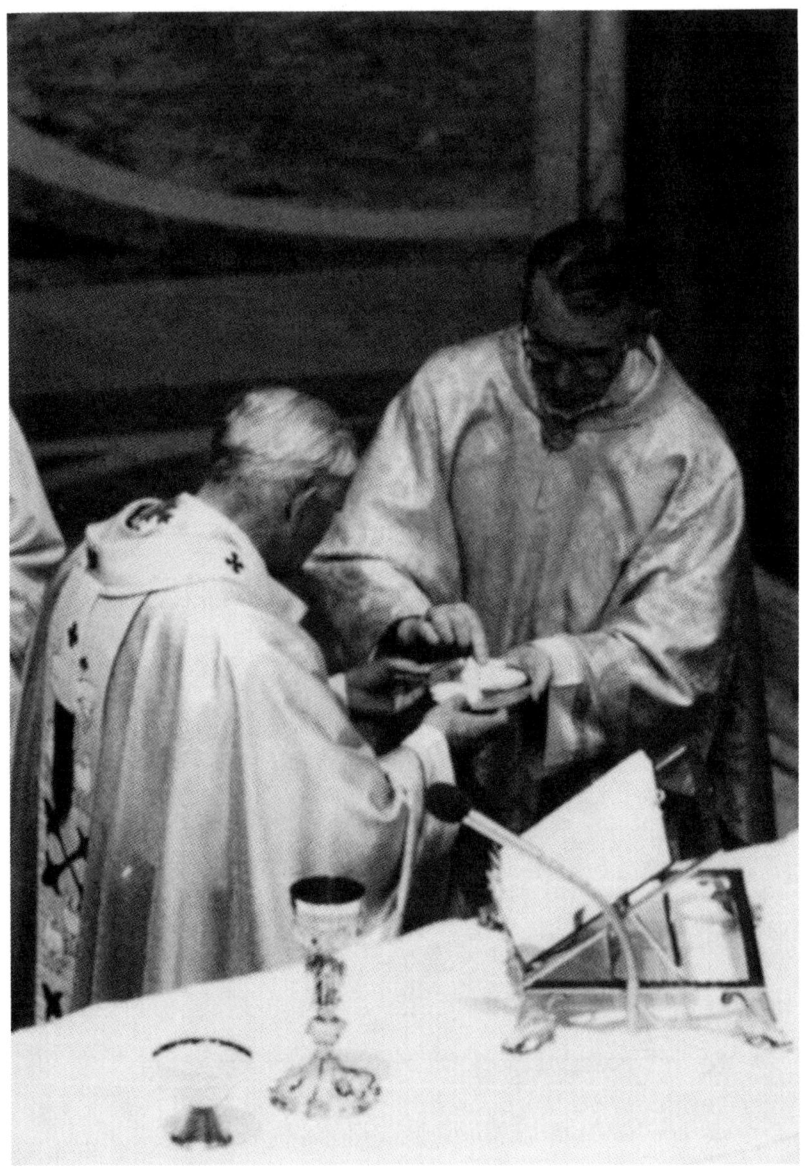

Cardinal Manning is shown here con-celebrating Holy Mass with Pope John Paul II in Saint Peter's Basilica.

"Priests should speak directly to the people at Mass on moral problems and let us know the Church's position in this area directly."

"Use the sermon time at Mass to explain and reinforce Catholic beliefs that are undermined daily in the media."

"Use cable television in color for religious education."

"Please use discretion in who is chosen to be lay ministers. Our pastor remains very detached from his parishioners. It worries me whom he may get because he doesn't really know them."

4. What helps to family spirituality would you like to see employed?

Personal prayer (108). Practice of virtues (135). Preparation for worship (73). Beatitudes (72).

Letters conveyed these suggestions:

"Have block Masses where neighbors can learn to worship together before meeting each other on Sunday."

"Provide stronger doctrinal classes that an entire family can attend."

"Have more solemnity in church. Do we have to clap after every Mass? The singers are no longer enhancing the liturgy, they are performing."

"When Catholics meet with Protestants at charismatic meetings the Protestants at times receive communion – the Body and Blood – and Catholics sometimes accept the bread and wine given by Protestants. Some priests say it is permissible. Other priests refuse. These questions are asked of me by my family."

5. What are the stress points that affect the relationship between husband and wife?

Lack of communication (273). Conflicting ideas (93). Work to make ends meet (65). Time (74).

Letters said:

The Synod of Bishops for 1983 is shown here in a plenary session. Whenever the Holy Father was not present, Cardinal Manning or one of the other two co-presidents presided.

Cardinal Manning felt that synods expressed the collegial nature of the Church in the fullest sense.

Cardinal Manning served as one of three co-presidents for the 1983 Synod on reconciliation and peace.

Over 200 delegates attended the Synod of 1983 at which Cardinal Manning was a co-president.

"We are not taking enough time to be with one another. There is too much stress on earning for material goods that are not needed but wanted."

"Our marriage was broken up by alcoholism."

"We have different viewpoints on how to discipline children"

"Stress comes from the influence of women's liberation, also when the woman's salary is equal to or more than a husband's."

"There is not enough time for couples to sit down and talk to one another."

6. What are the greatest stress points affecting family relationships?

Communication (148). Discipline (89). Time (72). Conflicting values (65).

"We tend to be too generous with our children. We need to communicate and spend more time with them."

"The cardinals, bishops, priests and nuns must get their act together and start teaching the same doctrine. There is so much confusion being taught that our young people are overwhelmed by the contrast in doctrine and find it easy to discount anyone's teaching, including their parents."

"Those in the single vocation seems to be ignored. Perhaps some focusing on how single people could help to serve the Church should be included in the document on family life."[42]

When the replies had been tabulated, the results were sent to Washington where an official for the National Conference of Catholic Bishops forwarded them on to the planners of the 1980 Synod of Bishops. Shortly before the synod opened, Manning sent a letter to the Catholics of the archdiocese asking their prayers for the synodal deliberations:

It will be especially opportune to underscore the need for conversion and renewal in family life. Our prayers and sacrifices during the time of the synod are requested. We ask

> you to observe on October 12 a particular emphasis in your parish communities according to the wishes of the Holy Father.[43]

Then, in 1983, Pope John Paul II named Manning one of the three copresidents of the Synod of Bishops concerned with "reconciliation and penance in the mission of the Church." Of the delegates attending the synod, forty-five were from Africa, forty-six from Latin America, thirty-three from Asia, six from Australia and Oceania and seventy-three from Europe.

Manning explained that "synods have their own internal rhythm:" The first week is devoted primarily to prepare speeches no more than eight minutes each, by the participants, who speak on whatever aspect of the theme they wish to emphasize. The second and third weeks are devoted primarily to discussions, with the synod fathers divided into eleven small groups by language. There will be three English and three Spanish-Portuguese groups, two French, and one each in German, Italian and Latin. The fourth week is devoted mainly to refining proposals through full assembly debate and voting.[44]

The cardinal felt that the theme "of each synod varies, but the constant intent is to give expression to the collegial nature of the Church in her exercise of teaching, her witness of unity and her exemplification of charity for the wide world."[45] He thought that the 1983 theme was especially appropriate since it coincided with that of the Holy Year of Redemption. His role was explained in graphic terms:

> The view from the delegate-Presidents' bench was like a microscopic view of the whole Catholic world. Each nation was represented. The realization begins to dawn that the complexity of the Church has shifted to the Third World. In numbers, in color, in local concern, the Church is clearly no longer a European entity. Always of course its center is Rome and its focal point the papacy. Once the missionary Church was colonial, now it is indigenous. Its leaders are articulate, cultured, Roman in loyalties yet protagonists of the local Church in its language, liturgy and traditions.[46]

Responding to the query, what did we do and what did we bring back from the synod? Manning said that it was a realization that:

In May of 1984, Cardinal Manning was invited to accompany Pope John Paul II to Asia and the Pacific.

Pope John Paul greets Cardinal Manning on his last trip to the Holy See.

there must reside in the community of faith that tender sense of the presence of a providential and caring father, waiting for the return of wayward children and reaching out, not to punish or reprimand but to embrace in love, reclothe with the garments of grace and celebrate with a joy that resonates in the choir-songs of the angels in heaven.[47]

Notes to the Text

1. *The Tidings*, March 26, 1976.
2. AALA, *Archdiocese of Los Angeles in California. Quinquennial Report* January 1, 1969 to December 31, 1973.
3. AALA, Timothy Cardinal Manning to Sebastiano Cardinal Baggio, Los Angeles, n. d. (1973).
4. *The Tidings*, November 1, 1974.
5. AALA, *Archdiocese of Los Angeles in California. Quinquennial Report* January 1, 1974 to December 31, 1977.
6. AALA, *Archdiocese of Los Angeles in California. Quinquennial Report* January 1, 1978 to December 31, 1982.
7. *The Tidings*, April 29, 1983.
8. Los Angeles *Times*, June 9, 1973.
9. *The Tidings*, November 30, 1973.
10. *Twin Circle*, December 21, 1973.
11. AALA, Timothy Cardinal Manning to Clergy, Los Angeles, August 20, 1974.
12. *The Tidings*, December 13, 1974.
13. *Ibid.*, September 26, 1975.
14. *Ibid.*, October 31, 1975.
15. *Ibid.*, August 11, 1978.
16. Irish *Times*, August 8, 1978.
17. Los Angeles *Times*, August 15, 1978.
18. *The Tidings*, August 18, 1978.
19. Los Angeles *Times*, August 28, 1978.
20. *Ibid.*, September 2, 1978.
21. AALA, Timothy Cardinal Manning to Faithful, Los Angeles, September 20, 1978.
22. AALA, Timothy Cardinal Manning to Faithful, Los Angeles, October 6, 1978.

23. *The Tidings*, October 6, 1978.
24. *Ibid.*, October 27, 1978.
25. *Ibid.*, November 17, 1978.
26. Los Angeles *Herald-Examiner*, May 18, 1981.
27. *The Tidings*, March 18, 1983.
28. *Ibid.*, March 25, 1983.
29. *Ibid.*, August 29, 1983.
30. *Ibid.*, April 29, 1983.
31. AALA, Timothy Cardinal Manning to Clergy, Los Angeles, March 8, 1984.
32. *The Tidings*, April 20, 1984.
33. *Ibid.*, May 25, 1984.
34. AALA, Karol Cardinal Wojtyla to Timothy Cardinal Manning, Los Angeles, September, 1987.
35. *The Tidings*, October 16, 1987.
36. *Ibid.*, September 30, 1977.
37. *Ibid.*, September 9, 1977.
38. *Ibid.*, September 30, 1977.
39. *Ibid.*, October 21, 1977.
40. Ibid., October 7, 1977.
41. *Ibid.*, November 11, 1977.
42. *Ibid.*, October 26, 1979.
43. AALA, Timothy Cardinal Manning to Faithful, Los Angeles, October 9, 1980.
44. *The Tidings*, September 30, 1983.
45. *Ibid.*, November 18, 1983.
46. Francis J. Weber (comp.), *Days of Change. Years of Challenge* (Los Angeles, 1987), p. 321.
47. *The Tidings*, November 18, 1983.

11. Priests and Religious

Of all Timothy Manning's distinctive characteristics, none was more admirable than his close relationship with priests. His door was open at home or at the chancery to priests and there was always time to listen, encourage, affirm or counsel them. He was a priest's bishop who personified the notion of shepherdship to his sacerdotal co-workers.

Manning was never more eloquent than when speaking or writing about priesthood. He once observed that "we are men, drawn from among men, extracted from each successive generation, not generating ourselves. We bring our weaknesses, our failings into the sanctuary. These may be covered over by the compassion and prayers of our people. We are but pilgrims going through a valley of shadows and of tears."[1]

Included in his concept of priesthood was the notion that "the priest is, first of all, the sacrament and the architect of unity for the people of God entrusted to his care. In biblical times the temple of Jerusalem, which was the national and religious center of all Jewish life, had multiple divisions in its structure. Walls separated priest from people, walls separated men from women, walls separated Jews from Gentiles. In the language of the apostle Paul, all these walls are torn down. There is no longer a validity for structural distinctions because we are all one in Christ. So it must be for the priest. In his person all racial, social and ethnic differences must disappear. He is the Christ-figure in whom all will find their unity."[2]

Manning never downplayed the challenges associated with the priesthood, but acknowledged that "suffering, contradiction, loneliness, heartache, frustration, misunderstanding - all of these things are the warp and woof of our priesthood. We cannot escape them. We must not try. We have to reach out and embrace them because they are the very garments that Christ Himself has worn. With these He cloaks us today in our vows of obedience, in our commitments to celibacy."[3]

In a commentary on the new *Code of Canon Law* which states that "clerics have a special obligation to seek holiness in their lives,"[4] he noted that "because the priest carries such an awesome title of consecration, he is ever conscious of being a vessel of clay. He is able to be faithful to his calling only in the measure of his personal spirituality by the prayers and sacrifices of the people of God."[5]

Manning addressed the notion of priestly celibacy openly and without reservation, saying that the Church had fashioned for him too, a cross, one beam against another, and in the loving embrace of that cross he offers up his human self, and his mortal days." One beam of that cross "is the white chastity to which he bonds himself, forswearing forever every carnal desire."[6] Nor did Manning foresee any change for the clergy in that regard, "Celibacy for the clergy is a closed issue," he said. Manning was no less outspoken about the ordination of women, saying that "it is important that the movement for liberation and equal rights will not include the ordination of women. Pressure is not a norm for altering Church doctrine. Vast opportunities of ministry, short of sacramental ordination are opening up to women."

Manning was aware that the vision of priesthood was suffering in his time. "It is obscured or contradicted. It is exposed to a danger of secularization. Its membership has diminished either by defection or by a lessening of the numbers reaching toward it. We call it the vocation crisis. It is a cause to which we must become painfully alert and to which we must apply our talents."[7]

Throughout his decade and a half at the helm of Peter's bark in Los Angeles, Manning supported and encouraged the ambitious vocation program initiated by Msgr. Lawrence Gibson and continued by Msgr. Gary Bauler. Weekend retreats at the minor seminary, recruitment drives among college students and home visitation of potential clerical candidates received top priority. Manning visited the three archdiocesan seminaries frequently and there mingled with students, listening to their viewpoints and identifying with their concerns. He made every effort to know each of the seminarians by name and often he asked them to assist at major liturgical events and to serve apprenticeships at the chancery or in other archdiocesan offices and agencies.

Manning spoke frequently about vocations and wrote several major pastorals on the need for involving the entire Catholic populace in the crusade for priestly and religious candidates. He was especially anxious that those who had left the seminary for one reason or another become involved in fostering vocations. In one of his pastorals, Manning identified three areas which he wanted emphasized:

> The first solution to the crisis is to be sought in the home. A new generation rises around us bred in the beginning of a

> new culture that is becoming one of the great divides in history. There is a bewildering gap between generations. The home must bridge that.
>
> Our second responsibility rests within the ranks of the priesthood itself. A joyous life is the best evidence of its genuine value. True priests are contented men, in love with God, serving Christ in their fellow-man, accepting all the built-in anxieties that go with it, together forming one presbyterate of charity with their bishop.
>
> Each family and each member of God's Church must be involved in this crusade. Teachers in our schools must be vigilant for signs of vocations among students and altar servers, and encourage them. Those interested should discuss with their pastors the requirements for entry into our seminary high school and seminary college. Our office and Director of Vocations, our senate committee, all interested lay organizations such as the Serra Clubs, together with all our priests, Sisters and Brothers are summoned again to this holy task.[8]

Three years later, noting that vocations were still in decline, Manning proposed, "to avert a crisis," the total involvement of all priests and faithful of the archdiocese. "We must begin with prayer," he said. The cardinal asked that every Prayer of the Faithful include an invocation for vocations. He asked that on a given Sunday each month the approved prayer for vocations be recited with the people at the end of Mass. He suggested that pastors urge families to have daily prayer in their homes for vocations and to foster in children a renewed sense of reverence and respect for the priesthood and religious life. The cardinal recommended that in schools first Fridays be dedicated to the subject of vocations and that devotions for that purpose be conducted before the Blessed Sacrament.[9]

Manning was also "available" to the Religious men and women of the archdiocese. During the fifty-five years of his priestly ministry, he gave no fewer than 200 retreats to different communities. He also pioneered a program whereby jubilarians in religious life were publicly saluted each year. On January 8, 1976, for example, 216 Sisters and Brothers gathered for a Eucharistic liturgy at Saint Vibiana's Cathedral where diamond, golden and silver anniversaries were observed. At that ceremony was a priest who had been ordained a year before the cardinal was born, Father Maxim Benso! In his homily, Manning said that "we live in the Church at a privileged moment of the Spirit. We are called to be its servants, bishops, priests and sisters, to witness to the transcendence of Christ and His Church." He calls them, the cardinal said, to witness to the reality of Christ today by voluntary poverty, self-denial, mutual charity, community living and prayer. This, the cardinal continued, can be done only within the framework of the Church. "It is inconceivable that anyone could love Christ and not His Church, could listen to Christ and not His Church, could follow Christ and not follow His Church. Jesus said, 'He who hears you hears Me.' There is authenticity." The cardinal asked the Religious to help bring about a restoration of many things discarded in the quest for purity of doctrine.[10]

Ever open to the need and desire for priests to pray, Manning gave his blessings for a House of Prayer in July of 1975. Placed under the direction of Father John McAnulty, S.J., it was located on the grounds of the motherhouse for the Immaculate Heart of Mary Sisters, the one-time estate of Bernardine and Daniel Donohue in Hollywood. Manning said that "the intent of this house is to allow for an opportunity for quiet prayer and for confession and direction. It may be used for an hour or a day, or for longer retreats." Trusting that this foundation would be "used to full advantage," he prayed that "God will send a benediction on all of us because of it."[11]

Many of the archdiocesan priests began affiliating with prayer groups in the late 1970s. In 1982, Manning sponsored the "Emmaus Journey" with 200 clergymen and he observed in a letter that "since that time, many have experienced a renewal in their lives through the grace of the Emmaus Retreat and the support they have been receiving from their fellow priests in the small reflection groups." He invited others "to join me in attending" the final sessions of the convocation in December, 1983. Observing that "in these challenging times, many priests here and elsewhere throughout the country have found that one of the greatest sources of strength in their lives is meeting with their fellow priests for prayer, reflection, discussion and social discourse."[12]

Early in 1977, after much consultation with canonical experts, Manning said that he was pleased "to call into existence" a Board of Conciliation and Arbitration which "had been designed for healing purposes in the archdiocese." Modelled after a program in Chicago, the board saw itself functioning to the point that it is first a means of reconciling differences between parties, priestly or otherwise, in a setting removed from the official management of archdiocesan affairs; that the process takes place only after the individuals have attempted to use all other channels of resolving the problem; that all procedures are totally confidential; and that arbitration is a last resort binding on the parties by their mutual consent. While he saw himself as "father of the family" and the "ultimate reconciler," Manning thought that the process would have "total freedom of intent and expression" if he took little or no part in it, noting that "the parties themselves are the ones who will select the conciliators or the arbitrators." He concluded by reminding the priests of the Lord's caution "that our gifts are not acceptable at the altar until we are reconciled, brother with brother." He prayed that the activities of the board would provide "healing" to hurt minds.[13]

A formal retirement plan for archdiocesan priests was inaugurated in January of 1972. It marked the first time that a standardized program was promulgated for the entire presbyterate. Initially, the funding was underwritten entirely from existing funds but, with the adoption of mandated priestly retirement, additional funds were needed to widen the support base of the fund. The plan as originally adopted was as follows:

1. The Age of Retirement will be as follows:

   Priests may request retirement at age sixty-five.
   Priests must request retirement at age seventy-five.
   The Ordinary of the archdiocese has the final authority to accept or reject requests for retirement after giving due consideration to the needs of the individual and of the Church in the archdiocese.

2. Pastor Emeritus:
   A pastor on retirement will retain the title of Emeritus of the parish from which he retires.

3. Place of Retirement:
   While it is understood that a priest may choose his own place of retirement, the most desirable place for retirement is in a rectory, and particularly for a pastor in the rectory of the church of his last appointment, or another rectory with the consent of the pastor.

4. Eligibility for Retirement:
   All priests incardinated in the archdiocese shall be eligible for retirement under this program.

   Priests of the archdiocese, who, on retirement are receiving pensions or retirement benefits from military or other services outside the archdiocese, shall receive a *pro rata* portion of retirement benefits in accordance with their years of service to the archdiocese, the details of which will be worked out on an individual basis.

5. Amount of Retirement:
   A. For priests retiring in a rectory: A priest retiring in a rectory will receive the following benefits:

   From the Parish: A pastor's salary (from the parish of his retirement or the parish where he resides);
   Total maintenance
   Appropriate arrangements for transportation;
   Blue Cross Companion Care and Priests' Relief benefits.

   B. For priests retiring *outside* the rectory: A priest retiring outside the rectory will receive the following benefits:

   From the archdiocese: $500.00 per month;
   Mass stipends in accordance with his need;
   Blue Cross Companion Care and Priests' Relief Benefits.

   (In addition, priests retiring outside the rectory will also be afforded every opportunity to engage in priestly work for which they will be compensated in accordance with current procedures.)

6. Sources of Funds:

   Over and above retirement benefits provided as described above from the parish, the archdiocese has provided funds for the support of this retirement program. This obviates the need for individual or parish assessments.

   Mindful of the needs of priests who have retired from administration and of their desire to continue to exercise as far as possible their priestly ministry, the Senate of Priests has established a Standing Committee for the continuing ministry of retired priests.[14]

At first Manning was hesitant about inaugurating the notion of team ministry. He finally agreed in the early 1970s to a pilot program for Nativity (Los Angeles) and Guardian Angels (Pacoima) and, later, Immaculate Conception (Monrovia). In a letter to the clergy, Manning

Mungret Graduates and cardinal - c. 1967.

First ordination class of Bishop Manning at Santa Barbara Mission.

Faculty Members of Saint John's Seminary.

Cardinal Manning with classmates at Saint Patrick's Seminary in Menlo Park - 1974.

indicated the advantages of the program as better communications and sharing, co-responsibility, mutual decision-making, mutual support and accountability and greater fraternity. It was his hope that those positive results would bring greater service to the people. He was even able to give the program a scriptural spin by observing that Christ had sent forth his disciples two by two. Though the program fell short of its ambitious goals, it did indicate Manning's willingness to listen to and be guided by the goodwill of his priests.

The establishment of the clerical Placement Board in 1972 was a further indication of the archbishop's eagerness to engage in co-responsibility. Its purpose was that of assisting "the Ordinary in the selection and assignment of pastors, associates and priests in special ministry." The board was a consultative body charged with making recommendations to the Ordinary. It was composed of seven members, five selected by the presbyterate and two by the Ordinary. The chancellor and a religious priest chosen by the archbishop would attend the meeting as auditors. The board would ordinarily meet twice monthly. In a newsletter circulated by the board, its duties were spelled out rather carefully:

> While the board lists no one area as a priority, the recommended assignment for the newly ordained has become a special concern. The board has made every effort to consult with the seminary staff, with the *ordinandi* and with their future pastors in order to insure a suitable first assignment.
>
> As regards the recommended assignment of priests as pastors, the board has tried to adhere to the following policy. All incardinated priests are eligible to apply for the pastorate of a vacant parish. The board will try to evaluate the applicant by taking into serious consideration his previous pastoral experience, his ethnic or cultural aptitude, his willingness and ability to cooperate with others in parochial administration, his sense of collegiality and shared responsibility and his seniority. These criteria have been emphasized by the Ordinary and also by the Priests' Senate as particular norms for assignment.
>
> Each applicant is encouraged to have an interview with the board or some members of the board. In addition to the above, the board will make use of profiles of the vacant parish drawn up by the board, utilizing information from the retiring incumbent, and/or administrator, associates and in-

volved religious and laity. This profile is given to any priest applying for the pastorate. The board also receives from the applicant a personal evaluation profile. This latter profile was adopted by the Priests' Senate and approved by the archbishop. The board at times solicits information about an applicant from other sources, such as fellow priests, previous pastors and interested religious and lay persons. Once all of the above is gathered and evaluated, then a recommendation is made to the Ordinary who is free to accept or reject the recommendation. Once the Ordinary has accepted the recommendation and made the appointment, he alone can initiate a review of it.

Priests are reminded that they do not have to limit their application for a vacant pastorate to one request. They may request consideration for every pastorate which becomes vacant. The request will be carefully considered.

With regard to associates' assignments or the assignment of those in special ministries, the board tries to act in the following manner. The tenure of appointment for associates ordinarily is four years. This policy has developed more out of necessity than choice. There has been an increased shortage of priests due to death, retirement, illness, special assignments and departure from the active ministry which necessitates changes as an ongoing process. When requested by the Ordinary, the board recommends priests for special ministry. The transfers within that ministry are normally handled by the respective department heads, with the approval of the Ordinary.

Whenever a transfer is to be made of associates, the Placement Board tries to practice the following policy:

1. The use of personnel profiles.
2. Consultation with the pastor of the parish in question to determine the nature of parochial work for which the prospective associate will be responsible.
3. It is the policy of the board to encourage priests to be interviewed by members of the board. This interview is normally held near the time of a change. The proce-

dure is as follows: the cover letter and profile is sent out; after its return, a phone call is made to encourage an interview and this takes place either at a regular Placement Board meeting or in a regional area. The board asks a priest if he would accept a particular assignment while respecting his right to refuse for good reasons.

4. Advance notice of transfer is the jurisdiction of the chancellor not the Placement Board.

> At times there arise unexpected and urgent needs which require an earlier transfer than is customary or a transfer to a less desirable situation. In these instances, the board recommends to the Ordinary that the situation be improved. Every individual priest is welcome to speak with the board or an individual member of the board concerning his assignment.
>
> The policy of the Placement Board is to bring to all assignments a humane consideration of the needs of each priest as a person, as well as a desire to respect the needs of the People of God. The board welcomes suggestions from the priests on how to develop procedures for all assignments. We are grateful to those who already have shared with us their suggestions and honest criticisms. While we have a reverence for the virtue of trust and confidentiality, we do wish to remain open as to our present policy. Our sole purpose is to serve all in justice and charity.[15]

As the years moved on, the overall program was fine-tuned and made even more responsive to local needs. It was one of the more substantial developments in Manning's tenure as archbishop.

In a message to the priests of the archdiocese issued on Holy Thursday, 1981, Manning said that it had been a priority for him, as archbishop, "to be present as much as possible to priests and people." He said that "the hopes and joys, the anxieties and the sorrows of my brother priests have been an intimate part of my own." He reminded them that "as a matter of strict policy, every priest in the archdiocese has free access to me and is welcomed as a brother." Noting that of late, "some concerns have been presented to me that express a desire for more such dialogue and the need for affirmation in the work of our ministry," he decided to establish a group of eleven priests who would function as "Visitors to the Clergy." Each would be available for contact and dialogue in his name and with his full support.

> In due time, you will be contacted by one of these, your fellow-priests. He will visit with you and be open to sharing your concerns, whether personal, domestic or diocesan. Each priest is pledged to total confidentiality, unless authorized by you to share your concerns with me. The principal reason for the visit is not, however, to confront your problems as much as to recognize the heroic and often inconspicuous dedication of your fellow-priests. Each visitor is an extension of myself, and will bear my appreciation for your co-working and the assurance that a personal visit from you is always an open invitation.[16]

Few priests availed themselves of this program which eventually fell into desuetude. Those who wanted or needed to see Manning personally continued to knock at his door and the latch always remained ajar.

Consistently supportive of his priests, even when one or two took advantage of his kindness, Manning tolerated no criticism of his clergy. And he was equally quick to stand by clerical friends. An example would be his long-time friendship with Scripture scholar, Father Raymond Brown. In April of 1980, when Brown was being attacked by a group calling itself "Catholics in Defense of Truth" at the Religious Education Congress in Anaheim, Manning issued a statement which said: "Do not be led astray by the venomous critics of Father Brown. He is a good and holy priest, and loyal to the Church. He is a scripture scholar and limits his skill to his Scripture experience. Father Brown, as a follower of Christ, is in good company when it comes to being criticized."[17]

Near the end of his archiepiscopate, Manning reported that "here in this jurisdiction there are about twelve hundred of us at the service of some two million Catholics. More than half of that number are members of religious communities. Forty-six communities of priests are represented here. We are drawn from many nations. Vocations from the local Church are never adequate for our needs and so we go begging across the globe. From Asian countries, the Philippines, China, Vietnam and Korea come native priests to serve their language groups here. Spain, South America and Mexico loan us priests to care for the Spanish-speaking. Some parishes are totally served in that language. For a century the burden of care for the English-speaking was carried mostly by Irish priests. Now, thank God, the alumni of our own seminary outnumber those from any of the other institutions that have supplied us in the past. Italians, Poles, Czechs, Hungarians, Dutch — all have worthy priests at their service."[18]

While acknowledging that as priests, "we are oftentimes misunderstood and misrepresented by those we serve," Manning liked to point out that "our priestly fraternity means everything to us."

> Time and time again the Senate of Priests attempts to regulate for this confraternity. To so attempt is redundant for, like water, it seeks its own level. Among ourselves we are uniquely our own men. We can be silent in one another's company. We may simulate abuse and condemnation, but we come from behind them as from a mask. We confess to one another — an open, heart-rending experience that brings the enfolding and merciful arms of our dearest Lord around us. We pray together, perhaps more so now than before, for it is only in prayer and in the togetherness of our singular lives that we shall live. We laugh together. It is fun, not coarse laughter. We laugh at ourselves. No one gets hurt. And we go gladly alone when we must go alone. The hearts we pledged in love to our people we do not divide for another. This would be betrayal. And when we die we lie in death together. Men will walk over our graves, talk in whispered tones, recall an incident of our lives, breathe a prayer for our eternal rest, and perhaps a tear may fall and be a benediction on our resting place.[19]

PRIESTS' SENATE

The relationship of a bishop to his priests has been spelled out since earliest times, especially in liturgical texts wherein God is called upon to pour His graces on candidates for ordination that they may assist the bishop in governing the People of God.

The movement towards establishment of the Priests' Senate in the various archdioceses and dioceses of the United States can be traced to the Decree on the Bishop's Pastoral Office, issued by the Vatican Council II on October 28, 1965. Therein it was stated that "included among the collaborators of the bishop in the government of the diocese are those priests who constitute his senate or council, such as the cathedral chapter, the board of consulters, or other committees established according to the circumstances or nature of various localities."[20]

One of the few decisions Manning had made well before he advanced from coadjutor to residential archbishop, was to allow formation of a Priests' Senate, something that had surfaced in his discussions with clergymen at every level of service in the archdiocese. At a meeting of the Board of Consulters, on February 9, 1970, Manning appointed a committee to survey the documentation on senates and "then to present to me and to the consulters recommendations as to the form and procedures that will best suit our purposes." It had been emphasized by the consulters "that this senate would be a presbytery of charity through which the common cause of our priesthood and the well being of the faithful can be more successfully pursued. If at any time such a body would become polarized from the archbishop, or a pressure group, it would be deficient in the prime charity which we are seeking."[21]

In that week's issue of *The Tidings*, the announcement about the proposed senate pointed out that Roman authorities had left to the local bishop the "method and plan" whereby the council or senate of priests would be constituted. Manning wanted it clear from the outset that such a consultative body would be supportive and collaborative, not independent and divisive.[22]

The drafting committee was empowered on March 16. It was to draw up proposals for a senate whose main purpose would be "to insure a bond of unity between the bishop and the priests, through which all of us can engage more effectively in the welfare of the souls committed to our care. This has primacy, and it is for this that we sanctify ourselves and become professionally skilled." Manning asked all the priests of the archdiocese to communicate suggestions that "might further the intent and purpose of the senate."[23]

By September, the committee had drafted a proposed constitution and by-laws which were sent out to the presbyterate for examination and discussion. In his cover letter, Msgr. Raymond J. O'Flaherty, the chairman of the committee, said that the aim of the document was "to provide the priests of the archdiocese with effective machinery for sharing with one another the concerns of their ministries." He hoped that the senate would be instrumental in solving "many of the problems confronting us as priests today." He proposed a system of standing committees so that in developing programs of action non-members as well as members could contribute their talent and efforts. He asked the clergy to consider five questions that needed resolution, namely:

1. Is a senate of thirty-five members too large?
2. Why choose the senators for age groups, areas and special apostolates?

JULIBEES FOR RELIGIOUS WOMEN

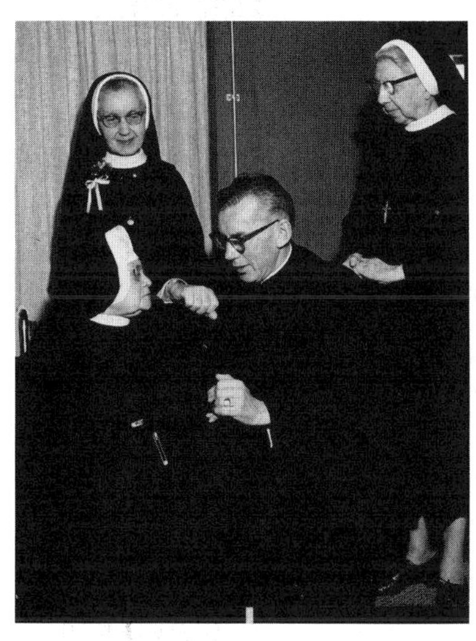

Cardinal Manning with Auxiliary Bishops, John J. Ward, Thaddeus Shubsda, Manuel Moreno and Juan Arzube.

Archbishop William Baum of Washington, D.C. greets Cardinals Timothy Manning, John Carberry (Saint Louis), Terence Cooke (New York), John Krol (Philadelphia) and Humberto Medeiros (Boston).

3. Why hold two preliminary elections for nominations?
4. Why should all priests vote for all senators?
5. Will the Senate really help solve basic problems?[24]

A series of clergy conferences was announced at which the theme for discussion would be "cooperation between priests and their bishop in the service of the People of God."[25] The conferences would focus on the proposed constitution and by-laws recently circulated among the clergy. Shortly thereafter, the priests were asked to vote by mail. The results were as follows:

> Total priests voting: 697 (of these: 490 - Diocesan, 207 - Religious)
>
> Voting for approval of the Constitution and By-Laws: 679 (negative votes - 18) [26]

An article in the constitution stated that it "shall be adopted and take effect when, having been submitted to the archbishop, it is approved by a two-thirds majority of the priests of Los Angeles eligible to vote and voting and ratified by the archbishop." It was ratified by Archbishop Manning on November 9, 1970 and thus became effective on that date.

Election of the first slate of senators then took place. The first stage involved writing in the name of any two priests in the various categories - geographic areas, age groups and Religious. The four highest candidates for each of the thirty senatorial positions were placed on the second ballot and the two leading candidates on the final ballot. On February 9, 1971, Manning announced, "with much pleasure," the names of those elected to serve in the first senate:

> The purpose of the Priests' Senate, as stated in the constitution, were:
>
> To unite and represent the priests of the archdiocese in the spirit of charity;
> To assist and advise the archbishop as his co-workers in one common pastoral work;
> To provide for the full and free discussion of all matters concerning the priestly ministry in the archdiocese;

AREA

1. Rev. Francis Roughan
2. Rev. George Niederauer
3. Rev. Joseph Schnieders
4. Rev. Msgr. Edward Wade
5. Rev. Msgr. John Sheridan
6. Rev. Thomas Acton
7. Rev. Robert Pierce
8. Rev. Joseph Francis, S.V.D.
9. Rev. James Hansen
10. Rev. John Fosselman
11. Rev. Gary Bauler
12. Rev. Royale Vadakin
13. Rev. Msgr. William Barry
14. Rev. Joseph Sartoris
15. Rev. John Sammon

APPOINTEES OF THE ARCHBISHOP

Very Rev. John J. Danagher, C.M.
Rev. Msgr. John Chedid
Rev. Alfred Hernandez
Rev. Charles O'Gorman

AGE GROUP

1. Rev. Msgr. Raymond O'Flaherty
2. Rev. Henry Alker
3. Rev. Msgr. Patrick Roche
4. Rev. James O'Callaghan
5. Rev. Vincent Barrett
6. Rev. Roddy Gorman
7. Rev. Patrick Thompson
8. Rev. Gerald Tellers
9. Rev. Patrick Ziemann
10. Rev. Helmut Hefner

RELIGIOUS

Special Apostolate -
Rev. Joel Gromowski, C.P.
Education -
1. Rev. Charles Casassa, S. J.
2. Rev. Augustine Carter, O. Carm.

Parochial -
1. Rev. Jesus Alonso, O.M.I.
2. Rev. Luis Valbuena, O.M.I.[27]

> To promote a more effective priestly life and ministry by studying, proposing and helping to implement specific policies and programs, especially in regard to the priestly apostolate, the education and the spiritual growth of priests, and their personal welfare;
>
> To seek with priestly concern for just solutions to the problems of the entire community;
>
> To undertake each and every other activity necessary and proper to carry out the above purposes.[28]

At the inaugural meeting, Msgr. William Barry was elected president, Fathers George Niederauer, vice-president, G. Patrick Ziemann, secretary and Joseph Sartoris, secretary. Concerns surfacing at the first meeting set the pattern of subsequent discussions. They dealt with the implementation of programs for instruction of the laity, the deepening of the spiritual lives of priests and religious, the extension of interparochial cooperation, the care of children, youth and young married couples, the formulation of means of reinvigorating the Church's teachings on the sacraments and enriching the practice of the liturgy. Standing committees were set up for pastoral ministry, apostolic research, priests' personnel, social action, priestly formation and education and minority issues. Initially the senate met weekly and later monthly.[29] Area meetings were begun in March, each presided over by a local senator.

Appearing at one of the first sessions, Manning outlined the chain of communication through which the suggestions of the priests could be funneled to the nation's hierarchy then preparing for the world-wide Synod of Bishops whose focus was on priestly ministry and world justice and peace. The archbishop used that opportunity to renew his commitment to the work of the senate and its responsiveness to the suggestions made by individual clergymen. He said "we love the priesthood to which we have given our lives and we must share our efforts to achieve the greatest strength possible in serving the People of God."[30]

A cursory glance at the reports and minutes of the senate sessions during the ensuing years indicates the wide range of interests and concerns of the archdiocesan clergy. In September of 1971, for example, the senate issued its first official resolution which read:

> In the spirit of Vatican II and out of reverence for the human person, we, the Senate of Priests of the Archdiocese of Los Angeles, condemn the crime of abortion. Reverence for life demands freedom from direct interruption of life once it is conceived. For through conception begins a process the purpose of which is the realization of human personality. This crime not only poisons human society but harms those who practice it and is a supreme dishonor to the Creator.[31]

In 1976, Father William Levada, retiring as president of the Priests' Senate, categorized seven functions performed by the Senate up to that time:

1. A forum for the discussion of various issues;
2. A listening post for outside speakers on various issues;
3. An agent for accomplishing specific programs or tasks;
4. A representative group addressing its own internal concerns;

5. A consultative council to the archbishop generating policy proposals;
6. A means of gathering information, and
7. A resolution-making body to focus on important concerns.[32]

During the years that followed, Manning's relationship with the Priests' Senate was cordial and productive. He regularly attended the morning sessions of their monthly meetings and always had words of encouragement and affirmation. He was most pleased when the day opened with a con-celebrated Mass and his homilies covered a wide variety of topics as they related to the Gospel reading of the day. Just before lunch, the president would ask the cardinal for his observations which generally centered around current problems and challenges facing the archdiocese.

There were few if any confrontations, mostly because Manning had an innate gift of avoiding and sidestepping controversies. He insisted on reading (and occasionally changing) the minutes of the meetings and often used them as departure points for subsequent gatherings. Once, when he returned to the Chancery Office, he was heard to say: "They gave every indication of renewing me for another year." Though he was impressed by the suggestions and proposals made by the senate on almost every imaginable topic, Manning felt that members often took themselves too seriously. He knew by experience that the passage of time solved more problems than did hasty decisions.

Though he had no credentials in the academic world, Manning knew that most priests, overly educated for what they were called to do at the parochial level, needed a forum in which to vent their views. He envisioned the Priests' Senate as an ideal "safety valve" for those who had no other means of expressing themselves about the needs and ideals of the ministry as they envisioned them.

Notes to the Text

1. Timothy Cardinal Manning essay taken from a series that appeared in *The Tidings* during June of 1984.
2. AALA, "Homily for Msgr. John Cosgrove," February 9, 1989.
3. *The Tidings*, June 2, 1978.
4. Canon 276.
5. *The Tidings*, February 17, 1984.
6. AALA, "Sermon Preached at the First Mass of Rev. Thomas Gannon, May 4, 1946."
7. Francis J. Weber (comp.), *Times of Tension. Moments of Grace* (Los Angeles, 1990), p.393.
8. *The Tidings*, August 20, 1971.
9. *Ibid.*, January 25, 1971.
10. *Ibid.*, January 16, 1976.
11. AALA, Timothy Cardinal Manning to Clergy, Los Angeles, November 2, 1976.
12. AALA, Timothy Cardinal Manning to Clergy, Los Angeles, November 10, 983.
13. AALA, Timothy Cardinal Manning to Clergy, Los Angeles, January 3, 1977.
14. AALA, "Retirement Plan," Los Angeles, 1972.
15. AALA, "Placement Board Proceedings," Los Angeles, 1972.
16. AALA, Timothy Cardinal Manning to Clergy, Los Angeles, April 16, 1981.
17. *The Tidings*, April 4, 1980.
18. Francis J. Weber (comp.), *Times of Tension. Moments of Grace* (Los Angeles, 1990) p. 393.
19. *Ibid.*, p. 394.
20. Walter M. Abbott, S.J., *The Documents of Vatican II* (New York, 1966) p. 416.

21. AALA, Timothy Manning to Raymond J. O'Flaherty, Los Angeles, February 12, 1970.
22. The members of the committee were: Monsignors Raymond J. O'Flaherty, James Hourihan, William J. Barry and Fathers James A. O'Callaghan, Joel Gromowski, C.P., Wilbur Davis, Louis A. Gutierrez, Donal Mulcahy, G. Patrick Ziemann and George H. Niederauer.
23. AALA, Timothy Manning to Clergy, Los Angeles, March 18, 1970.
24. AALA, Raymond J. O'Flaherty to Clergy, Los Angeles, September 1, 1970.
25. *The Tidings*, September 11, 1970.
26. AALA, Raymond J. O'Flaherty to Timothy Manning, Los Angeles, November 4, 1970.
27. AALA, Timothy Manning to Clergy, Los Angeles, February 9, 1971.
28. *The Tidings*, February 12, 1971.
29. *Ibid.*, February 26, 1971.
30. *Ibid.*, March 12, 1971.
31. *Ibid.*, September 24, 1971.
32. *Ibid.*, August 20, 1976.

12. Ireland

Though he spent the entire fifty-five years of his priestly ministry in California, Timothy Manning really never left Ireland. He brought with him all the charming aspects of his motherland and few of its shortcomings. One who visits Ballingeary and Gougane Barra can readily understand what he meant by saying that "people who die there have no place to go - they already live in paradise."

The clerical wags who contended that Manning's talks, sermons, addresses and homilies "reeked of Ireland" meant that observation as a compliment, not a put-down. In practically all of his utterances, there was some reference to that "small island in the North Atlantic" where people are "baptized anew each day by holy water from heaven." Those who want to know the cardinal need to walk in his footsteps and pray at his priedieu in the beautiful chapel of Saint Finbarr's hermitage on the picturesque island in the headwaters of the River Lee.

Manning was a keen student of his country's historical heritage as it related to the world at large. On June 24, 1952, the then Auxiliary Bishop of Los Angeles gave an address to the Maynooth Union in which he spelled out "the story of the Gael in the land rising beyond the rim of the western seas."

> We wish to speak of currents of Irish influence within the Church in America. A current is a concealed movement within a body of water. It has the surging flow and the dominating control of a river; yet it is integral to the sea, not alien to it. It is imperceptible to the casual observer, yet to the trained authority its course may be charted, its intensity measured and its variations recorded.
>
> We propose that the story of our race in America is best evaluated under such a concept. Undoubtedly there have been individual Irishmen whose names are written large into the history of the United States. They have given glory in the civic and religious records of that nation. Yet their true great-

ness may not be divorced from their times nor from the trends to which they were as rudders to a ship. Their histories are available and he who runs may read them. Our purpose here is rather to emphasize that the story of our people is not a record of a foreign and alien element in the American way of life, never completely absorbed into it, but rather that it is a blending of waters, a distinctive current that is fluid enough to form a part of, and cohesive enough to show a directing influence that helped to create the essence of the American tradition.

There are three main reasons to support this assertion. First of all the Irish, without prejudice to the claims of their native tongue, were English-speaking. The American population springs from European origins. Each wave of migrants from continental Europe was isolated by the barriers of language and could not become entirely absorbed until a second and a third generation was bred from that original stock. They did not quickly take their place in the public life of the whole community and remained long anchored to the particular locality where the first settlers made their homes. The Irish on the contrary were unimpeded on that score. They could flow with the tide of population within the country and could quickly assume their part in its public life.

The second reason was a love for liberty. Long centuries of oppression had accentuated their aspirations for freedom and like a growth contained within itself for lack of proper environment, they burst freely into bloom in the free air of a nation "conceived in liberty and dedicated to the proposition that all men are created equal." They will be remembered forever for the strength they gave to Washington in the great and successful war for independence and their names are written for their gallantry in every struggle that our nation has endured to preserve her dauntless glory.

The third reason is born of the faith of the Irish. It is that Christian gift of "piety," which expresses itself in a tender devotion to house and family and home, and when expanded to embrace the country of adoption becomes the virtue of patriotism. The backbone of any nation is the home where respect for authority is inculcated, where domestic virtues flourish and where a content with the providential will of God creates a tranquillity of order. This is the glory of the Irish home and this spirit was transplanted with the great migrations. Much of the stability of the American way of life is due to it, and in the current domestic unrest festering in the open sores of divorce, and likewise in the related national unrest manifested in the surprising extent of disloyalty, it is not saying too much that the love of home and fatherland, so characteristic of the Irish, may well be the inspiration once again for the return to the true nobility of a house in order.

There is a tendency yet lingering to consider the United States in terms of the cities along the Atlantic coast, New York, Boston and Philadelphia. There is a complacent conviction even among the residents of those cities that the ultimate limits of the country halt at their farthest on the banks of the Mississippi. Yet the country must be understood as stretching in vastness for two thousand miles west of Chicago, through the fertile farmlands of Iowa, across the grainfields of Kansas, over the rolling prairies, the deserts of sundown splendor, over the Rocky mountains, through the Mohave deserts, up the slopes of the Sierras and then cascading down in verdure and plenty to the silver shores of the Pacific.

The trend of population is forever westward and now with the orientation of world politics to the far east. The cities of the west, Los Angeles, San Francisco and Seattle are but now entering into that strategic importance they will play in the new order of things. Those cities are growing by the hour and presenting the greatest challenge to the Church in the history of our people.

Coupled with this geographical expansion we should likewise show the pathways of the Irish within that expansion. An old proverb reads that "God writes straight with crooked lines." In the great sweep of history by which the providential will of God is executed in time, the terrible disaster of the Irish famine was the source out of which God would harvest the seeds of the faith to be sown in the fertile fields of the new countries beyond the west most seas; the source from which as from a broken artery Irish blood would flow out to be transfused into the blood stream of America. The census records of the United States government give us the startling totals of immigration from Ireland and yet they are below the real figures because they do not take into account the vast number who came in through Canada and England nor those who came in without benefit of legal endorsement.

> Already by 1790 the census shows that 3.7% of the national population was of Irish stock. By 1840 there is a record of 506,719 immigrations. Over a million and a half migrated during the margin of the famine years from 1841-1860; two and a half million from then until 1910. All told in the space of 110 years from 1820 to 1930 the official figure of the census bureau records the startling number of 4,585,080, a figure exceeding the total present population of Ireland.[1]

After attempting to give some idea about the contributions of the Irish people to the formation of the American traditions and, further, indicating the force of the flow of immigrations, Manning felt compelled to complete the picture by showing the two great tragedies latent in the story of their progress.

> The first is that because the Irish as a general rule concentrated in the big cities, they were doomed in their descendants to the sterility of city life. There was good reason for the gravitation to the cities: work was plentiful, money was quick and the associations of home by family, town and county were perpetuated. They followed the law of "birds of a feather." This congregation into the city was of course for the while of immense benefit to the Church; the Irish were loyal and generous to their priests and they supplied the vocations, as no other nation did, for the abundant shepherding of their own flocks. Yet it is an established fact that urban life has a sterilizing effect upon a people and will not reproduce itself. The city must be constantly populated from the outside. For this reason there is a marked decline manifesting itself in communities that were once predominantly Irish. The comments of Father John O'Brien are an alarming warning not merely for the Irish in America but for those in the homeland. It is his considered judgment that if the present trend continues, in another century the Irish will have vanished much like the Mayans, leaving only their monuments behind them.
>
> The second historical tragedy lies in the fact that the rural districts of the United States were largely lost to the Church. The Irish should have loved the soil with a native zeal, but they lacked the patience to wait out the seasons and the uncertainties of harvests. The relatively few who did venture into country life were not followed by their priests, and in

> their hunger for things of God, they drifted inevitably into sectarian Protestantism and today you will find their names popular in the rolls of the Methodist and Baptist churches.[2]

Manning was also a keen student of American history and that's why he felt constrained to point out that the west must be considered apart. California was bred from Spanish stock.

> Its early history and colonization was through Mexico and today its place-names from San Diego in the south to San Rafael across the bay from San Francisco form a veritable litany of saints decorating the great *camino real*, the king's highway. With the discovery of gold in Sutter's Creek in 1849 the fortunes of California changed. It awoke like a giant from a long slumber and was quickly absorbed into the Federated States. The Irish were in the vanguard of the great gold-rush westward and their names are still legendary in the absorbing history of the coast. They caught up the fires of the faith relinquished by the vanquished colonials and by that strange affinity between Ireland and Spain were able to fill the vacated places of the Spanish *padres.*
>
> One of the unwritten glories of our race is the payment of our debt to Mexico under the dauntless leadership of the late Archbishop Cantwell. When the ugly head of persecution rose in Mexico, the exiles for the faith flocked across the border into California. More Mexicans were located in Los Angeles than in any city of Mexico save the *Distrito Federal* itself. Instantly our priests met the situation and churches and community centers were established to serve them. Our priests studied the language and became the cherished shepherds of this forlorn people. This work still carries on. The present incumbent of Los Angeles in the brief period since his arrival has erected over seventy schools, largely to serve the Mexican descendants, so that they will be able to take fitting and full place in the community as Catholic American citizens. All the dioceses of the southwest are now linked together in a movement to better the condition of these people and to care for the constant flow of migratory labour crossing the border for the harvesting each year. We believe that in the details of this movement there is a model

> for the handling of all such displaced and migrated people and perhaps also some suggestions that may help in the handling of a problem where our own Irish people are migratory from the homeland.[3]

The Auxiliary Bishop of Los Angeles, an inspiring speaker and informative lecturer, felt that the most convincing proof for the Irish character within the Church of the United States was in its leadership.

> The priesthood and the episcopate do not perpetuate themselves as in the house and family of Levi but they spring from the midst of each succeeding generation. They will be the best indication of the character of the people. A glance at the index of priests in the *National Catholic Directory* will tell that the origins and their names are echoes of all the clans of Ireland. Even when the popular motion pictures wish to portray the typical priest, he is always hallowed with an Irish name and given unmistakable shades of accent that a director thinks should emphasize his nationality.[4]

Like his episcopal predecessors since the days when Joseph Sadoc Alemany wore the mitre in California, Manning championed the importation of Irish priests and religious to the Golden State.

> The faith is perpetuated through the priesthood and the priesthood is the flowering of each succeeding generation. As long as priests come to America from Ireland they will forever bring that freshness of faith and its simplicity to penetrate the growing subtlety of a post-Christian world. Priests are germ-carriers, bearing the life-preserving antibodies that will counteract the germicidal diseases that this day affect men's minds, and the incubators for those preservatives are the holy homes of Ireland and their counterparts in America. The United States still needs the priests of Ireland, men of vision and faith like those who came before them, men of missionary zeal and humble origins, who will be the stuff out of which the last great nation of the Church will grow. As an ambassador without portfolio, I would presume to express to the homes and seminaries of Ireland the gratitude of the American dioceses for the inestimable

Cardinal Manning receives the Medallion of Merit from the Friendly Sons of Saint Patrick.

Cardinal visits President Eamon de Valera in 1973.

Connraḋ na Gaeḋilge
Tír is Teanga

Naoṁ Fionn-Barra

Naoṁ Columcille

Dileagra Aḋnóiḋ
don
Monsignor Ró-Oir. Taḋg Ó Mongáin
ó
Ċonnraḋ na Gaeḋilge
ar ócáid a ċeapṫa ina Easpog Ċonganta ar Los Angeles

Mór an scéal
againn a ċlos gur togaḋ tú féin
id aoḋaire ar ṫréadaib Ċríost
's id ċomarba fíor ar aspail Dé.

Mór fá ḋó
an gradam so do ḋul i dtreo
pearsan dár muintir féin –
Gaeḋeal ón nGaeḋealtaċt is ó pór.

Oiḋre tú
ar ṡluaġ na nGaeḋeal a ġaib ar siubal
ó Éire amaċ go tíorṫa i gcéin
le briaṫar Dé do ċur in iúl.

'Sé ár nguiḋe
gaċ grást ó Dia do ṫeaċt id líon
is eagna ċun riarṫa ar do ṫréad
i gcéimib t'aṫarḋa 's i ngaois.
-Aindrias Ó Muimhneaċáin

Uaċtarán

León Ó Dubġaill
Tánaiste

Árd-Rúnaiḋe

support and supply which they have received from the new harvesting of modern Ireland's vocations. May God always fructify this "teeming womb" of Levites for the well-being of the world.

What is true of the priesthood is likewise true of the sisterhood and the teaching community of brothers. Let it be said that without our teaching sisters in America the superstructure of the Church's organization would collapse. And outspoken Catholicity of the members of our American forces during World War II should know that such training is totally due to the tireless dedication of our sisters. On behalf of these sisters who solicit vocations in Ireland we would gladly be a beggar at your door. Eight sisters will teach a school of five hundred pupils and the destiny of Catholic America lies with them. As an example of the gigantic nature of our task, in the Archdiocese of Los Angeles alone in the last three years, our archbishop has erected over seventy schools at a cost exceeding nine million dollars. Seventy thousand children are enrolled in our diocesan schools and as many more waiting for the schools and sisters that can accommodate them.

Over and above the export of vocations from Ireland there is, we believe, another sphere where the Irish influence can be most potent for good. We mean in the realm of thought and studies. There are great issues confronting the Church in America today. We seek a new defining of the relationship with the Church to civil society; a new approach must be made to the accommodating of the encyclicals of the Holy Fathers to the labour and economic problems of the modern age, a fresh orientation must be given to theology to embrace a secularist world, a fathoming should be given to the interpretation of the liturgical life to society, a re-wording of our doctrines for the modern adolescent mind. We of America are perhaps too close to the problems to see all their implications, too hurried in our activities to give the required attention. The schools of Ireland have the talent and the perspective and the leisure. Those works in scripture and social studies and civics that have emerged from Ireland have avid readers. How we wish that there would be a constant flow of exportation from the scholars of home that

> in their words and virtues we might "whet the chisels of our minds on hastity, and lick the basalt of learning."[5]

That Manning loved and extolled his native parish of Iveleary, with its two parochial churches and shrine of Gougane Barra is obvious from an allocution in which he stated that "there are no adherents of an alien faith within the limits of this parish. Few parishes in the whole world can boast such a record. There is no known instance of anyone having lost the faith here, or even in all the migrations out of here, or anyone who has forfeited his ancient birthright. Such a record is not accidental. What secret covenant with God and St. Finbarr we know not, but we are acutely conscious that his merits before God and the trials, tears and prayers of our forefathers surround us like the hills and are barriers and bastions against the noonday devil and the terror that rides the night." He further observed that "like the waters of the Lee we shall inevitably journey toward the ocean of eternity. But look up always, for there is a star, bright in the firmament to guide us and to give us hope. The luminous star is Finbarr, hermit of Gougane, Apostle of our beloved Cork."6

Always and everywhere, Manning had utmost confidence in the Irish people and the depth of their faith. He often related that faith to the story of how the Irish came to the New World. He pointed out that "the great migrations to the United States in the half century after the famine give abundant testimony to this dominating force of the faith. Unlettered men and women, yet rooted deep in the oral traditions of the faith were such a decisive force in the development of the American religious and civic thinking that the vigorous, healthy and reproductive Catholicism of America today is due almost in its entirety to the strength and loyalty of a faith bred in these hillsides and among these glens. What happened in America fifty years ago, what is already accomplished in Australia, will be done again in the great rebirth of faith in our sister island across the Irish sea."

> Have no fear for the fidelity of our immigrants to the faith. True there will be alarming stories now and then of asserted defections from the faith, but by and large the strong bulwark of the faith will hold. The meshes of tradition, the holy memories, the strong blood, the merits of their persecuted forefathers will hold, and not only hold, but turn the tide against the secularism and post-paganism that is now inundating the remnants of a Christian Europe.

> In the city of Rome there is a street called the Street of the Marble Foot. On a pedestal by its side is a marble foot of immense proportions. It is all that remains of a colossal statue of pagan times. From the dimensions of the foot we can get some indications of the size of the statue. What we envision is of the same character. The fidelity and devotion of our people is like a footprint in this mid-century and from it we can gauge somewhat the immense statue of the holy Patron who first spoke the words of faith among these hills, and who by his prayer and penance should have merited its preservation unsullied through centuries of persecution and famine, and exile and despoliation.[7]

In August of 1959, Manning was asked by the Bishop of Cork to speak about the "Church in Silence and in Chains." Though nothing much beyond its title[8] refers strictly to Ireland, it abounds in the simple deposit of faith that Timothy Manning learned at his mother's knee. And, happily she was there to hear him.

> Here on the banks of our own lovely Lee, the waters which flow from the hills and valleys are met and mingled with the tide-waters of the universal sea which reach deep into the inner land. So too, we for a moment drawn from the surrounding hills and valleys, restless and rippling with the anxieties of our daily cares, are met and mingle with the eternal. Heaven has been let down among us and the soul surrenders to the great mystery of God's way with us.
>
> In our time we have seen the persecution of the Church, the desolation of two world wars, the holocaust of human life destroyed at all the frontiers and barricades of freedom on the earth, in the sky and beneath the sea, the untold millions burned like refuse in the gas chambers of concentration camps – then the aftermath of war, the materialism, the sensuality, the glorification of the human flesh.
>
> The Blessed Mother is eminently the symbol of the Church – the Woman clothed with the sun, the moon at her feet; on her head a crown of a dozen stars. She is the first trophy of the glory and the resurrection of Christ. She was assumed, body and soul, into heavenly glory. It was not a singular privilege like her Immaculate Conception, which no one else would merit – but she is the first fruits of the triumph of Christ.

> So it is that in her Assumption, defined in mid-century, there is injected into the world again the seed of hope, the certainty of triumph. The Church will rise again. "Ought not Christ have suffered and so enter into His glory?" – In God's good time and in the measure of our prayers, the bruised and buried Church will rise again, will be clothed in glory, assumed into heaven. Like a lover with his bride, Christ will sweep His Church across thresholds of heaven, and there shall be tears no more and mourning and sorrow not again. This is our faith – this is the hope in which we live – the tranquility in which we die.[9]

During the summer of 1961, Manning wrote what he entitled "A Reverie on Ireland." Apparently it had been intended as a talk but there's no indication that it was ever delivered. In any event, only in 1977 was the essay made public in a series of newspaper articles entitled *Signs of the Times*. He observed that "for those of us who were there (in Ireland), its remembrance binds our minds in haunting captivity. For those whose ancestors came from there, a strange magnetism possesses them."

> Like the migration of whales along the Pacific shore-line to a spawning spot in Baja California, there is this inexplicable pull to the places of their origins in that mystic land. Some, with no ancestral links to its shores, have visited it and forevermore plan and presume to return. Why is it so?
>
> It is certainly, but not totally, the country itself. The land is bathed in lights and half-lights. An incessant sequence of sunshine and shade drift, like a benediction, across its surface. Little fields, boxed in by stone fences, make a patchwork of every shade of green that nature possesses in her store houses. Rivers run noisily homeward to the sea. No town nor hamlet could exist without one. They are parables of life. They exemplify the irresponsibility and innocence of youth, the burdens of adulthood to be carried on the back, the indistinguishable blending with the tide-waters of eternity at life's end. Enticing little roads beckon the visitor to come and see what wonders may be spread beyond that nearest turn. Heather-dressed hills echo back the lonely cry of lamenting sheep. Mountain lakes bide their time for the still mornings when they can mirror their surrounding realities and bewitch the viewer with the puzzle of where sub-

> stance ceases and reflection begins. Long fingers of land jut out to the wild sea and dare its waves as they heighten and foam against the unyielding cliffs. Sometimes, as the waters rise and fall in the long and fiord-like bays, arms of land reach out and trap the sea waters in little coves with silver strands. Then they cry across the hills to the mothers and children in the little towns to come and play there until the setting sun makes fantasy of it all. Rain is inseparable from Ireland. Its gentle fall fills the rivers and greens the fields. Perhaps too it distills that quality of moodiness that possesses the Irish mind in life, literature and love.
>
> The story of Ireland is written in blood and tears. It is one of conquest, banishment, exile, torture, fragmentation, famine and betrayal. Even now her fair name is tainted by brothers' blood. Anguish rises from her northern homes and hill-sides. Innocence is swallowed up in hatred and vengeance. Religious allegiances are a mockery of reality. All proposed solutions are ineffectual. A cry must go up from all the land and from the distant countries that a merciful God would allow peace to descend into its broken hearts.[10]

In 1973, at the behest of the Lord Mayor Patrick Kerrigan and other corporation officials, Manning received the rarely-bestowed and highly-cherished "Freedom of Cork" in a ceremony attended by a host of Ireland's top leadership. The scroll attesting to the honor was placed within a richly-ornamented golden sepulchre executed in the studios of William Egan & Sons and mounted on a piece of Irish marble. Two cloisonne seals, one bearing the coat-of-arms for the Manning family and the other the shield for the Archdiocese of Los Angeles, are attached to the lid of the sepulchre. The scroll reads:

> In token of our joy and pride at his elevation to the Sacred College of Cardinals, in recognition of his special care for the underprivileged of his Archdiocese and in appreciation of his abiding affection for and interest in the welfare of the people of the City and County of Cork, November 12, 1973.[11]

While he was in Ireland, in 1973, the cardinal took the occasion to bless the newly-opened parochial church of Saint Brendan the Navigator at the Glen, Cork. A local newspaper reported that this was the first time an edifice in that area had been blessed by a cardinal. In his homily, Manning made special appeal for the exercise of charity through the

Bishop of Fresno arrives at Shannon Airport, 1969.

Cardinal Manning welcomes San Francisco's Archbishop Joseph T. McGucken to Gougane Barra.

love of fellow men and women, the sick, the imprisoned or those on the street, each one of which, he said, "was made to the image of Christ." The local bishop thanked Manning, noting that the "Cork-born, Cork-reared and Cork-blooded" cardinal was "the first Corkman to reach such a position of dignity in the Catholic Church."[12]

Manning's relation with Eamon de Valera stretched back several decades to the regime of Archbishop John J. Cantwell, when the Irish patriot visited Los Angeles and stayed at the archiepiscopal residence. In April of 1974, de Valera, by then President of Ireland, conferred an honorary doctorate on Manning *(in absentia)* in Iveagh House, Dublin. The Archbishop was described as "a distinguished Churchman and Irishman who, following in the great Irish missionary tradition, had given his life to the service of the Catholic Church in the United States."[13]

Cardinal Manning rarely journeyed to Ireland without delivering at least one major address. His visit in 1975 was arranged around ceremonies marking the 500th anniversary of Holy Cross Abbey in County Tipperary. Manning used the opportunity to extol the influence of monastery life on Ireland and its people.

> The history of our nation is the long, sad story of a people bent beneath the weight of a cross. Even at this hour the fair head of our land is crowned with thorned wire. Facing westward to the sea, she has suffered from every wayward wind and weather. Orphaned from the continent of Europe, she has clung to an ancient faith though dungeon, fire, famine and the sword.
>
> All the implications of the Way of the Cross are verified in her pilgrimage through time. Representatives of alien masters stood in judgment over her. She became a laughing-stock for the head-shaking of the passerby. Her betrayals were from those who dipped their bread in the same dish with her. She was stripped of all her garments and no title to land nor honor was left to clothe her shame. Time and again she was pronounced dead, was promised life in exchange for the forfeiting of her faith, but always, like returning spring, hope sprung to life within her. Her one abiding comfort of that *Via Dolorosa* was the presence of the Mother – silently comforting and sharing in the sorrow of those in the valley of tears.
>
> The history of Holy Cross Abbey is a parable in stone of this way of God with us – the royal road of the Holy Cross. It ranked in the primacy of the abbeys of Ireland. For the Irish

> the Church itself was in essence, monastic. The pope was the abbot of the Church in Rome. Jesus was the Abbot of the Church in heaven. Kings and earls and archbishops were familiar to it. They journeyed here to swear their treaties on the wood of the cross. Rich endowments and offerings were its patrimony. Then its destinies changed. Patronage placed unworthy men at its head, covetousness took away its lands and endowments, Cromwellian forces devastated its proud bearing, neglect and vandalism did the rest, until it became utterly empty of any glory, a by-word to the passerby – a ruin and no more.
>
> From these depths God raised it up. Through the ministering judgment and husbandry of the Prelate of Cashel and Emly, through the genius of artist and artisan, it enters into its resurrection, it lives again, radiant, ever enduring, witnessing to the design of God in our lives, a sermon, a parable in tone. The deed we do this day then must be an awakening and a commitment to the things of faith, to Christ the center of that faith. The altar in the restored abbey church bears on its marble slab the Latin inscription: *"Ut non evacuetur Crux Christi."* That the cross of Christ be not made void, a quotation from Paul's first letter to the Corinthians.[14]

In August of 1979, Manning presided at an open-air Mass honoring Edmund Ignatius Rice in Waterford. The remains of the famed educator were transferred to their final resting place in the new Chapel of the Blessed Sacrament at Mount Sion Monastery. Speaking in the presence of a thousand Christian Brothers from all over the world, the cardinal warned that Ireland was no longer insulated from attacks on family life.[15]

> Today I stand in surrogate for unnumbered thousands of alumni of the Christian Brothers' schools and Presentation Brothers schools throughout the English-speaking world. Echoing through my voice is the gratitude of men, most of us from origins of poverty, who owe our initiation into learning, our doorway to the wider world, to Edmund Ignatius Rice and the communities which he founded for the gratuitous instruction of the poor. It is not our intent on this occasion to narrate the life and times of Ignatius Rice. He who runs, may read the sequence of events that measure his life-span.

> Rather would we wish to share some reflections on that life that give a pertinence to our own day and time.
>
> It would seem safe to say that each time the Church defines a doctrine to be accepted on faith by all the members of the Church, and each time she elevates to the honour of the altars one of her members reputed for heroic sanctity, that she does so in virtue of a specific plan of God. The dogma of the assumption, for instance, is defined, not only to exalt for the veneration of the people the immaculate Virgin Mary, but more so by declaring that she was assumed body and soul into heavenly glory to give a needed healing to a wounded world.
>
> We are in no way anticipating here the ultimate judgment of the Holy See regarding the heroic sanctity of Ignatius Rice. Certainly we should pray that he will be given that high honour from the Church. Everything we can do to advance his cause should be generously done. He was a holy man. He was a man of great consequence for his times. Together with Daniel O'Connell and Father Matthew of temperance fame, we believe that the three of them were the outstanding figures of influence in the Ireland of the early 19th century.
>
> Ireland is not insulated from the attack on family life that is coming this way from overseas. Its symptoms are successive polygamy, live-in spouses without benefit of ceremony, independence of children from parental authority, abortions and artificial interception of the flow of life. Like a hurricane this inflow will leave havoc in its trail. One of the resistants to it is the life and conduct of exemplary laymen and women. One such was Ignatius Rice. He is a man for our times. Let us honour him as such.[16]

In August of 1980, Manning joined four other cardinals to commemorate the centenary of the apparitions at Knock[17] in County Mayo. The cardinal was always supportive of that shrine which has drawn a steady stream of pilgrims over the years, though he acknowledged that the significance of the apparitions has been difficult to assess since no words were spoken and no message given.

Whenever possible, Manning used the influence of his office on behalf of his motherland. In 1981, he sent a cable to Mrs. Thatcher,

Prime Minister of Great Britain, in which he said that "the situation on Northern Ireland had deteriorated to an extreme degree:

> The events there in recent days forebode social chaos and bloodshed among a precious people who have suffered too much and too long. We invite all Christian people to beg God's healing benediction on the Province and we urge the civil authorities to allow such measures as may avert the Province's collapse into civil war.
>
> As the Irish-born Cardinal Archbishop of Los Angeles with its nine million people I earnestly urge you in the name of all concerned with human rights to adopt the recommendations of Cardinal O'Fiaich and Bishop Edward Daly regarding prison dress and prison work of the prisoners held in the present crisis. We urgently petition a prayerful remembrance for an ending to the violence and hatred which is ravaging people and countries throughout the world.[18]

In mid 1981, Cardinal Manning was informed that Pope John Paul II had appointed him as a "Special Envoy" to the celebration in Drogheda commemorating the third centenary of Saint Oliver Plunkett.[19] An eloquent homily for that occasion was preached by Basil Cardinal Hume of Westminister. Manning prefaced the event by conveying the Holy Father blessings to Ireland and its people.

The ceremonies were held on July 3, the feast of Saint Thomas the Apostle. In his report, Manning told the pontiff that he had been "received with warm hospitality in a public ceremony which took place at Saint Peter's Church." The local mayor presented greetings as did the other religious and civic dignitaries. Over 12,000 people, including twenty-five bishops, took part in the principal Mass which was celebrated by Thomas Cardinal O'Fiaich.[20]

Concern over serious inroads being made into the sanctity of the family was expressed in Cork by Manning who preached the homily at the traditional Eucharistic procession in Cork City on June 1, 1986. More than 25,000 people gathered to take part in the ceremony. In an obvious reference to the debate about divorce then underway in Ireland, Cardinal Manning stressed the importance of the family or "domestic church." To properly understand the meaning of the family a person needed to understand the Church, "of which it is an image." And the defining quality of that family was togetherness, something that was being tampered with because of other distractions.[21]

GOUGANE BARRA

The world possesses few lakes more picturesquely situated than Gougane Barra, near the headwaters of the River Lee, in County Cork. It is environed by mountains on all sides except the east and from there a stream makes its way through a rocky gap on its rapid way to the ocean.[22] On the top of the mountainous precipices, eagles, hawks and other birds of prey breed and live in great security. It is indeed a most elegant and romantic spot. Since the 7th century, holy pilgrimages and miraculous cures have occurred on the island amidst the ruins of a hermitage erected by Saint Finbarr, the patron of Cork, and his companions.

The tiny chapel or oratory now on the island was erected in the early years of this century. Measuring forty-five by twenty-four feet, it is built in a Hiberno-Byzantine style, modelled after the one at Cormack on the rock of Cashel. The chapel's external elevations are simple and in harmony with the traditions of the site. The walling is of mountain stone, relieved by dressings of limestone. Over the doorway is a narrow circular-headed light in the high-pitched gable. The eastern end of the chapel has a neatly worked couplet window of limestone, with a circular-headed light above. On the apex of each gable is a small cross or Irish character.

The altar in the small oratory is fashioned principally of St. Maximin creamy-toned marble from the Jura. The *mensa* is made of blue Hainault limestone and the white columns of the arcades are richly veined red African marble from the quarries of Jugurtha in Numidia. The interior is lighted by eight stained glass windows, each featuring some saint connected with Saint Finbarr's life. Above the altar is the Blessed Mother after the style of Murillo and, to the side, is Finbarr vested in episcopal vestments.[23] This chapel had special meaning to Cardinal Manning and a white marble plaque on the south wall attests to his association with the artistic and devotional house-of-prayer. The Stations of the Cross were purchased by Manning in Mexico and erected in the 1970s.

For several generations Gougane Barra has been owned and cared for by the Cronin family, into which the cardinal's sister, Joan, was married. Following the death of his mother in 1964, Manning adopted the Cronin homestead, which is located about two miles from Ballingeary, as his own and it was there that he spent his vacations for the next two decades. Even as a youngster, Manning exhibited a love for Gougane Barra which was and is a shrine known and frequented by people from all over Ireland and the world. A priest from Cork customarily offers Holy Mass there on Sundays. The Cronin-Lucey family still

View of Shrine of Saint Finbarr.

Reportedly the cardinal's favorite swan at Gougane Barra died the same day he did.

James Manning (1911-1980) is shown here with his wife, Doreen (McCarthy) and their son, a pilot for Aer Lingus on November 20, 1970.

Prime Minister Lynch of Ireland at Gougane Barra.

operates the Gougane Barra Hotel and its adjoining sheep farm. Several hundred people flock to the shrine each week and no one leaves the area without a renewed implant of faith.

On the Sunday nearest to the feastday of Saint Finbarr in 1955, Manning told the people of Gougane Barra how it was the "destiny of our people particularly of mountain men, to migrate, to yearn for the far-off hills, to sail over the vast horizons. This wanderlust is part of the inheritance of the Gael, and not unintended in the Divine plan. When such a man goes out into an alien world, either he will submerge beneath its culture which is of the very fabric of his own existence or will dominate over the alien one." He went on to say that "in ancient Jewish dispensation, it was required each year that the people should gather by families to celebrate the great paschal meal. In the course of the ritual the father of the household was obliged, on the request of his son, to narrate the events of history which were commemorated at the annual feast. So it happened that in the great stream of the Jewish tradition, there was passed on from father to son, for unnumbered generations the great saga of the deliverance of God's chosen people from the bondage of Egypt and their stupendous crossing, dry-shod, through a corridor, miraculously created between the waters of the Red Sea."[24]

SAINT PATRICK'S PURGATORY

There are records of pilgrimages to Lough Derg in County Donegal from France, England, Hungary, Portugal and other places that date from the 12th century and the extent and severity of the penitential exercises were even more exacting in earlier times. That Saint Patrick was the founder of Lough Derg is one of the oldest and most tenacious of Irish traditions. Even when persecution destroyed all the buildings on the tiny island, the pilgrimages never ceased. Since 1613, nothing has changed.[25]

About the size of a city block, Lough Derg is an unattractive, craggy knoll less than an acre in extent. It is set in a grey, quiet lake, enfolded by a chain of low, rolling, barren, gray mountains. On the island is a giant basilica which accommodates 1,200 people. There is a hostel for men with facilities for bunk beds, and another larger one for women. A smaller church is used for confessions and nearby is a residence for the priests that staff the island.

Because of the severe weather limitations, pilgrimages to Saint Patrick's Purgatory are conducted only from May to mid-August. Numerous people journey to Lough Derg every year. The pilgrimages last for seventy-two hours and consist of prayer, penance and fasting. There is a light repast of dry bread and black tea or coffee each day. On arrival, pilgrims remove their shoes and stockings and go bare footed for the length of their stay. Sleep is replaced by prayer vigils on the first night. The prayers are simple, but long. The posture of kneeling and standing at prayer near the water's edge makes an indelible impression on a person's consciousness. Holy Mass is offered in the morning and evening, with Stations of the Cross recited in the afternoons.

Pilgrims leave the island hungry, tired and sore-footed. It is a unique experience in the Church and one that Cardinal Manning made no less than twenty-six times in his eighty years. He once observed that while he dreaded nothing more than going to Saint Patrick's Purgatory, it was a spiritual experience that he cherished above all others. It was his first priority upon arriving in Ireland.[26]

After his return to Los Angeles, in 1983, Cardinal Manning wrote the following memoir about his long association with Lough Derg:

> There is one witnessing to the practice of penance to which we would like to draw attention. It is unique in the experience of the Church. It is a place of pilgrimage located in the north of Ireland and an experience of penance as ancient as Christianity is in that island. We refer to Saint Patrick's Purgatory located on an island in a lake of Donegal called Lough Derg.
>
> The routine of the pilgrimage is not easy. It is not meant to be so. It is fulfilled within a space of seventy-two hours and consists of prayer, penance and fasting in a relentless sequence. The fasting begins on the midnight prior to the arrival on the island. It is broken once only in each of the twenty-four hours of three days.
>
> The solitary meal consists of dry bread or barley cake, and black tea or coffee – no more – and no more again until a corresponding time next day. One of the forms of penance is going barefooted. On arrival at the island shoes and socks are removed and the feet are left pitiless to the inhospitable surfaces and the uncaring chill of the water-cooled winds.
>
> There is a twenty-four hour vigil which extends from ten o'clock on the evening of the first day to the same hour of the next, so that sleep is also sacrificed to the demanding penance. The routine of prayers is mainly a vocal exercise. There is a body language of circling designated areas, kneel-

ing at specified spots that were once the entrance or center of a monk's cell; the renunciation, with outstretched arms, of the world, the flesh and the devil, and a posture of kneeling and standing in prayer at the water's edge. The prayers are the simple ones of God's little people, the Our Father, the Hail Mary and the Apostles Creed.

Because of the large number of pilgrims it is necessary to queue up in rows of five waiting one's turn to begin the ritual of exercises. When the queue is broken for a function, you are given a tag which entitles you to return to the same spot after the conclusion of the ceremony. Coupled with these penitential practices the community exercises in the church consist of a morning Mass at 6:30, a noon renewal of baptismal promises, the Stations of the Cross at 3:00 p.m., another Mass at 6:30 p.m. and evening prayers at 9:00.

As is evident from this summary, there is no surcease from the sharp edge of penance. You are either hungry, tired, sore-footed, or aching in body the whole time. When the vigil is completed on the second day you are allowed to drop into bed for that blessedness of sleep which Shakespeare called "Sore labor's bath, balm of hurt minds, chief nourisher in life's feast." How true![27]

Notes to the Text

1. *The Irish Standard*, June 27, 1952.
2. *Ibid.*
3. *The Furrow* III (December, 1952) 631-632.
4. The Tidings, March 13, 1953.
5. Timothy Manning, "Currents of Irish Influence on the Church in the United States," *Maynooth Union Record*, 1952, Pp. 13-14.
6. Francis J. Weber (comp.), *Times of Tension. Moments of Grace* (Los Angeles, 1990), Pp. 155-156.
7. *Ibid.*, Pp. 154-155.
8. "Irish Memories."
9. *Times of Tension. Moments of Grace*, Pp. 175-177.
10. *The Tidings*, March 11, 1977.
11. The custom of awarding this honor is one of Ireland's most distinguished activities. The tradition goes back to the 14th century. Others so honored are Woodrow Wilson, John F. Kennedy and Eamon de Valera.
12. *The Irish Independent*, December 3, 1973.
13. *The Irish Standard*, April 4, 1974.
14. *The Tidings*, October 10, 1975.
15. *Cork Examiner*, August 27, 1979.
16. This digest is taken from the *Waterford News & Star*, August 31, 1979.
17. *Evening Echo*, August 16, 1980.
18. *The Tidings*, May 1, 1981.
19. AALA, John Paul II to Timothy Cardinal Manning, Vatican City, June 20, 1981. Oliver Plunkett, former Archbishop of Armagh and Primate of all Ireland, was executed by the British in 1681 as a leader of "the horrid Popist Plot." Cardinal Manning was present in Rome for his canonization in 1975.

20. AALA, Timothy Cardinal Manning to Eduardo Martinez Somalo, Los Angeles, July 10, 1981.
21. *Cork Examiner*, June 2, 1986.
22. Charles Smith, *The Ancient and Present State of the County and City of Cork* (Cork City, 1815), Pp. 192-193.
23. See C.M. O'Brien, *Life of Saint Finn Barr* (Killarney, 1985), Pp. 5-11.
24. *Times of Tension. Moments of Grace*, Pp. 153-154
25. See Joseph Duffy, *Lough Derg Guide* (Donegal, 1978).
26. See Francis J. Weber, *Catholic California* (Mission Hills, 1992), Pp. 7-8.
27. *The Tidings*, September 2, 1983.

13. Ecumenism in Los Angeles

Manning could best be characterized as *Pontifex Maximus*, "a bridge builder," a link between the old and the new, between problems and solutions and between theory and practice. Nowhere is that role more evident than in his relationship with non-Catholics. And it is indeed ironical that a man who was nineteen years of age before he ever met a non-Catholic would preside over an archdiocese where ecumenical relations became a model for the American Church.

Though he was and remained a staunch believer and practitioner of everything Catholic, Manning was among the first American Bishops who seriously attempted to implement the directives of Vatican Council II on ecumenism. It was probably because he was so committed to his Catholic faith that Manning sought to share that gift with others, if only by a gesture, a kind word, a pleasant smile.

After conducting an exhausting search for an ecumenical officer for the archdiocese, Manning selected Father Royale Vadakin to chair the Ecumenical Commission which he reorganized and elevated in stature. From that moment onward, it is clear from copious evidence that Manning allowed himself to be guided almost entirely by Vadakin's recommendations. And, even when there were disagreements, as was the case with the initial draft of the "Guidelines for Marriages between Roman Catholics and Episcopalians," Manning told Vadakin: "Do not be discouraged about this. I think the ultimate document will be for the good of souls."[1]

That Manning envisioned ecumenism as an integral part of his archiepiscopate is evident from various sources. An example would be an interview he gave to a local newspaper during the first month of his incumbency. When asked about his relationship with other churches, Manning responded that "we will be as cooperative as possible." He said that the Church's voice "must be in tune with the times, trying to apply the eternal truths and those of the Gospel to changing situations." Manning "foresaw more unity in the Church of the future than in the past." He said that "the Church has a tremendous future in that regard.[2]

Even before he could visit all his own parishes in the archdiocese, Manning was busy calling on his non-Catholic neighbors. In March of 1970, he participated in a Lenten series on "Adventures in Theology" which was offered at Saint Paul's Episcopal Cathedral. His topic was "Vatican I: 1870-1970."[3] The following year, on Good Friday, he delivered a meditation on the Second Word: "Son; behold thy Mother, Mother, behold thy Son" at the Episcopal cathedral's parish house.[4]

On May 6, 1970, Manning delivered a major address in the Great Sanctuary of the Wilshire Boulevard Temple on "A Common Parentage." As he stepped to the podium, the archbishop explained that "this is one of a series of ecumenical appearances which I am making here in Los Angeles," noting with a smile that he was sure that his "ancestors were turning in their graves."

> In 1960, the great French Jew, Jules Isaac, went to Rome to see Pope John, and he gave him a brief containing three requests. These were, first, that there should be a correction of the false and unjust statements about Israel in the Christian teachings; secondly, the elimination of the myth that the scattering of the Jews was a punishment for the crucifixion of Jesus; and thirdly, renewed proclamation of an extract from the catechism of the Council of Trent, which taught very clearly that the Passion of Christ and the death of Christ was due to the sins of all men, that all were responsible, all guilty for that atoning death of Christ. He asked Pope John for hope that something could be done about it, and Pope John said, "You have reason for more than hope."
>
> Again in 1960 there was a famous meeting of about one hundred American Jews, who went to see the Holy Father. When he was Papal Nuncio in Bulgaria and Legate in Turkey, he had been known to be very effective and very friendly in preserving the Jews who were refugees. When this delegation of one hundred Jews came to see Pope John, he stretched out his hands. Using the expression of Joseph meeting his brothers, he said, "I am Joseph your brother." That became almost a slogan of all of Pope John's reign.
>
> We have the great journey of Pope Paul to the Holy Land and which again brought into focus the efforts, the anxieties and the urgencies of proclaiming once more the fellowship and the origin that was ours. So the Vatican Council wrote this very brief, very distinct document on the relation to the church, which calls for mutual respect and theological col-

> laboration. It cautioned against all faulty preaching, inaccurate catechism, and the elimination of all the offensive terms that had entered into our tradition.
>
> This presence of mine tonight here is in response, really, to that mandate of the Vatican Council for more than mutual respect. I think it's love. Certainly I have loved deeply through the years Rabbi Magnin whom I have known and cherished, who as the leader of this community, has been part and parcel of our mutual concern for God's people here in this city. We have gone beyond respect. I think we are in the area of love. Theological collaboration will come.[5]

In May of 1970, Manning joined with seven other prominent southland leaders of religious denominations[6] in an unprecedented plea to the community to halt trends they described as "destructive of what is human." These trends, they said, "repudiate values in which human dignity is rooted." The statement expressed a deep concern at deteriorating conditions in the community, particularly to the extent which citizens resort to violence, drugs and pornography." They called these "an unholy trinity" whose use is symptomatic of an irrationalism, an escape into unreality, as deceptive as it is dehumanizing. They appealed strongly for fidelity to Judaeo-Christian values on which human dignity is bedrocked and assert that "it is religion that activates our inalienable bonds with our fellow humans." The eight churchmen declared that neither God nor history would forgive their silence if in this hour of hope and travail they failed to enunciate "the indispensable spiritual principles for authentic humanism." They acknowledged the redeeming features of contemporary humanism: recognition by men of the cruelty and inhumanity of war, racism and poverty.

But the churchmen also took note of the counteraction of morally permissive homes, of justifying anti-human conduct on the grounds of "doing one's own thing."

> We are all aware of the dehumanizing features of the generation that seemed to make stainless steel and tinsel the measure of the good life. But we cannot accept the premise that the newer generation has a special edge on authenticity or a special immunity from self-deception.
>
> Now, as ever, the strong thrust to do one's own thing has merit only to the extent that one's own thing is the right thing. And the right thing, as ever, must stand the test of something that transcends the person doing it; it must stand the test of

> the community, of history, of experience, of the moral sense, of God's word.[7]

Manning kept travelling along the ecumenical trail. On April 18, 1971, he spoke at Temple Judea in Tarzana and, a few days later, he accepted an invitation to address a meeting of the Southern Baptist Association in Downey. In April of 1973, Manning spoke to 300 students at Fuller Theological Seminary in Pasadena about the "turmoil in the Church." He told his listeners that turmoil "is a healthy sign of life" and indicated fresh beginnings for the Christian message. Afterward, the cardinal fielded questions from the seminarians on a host of subjects, including the charismatic movement, the Roman Curia, rock Masses, the Reformation and Bible study among Catholics. A final question had to do with inter-communion and when it would take place in Los Angeles. Manning's answer cut to the central point of the query.

> As I understand it, a sharing of Communion is the final climax of oneness. We're a long, long way from that. This is not a matter peculiar to this diocese. We have many, many roads to go for that. We must pray together for that, but it is not in the visible future.[8]

In his Quinquennial Report to Rome for 1973, Manning outlined the work of ecumenism in the Archdiocese of Los Angeles as it then existed:

> The seven members of the Archdiocesan Commission for Ecumenical and Interreligious Affairs are involved in interfaith, action-oriented programs such as the Los Angeles/ARC Committee, which cooperates with the Episcopal Diocese of Los Angeles. A major portion of time and effort is given to the Interreligious Council of Southern California, whose members (Christian, Jewish, Moslems, Hindu, Buddhist and Sikh) represent those faith traditions in common dialogue.[9]

During October of 1974, Father Vadakin conducted an ecumenical leadership tour to Rome, Israel, Geneva and Taize composed of eighteen rabbis, ministers and priests. Cardinal Manning, who was in Rome making his *ad limina* visit to the Holy See, joined the group for a personally-guided tour of the Eternal City and an audience with the Holy Father, Pope Paul VI.[10] It was disclosed in a local newspaper that the cardinal also arranged interviews for the clergy group with Johannes

Cardinal Willebrands, president of the Secretariat for Promoting Christian Unity and with Archbishop William A. Carew, the Apostolic Delegate in Jerusalem. His Eminence remarked that "the pilgrimage speaks loudly for the interreligious concerns of the churches in greater Los Angeles."[11]

A meeting of the executive board of The National Council of Churches was held in Los Angeles on March of 1974. Manning was asked to speak on that occasion and as usual, he had something to say for everyone.

> When any city is chosen in the United States to host a National Council of Churches, it must surely have a religious heritage. It might even have been a haven of religious tolerance, where, in a fresh land, new expressions of faith were given freedom to live and grow. Just a very short distance from this hotel, in the center of Los Angeles, stands the Plaza Church, *Nuestra Señora de los Angeles*, founded here in 1784. Los Angeles began in a quiet, warm and hospitable land. *La Plazita* Church is not a museum and is not an historical hand-down. If you visit it today, you will find a faith community that is vibrant and strong, acknowledging in prayer and liturgy Christ our Lord.
>
> Yet to be authentic, warmth, hospitality, and peace are not the total lot of any church community. Tensions in areas of deep concern fill each of our faith commitments. However, as in the school aid issue, tensions are an able force. In the re-establishment of communications between the United States Catholic Conference and the Interreligious Committee of General Secretaries, we see the strength and depth of true ecumenical growth and understanding which has taken the place of tension and proved a creative force for further growth and understanding.
>
> In the abortion question, many find an issue deep in conscience. For many, the Catholic community is one for whom this issue is of great import. In the issue as you so well know it, there remains deep agony. However, we accept and acknowledge that Christians are all a part of the same family; and there are many positive agenda which present themselves to us in this year. One, very close to me, is the Holy Year.

> To Pope Paul VI, the Holy Year Theme of reconciliation strikes as a common effort and concern of all churches to witness by action this new testament theme to the reconciliatory thrust that Jesus was teaching. As the chairman of the National Conference of Catholic Bishops for the Holy Year in the United States, let me extend an invitation for the National Council of Churches throughout the United States to share in many areas this jubilee with the Roman Catholic community.[12]

The ecumenical momentum generated by Manning was felt at all levels of the archdiocese. For example, in 1975, new guidelines were handed down regarding burials:

> *Non-Catholic in Catholic Cemeteries:*
>
> The Catholic cemeteries in the Archdiocese of Los Angeles are available for burial to those not of the Roman Catholic religion, such as parties to a mixed marriage and close relatives. In such cases, clergymen of other religions may conduct graveside services.
>
> *Catholics in Other than Catholic Cemeteries:*
>
> The most recent synodal decrees for the Archdiocese of Los Angeles direct that "the bodies of the faithful must not be buried in secular cemeteries." Only for compelling circumstances, and with specific permission of the archbishop or his delegate, are priests allowed to perform graveside services in other than Catholic cemeteries. Exceptions are made for veterans wishing to be interred in a National Cemetery or converts utilizing property acquired before the profession of the Catholic Faith.
>
> *Burial Services in Other Christian Traditions:*
>
> When requested by the family, priests may officiate at the funeral services of other traditions in funeral homes and at the graveside. By the same token, they may, if invited, participate in the funeral services conducted by the decedent's minister. Whenever a priest officiates at or takes part in such

> a funeral, he should use prayers and Bible readings suitable for the occasion. Priests may not officiate at church funerals of other communions but, when asked by the family and the resident pastor, they may be present in the sanctuary or chancel to offer prayers and expressions of sympathy.[13]

After several years of intensive preparation and revision by Vadakin, his staff and commission members, a thirty-six page booklet containing the *Guidelines for Ecumenical and Interreligious Affairs* was promulgated by Cardinal Manning on September 1, 1976. Over 2,000 copies were mailed to priests and convents of the archdiocese, to education department personnel, to master catechists and interfaith leadership persons in the Los Angeles area representing Protestant and Jewish communities. Vadakin characterized the guidelines as "primarily pastoral, with the pages developed along a sacramental theme." He said that the guidelines reflected "the here and now in Los Angeles" and were intended "to be refined and added to as developments in the ecumenical life of the Church takes place." Containing directives on baptism, confirmation, reception into the Catholic Church, the Eucharist, marriage, burial and dialogues with various faiths, the book also included an ecumenical directory and the text of a service for Christian unity.[14]

In his preface to the booklet, the cardinal noted that the "implementation of the teachings of the Second Vatican Council in the church of Los Angeles remains an overriding pastoral concern."

> We are happy to promulgate officially these updated guidelines to the priests, religious and laity of the archdiocese. Developed by the commission, they express the authentic statements of the Universal Church and touch the unique pastoral needs of this archdiocese. May these guidelines assist the clergy and people of the archdiocese to strengthen the ministry of ecumenical and interfaith life which has been so rich and strong in the history of the Church in Los Angeles.[15]

This publication, more than all the other accomplishments of the Commission, served to enshrine the Los Angeles jurisdiction in prime place ecumenically throughout the United States and the world. Even Vatican officials were impressed and thereafter the focus was on Los Angeles in all matters ecumenical. Vadakin was acclaimed and Manning was pleased.

Not long after, as if to reassure those who felt compromised by all the ecumenical gestures, Manning wrote a Lenten meditation for *The Tidings* which received wide circulation.

> A friend of long-standing has a refrain in his conversation which asks for "the truth in small words." This is needed particularly today. There is a growing interest in the teachings of our holy faith. There is an avalanche of learned and supposedly learned books and articles in every aspect of our faith. Even the secular magazines dip into our deposits and give popularity to some deep or undigested theory or explanations in a matter of our beliefs. The common man is confused. He yearns for the security of the old, for the uncontested truths that he inherited at childhood, for the devotions that were his solace in the humdrum thoroughfare of his life.
>
> Are they all swept away? Has the field been ploughed over and converted to another crop? Is the familiar landscape of the truths we cherished bulldozed away? We hope not. It may be to our advantage, during this Lenten season especially, to restate our faith in familiar things and, by restating it, to vivify it and hopefully keep at a distance the doubt and confusion that menaces us all around. A good place to start is our faith in the Church. It was condensed in the formula. "I believe in one, holy, Catholic and apostolic Church." What has happened to that belief?
>
> A false ecumenism has tampered with that word "one." You get the impression that our Church is only one of many "rooms in our Father's house" where we find His truth and grace in adequate measure. The fall-off in conversions is probably due to this. The inter-religious concessions in the celebrations of marriage, the exchange of pulpits, inter-communion and such give the idea that it really does not make much difference what church you belong to. We have had even the spectacle of an Anglican woman, assertedly ordained in her own religion, concelebrating a Catholic Mass. No one seems to be greatly disturbed.
>
> Yet, I believe that the Church is one. We do recognize "that in many ways she is linked with those who, being baptized, are honored with the name of Christian, though they do not profess the faith in its entirety or do not preserve unity of communion with the successor of Peter." So says the teaching of Vatican II.

Ecumenical leaders of Los Angeles discussing integration challenges, March, 1977.

Fifteenth anniversary of Nostra Aetate.

Academic Convocation at Wilshire Boulevard Temple in 1979.

Manning releases book on The Religious Heritage of Southern California for the Interreligious Council.

> In another place it says, "our separated brethren, whether considered as individuals or as communities and churches, are not blessed with that unity which Jesus Christ wishes to bestow on all those whom He has regenerated and vivified into one body." Having said these things, and quoted from the documents of the Vatican Council, it is of course necessary for us to add certain corresponding and compensating truths. The Church rejects nothing which is true and holy in other religions. She has a sincere respect for their ways of life. She admires the honor that is paid to sacred Scripture; acknowledges the validity of some of their Sacraments, such as baptism; and particularly admires, wherever it is in use, the devotion to the Virgin Mother of God.
>
> Without question, there is evidence of a movement of the Holy Spirit within these bodies for the restoration of unity among all Christians. It is true that we need God's forgiveness for our part in the alienation of men from His Church. It is imperative that we be united in prayer for petitioning the grace of unity.
>
> It is in this spirit that I profess the Catholic Church to be the one true Church of Christ. Doing so, I incur a double obligation. First, I must grow in the knowledge of the truths of my faith, so that I will be not only enriched myself but I will also be able to give others a reason for the faith that is in me – that I will help to bring other minds into the captivity of the knowledge and love of Christ. Secondly, my whole life must be a witness to that truth. This will be done by a holy life, by sharing in the holiness of the Church.[16]

There was yet more to be accomplished. The cardinal continued to use every opportunity to impart an ecumenical overtone to major events. An example would be the Los Angeles Police Week Interfaith Service which he personally attended every year. The theme for that occasion was "Service to Others is Service to God." In his opening prayer, Manning emphasized the duty of leaders to cooperate in the exchange of ideas and works.

> The dearest thing I own is my life. Every instinct within me is alerted to preserve it. I will spend the last substance in my purse to prolong it. I will sacrifice every human ambition to defend it. My life is my blood, is me. There is only one altar at which I will sacrifice my life's blood. I will do so gladly and

> without reservation. It is the altar of love for my fellow man. I will give my life in defense of his and greater love than this no man has. I have a rendezvous with death and I will not fail that rendezvous. I speak from the grave - my name bears testimony on this monument. I ask our heavenly Father to regard with love this community we are dedicated to serve, to bless all those whose lives are pledged to its service and to hold in dear and grateful remembrance the names of those herein inscribed that a new Spring of peace may rise from our graves and bring benediction on us all.[17]

The relationship between Rabbi Edgar Magnin and Cardinal Manning stretched back many years to the Cantwell regime. They shared common objectives and each was willing to look beyond the needs of the moment. In April of 1976, Manning responded affirmatively to Magnin's offer to host a Seder celebration of the Passover at the Wilshire Temple for high school students. Representatives from thirty-five Catholic schools gathered at the Temple to hear Magnin explain the exodus of the Israelites from their captivity in Egypt. Cardinal Manning recalled a former parishioner who went back to her old home, to see once more the stairway she came down as a bride. "Something like this is happening to us," the cardinal said. "We speak of the Church as the bride of Christ. We are going back to our Father's house, our dowry, our inheritance. It is a joy for us and an education . . . Our religion will be more meaningful to us for visiting the place where we became a bride."[18]

Manning never hesitated to express the Catholic Church's view openly and forcefully, but always in a gracious and non-threatening manner. He felt obliged, for example, to register his disappointment when the Episcopal Church in the United States voted to permit the ordination of women. In response to a question at a press conference in Spokane, Washington, the cardinal said that Catholics are "officially and, I think, irrevocably, opposed to the ordination of women." He added that such an action would cause "considerable hazard" to dialogue between the churches.[19]

Another joint action by the "Big Eight" of Southern California's religious leaders occurred on March of 1977 when an "open letter" was issued to the community counseling prayer, patience, peace and understanding as the city attempted to comply with a court order integrating its public schools. The cardinal transmitted the letter to his own clergymen, noting that " when a plan is approved by the school board and accepted by the courts, then it becomes law. Our role as priests is to uphold the law and maintain peace in the community." He solicited "the prayers of our people that this issue, so charged with emotion, will be resolved in peace."

> As religious leaders of the community, we wish to speak to the people of Los Angeles. Our concern deals with a moral issue – the desegregation of our public schools.
>
> The facts are these:
>
> 1. Desegregation has been ordered by the California State Supreme Court decision of June 28, 1976.
>
> 2. To arrive at a process for integrating schools, a plan is necessary.
>
> 3. A citizens' committee has submitted a plan which is being studied and revised by the Board of Education and when approved by them it will be presented to the court for final approval.
>
> We believe that it is right that children be able to gain their education under peaceful and assuring circumstances.
>
> In order that there be no confusion or misunderstandings, we urge all citizens to be sure of the facts and avoid spreading rumors. We, on our part, will cooperate in those schools that are under our jurisdiction and will not allow them to become havens for those who wish to avoid the integrated public schools.
>
> We ask the children of Los Angeles to lead us, their elders, in showing love toward others and respect for the law. We call upon parents to encourage their children in those principles. We should insure equality as well as the highest standards of education for all children. We ask the people of our city to join us in our prayer for patience, peace and understanding. Let us fulfill this difficult task by proper planning, good communications, wholesome community involvement and genuine care for the welfare of our children.[20]

Later that year, Manning called upon southland Catholics to pray for the Jewish community during the period of Judaism's High Holy Days. He asked that a petitionary prayer be included at all Sunday Masses on September 18:

> We pray that our Jewish brothers and sisters be richly blessed by Almighty God as they celebrate in faith these holy days. May Rosh Hashana and Yom Kippur bring peace, love, joy and justice to their families and their communities. We pray to the Lord.[21]

The cardinal also cautioned against any attempt at proselytism among the Jewish community, saying that the "mission and witness for the Catholic includes neither proselytism nor crusade."[22]

Manning and Magnin pushed the horizons of ecumenism still further in December of 1977 when they welcomed Grand Imam of Islam, Shaykh Abdel-Halim Mahmoud of Cairo, Egypt to Los Angeles. The spiritual leader of the world's 800 million Muslims was hosted at a luncheon in Wilshire United Methodist Church sponsored by the Interreligious Council of Southern California.[23]

Nearly a thousand Lutherans and Catholics prayed together, renewed their baptismal promises and expressed sentiments of their hope for the future at Saint Vibiana's Cathedral on June 17, 1980. Participants represented twenty-three paired Lutheran and Catholic parishes that had conducted Lenten dialogues. The cathedral Vesper ceremony commemorated the 450th anniversary of the Augsburg Confession. In his homily, Cardinal Manning said, "let us put behind us the things of the past that alienated us and tonight gather together as one family to reflect upon the face of Christ." He spoke of the search for faith by Nicodemus who came to Christ seeking a teacher and of the discovery of God's love, "the compulsion of the infinite love of God that wishes to appear among us." There is no neutrality as far as Christ is concerned, "He who is not with me is against me. If our faith is strong we will radiate that love of God to our fellow man . . . Let us go to Him together in truth and love."[24]

Manning joined Episcopal Bishop Robert C. Rusack in issuing a series of *Guidelines on Marriage* which he described as sharing our "common pastoral concern for couples entering into marriage." He noted that it is "in the pastoral area of the Sacrament of Holy Matrimony and family life that both our churches most closely and intimately touch one another. The nurture of Christian families is critical to the continued vibrant life of both our churches as well as the people for whom we have responsibility."[25]

The cardinal authorized Monsignor Vadakin and his commission to engage in a collaborative dialogue with the local Jewish community on various topics. He wrote to his clergy saying that he was "pleased to bring to your attention the third joint statement of the Los Angeles

Catholic-Jewish Respect Life Committee." He sent along a copy of the booklet on *The Single Parent Family* with the observation that pastoral issues involved "challenges both parish and synagogue." The statement identified many critical areas and encouraged common directions which could be undertaken by congregations of both faiths.[26]

The cardinal visited Wat Thai Buddhist Temple in North Hollywood where he participated in a conference on "suffering" at which he presented the Catholic viewpoint.

> We, believing in the history of salvation, believe that in the primitive time God who made everything in the world and saw that it was good, made man. He gave man the option, the choice of saying yes or no in the testing that was necessary to see the kind of man he was. Man said no. Because of that "no," God then laid upon mankind a curse that he would live by the sweat of his brow, and that the woman would suffer through child bearing. In salvation history, the cardinal said, the puzzle begins, Why suffering? Why do good people suffer and the bad seem to prosper? Is all suffering the result of one's personal sin or personal evil or does it remain with that initial alienation from God?

The cardinal told the gathering of some 300 persons that the nobility of the Hebrew people is not often appreciated. "They had no revelation or awareness of an after-life. They had to live out this mystery of suffering without any concept of an after-life where things would be rectified." The nobility of their character lay in total trust in God in living that mystery and remaining faithful to the primitive commandments of God."[27]

In an article prepared for the local Catholic newspaper, Manning said that Vatican Council II's declaration on relations with non-Christian religions dramatically called the "Roman Catholic Church into dialogue with the non-Christian faiths of the world. Most significant of these dialogues are those with our brothers and sisters of Judaism and Islam."

In Los Angeles we have enjoyed a varied and sustained dialogue with both the Jewish and Islamic communities. These two encounters have brought growth and enrichment to our faith as Roman Catholics. Today the anguish of the Middle East creates tensions. The impact of war, suffering, anger, displacement and wanton death affect us all. Our human encounters rebel at the suffering they see and feel so intensely.

Cardinal Manning visited the Wat Thai Buddhist Temple in 1980.

Felicitations from Pope John Paul II are given to Rabbis Edgar Magnin and Alfred Wolf at the Wilshire Boulevard Temple by Msgr. Jorge Mejia from the Vatican.

Over the course of his archiepiscopal tenure, Cardinal Manning received numerous ecumenical plaudits.

> Anguish and shock must not paralyze the partners in dialogue. Thus we elect at this moment to state and restate our commitment to friendship on the local level with both the Jewish and Islamic communities. With the Islamic community we have locally enjoyed a strong and cordial bond which has included formal discussions and has placed great emphasis on secondary education. We have welcomed representatives of the Islamic community into our schools and educational programs.
>
> We of the Catholic community feel and understand the deep emotions caused by the events of the moment in the Jewish and Moslem communities, as well as our own Catholic community. It is our hope and ardent prayer that our continued friendships with both these faith groups may help our three faith communities in creating an atmosphere of heightened respect, confidence and trust.[28]

A revised copy of the booklet Guidelines for *Ecumenical and Interreligious Affairs* was released in 1982. Its purpose was to update and expand the earlier edition. In his preface, Manning observed that since 1976 there had been substantial exchanges, programs and agreed statements - internationally, nationally and locally:

> I am happy to promulgate officially these updated guidelines to the priests, religious and laity of the Archdiocese. As always guidelines are simply aids. The implementation of these must involve ourselves actively and creatively in responding to the promptings of the Holy Spirit. Pope John Paul II certainly offers us a vital witness to ecumenical and interreligious concerns, as he has tirelessly involved himself in the search for Christian unity and understanding among the great non-Christian religions of the world.[29]

In March of 1985, the Jewish and Catholic people of Southern California observed the twentieth anniversary of *Nostra Aetate*, the Vatican Council's document redefining the relationship of the Church with non-Christian religions. Cardinal Manning pointed out on that occasion that the conciliar fathers "burst through all of the confines of our traditional religious experience."

> Rethought were attitudes handed down framed in rigid formulas or traditional concepts, inherited prejudices or whatever they may be. The documents of Vatican II opened the Church up to the whole world. It was one of these experiences in history that transcends a human development . . . There was some presence that brought together from all the nations this immense group of people. *Nostra Aetate* put behind us so many things we were ashamed of, reparative for, opening up new relationships.
>
> The years since *Nostra Aetate* have been ones of linking its ideals with the lives of ordinary people. Here in Los Angeles is a perfect example of that process. We have a movement to open up the minds and hearts of people to mutuality, understanding, and the concept of one family. As a remnant of those who engaged in the discussion twenty years ago, I assure you of the pleasure and gratitude that I have lived to see this day of celebrating the anniversary of *Nostra Aetate*.[30]

Few if any areas of the world "could hold a candle" to the ecumenical progress made in Southern California during the fifteen year regime of Timothy Cardinal Manning. With his enthusiastic endorsement and unqualified encouragement, Msgr. Royale Vadakin and his commission moved onto center stage for a series of unprecedented theological discussions, joint statements, bilateral dialogues, structured interchanges and shared praying. As he neared the end of his archiepiscopate, Manning wrote an article for *Christian Jewish Relations* where he acknowledged that "surely we have come a long way in so short a time. Dialogue born of personal friendships, common concern for the well-being of our citizens, meeting our God in the pages of Holy Writ, sounding the depths and roots of our beliefs in the Hebrew inheritance, all of these have created a bridge of understanding over which we confidently cross and embrace one another in peace and love."[31]

Notes to the Text

1. AALA, Timothy Cardinal Manning to Royale Vadakin, Los Angeles, August 7, 1979.
2. Los Angeles *Times*, January 22, 1970.
3. *The Tidings*, February 13, 1970.
4. *Ibid.*, April 9, 1971.
5. Francis J. Weber (comp.), *Days of Change. Years of Challenge*, (Los Angeles, 1987), Pp. 144-147.
6. Including Rabbi Edgar F. Magnin, Methodist Bishop Gerald Kennedy, Episcopal Bishop Francis Eric Bloy and Lutheran President Carl Segerhammer.
7. Los Angeles *Times*, May 15, 1970.
8. *The Tidings*, April 6, 1973.
9. AALA, *Archdiocese of Los Angeles in California, U.S.A. Quinquennial Report*, January, 1969 - December, 1973, p. 40.
10. Los Angeles *Herald-Examiner*, October 17, 1974.
11. Los Angeles *Times*, October 20, 1974.
12. Francis J. Weber (comp.), *Times of Tension. Moments of Grace*, (Los Angeles, 1989), Pp. 282-283.
13. AALA, "Burial Guidelines" draft, Los Angeles, July 15, 1975.
14. *The Tidings*, September 3, 1976.
15. AALA, Timothy Cardinal Manning to Priests, Los Angeles, September 1, 1976.
16. Francis J. Weber, *Days of Change. Years of Challenge*, Pp. 192-194.
17. Francis J. Weber (comp.), *Hours of Consecration. Minutes of Prayer*, (Mission Hills, 1990), p. 64.
18. *The Tidings*, April 16, 1976.
19. *Ibid.*, September 24, 1976.
20. *Ibid.*, March 4, 1977.

21. AALA, Timothy Cardinal Manning to Priests, Los Angeles, September 1, 1977.
22. *The Tidings*, September 16, 1977.
23. *Ibid.*, December 2, 1977.
24. *Ibid.*, June 20, 1980.
25. AALA, Timothy Cardinal Manning to Friends, Los Angeles, September 10, 1980.
26. AALA, Timothy Cardinal Manning to Priests, Los Angeles, October, 1981.
27. *The Tidings*, March 4, 1983.
28. *Ibid.*, October 8, 1982.
29. AALA, Timothy Cardinal Manning to Priests, Los Angeles, January, 1982.
30. *The Tidings*, March 20, 1985.
31. XVIII (September, 1985), 31.

14. Immaculate Heart Institute

IMMACULATE HEART CONTROVERSIES

Among the most unpleasant chapters in the lives of both James Francis Cardinal McIntyre and Timothy Cardinal Manning were those dealing with the California Institue of the Sisters of the Most Holy and Immaculate Heart of the Blessed Virgin Mary and attempts made to "modernize and update" the religious practices of members in the aftermath of Vatican Council II.

IMMACULATE HEART INSTITUTE

From the onset of the difficulties between the Immaculate Heart Sisters and the Archdiocese of Los Angeles,[1] there was a small cadre within the community who remained loyal to their vows and strongly objected to the so-called modernization programs advocated by Sister Anita Caspary and her sympathizers. As the scenario unfolded yet further, the minority was drawn together in a desperate attempt to retain the essentials of religious life to which they were committed.

In a request by James Francis Cardinal McIntyre, on May 6, 1968, to the effect "that a decision be made promptly concerning the status of the Sisters of the Immaculate Heart community who desire to remain in the community and continue serving in our schools,"[2] the cardinal pointed out that there already was a "*de facto*" division in the group which needed to be looked after and provided for.[3] In response, the Bishop's Committee serving as a Pontifical Commission issued a preliminary ruling in June which said that "those sisters who intend to follow the constitutions in effect previous to the Ninth General Chapter of the community, are placed under temporary direction of Sister Eileen MacDonald . . . who is given faculties for their government and work and may proceed to agreements regarding the schools within archdiocesan authority."[4]

Each member of the overall community was given a form on which she was "to declare her intention regarding the group to which she wishes to belong."[5] There were also provisions made for members to change their affiliation before the choice became definitive. On June 24, the Apostolic Delegate thanked Sister Eileen MacDonald for reporting that fifty-four had reaffirmed their commitment to observing the traditional constitutions. He concluded by saying that "your community is the object of the personal interest of the Holy Father. Each day His Holiness prays for the welfare of the group and that all decisions for the future may be made out of love of Christ and the service of the Church."[6]

The next month, the local Catholic newspaper reported that the group of Immaculate Heart Sisters who had been authorized by the Holy See to contract to remain in the nine schools of the Archdiocese of Los Angeles "intend earnestly to uphold the values of Religious Life as defined by the Church and updated by Vatican Council II." Sister Eileen told the paper that "the group is relatively small but its quality is distinguished. Every Sister assigned to administration and teaching has at least her Bachelor's degree and appropriate California State credential for her field."[7] Another report indicated that eleven of the Sisters had Master's degrees and three held doctorates.[8]

In a story released by the NC News Service, Sister Eileen said that "we are grateful to be able to serve the children of the schools we are to staff. Love for them was an important factor in our decision to seek permission to continue as teachers in these schools." She expressed gratitude to the parents and pastors "who have so generously received us back into their schools." Sister Eileen was no dinosaur nor were her compatriots. Asked whether the group contemplated any changes in its educational and spiritual apostolate, she replied: "We firmly believe that life means change; therefore this group is marked by an enthusiastic desire to improve its Institute through a deeper spirituality. And this revitalization is not limited to a mere revision of the Constitutions under which we live, important though that effort may be, but also to promote a greater love for God and His Holy Church, which is basic to all progress and renewal."[9]

During that summer a delegation visited Rome where they were received by Pope Paul VI on July 24. They also met with Ildebrando Cardinal Antoniutti, Prefect of the Sacred Congregation for Religious. The cardinal told them that some sort of distinctive attire "must be a sign of consecration so that Sisters can always be recognized as persons of one community."[10]

In the fall of 1968, the Los Angeles *Examiner* proclaimed to readers that the "Nun Revolt Fails - L.A. Catholic Schools Open." According to that source, the "threatened crisis . . . has been resolved quietly - if not to everyone's satisfaction." The paper also described how "a few IHM nuns, who conformed with the cardinal's wishes, still are teaching in the schools of the archdiocese, which runs the second largest school system - public or private - in California."[11]

Sister Eileen MacDonald's group, known thereafter as the Immaculate Heart Institute, had its own special chapter in December of 1969 wherein they adopted "Interim Constitutions" which would govern their communal religious life. In the foreword to that twenty-two page document, the Sisters declared that in addition to updating their earlier rule, "we have adopted the articles of our Constitutions to reflect the norms of the conciliar decrees: *Lumen Gentium, Sacrosanctum Concilium, Christus Dominus, Perfectae Caritatis, Gravissimum Educationis,* the motu proprio *Ecclesiae Sanctae* and the instruction *Renovationis Causam*. They promised to revitalize their religious institute and personal lives "through a deepened pursuit of the imitation of Jesus Christ by the study and meditation of Holy Scripture, of ecclesial documents and of the writings of our Father Founder." Finally, they expressed "fidelity to Holy Mother Church" and ready obedience to the guidance of Our Holy Father."[12]

Early in 1970, members of the Institute elected Sister Eileen MacDonald superior general, a post she had held on an interim basis since June of 1968. Auxiliary Bishop John J. Ward presided at the elections and, in a brief but optimistic homily, he "pointed out the place and need for religious women in the Church and expressed the strong hope for a vital resurgence of religious vocations as a result of a correct call for renewal among religious communities."[13]

Since the members of the Institute had virtually no operational funds, a group of supporters organized the Auxiliary of the Sisters of the Immaculate Heart of Mary with the following objectives:

1. To unite all who sustain the Sisters in their decision to remain faithful to their vows as religious;
2. To offer daily prayers in their behalf;
3. To give moral support and to render practical assistance in their needs;
4. To work toward the establishment of a home for the old and infirm of their own Community;
5. To provide a novitiate for the preparation of young religious to carry on the work of the Church as mem-

> bers of the institute of the Sisters of the Immaculate Heart.[14]

Archbishop Manning was anxious to provide a motherhouse for the Institute which received no property in the final settlement. Accordingly, he approached Daniel Donohue about the possibility of obtaining Villa San Giuseppe, the old Earle C. Anthony estate in the Hollywood Hills for a pittance of its real worth. Manning wrote to the Apostolic Delegate that "the archdiocese is providing the necessary funds for the purchase of the residence, previously the home of Sir Daniel and Countess Bernardine Donohue, which will now be the official headquarters of the canonical community of the Sisters of the Immaculate Heart."[15] After some modifications to the eight acre estate, the Sisters took up residence there in the fall of 1971. At the same time, Sister Eileen MacDonald announced the opening of the estate for retreats and days of recollection. The area included a Gothic chapel, dining hall, lounge, library and extensive gardens.[16]

Writing in a Catholic newspaper, Edwina Bowe called Villa San Giuseppe "the perfect site for a fresh beginning." She said that "the fires of dissent that rent the community asunder are banked. Out of the crucible has risen a promising future for the sixty Sisters who remained faithful." There were many lean days for those who stayed. Divested of all property, including their motherhouse hospital and college by the departing dissidents, they were scattered throughout nine parochial schools in the archdiocese. But the long, dry months of exile were over thanks to the generosity of the I.H.M. Auxiliary, Daniel Donohue and Archbishop Timothy Manning who suggested Villa San Giuseppe as the novitiate site.[17]

IMMACULATE HEART COMMUNITY

By the time Manning became Archbishop of Los Angeles, those Sisters of the Immaculate Heart of Mary under the direction of Sister Anita Caspary were well into a meltdown mode, far beyond the arena of compromise at which Manning excelled. The jubilation heard within the walls of the motherhouse in Hollywood over the retirement of James Francis Cardinal McIntyre was short-lived. With McIntyre off the scene, the Sisters lost their "villain" and were reduced to arguing their case on its own merits and that proved a hard sell to rank and file Catholics of Southern California, to say nothing of the Sacred Congregation of Religious in Rome.

After January 21, 1970, Anita Caspary and Helen Kelley, who had shrewdly focused their attempts "to push back the boundaries of religious life"[18] on the intransigence of an aged cardinal already under siege by a hostile press, were confronted by a popular and patient new archbishop who was willing to accommodate their wishes, but only within the confines of Roman guidelines. Though Manning, ever the gentle and kind shepherd, had his own views on religious life which leaned towards the traditional interpretation of that calling, he never injected his own views into the conversations and deliberation in which he engaged during the ensuing months.

While those who had decided to remain with the Immaculate Heart Institute were already in total compliance with the directive issued by Archbishop James Casey of Denver and the other members of his episcopal committee on June 6, 1968, the future of the Immaculate Heart Community under Sister Anita's leadership was still very much unsettled. Archbishop Manning gingerly reminded Sister Anita several times that "the clock is ticking."

In January of 1970, the Sacred Congregation for Religious informed the Immaculate Heart Community that all the appeals had been exhausted and that the "reasonable time to reflect and come to a definitive decision" was over. They were told that the role of the Apostolic Visitator, Father Thomas R. Gallagher, and the work of the Bishop's Commission had been terminated. The Apostolic Delegate deputized Archbishop Manning "to assist the Sisters in their choice for the future," empowering him to grant dispensations from religious vows, to authorize transferral of any religious to another institute and to approve any agreements of an economical-financial nature that might arise.[19]

While Manning was not pleased with this distasteful task, he was optimistic that "this matter would soon be brought to a peaceful conclusion." He made arrangements to meet with Sister Anita Caspary and their subsequent relationship proved to be "very cordial and cooperative."[20] Sister Anita was receptive to suggestions of how best to facilitate the granting of the dispensations. It was decided that each one seeking a dispensation from vows would present a written application along the lines of a draft prepared by canon lawyers. Sister Anita also consented to meet with lawyers "to discuss the various problems in the financial and economic matters affecting the community." She also concurred that any publicity should be kept in "a low key." Manning told the Apostolic Delegate that "seemingly the membership of the community will retain some cohesion after the dispensations are granted. Each member who remains will sign a contract for services completely as a lay group with no implications of secular institute involved." Finally,

Manning said he would keep the bishops of the other eight areas serviced by the Sisters updated.[21]

Later that month, the cardinal sent Sister Anita the form that each Sister would fill out in petitioning for her dispensation:[22]

Most Reverend Timothy Manning
Archbishop of Los Angeles
1531 West Ninth Street
Los Angeles, California 90015

Your Excellency:

I, ______________________________, known in religion as
(family name)
Sister ________________________________, a Temporarily/Perpetually Professed member, with simple vows, in the California Institute of the Most Holy and Immaculate Heart of the Blessed Virgin Mary, humbly implore an Indult of Secularization, so that I may return to the lay state.

I made my first Profession of Vows on _________________. The reason for my request is the desire to terminate my commitment to religious life.

I have prayerfully considered this request, and I now freely seek a dispensation from the obligations incurred on the occasion of my Profession of Vows. This petition is presented with the approval of Sister Anita Caspary, the Provincial.

Sincerely,

____
Signed

____
Address

Approved:

____
Sister Anita Caspary

The verbal pledge that the negotiations would be "kept in a low key" was not honored by Sister Anita. Leaks to the press included all sorts of fanciful scenarios about the future of the Sisters. One report in a Catholic paper said that many members of the Immaculate Heart Community fully expected to "take some sort of private vows or promises" and continue in whatever ministry they wanted. Sources close to the Sisters said that "moving to a lay community" would be a "creative opportunity for desperately needed new forms of religious life."[23]

That there was some truth to the above story seems evident in several petitions sent to the cardinal in which Sisters were reluctant to change their "esteemed status as women religious." Manning pointed out that "it was for them that the Sacred Congregation granted him authorization" to give Sisters wishing to live their public vows permission to transfer to other religious communities approved by the Church. Manning carefully explained that "religious vows oblige in conformity with the Rules and Constitutions of the particular Institute." Since the decrees of the Extraordinary Chapter of 1967 were never approved by the Holy See, there were no Rules and Constitutions left to which "the members may conform their lives." Manning emphasized that a "Religious Community cannot be a free-floating body independent of the Church. It exists in the Church." As Manning understood it, the Immaculate Heart Community under Sister Anita's direction wanted to establish "a Community of hope, for which ecclesiastical approval will not be sought."[24]

On February 2, Manning released a letter to the public in which he thanked Sister Anita and those in her group who plan "to form a new community apart from and outside the jurisdiction of the Catholic Church." The lay community would be "open to both married and single persons, committed to the service of man in the spirit of the Gospels." Non-Catholics were also welcomed into the community.

> On behalf of the Archdiocese of Los Angeles, we wish to express to Sister Anita and her companions our gratitude for the many years of service rendered as members of the Sisters of the Immaculate Heart of Mary. A free decision has been reached by each member to solicit a dispensation from the canonical vows and to join together under another commitment to apostolic activity. It is the action of the Chapter and thereby becomes a non-canonical lay grouping. We are confident that the service to God and to people will be continued by them as they pursue this new form of life. Our prayers will follow them on the pathway they have chosen.[25]

On the same day, Anita Caspary distributed a statement from the motherhouse on Franklin Avenue in Hollywood.

> The Sisters of the Immaculate Heart of Mary today announced that they have begun procedures to form a lay community open to both married and single persons who are committed to the service of man in the spirit of the Gospels. Anita Caspary, president of the former order of sisters, will continue as the head of the new lay group, which will be based in Los Angeles.
>
> Nucleus of the new Immaculate Heart Community will be those Immaculate Heart Sisters who have asked to be dispensed from their canonical vows and from the prescriptions of the Sacred Congregation of Religious in Rome in order that they might fully develop the experiment in contemporary community life which they attempted to set in motion two years ago. Repeated efforts of the sisters to expand the structure of canonical religious life did not meet with the approval of the Sacred Congregation.
>
> The underlying philosophy of the experiment was promulgated in the Documents of Renewal issued by the Immaculate Heart Sisters in October of 1967. Community is approached primarily as a spiritual kinship rather than as a matter of surface uniformity or regimentation. Individuals are free to be and to develop as individuals, but form a body knit together by common goals and consensus on the most effective means of achieving them.
>
> The new group has not defined itself as a secular institute or sodality, forms already approved by the Church. However, the members of the non-canonical group intend to continue their life of dedication and service. The new community will encompass differing life styles and living arrangements, differing ways of seeing mankind and his needs, differing intensities in the individual member's need to belong with others and anxiety about loss of identity within the group.
>
> The community expects to continue its long-term commitments to education, health services, social concerns and the fine arts. Members of the community will continue to staff Immaculate Heart College, Immaculate Heart High School, Queen of the Valley Hospital and Montecito Conference Center. Individual talents, convictions, and interests of mem-

La Casa de Maria - Montecito.

Immaculate Heart College.

"We must point out the other side of the obligation of protecting (institutional) goals and of the chaos which follows from failing to do so. That is the equally destructive, equally tempting course of suppressing genius or the prophet by taking refuge in stated aims.

"I speak of the prophet here as the man singularly in touch with his times who senses the implications of certain trends and movements before they become obvious to others, the man with a vision not so much of the future as of the present.

"The best and most radical departures from accepted educational practice have been suggested by prophets whose skins were thick enough and personalities forceful enough that they were able to join the ranks of the administrative enemy to make it happen.

"The listing of such men would include many of the world's great teachers and their life stories would include some brutal accounts of the resistance they met from men of good will who didn't have the courage or insight to live in the present moment."

Sister Helen Kelley, I.H.M.
President

(taken from the Immaculate Heart College Catalog, 1970-1971.

> bers will be considered, however, in determining other community apostolates.
>
> The community will continue, as it has in the past, to support itself by its own labors. Individual members will be assessed to provide the financial base which will make possible the group projects which individuals would be powerless to set in motion on their own. Formal agreements between the individual members and the community will be the basis of community membership. Promises or testimonies of dedication to religious witness may also be made by the members.
>
> Those former sisters who will found the new Immaculate Heart Community are expected to have signed their agreements by the end of March. A day of prayer and celebration is scheduled for Holy Thursday, March 28, to mark the community's new beginning.[26]

News releases abounded from Hollywood. Sister Mary Mark Zeyen, Vice President of the Immaculate Heart Community stressed to a reporter from the Los Angeles *Times* that "we are not leaving the Church" but would look for "new forms, new styles" of service as "are called for in every age."[27] She explained that thirty-seven members had chosen to leave religious life altogether and 315 would form the new lay community. "Such a move by so many is unprecedented in Church history" according to Zeyen.[28]

For his part, the archbishop found his role in the whole process "distasteful." He told Father Edward L. Heston, the Holy Cross priest acting for the Sacred Congregation for Religious, that "the stark reality and finality of their decision is now striking home to a goodly number of the Sisters. Many of these fine women will not transfer to Sister Eileen's community and would be misfits in any other community if they were accepted. Suddenly they realize that, as of a certain date, they are no longer religious. One by one, and sometimes in groups, they are coming to me, tearfully." Manning went on to say that he had "a suspicion that many of them thought that they could retain their vows in a manner like exclaustrated religious, and yet serve with Sister Anita. They are finding out that this is not so. Two of them have begged me to inquire if they could not retain some form of public vow, even though they are working directly under the bishop in a religious program for adults in a given parish. Lurking in the back of the minds of many is the hope that even at some remote day some diocesan community might be formed into which many of these dedicated women could be regrouped."[29]

To each of the Sisters applying for dispensations, Manning made it clear that there was to be "a total separation from the religious and canonical community of the California Institute of the Sisters of the Most Holy and Immaculate Heart of the Blessed Virgin Mary." He went out of his way to emphasize that "whatever aggregate is formed by those who are dispensed does not constitute in any way a secular institute, a pious society, or sodality, or any organization in which public vows are recognized by the Church. Only by the public acceptance by the Church, in a manner determined by the Sacred Congregation of Religious, can a community have canonical status." Though that message had already been communicated to the Sisters, Manning repeated it so "that there will be no misunderstanding of the consequences of acceptance of the dispensation." There was to be "no middle ground in which the vows may be retained."[30]

In a communication written on the same day to Father Heston, the archbishop observed that many of the requests for dispensation added a qualifying statement which requested the dispensation "is the desire to terminate commitment to religious life as defined by the Sacred Congregation." He felt that such a reservation, "expressed bitterness . . . that they were forced out of religious life by the Sacred Congregation." That was why he had been so explicit in his letter to Sister Anita.[31] Heston replied from Rome that "we agree completely with your handling of the dispensations" as well as with "the necessary clarifications you made in the letter intended for each of the Sisters requesting the dispensations."[32]

TEMPORALITIES

The question of dividing the temporalities was still to be solved. Manning discovered that "the properties owned by the Community are held in five separate corporations and owned by the members of those corporations." At that time no real estate had "passed to the control of Sister Eileen and her religious residue." She had petitioned for the property at Montecito and the archbishop wanted her lawyers to meet with those of Sister Anita. He acknowledged that his "authority seems to be limited to approving whatever economic agreements are mutually arrived at."[33]

Father Heston and other members of the Congregation wanted Manning to assist "the two groups to come to just and equitable settlements." While realizing the difficulties involved, Heston felt that "someone with first-hand knowledge must intervene to protect the rights of Sister Eileen's group." He noted that the dispensations separated the petitioners not only from the religious and canonical community but also "from anything that belongs to that Community, no matter in what corporate name the property may be held." He emphasized that "the plain fact of the matter is that the dissident group has no right whatsoever to any of the goods of the California Institute." He thought it was "imperative that this group be brought to recognize as a strict minimum the right of Sister Eileen's Community to sufficient assets to satisfy their immediate needs, to assure the retirement of the elderly and aging Sisters and to allow for expansion." It was a matter, he said, "of not merely of equity but of fundamental justice."[34]

During the ensuing months, the lawyers labored assiduously to arrive at an acceptable settlement. Anticipating that an eventual financial settlement with the smaller group would eventually be necessary, Sister Anita and her advisers had sheltered the community's holdings in such a way that legally favored the Community over the Institute. She wanted to retain Immaculate Heart College, Queen of the Valley Hospital, Immaculate Heart High School and La Casa de Maria in exchange for a proportional cash payment representing a value of one-sixth of the overall holdings.

Manning, desperately wanting to avoid a protracted and nasty lawsuit, sought advice from several of the archdiocesan "elders" whose opinion he valued. Eventually, he sided with the one submitted by Msgr. Benjamin G. Hawkes, Vicar General for Finance:

> We have here a case not of what is right or wrong, but what is less wrong. Sister Anita holds all the cards because what is plainly erroneous canonically is less so legally. If we go to trial, there is little likelihood that we can win. By statutory law, she has cleverly stacked the deck. To pursue the matter would cause unnecessary scandal for everyone. It would be better for us to provide for Sister Eileen's group than to engage in a long and painful legal fight. Also, from a practical point of view, Sister Eileen's group doesn't have the personnel or resources to operate either the college or the hospital. My advice would be to take what has been offered.[35]

Manning finally agreed to an arrangement whereby the Community would pay the Institute $150,000 on December 22, 1970 and another

$125,000 at the end of six months. These payments were "paid to the Institute not only in satisfaction of any claims now known but also in full and complete satisfaction of every claim and demand."[36] The heart of the statement was reproduced in *The Tidings*:

> By this letter, notice is given that the affairs of the Sisters of the Immaculate Heart of Mary have been brought to a conclusion insofar as Church and civil law are concerned. The canonical community still resides in the California Institute of the Most Holy and Immaculate Heart of the Blessed Virgin Mary, of which Sister Eileen MacDonald is Mother General and with headquarters at 6636 Selma Avenue, Los Angeles 90028.
>
> A number of Sisters, previously members of this community, have received dispensations from their canonical vows of poverty, chastity and obedience. This aggregate has grouped together to conduct certain educational and welfare enterprises. It does not constitute a religious community in the Church but nevertheless elects to use the name "Immaculate Heart Community." Its President is Anita Caspary and the headquarters are located at 5515 Franklin Avenue, Los Angeles 90028.
>
> The assets of the non-profit corporations existing under California law, including Immaculate Heart College, Immaculate Heart High School, Queen of the Valley Hospital and La Casa de Maria, continue to be administered by members who have received dispensations. An equitable transfer of funds from the "Immaculate Heart Community" to the residual Sisterhood has been approved in the name of the Church. Other contingent provisions are likewise approved. In view of these negotiations, we are happy to write a terminus to these anxious events and to pray God's benediction on all those who so charitably sustained the members of both groups unto this end.[37]

The local newspapers had a field day with the announcement. One said that "the amount of the cash settlement was not divulged, although Sister Anita conceded it had been necessary to convert to cash most of the liquid assets of the Immaculate Heart Community in order to meet the amount agreed upon."[38]

From Rome, Father Heston hastily wrote to say "we feel with you that the best arrangement possible under existing circumstances has been made." He did feel that it was regrettable that "the small group . . . is not able to get even one piece of property which in all justice belongs to it and for which many of the faithful undoubtedly made contributions over the years with the intention of benefiting the Institute and its works." But he thought "it was evident that the Immaculate Heart Community profited by the formation of civil corporations to assure ownership of the property for themselves, not as members of the Institute, but as members of the corporations." He concluded by saying that "it is most generous of the archdiocese to undertake to help the small group financially and we are grateful to you for this."[39]

For some unexplainable reason, E. B. Durate, news editor for the NC News Service, after interviewing Sister Anita by telephone, released a story on January 6, 1971[40] indicating that "an invitation" had been extended by Archbishop Manning to the Immaculate Heart Community suggesting that they "resume teaching in archdiocesan schools." The release also referred to Anita Caspary as "Sister," a title she and the others had forfeited by asking for their dispensations. Manning was extremely irritated and complained to Bishop Joseph Bernardin, Secretary of the NCCB, that no part of the settlement "constituted an invitation by me to resume teaching in the parish schools." The archbishop reiterated that his "release was very careful to avoid any semblance of any endorsement of a 'community' and any reference to Anita Caspary as 'Sister.' She was aware of this in the drafting of our statement."[41] After looking into the matter, Bernardin indicated that the News Service "was fully responsible for the error" and that the director would thereafter exercise "more vigilance."[42] The director also wrote to Manning, apologizing for "the sloppy and unprofessional reporting of this story."[43]

Some days later, Manning sent Caspary, whom he thereafter referred to as "President," a draft of a document on the status of chapels in institutions operated by the Immaculate Heart Community.

DECREE

WHEREAS, Anita Caspary and her associates have freely sought and received dispensations from their Canonical Vows of Poverty, Chastity and Obedience in the California Institute of the Sisters of the Most Pure and Immaculate Heart of the Blessed Virgin Mary, a Pontifical Institute, and have returned to the status of laywomen in the Church, and,

WHEREAS, in the acceptance of the aforementioned dispensations, Anita Caspary and her associates voluntarily relinquished all rights and privileges awarded in the Code of Canon Law to women religious, and,

WHEREAS, among the rights and privileges of women religious is the right to have a Chapel and the reservation of the Most Blessed Sacrament in their Institutions

WE

Archbishop Timothy Manning, Archbishop of Los Angeles in California and in virtue of the Apostolic Mandate from the Sacred Congregation for Religious and Secular Institutes, Prot. 493/65 do, with these presents, decree and declare that the Chapel at La Casa de Maria in Montecito, California, the chapel at Immaculate Heart Convent at 5515 Franklin Avenue, Los Angeles, California and the chapel at Queen of the Valley Hospital in Covina, California, are in accordance with Canon 1170 no longer to be regarded as sacred edifices for the offering of the Holy Sacrifice of the Mass and the reservation of the Most Blessed Sacrament. The aforementioned chapels, heretofore sacred by reason of blessings, are now reduced to secular status.[44]

REACTION TO SETTLEMENT

In most areas, the decision was accepted if not joyously, at least as inevitable. Msgr. Francis Maurovich wrote that all sides were "to be commended for the way in which the case was resolved." He considered it "a tribute both to the Los Angeles Chancery and to the Sisters that the decree was received in a spirit of mutual cooperation."[45] Father Heston was quoted in *Time* Magazine as saying that "one good thing in the rebel's departure is that the Church has demonstrated the limits of innovation." Heston explained the Vatican's refusal to back down in these words. "When it became obvious that these ladies no longer wanted to operate within the framework of the religious community, there was nothing else to do put permit them to get out."[46]

There was some displeasure. The editor of the Louisville *Record*, for one, said that the decision was "a way out and not a solution" and hoped that it would not become a pattern for other religious communities, because, as he said, "splitting up seems to be a very uncatholic solution for a Church that is committed to finding within itself room for all kinds of views."[47] Others criticized the whole settlement. Sister Margaret Ellen Thaxler, chair of the National Coalition of American Nuns, charged that in allowing this hour to come, the Conference of Major Superiors of Women and the American Bishops had exposed "a renunciation of leadership."[48] Father Andrew Greeley had much the same view. He blamed the "leadership of the American Church" who had permitted the sisters to be "driven to the fringes." While acknowledging that the Immaculate Heart Community did make some tactical errors, Church officials "made more serious mistakes rooted in astonishing incomprehension of what was going on."[49]

In its reference to "the grief-laden passage of a great majority of the California Immaculate Heart Sisters," the editor of *America* said that "their fragmentation and dissolution as a canonical group cannot, of course, be traced to any one person or any single cause. Gradually but inexorably a mentality gap about the nature of religious life appeared. It grew so wide and deep that seemingly nothing could heal the breach." The editor "admired the Sisters' efforts in the past and wished them well in their venture into an unknown future. Whether they are long-term losers will depend on their ability to impregnate their new community life with something of the same religious spirit they have so often manifested."[50] Frank Morris, writing in the Saint Louis *Review*, noted that "one thing seems inescapable." The Immaculate Heart Community were "victims of the cult of change, which has as its principal doctrine that all values are temporary and fleeting." He offered "the Los Angeles incident as proof positive of the mischief the cult of change can work. Religious life has succeeded so remarkably well because it has always put its trust in the unchanging and unchangeable nature of true piety."[51]

As for Archbishop Manning, he felt, as did many of his contemporaries, that much of the blame rested with Roman Officials who allowed open-ended experimentation but made little if any attempt to monitor or limit it. Always guarded in what he said, especially publicly, Manning's chief goal was to bring closure to this most distressing controversy. But his letters are more revealing. On one occasion he told Father Heston that "it is becoming evident, I think, that the intellectuals in the community masterminded this dissolution of the sisterhood."[52] He said that every night he went to bed, he prayed that the perfect solution would come the next morning. It never did and he agonized over this issue more than any other he confronted in his archiepiscopate.

DEMISE OF A COLLEGE

Among the more tragic casualties of the Immaculate Heart conflict with ecclesial officials in Southern California was the eventual closure of the liberal arts college which the Sisters had established in the strikingly beautiful Hollywood foothills in 1916. By the 1960s, Immaculate Heart College was described by Father Andrew Greeley as "the happiest and, I think, the most Christian."[53]

That the highly publicized campaign launched by the Sisters for total autonomy within the Church was not well received by the general Catholic public is clear from several sources, the most obvious of which was a discernible diminishing of confidence in Immaculate Heart College. As the enrollment began dropping, officials lowered entrance requirements. At the same time, fund raising, essential to the well-being of any educational institution, public or private, became an increasing difficult and frustrating challenge.

Initially, college administrators attributed the downsurge to the smallness of their institution on North Western Avenue. In 1965, Helen Kelley told a reporter that facilities "were inadequate, the campus too small and, in addition isolated from other colleges."[54] As a result, plans were formulated to relocate on a twenty acre plot near the affiliated Claremont colleges. The proposal to join the Oxford-like cluster was hailed as "a kind of academic ecumenical movement. It was believed to be the first time in the history of higher American education that a Catholic college had allied itself with non-Catholic institutions."[55]

From the outset, doubts arose over financing the move of the college to Claremont. But, in mid July, 1968, Anita Caspary told 700 persons at Beverly Hills High School auditorium that "we should be there by 1971."[56] In April of the next year, Mr. & Mrs. Bing Crosby pledged a million dollars towards construction of a science building and, several months later, another promise of the same amount was received for a learning resource center on the new campus. Under terms of that grant from the Department of Health, Education and Welfare, the college would provide an additional $3,285,000 within a calendar year.[57] Delay after delay plagued the project and, in January of 1970, an article in the Los Angeles *Times* admitted that "the controversial renewal programs within the order of nuns" had taken "its toll."[58]

At the same time, it was disclosed that "conversations" were underway between Caltech and Immaculate Heart College that "could lead to a future alliance" between those two institutions. Courses had already been offered at the two schools for students of both. The report noted that "the possible linking between the celebrated science and

Chapel at Villa San Giuseppe in Hollywood.

Auxiliary Bishop Timothy Manning blesses the coffin in which are the restos of the Right Reverend Francis Mora who brought the Immaculate Heart Sisters to California in 1870s.

engineering school and the Catholic liberal arts college for women has set off a major stir on both campuses." Student publications showed enthusiasm for the alliance, but administrators remained cautious about discussing the matter. The newspaper account also disclosed that Immaculate Heart College and the Claremont colleges are "no longer joint ventures" in construction of a science complex going up on the campus of Harvey Mudd College, directly across the street from the Immaculate Heart property." All the while, much of the objection from officials at Caltech may have been "fear at Caltech, perhaps unjustified, that Immaculate Heart College academic standards are not on a par with those at the prestigious Pasadena campus." In an effort to inject a little humor into the deliberations, Helen Kelley doubted that many Immaculate Heart girls were interested in nuclear engineering, though "they might well be interested in nuclear engineers."[59]

A few months later, Caltech and Immaculate Heart College ended speculation that the Catholic women's liberal art college might move to Pasadena. Throughout the deliberations, "students and numerous faculty members at both institutions exhibited more enthusiasm for alliance than did their administrators." It was also admitted that "the romance may have cooled partly because of the feeling of some at Caltech that the womens' college was not on an academic level with the science institution."[60]

Plans inched ahead for relocating at Claremont. Ground was to be broken in August of 1971 for two buildings; a basic academic building and a dormitory. Then, abruptly, the whole transferral proposal was called off. Immaculate Heart officials announced that they would not move, but would concentrate their efforts on updating facilities in Hollywood. The funds already collected would be used for "all the urgent basic needs" of existing structures. A letter was sent to donors saying that "the current state of the nation's economy and its implications" had affected the ability of donors to remain on schedule with their pledges." Actually the biggest donor had defaulted completely. Interestingly the word came "just ten days after the Claremont baccalaureate ceremony in which the IHC banners flew with those of the other six colleges." Alumni were told that "expansion by high-rise" was among the possibilities that will be explored by trustees."[61] Helen Kelley admitted to one reporter that "the fund drive wasn't very successful."[62]

In a letter to college graduates, Kelley explained that IHC trustees, faculty and students had met and discussed "how and where the college could best fulfill its obligation to educational and spiritual values while remaining simultaneously faithful to its traditions and fully in the world." Accompanying the letter was a copy of the statement issued by the Board of Trustees which said that "prudence forces us for a few weeks to call a moratorium on construction plans - literally on the eve of ground-breaking."

The lengthy statement also revealed, for the first time, that Helen Kelley and others had "concluded with Dr. Carl Rogers and his staff a two year study of the impact the ideas and techniques of sensitivity training might have on the creation of a climate for self-directed change within a college." The statement concluded with the "decision to keep IHC within the limits of the City of Los Angeles," something which the trustees felt was "mostly compatible with the college's own nature and society's need."[63] In retrospect, the long, six page document was clearly the initial draft of the eventual obituary for the college. Clearly neither Helen Kelley nor the trustees knew where they were going or how they would get there. Several of the trustees had, in fact, resigned in recent months.

Helen Kelley sent a copy of the statement to Archbishop Manning, along with an offer "to discuss with you the implications"[64] for the future of the college. Privately, the archbishop expressed his view that "there was no future for the beleaguered institution." He and others felt there had been a terrible betrayal of the initial purposes of the institution's founders. Though he disagreed with Kelley in many areas, Manning was always friendly and willing to listen. For example, he asked Auxiliary Bishop Joseph Dougherty to attend the commencement in 1970, even though the college was no longer considered "Catholic."

The financial status at IHC continued deteriorating. A large bank loan was acquired, but the college officials were unable to service the debt which grew annually. The loan was renegotiated in 1975 through "the efforts of Governor (Edmund G.) Brown, who put together a fund raising effort for the school at the Hollywood Palladium."[65] A few months earlier, Cardinal Manning had been approached by Martin Gang on behalf of the Board of Trustees for the college.[66] The board admitted that "we have reached the end of the road and feel it would be tragic for such an outstanding institution to disappear." Gang had been asked to find out if the cardinal could "aid us in securing help from the Catholic community to enable us to weather the present storm and to put the school on a viable basis." Manning wrote his reply on the bottom of Gang's letter: The Archdiocese of Los Angeles "would do nothing to bail-out the college. It was a branch cut from a tree and inevitably would die. It did not qualify, as a 'Catholic' college."[67] The cardinal had no objections about the board approaching "individual Catholic laymen" but he would not be part of any such actions.

In November of 1979, "faced with insurmountable indebtedness and rising operational costs, officials of Immaculate Heart College announced that the landmark sixty-four year old, independent liberal arts college will close next August." The board of Trustees had voted, on November 20, to terminate the college which then had 700 undergraduates and graduate students and ninety-five full-time and part-time faculty members. To the very end, Mary Jean Pew, the acting president and others "discounted the belief, held by some, that a 1967 rift between the Immaculate Heart community and the late James Francis Cardinal McIntyre over the school's increasing liberalization caused a major cut-off of funds."[68] That contention was correct insofar as the Archdiocese of Los Angeles had never provided any funds for the operation of the institution.

The last commencement took place on June 7, 1980. An article in the local newspaper said that "the college property is for sale" and that "the college will continue to offer a limited program of summer classes for students who need only a few units for their diplomas."[69] Eventually, after some complicated litigation, the property was purchased by the American Film Institute as a research center.[70] The college library was sold to a young businessman who later became Mayor of Los Angeles.[71]

In an article for *America*, Mary Pjerrou Huckaby, a former professor at Immaculate Heart College, said that "the death of a college is the death of an idea, the death of a social milieu and the end of a substantial effort to educate people in a particular way." She admitted that something went wrong for the "independent, energetic and smart" Sisters. Perhaps they "were too well educated, perhaps too creative and too independent." She acknowledged that there were "head-on confrontations in which no one could save face, and everybody lost." Whatever one thinks of Huckaby's interpretation, she certainly spoke for many with her observation that Immaculate Heart College was "a unique, valuable and irreplaceable educational institution."[72]

Notes to the Text

1. For the earlier phase of this controversy, see Francis J. Weber, *His Eminence of Los Angeles. James Francis Cardinal McIntyre* (Mission Hills, 1997). Pp. 416-442. Ann Carey, author of *Sisters in Crisis* (Huntington, 1997), said that she had "found nothing that would contradict the material in your chapter on the Immaculate Heart Sisters." She also noted, for future researchers, that "there is even more material about the IHM and Cardinal McIntyre conflict in the archives of the University of Notre Dame." See AALA, Ann Carey to Francis J. Weber, South Bend, September 4, 1997.
2. AALA, Memorandum, James Francis Cardinal McIntyre, Los Angeles, May 6, 1968.
3. AALA, Memorandum, James Francis Cardinal McIntyre, Los Angeles, May 7, 1968.
4. AALA, Decree of Bishops' Committee, Los Angeles, June 6, 1968.
5. AALA, Ballot, Los Angeles, June 6, 1968.
6. AALA, Luigi Raimondi to Sister Eileen MacDonald, I.H.M., Washington, D.C., June 24, 1968.
7. *The Tidings*, July 19, 1968.
8. Los Angeles *Times*, July 20, 1968.
9. *Southern Cross*, July 25, 1968.
10. *The Tidings*, August 16, 1968.
11. October 6, 1968.
12. AALA, The California Institute of the Sisters of the Most Holy and Immaculate Heart of the Blessed Virgin Mary, Special Chapter, December, 1969.
13. *The Tidings*, January 16, 1970.
14. *Ibid.*
15. AALA, Timothy Manning to Luigi Raimondi, Los Angeles, July 19, 1971.
16. *The Tidings*, September, 17, 1971.
17. *Twin Circle*, October 17, 1971.

18. *Newsweek* LXXV (February 16, 1970), 84.
19. AALA, Luigi Raimondi to Timothy Manning, Washington, D.C., January 12, 1970.
20. AALA, Timothy Manning to Ildebrando Cardinal Antoniutti, Los Angeles, January 19, 1970.
21. AALA, Timothy Manning to Luigi Raimondi, Los Angeles, January 18, 1970.
22. AALA, Timothy Manning to Anita Caspary, I.H.M., Los Angeles, June 23, 1970.
23. *Catholic Voice*, January 28, 1970.
24. AALA, Timothy Manning to Anita Caspary, I.H.M., Los Angeles, January 30, 1970.
25. *The Tidings*, February 6, 1970.
26. This statement also appeared in *The National Catholic Reporter*, February 11, 1970.
27. February 2, 1970.
28. *Catholic Voice*, January 28, 1970.
29. AALA, Timothy Manning to Edward L. Heston, C.S.C., Los Angeles, March 2, 1970.
30. AALA, Timothy Manning to Anita Caspary, I.H.M., Los Angeles, July 6, 1970.
31. AALA, Timothy Manning to Edward L. Heston, C.S.C., Los Angeles, July 6, 1970.
32. AALA, Edward L. Heston, C.S.C. to Timothy Manning, Rome, July 22, 1970.
33. *Ibid.*
34. *Ibid.*
35. AALA, Statement, Benjamin G. Hawkes to Timothy Manning, Los Angeles, November 2, 1970.
36. AALA, Settlement Agreement and Mutual Release, December 11, 1970.
37. *The Tidings*, December 25, 1970.
38. Los Angeles *Times*, December 26, 1970.
39. AALA, Edward L. Heston, C.S.C. to Timothy Manning, Rome, January 18, 1971.

40. AALA, NCNews Release (Domestic), "IHM Settlement Apparently Ends Dispute," January 6, 1971.
41. AALA, Timothy Manning to Joseph Bernardin, Los Angeles, January 11, 1971.
42. AALA, Joseph Bernardin to Timothy Manning, Washington, D.C., January 15, 1971.
43. AALA, Richard Guilderson to Timothy Manning, Washington, D.C., January 13, 1971.
44. AALA, Decree, Timothy Manning, Los Angeles, January 15, 1971.
45. *Catholic Voice*, June 19, 1968.
46. XCV (February 16, 1970), 50.
47. June 20, 1968.
48. *National Catholic Reporter,* February 11, 1970.
49. *The Monitor*, February 19, 1970.
50. CXXII (February 14, 1970), 146.
51. February 13, 1970.
52. AALA, Timothy Manning to Edward L. Heston, C.S.C., Los Angeles, March 2, 1970.
53. *Catholic Voice*, November 29, 1967.
54. Hollywood *Citizen News*, June 20, 1970.
55. Los Angeles *Times*, January 11, 1970.
56. *Ibid.*, July 15, 1968.
57. *Ibid.*, July 24, 1969.
58. *Ibid.*, January 11, 1970.
59. *Ibid.*
60. *Ibid.*, January 28, 1970.
61. *Ibid.*, June 19, 1970.
62. Hollywood *Citizen News*, June 20, 1970.
63. AALA, Helen Kelley to Graduates, Los Angeles, June 19, 1970, Statement attached.
64. AALA, Helen Kelley to Timothy Manning, Los Angeles, June 15, 1970.
65. Los Angeles *Times*, November 22, 1979.

66. AALA, Martin Gang to Timothy Cardinal Manning, Los Angeles, July 2, 1979.
67. AALA, Chet Lappen to Martin Gang, Los Angeles, June 22, 1979.
68. Los Angeles *Times*, November 22, 1979.
69. *Ibid.*, June 8, 1980.
70. *National Catholic Reporter,* August 29, 1981.
71. *V.g.*, Richard Riordan.
72. September 20, 1960, p. 134.

15. Controversies [1]

Though he avoided confrontations wherever possible, Timothy Manning refused to compromise his principles. He was gracious, kind and gentle by nature, but those few who pushed him into a corner generally regretted their presumptuous behavior. Nolan Davis, a free-lance writer, was the first to test the waters after Manning had become Archbishop of Los Angeles.

Early in 1972, Manning had agreed to be interviewed for an issue of *West* magazine, issued as a supplement to the Sunday edition of the Los Angeles *Times*. In his essay, entitled "The Archbishop in Motion," Nolan described Manning as "thin and self-effacing," his "well-groomed salt and paper hair a pleasing counterpart to his black and white attire."

The upbeat report about Manning began by proclaiming the new Archbishop of Los Angeles as "something of an ecclesiastical superstar" who had "revitalized the Church in Southern California, becoming renowned as one of the most socially progressive Catholic officials in America." Throughout the long article, Manning was portrayed as "a gifted orator and preacher" who was "retiring and soft-spoken in private." Seen by "many as a virtual saint," he knew "most of the priests in his vast province by their first names and has followed an aggressive policy of visiting a new church each Sunday."

Then, ever-so-cleverly, the direction of Nolan's essay shifted to Manning's predecessor, James Francis Cardinal McIntyre who, the author claimed, had administered the archdiocese amidst an "atmosphere of sheer terror." On and on the journalist went, repeating the usual laundry list of complaints contrasting McIntyre to the "quiet-spoken, youthful-looking Manning" who had "made it clear from the start that there would be some changes made."[2]

When the article appeared, the archbishop was livid. He fired off a letter to Otis Chandler, publisher of the Los Angeles *Times*, explaining that "when consenting to an interview by the writer, the article was to deal with a description of my own experiences since taking office as Archbishop of Los Angeles in January of 1970." Insofar as the article touched on that theme, he was deeply appreciative of the sympathetic treatment accorded him, "but not at the expense of Cardinal McIntyre." He said it was "reprehensible that this theme was employed to launch a totally unsympathetic and distorted attack on the stewardship of James Francis Cardinal McIntyre, my predecessor in this office and now retired. I protest to being used in that way."

Then, to set the record straight, Manning said:

> I have been closely associated with Cardinal McIntyre since his arrival in this archdiocese in 1948, and have esteemed him in all these years as a model churchman, a priestly priest, and a warm and personal friend. That esteem is shared, as I know from personal experience, by the vast body of priests, religious and laity whom he has served.
>
> Few better than I know the burdens he has carried, the accomplishments he has undertaken, and the injustice of the caricature which a few malcontents, both clerical and lay, as well as shallow and sensation-seeking journalists, have tried to fasten upon him. That character, developed upon innuendoes rather than truth, gossip rather than facts, rumor rather than reality, is substantially reflected in the treatment of the cardinal in the article in last Sunday's West Magazine. To rely upon such material rather than upon objective research in composing this section of the article questions a responsible journalism.

Manning concluded by noting that his "personal protest echoes the scores of protests which have poured into my office since last Sunday." He charged that "in publishing such materials," the *Times* had "done an injustice to a great citizen of this community, and to the loyal people whom he faithfully shepherded for over twenty years, and has offended the citizens of Los Angeles who have held him in high esteem."[3]

In his editorial for *The Tidings*, Msgr. Patrick Roche chastised Nolan Davis who, for "some strange reasons of his own, felt it appropriate to embellish his story with a tapestry of inaccuracies, slanders and misconceptions relating to the archbishop's predecessor."

> In so doing, he dragged out every tired and sick tale which has wagged the tongues and titillated the fancies of the idle rumor-mongers of our day. Some of them are so laughable that they border on the hysterical; some of them are so vicious that they defy definition. When a reporter adopts as

> his sources the casual observations of a handful of wandering minstrels, and discontented ones at that, he sacrifices credibility and reduces journalism to an exchange of backstairs gossip.[4]

Unpleasant though it was, the incident had the positive effect of putting the local journalists on guard that Manning would not tolerate any continuance of the decade-long press campaign against McIntyre. Just a year later, Manning told reporters that "the passage of time and actions by the Church have eased the tensions of the late 1960s." But, he reiterated for the record that he had "never differed on any issue" with Cardinal McIntyre.[5]

Manning snapped back at the Los Angeles *Times* on several other occasions. In the February 27, 1975 issue, staff writer Jerry Cohen cited various studies indicating that dissatisfaction with celibacy was a major reason for the departures of priests from the ministry.[6] Interpreting Cohen's article as a frontal attack on the priesthood, Manning wrote to the paper:

> This intervention is to record the indignation and the hurt of the Catholic people of Los Angeles, and of all honest-minded and concerned religious people over the article spread on the pages of the *Times* "The Celibacy Crisis Grips Catholicism."
>
> The impulse and intent behind this article, the extensive space devoted to it, the absence of any consultation with those who choose to be faithful to their celibate commitments and the ignoring of significant news events which are sources of edification within the Church – all these give us cause to wonder and a cause to protest. It ill-becomes the *Times* to discredit the Catholic priesthood before its public.[7]

Manning brought the matter to the Priests' Senate and suggested a formal intervention on their behalf. Working with several priests, the following criticism was sent to the *Times*:

> As a fraternity whose members serve in every country and every culture, the two-thousand-year-old Catholic priesthood is not a monolith. Its members do not agree on every theological nuance nor on every aspect of their ministry; nor do they reach the same level of sanctity or heroism. We have our tensions and our challenges to which all of us do not

react alike. But our fundamental commitment is, was and continues to be the proclamation of Christ's Gospel within the authority and framework of our Church's teaching ministry.

We do not expect the press to be a vehicle of propaganda for our way of life or our beliefs. We only expect the kind of fairness that just people extend to each other in every walk of life and the quality of reporting the press is expected to give the responsible professions it chooses to cover.

We have among our ranks men trained and experienced in every field, including the press. We are thus familiar and sympathetic with the reporter's thirst for news, especially in these days when the press has so little space and so much competition; we are sympathetic with the reporter's search for the "news angle," the thing he thinks will sell his story. But we unqualifiedly repudiate articles or commentaries that cast us, who are trying to serve humanity in our own weak way, in an unjust light.[8]

TEACHERS' STRIKE

The cardinal purposely kept a low profile in the dispute that arose in 1975 over those who wanted to launch a union for Catholic teachers in archdiocesan high schools. In May, organizers reported that 60% of the teachers at twenty-six schools had formed a United Catholic Secondary Teachers Association which would affiliate with the American Federation of Teachers, AFL-CIO. A spokesman told reporters that "teachers were primarily concerned about lack of job security. They were not protected by due process or grievance procedures to prevent arbitrary or capricious dismissals, transfers or assignments."[9]

From the outset, the Archdiocese of Los Angeles refused to recognize the union as representing any or all of the teachers in question. In March of 1976, the National Labor Relations Board called for oral arguments in a case involving the rights of the California Federation of Teachers to bargain collectively for about 500 teachers at parochial high schools. It was regarded as " an usually sensitive and controversial" case which was part of a mounting trend toward efforts to organize lay teachers.[10]

The archdiocese was adamantly opposed to the position for several reasons. It said that the First Amendment to the constitution exempted its schools from the Labor Relations Act. In addition, it also said that, should representational elections be necessary, each high school should be treated as a separate unit, with a separate election for each. Finally, the archdiocese argued that nuns and other members of religious orders teaching at the schools should be permitted to vote in the elections. During the ensuing proceedings, the NLRB alleged that schools operated by the archdiocese illegally spied on teachers and fired ten of them for backing the union, a charge which the archdiocesan attorney said was "without merit." The archdiocese was also accused of cutting back the length of school days from eight to seven class periods "to discourage the lay teachers from engaging in union activities."[11]

Understanding the importance of having strong support for the schools among the faithful, Manning wrote a letter communicating "the position of the archdiocese in relation to the current issue with the secondary teachers." After expressing the "gratitude through the years for the dedication, sacrifice and service of the many teachers" in the schools, he felt that the following facts "must be on record:"

1. The United Catholic Secondary Teachers Association, which is the title adopted by some teachers, is a local affiliate of the American Federation of Teachers. This American Federation of Teachers has been in the past irrevocably opposed to federal aid to private schools. At the present time, its president, Albert Shanker, has joined in a lawsuit in New York Federal District Court in an effort to remove federally supported compensatory education services to children in New York Catholic, Hebrew and Protestant schools. This is being done with the American Civil Liberties Union, and a coalition known as PEARL. It means if the American Federation of Teachers prevails, even the crumbs that fall from the federal table are being snatched from us. This is the parent of the union that would now like to become the sole bargaining agent for some of the private Catholic schools in the archdiocese.

2. The United States Supreme Court has ruled that our schools are religious institutions and, therefore, ineligible for supporting funds from the government. If we are discriminated against because of "excessive entanglement" between state and Church, then we therefore believe that the federal government has no right to

entangle itself in our schools in response to a demand by some of our lay teachers.

3. The arbitrary selection of twenty-six of the sixty-eight high schools as a single union unit could result in an umbrella of control and interference which would seriously handicap the purpose of the Catholic schools. Our school system is an aggregate of independent high schools. Individual schools are autonomous. In each school, the principal employs the teachers and generally sets school policies; in many schools, the principal is appointed by a provincial of an Order. Tuition and other related matters are independently handled by separate schools.

4. The Archdiocese of Los Angeles has consistently endeavored to escalate its remuneration to our teachers, even though we can never compete with the public schools. We will, as long as we are able, endeavor to continue conducting our schools relying on the sacrifices of so many who sustain us. From February 1974 to February 1975, over $2.5 million dollars were spent in the service of our high schools. The intervention of a union would create pressures for escalating this figure. We are dependent totally on the free offerings of our people for the sustenance of our schools. Four percent of the ordinary income of each parish is diverted for the high schools. We believe it would be an excessive demand on the generosity of our people to ask for consistent sums each year in excess of this amount.

5. The union has stated in writing that it anticipates calling a strike on April 2. We believe that a strike can only be disruptive and divisive and would be an irresponsible act which could only redound to the detriment of the students. The union filed a petition with the National Labor Relations Board, a federal agency, in April of last year. Hearings were held in June and July, and written briefs were filed by the parties in September. We are now awaiting a decision by that agency, which could arrive at any time now. We have done nothing to delay that decision. The union decided to involve the federal

> agency by asking that it decide various issues. Now, for some reason, the union has taken the position that it does not want to wait for that agency decision and that the schools must not begin to negotiate. We have taken the position that since the matter has been submitted to that agency, its decision should not be anticipated.[12]

California's professedly Catholic governor and presidential candidate, Edmund G. Brown Jr., gave his support to the teachers and their collection basket boycott in an appearance at a California Federation of Teachers convention. Wearing a "Catholic Teachers Have Rights" button, Brown suggested a "colloquy" between himself and Cardinal Manning in which to give the cardinal "a homily on the rights of teachers," according to the teachers' union newsletter. Brown also spoke favorably of the union's "teacher bucks," which were distributed to conventioneers for use in lieu of contributions to Sunday collections.[13]

In a letter read in all parish churches April 4, Manning told the archdiocese's two million Catholics that a strike by teachers would be "disruptive and divisive . . . an irresponsible act which could only redound to the detriment of the students."[14] Manning noted that the NLRB's decision on the unions' petition is expected at any time. He did not say whether the archdiocese would begin a court fight if the NLRB ordered an election.

On June 8, in a settlement between the archdiocese and the putative union, Catholic officials agreed to pay an estimated $12,000 to five teachers allegedly fired for union activities. Also the archdiocese promised to post notices about refraining from such conduct as spying on union supporters. Still unresolved, at that time, was the basic issue of whether the archdiocese had to recognize and bargain with the union. The Church held out for a court test of the NLRB decision "because it involves fundamental rights which the (Catholic) schools cannot surrender without serious damage to themselves and to the larger Church community of which they are a part." If the larger Church accepts the government order, he said, it would mean agreeing that the government has a right to "interfere and entangle itself" in Church affairs, and that could lead to the "destruction of the local administration and autonomy of Church schools . . . "He said it would also mean acceptance of a union "which has openly declared its hostility to Catholic moral principles in the area of abortion and contraception . . ."[15] Though contrary charges were made, Msgr. Donald Montrose, speaking for the archdiocese, said that "the settlement specifically states there is no admission of guilt or

Poster carried by protestors during the Holy Name Society procession to the Palladium in January, 1985.

The campaign to keep Cathedral High School open was carefully orchestrated.

Manning celebrates Mass at Cathedral High School.

liability by the archdiocese. It was, he noted "a gesture of good will to these teachers and to the others."[16]

Teachers in the union, frustrated by their inability to win points with the archdiocese, decided to go on strike in March of 1977. On its part, the archdiocese continued to claim that it could not recognize the union "without jeopardizing litigation in federal courts."[17] Teachers at twenty-four Catholic high schools walked out on March 10th. Officials were able to keep the schools operational, though some went on half-time sessions. According to Marian Hull, president of the striking American Federation of Teachers, the key issue was that "the Church argues that the U.S. Supreme Court and Congress refuse to give federal aid directly to Catholic schools on grounds that the schools are religious institutions and that the constitution mandates a separation between Church and state." Hence, the government cannot insist on applying federal laws to Church schools.

At this juncture, Manning once again expressed himself about the facts of the case, this time in a letter to a lay teacher at Pius X High School:

> First: an open door policy exists at each of our schools and our teachers have been notified again of this policy. Each principal welcomes the opportunity of meeting with teachers from his or her school to improve communications, receive suggestions, and discuss problems and concerns of those serving the Church in our schools.
>
> Second: in further hope of improving communications and providing an additional opportunity for exchanging views in an attempt to improve understanding and relationships between our schools and teachers, representatives from the Department of Education are available, as they have been in the past, to meet with representatives of the United Catholic Secondary Teachers Association, Local 3448.
>
> I strongly urge an early initial meeting of representatives of the United Catholic Secondary Teachers Association and of our Department of Education in order that agenda items for discussion may be explored. In order to eliminate any misunderstanding as to the mutual desires of the parties, a memorandum is attached for signature by the parties before such meetings begin.[18]

Several months later, the cardinal felt compelled to speak on the matter to the clergy of the archdiocese. He felt that such information might be useful in case "it becomes necessary to explain the policy at the Masses on Sunday or in any other context:

> There is a constitutional law question.
>
> a. By decree of the Supreme Court of the United States, Catholic schools do not qualify for Federal aid, because they are *religious schools* - "an integral part of the mission of the Catholic Church."
> b. Another branch of the government, the National Labor Relations Board, decrees that it has authority over the labor practices of our schools because it holds that our schools are non-religious - "not intimately involved with the Catholic Church" - and therefore are subject to governmental entanglement.
> c. The constitution says government shall not interfere with religion. The only recourse left to the Church in this instance is to seek a ruling from the courts as to where we stand in relation to Federal intervention. We are victims caught between two contradictory governmental positions. The government cannot have it both ways. The only way to obtain Federal court review of the important constitutional issues is by refusing to bargain.
>
> The second issue facing the archdiocese is the welfare of our teachers in all of our schools. We recognize their contributions; we respect their loyalty and good intentions; we do not dispute their right to collective bargaining; we do not dispute their legal right to strike. We do dispute the right of the government to interfere with the operation of our schools.

A written agreement was reached between representatives of the union and the schools on January 14, 1977 in which precautions were taken to preserve our right to test the constitutional issues in Federal court. We agree to discuss informally the needs and the concerns of teachers. Under this agreement the schools were and are willing to discuss and attempt to resolve any matter presented by the union representatives. Three such meetings in an atmosphere of goodwill have taken place. There seems to be no reason why this could not continue. We made the agreement in good faith. We wanted to avoid a strike and resolve the issues.

Manning then said that "there were other factors that must be considered:"

a. The parent labor organization of the local affiliate union is the American Federation of Teachers which is on record against Federal aid to parochial schools and is likewise a proponent of abortion information to schools.

b. We affirm the distinctive nature of each of our Catholic schools and believe that collective bargaining must be limited to each school separately. Some of our schools are large, some small, some coed, some all boys, and some all girls. Some are located in the inner city, others in outlying communities, and all have varying racial and ethnic mixes. Each school has important individual differences.

c. We have a deep concern for all our students. They will be injured by any interruption of their education; particularly the seniors, who are preparing to graduate and to enter college this fall, may be seriously affected. Every effort will be made to keep our schools in operation. Preparations have been made and are being carried out to attempt to insure the efficient operation of our schools during this crisis.[19]

A Church spokesman said officials had not only agreed to meet informally with the teachers, but urged that the meetings be held before the strike "takes place in an atmosphere of good will . . . while at the same time safeguarding our right to test the constitutional issues in court by not negotiating or signing a contract with the union."[20] Advertisements in local newspapers, "occupation" of the Chancery Office and picketing the cardinal's residence did little to influence Manning who pointed out the inconsistency of the federal government which denied Catholic schools federal aid but wanted to intervene in their labor affairs.[21]

A moratorium in the twenty-one day strike was reached on March 30, when Cardinal Manning agreed to engage in informal talks with representatives of the United Catholic Secondary Teachers Association. Labor leaders called it a "*de facto*" victory, but Church leaders "continued to say that the talks were informal and did not represent negotiations."[22] After meeting with representatives of the strikers, for two hours, Manning announced an unusual "reconciliation Mass" to be celebrated by the cardinal himself. Marian Hill, President of the striking United Secondary Catholic Teachers Association, said the tentative settlement was "an enormous victory" for the strikers, and she said agreement was reached in large part because of Manning's "openness, warmth and understanding." Manning called Mrs. Hull "an absolutely gracious lady," and said that the discussions with the union representatives were "exceptionally cordial, open and cooperative."

The tentative agreement actually provided only for further "talks" but according to union officials represented a major victory because it gave them "*de facto*" recognition as bargaining agent for the teachers, which was a key issue in the strike. Msgr. Donald Montrose insisted that the Church has not changed its basic position as a result of the settlement, but did agree to intensified "informal talks" with the union on many issues in dispute. Both Montrose and Mrs. Hull agreed that the tentative strike settlement agreement would allow the Church to continue its test case in the courts.

Manning promised that the renewed "talks" with the union would deal with all of the "fundamentals and basic concerns of the teachers." Then whatever agreements were reached in the talks between the union and the principals "would be presented for inclusion in the (individual) contracts which the teachers will make with the separate schools."[23]

Eventually, in March of 1979, the United States Supreme Court ruled that the Roman Catholic Church "need not recognize parochial school teachers' unions." The precedent-making ruling in effect said that the government could not regulate labor relations in Church-operated schools because to do so would violate constitutional guarantees of religious freedom. Hence groups of all faiths were given the option whether to recognize teachers' unions or not. Despite this, union officials promised to press on "for better wages and working conditions." Immediately after the court decision, Manning extended an olive branch to the teachers, promising to work closely in responding to their needs and aspirations in the years ahead. His spokesman expressed the cardinal's views when he noted that "a religious school should have other ways than an adversary labor-management position to communicate and solve problems.[24]

CONFLICT IN SAN BERNARDINO

The creation of the Diocese of San Bernardino in 1978 occasioned a hostile article in the *National Catholic Reporter* by Father James Pawlicki in which he vented his anger and that of others about the non-appointment of an Hispanic bishop for the newly-created jurisdiction. Ignoring history and the fact that the proto-bishop of California was a native of Mexico and that his three successors were Spanish-born, the activist priest complained that the incumbent in Los Angeles, "the second biggest Mexican city in the world," is Cardinal Timothy Manning, "an Irish import who has repeatedly blocked the idea of a regional office of Hispanic Affairs for Los Angeles.[25]

Msgr. Joseph Pollard, a spokesman for the archdiocese, wrote a letter to the *National Catholic Reporter* which deserves to be repeated in his entirety:

> Pawlicki introduces us to Manning as "an Irish import." The phrase, in context, is a racist slur and an attempt to isolate Manning in a "special" category. It is also an insult to the thousands of Irish priests and Religious who have served the southland and all its peoples in this century with a measure of Gospel greatness.
>
> Pawlicki's concoction of [Apostolic Delegate] Jadot and Manning "in a corner" at an "inner circle party" discussing "replacements for the bishops who were retiring in California" is aimed at showing up Manning as a sinister Hispano-bishop-blocker. For such a libel, Pawlicki makes use of nothing more substantial than the terms "allegedly" and "reportedly." These "sources"only highlight the farce that is Pawlicki's scenario and the nakedness of his injustice to Manning. Another of Pawlicki's allegations is his lie, pulled from the nearest wall, that Manning has stated he would never have an Hispano Ordinary in his metropolitan area.
>
> Thus far, one-half of the number of auxiliaries ordained by Manning have been Hispanic. None has come from the largest clergy group, the Irish. This record of Manning's speaks to the present and indicates the future, but Pawlicki doesn't know or like favorable marks for Los Angeles's cardinal.
>
> Pawlicki projects himself as a promoter of justice and a defender of the immigrant poor. He is very short on the one and highly selective about the other. Obviously, immigrants such as Manning rate only character extermination in Pawlicki's corrupt version of justice and the Gospel to the poor.[26]

OTHER ISSUES

In mid 1980, Manning went on the verbal warpath, attacking "popular professors and conceited columnists" who object to the decisions of the Vatican Council. He reasserted in strong terms that the Roman Catholic Church is not a club whose teachings "are subject to selective acceptance."[27] Writing in *The Tidings*, the cardinal declined to identify what professors or columnists he had in mind. But he observed that words such as "hierarchy," "institution" and "*magisterium*" (the Church's teaching authority vested in the pope and bishops) were unpopular. By contrast, he continued, the favored words are "community," "people of God" and "charismatic" and the literature is preoccupied with such themes as freedom of conscience, religious liberty, ecumenism and human dignity.

> There is abroad a free and easy attitude toward the Church. Her teaching is subject to selective acceptance. Popular professors and conceited columnists criticize, contradict or deride norms and decisions coming from the Holy See. The Church is regarded by critics as a sort of club in which one has membership. You may take advantage of it as you will. You are free to give democratic expressions on its regulations and policies. You don't have to leave it when you have a basic disagreement with it.

The demands of Church loyalty may seem hard, Manning wrote, "but as offspring should respect their seemingly old fashioned, old-world mother, so should members dutifully listen to their Church."[28]

Manning took the unusual step of devoting a whole essay to Father Hans Kung in *The Tidings*. Therein he endorsed and proclaimed a Roman decision that "Kung can no longer be considered a Catholic theologian." The cardinal said there should be no panic or alarm, noting that "he who succeeds Peter in the shepherding of God's flock is fearless in his guarding of the sacred trust given to him." In fact, Manning saw "a certain advantage" emerging from this course of events insofar as it allowed for a better understanding of a particular tenet of faith. Manning concluded by reminding his readers that Jesus was walking on the troubled waters of our times. Over the tumult He speaks to us through Peter – "it is I – do not be afraid."[29]

CATHEDRAL HIGH SCHOOL

For several years, school officials in the Archdiocese of Los Angeles had been studying the changing demographics of its 265 elementary and secondary schools. It was noted that enrollment had declined at three boys high schools – Cathedral, Pater Noster, and Bishop Mora

ADVERTISEMENT

An Open Letter
to Timothy Cardinal Manning

Re: Cathedral High School

Cardinal Manning:

The crescendo of public outcries from all segments of the Los Angeles community regarding the sale of Cathedral High School continues to fall on the deaf ears of the Church.

Why?

★ Does the Los Angeles Catholic Archdiocese still adhere to the medieval practice of acting unilaterally with no accountability to its constituency? If so, it sets itself far apart from all other major institutions in this country, including business and government, which consider it socially responsible to operate in concert with, rather than against, their constituencies.

★ Is the gain from the sale of this valuable property so attractive as to overshadow the great social contributions this school has made for 60 years to the academically qualified youth of the inner city? Perhaps it is this very business orientation that has made the Los Angeles Catholic Archdiocese one of the world's largest and wealthiest, with estimated assets of nearly $1 billion.

★ Why the secrecy surrounding this transaction? Despite repeated pleas, neither the Church as seller, nor the Hong Kong based buyer will reveal any aspect of the deal—not even a basic description of the firm buying the property. Such mystery is highly unusual and unworthy of the Church.

★ Is your recent proposal of a two-year extension a true concession or merely a public relations ploy? Such an extension has little meaning. It would still leave current freshmen out on a limb. Could it be, Cardinal, that through the action of the City Council and Cultural Heritage Board, the property is tied up for about two years, anyway? And during this extension period, wouldn't the Church as owner reap tax benefits because the property will have been used as a school rather than commercially?

★ And, lastly, Cardinal Manning, how does the Church justify selling (at a multi-million dollar profit) property donated by the City of Los Angeles, without considering the intentions of the donor? In 1844, the City donated to the Church the land on which Cathedral stands. The donation had a public purpose: First, to maintain a cemetery (the original Calvary Cemetery) on the site; then to operate Cathedral High School, which opened there in 1925 when the cemetery was transferred to its present location. The apparent purpose of this property, if sold, has no public components—only the private gain of buyer and seller.

So you see, Cardinal Manning, that the Archdiocese faces a variety of serious ethical questions regarding the sale of Cathedral.

As you prepare to leave office, you can be remembered as the Cardinal who placed Catholic education of our inner city ahead of short-term profit—or the one who disregarded the will of the Los Angeles community for the sake of institutional financial gain. We urge you to leave a fitting memorial and rescind the sale.

Sincerely,

Friends of Cathedral, Inc.

Concerned Catholics and citizens of Los Angeles: In order to establish meaningful dialogue with the Archdiocese leading to a resolution of this issue, please write to Cardinal Manning expressing your views at the Catholic Archdiocese, 1531 W. 9th St., L.A. 90015 or call (213) 251-3200.

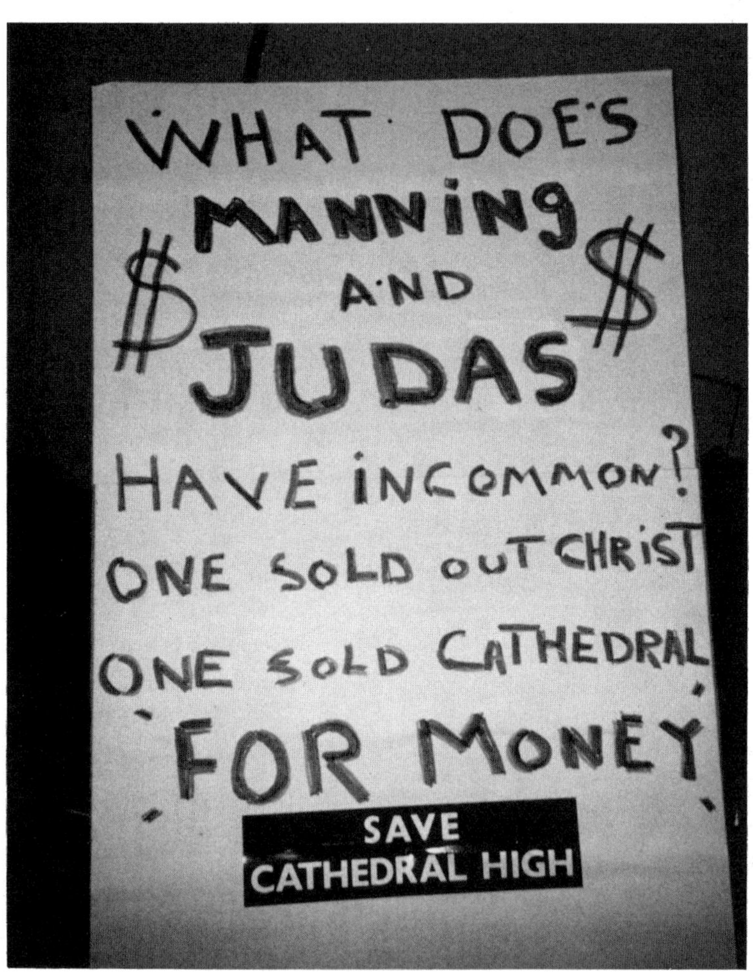
WHAT DOES
MANNING
$ AND $
JUDAS
HAVE INCOMMON?
ONE SOLD OUT CHRIST
ONE SOLD CATHEDRAL
FOR MONEY
SAVE
CATHEDRAL HIGH

Salesian – all located within a three mile radius of one another. These three schools with a combined student capacity of 2,300 students, had an anticipated combined enrollment of only 1,200 students for 1984.

Further research indicated that the closing of one of the three schools and the consolidation of its student body with the other two would enable the archdiocese to allocate its resources more equitably and increase substantially the student enrollments at the remaining two schools. In deciding which school to close, it was determined that Pater Noster and Bishop Mora Salesian were situated in the center of large Hispanic residential areas, while the area around Cathedral, located in Chinatown, was rapidly becoming commercial and industrial. Many of the students attending Cathedral lived closer to the other two schools.

Cathedral was the oldest of the three schools and two of its existing buildings did not comply with the city's Earthquake Safety Ordinance. To bring them into conformity would require a substantial capital outlay. Students at Cathedral could continue their education at either of the two adjacent schools with minimal interruption of their academic programs. In March, 1982, archdiocesan officials met with representatives of the Brothers of the Christian Schools to inform them, in confidence, that because of continuing under-enrollment, the archdiocese intended to relocate the students at Cathedral to either Pater Noster or Bishop Mora Salesian.

On July 11, 1983, the Brothers of the Christian Schools were informed that the school site would be sold. Negotiation with a potential buyer had begun and the archdiocese would keep the Brothers informed. On August 25, 1983, the escrow was signed by the archdiocese. On both occasions, there were offers to relocate the Brothers to another inner-city school where they could continue their teaching apostolate.

On April 30, 1984, the archdiocesan Superintendent of Secondary Schools notified Brother Dominic Berardelli that the conditions of the escrow with the potential buyer had been fulfilled and the Cathedral High School property escrow would close effective July 1, 1985. Three months later archdiocesan officials met with five representatives of the Brothers to discuss how parents would be notified of the consolidation and what procedures should be instituted to effect an orderly academic transition. Cardinal Manning repeated his offer to have the Brothers administer and staff another high school with predominantly Hispanic enrollment. Throughout the discussions, it was repeatedly emphasized that the over-riding concern in this action was that of providing cost-effective, quality education for inner-city and Hispanic students.

Though they had been asked to keep the deliberations private until everything had been finalized, the Brothers began leaking information to the press. Two staff writers from the Los Angeles *Times* broke the news in July that the archdiocese was "selling Cathedral High."

> In an unannounced move that has shocked and angered alumni of one of Los Angeles' oldest Roman Catholic schools, the Archdiocese of Los Angeles has arranged to sell Cathedral High School to a developer. The school, a cluster of old stucco buildings tucked into a corner of Chinatown, is a college preparatory institution with high educational standards. It has primarily served inner-city youths.
>
> According to the Los Angeles Community Redevelopment Agency, the property is in escrow for sale to Wing Ming Properties, which filed an application two weeks ago to build low - and moderate-income housing on the site. News of the sale surfaced inadvertently this week when alumni involved in a fund-raising effort for the school heard about it through business contacts. Alumni, as well as faculty, students and parents, were not informed of any plan to dispose of the sixty-year-old school.
>
> "The kids are just going to be devastated by this," said Brother James Meegan, school principal. He said he had learned of the transaction "very recently," but would not elaborate.

Some alumni expressed bitterness about the handling of the sale, saying that it had been "carried out in secret and complaining that the archdiocese did not return calls." Dominic Ferrante and others served notice that "there's going to be a battle. We're not going to lie down and let this happen. The school has meant too much to us and our families. And it's meant too much to the inner-city."[30]

In its press release, the Catholic Department of Education emphasized that "throughout Southern California both private and public school systems have had to face the facts of changing demographic patterns and shrinking school enrollments:"

> The resulting closure of schools and consolidation of student bodies have caused concern and in some cases an emotional outcry which, while understandable, does not recognize the reality of the changing situation. It is hoped that those who are so openly concerned about the closing of Cathedral High School would channel these same energies and talents into working for the success of Pater Noster and

> Bishop Mora Salesian and all of the students who will attend these schools. The archdiocese is grateful to the Brothers of the Christian Schools for their dedicated service to Cathedral High School and its students. Archdiocesan officials hope that this long and beneficial relationship can continue.[31]

Meanwhile, in response to an inquiry from the Apostolic Pro-Nuncio, Manning wrote to say that "the closing of the high school would in no way compromise or diminish the educational opportunities for Hispanic and inner-city youth."[32]

Because a number of pastors in the archdiocese had received erroneous information about the closure, a letter was dispatched which reiterated the archdiocesan position. It noted that merging Cathedral with its two neighbors would "enhance quality education and cost effectiveness by merging resources and optimizing the redeployment of facilities." Both Pater Noster and Bishop Mora Salesian had newer and more modern facilities. Also pointed out was the fact that Cathedral "did not enjoy the support of an alumni organization until consolidation plans were underway." The superintendent of High Schools and Colleges for the archdiocese concluded by saying that it was "important to view this situation not from a single school perspective, but from an overall vision of what is best for the entire Catholic community which we serve."[33]

The cardinal then sent out an "open letter" which further attempted to enlighten those affected by the envisioned closure:

> The Archdiocese of Los Angeles in fulfilling its pastoral ministry owns and operates twenty-eight archdiocesan and six parish high schools. Decisions concerning these schools are made in the context of support for the total educational mission of Catholic secondary schools and in light of the common good. In practice this means that when a decision is made which affects more than one school, then the good of all the schools is the controlling principle.
>
> In response to the decision to consolidate Cathedral, Pater Noster and Bishop Mora Salesian High Schools, current and past members of the Cathedral High School community, understandably, perceive and regard this decision as detrimental to them. In fact, the negative experience of the Cathedral High School community has been a primary public focus. Virtually no public comment has been made concerning any positive, renewing effects of consolidation, for exam-

> ple, the enabling of the archdiocese to allocate resources more equitably and to improve overall quality and cost-effectiveness of inner-city Catholic secondary education.
>
> Cathedral High School will close on July 1, 1985. On this day the escrow will close and the property ownership will be transferred. Pater Noster and Bishop Mora Salesian High Schools are involved in planning for increased enrollment and for providing quality education programs that will meet the needs of their expanded student bodies.[34]

The bitterness felt by certain of the Christian Brothers spilled into their relations with Manning. Late in 1984, Brother James Meegan, principal, wrote to the cardinal recalling the cherished tradition of having him celebrate "the liturgy for us on the Feast of Our Lady of Guadalupe," something which, he said, had been "a source of joy and strength for us." But this year, due to the "great sorrow and hurt at Cathedral as a result of the decision to sell the property and close the school,[35] it does not seem appropriate to extend an invitation to you to celebrate with us." Manning replied that "I understand. May Our Lady show us a way."[36]

A series of letters began appearing in the southland newspapers, many of them attacks on the person of the cardinal. The "Friends of Cathedral High" appear to have instigated the campaign. Early in 1975, the Los Angeles City Council heeding "the plea of 400 Cathedral High School students" passed a resolution asking the archdiocese to keep the school open. Councilman Art Snyder, in whose district the school was located, declared that the site "was donated by the city in 1844 with a public purpose in mind." (Snyder apparently didn't know that the "public purpose" was a cemetery!) Councilman Ernani Bernardi, who voted to oppose the resolution, called the city's demand "the height of arrogance."[37]

At a meeting with the provincial of the Christian Brothers, Manning verbally agreed to a two year moratorium on the closing of the school, stating that if the potential buyer were to withdraw, the school would remain as it is. Looking ahead to his pending retirement, the cardinal decided to leave the final decision to his successor.[38]

The provincial of the Christian Brothers was considerably more incisive than his confreres on the scene. He obviously felt that if the school could survive beyond Manning's tenure, it had a chance of lasting even longer. Hence, when the "Friends of Cathedral High" sponsored a march on March 24, 1985, Brother Norman Cook quickly disavowed "any relationship or connection of myself or the Christian Brothers to these expressions." He asked organizers to refrain from marches, civil actions, suits, demonstrations, protestations, *etc*., because the Christian Brothers are pursuing solutions to our differences with the Archdiocese of Los Angeles within proper and ordinary avenues provided by the Catholic Church."[39]

Despite the wishes of the provincial, supporters of Cathedral High School filed a lawsuit in Superior Court on April 30, 1985 in an attempt to stop the transaction. According to a local newspaper, "We have filed this suit because we believe in our hearts that the sale of Cathedral High School is unlawful, unethical and contrary to the educational interest of the youth of the inner-city," said Mike Cimino, a spokesman for Friends of Cathedral Inc. He said the suit was filed only after months of sporadic talks with the archdiocese had broken down. "Nobody takes any delight in filing this lawsuit,"[40] he added.

The lawsuit was subsequently dropped when Manning's successor, Archbishop Roger Mahony, "after extensive consultation and reflection," reached the decision "that Cathedral High School should not be closed, but that it should continue to serve the high school students of this general area of the archdiocese." He said that a task force appointed to study the matter had come "to the unanimous conclusion that the school is needed by youth in the area and that its enrollment can be increased to meet its full potential with the support of the local community, the alumni and all friends of Cathedral High School." Archbishop Mahony also noted that his decision "is fully concurred in by Cardinal Timothy Manning, whom I have kept fully advised of the evolution of these developments."[41]

Notes to the Text

1. Since this treatise is primarily a biography of Timothy Cardinal Manning and only secondarily a history of the Archdiocese of Los Angeles over which he presided from 1970 to 1985, only those controversies have been treated which related directly to Manning or over which he exercised significant influence. Hence, the charges made by a reporter for the *National Catholic Reporter* in 1982 that the priest director of the Religious Education Department was involved in a "conflict of interest" because he "promoted the textbooks of a publishing company for which he had acted as a paid consultant and author" are not here examined. Not only did Manning refuse to get involved in that issue, he made it known that he considered the charges as journalistic gobbledy-gook.
2. Los Angeles *Times*, March 12, 1972.
3. AALA, Timothy Manning to Otis Chandler, Los Angeles, March 15, 1972.
4. *The Tidings*, March 17, 1972.
5. Los Angeles *Times*, February 14, 1973.
6. *Southern Cross*, March 20, 1975.
7. Los Angeles *Times*, March 9, 1975.
8. *The Tidings*, March 21, 1975.
9. Los Angeles *Times*, May 1, 1975.
10. *Ibid.*, March 4, 1976.
11. Ibid., March 9, 1976.
12. AALA, Timothy Cardinal Manning to Faithful, Los Angeles, March 30, 1976. This also appeared in *The Tidings*, April 2, 1976.
13. *National Catholic Reporter*, April 30, 1976.
14. AALA, Timothy Cardinal Manning to Faithful, Los Angeles, April, 1976.
15. Los Angeles *Times*, June 23, 1976.
16. *National Catholic Reporter*, July 16, 1976.
17. *Ibid.*, March 18, 1976.

18. AALA, Timothy Cardinal Manning to Thomas Hale, Los Angeles, January 26, 1977.
19. AALA, Timothy Cardinal Manning to Clergy, Los Angeles, March 10, 1977.
20. Los Angeles *Times*, March 18, 1977.
21. *National Catholic Reporter*, March 25, 1977.
22. Los Angeles *Times*, June 21, 1977.
23. *Ibid.*, March 31, 1977.
24. *Ibid.*, March 23, 1979.
25. *National Catholic Reporter*, September 29, 1978.
26. The *Tidings*, October 6, 1978.
27. Los Angeles *Times*, May 31, 1980.
28. *The Tidings*, May 23, 1980.
29. *Ibid.*, January 4, 1980.
30. Los Angeles *Times*, July 13, 1984.
31. AALA, Press Release, Los Angeles, July 17, 1984.
32. AALA, Timothy Cardinal Manning to Pio Laghi, Los Angeles, July 30, 1984.
33. AALA, Jeremiah T. Murphy to Clergy, Los Angeles, August 13, 1984.
34. *The Tidings*, November 30, 1984.
35. AALA, James Meegan, F.S.C., to Timothy Cardinal Manning, Los Angeles, n.d.
36. AALA, Timothy Cardinal Manning to James Meegan, F.S.C., Los Angeles, December 7, 1984.
37. Unidentified news-clipping, February 2, 1985.
38. AALA, Norman Cook, F.S.C. to Timothy Cardinal Manning, Moraga, February 22, 1985 and Timothy Cardinal Manning to James Meegan, Los Angeles, February 25, 1985.
39. AALA, Norman Cook, F.S.C. to Timothy Cardinal Manning, Moraga, March 28, 1985.
40. Los Angeles *Times*, May 1, 1985.
41. *The Tidings*, December 6, 1985.

16. Catholic Education

According to a viewpoint he first expressed in December of 1950 and repeated on several occasions, Timothy Manning felt that there was "only one Catholic position on education."

> It must lead with certainty and with finality to God in the manifestation of His ways and purposes. It must view life in its totality; here on earth as a condition and antechamber and correlative of eternal life. It is not merely the knowledge of the penny catechism nor the *Summa* of St. Thomas, but a living vibrant faith embracing all sciences and all aspects of life, making the mind large and fertile by synthesizing knowledge into its ultimate first-principles and blending the social, political, economic, aesthetic and recreative departments of human living into a harmonious whole that revolves, like a planet around a sun, around the Infinite Origin of all truth and goodness and beauty.
>
> It is not merely the external fidelity to the sacramental system of the Church, but also the opening up of the soul to the requisite conditions for the fruitful reception of sacrament and sanctity. It calls for heroism! It demands unwavering obedience to the voice of Peter, vocal over the crucial issues of every age in the condemnation of error and the proclamation of truth. It demands discipline, the pruning of unproductive digressions, the upturning of the soil by study, the atmosphere of prayer for divine guidance, the humble recognition of personal limitations, the aspiration of the human mind for truth and the reaching out of the will to embrace goodness until mind and heart and will are brought captive to the obedience of Christ.[1]

In another context, while speaking on "Catholic Education and Modern Youth," Manning proclaimed that "the ultimate and central mission of the Church, through education, is to put Christ" at the center of life and "through Him and in Him to give cohesion and depth and meaning and beauty and dignity to the mystery of life.

After his arrival in the southland as archbishop, Manning lost no time in pledging that the school system which he inherited, the fifth largest of its kind in the United States, would remain in place, except in those cases where demographics demanded a shift of emphasis. There were sixty-nine high schools and 272 elementary schools with enrollment of 140,298. The schools were staffed by a dedicated corps of 5,163 lay and religious teachers. At the time there were representatives of sixteen communities of priests, seven communities of brothers and sixty-two communities of Sisters working in the schools. Another forty-two archdiocesan priests were engaged full-time in Catholic education.

Although the schools in the archdiocese received no direct financial support from the public treasury, the children attending those institutions did benefit from a variety of government programs. Under Title I of the Elementary and Second Education Act of 1965, for example, some 4,700 inter-city children needing remedial instruction in reading and mathematics were assisted by teachers from local public schools. By 1974, eighty of the elementary schools were participating in the Instructional Television System operated by the archdiocese. Los Angeles was the first education system, public or private to own and operate television channels. Programming consisted almost entirely of pre-recorded materials produced for national distribution by educational television libraries.

Manning liked to tell his episcopal confreres that the education department for the Archdiocese of Los Angeles was totally professional. For example, there was a 146 page *Administrative Handbook for Elementary Schools* which was a compilation of policies and regulations governing the primary schools. And there was a corresponding book for secondary schools, which made policies known under one cover so that pastors and other concerned persons could have them for ready reference.

In a pastoral letter issued in mid 1973, Cardinal Manning made clear "that our planning for Catholic schools must be based on our own efforts and sacrifices." He praised parents who the previous year had contributed $20,667,931 toward the education of their children in tuition and other instructional fees. He was also appreciative to "the Catholic community at large: which through donations, fund raising activities, and extraordinary gifts, had provided another $10,700,000 to the school system." But more was needed. In order to make Catholic schools even more effective additional steps had to be taken. The cardinal recommended a number of steps - clear explanation of the distinctive goals of Catholic schools; closer association with other non-public and public schools; increased efficiency of operation, fiscal professional, academic and civic accountability; vigorous student recruitment; wholehearted parental involvement and full participation in the search for solutions to the racial crisis in American education. Manning said that the "task is large. So are the rewards. We invite every Catholic to consider the specific role he or she will play in helping to meet the challenges which face us all."[2]

At no time did Manning ever involve himself at the operational level of the school system. He envisioned his role as that of defining and continually readjusting the spiritual tone and objectives of Catholic education in the Archdiocese of Los Angeles. He made himself ever available in that role. An example would be the opening of the 74th annual National Catholic Educational Association convention in San Francisco. There he told the 2,000 educators "unless at the core of our lives in all that we do, is the transforming belief in Christ, we are only offering alternate means of selective education."[3]

Manning was extremely effective on a person-to-person basis. He once told newly-appointed principals of Catholic schools that "the competition you're up against as principals and teachers is overpowering and overwhelming. Television is the major teacher of our times. It has a position you'll never have. Children look at television six hours a day. Your competition is the values promoted on the TV screen. You have to counter them with gospel values. In television," continued the cardinal, "no activity is demanded of the pupil. Nothing is asked of the child."

When queried as to why the Church needed to have its own schools, Manning said "We have our own schools because we believe the whole person must be educated. Everything in creation must have an orientation to one's eternal destiny. This orientation is done not only through communication but through a process of exemplification. A teacher must be the incarnation of those values as a priest must. Therefore, there must be an element of prayer in our work." As to how he viewed Catholic schools in the 1970s, Manning responded that he had seen a great change for the better, "I am happier with the educational system than ever before."[4]

In an interview with a reporter from the Los Angeles *Times*, Manning said that the reason why Catholic schools were not expanding "is the Catholic Church's commitment to the inner city." He put the archdiocese on record as opposing "white flight," the so-called phenomenon of parents seeking to enroll their children in private and religious schools to escape court-ordered busing to achieve racial integration.

> We take seriously the fact that there are suburban parishes without a school or with a school which could be filled several times over. We are also sensitive, however, to the needs of the central city. The economically deprived have to enjoy a high priority for us . . . We feel that for the present their needs must take priority over any move, however desirable it might be, to expand schools in other areas of the archdiocese.

Manning and his advisors had decided that urban areas deserved parochial schools "not only for their sometimes dwindling Catholic population, but also for those outside our faith, who prefer a religious education for their children. The school is a way of maintaining the Church's presence in the inner city." In parochial schools of the archdiocese, the cardinal noted that two-thirds of the teachers were lay persons and only one-third belong to religious orders, a reverse of just a decade earlier. Sharply higher salaries must be paid lay teachers than religious ones who take vows of poverty when they enter orders. "We have an ideal, perhaps difficult to maintain given the economics of the day." He said, "that no child will be deprived of a parochial school education for want of money . . . Catholic schools could not operate on a purely business basis."[5]

By 1982, the statistics and demographics had changed even more. As he prepared the quinquennial report for the Holy See, Manning drew up a profile of the Catholic schools in the archdiocese.

> There are three types of Catholic schools in the archdiocese: archdiocesan, parochial and private. The Archdiocese of Los Angeles Education and Welfare Corporation owns, maintains and operates the archdiocesan and parochial schools. Private Catholic schools are those owned and sponsored by religious communities or duly authorized governing boards.
>
> The archdiocesan Department of Education reported that the 1981-82 enrollment in sixty Catholic high schools in the archdiocese was 35,925 pupils. Of that number 85.36% were Catholic students. Ethnic diversity encompassed 30.50% His-

> panic, 13.45% Black, 4.45% Asian, 0.83% American Indian, and 50.68% all other categories.
>
> Full time professional staff in the high schools numbers 739 lay women, 694 lay men, 269 sisters, 106 religious order priests, ninety-five brothers and thirty-three diocesan priests. The 232 Catholic elementary schools during 1981-82 enrolled 74,990 students. Ethnic makeup consisted of 44.34% Hispanic, 9.93% Black, 6.48% Asian, 0.31% American Indian and 39.10% all other categories. Full time elementary school professional staff included 1,592 lay women, 679 sisters, 243 lay men, five brothers and one diocesan priest. Financial reports for the schools disclose that only five archdiocesan secondary schools were supported by advances from the Chancery totalling $266,798. Several parish secondary schools were supported by advances from the parishes totalling $50,295.
>
> Although lay staff salaries increased $1,886,984 in the elementary schools, their operating deficit was $844,213 less than last year. Archdiocesan and parish secondary schools were able to meet annual operating expenses and to allocate one million dollars to the major summer maintenance program required by hard-use buildings and facilities. Total cost of maintenance performed during the summer was $2.7 million. The Chancery Office supplied the additional funds to meet the total cost.

"With God's help, our schools will strive to be communities whose members learn incarnate gospel values particularly through the integration of faith, knowledge and culture in their lives," the cardinal said. "May the Catholic schools of the Los Angeles archdiocese continue to find support for the belief that they have in themselves and in the value of their ministry and mission – to teach as Jesus did."[6]

By 1982, the Catholic secondary school system in the archdiocese was the largest system in terms of schools and students of any of the Catholic jurisdictions in California and second largest of any system public or private. The Department of Education exercised varying degrees of responsibility to sixty secondary schools. There were thirty archdiocesan and six parish high schools that were directly accountable to the superintendent, while twenty-four were answerable in matters of religious instruction. All shared equally in the services provided by the archdiocese.[7]

In a message to the archdiocese, one of his last relating to education, the cardinal portrayed the schools as "communities of faith:"

> Our pilgrimage toward the Lord is constantly lived out in the faith community which comprises each of our Catholic schools. The unique character of this ingathering is rooted in the values of the Gospel. We must always be a forum in which the Word of God is clearly spoken, and the teachings of the Church are proclaimed with reverence, respect and true conviction.
>
> The teachers and co-workers are challenged to model a living faith. We assert that our schools are indeed such communities of faith, constantly reaching out for a deeper understanding of the Gospel and invoking the strength of God's spirit. We speak the gratitude of a great multitude of parents who support our schools at great personal sacrifice. We assert also in our sentiments of thanksgiving all those who have graduated from our Catholic school system and look back in profound appreciation. The kindness of God has been bountiful to us through those who labor with love and generosity in our Catholic school system.[8]

YOUNG PEOPLE

Among Manning's goals as archbishop was that of visiting each of the seventy high schools operated by the archdiocese and there listening to, instructing and challenging the students. The archbishop interacted well with young people and he never tired of being with them and sharing their goals and aspirations. Customarily, he met privately with the senior class with no faculty member in attendance. He asked them to express their feelings about the Church and how it could better serve them. Usually the discussions centered on confession, Christ's love and relationships with the neighbor. Later he would celebrate Holy Mass for the entire student body.

In his homily at Cathedral High School, Manning complimented the students for their sense of pride, loyalty and belonging to the school and told them that "our day has been uplifted by being among you." He spoke of Apollo 17 and its journey through space to the moon which like many other planets seems a burnt out cinder. "Yet this tiny earth in space, like a speck of dust in this room, has been favored by the Creator

It was during Manning's time as archbishop that the archdiocesan clergy assumed administrative charge of Queen of Angels Seminary.

Cardinal speaking to high schoolers in 1983.

Manning receives a plaque from students.

with life. All other planets seem to be like lamps to it. Earth has color, life, warmth. "The sun," he said, "ninety-three million miles away sends its fire and warmth to drench the earth's soil, a soil that always springs with new life. Around the earth," the archbishop continued, "there is a halo, the atmosphere, that modifies the intensity of the sun.

> This halo, this blue atmosphere around the earth, reminds us of the Blessed Mother through whom God reaches us. If God's justice were to fall on us we would wither away. But she is the one through whom God's justice comes, through whom we learn to be humble and poor, to forgive our brothers, to be clean of heart, to bear with one another, to know how to love. Go to her on your way to Christ. Every day say a Hail Mary with love, with feeling. She will change your life, this lovely Lady of Guadalupe.[9]

During his visit to Saint Bonaventure High School, Manning discussed such current issues as the role of women in the Church, changes in the Liturgy, opportunities for Confession and Reach-Out programs for teenagers. In his homily he told the youngsters that "it is impossible for me to put into words the joy and satisfaction that I have experienced here." If the senior class is typical of the school, it certainly rates very high. I know your parents must be very happy and proud of this school as you are of the Christian Church." Cardinal Manning developed the Gospel theme, "I am the Way and the Truth and the life," with emphasis on truth. He pointed to Watergate as a sad example of modern lies and told the students: "If you tell the truth you are ten feet tall."[10]

Speaking to three thousand young Holy Year pilgrims on the campus of Queen of Angels Seminary in Mission Hills, the cardinal offered a clear, simple exhortation to renewal and reconciliation in concrete, practical ways. In a reflection on a letter of Saint Paul, Manning explained the pitfalls of anger:

> All across the world there are divided nations, North and South Ireland, North and South Korea, North and South Vietnam, East and West Germany, because anger which derives from Cain and Abel has found its sway. Forgiveness, a sense of reconciliation, must be very much indicative of you, just as truth is something you owe your fellow man. We are begging you for that sense of fraternal love that is the peculiar mark of your years, of your time.

Then he spoke about cleanness of speech, noting that "there is in our entertainment today a vulgarity that is sickening. We would hope that through your dedication to the sanctification of your tongue and lips by the Eucharist you would vow never to allow an unclean word to pass your lips. Be apostles of cleanness of language."[11]

The growth of gangs in Los Angeles was a worrisome issue to Manning. He wrote to the clergy of the archdiocese on that matter, saying:

> Over the last year there has been a growing concern for the problems that result from youth gangs. Three hundred such gangs exist in the County of Los Angeles at the present time. They have resulted in deaths, community problems and alienation from the people who live and surround these young people. A major concern for us is to help those who are presently in these youth gangs, and also to help those young people who are on the brink of decision-making. They are looking and searching for a value in life and, unfortunately, find encouragement to enter into membership with these troubled youths.
>
> We urge your constant care and help in this serious matter and we also commend to you the support of the priests, Brothers and Sisters, who are working in the many parishes of this archdiocese with these troubled youths. Two Brothers from the East-side are particularly dedicated to the solution of these gang problems. Should they contact you or invite you to any meetings, I would wish to encourage you most sincerely to cooperate with them. This is a sensitive apostolate and has our deep interest and priority.[12]

Manning called upon his experience with youth for the text of an address delivered before the World Synod of Bishops at Rome in 1977. He recalled that on that occasion Pope Paul VI had encouraged young people to practice the virtue of generosity, purity, respect and sincerity as ways to build a better world than that of their elders. He called that "a catechesis of love, a ground plan of action, a program of holiness." He then went on to say:

> The signs of the times show us young people looking to relationships and a return to the two great Commandments of Christ as a God of love and to love their neighbor as themselves, rather than duty or observance only out of dis-

> cipline. They are showing a profound hunger for the spiritual. It must be realized that the catechesis of youth can take place adequately only within the wider concept of ministry to youth. This ministry begins with the adult who must be trained to deal with youth and to transmit authentic values. Adults must live the Gospel message so that young people not only understand it but see it exemplified.
>
> The next recognition is the place for youth-to-youth ministry. The training of natural leaders is vital. Some Protestant churches are ahead of us in this. Youth has a unique call by Christ to serve in the Church. Perhaps even a ceremony of commitment would be desirable. The ministry we speak of is threefold:
>
> (a) The message must be proclaimed. Doctrine and discussion suitable to youth's intellectual needs and questions must be provided. This will include the study of Scripture, the Church, the Sacraments and morality.
>
> (b) Community must be established. This gives a sense of security and of being cherished. The family and the parish are the basic models. The elements of smallness, knowing by name and participation must be present. Week-end prayer, search, encounter or retreat experiences provide a context for liturgical observance in a communal setting of acceptance and exchange.
>
> (c) Mission and service opportunities must be given. These must be substantive and adult in their challenges. Missionary call and activities must also be presented.
>
> We believe it is the duty of this Synod to read these signs of the times and to show further awareness that these youths are a substantive part of the Church. We believe it of vital importance that the youth of the world be addressed again through a vehicle of communication which is accommodated to their life-style.[13]

Speaking to 2,400 members of the Archdiocesan Council of Catholic Women, Manning said that "every child is a unique and irreplaceable gift of God. Every child is a unique masterpiece in the mind of God. In each child there is a destiny, a service, a praise to our heavenly Father that only that unique irreplaceable person can give. There is a theology of childhood," continued the cardinal, "in which Jesus relates the whole kingdom He's going to give as a gift from His heavenly father in terms of childhood." The cardinal cited scriptural reference to children like

ARCHDIOCESAN SCHOOL SUBSIDY

(Funds allocated over and above tuition)

1971	5.7 million
1972	
1973	
1974	
1975	9.8 million
1976	8.9 million
1977	7.1 million
1978	7.5 million
1979	6.8 million
1980	6.1 million
1981	6.1 million
1982	5.1 million
1983	6.3 million
1984	6.5 million
1985	6.5 million

SCHOOLS CLOSED IN THE ARCHDIOCESE OF LOS ANGELES

(During the archiepiscopate of Timothy Cardinal Manning)

Villa Cabrini Elementary - Burbank	1970
Villa Cabrini High School - Burbank	1970
Our Lady Queen of Angels - Lompoc	1970
Lasuen High School - San Pedro	1971
Saint Leo Elementary - Los Angeles	1972
Nazareth School - Van Nuys	1972
Marymount High School - Santa Barbara	1972
Pelletier High School - Los Angeles	1973
Little Flower of Jesus - Los Angeles	1974
Our Lady of Guadalupe - Santa Barbara	1974
Saint Brigid Elementary - Los Angeles	1974
Saint Victor Elementary - West Hollywood	1975
Marymount Preparatory - Palos Verdes	1975
Saint Bartholomew Elementary - Long Beach	1976
Sacred Heart - Altadena	1978
Saint Andrew High School - Pasadena	1980
Our Lady Queen of Angels Middle School	1982

olive branches about a father's table. The concept of praise is wrapped up in childhood: "Out of the mouths of babes and sucklings will come praise."

> Jesus inaugurates the kingdom by Himself becoming a child. He enters the human story, sanctifies the human family, ennobles all it stands for in terms of childhood. Then he challenges us that unless we become as little children we cannot enter into the kingdom of heaven. We, even though we have lost our innocence, must somehow again reclaim it before we can enjoy the kingdom. There is this mysterious call for reconciliation and the undoing of every perversity and waywardness that is in our human fallen nature striving out to reach that cleanness of heart . . . so that we can become totally a child. This mild, merciful Jesus was ruthless when it came to those who scandalize a child. He said it would be better for a man to have a millstone put around his neck and be carried out to deep water and dropped into the sea rather than scandalize the least of my little ones.[14]

Speaking in Spanish, at the conclusion of the 48th annual Guadalupe procession, Manning addressed a moving plea to Our Lady of Guadalupe:

> Bless our young people. Protect our young men and free them from all temptation to violence and hate. May their hearts be pure, may their conversations be full of rectitude and may their conduct be irreproachable before your eyes. Look with love on this city that loves you and intercede with your divine Son so that all of us who venerate you in this place may be together with you in the celestial city where you will be revealed in all your glory as our heavenly queen.[15]

In the nearby city of Bell, the cardinal received a gift of a black club jacket with his name stitched on the front. On the back were the words: *Los Hermanos Unidos*. To them, Manning said:

> The Church asks two things of you. First, that you not be phony, that you be for real, sincere. That's the basic thing we're asking of you. When you look your mother and father in the face, they should be able to see that you're for real. The second thing asked of you is respect. Respect begins

> when we take a second look at something. That's the meaning of the word. Take a second look at the beauty of the Church. But above all take a second look at the boy or girl next to you. Discover in them the beauty and dignity given by God. Never will God's design represented in them be repeated in any other human being. Give respect.[16]

At Hacienda Heights, where he celebrated a Mass honoring Saint John Bosco, Cardinal Manning said that Don Bosco still summoned young people to resist the technological culture characterized by "total indifference to God and Church."

> St. John was born in times of war and anti-religious strife. But there is a different kind of enemy today in our culture and our world. It's not hostile. It's just that total indifference to God and the Church . . . We live in a technological age where we don't need God. We have all that we need. And so, there is this pursuit of materialism and secularism – having things that our whole lives are consumed by. It is that particular enemy – and it is an enemy – that St. John Bosco's spirit calls on the young people of our day to resist.[17]

RELIGIOUS EDUCATION

Manning's close relationship with the work of the Confraternity of Christian Doctrine stemmed from his realization that most Catholic young people were unable, for a host of reasons, to attend the schools operated by the Archdiocese of Los Angeles. He enjoyed explaining biblical passages to those youngsters because, as he often observed, God "hides in the Holy Scriptures and gently shows us Himself, beginning with Moses and the prophets, suggesting the while that suffering is the prelude to entrance into glory."[18] Each year as fall classes for the C.C.D. began, Manning called on the priests and religious to preach on the importance of the Word of God and the duty to communicate it to others:

> With all the conviction and concern that we possess, we beg for the unstinting support of this whole catechetical program so that at least the morsels of our holy faith and the habit of simple prayer will be communicated to another generation made to the image and likeness of God.[19]

Students at Saint Michael's High School greet their chief shepherd in 1974.

Manning is welcomed at Bishop Mora Salesian High School in 1970.

Cardinal receives a spiritual bouquet from students of Saint Cyril School for his fiftieth sacerdotal anniversary.

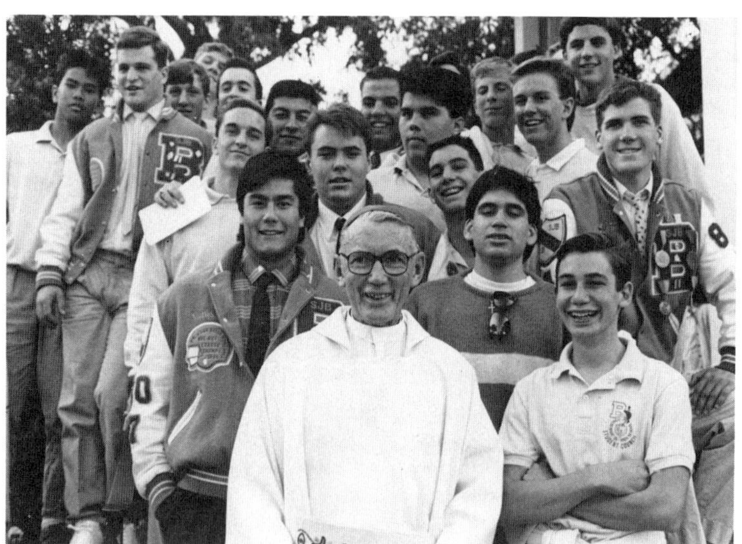

Cardinal Manning continued visiting schools even after his retirement.

Manning never missed the annual Religious Education Congress which was held at the Anaheim Convention Center. In 1972, when the golden jubilee of the Confraternity of Christian Doctrine was commemorated, the cardinal expressed "through our unworthy lips, an act of thanksgiving for all the graces of the past fifty years," for the countless thousands who have consecrated themselves to this great task of proclaiming God's message: He reiterated that "Christ is our message. We have to live, know, pray, fast and go into the desert with Him. We have to be crucified with Him. If we are to turn our faces to those to whom we would say, 'This is He,' our minds must be captured by Him and our souls drenched in Him."[20]

Manning used his homily for the young people in 1974 to report on the "listening" sessions he had been having with teenagers for the previous two years. He said it was a message of hope, of reassurance, of joy, of gratitude for such a wonderfully, generous young people, assurance that the Church of tomorrow is secure and in love. He selected five areas that surfaced in those sessions.

> The *first* of these is the liturgy. We have found among you a certain tiredness with the liturgy. Its anonymity, its monotony, the poor sermons which you hear, a lack of warmth in large congregations – all of this you have told me and, in so far as we are guilty, we priests apologize to you. And very often it is true. But at the same time, we want you to realize that Jesus declared Himself to be the temple, the altar the priest, the victim and it is through Him and with Him and in Him that we give praise and honor to our Heavenly Father. The means that He has chosen is the Mass. And, therefore, we must not ask merely what the Mass can do for us, but we must ask what we can bring to the Mass. The total surrender of ourselves to our Heavenly Father and the uniting with Christ in this great act.
>
> The *second* area that we wish to report to Jesus about is the area of confession. Your voice has been heard in the heart of the Holy Father and today has been issued an updated liturgy for confession. It is no longer a sacrament of penance, it is the sacrament of reconciliation and mercy. And for the times that we have been abrupt with you, the times that we have been unlistening to your hunger for dialogue, the anonymity behind the darkened screen in a closed box – for all of these things that have kept you away from God's mercy, we say *mea culpa, mea maxima culpa.*

> The *third* thing is the fact that both the liturgy and penance imply a deep knowledge and love of Christ; Christ, unfortunately for many of us, is simply lost in the forest of things we have learned about Him. Christ has been used on stage and screen for messages that are valid but are not the total Christ. There is only one teacher of Christ and that is the Church, the only authentic teacher; and therefore, we must try to find Him in the pages of the Gospel as He is proclaimed to us by His official ministers. When we do that, then there will be a deeper meaning to all our activity, our devotion and our relationships with one another in Christ.
>
> The *fourth* area about which you have spoken to us is the area of social concern for your brothers, Christian involvement, and we have found that in affluent areas and schools there is only an academic knowledge of poverty, of social injustice, of the things that are eating the hearts out of the poor and the lonely. And there is the danger that when we give something or do something that we have thereby satisfied our consciences, that we have quieted their claim.
>
> *Finally*, there is your relationship with the priesthood. There has been an attempt to secularize the priesthood and in that attempt something of the reverence for the priest has been lost. Now, we can assure to you, and in front of you, no greater affirmation of our concern and of our love than the presence here today of this large number of young priests whom you know and whom you know are dedicated to your services. And they are a happy band of men and that is the one assurance we can give you of the validity of our priesthood, of our joy and of our welcome to those who might be thinking about it, that it is the finest and most perfect completion of a man's destiny as he walks in this pilgrim journey toward the Lord.[21]

In his greeting to participants at the 1977 congress, Manning portrayed the event "as dear to the heart."

> It is a time of spiritual significance: laity and priests and religious - the Church itself - coming together to share in learning processes, more fervent prayer experiences, and that indescribable inner peace and joy wherein we are called to dwell by the Spirit of the Lord. It is an all too brief three days in which to refresh the soul before returning to our

HIGH SCHOOL ENROLLMENT

YEAR	Archdiocesan Schools	Parochial Schools	Total Schools	Archdiocesan Students	Parochial Students	Total Students
1970	28	11	39	21,458	6,141	27,599
1972	27	11	38	19,620	5,635	25,255
1973	27	11	38	18,872	5,431	24,303
1974	27	11	38	18,910	5,501	24,411
1975	27	11	38	18,793	5,416	24,209
1976	27	11	38	19,204	5,435	24,639
1977	25	11	36	17,107	5,484	22,591
1978	25	11	36	17,314	5,559	22,873
1979	25	11	36	18,370	3,985	22,355
1981	27	6	33	18,216	3,861	22,077
1982	27	6	33	18,190	3,836	22,026
1983	27	6	33	17,785	3,783	21,568
1984	27	6	33	17,721	4,355	22,076
1985	27	6	33	18,090	3,748	21,838

ELEMENTARY SCHOOL ENROLLMENT

YEAR	SCHOOLS	ENROLLMENT
1971	264	107,064
1972	264	106,877
1973	264	97,981
1974	262	93,402
1975	262	92,610
1976	262	90,858
1977	231	75,954
1978	228	76,032
1979	226	75,209
1980	226	74,356
1982	226	83,801
1983	226	72,919
1984	226	71,938
1985	226	70,942

> homes, our offices, our classrooms. It is a moment of time, focusing on a love so great that we are awed by its beauty and humbled by its message. It is a time when dedicated people renew their determination to pursue Jesus' command, "come, follow me."[22]

Manning told the teachers attending the 1978 congress that "the single, credible potency of what we say is the fact that we ourselves in our personal lives have encountered Christ, have listened to His words and have loved His person. Then and only then," the cardinal observed, "can we turn to our classes and to our people and say: 'Be followers of me as I am of Jesus and Him crucified.'" He also noted that the recent Synod of Bishops had proclaimed that the work of catechesis was of the highest priority in the Church and that it required the primacy of three elements:

> The *first* was that catechetics could adequately be performed and fulfilled only in terms of community, the original cell of which is the family, and then within the larger community, the parish, but not independently of it. In that community, everyone, priests, bishops, parents, adults, everyone is involved in the totality of catechesis.
>
> The *second* essential of catechesis is that the core of catechesis is the mystery of the Person of Christ as found in the institution of the Church. The core of catechesis is knowing Christ, His Person, His mystery and His mystic involvement.
>
> The *third* element in catechesis is that for the promulgation of its content there must be personal commitment to Christ. The effectiveness of catechesis requires a witnessing of Christ. Catechetics may involve the skill of words and a great knowledge of truths, but the total force of our catechetical vocation is in giving witness to Christ and to Him crucified.[23]

In 1979, the cardinal asked religious educators to renew their affection and loyalty to the teaching authority of the Church. He also asked them to bring back to young people a sense of reverence for God, saying that "it's missing. It's missing from our communities, from our gatherings. We're taking God and His holy things for granted. By that I mean that there must be a reverence for silence; there is a reverence of modesty."

> Sometimes we're shocked through and through at the lack of that sense of modesty today by those who are pursuing the fashions of the world. For God's sake, bring back that sense of awe and wonder and reverence in the presence of God. It cannot come except you yourselves walk daily in God's presence. You are the custodians of His word. Walk before Him humbly, gratefully and in that sense of wonder at God's Holy way with us.

At that gathering there were 1,500 men and women presented for commissioning as catechists, 700 were Hispanic and 200 were trained in classes conducted in Spanish. They had qualified for their commission by completing fifty hours of instruction and finishing two sessions of supervised teaching and two of teacher observation. Among that group were twelve young men who were seniors at Loyola High School. "Christ has a very special place for those who are going to be His witnesses," the cardinal told the catechists who filled the cathedral on that unseasonably warm evening. "He has reserved in His heart a particular place for those who are witnesses to Him in the world."[24]

Two years later, Manning spoke about the need for healing the wounds in American society. In particular, he singled out the pornography industry that was pouring millions into the hands of abominable people in our culture, "thus defiling the souls of our young people."

> For God's sake, let's cut that out of our lives, out of our homes, so that we're not tainted with that surge of passion and sensuality. Lust is what Jesus called it. Lust is what John Paul II called it, and the world laughed at him . . . Only the clean of heart can see God.[25]

The cardinal, before beginning his spoken homily, turned to a section of the arena where hard of hearing persons were gathered with their interpreters. Manning spoke to them briefly in sign language. The hard of hearing men and women gasped with surprise and joy as they suddenly recognized that the cardinal was signing to them.

In announcing the congress for 1982, Manning said that it had "a dimension which distinguishes it from any other religious, social or educational gathering. It has a primacy of importance. On its outcome much of the spiritual well-being of the whole local Church exists. He said: "Let there be prayers for its success, attention to its proposals and gratitude to God for the wonderful servants of the truth who inspire and

Cardinal honored as "home-boy" in South Central barrio.

Cardinal Manning at his annual Christmas party, 1980.

Manning shown among students from Bishop Mora Salesian.

The cardinal was always at ease with children.

direct its posture."[26] Two years later, in his last message, Manning offered "thanks to God for the gift of the Religious Education Congress. It is an affirmation and a witnessing to the abiding truth that the Lord is with us." At this gathering, "the Lord walks among us once more."[27]

Notes to the Text

1. *Catholic High School Quarterly Bulletin* VIII (January, 1951), 41-42.
2. *The Tidings*, August 24, 1973.
3. *Ibid.*, April 15, 1977.
4. *Ibid.*, June 22, 1979.
5. Los Angeles *Times*, September 4, 1979.
6. *The Tidings*, August 27, 1982.
7. *Ibid.*, January 29, 1982.
8. *Ibid.*, January 28, 1983.
9. *Ibid.*, December 15, 1972.
10. *Ibid.*, May 10, 1974.
11. *Ibid.*, November 8, 1974.
12. AALA, Timothy Manning to Clergy, Los Angeles, June 28, 1976.
13. *The Tidings*, October 14, 1977.
14. *Ibid.*, October 19, 1979.
15. *Ibid.*, December 14, 1979.
16. *Ibid.*, December 21, 1979.
17. *Ibid.*, January 29, 1988.
18. AALA, Taken from an address given at the 65th annual meeting of the National Catholic Educational Association, April 15, 1968.
19. AALA, Timothy Manning to Clergy, Los Angeles, n.d. (1970).
20. *The Tidings*, February 25, 1972.
21. Francis J. Weber (comp.), *Times of Tension. Moments of Grace* (Los Angeles, 1990), Pp. 280-281.
22. AALA, Timothy Cardinal Manning to Friends, Los Angeles, February, 1977.
23. *The Tidings*, February 10, 1978.
24. *Ibid.*, May 18, 1979.

25. *Ibid.*, February 20, 1981.
26. *Ibid.*, March 5, 1982.
27. AALA, Timothy Cardinal Manning to Lloyd Torgerson, Los Angeles, January 17, 1984.

17. *Devotional Matters*

Throughout his eighty years, Cardinal Manning lived a very carefully ordered life and he endeavored to imprint the advantage of such a lifestyle to others. Especially did he feel the need for structure in the spiritual realm. He often referred to and endorsed the Pauline injunction about the need for doing all things according to order.

LITURGY

Cardinal Manning once observed that "my whole life is liturgically-orientated and I have great love and respect for the liturgy."[1] That appreciation for the liturgy dated back to the days when Manning served as Master of Ceremonies for Archbishop John J. Cantwell. One of the clerical elders recalled that "ceremonies conducted under Manning's direction were always letter perfect" and that "attention to detail characterized his own future life as bishop, archbishop and cardinal."[2]

The 1970s were critical times for the liturgy and Manning wanted to codify and unify its performance in the Archdiocese of Los Angeles. He felt that the new constitution was "too much of a culture shock. Had it moved along more slowly, there would have been less opposition."[3] Another clerical observer credited Manning with having "a very good instinct for how much change people can handle. He introduced the reforms slowly, so that the people had a chance to adjust."[4]

One of Manning's first actions as archbishop was to issue a pastoral letter in which he proclaimed "the primacy of the liturgy in our pastoral administration." He pointed out that "pastors of souls" should realize that it is "their duty to ensure that the faithful take part knowingly, actively and fruitfully" in the liturgical life of the Church. He looked upon his own role as that of "principal dispenser of the mysteries of God . . . the governor, promoter and guardian of the entire liturgical life in the Church."

He said his "first concern" was to quiet the anxieties of those, whether clergy or laity, who are disturbed by the liturgical changes mandated by Vatican Council II. He invoked, "with Pope Paul, a punctual and unanimous observance" of the new reforms. At the same time, he denounced "any arbitrary abuses of these norms, any unauthorized experimentation." Only careful observance of approved and "authentic traditions of the Church are preserved, what is immutable remains, the validity of the Mass and sacraments is untouched." He concluded by saying that "whatever is permitted by our National Conference of Bishops and authorized by our own Liturgical Commission, is hereby heartily approved and encouraged."[5]

Under the chairmanship of Auxiliary Bishop John J. Ward and the watchful eye of Msgr. Lawrence Gibson, the Archdiocesan Commission for the Liturgy issued a series of twenty-two newsletters and fifty Liturgical bulletins between March 15, 1970 and December 15, 1973, the tenth anniversary of the conciliar Constitution on the Sacred Liturgy. No fewer than fifteen clergy conferences devoted to discussions and instructions on the liturgy were held during that period.

Manning had something more in mind and in mid 1972, he appointed a Task Force "to provide for the description and organization of a revised Liturgical Commission." The document produced by the Task Force went through the usual channels, with Manning making only some minor additions. As revised, the document was "in accord with the mind of the Church" and expressed "the active concern of the presbyterate for sustaining and growth of the liturgical life" in the local Church. The structure of the committee, which was to be advisory and executive, had both an educational and catalytic style:

> It shall consist of twelve members including priests, men and women religious, laymen and laywomen, ethnic and language groups, as well as students. Members will be appointed by the archbishop from a list supplied by a nominating committee. The term of office is three years, renewable once consecutively at the option of the archbishop. The chairman should be elected by the members, subject to confirmation by the archbishop. The commission shall have an executive secretary appointed by the archbishop. It should meet regularly once a month, except July and August. It will have three standing subcommittees on music, art and liturgical building. It will maintain constant liaison with the Priests' Senate.[6]

Late in 1974, the cardinal made his move. As a means of emphasizing the growing importance he attached to correct "modes of worship," he implemented the full reorganization at the Archdiocesan Commission for the Liturgy in such a fashion that he personally occupied its chairmanship. He defied and thereby altered local tradition by selecting a veteran school teacher, the highly respected Sister Miriam Joseph Larkin, to act as executive secretary. Her duties were to coordinate the office work, training programs and major liturgical celebrations. She was to be the liaison with the educational departments and prepare agenda and input collated from consultants for consideration by the cardinal.

> Among her educational, executive and advisory functions were:
>
> 1. to be informed on pastoral liturgical action and the needs of the people;
> 2. to implement official documents carefully throughout the archdiocese, to coordinate liturgical directives from different commissions and education offices for a unified archdiocesan policy, to keep abreast of current liturgical, spiritual, and pastoral research and obtain information on studies and programs for an ever-enriching, vital, and ongoing program of archdiocesan renewal and catechesis;
> 3. to provide liturgical and spiritual formation for the clergy, religious, and laity through workshops, seminars, conferences, aids, in-service education, and curriculum for each area;
> 4. to train and educate parish worship personnel and religion educators, and prepare a general liturgical catechesis and ministry formation to enable all pilgrim people to live the mystery of Christ with an ever-fresh perspective and to be a sign of hope in their concern and love for all.

Manning thereafter used the medium of the commission's newsletter "to communicate the progressing spirit of the liturgy and items of information that assist in this worthy exemplification." In the issue for October, 1976, for example, he thanked the faithful for their reception of the catechesis for the Revised Rite of Penance. Then he listed some of the projects which would be discussed and promulgated by the commission in the years ahead, noting that sub-committees had already been formed in the areas of children's liturgy, youth ministry, parish worship and spirituality. He recommended the use of the Liturgy of the Hours for parish worship, the better training of lectors, the need for quality daily and Sunday homilies, the norms for reading the Gospel and preaching, the abolition of Ember days and the retention of paraliturgical celebrations.[7] For each of the sets of guidelines issued between 1974 and 1985, Manning appended a personal letter.

Though he disliked making negative statements, the cardinal felt the need for speaking out about liturgical abuses when they surfaced. He was especially upset by the "orthodox Roman Catholic Movement, Inc." which advocated using formats for confecting the Eucharist which were either outdated or abbreviated. Appealing to a decision from the Congregation of Divine Worship, which states clearly that henceforth only the Order of the Mass as contained in the 1969 edition of the Roman Missal of Pope Paul VI would be allowed, he cautioned Catholics "that they may not participate in liturgies that are contrary to this instruction" noting that "to do so involves contempt for the Holy See."[8]

In the first year of operation, the secretary established what became a state-of-the-art-library of liturgical resources which were made available to parishes and other interested parties. Upwards of 2,400 written requests were processed and monthly mailings were begun for 3,500 recipients. Fifty-four consultants were involved as resources for the commission, parish workshops and seminars, in-service training, institutes and conferences were sponsored, some of them for an inter-diocesan audience. Among the topics discussed in the newsletter were directives for Catholic burials, Rite of Anointing, catechesis on Penance, celebration of the Eucharist, training for cantors and instructing special ministers of the Eucharist.

Writing in the first of a long series of newsletters, he told the faithful that this valuable "link" between him and his people had as its purpose "to keep abreast of the enriching lights that will be shed for the better understanding of the liturgy, to supply information and direction as requested and to set a time of dignity through which we shall be nourished."

Manning was careful to note that no newsletter, commission, or directive would achieve its purpose unless there be in the recipient a prior profound faith in the Eucharist and a daily striving for holiness through the Mass and the Liturgy of the Hours. Otherwise, we are but sounding brass. Liturgical renewal is counterfeit unless it is a correlative of personal renewal. Then the people of God and His ministers will give proper glory to the Almighty. We make our own the opening words of the Constitution: "It is the goal of this most sacred Council to intensify the daily growth of Catholics in Christian living." [9]

Members of the commission provided weekly articles for *The Tidings* on various liturgical themes. Late in 1974, Sister Miriam Joseph suggested to Manning that Father Charles Miller be commissioned to write a permanent weekly essay on some aspect of the liturgy, a proposal that Manning[10] readily endorsed and which continued until 1995.

The cardinal encouraged the commission to prepare a set of guidelines for children's liturgies which he envisioned could be celebrated at regular intervals during the school year and on such occasions as First Communion and other sacred times. In his letter accompanying the guidelines, Manning cautioned that:

> Great care and sensitivity must be exercised in the preparation and exemplification of these rites. They must lead naturally to ultimate participation in the adult Sunday liturgies. Class Masses, therefore, and student body Masses should acquire a dimension of grave importance in the eyes of the children. These smaller units must lead to more comprehensive liturgies which parallel the Sunday liturgy.[11]

With the appearance of the weekly liturgy columns in the pages of *The Tidings*, the cardinal preferred to let the "experts" speak on the various aspects of divine worship. Occasionally, he would offer a reflection, such as the one he wrote on "Why the Church Blesses Throats." After asking if "it is an outmoded and superstitious practice, totally irrelevant to the well-being of our throats," he suggested that, in reality, the blessing contained "a gem of truth that is conducive to our spiritual relationship with our Creator."

> All blessings are under the control of the Church. They are sacred signs, a language of signs that render holy various occasions of life. All created things must be surrendered to the Creator as their author. What a complex and wonderful part of anatomy is the throat. A casual glance at a medical book awes us with the complexity, the control, the "engineering" of this organ. Reflect on the astounding gift of voice alone. These considerations convince me of my duty to thank my God for this gift, to so exercise and use it that it gives praise to my Creator and not insult by its abuse.
>
> Is there a better way in which to show this gratitude than to go on my knees, let priestly hands hold blessed candles to my throat, invoke a saint who is my surrogate before the Lord and, in that dependency of posture and sign, surrender

> this organ to the will of my Creator and ask Him to bless it? My life vibrates in my throat. The pressure of a few fingers into its structure could snuff out my life. As a free man, I bow my head before my God and once more affirm in His sight my dependence on Him and my grateful love.[12]

In 1976, the distinguished Dominican theologian, Father Yves Congar, a member of the International Theological Commission, suggested that the Holy See re-allow the celebration of the Tridentine Mass as a mark of "reconciliation" to the followers of Archbishop Marcel Lefebvre.[13] Rome moves slowly and it was another decade before Pope John Paul II, on October 3, 1984, issued an indult whereby the Tridentine Mass could once again be celebrated. Manning arranged to have one Mass offered weekly at different locales in the archdiocese. In every case, a non-parochial church or chapel was selected and, initially, only those who petitioned directly to the cardinal were allowed to attend the services. Petitioners were asked to sign the following declaration:

CLERGY REQUEST FOR THE USE OF THE ROMAN MISSAL OF 1962

Your Eminence:

May I respectfully request to take advantage of the indult to attend the Holy Sacrifice of the Mass using the Roman Missal issued March 2, 1962. In consideration of this request and in order to comply with the conditions contained in the Instructions from the Congregation of Divine Worship, I make the following statement of facts:

1. I solemnly declare that I do not share the position of those who reject the legitimacy and the doctrinal integrity of the Roman Missal promulgated by Pope Paul VI in 1970 and now in use.
2. The Roman Missal of 1962 will be used exclusively together with its assigned texts and its General Rubrics. There is no intermingling of the assigned texts of the Roman Missal of 1962 with the Roman Missal approved in 1970.
3. Celebration of the Holy Sacrifice of the Mass using the Roman Missal of 1962 will be made only for the benefit of my group requesting it.
4. My reasons for the petition are:

Signature [14]

This statue of our Lady of Angels looks out on Wilshire Boulevard from Saint Basil's church.

This Byzantine panel portraying the Annunication, executed in mosaic by Isabel Piczek, was placed above the entrance of the old Plaza Church as part of the Los Angeles bicentennial celebration, 1981.

At San Fernando Mission, one of the places designated for the Tridentine celebration, the first Mass was held on May 5, 1985. About 350 people turned up to take part in the Mass offered in accordance with the March 2, 1962 printing of the *Missale Romanum*. Manning authorized the return of the Tridentine Mass with little enthusiasm, because he felt personally that the advantages of a vernacular liturgy far outweighed the return of the Latin.

During the ensuing years, the Archdiocesan Commission for Liturgy gained a national reputation and its executive secretary was frequently called upon to conduct workshops and training sessions throughout the country. She was also elected to the Federation of Diocesan Liturgy Commissions for Liturgy representing Region XI. The bulletins and newsletters of the commission were widely circulated and, on more than one occasion, Cardinal Manning was commended by Roman officials for the efficient manner in which the Archdiocese of Los Angeles had implemented the liturgical spirit of Vatican Council II.

A measure of the thoroughness and breadth of the commission's activities can be gauged by the bound volume of the archdiocesan Quinquennial Report for December 31, 1982. The appendix to that 134 page report, devoted entirely to a summary of liturgical activities, amounted to an additional 130 pages!

Through all those years, the cardinal retained his position as chair of the commission. His view of liturgical renewal could be summed up in a little-known "decalogue of suggestions" which Pope Paul VI released from Castel Gandolfo on August 22, 1973. Manning referred to this decalogue in many of his talks and it is worth repeating in its entirety:

> The first rule is to follow the Second Vatican Council's liturgical reforms faithfully, intelligently and diligently.
>
> The second is to learn the scriptural, theological and pastoral teachings of the Church about divine worship.
>
> The third law enjoins great caution in reforming traditional religious customs of the people. Otherwise, one might extinguish religious feeling in the very act of clothing it with new and more authentic religious expressions.
>
> The fourth says: The family must be a great school of piety, of spirituality and of religious fidelity. The Church has great trust in the delicate, authoritative action of parents in the field of religious education. For their action there is no substitute.
>
> The fifth states: The precept of Mass on Sundays and holy days maintains, more than ever, its gravity and its basic

> importance. The Church has made concessions to make its observation easier. Whoever realizes the content and role of this precept must consider it not only a primary duty but a right . . .
>
> The sixth reaffirms the right of the constituted community – by which he meant the parish – to the presence of all its faithful.
>
> The seventh, directed to priests, declared that the celebration of Mass must be prepared and carried out with great care, under every aspect.
>
> The eighth, directed to those hearing Mass, urged punctuality, quiet dignity, and, above all, participation.
>
> The ninth noted that the fullness of prayer should be both personal and collective.
>
> The tenth exhortation preserving the Gregorian chant in Latin for some of the principal parts of the Mass: the *Gloria*, the *Credo*, the *Sanctus* and the *Agnus Dei*.[15]

Though priest members of the commission occasionally attempted to undercut Sister Miriam Joseph's work, she remained at her post until the end of the Manning regime. In a final letter, the cardinal said that "since February, 1974, you have unceasingly dedicated yourself and your exquisite talents in the service of the Church in our office. The nobility of our liturgical occurrences derives from your inspiration and preparation. We will not again experience its like."[16]

MARIAN DEVOTION

Timothy Manning's devotion to Mary, the Mother of God, was expressed by a single word which he had emblazoned on his episcopal shield in 1946 and which is the title of this book - *Magnificat*. Just as Mary portrayed herself as the handmaid of the Lord, so did Manning see his ministerial role as one of service to God and His people.

During his years as archbishop, Manning used every opportunity to speak and write about Mary and her place in the contemporary Church. His first and last utterances as Chief Shepherd of the southland were tributes to Mary. His initial pastoral "to the beloved clergy, religious and faithful of the archdiocese" was a reminder that during May "our hearts are stirred with the instinct of an ancient faith to do her honor. A tenderness enters our weary souls and we yearn to be enfolded within her maternal arms:"

> We are surfeited with human wisdom and computerized knowledge. Novel theologies and self-accredited moralists leave us but bewildered. We are the poor of Yahweh, the foolish and the weak things of the world, and we cry for the comfort of our heavenly Mother. Let us gather around her to sing her praises and plead her intercession.
>
> We assent to all the beautiful truths told about her in the lovely Eighth Chapter of the Decree on the Church issued by the Second Vatican Council. The Fathers of the council wove a robe of light and beauty for her with texts from the Sacred Scriptures and truths from the deposit of faith. Our Holy Father has proclaimed her to be the Mother of the Church and we in this city invoke her in the endearing title of Our Lady of the Angels.
>
> She is the first-born of the redeemed, the archetype of the pilgrim Church, the model of the Beatitudes, more blessed in hearing and keeping the word of God than housing Him in her womb and nursing Him at her breasts. She is the Bible; the Old Testament, pregnant and heavy with His promise and His coming; the New Testament in which He is revealed and known. Her *Magnificat* is the song of the beloved to her lover, which is the voice of our liturgy. She is the ultimate sign of orthodoxy and no unity will occur until the knowledge and love of her is clearly admitted.
>
> Her icons are pawns for the full return of the eastern churches. She is first witness that Christ is the Lord. All education is but the revealing love of Christ, just as a mother's self is known and loved by the child in her arms. All truth of revelation is summed up in her and it is this truth only that makes men free. Devotion to Our Lady is mandatory. It is a mandate of our love. This letter of ours is an anguished cry for a return to a childlike regard for her.[17]

Each May for the remainder of his tenure, Manning wrote a pastoral reflection on Mary. The one for 1971 told how every Catholic is summoned to give unreserved assent to truths taught by the Church, to respect ecclesial authority in moral and disciplinary matters and to emulate Mary as a model of religious vocation.

> Our Blessed Lady is the personification of the great charter of the Church formulated in the Sermon on the Mount and fulfilled in the invitation to follow Jesus. The only approved way is to take up the daily cross and walk in His footsteps. Suffering is the prelude and condition to glory. The seed must die before it brings forth fruit.
>
> As the chief shepherd of the archdiocese, we are urged from many segments to proclaim certain devotions to Our Lady for the month of May. With no misgivings we have shied away from the mass gatherings that were formerly a sign and ornament of our faith. Rather do we urge the regional or parish celebrations which will involve more of the faithful, need less of the artificial preparation, and give ventilation to the spontaneous love in our hearts for our dearest Mother. Finally, we ask for the charity of our people' s prayers to Our Lady for the one who must bear the lonely and awesome burden of shepherding God's people. May he be faithful and constant in proclaiming the Gospel of Christ, loyal in obedience to the successor of St. Peter, the Apostle, a devoted father to the priests and deacons, a man of kindness and compassion to the poor and to the stranger and to those who stray. May he be a lover of Our Lady and, in being so, be all else besides.[18]

Manning was among those who felt that the conciliar Fathers of Vatican II should have issued a separate document on the Blessed Mother, rather than include mention of her in the dogmatic constitution on the Church.[19] There were those who seized upon that omission as a rationale for downgrading Marian devotion. Speaking at Saint Therese church in Portland, Oregon, Manning noting that "many truths of the church are centered on the Blessed Virgin." He thought it was "a tragedy that Mary has been removed from some religious devotions." At an outdoor Mass, he declared that "love for her has been stolen out of the hearts of little children." He worried that many Catholics attending the ceremonies didn't even own a rosary. "What better way to go to eternal life than as a child of Mary," he asked. He concluded by saying that "when you think about our Blessed Lady, you think of all the truths of the Church.[20]

In a statement issued a few days later, Manning asked each Catholic family in the archdiocese to pray the rosary every day during October:

> The recitation of the rosary is urged earnestly in each home and community during the month of October. As a special intention we propose the return to a sense of modesty in dress, especially in church and in the approach to the Blessed Sacrament. Mary having entered intimately into salvation history, in some way unites and echoes the great teachings of faith, and while her glories are preached and she is venerated, she calls the believers to her Son and His sacrifice and to the love of the Father.[21]

Wanting to make a major, public gesture of his devotion to Mary and the place of Our Lady of Guadalupe in the spiritual heritage of the Golden State, Manning decided to lead a pilgrimage to Our Lady's National Shrine in Mexico City, where California's first bishop, Fray Francisco Garcia Diego y Moreno, was consecrated. He said that the purpose of the pilgrimage was to pay homage to Our Lady and to thank the Mexican people for their role in bedrocking the faith in California. This pilgrimage would be an acknowledgment of the affinity of this archdiocese and its people with Mexico "from which we drew our origins."[22] It had been exactly thirty years earlier that young Father Timothy Manning had accompanied Archbishop John J. Cantwell to Mexico City for a similar manifestation of solidarity with the Mexican people.

Almost 200 pilgrims joined Manning, his two auxiliaries and dozens of priests who left Los Angeles on December 8 to thank Mary "for her maternal blessings upon California and to pray for a new springtime of faith rooted in California from Mexico." In his homily that evening at the historic Metropolitan Cathedral in the *Distrito Federal,* which was outfitted with thousands of Christmas lights and a seven story tableau portraying children at the crib in Bethlehem, Manning said "Our Lady of Guadalupe told Juan Diego to go first to the bishop. It is very important for us that before we go to her shrine we go first to the Chair of the archbishop to make our profession of faith, to profess our belief on this day in the Immaculate Conception. We have come here to venerate Our Lady as the most beautiful woman in all creation."

Next morning, the pilgrims went to the Basilica of Our Lady of Guadalupe and it was there that a five year old youngster from Los Angeles, Jimmy Powers, was confirmed and given the name "Timothy" after the archbishop. Manning's homily touched all the bases:

> When Our Blessed Lady appeared, she appeared as the mother of all America and all its peoples – and she was so

> designated by the Holy Father. No matter where we come from, we come as members of one family to lay our hearts at her feet. We of Los Angeles have special reason for coming to her because this is the cradle of the Church in California. Here in this basilica in 1840 the first bishop of California, Francisco Garcia Diego, was consecrated a bishop. His diocese included all California, Arizona, Utah and Nevada. Prior to that a total of 127 priests came from the College of San Fernando in Mexico City to evangelize California. So the faith we profess and love in California began at her feet.
>
> When she came she approached the poorest of the Indians. Today we have what the pope has called a "hellish circle of poverty." We ask her to look compassionately on the poor. We beg her to look pityingly on us and protect our priests, for too many have left the active service with broken hearts for other fields. We ask her to have pity at what is happening in our ranks. We present to her our petition that we have a hopeful springtime through her intercession to move young hearts to come and serve her Son.

The rest of the pilgrimage was equally spiritual in tone. Everyone made the climb to Tepeyac, visiting all the beautiful chapels on the mount. Manning was heard to say "all children should be born Mexican and remain so at least until age fifteen."[23]

Some of Manning's most insightful utterances were simple observations that went unrecorded. One that received wide coverage in the Catholic press was entitled simply "*Ave Maria*."

> She herself proclaimed that all generations would call her blessed. Every land and tongue give praises to her. The wonder and beauty of nature are borrowed for images to convey her loveliness. Words cascade in poetry and prose to honor her. Months and times and seasons are set apart for her dowry. Her name is appropriated by men and women to insure her care. Art in all its forms is summoned to portray the longing for her which lies at the heart of a pilgrim in a passing world. Prototypes from the history of salvation are accommodated to her.
>
> But nothing can quite reach the essence of the honor which is her due. The Divine Majesty sent an archangel-ambassador to do her homage. All mankind's genius cannot

> outdo the greeting of God on His messenger's lips – "*Ave Maria.*" And so we repeat it again and again, told fifty times over. We punctuate its decades by outbursts of glory to the Blessed Trinity. We look at mental pictures of her and her Son in the mysteries of joy and sorrow and glory that reveal His way with us.[24]

The Feast of Our Lady of the Angels, known throughout the Catholic world as "Portiuncula Day" was celebrated in the Seraphic calendar on August 2. It is important to Los Angeles because it was on the vigil of that feastday in 1769 that European explorers first arrived in the area. Fray Juan Crespi recorded in his diary that "the explorers crossed an *arroyo* of muddy water and stopped a little further on in a wide clearing." Crespi stated that the next day was one of rest "for the purpose of exploring, and especially to celebrate the jubilee of Our Lady of Los Angeles de Portiuncula."[25] First the river and then the village came to be known as Los Angeles and thereafter the titular feastday of the city of *Nuestra Señora de los Angeles* was observed on August 2.

Manning thought it would be appropriate to change the feastday of *Nuestra Señora de los Angeles de Portiuncula* to September 4 which, since 1781, had been observed as the city's birth date. He petitioned the Sacred Congregation for the Sacraments and Divine Worship to that effect and, in 1981, received official authorization.[26] Manning happily told press that "on this bicentennial year to perpetuate the sacred origins of the founding of our city, the "feast of Our Lady of the Angels will be hereafter observed each year on September 4."[27]

It was also about this time that Manning asked for and received authorization to restore the Feast of Our Lady, Refuge of Sinners, to the local calendar on July 5. Bishop Francisco Garcia Diego had declared that Our Lady under that title was to be the Patroness of the Californias on January 4, 1843.[28]

Manning rarely missed occasions to speak about Mary. He told an annual conference of the Los Angeles Archdiocesan Council of Catholic Women that "it is time to bring back the old devotion to Mary." He singled out "Mary's title Ark of the Covenant," which he said was "a sign of God's presence among His people. She is the perfect evangelizer. Without her presence, we cannot reach out with the arms of the Lord to all people." Noting that Marian devotions had faded in recent years, the cardinal urged the women to help revive them, particularly regular praying of the Rosary. "We must teach our children to venerate her," he added. Mary's benign presence, he concluded, can counter the evils of the present day.[29]

While in Mexico City, on his pilgrimage to the Shrine of Our Lady of Guadalupe, Archbishop Manning met members of the Garcia Diego family. Fray Francisco Garcia Diego y Moreno, the first Bishop of Both Californias, was consecrated in the shrine of Our Lady in October of 1840.

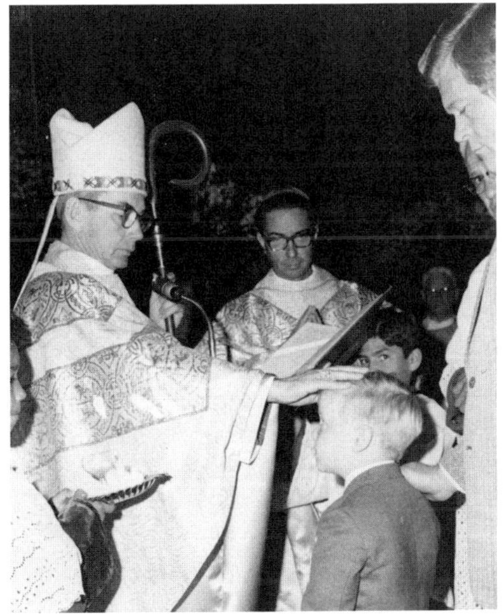

Archbishop confirms at Tepeyac.

In one of his first pilgrimages, Archbishop Manning led a group of several hundred people to the Shrine of Our Lady of Guadalupe in Mexico City.

Los Angeles pilgrims are met at Tepeyac in Mexico City.

In his homily at a meeting of the Institute of Religious Life held at San Marino, the cardinal spoke on the encyclical *Redemptoris Mater* which had just been released by Pope John Paul II for the Marian Year.. He noted that the most important teaching in that encyclical was Mary's obedience of faith. At the Annunciation, the Visitation, the Presentation in the Temple, at Cana in Galilee and on Mount Calvary, it was Mary's obedience of faith, her total trust in and submission to the will of God, which the Church praises and calls on Christians to imitate. Religious, he said, by their consecration to God by vows of poverty, chastity and obedience make a special act of entrustment to God's divine Providence and His holy will. "Mary is the special model who will help them carry out their consecration in the love of God."[30]

In 1985, in response to a query as to "why the Assumption of Mary is a Church dogma," Manning wrote a brief message for the archdiocesan newspaper:

> The Assumption of Our Blessed Lady into heavenly glory was defined as a dogma of faith by His Holiness, Pope Pius XII, on November 1, 1950. The fact of her bodily assumption was a constant belief among Christian people. Like a seed in the ground, it was part of the original deposit of faith given to the apostles but came to full flowering only in our own time. The date of the definition is significant. It was at the midway point of the twentieth century. This, our century, has been one of unceasing wars, two of which were classified as world wars. A sense of despair had entered our time. Human life was sacrificed to the gods of war. Men and women in military services were shattered to death on the earth, on the sea and in the sky. Civilian populations were annihilated or devastated by the instruments of war. Life was cheap, expendable and aimless.
>
> While the definition of her Immaculate Conception was designated as a "singular" privilege, unique to her, that word was not used in the definition of her Assumption, because it is a privilege that will be given to all who die in God's favor. She is the first of the redeemed. How good God is to us, to invest in her this gift which becomes the dawning of our hope of resurrection.
>
> Another latent reason for the definition was to counteract the debasing of the flesh of womankind in our modern culture. Grasping the sensuality of fallen nature, her body has been used as a vehicle for commercial advertising and a lure

> for the flesh magazines that drag her down. To restore this sense of dignity, the doctrine of the Assumption upholds the glory of womankind through whom the all-holy God became incarnate, flesh from her flesh. Blessed is the womb that bore Him and the breasts that nursed Him. In her too, all her sex is blessed, blessed as the source of our bodily lives, the inspiration of all that is good in an unholy world and the certain hope that in this flesh we too shall see our God as He is.[31]

As the years rolled on, Manning noted a gradual resurgence in devotion to the rosary "because confusion has been cleared up about whether praying to Mary was considered appropriate. People have gotten wise to the fact that there was no downgrading of Mary, the Mother of God, in our religious life." He observed that "now people are beginning to realize the inherent beauty of the rosary, it is contemplative, vocal and brings people together, especially in community prayers."[32]

Fittingly, Manning's last address was at Mary's Hour which was held at the Hollywood Bowl on May 21,1989. His listeners knew he was dying and their response was truly moving:

> In response to the theme of this Mary's Hour, namely a reflection on the Immaculate Conception, and also the discipleship of our baptism, we would invite you for a few moments to reflect with me on the meeting of Christ and His mother which we celebrate on the fourth Station of the Cross. To human eyes this was a very, very sad and mournful occasion, the earthly mother seeing her innocent Son led to His execution.
>
> She who had seen Him grow from childhood, through adolescence into young manhood remembered all the endearing things of their life together, kept them all in her heart as the scripture said. Now without complaint she follows Him to His death. From the eyes of Christ there is something much more beautiful. We are told in the doctrine that defines the Immaculate Conception that the Lord God anticipated the sufferings of Christ and applied them to Mary at the moment of her conception. So that when she was conceived she was free from any stain of original sin and the power of evil had no force over her.
>
> When Jesus' eyes rested on her there on that sad journey, what He saw was not only the Sorrowful Mother, but He saw

that single solitary radiance, eternal beauty shining from her soul, created there by God. The painter Murillo in the Prado in Madrid had tried to capture some of that in the great painting of the Immaculate Conception, seeing her as God might have seen her before the foundation of the world, a surpassing beauty that was ready for her because of the passion of His son.

Mary is the model of the Church. Just as she conceived Christ without human intervention, without human agency, so also the Church our mother brings us into the life of grace without human intervention because we accept and believe something that comes from God. That is how we become her children. That is why she is presented to us as our mother at the foot of the cross. Therefore each member of the Church, each one baptized, has to walk behind the Lord on that journey to the cross believing, loving, hoping, trusting in His all holy wisdom, His all holy providence, holding our hands in hers and crying out to her from the depth of our being: Holy Mary, Mother of God, pray for us sinners now, and at the hour of our death. Amen.[33]

HILL OF HOPE

Among the more colorful but aggravating ecclesial problems that surfaced in Southern California during the early 1970s related to Frances Klug, "a Placentia housewife of unpretentious manner and simple dress" who claimed that she was receiving "messages from heaven," especially from Saint Joseph.[34] According to her own testimony, made in a series of interviews, "God, Jesus and the saints began speaking through her about 1967."[35] She envisioned herself as "the vehicle for the admonition and advice" to her contemporaries. Interestingly, she soon had gathered a considerable following of supporters, most of them Catholics.

When her "locutions" began to draw overflow crowds to her home early in 1972, the meetings were transferred to a local clubhouse and, later, to a 440 acre Carbon Canyon Site where, on Sunday and Wednesday mornings, she engaged in her "locutions." Eventually, a hilly, oak-dotted parcel of land in the Chino hills was purchased and Frances unveiled an ambitious program for constructing a religious/medical complex within the next five years. A non-profit corporation was established under the name of "Saint Joseph's Hill of Hope."

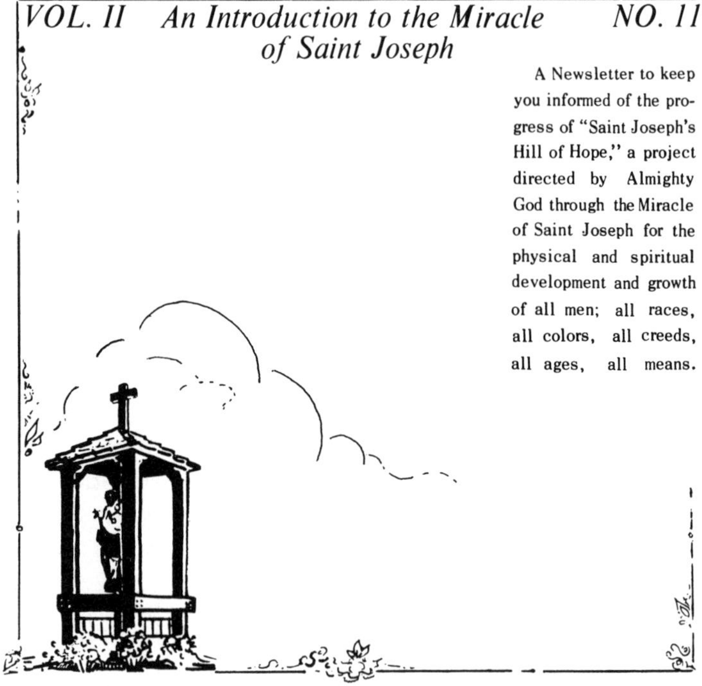

SPECIAL ISSUE

VOICE OF HOPE

VOL. II *An Introduction to the Miracle of Saint Joseph* *NO. 11*

A Newsletter to keep you informed of the progress of "Saint Joseph's Hill of Hope," a project directed by Almighty God through the Miracle of Saint Joseph for the physical and spiritual development and growth of all men; all races, all colors, all creeds, all ages, all means.

Proposed basilica at Hill of Hope.

Hill of Hope followers in Rome.

Carbon Canyon, which stretched over San Bernardino, Orange and Los Angeles counties, was in both the Archdiocese of Los Angeles and the Diocese of San Diego. Early on Bishop Leo Maher reported that "a new effort is being put forth by individuals purporting to have personal revelations from God." He warned that "no credence should be given to these claims unless and until authenticated by the Church."[36]

A member of Saint Joseph's parish in Placentia, Mrs. Klug was a lifelong Catholic who always professed a willingness to submit "to the authority of the Church."[37] Her subsequent activities cast some shadow on that allegation. As her influence continued to grow, Mrs. Klug began issuing printed and taped versions of her "locutions" to followers.[38] She inaugurated a giant fund raising campaign called "Pennies from Heaven" to pay for the land and to begin construction of her contemplated complex of buildings.

A reporter from the Los Angeles *Times* said that "attempts to get some recognition from the Los Angeles chancery or an interview with Archbishop Manning have failed."[39] Actually, that wasn't true. Manning responded that representatives from the Hill of Hope had visited his office on March 21, 1972 and they had "received very definite information as to my frame of mind."[40] However, to make his views crystal clear, Manning had a notice placed in *The Tidings* which read: "The Saint Joseph Hill of Hope, its proposed religious communities and building programs have no endorsement from the Roman Catholic Archbishop of Los Angeles. Appeals for funds for these projects do not have the approval or encouragement of the Archdiocese of Los Angeles."[41] Others were even more outspoken. The editor of the San Diego *Southern Cross* wrote that after hearing Frances and reading her transcribed locutions, he felt that they were "naive and simplistic, and written in a stilted, awkward style of language."[42]

Observers admitted that though the "chances of recognition and endorsement are probably slim,"[43] they went ahead with preliminary work of leveling and preparing the Hill of Hope for its contemplated buildings. One local newspaper reported that the overall plans for her building project "came directly from God" and would cost 200 million dollars.[44] In addition to a bridge of saints, there would be a 5,000 seat amphitheatre, a two story underground parking structure and a magnificent shrine in the first building phase. Plans for the "Biblical City" grew to gigantic proportions. The shrine would accommodate 20,000 pilgrims daily. And a hospital was added, as was a seminary for her two sons.[45]

On June 26, Mrs. Klug met directly with Manning. The cardinal described the meeting in a letter to the Vatican Secretariat of State: "I made it clear to her that at no time had she been refused access to me, though she did assert that she could not see me." And he also emphasized that he could "not approve, or bless in any way the program that she has inaugurated and which she bases on her asserted revelations." He said "she left, indignant at my pride and my injustice, but she does clearly understand that there is no approval."[46] Meanwhile, Mrs. Klug was making arrangements to take her cause directly to Rome where she hoped to gain the endorsement of the Holy Father. She did manage to receive Holy Communion from the Pope, using a falsified name. Afterwards she circulated photographs of that occurrence widely among her followers as if to indicate papal approval.

A year later, with no approbation coming from Rome, the following press release "was issued through Frances Klug by Our Blessed Mother" at approximately 3:15 p.m., May 9, 1974:

> Due to the lack of interest by the hierarchy of the Roman Catholic Church in the greatest miracle in the world, the teaching miracle of Saint Joseph, men have been requested to stand in defense of God's will so that Christianity can be seen once again and that political men will have to bend to the gift of faith so that souls will be saved.
>
> There are so few men in the world who are spiritually oriented. Most men are following the written word of others and are forgetting that prophets of sound truth were evident at the birth of the son of God and they had no books. It is through the soundness of wisdom that Christianity was formed and permeated the earth.
>
> Now in our time, the wisdom of the heavens resounds through the earth through the miracle of Saint Joseph. Men shout it is too simple to follow, but bear in mind, the wise men followed a star which was truly the light from the divine. The heresies men are accepting will only lead all mankind to perdition to the ugly pits of hell. It is time now for that "simple teaching," the "light of wisdom" to be shown to the world as it once was one time.[47]

Commenting on an identical telegram sent to Bishop Leo Maher, the editor of the *Southern Cross* said: "Now I've seen it all." He went to observe that "after close to forty years in the writing business and having handled, written or read thousands of news releases and p.r. handouts, the classic example has now arrived. No less than a press release from the Blessed Mother herself." And her press agent is none other than Frances Klug, the guiding force behind the "miracle of St. Joseph" which operates from a site on the border of our diocese near Brea. "Due to the lack of interest by the hierarchy of the Roman Catholic Church in the greatest miracle in the world," states the message, "men have been requested to stand in defense of God's will . . ." Nothing like getting a dramatic impact, is there? Strange that Our Blessed Mother should have used a modern American advertising gimmick in claiming "the greatest." She was formerly so retiring, according to the gospels. And I always thought the Incarnation was the "greatest miracle." Funny, how wrong we all were. What is so interesting about the St. Joseph's Hill of Hope business – and I use the word advisedly – is that it is not Catholic, since it is not approved by the hierarchy, yet the organizers continually use the Catholic Church to promote their operations and solicitations for financial support. It is in no way affiliated with the Church, although the leaders are trading on the devotion of the Church to Mary and St. Joseph.[48]

Throughout the following months, Manning kept the Holy See advised. In a letter to the Apostolic Delegate in 1975, he reiterated the background of the Hill of Hope. After describing her "colloquies with God the Father, and with several members of the heavenly court," Manning expressed his belief that "the woman herself is honest and devout, but the movement is totally unacceptable." It was his judgement that "none of this should receive any encouragement whatsoever."[49] Later that year, Archbishop Giovanni Benelli reported to Manning that Mrs. Klug had left a gold watch in Rome for the Holy Father's acceptance. It was being returned, along with Benelli's assurances that "the Holy See has no intention of entering into direct contact with Mrs. Klug or of giving either approval or recognition to her institution."[50]

By July of 1976, the only permanent structure at the Hill of Hope was a statue of Saint Joseph and a half-finished grotto. Many of Klug's followers had tired of her antics and were disillusioned. In a memo to Manning, the chancellor for the Archdiocese of Los Angeles said emissaries from the Klug organization had come to his office complaining about financial expenditures that were, at best, questionable. Creditors were calling about past due bills and the corporation's credit rating had declined measurably. "The visionary seems to be running low on locutions of recent date."[51] When, in January of 1977, the chancellor reported that the Hill of Hope was "now closed" and that Mrs. Klug was "selling pillow cases and sheets in her downtown location," Manning wrote onto the bottom of that memo: "*Sic transit* . . ."[52]

In 1990, a story ran in the Los Angeles *Times* under the masthead: "Self-Described Visionary's Hill of Hope Dream Ends." The property had been placed on the market and Frances Klug had become a decorating consultant for the Frances Roberts Interiors Design Company.[53] Earlier, Molly Bickford asked her readers whether Frances Klug was a "person truly touched by God and His saints, as her followers devoutly believe? Or is she, as others suggested, merely a talented actress playing with those who want to believe." She answered that "only time will tell."[54] And it did.

Notes to the Text

1. AALA, Biographical Interview with Timothy Cardinal Manning, Mission Hills, August 24, 1981.
2. AALA, John J. Devlin - interview, Los Angeles, October 13, 1968.
3. AALA, Biographical Interview with Timothy Cardinal Manning, *Op cit.*
4. John J. Sheridan quoted in "Power and Glory," 1986.
5. AALA, Timothy Manning to Faithful, Los Angeles, March 10, 1970.
6. AALA, Timothy Cardinal Manning to Clergy, Los Angeles, October 1, 1973.
7. Reprinted in The Tidings, October 15, 1976.
8. *The Tidings*, December 19, 1975.
9. AALA, Timothy Cardinal Manning to Faithful, Los Angeles, November, 1974.
10. *The Tidings*, December 27, 1974.
11. AALA, Timothy Cardinal Manning to Faithful, Los Angeles, August, 1979.
12. *The Tidings*, February 1, 1980.
13. *Ibid.*, October 29, 1976.
14. AALA, Timothy Cardinal Manning to Faithful, Los Angeles, n.d. (March, 1985). Happily, this stipulation was never enforced and was soon discarded altogether.
15. *The Tidings*, August 3, 1973.
16. AALA, Timothy Cardinal Manning to Sister Miriam Joseph Larkin, C.S.J., Los Angeles, August 15, 1985.
17. AALA, Timothy Manning to Clergy, Los Angeles, April 17, 1970.
18. Extracted from *Our Lady's Digest* XXVI (July-August, 1971), 47-49.
19. The chapter on Mary was appended to the one on the Church as a result of a vote taken on October 29, 1963, in which the conciliar Fathers, by a small majority, decided against issuing a separate document on Mary, as had originally been planned.

20. *Central California Register*, September 30, 1971.
21. *The Tidings*, October 1, 1971.
22. *Ibid.*, October 29, 1971.
23. *Ibid.*, December 17, 1971.
24. *Ibid.*, April 25, 1980.
25. Francis J. Weber, *El Pueblo de Nuestra Señora de los Angeles* (Los Angeles, 1968), p.4.
26. AALA, John Cardinal Knox to Timothy Cardinal Manning, Rome, February 10, 1981.
27. *The Tidings*, June 12, 1981.
28. AALA, Memo to Bishops of California, Los Angeles, n.d.
29. *The Tidings*, November 2, 1984.
30. *The Wanderer*, February 11, 1985.
31. *The Tidings*, August 9, 1985.
32. *Catholic Sun*, October 2, 1986.
33. *The Tidings*, May 26, 1989.
34. Los Angeles *Times*, July 29, 1973.
35. *Ibid.*, September 4, 1990.
36. *Southern Cross*, August 24, 1972.
37. North Orange County *Daily News Tribune*, May 15, 1972.
38. The first of the printed locutions was issued on August 10, 1969.
39. October 1, 1972.
40. Los Angeles *Times*, October 7, 1972.
41. *The Tidings*, November 3, 1972.
42. *Southern Cross*, August 24, 1972.
43. "Enthused Catholics Launch Monumental Project," *Earth* XVII, (June-July, 1973), 7.
44. La Habra *Daily Star Progress,* June 18, 1973.
45. Los Angeles *Times*, July 29, 1973.
46. AALA Timothy Cardinal Manning to Giovanni Benelli, Los Angeles, June 26, 1973.
47. AALA, unsigned telegram to Timothy Cardinal Manning, Brea, California, May 20, 1974.

48. *Southern Cross*, May 30, 1974.
49. AALA, Timothy Cardinal Manning to Jean Jadot, Los Angeles, April 25, 1975.
50. AALA, Giovanni Benelli to Timothy Cardinal Manning, Rome, October 25, 1975.
51. AALA, John A. Rawden to Timothy Cardinal Manning, Los Angeles, July 14, 1976.
52. AALA, John A. Rawden to Timothy Cardinal Manning, Los Angeles, January 6, 1977.
53. September 4, 1990.
54. North Orange County *Daily News Progress*, May 15, 1972.

18. Outreach Ministries

In the years after Vatican Council II, the term "ministry" took on new significance in Catholic parlance. No longer restricted to strictly clerical functions or pursuits, "ministry" became an umbrella for any activity relating to the furtherance of the Gospel message.

THE PERMANENT DIACONATE

When Pope Paul VI restored the order of deacon as a permanent ministry in the Latin Church, on June 18, 1967, James Francis Cardinal McIntyre was heard to say that "we will leave the implementation of that directive in Los Angeles to my worthy successor." That the cardinal was enthusiastic about the potentialities of that ministry is obvious from the positive vote he cast when, on April 23, 1968, the American bishops petitioned the Holy Father for its use in the United States "both to complete the hierarchy of sacred orders and to enrich and strengthen the various ministries of work in the United States with the sacramental grace of the diaconate."[1]

The following October, the Holy See granted the request of the NCCB "to establish in the United States the permanent diaconate for married and unmarried men of mature years in those areas where they are needed."[2] Bishop Fulton J. Sheen ordained the first permanent deacon, former Anglican priest Michael Cole, in June of 1969.[3] On September 22, 1971, the Bishops Committee on the Permanent Diaconate issued a series of guidelines for the formation of that ministry in the United States.

As was the case with many of his episcopal contemporaries, Archbishop Manning was not initially enamored about establishing the permanent diaconate in Los Angeles. He felt that the chief relevance of restoring that ministry would be in missionary areas of the world where it would sacramentally enhance the office of catechist. He wondered whether it was really needed in the United States, noting that, with the exception of witnessing marriages and conferring baptism, most of diaconal functions could be performed by any delegated lay person. In any event, the archbishop remained open-minded on the notion and asked the newly established Priests' Senate to look into the matter and report back to him with suggestions.

In May of 1971, a subcommittee of the senate commissioned Fathers Joseph George and Mario Antoci to study how best to organize and administer the permanent diaconate in the Archdiocese of Los Angeles. Seeking the advice of prominent, local clergymen and lay people, they proceeded to draft a series of proposals. At that juncture, Manning signalled his unequivocal endorsement by appointing Father Peter Healy to be director of the diaconate ministry in Los Angeles. It was one of the wisest and most important appointments of his archiepiscopate.

Working with George, Antoci and their collaborators, Healy drew up a "position paper" in March of 1972 which defined the program's academic, spiritual and outreach objectives. The draft was reviewed by the archbishop and his staff and, finally, in April, a thirty-five page booklet on *The Permanent Diaconate* was completed and distributed. That booklet was further fine-tuned and, on December 14, Manning wrote to the *pro tem* President of the Priests' Senate complimenting members for the "immense zeal of energy" which they had expended in the "superb master plan." The archbishop accepted the draft as a "working document, recognizing the validity of the suggestions and recommendations contained therein." He appointed a committee of priests to assist Healy, comprising Fathers John Danagher, Michael Lenihan, Armando Ochoa, James Nash and Anthony Leuer. The archbishop envisioned selecting twelve candidates for the initial program which would stretch over two and a half years. There would be an additional year to "evaluate the effectiveness of their position" and, with that done, "we would then be in a position to consider the next class of candidates and the successive classes thereafter on a regular basis." He designated the parochial hall at Immaculate Conception Church as the headquarters for the training sessions.[4]

The archbishop was later to note that "one of the beauties of the Church since the Second Vatican Council is the visible and in-depth meaning given to the hierarchy which Jesus established for the service of His people in the Church. It was always true in the ranks of bishops and priests, but lacked the completion of the permanent order of the diaconate. This is now established and the Church is thereby enriched." Manning further observed that "in the Church of Los Angeles we have inaugurated and pursue a program of training that is discreet, profoundly spiritual and coordinated to serve the needs of the local Church. This demands a measure of sanctity and sacrifice from each ordained deacon."[5] Manning wanted the Catholic people in the archdiocese to understand that Vatican Council II had not simply restored the diaconate but, drawing on the roots of the early Church, it re-created a precious channel for better and more fully serving the needs of the Church in the modern world.

In a booklet written in 1977, Father Royale Vadakin outlined eleven duties entrusted to deacons:

1. To assist the bishop and the presbyters in the liturgy;
2. To administer baptism solemnly;
3. To be custodian of the Eucharist and to dispense it, to carry Viaticum to the dying and to give the Eucharistic blessing;
4. To preside at marriages in the name of the Church;
5. To administer sacramentals and preside at funerals and burial services;
6. To proclaim the gospels liturgically and to preach;
7. To preside at the worship of the people (presumably the public celebration of the Divine Office);
8. To direct the liturgy of the word;
9. To fulfill the obligations of charity and administration, as well as social assistance;
10. To guide scattered Christian communities;
11. To support and promote the lay apostolate.[6]

The process for choosing candidates would entail the following objectives: (1)1 to select candidates who exhibit qualities of faith, moral integrity and adequate intellectual ability; (2) to replace in some way the ethnic, cultural and social fabric of the Church community of Los Angeles and (3) to provide men capable of ministering to the needs of the Church at Los Angeles.[7]

A breakdown of the original class indicated how well Father Healy and his advisers had done their work. It was truly a "catholic" group of twenty-five people.

Community Represented

3 Represent the Black Community. (All are converts)
5 Represent the Mexican-American Community.
(All speak Spanish fluently)
1 Represents the Japanese-American Community.
1 Represents the Philippine-American Community.

Marital Status

19 are married. (7 have children under 13 yrs. of age)

5 are single.

1 is a widower.

Education

11 have completed high school. (5 have had 2-3 yrs. college)

14 are college graduates. (8 have had at least 2 yrs. post graduate study)

7 candidates speak Spanish fluently.

Religious Background

7 are converts. (1 was a Congregational Minister)

3 were Brothers. (1 for 13 yrs., 1 for 11 yrs., 1 received temporary vows only)

4 studied for the priesthood. (1 with the Jesuits 5 yrs., 3 for the Archdiocese of Los Angeles)

Age and I.Q.

Youngest candidate is 37, the oldest is 69. Four are over 60.
Average age is 49.
Average I.Q. seems to be about 120.

Work or Profession

The highest percentage would be engaged in what could generally be termed Engineering or Technical skills.
The second highest would be school teachers.

Representation by County

20 Los Angeles County.

4 Orange County.

1 Santa Barbara County.[8]

Even in its earliest format, this academic program was tailored to provide candidates with maximum exposure to all areas of theology. This was in response to a directive from the NCCB which stated that "to be effective as an ordained representative of the Church, the deacon should have enough knowledge of theology to be competent in the specific ministry he exercises."[9]

Sacred Scripture	(69 hours)
Dogmatic Theology	(60 hours)

Moral Theology	(73 hours)
Liturgy	(12 hours)
Pastoral Theology	(106 hours)

In May of 1974, Bishop William R. Johnson, a member of the advisory board, wrote an interesting letter to the Archbishop of Louisville describing the program as it existed in Los Angeles. He admitted that when the program began, he was "very concerned about it," but he said that his "attitude had changed to one of optimism and great hope for this development in the Church." He felt that apart from their liturgical functions, the permanent deacons "will touch the lives of their neighbors" in many ways that are new and exciting. Johnson told how, "with a minimum of publicity," there were one hundred applications for the initial twenty-five slots. A special effort had been made to recruit Mexican-Americans and others with a Spanish language background as well as blacks. He described the academic staff as being "made up of diocesan as well as religious personnel, some from the seminary and some who are engaged in pastoral work in offices and parishes." Classes met twice weekly from 7 to 10 o'clock in the evening. Candidates and their wives participate in monthly days of recollection and candidates were visited by Father Healy and other members of the board in their homes. He concluded by saying that "their enthusiasm and participation in all aspects of the program is truly remarkable. Priests, religious and lay people who have had the opportunity of meeting these candidates are very much impressed with them and with the potential contribution they can make to the Church."[10]

On September 29, 1974 Manning, by then a cardinal, ordained the twenty-five initial candidates as acolytes and lectors. In his homily, the cardinal explained the requisites of their office "to fulfill the obligation they have to the last man in the last pew who has a right to hear the Word of God from their lips in a skilled and effective manner." Ever-so-gradually, the men were "drawing closer to the mystery of the Eucharist." Their acceptance of the ministries of acolyte and lector implied "a new dimension of reverence for the Word of God and the obligation to witness it by their lives."[11]

Over the following months, most of the diaconal candidates were interviewed by *The Tidings*. In a feature story about Roy Murvin, the retired insurance company executive said that as a deacon he would "be able to baptize, to witness marriages, read holy scripture in church, instruct inquirers on the faith, lead worship and prayer services, give communion to the sick and dying and lead funeral and burial services." Roy felt that his special education in the diaconate program had given him "a new understanding of human problems."[12] Msgr. Peter Healy was also interviewed and he explained that "upon ordination the deacon becomes a public and life-long minister of the church." He emphasized that the vocation of the deacon is distinct from that of the priest insofar as "he cannot celebrate Mass or hear Confessions." He may be married or single and he continues his secular work or profession. "His first responsibility is to his wife and family."[13]

Ordination for the proto class of deacons was scheduled for October 7, 1975 at Saint Charles Borromeo Church in North Hollywood. One newspaper told how "in recent centuries the diaconate was reserved for men preparing for the priesthood but the permanent diaconate, open to married men, was restored by Pope Paul VI in 1967."[14] It was clear in Manning's homily that his initial skepticism for the diaconate had turned to enthusiasm.

> This is one of the most historic days in the history of the archdiocese. For a thousand years in the Catholic Church, the diaconate has been regarded only as a transitional step to the priesthood. Something very important and beautiful was lost in the service of the Church.
>
> The first indication of change came from Pope Pius XII. This was picked up by the Fathers of the Vatican Council. When they finalized the momentous decree, *Lumen Gentium*, on the Church. In article 29 they asked that the diaconate be restored to a permanent position in the hierarchy of the Church. Pope Paul, taking that indication upon the action of the Holy Spirit, in the Apostolic Constitution of 1967 regulated that the diaconate should be restored and that it might be enjoyed by men who were married, with the consent of their wives, at the age of thirty-five and upward, that those who were not married might also receive the diaconate, but there was to be attached to it the vow of permanent celibacy to the Church.
>
> That authorization by the Supreme Pontiff has had ripples to the ends of the earth. Today for the first time that is exemplified here in our midst in this archdiocese. These men are called now to the ministry of the Liturgy of the Word and of charity. To the inquiring as to their worthiness, the answer is given that, so far as human knowledge allows us to know, these men are deemed worthy. How well we can testify to that worthiness. Of the eighty or more applicants who desired this service through a very, very grave process

> of screening and through the indoctrination of two years or more, these men have been subjected to a scrutiny and to the training and to an inservice of love which validates the statement made by Msgr. Peter Healy, their director, that they are indeed worthy of this promotion.
>
> And so they come forward into the sanctuary to receive the laying on of hands. Some come with the premeditated consent of their wives. But others are a spectacle for angels and for men, because six of them will pronounce the vow of permanent celibacy in the service of the Church. Such a thing has not been heard of before. It is the abiding presence of the Holy Spirit inflaming the hearts of these men that by this commitment they are giving witness to the totality of love and service which the Church gives to the people of God.

As to why the Church had decided to revive the permanent diaconate, Manning noted, first of all, it was for pastoral reasons:

> In the course of time many of the duties that normally belonged to the ministry were appropriated by the priests. So the Church desired that these should be disengaged from the priests and given to those who, by the laying of hands and by the in-rush of the Holy Spirit would have a hierarchical status in the Church for this service. And providentially the diminishing number of priests allowed that this truth should shine forth in the Church and give that margin of cause for the advancement of the permanent diaconate.
>
> The second reason is theological. The bishop is the principal servant of the Church. He has the counsels particularly to avoid the word of primacy or priority. But he has the fullness of the Sacrament of Orders. The bishop of necessity has that. That fullness is shared with other men, with priests and with deacons, so that they can localize him to the various communities and so that they can exercise his duty of charity to the people at large.
>
> The third reason is this, that even though all of the ten particular duties that are listed for the permanent deacons could be exercised by any lay person in the Church, yet these men are to receive the Sacrament of Orders and go back into their professions, their duties, their lay vocations, so that they

impregnate that particular level of society with the love of God. That is the necessary kind of service, not their preaching, not their ministering of the sacraments, but their very existence there among the people of the world with that force that is in them of God's spirit. Through the dynamism of that spirit, exercised through them as a leaven, the whole community is purified and lifted up because of their very presence.

They are to be specifically charged to preach the Word according to the Gospels and according to the tradition of the Church. Bishop, priest and deacon must vow fidelity to the teaching of the Church.

We come, then, to the precise moment when they will come one by one and kneel before the ordaining bishop and he will place both his hands upon their heads. At that moment, coupled shortly afterwards with a brief prayer, this mystery of grace occurs in their souls. They become members of the hierarchy. They share in the Sacrament of Orders. For all eternity, they are marked men. They are God's men. Afterwards they will be given the garments that identify their rank for cultic service. They will be asked to give to the bishop a pledge of reverence and obedience so that, wherever they go, whatever assignment they take, is done by virtue of this mandate from the bishop.

Finally, there is peace. There is attached to this entry into the sanctuary here a measure of peace that only we know. We cannot define it, explain it, analyze it, but it is an embrace of Christ that fires the heart and brings that person so much closer to the priestly heart of Christ. So now we proceed with this holy task. We commend these generous people to our Heavenly Father and to your holy prayers.[15]

The assignment of the new deacons was anything but haphazard. Lengthy interviews with the candidates and prospective pastors and/or agency directors were held and every effort was made to maximize the special talents of the newly ordained. A review process was also introduced whereby questionnaires were filled out annually by everyone involved in the appointment.

I. Deacon | Placement
Address of Placement | Phone

II. PASTORAL TASKS

Community Service (hours per month)

_____ Community Organizer
_____ Working Life
_____ Public School
_____ Mental Health
_____Police
_____ Youth Work
_____ Drug Addiction
_____ Correctional Institutions
_____ Welfare
_____ Juridical System

Other (Specify)

General Parish (hours per month)

_____ Aged
_____ Sick
_____ Social Groups
_____ Poor
_____ Youth
_____ CCD
_____ School Board
_____ Parish Council
_____ St. Vincent de Paul
_____ Marriage Practice

_____ Ordinary Minister of Communion
_____ Deacon at Wake Service
_____ Deacon at Burial Service
_____ Deacon at Para-Liturgies
_____Deacon at Baptism
_____Preparation for Baptism
_____Preparation for Marriage, etc.
_____Holy Communion for Sick & Dying

Other (Specify)

Specialized Ministry (hours per month)

_____ Business Men
_____ Hospitals
_____ Campus
_____ Handicapped
_____ Unions
_____ Catholic Charities
_____ Parish Clusters

Other(Specify)[16]

Always a canonical stickler, the cardinal gave each new deacon a carefully prepared set of "faculties" which outlined his ministry and its limitations.

> Confident of your character, doctrine, and good judgment, by these presents, We approve the exercise of your diaconal service within the Archdiocese of Los Angeles in California.

In virtue of our own authority as archbishop, and in virtue of the authority delegated to us by the Holy See, We grant to you the faculties to use the authorization conceded to your office in the Code of Canon Law and declare that you may exercise these faculties in accordance with the norms of Canon Law. These faculties are to be used within the territorial limits of the parish to which you are assigned. Whenever there is need for the exercise of your faculties outside of the parish to which you are assigned, the permission of that pastor and the pastor of the parish in which you wish to exercise your faculties must be obtained.

I. -WITH REGARD TO THE SACRAMENT OF BAPTISM,

1) you may administer Baptism solemnly and may supply ceremonies which have been omitted when conferred on children or adults;

2) you may assist the pastor in the recording of the fact of Baptism in the parochial books, observing accurately the Provisions of Canons 777, 778 and 779 of the Code of Canon Law.

II. -WITH REGARD TO THE SACRAMENT OF THE MOST HOLY EUCHARIST AND THE SACRIFICE OF THE MASS,

1) you may assist the bishop and the priest during liturgical actions in all those activities which the ritual assigns to the office of deacon;

2) you may reserve the Holy Eucharist and may distribute to yourself and to others the Most Blessed Sacrament;

3) you may bring Viaticum to the dying and may impart to the people Benediction with the Most Blessed Sacrament in the sacred ciborium.

III. -WITH REGARD TO THE SACRAMENT OF MATRIMONY,

1) in the absence of a priest you may assist at and bless marriages in the name of the Church by this specific delegation having first complied with the requirements of the Code of Canon Law on all those matters that are preliminary to the licit and valid assistance at marriage;

2) in order to comply with the provisions of the Civil Code of the State of California regarding marriage, you are to

sign the civil document in this instance with the prefix "Reverend";

3) you may assist the pastor in the recording of the fact of marriage in the parochial books, observing accurately the provisions of Canon 1103.

IV. -WITH REGARD TO THE LITURGY,

1) you may read the sacred books of scripture to the faithful and preach and instruct the people;

2) you may preside over the offices and prayers of religious worship whenever a priest is not available;

3) you may conduct bible studies.

V. -WITH REFERENCE TO THE SACRAMENTS,

1) you may administer the Sacramentals following the formulas found in approved liturgical books;

2) you may preside at funeral and burial rites.

VI. -WITH REGARD TO SERVICE OF CHARITY,

1) you may carry out in the name of the hierarchy the duties of charity and administration as well as the works of social assistance under the direction of the pastor;

2) you may promote and sustain the apostolic activities of laymen.[17]

In the fall of 1975, a second class was begun, this time with thirty-two new candidates. The following April, a program for Spanish-speaking candidates was launched with Bishop Juan Arzube as consulter and Father Armando Ochoa as director.[18]

A newsletter was established in December of 1976. Msgr. Healy said that the publication would give "each of us another meaning through which we may share in the growth of the ideals in the program. Through the sharing of experiences, of hopes, of successes, of failures these ideals take on flesh and blood in the living service of God's people." A letter from the cardinal was featured on the first page in which Manning noted that the permanent diaconate in Los Angeles had "been most rewarding." He said that the deacon is "providing a staunch witness to the values of the Gospel not only in the assignment which he fills, but specifically in his way of life."[19]

The first permanent deacon to die was Joaquin Fraters who succumbed on July 16, 1977. A life-long teacher in the public school system, Joaquin fulfilled his ministry at Saint Ambrose parish, Saint Vincent's Hospital and the De Paul Convalescent Home.[20]

In a reflection on the diaconate program as it had evolved in the first five years, Cardinal Manning said: "Thank God, the results have justified the intensity of preparation to which each candidate was subjected," a view held by all who were in any way connected with the diaconate ministry in Los Angeles.[21]

In a homily for the Mass at which thirteen Spanish-speaking men were ordained to the permanent diaconate, June 3, 1978, Manning, "recalling uneasiness in the early Church because of dissension among peoples speaking diverse languages," said that centuries later the Church is "again resolving problems by ordaining men firmly rooted in faith" to the diaconate.

> We have judged these men worthy to carry out the ministry. They will be efficient servants to their own language group...They will draw new strength from the gift of the Holy Spirit. They will provide help for the bishop and his priests as ministers of the Word, of the liturgy and of charity, making themselves servants to all men . . . They will proclaim the Gospel, make all preparation for the sacrifice and distribute the body and blood of the Lord to the faithful.

Commenting on the preparation "in all its phases" of the training program for deacons, Manning said that "no other program in the United States, perhaps in the world, is as thorough and perhaps as effective."[22]

CURSILLO

The first *Cursillo* was held in Los Angeles in 1962[23] and, within four years, thirty-three sessions had been conducted. By 1967, nearly 1,200 persons had made the *Cursillo*. The movement was warmly endorsed by Manning when he became archbishop. He described the experience as reflecting "the flame of the fire of Christ's charity, in which there is no contestation, no antagonism, no dispute." Early in February of 1970, the archbishop issued an official mandate for its work and appointed three priests, Father Luis Valbuena, Enrique Parisi and Manuel Moreno as directors of the movement. A special department was set up in the curial offices and two vacant dormitories were set aside at Queen of Angels Seminary in Mission Hills for the weekend sessions.

Described as "a little course in Christianity and Christian living," the movement involved an intensive, three day program of prayer, study and discussion of the Faith conducted largely by laymen under the guidance of priests. It was designed to motivate *Cursillistas* to make their lives more God-centered and to inspire them to be more active in apostolic works.

Manning had observed its marvelous effects for several years and declared himself "totally behind the movement," provided only that it retain its close link with him as archbishop. He noted that "the bishop, in the design of Christ, is the center of unity in a diocese: there is no cohesion without him." He went on to stress the necessity and value of the follow-up program by which *Cursillistas* provide a valuable sequence of contacts with other members. The archbishop said that "the age in which we live cries for the recognition that each person is a unique image of God and because of that, has a supreme dignity and innate potency for goodness which no other man can downgrade or diminish."[24]

Late in March of the following year, Manning made a *Cursillo* himself, along with forty-two men and six priests. In an interview with the archdiocesan newspaper, the archbishop said that he had "never been so moved spiritually" in his life. He was "drawn into an experience of the love of Christ in the Blessed Sacrament in the company of people" he had never known before. When asked to define the movement, Manning advised: "Compare it to nothing. In the *Cursillo* you become yourself. I went there as archbishop. But the second day, you become yourself. There is no suspicion of sensitivity session in the *Cursillo*, no pentecostalism, no gimmicks, none of the popular fads, no self-revelation. The only revelation is between yourself and God." He said that the *Cursillo* "is an extremely orthodox, solidly structured process. For years," the archbishop continued, "I've seen the goodness of this work. I wanted to find out what the source of it was. There was only one way to do it and that was to make the *Cursillo*. From my experience I must say that it has my 100 percent plus - not only approval but enthusiasm."

When asked, if the *Cursillo*s were so effective in the spiritual life, why they are not epidemic so that the good results might be widespread. The archbishop responded that "the twelve apostles were not epidemic."

> Sacrifice can never be epidemic. This calls for tremendous sacrifice of time. *Cursillistas* devote themselves to nothing

Manning is engulfed by high school students at Anaheim Convention Center where he participated in youth day of Confraternity of Christian doctrine.

Manning greets Cursillistas at Anaheim Convention Center in 1981.

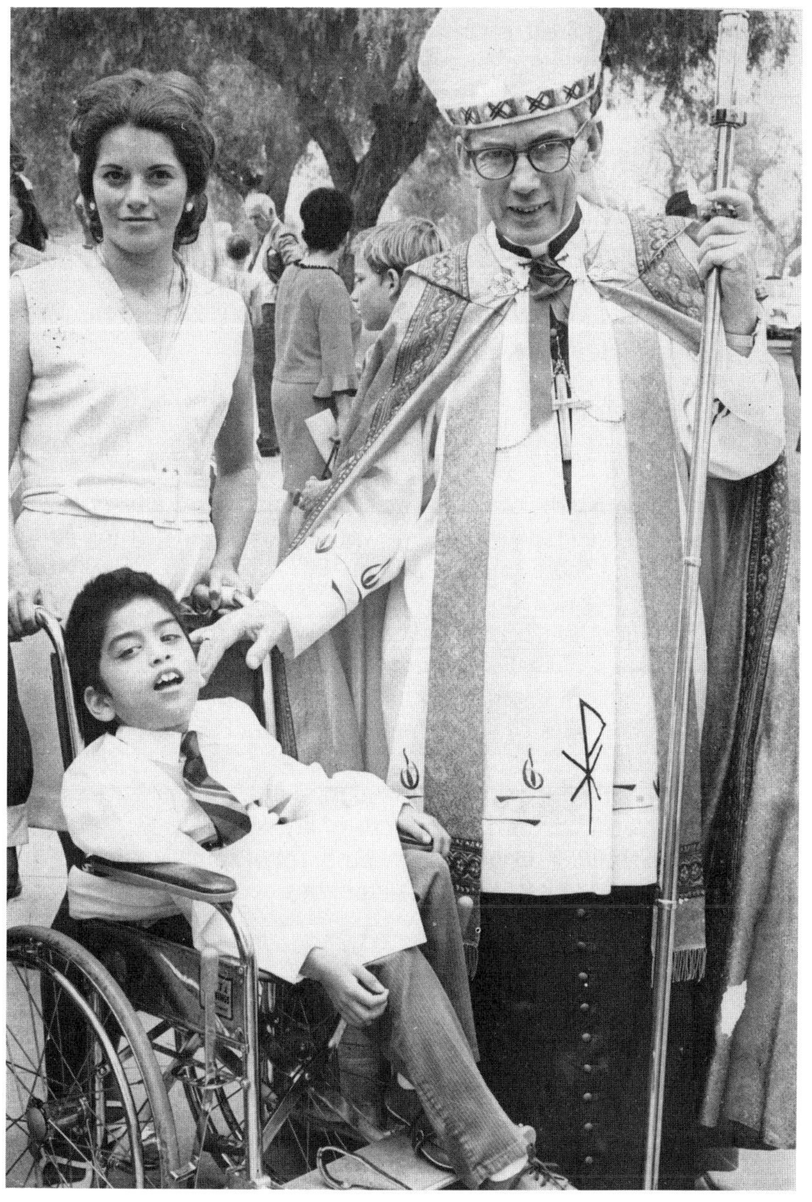

> but the thought of Christ. In many instances they have to give up a day's work for the *Cursillo.*
>
> The *Cursillo* postulates the natural qualities of leadership of those who make it. It's not for everybody. It's for those who have the God-given charisma of leadership. Prepared soil responds to grace and affects all it touches.

He concluded his observations by comparing the potential of the *Cursillo* to "the hidden wells reported to exist in San Fernando Valley. If these were tapped, it would transform the valley" into a paradise.[25]

Throughout the rest of his life and even into his retirement, the archbishop would return to Mission Hills each time a *Cursillo* was held. Truly that week in early 1971 was an experience that profoundly influenced the remainder of his earthly sojourn.

CHARISMATIC RENEWAL

Among the earliest challenges facing Manning as archbishop was how to deal with the charismatic renewal that had been gaining popularity in the United States since early in 1967 when it reached Notre Dame University from Pittsburgh.

Based on rather liberal interpretations about certain phases in the Acts of the Apostles, as well as allusions to the Holy Spirit gleaned from documents of Vatican Council II, the loosely-knit program placed its major thrust on the nine gifts enumerated by Saint Paul:

> *Sign Gifts* - faith, healing, working of miracles;
> *Teaching Gifts* - wisdom, utterances of knowledge;
> *Revelational Gifts* - prophecy, discernment of spirits, tongues (glossolalia) and interpretation of tongues.

These "community-orientated" favors, supplementing to the usual gifts of the Holy Spirit, tended to relate towards the activated plane. Affiliates prayed for the "Baptism of the Holy Spirit."

Manning asked a member of the Board of Consulters to submit a report on the matter. In that report, the priest told the assembled board that the movement had "no format, few if any acknowledged leaders and little organized thrust. The whole phenomenon is badly in need of direction and, it is altogether within the realm of possibility, that if Catholicized, it could prove to be a spiritual palliative to a portion of God's people. In its existing state, however, even well-balanced and honest-intentioned participants are venturing onto psychologically thin ice." He concluded by saying that, for the present, he would be inclined to agree with Andrew Greeley's appraisal of "Catholic" Pentecostalism as "a transitional phenomenon (which) will last no longer than the transition lasts!"[26]

That there were others who frowned on the movement is apparent in a report published in *Time* magazine:

> The squeaky-clean image of singer-actor Pat Boone is no stage illusion; he is an all-out, 24-hour-a-day Christian and a dedicated drum beater for the growing "Jesus movement" among the young. All the more surprising, then, that Pat and Wife Shirley have just been dropped by the fundamentalist Churches of Christ. The reason: they have been practicing faith healing and *glossolalia*, the "speaking in tongues" that is mentioned in the biblical account of Pentecost and in Paul's first letter to the Corinthians. Boone, who has personally baptized about 100 Christians in his heated Beverly Hills swimming pool, does not know where he and Shirley will end up, denomination-wise.[27]

The spectre of the fundamentalist (and liberal) Church of Christ taking the extreme measure of excommunicating its most prominent members over the question of pentecostal involvement was a forceful example of principle versus expediency that Roman Catholics could hardly ignore.

In the absence of any firm directive from either Rome or the National Conference of Catholic Bishops, Manning issued a pastoral letter "to the beloved clergy, religious and faithful of the archdiocese."

> The Council Fathers insisted, against efforts to the contrary, that the faithful receive from the Holy Spirit, together with ministry and Sacraments, special gifts as well. These must be used in the Church and in the world for the good of mankind and for the up-building of the Church. "In so doing believers need to enjoy the freedom of the Holy Spirit who 'breathes where he wills'. At the same time they must act in communion with their brothers in Christ, especially with their pastors. The latter must make a judgment about the true nature and proper use of these gifts, not in order to extinguish the Spirit, but to test all things and to hold fast to what is good".

> It is in the exercise of this pastoral responsibility that we take note of the growing devotion to the Holy Spirit within the Church. This is good and timely. Certainly the striving toward individual perfection, the loyalty to the visible Church and its leaders, the fulfillment of the duties of one's state in life - for religious and laity, the depth involvement in the liturgy, the awareness of the missionary nature of the Church, the gravitation toward the Sacred Scriptures, the spontaneity of private prayer, and above all the regard for our fellow-man and the bearing of his burdens, these are a splendid flowering of the Spirit in our times.
>
> We earnestly invoke the cooperation of our priests in the watchful guidance and direction of this particular devotion in the Church. No so-called Pentecostal activity should be held without the knowledge and guidance of the local pastor, who, in cases of doubt, will have recourse to the Ordinary. Some dangers cause us concern. Any effort beyond the liturgy, the fountain of all prayer in the Church and the summit of her activity, is a signal for concern. Again, while it is true that some of the endowments of the Spirit and His interior gifts and visible elements do exist outside the boundaries of the Catholic Church, any activity tending toward equation with other denominations, as one sect among many, must be scrupulously avoided. Excessive emotionalism, credulity and sought-after charismatic displays question the genuineness of the activity of the Spirit and open the devotion to people of peripheral stability. Finally, we must insist, with our Holy Father, that the Holy Spirit cannot be separated "from the hierarchy, from the institutional structure of the Church, as if they were two antagonistic expressions of Christianity."
>
> So, we issue these interim words in answer to the anxieties brought to our attention. "May all of us who share in the body and blood of Christ be brought together in unity by the Holy Spirit". May we grow in love together with Paul our bishop, so that in the fullness of time we may become a fitting gift which Christ our Lord will present to His Heavenly Father.[28]

Unbeknownst to Manning, the Holy Father was busily crafting his own document on the charismatic movement. Word trickled down from the "Upper Chambers" that Rome was "not pleased" with Manning's pastoral. Interestingly, Manning was not overly concerned about the pontiff's displeasure, perhaps as a result of an unsigned note from a friend which said that "Old Hamlet had delayed too long, as usual, in speaking out on a matter which surely needed his attention. You scooped him!"[29]

Manning's pastoral was received "with great relief" on the local scene by a number of active Catholic Pentecostals, including a group at Loyola University which had been organized in the fall of 1970. Until then, "most Catholic Pentecostals kept their activities quiet in the face of suspicion and sometimes hostility." That same report indicated that "Catholic groups in the Los Angeles area appear dedicated to the Church, and have appealed for more guidance in doctrine."[30]

Not all the country's Catholic bishops agreed with Manning's viewpoint. His long-time friend, Archbishop Robert Dwyer of Portland, sent a copy of a strongly worded article he had written in which he described Pentecostals as the "oldest of heresies" and the "newest of aberrations."[31] In a later essay, Dwyer said that the movement may "pose a real threat to the integrity of the Catholic Church today," because it did not "need the Church, her authority or her sacraments."[32]

Those who read Manning's pastoral carefully can readily perceive that he stopped far short of giving the charismatic movement a blanket endorsement. An essay in *Catholic Currents* pointed out that "a new warning has been sounded against the Catholic Pentecostal movement" by Manning. He said that "excessive emotionalism, credulity and sought-after charismatic displays question the genuineness of the activity of the Spirit and open devotion to people of peripheral stability."[33]

After the "Charismatic Renewal Conference" which was held at Loyola-Marymount University in July of 1972, Manning received a number of negative comments that bothered him. One writer, agreeing that the archbishop "can't keep up with them all," was nevertheless upset at the whole tone of the gathering. She sent a blow-by-blow report of the activities.[34] It was then that Manning asked Father Ralph Tichenor, a member of the Jesuit faculty at the university, to describe his experiences with the Catholic Pentecostals. Manning was greatly impressed with the balanced and erudite reply to this and other inquiries. Tichenor said that "it is an exciting period in the local Church, and while there are dangers I feel sure that if it is wisely guided it can truly continue to be a chosen vehicle for bringing the Spirit in a renewed way to all of the parishes of the archdiocese. He noted that "wherever this renewal has taken place, there is a resurgence in the use of the sacraments especially the sacraments of Penance and the Eucharist." He was "very aware of the evil around us, but we know that where evil abounds, good also abounds and can, if we have faith, destroy the evil for God is not overcome by evil, but using the weak things of the earth, conquers it."[35]

In subsequent months, the archbishop referred many queries to Tichenor. The Vicar General and others on the curial staff replied to inquiries that "with reference to the policy of the archdiocese on the Pentecostal movement, Archbishop Manning has advised all pastors that the bishops of the United States have not approved or disapproved of this movement. They have taken the position of wait-and-see. If a group is under the direction of its own pastor, and if the pastor approves, they may use the parish facilities, with the exception of the church, for prayer meetings . . ."[36]

In January of 1973, Manning commissioned another "Survey of the pentecostal (Charismatic) Movement." Therein were many useful observations. For example, it indicated that there were already "from sixty to eighty groups in the archdiocese" and that the participants "vary in age (children of preschool to old age), in culture, profession, background and social status." Most of those interviewed had "been very respectful and enthusiastic, and seemingly docile." Customarily, at the end of the meetings, members adjourn to the church for the celebration of the Eucharist. And that ceremony appeared "to be very orthodox and devotional, with the exception of some prolonged period for the exchange of the sign of peace." The author of the report felt that "the whole charismatic phenomenon" will "stand or fall with the spiritual guidance and direction by the concerned and qualified priest." For that reason, he advised that there was a "great need for qualified direction to assist the local priests wherever these persons or groups are present."[37]

In April of 1973, Manning, by now a cardinal, addressed a group of Protestant seminarians at Fuller College in Pasadena, in which he said that there should be no condemnation of the charismatic movement. "If we are dealing with a movement of the Spirit, we must not run the risk of quenching the Spirit." The cardinal said that "he had observed the movement closely and kept certain cautions because sometimes such movements attract fringe people." He felt that "there are certain things like the laying on of hands and speaking in tongues that are not necessary to such a movement." He concluded by saying that he was making "no endorsement, just a cautious observation."[38]

Manning wrote to the archdiocesan clergy in April of 1974 about a "forthcoming conference" at Loyola-Marymount University which would include addresses, workshops and seminars by prominent, national leaders in the movement."

> There has been a remarkable growth of renewal communities in the archdiocese. There are sixty such registered groups of an average attendance of 100 in each group. Regretfully, only a small percentage of our priests have become involved in this, and it is quite important that there should be a relationship between the priest and the separate groups. Priestly counsel is necessary and looked for. There is a deep awareness of the Holy Spirit active in our lives and its direction needs the help of the priest. We will be very happy if there is close association between the parish priest and each group.[39]

An article in the Los Angeles *Times*, late in 1974, reported that "prayer meetings of Catholic Charismatics are becoming commonplace in the Los Angeles archdiocese. The Roman Catholic Church has taken a cautious, tolerant and sometimes interested attitude toward the phenomenon which took Catholicism by surprise in the Midwest." By then, according to the essay, there were 100 prayer groups registered in Southern California, sixty-four percent of which had received pastoral approval to meet in parochial facilities. "Priests are either advising or leading 45% of the groups." Father Tichenor had told the reporter that Cardinal Manning wanted the movement to "keep within the theological and scriptural" lines of the Church's teachings. Tichenor reminded readers that the aim of the movement is "renewal of the local and universal Church through a rediscovery of the fullness of life in Christ through the Spirit which includes the full spectrum of gifts."[40]

To the relief of the country's bishops, Pope Paul finally addressed the movement in October of 1974, noting that "the Church lives by the outpouring of the Holy Spirit, which we call grace, that is to say, a gift *par excellence*, charity, the Father's love, communicated to us by virtue of the redemption operated by Christ, in the Holy Spirit." He concluded by saying that "the miracle of Pentecost should continue in the history of the Church and of the world."[41] From there onwards, Manning felt totally comfortable with the charismatic movement. As time progressed he relied more closely on Father Tichenor who became the founder-president of the "Serving Catholic Renewal in the Church," or SCRC. In 1983, Manning issued a statement which said:

> The Charismatic renewal enjoys the highest ecclesiastical approval. It also provides guidance and solid Catholic teaching to parish prayer groups. In this area particularly we ask your pastoral assistance. We ask your support of the Charis-

> matic Renewal. It has been a powerful influence in the sanctification of its members. Its essential requirement is the support and blessing of each pastor.[42]

Those who question Manning's abilities to sail on uncharted seas might reflect on his track record in the charismatic renewal movement. He ventured into the fray well ahead of the NCCB and the Holy Father himself and, in that sense, could be regarded as one of the movement's courageous pioneers.

NEW MINISTRIES

That Timothy Manning allowed things to happen is amply documented in this book wherein the cardinal is portrayed as using, endorsing and promoting the talents of his co-workers. And, more remarkably for a bishop, Manning didn't mind sharing the accolades or directing them to others. Like his predecessor, Manning had no identity problem.

Manning enjoyed reading scripture, examining concordances and studying biblical commentaries. He felt the need for growing intellectually and he wanted his priests to do likewise. Hence it was an "easy sale" for the Priests' Senate when they proposed a Continuing Education program for the clergy. When announcing the schedule for 1972-1973, Manning said that "much thought and discretion has gone into this planning and we should be enriched in knowledge and grace as a result." He recommended "strongly" that "adequate time be allowed in parishes so that all the priests who wish to do so may avail themselves of these opportunities." He even agreed, without being asked, that the Church should "subscribe toward the costs of attendance."[43]

FAMILY LIFE

When the Big Brother movement was expanding, Manning wrote to the priests highly recommending their services to fatherless boys in the Los Angeles area:

> Catholic Big Brothers are volunteers, devoted men of average endowments who offer a service of friendship and guidance to fatherless boys under the age of eighteen. These men offer their time because they appreciate the influence a man can have in molding the life of a boy in his developing years.

Cardinal greets developmentally disabled after Easter liturgy.

The cardinal was an avid supporter of the Handicapables Program.

First Diaconate Class - ordained June 7, 1975.

They are aware that the principles engendered in youth are those that remain throughout life and out of which spiritual, social and economic patterns of the future are formed.

The Catholic Big Brothers are attempting to establish a Parish Delegate System as a means of recruiting additional volunteers to serve in their program. The need is great because there are literally hundreds of fatherless boys in the area, the majority of whom need and can use the help of a volunteer Big Brother. Your cooperation with them will be a great source of encouragement to them in this charitable work and will ultimately provide an important and effective aid to boys in your parish.[44]

In January of 1972, Manning authenticated a new Family Life Bureau and asked the clergy "to solicit for it the unreserved cooperation of all parishes. Through collegiate action," the archbishop wrote," we hope to see in effect an appropriate marriage preparative program, the fostering of encounters to enrich married life, the zoning of areas where difficulties of married life can be exposed and healed. But above all, we look forward to a period of intense sanctification of the family so that the love of Christ for His Church, of which the love of man for his wedded woman is a sacramental sign, will shine with a new brilliance and meaning in our darkening time." At stake in the institution of marriage and the family, the archbishop said in his letter, are a litany of current and eternal values: the beginning and nourishment of human life, the dignity of the human person, the requirements of authority, the overlay of sex on love as source of life and happiness, the respect, reverence and modesty inherent in the regard for life, the rights of the elderly, the sense of community, the beginning of responsible patriotism and the raising of the mind and heart to knowledge and love of the Creator.[45]

Among the innovations inaugurated by the Family Life Bureau was an annual "jubilarians" day when couples observing anniversaries could publicly celebrate their love together. Early the following year, the cardinal told 600 couples in Hollywood's Palladium that "you are the last defenders that are left of our culture in our time." Marriage, he said, was the only institution preserved in the flood after "God repented of the creation He had made." Noah and his wife, his sons and their wives were spared so that the world might be renewed.

Once more it seems that a deluge is passing over the earth. The great tradition of Judeo-Christian culture is being swept away. Three out of four marriages are headed for divorce,

> and in this decade there will be ten million abortions in the United States. So it is extremely important that we come here to this church in the center of materialism, of glamour, of divorce, or remarriage and polygamy to make this affirmation, this commitment to married love. As we see the love Christ has for His Church, we understand something of the mystery of marriage – that a man should leave father and mother and cling to his wife and the two become one flesh. It is God's imagery that woman be at the side of her man.[46]

Manning was especially moved by the faith of the handicapped to whom he personally administered the Sacrament of Confirmation several times a year. He spoke about the need for more concern along those lines in a letter to the faithful early in 1984, pointing out that "Our Blessed Lord, in poignant ways, showed His love for not only the disabled people of His time, but for their families as well. He declared parents blameless for the disabilities of their children stating that they were granted life precisely to make manifest the glory of God:

> No family is really prepared for the birth and education of a retarded youngster. Fathers, mothers, brothers and sisters all need support, encouragement and assistance. They need understanding, not condescension; true compassion, not sentimental pity. Mentally retarded are a challenge to the Church itself, especially to the parish community, precisely because they have many more rights than merely to live.
>
> The parish in its census operation must, like the Good Shepherd, seek out all the families with retarded children and adults. It must offer catechesis, Catholic education, and preparation for the Sacraments; it must sensitize all parishioners to not only the problems involved, but as well the capabilities of the retarded, even to suitable employment.
>
> But in some ways even more importantly, the family must be given a warm welcome, a heartfelt acceptance into the parish community. They must be welcome and feel welcomed to participate as a family in the divine liturgy; to share in parochial activities. They too must learn that sacraments and prayer life are available to and important for the mentally retarded.[47]

In one of his last functions as archbishop, Manning blessed a new one-story, split level headquarters for the Church's expanding ministry to the handicapped and disabled. The building housed specialized staff members who directed programs for the deaf and hard of hearing, the visually impaired and people who were developmentally and physically disabled. Programs included religious education, liturgical celebrations, counseling, visitations, referrals, social activities, summer camp sessions, sign language classes, training courses and translations of devotional and educational publications into Braille.

In formal remarks before the blessing, Cardinal Manning told the small gathering that he had forty years of memories of association with the handicapped. There was one incident that conveyed how he would like to be remembered. "I was asked to have a picture taken on Ninth Street with a mentally retarded child and I put my zucchetto on his head. After the picture the child took off and I never got it back," the cardinal laughed. "That's the way I'd like to be remembered, that part of me remains here on Ninth Street." Using the analogy of a building and the different materials cut, shaped and altered to fit the master design, Manning said "all of us are part of God's building, part of the master plan Jesus has for the Church."

> Some have a special part and must be subject to a conditioning, a chipping away, in some human way a deprivation, so they have a special place in God's plan. This kind of apostolate is not horizontal. It is vertical, the dedication the people have for the disabled. This building is under the shadow of the archbishop in its solidity and permanence. Every time we look at it, it's an act of faith and love.[48]

Finally, Manning noted that "in recent years much emphasis has been placed on ministry to families" by the Church. He recalled that in 1978 the United States bishops issued a document calling for "a plan for pastoral action for Family Ministry." And it had named 1980 the "Year of the Family."

We recommend to you, therefore, an opportunity to support this effort. The Office of Religious Education is sponsoring, on behalf of those ministering to the family, "Hearings on the Family." These will be held in different areas of our archdiocese. In sponsoring these hearings our catechetical office hopes to model what parish communities are being asked to do: listen to their people and respond. We encourage you to invite those involved in leadership positions as well as your parishioners, to participate in these hearings.[49]

EPISCOPAL VICARS

The position of episcopal vicar is an outgrowth of Vatican Council II. "Its purpose is to bring the authority and responsibilities of the bishop closer to the people through a local representative or vicar." At the time, Bishop John Ward said that "the good of the faithful is the ultimate norm of the office."[50] In 1973, Auxiliary Bishop William Johnson was named Episcopal Vicar for Los Angeles county and for the Black communities and, at the same time, Auxiliary Bishop Juan Arzube was given that title for the Spanish speaking in the archdiocese. In April of 1974, Manning named Father Donald Strange Episcopal Vicar for Orange county and Father Patrick O'Brien Episcopal Vicar for Santa Barbara and Ventura counties.

Not long after, the cardinal established a multilingual apostolate for persons who spoke neither English nor Spanish. Father August Moretti was named to an *ad hoc* committee to poll all priests speaking languages other than English. They were then to be available so that everyone in the archdiocese could "take full advantage of sacramental, liturgical and pastoral life."[51]

MARRIAGE ENCOUNTER

The Marriage Encounter movement, introduced in the country in 1968, was enthusiastically welcomed to Los Angeles. In 1975, 5,500 participants gathered at California State University, in Pomona, in what was featured as the largest assemblage "of its type ever held in the western United States." Manning supported the movement, appointing Father Patrick Colleran as the archdiocesan coordinator. On June 26, 1977, he offered Mass for the final meeting of the Worldwide Marriage Encounter in the Los Angeles Coliseum which he said had been converted into a "ciborium of love" for the occasion. In his homily the cardinal said:

> The Catholic Church believes that the sign and instrument of the divine initiative to live according to the teachings of the Church "remains for the faithful of all ages in the gift of a ministry within the Church. This ministry is empowered by the Holy Spirit to discern, teach, and judge according to the mind of the Lord. This ministry is that of the bishops united with the successor of St. Peter."

Then he recalled Saint Paul's admonition to Timothy wherein he called for refuting error and correcting wrongs with obedience. He decried the "false teachers" then and now "within our own ranks, dressed in sheep's clothing, to present us a doctrine, a code of conduct and moral principles that are alien to the official magisterial teachings of the Church." He concluded by an exhortation:

> If marriage encounter has as its prime purpose the sanctification of the home, it follows as must night the day, and day the night, that if the famine of vocations is going to end, it will end in the homes of those who are here present today, and that the first result of this gathering, of this prayer, will be a new spring of vocations to the priesthood and the religious life once more in the glory of the Church.[52]

The ever increasing call by Catholics for marital annulments and dispensations triggered concern from the cardinal about the quality of the marriage preparation courses offered in the parishes. He expressed his thoughts on the subject in 1974:

> The need is felt, and strongly impressed on us, to reemphasize the importance and nature of the marriage preparation programs in the archdiocese. These courses are necessary and helpful, but they are so designed to help the parish priest, not to replace him. He has the ultimate responsibility for the couple's preparation. Courses offer general information, but cannot possibly cater to the specific needs and life-situations of all couples in attendance. Fears are being expressed by some moderators of the programs that for some priests, their total preparation of a couple consists in referring them to a marriage preparation course.
>
> Areas of great concern deal with the preparation of the young, those under eighteen years of age; inter-faith couples; couples lacking in knowledge of their faith; or without a faith commitment, and couples who attend the course reluctantly or with some hostility. Indeed in the area of marriage preparation, more attention must be given to parochial and educational programs, to provide long-range marriage and family life education. Our people and their life styles are being affected by the changing values of society regarding

> marriage and the family and the divorce rate among Catholics is climbing steadily.

Manning concluded by unequivocally endorsing Pope Paul VI's teaching on birth control: "We feel that special emphasis must be given to the teachings of *Humanae Vitae* so that there be a strict adherence to this official teaching of the Church, and that every Christian marriage is a lifetime commitment and always open to life."[53]

Two years later, the cardinal issued a new Marriage Preparation policy which required all couples to notify their parish priest three months before their proposed wedding "so that there will be an adequate time for proper preparation for married life."[54] It was a sound policy primarily aimed at helping young people understand their own strengths and weaknesses as they planned their futures together.

PARISH COUNCILS

By 1974, a fair number of parishes in the Archdiocese of Los Angeles had already established parochial councils. "Shared responsibility in the reality of a new age in the Church" was the theme of a message by the cardinal endorsing the movement. He said that such sharing "allows for the involvement of all the faithful" and was typical of the early Church. "No superficial attempt to capture this spirit will suffice" he said. "The parish council is an excellent forum for the development and expression of these gifts by which all things are restored in Christ."[55]

It was in 1971, that Manning encouraged the Catholic Welfare Bureau to look into ways of expanding senior citizen housing in the archdiocese. Those efforts led to the eventual establishment of the independent, non-profit Las Torres Corporation which was able to secure a $5.4 million loan from the United States Department of Housing and Urban Development (HUD) to construct a building. The property owned by the archdiocese was transferred to the Las Torres Corporation. The modern eight-story facility at 944 Gratten Street was finally opened in 1980. Each of the 108 units was approximately 57 square feet in size and contained a bedroom, a living room, kitchen, bathroom and private balcony. Six of the apartments were specially equipped for wheelchair handicapped people.[56] While Las Torres only addressed a minuscule portion of the overall needs, it visibly symbolized the concern of the Catholic Church for the poor.

PEACE AND JUSTICE

Cardinal Manning established the Commission on Peace and Justice in 1983 with six specific objectives:

1. Through peace and social justice education, to deepen the Gospel principles of all the people in the archdiocese;
2. To create at the parish and neighborhood levels a sense of concern for all who suffer from injustice and who are unable to find peace in their lives;
3. To act as a resource to the archbishop and, if he requests, in specific instances, to function as a resource for the presbyterate, religious and people of the archdiocese;
4. To assist and advise the archbishop in his proclamation of the principles of peace and justice in areas of concern within the archdiocese;
5. To bring to the attention of the archbishop selected passages or documentation from the Holy Father, the National Conference of Catholic Bishops and any other authentic and authoritative voice;
6. To promote sound Catholic peace and social justice principles in areas of public policy within the archdiocese.

Father Royale Vadakin, the chairperson of the commission said that:

> Since the overall mission of Christ within the Church falls to the pastoral leadership of the archbishop within the archdiocese, the commission will maintain close working contact with the archbishop in selecting areas of peace and social justice concern. The commission will keep the archbishop completely informed of its proceedings, discussions and the results of its study and will take no action without his explicit approval.
>
> Since many peace and social justice issues also have various theological, scriptural and pastoral dimensions, the commission shall confine its study and proclamations to the specific areas of its competency and mandate. The archbishop may refer theological and pastoral dimensions of

issues to other bodies within the archdiocese for study and possible action.[57]

Manning's penchant for peace and justice was likely a throwback to his youth when his native country was ravished by so many violations of those virtues. In his Christmas message for 1983, the cardinal said that "the heart hungers for many things. It is restless until it rests in God. The other name for this fulfillment is peace."

> Our global village has now no peace. Violence and fratricide are the patrimony of a world gone mad, gone astray from God. We have lost the way, we have abandoned the truth, we have smothered life. Yet there is a way back, a way known as conversion, reconciliation, forgiveness. It runs from Bethlehem to Calvary to the right hand of the Father. It is the glory road. Peace is the theme-song of Christmas. It is dropped down from heaven on angels' voices. It enters our own souls in the Sacrament of Reconciliation. Let us go over to that peace, no matter how heavy the burden on our conscience, no matter how petty our transgressions. Going there we will find our peace and finding it we will know the happiness of the Christ Mass – Christmas. This is a shepherd's wish for all his flock.[58]

In a commentary on the United States Bishops Peace Pastoral, the cardinal issued these moving words:

> To turn from war to peace is to be converted; to grow in our dedication to justice and peace is a process of ongoing conversion. The call to a change of heart is accepted by the bishops themselves and addressed by them to others in ministry in the Church: priests, religious educators, all who help form Catholic consciences.
>
> Political and military leaders as well must re-think their positions if the world is to be changed. Catholics who serve in the armed forces or who work in the arms industry will also have to search their consciences to discern how God is calling them. All of us who are citizens of this most powerful country in the world need to reflect and pray over the Gospel message and learn to apply it to the complex choices that face us. The bishops can speak as leaders of the Church: it is up to us to act.[59]

Notes to the Text

1. *The Tidings*, October 11, 1968.
2. *Ibid.*, June 6, 1969.
3. *Ibid.*, October 22, 1971.
4. AALA, Timothy Manning to John Sammon, Los Angeles, December 14, 1972.
5. AALA, Timothy Manning to Friends, Los Angeles, September 23, 1977.
6. *Permanent Diaconate. Five Years Later* (Los Angeles, 1977), Pp. 3-4.
7. *Ibid.*, p.5.
8. AALA, "General Background of the Twenty Five Candidates," 1973.
9. U.S. Bishops Committee, *Permanent Deacons in the United States* (Washington, 1968) p.28.
10. AALA, William R. Johnson, to Thomas J. McDonough, Los Angeles, May 13, 1974.
11. *The Tidings*, October 4, 1974.
12. *Ibid.*, February 21, 1975.
13. *Ibid.*, June 6, 1975.
14. Los Angeles *Times*, June 7, 1975.
15. *The Tidings*, June 13, 1975.
16. AALA, "Deacon Role Delineation," Los Angeles, n.d. (1975).
17. AALA, John A. Rawden, Chancellor, Faculties for Deacons, Los Angeles, January 7, 1975.
18. AALA, Peter Healy to Benjamin G. Hawkes, Los Angeles, April 6, 1976.
19. AALA, *Newsletter* I (December, 1976), 1.
20. *The Tidings*, July 22, 1977.
21. *Permanent Diaconate. Five Years Later*, p.1.
22. *The Tidings*, June 9, 1978.

23. AALA, James Francis Cardinal McIntyre - Memo, Los Angeles, April 14, 1962.
24. *The Tidings*, February 6, 1970.
25. *Ibid.*, April 9, 1971.
26. "Some Observations on Catholic Pentecostalism," Los Angeles, April 8, 1971.
27. 97 (April 19, 1971), 30.
28. AALA, Timothy Manning to Clergy, Los Angeles, June 7, 1971.
29. AALA, TRD to Timothy Manning, Los Angeles, August 4, 1971.
30. Los Angeles *Times*, July 11, 1971.
31. Monterey *Observer*, February 2, 1972.
32. *National Catholic Reporter*, September 9, 1973.
33. III (July 15, 1971), 6.
34. AALA, Betty Smith to John J. Ward, Los Angeles, July 20, 1972.
35. AALA, Ralph Tichenor to Timothy Manning, Los Angeles, August 31, 1972. For a short but accurate history and explanation, see Tichenor's *Reflections on the Charismatic Renewal* (Los Angeles, 1974).
36. AALA, Benjamin G. Hawkes to Thomas A. McDonald, Los Angeles, October 16, 1972.
37. AALA, August Moretti to Timothy Manning, Los Angeles, January 16, 1973.
38. *The Tidings*, April 6, 1973.
39. AALA, Timothy Cardinal Manning to Clergy, Los Angeles, April 1, 1974.
40. November 30, 1974.
41, "Address of Pope Paul VI," Rome, October 16, 1974. Quoted in *Statement on Catholic Charismatic Renewal* (Washington, D.C., 1974), Pp. 7, 9.
42. AALA, Timothy Cardinal Manning to Clergy, Los Angeles, September 15, 1983.
43. AALA, Timothy Manning to Clergy, Los Angeles, September 14, 1972.
44. AALA, Timothy Manning to Clergy, Los Angeles, May 26, 1970.
45. *The Tidings*, January 21, 1972.

46. *Ibid.*, October 19, 1973.
47. AALA, Timothy Cardinal Manning to Friends, Los Angeles, February 7, 1984.
48. *The Tidings*, September 6, 1985.
49. AALA, Timothy Cardinal Manning to Clergy, Los Angeles, February 19, 1985.
50. *The Tidings*, April 26, 1974.
51. *Ibid.*, January 4, 1974.
52. *Ibid.*, July 1, 1977.
53. AALA, Timothy Cardinal Manning to Clergy, Los Angeles, January 21, 1974.
54. AALA, Timothy O'Connell to Clergy, Los Angeles, September 24, 1976.
55. *The Tidings*, June 24, 1977.
56. *Ibid.*, August 1, 1980.
57. *Ibid.*, March 4, 1983.
58. *Ibid.*, December 23, 1983.
59. *Maryknoll* LXXVIII (March, 1984), back cover.

19. *A Trilogy of Concerns*

At the curial level, the Archdiocese of Los Angeles is composed of several dozen agencies, departments, apostolates, commissions and ministries especially crafted to serve the needs of its constituents. During his years as archbishop, Timothy Manning had a special interest in and relation to three of those services.

THE TIDINGS

Throughout his long ministry, Timothy Manning recognized and appreciated the role of the Catholic press in gathering, propagating and validating the Gospel message. He once observed that "newspapers are like the daily manna that sustained the Israelites on their pilgrimage through the desert. Like manna, the newspaper is good only for the day, but it is a necessary mental sustenance."[1]

Few issues of *The Tidings* published between 1946 and 1989 failed to reproduce a homily or address given by Manning as auxiliary bishop, archbishop or cardinal. In fact, that relationship stretched back even further because a fair number of Archbishop John J. Cantwell's utterances appearing in *The Tidings* were ghost written totally or in part by Manning who served as the prelate's secretary for eight years.

During the early 1950s, the editor of the paper inaugurated what became known as the annual Tidings Crusade. Contest were held in the Catholic schools of the archdiocese and prizes were awarded to students turning in the largest numbers of renewals or new subscribers. With the cooperation of the Sisters, the circulation of *The Tidings* hit an all-time high in 1966, with 120,356 paid subscribers. Manning took an active part in the crusades even before he became archbishop. In 1961, for example, in a talk to the Archdiocesan Council of Catholic Women, he pointed out that "the parish and diocesan life is the divinely constituted source of our spiritual life. The very voice of that parish and diocese is underscored in the diocesan newspaper, the means through which the bishop, the constituted teacher of the flock, speaks to us. His voice is the paper. It is the official voice, interpreter and molder of the Catholic faith."[2]

Manning's support for *The Tidings* became even more pronounced when he became the newspaper's official publisher. He often referred to the paper as the "indispensable mouthpiece" for the Church in Southern California. He expressed a profound disappointment when *The Monitor*, the Catholic paper for San Francisco, was closed down, promising that such would never happen in Los Angeles.

A measure of the prominence that Manning accorded *The Tidings* is evident in his annual appeals for the crusades. In 1970, for example, he urged every Catholic family to subscribe saying "our archdiocesan newspaper functions as an authentic extension of the *magisterium* of the Church, and as such, should be read in every Catholic home. Our people need correct information and balanced perspective in matters of their faith."[3] On another occasion, Manning described the paper as the "authentic voice of the bishop," noting that in Los Angeles *The Tidings* was "the communication of the bishop to the people of God who are on pilgrimage and cannot always safely follow in the rarified climate of the wise ones." Asking that a copy be in every home, he said "it will be a symbol of our shepherding in love of this wonderful people and it will be a touch of orthodoxy in our beliefs and in our loyalties."[4]

And, in a letter to pastors, Manning accorded *The Tidings* "prime place in the promotion of social dialogue in that it encourages people to think and stimulates the processes by which public opinion is formed. It is a glass that reflects the world and a light to show the way." He found it hard "to see how people can keep in touch with what is happening in the Church without the Catholic press."[5] In another exhortation for support, the cardinal noted that "all concerns that preoccupy the Church and society find a hearing in *The Tidings*. These are the social and cultural realities in which people live." The paper is "for young and old, for the multiplicity of our ethnic groups and for those who can scan the wider horizons of the world from the perspective of eternity."[6]

Though he left the daily operation of the paper to his editors, Manning monitored the contents of every issue. He made frequent suggestions about potential topics, especially to the writer of the column, "California's Catholic Heritage." He considered *The Tidings* his newspaper and he was proud of it. Among the most popular columns during those years was that compiled by Hermine Lees, "Files from *The Tidings*," wherein readers learned about the happenings of seventy-five, fifty or twenty-five years earlier. Early in 1976, *The Tidings* surveyed its readership about their expectations of what a Catholic newspaper should provide for its readers. Not surprisingly, the results indicated that most of what it was doing was on target.

Sixty-nine percent of readers wanted local news, sixty percent read national news and fifty-five percent liked the editorial page. Entertainment news, sports, school and women's news were next in order of reader preference. Columnists were also rated, with Archbishop Robert Dwyer being the most read (56%), followed by Dolores Curran (43%) and "California's Catholic Heritage" in third place (40%). Most people requested more attention to Catholic teaching and the viewpoint of the Church on current events. That *The Tidings* continued being highly regarded by the Catholic Press Association was confirmed by the steady awarding of citations given to the paper during the 1970s.

The cardinal had a close personal relationship with Msgr. Patrick Roche who edited the paper from 1957 to 1973. Those who followed Roche's *El Rodeo* columns were as impressed by his style as by their content. To the very last, the monsignor was a master of phraseology. The record needs to show, however, that Roche departed significantly from his predecessors insofar as he was exceedingly conservative, almost reactionary in many of his views. During his editorship, *The Tidings* lost much of its credibility among those imbued with the so-called "spirit" of Vatican Council II. Yet, when he retired, he was praised by Cardinal Manning for his "sensitive and capable management of the paper. *The Tidings* has reflected a true image of the Church and the archdiocese under your loyal priestly mind and heart." Manning went on to express the hope that "we can all call upon your experience regularly for the continued guidance of the official newspaper of the archdiocese." With Roche's retirement, Manning chose a veteran columnist and an outstanding Catholic layman as its editor. Alphonse Antczak had been with *The Tidings* since 1947 and was destined to remain at his post until 1989, leaving his imprint on no fewer than 2,210 weekly issues. The fifteenth editor continued and expanded the coverage of California's oldest and most distinguished Catholic newspaper.

During the Antczak years, *The Tidings* operated in the black and continued to help subsidize such projects as the construction of the Education Building, the Catholic Charities headquarters and Santa Marta Hospital. Substantial annual grants were also distributed to numerous inner-city parishes during the tenure of the post World War II editors. During those years, *The Tidings* won awards for reporting, editorials and layout. Among those citations, none pleased Manning more than the one given for the paper's editorial support of farm workers at Rancho Sespe in Ventura County.

One of the biggest stories during the 1970s was the creation of the Diocese of Orange. At Manning's behest, Antczak wrote to Bishop William R. Johnson offering the services of *The Tidings* to the new Diocese of Orange where the circulation was already 9,222. Antczak wanted to continue coverage of Catholic events in the diocese, even suggesting the possibility of a special section carrying a separate logo.[7] Several of the employees at *The Tidings* lived in the county and Antczak envisioned profiling the diocese in several tabloid sections. Happily, most of the subscribers in the area opted to retain their subscription to *The Tidings*, even after the establishment of the *Diocese of Orange Bulletin*.

In August of 1978, editor Alphonse Antczak summarized some of the programs underway, noting that *The Tidings* had already that year published eight tabloids related to various ministries. He pointed out that stories receiving priority coverage were those dealing with civil rights, the Church in Latin America, abortion, school support and the relationship of teenagers and young adults with the Church. In every case, this same mix was being featured by the secular press, but without any relationship to morality or religion.

Beginning in February, 1978, *The Tidings* launched a program whereby its weekly issues would be recorded on cassettes for the blind. The cassettes were made available to any handicapped person with an inability to use printed matter. For the first taping, Cardinal Manning personally recorded his Lenten message, declaring that "the taping of the archdiocesan newspaper, *The Tidings*, is another example of the use of the electronic media in our pastoral concern for handicapped people. This will keep our people better informed as to what is taking place in their Church and encourage their own involvement in it!"

> For four years we have been using very successfully a teletypewriter to keep contact with our hearing-impaired people. Although in many areas of their lives deaf and visually handicapped people might feel the isolation of their condition, we are hopeful that our efforts to communicate with them through these machines, will be an indication that the Church loves them and is reaching out to them in this way.[8]

After several years of study, Cardinal Manning announced, in September of 1977, a Retirement Plan for the staff of *The Tidings*. His Eminence noted that he and others had long been concerned for the financial security of workers in their retirement years. The parameters

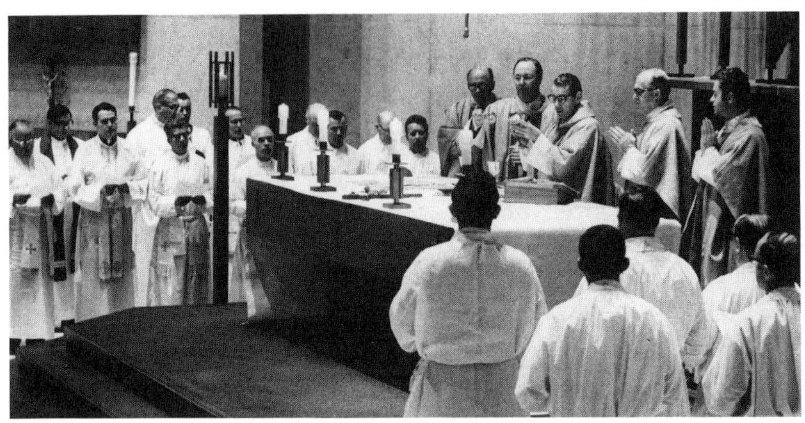

Manning offers Mass for the missions at Saint Basil's church in the mid-Wilshire district.

The cardinal pauses in the shack of a missionary in the Pacific.

Cardinal Manning visits with a Lay Mission Helper.

The cardinal exchanges his zucchetto with a youngster in the missions.

of the precedent-breaking plan were spelled out in a brochure distributed to employees.

Among the cardinal's innovations for *The Tidings* were his annual Lenten and Advent reflections, some of which were re-issued in pamphlet form after their appearance in the newspaper. An examination of the two volumes of his homilies, addresses and talks, which were published in book form between 1987 and 1990, together with the smaller selection of his invocations, blessings and dedications, reveal that many of those utterances first appeared in their entirety or in excerpts in *The Tidings*. Manning also wrote many short but penetrating pastoral letters which graced the pages of *The Tidings* and many of them also found their way into brochures and pamphlets. The Archival Center still gets requests for copies of those works.

In one of his last appeals for support of *The Tidings*, Manning once again demonstrated his support of the Catholic press as a vital part of the Church's ministry:

> The Church calls us to live our lives in fidelity to the Gospel. We must live with sensitivity for the teachings of Jesus. These must be the basis for our relationship to God and to our neighbor. To help us attain and maintain this sensitivity in the many dimensions of our daily lives, the Church publishes a weekly newspaper. Its purpose is to keep us up-to-date on the authentic thought, work and teaching of the Church.
>
> Each week *The Tidings* reports the guidance and instruction our Holy Father gives us on family life, personal spirituality, our obligations to social justice and work for peace. Each week *The Tidings* reports the counsel given by our bishops and pastors, the news and human interest stories of edifying apostolic work by an amazing number of lay persons here.
>
> *The Tidings* is not only informative but formative through the adult education material in its Question Box, liturgy column, commentaries on family life, television and movies. *The Tidings* makes a particular effort to appeal to the young in its editorial style.[9]

Though he left the everyday operations of *The Tidings* to its professional staff, Manning remained ever ready to lend his support and encouragement. He remained always the "wind beneath their wings" as the presses rolled out the weekly newspaper for the Archdiocese of Los Angeles.[10]

CEMETERIES

In 1941, when Bishop McGucken became auxiliary, the then Father Timothy Manning was given care of Catholic cemeteries. In addition to parochial cemeteries in such places as Santa Barbara, Oxnard and San Gabriel, there were two archdiocesan cemeteries, Calvary and Holy Cross. Resident directors residing at both locations directed daily operations. Even after becoming auxiliary bishop, Manning retained his position as "director" of cemeteries until 1952. He enjoyed celebrating the liturgy in the beautiful and artistic Mausoleum chapel at Calvary which was designed by the same architect who worked on the chapel at Saint John's Seminary in Camarillo.

In the summer of 1970, Archbishop Manning wrote that:

> Every church has a facility known as the "*sacrarium*." It is a disposal place into which is put the residue of holy things that have served their function. Sacred oils, the ashes of sacred objects that have been burned as required by ritual, the washings of sacred linens. The disposal empties directly into the earth and not into the common sewer. Such is the respect the Church has for material things that, when they have fulfilled their sacred purpose, they may not be profanely discarded, but reverently enfolded in the earth.
>
> If this be the measure of respect for material objects, we can have some concept of the regard which the Church has for the human body when it becomes a corpse. In life it was the envelope of the soul, anointed in baptism, a housing for the Eucharist, made sacred again in the oils of Confirmation, hallowed in suffering and pain. It lays down life in the hope of rising again in the same, but glorified flesh. For all these reasons the Church will not allow a profane discarding of human remains. She reverently incenses them, sprinkles them with holy water, blesses the earth in which they will lie and stands watch over their holy ashes, until doomsday and the resurrection from the dead.[11]

A few months later, Manning observed that "the liturgy speaks of a place of light, happiness and peace, which we wish for those who have gone before us marked with the sign of faith. Our Catholic cemeteries are in a way sacramental signs of that eternal blessedness. There is an abiding quality of repose and peace which descends over these holy acres. It is a wholesome thing for us to visit them, and there, in a communion of Saints, to pray for those from whom we are separated for a while." Then Manning suggested that the Catholic cemetery "offers us graphic evidence that the ultimate goal of our earthly lives is to prepare ourselves to go home to God." It is "a reliquary of the saints, just as surely as the catacombs were in the earliest centuries of the Church. Already in the next world, those buried there have left us something of themselves aside from their memory, love and prayers." He concluded by saying that a Catholic cemetery is "first and last and always a blessed sanctuary wherein rest the faithful, awaiting the fullness of Christ's redemptive action, on the day of our resurrection unto life eternal."[12]

The only cemetery opened during Manning's tenure was Assumption in Simi Valley which was dedicated by the archbishop on November 7, 1970. Property for the new cemetery, 160 acres, had been purchased in 1962. Only part of the area was dedicated to burial purposes in what was the fourteenth cemetery in the archdiocese.[13]

The question of allowing cremation for Catholics finally was addressed in 1972. Manning remained personally opposed to the practice, but he did notify his priests that exceptions to the general practice would now be permitted. In issuing this directive, he said that "it is not recommended that this be given any general publication, but merely be available for pastoral counseling in individual cases."

1. The practice of burying the bodies of the faithful is by all means to be kept; hence Ordinaries should, by appropriate instructions and exhortations, see to it that Catholics do not practice cremation and that, except in cases of necessity, they do not abandon the practice of burial, which the Church has always kept and which she consecrates with solemn rites.

2. However, lest difficulties arising from present circumstances be unduly increased, and lest the necessity of dispensing from existing laws in this matter become more frequent, it has been wisely determined to mitigate somewhat the prescriptions of canon law concerning cremation, so that the provisions of canon 1203 2 (prohibiting cremation) and those of canon 1240 1, 5 - (denying ecclesiastical burial to persons who ordered that their bodies be cremated) be henceforth binding, not universally, but only when it is certain that cremation was chosen because of the denial of Chris-

tian dogmas, or because of a sectarian spirit, or through hatred of the Catholic religion and the Church.

3. It follows that persons who chose to have their bodies cremated are not for that reason to be denied the sacraments or public suffrages, unless it is certain that they made that choice for the above-mentioned reasons inimical to the Christian way of life.[14]

In 1983, Manning once again wrote the priests, reminding them that the archdiocese "maintains cemeteries with a great deal of pride, effort and expense, so that there may be places of faith, hope and love for both the living and the dead." He worried that "many of our Catholic people do not seem to be fully aware of the importance of the Catholic cemetery in their life of faith."

> November, the month dedicated to the Holy Souls, gives us a perfect opportunity to remind our people that the blessed end of the earthly life of the faithful Christian resides within the Catholic Cemeteries. May we ask your support through preaching, announcements and education on the value and the necessity of burial in our Catholic Cemeteries?

The cardinal emphasized that "for many of us, as well as our people, these thoughts carry us to our own cemeteries where our dead have found their final resting place. These holy places give hope and inspiration for us pilgrims on our journey to be with our Heavenly Father."[15]

MISSIONARY APOSTOLATE

The Pontifical Society for the Propagation of the Faith is the official missionary outreach program established in each diocese and archdiocese of the Catholic Church throughout the world. Operating under the auspices of the Roman Congregation of the Evangelization of Peoples, it provides the material and spiritual support necessary to sustain missionaries and their programs around the globe. Since the days of Msgr. Anthony Brouwers, the Los Angeles branch of the society had been a model for other jurisdictions throughout the United States. In his early days as bishop, Manning had enlisted Brouwers as his master-of-ceremonies on his annual confirmation tours and the two became close friends, sharing similar viewpoints about the missions. Throughout his life, Manning considered "the missionary movement as the essential heart of the Church in the modern world.[16]

Organizationally, the Propagation of the Faith office in Los Angeles remained mostly unchanged during the Manning years. Already its track record was impressive and Manning saw no advantage in tinkering with what was already performing at maximum efficiency. That Manning took an active role in furthering the goals of the Propagation is evident from the letters he sent out announcing the annual appeals for support. In each of those letters, Manning stressed that the Church was "essentially missionary," as had been stated by the Vatican Council. That being so, then "the emissaries of the missions must claim attention from us that be not peripheral to our life interests but must touch its core."[17]

In 1975, Manning said that "it is time for harvesting and the fields are ripe. The cultures of the mission countries are precursors to the Gospel. The emergence of native hierarchies and priesthood usher in a new era of life-movement in the Church. All of us belong to that universal Church. All of us must share in the prayer and sacrifice required for the coming of the kingdom to all people."[18]

Manning's appeal in 1977 was especially pungent:

> Each dawn and sunrise is a miracle of God's fatherly providence for all of us. The mystery of Christ in God's plan is also a miracle of light flooding the world with each day's Mass. The more brilliant the light, the deeper are the shadows where it does not reach. We light our tapers from the sun to carry its light and push back the darkness. Likewise must we be illuminated by Christ, the Light of the World, so that we may be bearers of His grace and truth into the darkness.
>
> Mission Sunday gives us an occasion to meditate on our commitment to Christ and to His Church. Where we cannot go ourselves we must sustain those who do. Our cooperation is two fold. It is exemplified in prayers for the missions and in our monetary contribution according to our means. Mission Sunday is a day for reminders. It is not just a once-in-a year Sunday for our thrust must be missionary always.[19]

On another occasion, he said that "We salute the entire missionary Church, and we extend to all men and women who in their outposts of evangelization dedicate themselves to the care of their brothers, our encouragement and our most loving recognition. They should know

Cardinal Manning gets buckled in for a flight to a mission out-station in New Guinea.

Who's the man in the funny hat?

Cardinal Manning in a back station in Africa.

Cardinal shows his pectoral cross to youngsters in Africa.

that, among all who are dear to us, they are the dearest."[20] Manning felt that "an essential component of our faith is the joy of professing it. Surely it is proper that we should share this joy with the missions." He reminded his people that "the Holy Father looks to us to help him. We do this in many ways throughout the year. However, one Sunday it is set aside for a particular response to this need and we call it Mission Sunday."[21]

While appealing for material aid, Manning felt "we must be cautious, lest we would think that our duty is fulfilled in listening to a sermon or making a contribution on this isolated occasion. The Church is essentially missionary. We are, each one of us, missionaries to the world that does not know Christ. May our life and our love be a fulfillment of that responsibility."[22] Of all the dozen or more annual collections taken up in the archdiocese, the largest was always the one for the missions. Receipts from the offices of the Propagation in Los Angeles customarily ranked near the top for the nation, as indicated by the following chart.

YEAR	DIOCESAN OFFICE	NATIONAL OFFICE	TOTAL
1974	261,471	402,840	664,311
1977	514,153	404,806	918,959
1978	524,781	879,639	1,404,420
1979	751,371	387,741	1,139,112
1980	828,717	238,819	1,067,536
1981	995,656	294,941	1,290,597

The direct appeal to the faithful for missionary support was not just a once-a-year event. The archdiocese sponsored what was known as a Mission Cooperative Plan whereby up to eighty missions societies and dioceses were each invited to send preachers to three or four parishes.

A Sunday was set aside and the guest speaker explained the work of the Church in some desolate area and how that ministry needed to be assisted by prayers and material offerings. Generally those appeals were quite successful.

Also operating under the umbrella of the Society for the Propagation of the Faith were other missionary programs, including the Pontifical Association for the Holy Childhood, the only agency of its kind for young Catholics. Mostly this group sponsored programs that assisted youngsters to practice their faith better through learning, prayer and action, especially towards those who were sick, hungry or unloved. Appeals in Advent, Lent and other seasons provided youngsters with the opportunity of contributing to the Holy Childhood and traditionally, the Archdiocese of Los Angeles ranked first in the United States for total contributions to this worthy cause.

YEAR	AMOUNT
1969-1970	200,131
1973-1974	118,851
1974-1975	114,731
1975-1976	128,145

Of all the accomplishments that adorned the Manning years, he was happiest and most pleased with the Lay Mission Helpers. He claimed that "they are indeed the pride and ornament of our Church."[23] He once declared that he was "proud to be the archbishop from the jurisdiction that sponsors this work."[24]

The Lay Mission Helpers were founded by Msgr. Brouwers in 1955 and, by the time Manning became archbishop one out of every six long-term missionaries from the United Sates was a Lay Mission Helper. In one of his editorials for the archdiocesan newspaper, Msgr. Patrick Roche explained that "This organization is made up of Catholic laymen and women who, after undergoing an intensive and lengthy period of preparation, volunteer their services to help the Church in the missionary areas of the world. They commit themselves, their energies and skills, to serve God in those areas where He needs the human resources which they alone can supply."

Roche went on to say that Manning had returned from his first visit with the Lay Mission Helpers the previous week. "It was a journey suffused with all the arduous qualities which any long journey entails. It was a journey to a land which he had not seen before, among peoples whom he had never met, along pathways which few have encountered in the Western world. He returned from that journey rejoicing in the fact that he had gained a brief glimpse of the kingdom of God on earth. It was, in his own words, the most tremendous and warming experience in his entire priesthood. For he had traveled on a paternal visit to the Lay Mission Helpers who have gone forth from this archdiocese to the remote missions of eastern Africa."[25]

Each year Manning would preside at the commissioning ceremonies for the Lay Mission Helpers. He followed their travels with great interest, concern and prayer, often sending personal messages to them. In 1971, for example, he said that "God loves us with outstretched arms. His arms are nailed to love. This love must be made visible to each generation and in each place. This is the secret fire in the hearts of our Lay Mission Helpers. It is their driving force of love, and our gratitude rests with them."[26] In another communication, he noted that "The Spirit is moving quietly and forcefully all across the Church. Here in Los Angeles we are edified each day by new manifestations of dedication and of love. One of the most decisive evidences of the activity of the Spirit is the program of the Lay Mission Helpers. In the mission world their names are a benediction and our archdiocese is richly blessed in return. Every prayer and every sacrifice made for this cause is worthy of the great traditions of the Church of Los Angeles."[27]

By 1980, over 600 men and women had served in the Church's missions in thirty-two countries and their number continued to grow.[28] Four years later, there were 175 "mission circles" active in the archdiocese. They were "guilds" formed to support a particular mission materially and spiritually. The original notion of the Lay Mission Helpers was that they be self-sufficient and mostly they were. Manning rarely missed the annual luncheons for the Mission Circles which were held at the Embassy Room of the Ambassador Hotel.

Closely aligned with the Lay Mission Helpers was the Mission Doctors Association. That agency was desperately needed in mission lands where two-thirds of the world population knew little or nothing about medicine. Manning was also supportive of that group and never missed one of their gatherings. He once noted that there were "two abiding characteristics which our saving Lord announced for His kingdom" namely "that the sick would be healed and that the poor would have the Gospel preached to them. This must be verified in every generation if the credibility of the claim of the Church is to be vindicated. Too often it has been presumed that these activities are the responsibility solely of missionary priests and Sisters. It is not so. Everyone who has responded in faith to Christ must become a witness, a missionary. Our Mission Doctors Association is an eminent vehicle for such a response. We wish to emphasize our endorsement of its plan and program, and we solicit wide cooperation and support in its endeavors."[29]

In another context, Manning pointed out that "an essential part of this apostolate is the physical care for the needs and illnesses of the Third World. This is the vocation to which our Mission Doctors Association responds. As a preparation for evangelization, for receiving the Word of God, our Divine Lord healed the sick and cast out demons. He was forever pushing back the empire of darkness. It is in fidelity to this plan that our doctors dedicate themselves to so holy a cause."[30]

MISSIONARY JOURNEYS

During the final three decades of his life, Manning probably visited more missionary areas of the world than any other prelate, except perhaps the Cardinal Prefect of the Sacred Congregation for Evangelizing Peoples. Everywhere he brought the message of a kind and loving shepherd, intent on searching out the lost sheep. Manning's first trek occurred in 1965, while he was still Auxiliary Bishop of Los Angeles. On that occasion he visited stations in the South Pacific, the Far East and India.

Upon his return, Manning was interviewed by a reporter for *The Tidings*. He noted that "the Church is not a European thing, not a Roman culture nor language nor law. It is a leaven injected into every culture and country, redeeming it for the Lord." He predicted that the decree on missions, then being formulated at Vatican Council II, would "disturb the complacency of those who thought the peoples in the Third World were less than important in the sight of the Lord." He felt that "in due time God will give the increase" to the seed sown by contemporary missionaries. "The harvest follows the interstices of failure, suffering and awaiting."[31]

After he became archbishop, Manning took seriously his role as spiritual leader of the Lay Mission Helpers and the Mission Doctors. His objective was to visit every one of those dedicated people at least once during his incumbency. The first of those month-long journeys, planned for the summer of 1970, would take him to South Africa, Rhodesia, Kenya, Malawi and Uganda. In Rhodesia he would visit Mission Doctors who maintained a flying medical service in an area nearly the size of California. Manning explained the motives impelling him to visit Africa in these words:

> Our first is to meet as many as possible of the members of the Lay Mission Helpers of Los Angeles serving on the African continent. These are part of the flock of our archdiocese, and our pastoral concern follows them. They are indeed the pride and ornament of our Church, and surely much of the benediction that has reverted on our heads locally is due to the merits of this heroic band of volunteers, selflessly and zealously tithing their lives in Africa and elsewhere.
>
> We will be companioned on the journey with the spirit of Monsignor Anthony Brouwers. We shared the secrets of his great heart when he conceived this movement, and we witnessed the sacrifice of his young life for its cause. Secondly, we wish, by this pilgrimage, to subscribe to the whole missionary concept and essence of the Church as recalled in the Second Vatican Council. The Church is not the aggregate of local churches, but is one in its surpassing and contemporary witnessing to the lordship of Christ our Lord over all men and all creation.
>
> The pastors of the Church must affirm that truth and instill its meaning and responsibility into those who might otherwise remain closed in their own contented form of Catholic life. We must burst through all barriers and restrictions that the word of God be not inhibited in our times.[32]

His journey was exceedingly successful. When Manning returned he was once again interviewed for the local Catholic newspaper. He called the visit "the greatest experience of my priesthood."

> There you see the Church in a throbbing sense of charity. You see and read about the missions, but that doesn't begin to give you any concept of the great dedication there. You expect it from priests. It is radiant in the lay people. Why would a young doctor, his wife and four children, leave home and pledge to serve three years in the mission?

He was most impressed by the "great spirit among the missionaries. They're all happy people. There's a sense of happiness there that we have lost." He was pleased to report that time and time again he was told that the Lay Mission Helpers "were the best trained" of any in the field. And "there's a deep spirituality among them. There's not a single complaint. Joy is very obvious. I could not speak in more glowing terms of them, their total trust and love of God."

> The Lord gave two signs of His mission, that the poor would have the Gospel preached to them and that disease would be healed. These things are being done. Priests are preaching the Gospel and Mission Doctors and Lay Mission Helpers are healing disease and pushing back the darkness of ignorance.

Manning said that his journey "was taken to carry out the dictates of Vatican II that a diocese concern itself with the universal Church beyond its own boundaries. We must open our sights to the mission world. It's not charity, but an obligation."[33]

Two years later, Manning set out once again for Africa to visit twenty-five Lay Mission Helpers working in Ghana, Nigeria, Malawi and Kenya. This time he proclaimed that his "primary purpose was to make "a symbolic affirmation, to assert the essential missionary character of the Church." A second purpose was that of encouraging the Lay Mission Helpers "who are devoting their energies, skills and love to the poor and needy peoples of missionary territories."[34] A motion picture cameraman accompanied the party to shoot footage for use in promotional films about the Church's work in missionary lands.

Later, when queried by a reporter from the Los Angeles *Times*, Manning portrayed Africa as "poor, torn by tribal rivalries" but coming to age spiritually. He found the Lay Mission Helpers "hard at work, convinced of the value of what they are doing, and sweeping ahead with Christian efforts on the continent." As an aside, he noted that he found "no peer tyranny to dictate conduct, style, hair-do. The only Afro-do we saw was an American visitor at the airport at Nairobi." Though there was a color line and racism in Africa, he felt that "Tribal rivalry is more acute than black-white racism. Efforts are being made to temper these rivalries, while at the same time preserving the best of their inheritance. It is a good move." Manning was optimistic about Africa's future, feeling that "while the back of the white world is turned, the Holy Spirit is cultivating a garden of the Church that will be the joy and harvesting of a new dawning and a new day."[35]

Rose Princess Rabin Townsend and Cardinal Manning appear in 1979 to promote The Tidings.

Cardinal Manning and Alphonse Antczak at a rally for The Tidings.

Manning's 1973 trip to Papua, New Guinea was aborted midway by news that he had been appointed to the College of Cardinals. However, he was able to fulfill his earlier commitment in January of 1975 when he set out for Anchorage, Tokyo, Hong Kong and Port Moresby, returning by way of Sidney and Honolulu. Declaring those visitations "most rewarding," the cardinal said that "to see our missionaries at their appointed places, well-trained, happy and holy is an exhilarating experience. You feel unworthy to be close to them, they are so close to God and so unaware of the greatness of their lives."[36]

James Cardinal Freeman invited Manning to make three major presentations at the Sydney Marian Congress in 1976. Enroute to Australia, Manning visited Lay Mission Helpers in Pago Pago, American Samoa. Then, on his way back, he stopped on the island of Ponape in the Carolines. The eighteen day trek presented the cardinal with a panorama of the Church in the Pacific and provided insights into the work of priests, religious and lay missionaries "in lands of stunning sunsets, overwhelming skies, tropic downpours and gentle beauty." From island to island, he was able to observe people "whose lives were like stars fixed for pilgrim journeying to salvation." At each place, they welcomed the cardinal with flowers and songs, and the three hour royal kava ceremony reserved for high dignitaries. "This trip," remarked Manning, "had given me a great admiration for the Jesuit missionaries. They are in the great tradition of Xavier and are most dedicated men." At Ponape, he had great praise for the agriculture and trade school founded by Father Hugh Costigan. "It is a miracle of dedication, zeal and love, a joy for the missions in the Pacific." He compared Ponape to the scriptural pearl hidden in a field which a man discovers, sells all he has and buys the field."[37]

Manning's third trip to Africa and his seventh to the missions occurred during the summer of 1978 when he set out for the West African nations of Sierra Leone and Cameroon. Four years later, Manning was invited to accompany Pope John Paul II to Papua New Guinea where ten Lay Mission Helpers were busily at work at various apostolic tasks. Manning also travelled with the Holy Father to the capital of the Solomon Islands, Honiara on Guadalcanal, the site of prolonged fighting between the Allies and the Japanese in World War II.[38]

The cardinal's last missionary journey took place early in 1986, when he visited coastal Peru, "a dry weary land without water," where his home Diocese of Cork and Ross staffs and maintains four parishes and seventeen churches with eleven priests and an equal number of Religious women. It was estimated that in and around the City of Trujillo, where the Cork mission is centered, over a half million Catholics were being served by these Irish missionaries, people who otherwise would have no ministration by the Church. Manning said that "Cork may be a *statio bene fida* for ships at sea, but she is also a waterway of love opening to the western world where Irish men and women of God keep faith.[39]

Commitment to missionary work must be regarded as among Timothy Manning's most important contributions to ecclesial annals. He once said that "the sharing of the Archdiocese of Los Angeles in the missionary activity of the Church is a legend of admiration throughout the world."[40] Surely the cardinal himself deserves a prominent part in that credit line.

Notes to the Text

1. *The Tidings*, November 8, 1974.
2. *Ibid.*, January 20, 1961.
3. *Ibid.*, January 30, 1970.
4. *Ibid.*, February 5, 1971.
5. *Ibid.*, January 28, 1972.
6. *Ibid.*, January 29, 1982.
7. AALA, Alphonse Antczak to William R. Johnson, Los Angeles, April 15, 1976.
8. *The Tidings*, February 3, 1978.
9. *Ibid.*, January 23, 1981.
10. Francis J. Weber, *A Centennial History of The Tidings* (Mission Hills, 1995), p. 102.
11. *The Tidings*, May 29, 1970.
12. *Ibid.*, October 30, 1970.
13. Ibid., November 6, 1970.
14. AALA, Timothy Manning to Clergy, Los Angeles, April 27, 1972.
15. AALA, Timothy Cardinal Manning to Clergy, Los Angeles, November 2, 1983.
16. *The Tidings*, November 19, 1965.
17. *Ibid.*, October 13, 1978.
18. AALA, Timothy Cardinal Manning to Clergy, Los Angeles, October 1, 1975.
19. AALA, Timothy Cardinal Manning to Clergy, Los Angeles, September 26, 1977.
20. AALA, Timothy Cardinal Manning to Clergy, Los Angeles, September 12, 1978.
21. AALA, Timothy Cardinal Manning to Clergy, Los Angeles, September 15, 1982.

22. AALA, Timothy Cardinal Manning to Clergy, Los Angeles, September 10, 1971.
23. *The Tidings*, July 24, 1970.
24. Francis J. Weber (comp.), *Times of Tension. Moments of Grace* (Los Angeles, 1990) p. 293.
25. *The Tidings*, September 4, 1970.
26. AALA, Timothy Cardinal Manning to Lay Mission Helpers, Los Angeles, October 1, 1971.
27. AALA, Timothy Cardinal Manning to Lay Mission Helpers, Los Angeles, October, 1973.
28. *The Tidings*, December 19, 1980.
29. AALA, Timothy Cardinal Manning to William E. Lenahan, Los Angeles, January 8, 1973.
30. AALA, Timothy Cardinal Manning to Herbert Sorensen, Los Angeles, January 31, 1980.
31. *The Tidings*, November 19, 1965.
32. *Ibid.*, July 24, 1970.
33. *Ibid.,* September 4, 1970.
34. *Ibid.*, June 23, 1972.
35. Los Angeles *Times*, August 27, 1972.
36. Francis J. Weber (comp.), *Times of Tension*, p. 292.
37. *The Tidings*, October 15, 1976.
38. Ibid., August 4, 1984.
39. *Ibid.*, January 17, 1986.
40. AALA, Timothy Cardinal Manning to Herbert Sorensen, Los Angeles, January 31, 1980.

20. *The "Grey" Eminence*

Most contestants on "Jeopardy" would readily identify Jean Cardinal Richelieu as the Prime Minister who ruled France with an iron hand from 1624 to 1642. Probably fewer would be able to recall the monarch whom he served so loyally, Louis XIII. Like Richelieu, Msgr. Benjamin G. Hawkes will likely be treated more favorably by future historians than he was by contemporary journalists and loquacious clerics.

Born August 18, 1919, the son of Benjamin George and Mae E. (Hickler) Hawkes, at Lockport, New York, Benjamin received his early education in Buffalo at Saint Vincent's School. In 1927, the Hawkes family moved to Los Angeles, where Benjamin and his brother William enrolled in Immaculate Heart of Mary School in East Hollywood. Benjamin graduated in 1932 and entered Los Angeles College, the preparatory seminary for the Diocese of Los Angeles-San Diego. Following matriculation in 1936, he transferred to Loyola University where he majored in accounting. He received a bachelor's degree in Business Administration in June, 1940.

Later that year, he was employed at Douglas Aircraft Corporation, as an accountant in the Material Division. In 1941, he went to work in the Cost Accounting Department at Lockheed Aircraft Corporation. Following entry of the United States in World War II, young Hawkes was transferred to the Dallas Modification Center in Texas. Later he returned to the home office in Burbank where he worked as administrative accountant in the Engineering Department for about three years. After lengthy talks with Father Charles Casassa of Loyola University, he terminated his employment at Lockheed and, in September of 1945, entered Saint John's Seminary as a clerical aspirant for the Archdiocese of Los Angeles.

Benjamin Hawkes was ordained priest by Archbishop J. Francis A. McIntyre on the Feast of the Solemnity of Saint Joseph, April 26, 1950. He celebrated his first Solemn High Mass at Cathedral Chapel parish on

April 30 and, shortly thereafter, was named curate at Saint Michael's parish in Los Angeles, a position he held for two years. Upon the recommendation of Father Victor E. Roden, rector of the preparatory seminary, Father Hawkes was made a notary in the matrimonial curia on February 18, 1952 and, on March 5, secretary to Archbishop McIntyre. He remained on the chancery staff of the archdiocese for the next thirty-three years.

Hawkes was named papal chamberlain by Pope Pius XII on February 4, 1955 and a domestic prelate on January 15, 1960. Two years later, with the transfer of Bishop Alden J. Bell to Sacramento, Msgr. Hawkes became chancellor for the Archdiocese of Los Angeles. In 1966, he was appointed to the Board of Consulters and Chaplain Delegate for Area XI of the Military Ordinariate by Francis Cardinal Spellman. On December 19, 1967, be was advanced to the position of Vicar General. Early in 1969, he took up residence at Saint Basil's parish in the mid-Wilshire district and, on December 15, with the retirement of Msgr. Henry Gross, Hawkes became canonical pastor of Saint Basil's.

In the latter years of the McIntyre regime, Msgr. Hawkes became the "prime" minister of the archdiocese, a position in which he often crossed swords with his fellow priests and even with some of the clerical elders who successfully blocked his becoming a bishop. By the time of McIntyre's retirement in 1970, there was a general consensus that the new archbishop would consign Hawkes to a full-time pastorate at Saint Basil's.

Manning and Hawkes were not close friends and had often differed over matters of common interest. Though Manning was auxiliary bishop and, later, Vicar General during the McIntyre years, Msgr. Hawkes was clearly second-in-command after Bishop Joseph T. McGucken's departure for Sacramento. On the other hand, Manning was pragmatic enough to realize Hawkes' outstanding administrative abilities. Also, and this is pivotal to understanding the new archbishop's concept of shepherdhood, Manning did not want to be directly involved in the day-to-day decisions of "running" the archdiocese. He knew his strengths and weaknesses and he opted to restrict his efforts to those areas in which he excelled and they didn't include looking after temporalities.

Over the objections of some of those whose opinions he sought, Manning followed the advice of Msgr. James Hourihan and asked Hawkes to remain on the curial staff in a new role which he defined as "Vicar General for Finance." In retrospect, it was the wisest decision Manning ever made. The appointment of Hawkes read as follows:

> WE
>
> Timothy Manning, Archbishop of Los Angeles in California deciding to elect you as an assistant to share part of our pastoral burden, vigilance and solicitude, with these presents, appoint you, Monsignor Benjamin G. Hawkes, whose doctrine, integrity and prudence are known to us from long experience, our Vicar General in the administration of the Archdiocese of Los Angeles, *ad universitatem negotiorum tam spiritualium quam temporalium* in accordance with the provisions of Canon 366, Section 1 of the Code of Canon Law.
>
> With this appointment we grant to you all power, faculties, privileges, honors and precedence which are given to the Office of Vicar General according to the norms of the Code of Canon Law. In addition we hereby commit to you a special mandate in order to validly and licitly act in all those matters which require a special mandate according to the norms of the Code of Canon Law.
>
> In addition to the authority awarded to the office of Vicar General in the Code of Canon Law, we grant to you the Quinquennial Faculties according to the current formula awarded to us by the Holy See.
>
> Whereas, in addition to the aforementioned Quinquennial Faculties the local Ordinary has been awarded other faculties by the Holy See and the constitutions, decrees and declarations of the Vatican Council II, we do hereby award to you the Faculties set forth in the customary documents:[1]

Throughout the next fifteen years, Hawkes and the archbishop developed a unique and quite successful working relationship whereby Hawkes functioned as chief administrative officer in all areas except personnel. Manning occasionally heard "appeals" from disgruntled clerics and others, but rarely did he over rule Hawkes. For his part, Hawkes never appeared to mind being the "heavy."

So pleased was Manning with his arrangement with the Vicar General for Finance that he even explored the possibility of asking the Holy See to name Hawkes a titular bishop. The Holy Father knew Hawkes personally and likely would have been willing to grant such a request, especially from a cardinal. However, Manning was convinced by those at the local level that naming Hawkes as a Pronotary Apostolic would be more acceptable to the Los Angeles presbyterate. On November 14, 1975, it was announced that Hawkes would be only the seventh priest in the history of the archdiocese named to the College of Pronotary Apostolics. "The very rarity of the appointment bespoke the eminence and esteem associated with the person designated for that honor."[2]

In October of 1975, Msgr. Hawkes addressed the Catholic Press Council on what he called "the Los Angeles Plan." So important was that talk that it is here reproduced in its entirety:

> "The Los Angeles Plan" is the story of the response of the people of God to the needs of the community of faith. Technically it is the story of nine corporations that make up the structure of the Archdiocese of Los Angeles, comprising four counties covering 9,508 square miles, with a Catholic population of 2,099,749 - 22% of the total population. On each of these diocesan corporations an audit is made annually with certified balance sheets published in our archdiocesan paper, *The Tidings*.
>
> During the years that we have been an archdiocese we have had three Ordinaries, all of whom have been responsive to the needs of their times. We are doing our utmost to maintain our parishes and schools and welfare institutions they have built in the best possible condition. This necessarily requires a team effort, and we are all Church.
>
> For the various corporations the Roman Catholic Archbishop of Los Angeles, a corporation sole, is more or less the parent company. His Eminence is the incumbent, and yours truly the attorney-in-fact. As incumbent, the Ordinary is the owner of 1,700 automobiles. He owns and operates thirteen cemeteries, 260 elementary schools and thirty-seven high schools. He pays $2,000,000 in taxes and assessments annually. Including the school plants and welfare facilities, along with the churches and parking lots and rectories, the county assessors of our four counties have established for these a total market value of $340,000,000. The replacement value of our buildings and contents for the purpose of insurance is $578,000,000. For economy reasons, we are self insured on fire insurance for the first $100,000 of each individual fire.
>
> For some years now we have had no investment portfolio for stocks and bonds. However, we do own stocks with a current market value of less than $300,000. These stocks have been donated to the archdiocese with a restriction as to the use of income only. We own sites for future parishes with a cost value of $7,000,000. We have a franchise from the

Monsignor Benjamin Hawkes

Born August 18, 1919
Ordained April 26, 1950
Died September 22, 1985

Hawkes Residence
703 North Waterloo Street
Los Angeles, California 90026

DEDICATION CEREMONIES
of the
HAWKES RESIDENCE

(A transitional housing unit of Good Shepherd Center for Homeless Women, under the sponsorship of Catholic Charities and in partnership with Queen of Angels Medical Center.)

★ ★ ★

Monday, March 14, 1988

Mass of Thanksgiving 10:00 a.m.

Bishop John J. Ward — Principal Celebrant

State of California to sell annuities. We have $1,500,000 in annuities and a corresponding investment in income properties for the same amount.

This corporation operates its own little bank which we refer to as the "X" account. Parishes may borrow funds only from the chancery. Pastors are encouraged to deposit surplus funds with the chancery. We are currently paying 5% on deposits and charging 6% for loans. As you know, the current prime rate is 7%. Although prime did hit a high of 12% last year, the diocese has never charged more than 6% on loans to parishes. We are currently maintaining construction projects totaling $3,000,000. These consist primarily in renovations, new rectories and multipurpose halls for inner-city parishes.

The second corporation that we will consider is the Archdiocese of Los Angeles Education & Welfare Corporation. This corporation was established to include all the schools, welfare and youth center facilities, valued at $208,000,000, and now serving the civic communities embraced within the borders of the archdiocese. In addition, church buildings and related properties are valued at $132,000,000. These valuations represent market values according to the appraisals of the county assessors. They do not represent liquid assets since they are not readily saleable and constitute a grave liability in their operation and maintenance. It is interesting to note that 61% of the real property and equipment are devoted to education, welfare and youth activities. Only 39% of the assets represent Church properties in the 326 parishes of the archdiocese. All of these properties represent the donations made week by week and in concerted funding drives of the Catholic laity in this area. It should be further noted that facilities for education and youth work absorb more than one and a half times as much of the parishioners capital contributions as actual church facilities. The tax payers of our four counties have the benefit of $202,000,000 worth of educational facilities freely donated by the Catholic people for the education of 117,000 elementary and high school students. Over and above all this, $9.7 million was contributed last year by parishioners and the chancery to cover operating deficits in these schools and to keep their doors open.

The next two corporations are St. John's Seminary in Camarillo, our theologate and college, and Our Lady, Queen of the Angels Seminary, our 4-year high school, at Mission San Fernando.

St. John's Seminary is at the center of the four county archdiocese midway between Santa Maria and San Fernando. Nearly 600 alumni of the thirty-five year old seminary have been ordained priests for the archdiocese as well as for other dioceses and Religious communities. Two units of the three part archdiocesan system are located on the Camarillo campus. St. John's Seminary College provides four years of collegiate liberal arts studies with a major in philosophy. Graduates of the college complete their preparation for the priesthood with four years of theology study at St. John's Theologate. We now have 147 young men at the college and eighty-four in theology. The present campus comprises a total of 215.55 acres, with 85.63 acres in citrus and 11.20 acres in avocados. The income from this seminary ranch represents one of only two sources of unrelated business income on which we must pay taxes, the other being advertising income from *The Tidings*. The balance sheet published as the result of the current year's audit shows an investment of $11,000,000.

Our Lady, Queen of Angels Junior Seminary is located on forty-six acres, adjacent to the Mission San Fernando. We presently have 101 young men enrolled in our four year high school. This year's audited balance sheet shows an investment of $5,250,000 in this facility. On the same grounds are accommodations for 600 pre-school students, conducted by the Franciscan Missionary Sisters of the Immaculate Conception, as well as facilities for weekly *Cursillos* and retreats for seventh and eighth graders interested in the religious life.

Our fifth corporation is The Cardinal McIntyre Fund for Charity, a non-profit corporation established to assist with works of charity that cannot be funded by the United Way. This year the Fund had the greatest response in its twenty-four year history - an increase of 33% in the parish collections which totaled $281,000. To this was added $130,000 that came from direct contributions by the public. On August 25 of this year $430,000 was appropriated for disbursement in the following year.

Our sixth corporation is *The Tidings*, with which you are all most familiar. We are indeed most grateful to our editor, his predecessors and our excellent staff for the magnificent job they have done in fulfilling their commitment as an instrument of communication for the Ordinary.

The Saint Vincent de Paul Society constitutes our seventh corporation. I might add here that His Eminence is the president of all these corporations, and myself the treasurer. Employment and rehabilitation of marginal workers account for one of the largest expenditures by the society. Persons handicapped by age, mental or physical problems, lack of education or language barrier, are helped to become self-supporting members of the society. Many marginally handicapped persons are employed in the preparation, in sorting, repairing and sale of donated discards which in turn are sold at nominal prices to low income families. After their training and experience a majority of these workers find employment in private industries. Rather than a burden on society they become contributing members. Salaries and wages paid during 1974 totaled $714,000. The society helps in other areas. Thousands of men annually pass through the portals of St. Vincent's Center on Skid Row. They pause long enough for recreation, a bath, for a shave, a bed or a meal. Alcohol counseling is now available at the center. Each year hundreds of boys up to twelve years of age enjoy a week at the St. Vincent de Paul Summer Ranch Camp. The archdiocese provides facilities for the operation of the Society and subsidizes it for as much as $100,000 annually.

The Catholic Welfare Bureau constitutes our eighth corporation. Last year the bureau received $2,325,000 support from the public with the total revenue coming to $3,831,000 and expenditures of $3,788,000. Nearly one-half of these expenditures were expended to provide counselling services and financial assistance to families, children and single women. As a point of information, we might mention here that the bureau's resettlement program was responsible for the relocation of 5,000 Vietnamese refugees in four months, a percentage of slightly over 20% of the refugees resettled out of Camp Pendleton.

Don Bosco Technical Institute is a four year high school and one year junior college located in South San Gabriel, which after five years confers an Associate in Science degree. This was erected by the archdiocese with the assistance of industry. There are currently 1,000 young men studying at the school, which is directed by the Salesian Fathers. A separate corporation was formed for the ownership of this school so that industry might be encouraged to contribute to the maintenance of same. The archdiocese has invested $5,000,000 in these facilities, and industry and benefactors have been most cooperative in the maintenance of the school.

This is our corporate structure.

Back in 1962, this archdiocese established a policy of asking the "HAVES" to help the "HAVE NOTS." Parishes with relatively large surplus balances on deposit in our "X" account were asked to contribute to the poorer parishes of the diocese. Since that date $32,750,000 has been contributed by parishes with surplus funds and by the chancery office to pay off the debts of parishes that have been unable not only to pay their principal but even interest on the principal. Our parish debts in 1950 totaled $7.8 million dollars. In 1967 parish debts reached an all-time peak of $27,000,000. As of October 22, sixty-four of our 326 parishes have a debt totaling $5,418,000. No poor parish in this diocese has a debt. No property is mortgaged. We are presently subsidizing thirty-six parishes.

In order to assist in the financing of expenses of the diocese the following assessments are levied:

1% of ordinary income to assist in the operations of the Chancery Office;

2% of ordinary income to help finance the three seminaries;

4% of ordinary income to help finance the high schools.

In November of 1973 we inaugurated a two year fund raising drive in which we assessed each parish 10% of ordinary income per year for two years. The goal of this drive was for $5,000,000. The drive ends November 30, 1975, and to date we have collected $4,800,000 in cash.

The needs of the Church, of the people of God here, are great. Providentially, their response is also great.

Our primary purpose of existence is the worship of God through the parochial system which has made the faith flourish in America. We are also in various other works of religion. We are committed to Catholic education. We in-

> tend to maintain as many eight-classroom schools in as many parishes as we can afford to. We intend to maintain our thirty-seven diocesan supported high schools as long as we can afford. This year we have budgeted a $1,500,000 subsidy to our high schools. Each school charges tuition according to ability to pay. Our lowest diocesan high school tuition is $31.00 per month. Our highest diocesan high school tuition is $55.00 month.
>
> Here in the Archdiocese of Los Angeles we have been blessed with a magnificent people - a people of God who have been consistently responsive to leadership. We realize that religion lives on the free-will offerings of people. We believe that God will provide. Consequently we budget our programs from year to year. We believe that we will be able to give the people of God in this jurisdiction what they can afford to pay for.
>
> During the last twenty-five years, the ordinary income of our parishes has increased 400%. It has increased each year, always more than every preceding year. God has truly provided. At the end of each fiscal year, we budget for the program of the coming year. This includes one and a half million dollars for the summer repairs of our high schools and one and a half million dollars for the maintenance of our inner-city parishes and schools. Remaining surplus funds are applied annually to parish debts. God has indeed been good to this mission area on the far Pacific.[3]

Hawkes consistently shunned all sorts of honors and accolades, including honorary doctorates, several of which were offered. He did relent once, in 1980, to receiving the prestigious Loyola Marymount University Distinguished Leadership Award. The citation, given for "his long and dedicated service to the Catholic Church in Southern California," was bestowed by Father Donald Merrifield, S.J., university president. Presented on the occasion of the fortieth anniversary of his graduation, the award credited Hawkes with "playing a key role in the planning and development of the facilities of parochial schools and parishes of the Archdiocese of Los Angeles and the Diocese of Orange."[4]

Despite the fact that from the outset of Manning's regime, minute financial reports of all the agencies and corporations of the archdiocese had been publicly printed annually in *The Tidings*, there was a handful of priests who complained to the press about the management of the archdiocesan finances. Mostly they were concerned about the manner in which they were allegedly treated by Hawkes. One recalled that when people were called in, "they were made to stand in front of his desk, without being offered a chair." Another complained that he "felt just like the cowardly lion in the Wizard of Oz." And a former associate of Hawkes told how "he left people shaking their heads. The cardinal is much more compassionate than he is."[5]

In any event, an investigative team from the Los Angeles *Times*[6] began sniffing around the parishes and agencies of the archdiocese, much to the annoyance of Cardinal Manning who, on July 16, 1982, issued a "notice" to the faithful which read:

> In recent weeks numerous reports have reached the Chancery Office of efforts to secure information concerning the internal operations of the archdiocese. The persons making these inquiries, who identify themselves as newspaper writers, have queried priests, sisters, real estate enterprises, members of the construction industry, school personnel and others, probing for information on the archdiocese and its management. The tone of the questioning evidences a purported intention to indicate dissension in the Church and implies misconduct by archdiocesan personnel. The purpose of this notice is to thank all priests, religious and laity, of our appreciation for advising us of any comments or questions by media representatives that impugn the good name of the Church or the archdiocese.[7]

In July of 1982, in an effort to answer some of the queries that had been circulating around the archdiocese, Msgr. Hawkes wrote an editorial for *The Tidings* in which he outlined how "Church, Faith, Property and Money" are inter-related in the administration of the archdiocese. Again, because of the relevance of this essay to the overall working of the Church in Southern California between 1970 and 1985, that essay in here reproduced:

> Thirty-six parishes of the archdiocese are subsidized by the archdiocese. They serve neighborhoods too poor to be able to maintain fully the staff and facilities of a parish. Over the past ten years the 261 schools in the archdiocesan educational system have incurred a deficit of $80 million, now an average yearly loss of $6 million. Through the generous

response of the people and the support of education by foundations the archdiocese has been able to finance this deficit.

Despite these losses, parishes and schools are kept in operation because the guiding principle is a faith commitment of service. The economy of faith is based on different motivations than that of the marketplace yet it is subject to all the hazards and problems of a marketplace economy.

The Church honors the faith of the people. That is the priority. The operating principle is faith in providence. Parishes, schools and other church entities are kept in operation because of faith considerations.

Stewardship and accountability of the strictest kind are required in managing funds freely and charitably given for support of the temporal needs of the Church. The Church is a community of faith, made up of men and women who respond to faith, and who freely accept and abide by the teachings of the Church. Accordingly, they recognize in a temporal society it has material needs to be met if it is to fulfill its mission. This translates into churches for worship and schools for education, as well as provision of services for social needs – plus all the personnel that these institutions require.

Church members expect their churches to reflect the dignity, esteem and beauty of an edifice devoted to worship, the expression of a community's prayerful relationship to God. High building and material costs have, of necessity, resulted in modification of what is desired. Schools are an essential part of the Church's mission. Education can no longer be carried out by a teacher under a tree as in biblical times. There are now educational, building and safety codes. These are reasonable. They also add to overhead; there is also the maintenance needed in buildings subject to heavy, hard usage. Financing construction, maintenance and operation of the Church's work in a temporal society involves the Church in property management and maintenance – and, of course, money.

Through the long experience of the Church in the archdiocese follows organized methods and procedures for fulfilling its obligations to the people – and to its own doctrines – by careful policies of building and maintenance and of funding.

The archdiocese employs a bidding system in construction. The general rule is that bids are accepted on all construction. There is an approved listing of contractors whose financial condition and experience are determined by the archdiocesan lay construction coordinator. Due to particular or individual circumstances a contract may be negotiated provided the contract price does not exceed the architect's estimate. The contractor responsible for maintenance and remodeling work obtains three bids on all major subcontractors' work, such as painting, plumbing, grading, concrete, asphalt, electrical work, etc. In most projects there are many subcontractor bids. It is the policy to try to obtain bids from the locality in which the work is to be done. The diocese presently has a total of five and one quarter million dollars worth of new construction and maintenance work under contract. Four different contractors are doing the new construction in ten different locations totaling over $3,600,000 – sixty-nine percent of all work presently in progress. The remaining thirty-one percent is for maintenance and remodeling work contracted for with one other contractor.

The reality ever present to those responsible for meeting the day-to-day temporal needs of the Church is that the basic source of funds is in the good will, freely given charitable donations of the people. This imposes an obligation of strict stewardship and accountability, and of verifying these qualities through use of reputable outside auditors. The reports on all archdiocesan corporations are regularly made public in *The Tidings*. The financial reports for all eight corporations have been published annually since 1970 in *The Tidings*. The balance sheet for the corporation sole is also given to the Los Angeles office of Dun & Bradstreet.

For over thirty years the archdiocese has been assisted by a financial advisory committee made up of community leaders from the following professions: banking, insurance, legal, real estate development, industry and government. The expertise of the members of this committee has always been readily available. There are in the archdiocese eight corporations. The principle corporation is The Roman Catholic Archbishop of Los Angeles, a corporation sole. This corporation has a Board of Consulters made up of twelve priests. All financial transactions are submitted to this board regularly for approval. Each of the other seven corporations has a

"Christ on Wilshire Boulevard"

Interior view of Saint Basil church.

Ground breaking - Saint Joseph's Church - 1985.

Msgr. Hawkes in the Estelle Doheny Collection - 1973.

> board of directors comprised of priests and members of the laity. Each of these boards approves the annual budget and receives a copy of the audited financial statements.
>
> To summarize: The Church exists in a temporal society. It has temporal needs. These are provided for by the generous charitable giving of the people. This in turn makes incumbent strict, conscientious management and compliance with all requisites of Church law and of civil laws governing a corporate entity as complex as the Church in its mission of spiritual, educational and social service.[8]

The "exposé," by the Los Angeles *Times* reached the newsstands on October 18, 1982. It revealed that Hawkes was indeed a priest who "controls vast power as a fund caretaker." It told how, to the 1,200 priests in the three county archdiocese, Msgr. Hawkes "stands out as a legend - a priest who for years has wielded immense power for two cardinals." The writers said that "so commanding a figure is Msgr. Benjamin G. Hawkes that actor Robert De Niro chose to observe him saying Mass before the actor's portrayal of a monsignor in the motion picture "True Confessions" released last year."

Russell Chandler and Robert Welkos related how as archdiocesan vicar general, Hawkes "had guided its finances for nearly two decades - first under his mentor, James Francis Cardinal McIntyre during the post World War II boom era of parish and school growth, and, since 1970, under the soft-spoken, spiritually-minded Manning. While Manning and McIntyre made the headlines, Hawkes directed their building programs, purchased and sold huge parcels of land, managed a swelling array of investments, courted Church benefactors and dealt sternly with priests whom the cardinals wanted disciplined." With the growth of his almost unlimited power - McIntyre gave him power of attorney in 1965 - "Hawkes today finds himself perhaps the most respected yet feared official in the archdiocese. To priest and parochial school administrators who must come to him for money for their building programs, Hawkes can be an imposing figure."

Hawkes made no secret of his friendship with certain wealthy people of the archdiocese, claiming that "the rich have souls too." When asked how he could afford to wear "expensive black suits and gold cufflinks, " he said that "people have been good to me." By saving $200 a month of his salary, he invested in government bonds. "I own no stocks. I own no personal property. And what I had given to me has been invested and I get income every month." He was able to vacation in Diamond

Head because of the generosity of Fritz Burns at whose residence he and other priests stayed.

One subject, which had been an annoyance to priests was the construction company which the archdiocese used for its repair work. It was headed by a prominent Catholic layman, Michael Bolger, and it was alleged that other contractors got few if any opportunities to bid on jobs. The M.T. Patrick Company had indeed been receiving most of the repair work and Hawkes made no effort to disguise the fact that Bolger's company performed exceedingly efficiently for the Church. "They do superb work, they stand behind what they do, and their prices are competitive." When asked to comment, Bolger said that he did "a lot of jobs big contractors wouldn't want to fool with." Almost every Saturday, Hawkes and Bolger toured the archdiocese checking on jobs in progress and planning for work to be done. When asked if it was true that M.T. Patrick grossed $1.6 million in renovation work in one summer, Hawkes said that "I think I'm getting the best deal . . . We have never bid repairs and maintenance unless they are (for) a large amount of money."

As "chief moneyman for the archdiocese, Hawkes had a principal role in building the Church corporation's investment portfolio and buying and selling land." People "credit Hawkes with getting the archdiocese into the black financially, eliminating much of the debt incurred by McIntyre during the boom era of building." Hawkes said that "in 1967, the parishes of this archdiocese owed $27 million. And today, there are five parishes in debt and no poor parish has ever been in debt since 1969." Moreover, between 1971 and 1982, investments leaped from a mere $1.2 million in certificates of deposit to more than $115 million in stocks, government bonds, certificates of deposit and savings, chancery office balance sheets show.

Oh, there were some problems, one of which involved Michael Purcell, a real estate developer and consultant for the archdiocese. When the archdiocese sold a three-acre parcel of vacant land several years earlier in Solvang, "Hawkes found to his dismay that the Church had let the land go for hundreds of thousands of dollars less than market value. Purcell had a principal role in counseling the monsignor to sell the Solvang land for $397,000. What Hawkes did not know until escrow closed, according to a lawsuit, was that Purcell was a secret buyer in the partnership that purchased the property. At no time prior to the opening of... escrow did Purcell advise (Hawkes) that this was a grossly inadequate price or that he was an undisclosed buyer of (the) property," the lawsuit, filed in Santa Barbara County Superior Court in Santa Maria, stated.

Cape Pacific Partnership, which Purcell formed with three other businessmen, in turn sold half the property for $450,000 to a second partnership called Solvang Mission Inn. That partnership intended to develop the property, just south of the town's main tourist area, into a mini-convention center. Escrow closed on January 2, 1979, and the Church did not learn of Purcell's role until the following month, when word got back through a Catholic parishioner in Santa Ynez. By the following month, Purcell had unexpectedly signed over all his interest in the property to the Archdiocese of Los Angeles. Purcell said he did so after Hawkes took him into the cardinal's conference room. "Hawkes can be charming and he can be ruthless," Purcell said. "Literally, I was forced to sign that document. Hawkes told me he was personally going to get me. It scared me." When asked whether he had told Hawkes prior to the sale that he (Purcell) was a party to the purchase, Purcell said: "I had mentioned if off the cuff. Well, I may not have done it. In my mind I was totally convinced (I had told Hawkes)."

Hawkes denied to the reporters that he threatened Purcell, adding: "I do believe in conflicts of interest and I thought this was one." The dispute was settled out of court. All parties went back to square one: The investors got back their money. The Church got back the land. Purcell lost his job under Hawkes. And Hawkes wasn't duped after all. Then Hawkes turned around and sold the same land to most of the same partners (minus Purcell) for $1.2 million.[9]

The staff at the *National Catholic Reporter* had also launched its own investigation. Two members of the NCR staff roamed the southland looking for evidence of misdeeds. In the end they were reduced to commenting on the Chandler-Welkos article, concluding that it showed Hawkes as "immensely powerful as well as clever, cunning and at times ruthless." They quoted Hawkes as asking "who is it that is complaining? It's not the lay people; its just a few disgruntled priests . . . who think they could do a better job at running the archdiocese."[10] Probably the best commentary on the "exposé" was that written by M. Joyce who wrote to the Los Angeles *Times* that "after columns of innuendo, the bottom line of Chandler and Welkos tirade is that Msgr. Hawkes, whose responsibility in the archdiocese is vicar general (for finance), has done an excellent job. There is many a corporate board room in America today which would be delighted to be in that posture."[11]

During all these years, Hawkes was also a very active pastor of Saint Basil's in the mid-Wilshire district. He enjoyed being the spiritual leader of the elegant, modernistic church on Wilshire Boulevard. He once told an interviewer that "I have 6,000 people every weekend from Saturday night to Sunday night. Show me a church of any denomination that has this size congregation." There were five Masses every day and six during Lent. In 1981, there were 226,000 communions at Saint Basil's.

Though not a great preacher, Hawkes was better than most. He always spoke from a script and never fell into the practice of ad-libbing. He thought too much of his congregation to do that. Since he didn't have a school, the youngsters living in his parish had their tuition at other local Catholic schools paid for by Hawkes. In addition, he occasionally gave financial grants each to neighboring pastors. He personally financed numerous teenagers at local Catholic high schools. More confessions were heard at Saint Basil's than anywhere else in the archdiocese. Hawkes required every priest to be in the "box" before, during and after the daily Masses. When told that such a practice was "unliturgical," Hawkes responded that he would personally take responsibility for that decision before God's throne in heaven. There was always a priest "on duty" at the rectory and the number of annual converts to the faith exceeded any other local parish. As one of his associates observed: "And there, in the box, on the predella and in the pulpit, was old Ben taking his place with the rest of us."

On December 15, 1983, Hawkes was appointed to the Board of Trustees for The Catholic University of America. He was one of the four non-bishops on the board, along with twenty lay people. In his letter of appointment, the university president said that "we want to become more aware of our national responsibilities. We want to reach more effectively our national Church constituency. And we want to link ourselves more directly to the most populous archdiocese of the United States. You can help us on all three of those fronts."[12] There were four meetings held each year and Hawkes was diligent in attending them all.

Two years later, Father Thomas J. Reese interviewed Hawkes for his book *Archbishop, Inside the Power Structure of the American Catholic Church*. In his penetrating study Jesuit Reese explained how the McIntyre influence stretched beyond his own tenure into that of his successor, Timothy Manning. By carefully considered design, Manning, who cared little for administrative duties, designated Hawkes to act as his Vicar General for finance or chief operating officer, a role in which Hawkes supervised and coordinated all archdiocesan agencies. While technically only in charge of finance, Reese pointed out that "since most things cost money, Hawkes exercised sweeping power in Los Angeles." Though they held little affection for one another, Manning and Hawkes respected each others talents and they devised a working relationship that was unique and effective in American ecclesial annals. While everything related to finance and administration was completely entrusted to him, Hawkes did nothing of any magnitude without advising the archbishop before he did it.

In many ways, Hawkes was a clone of McIntyre. He believed, for example, that the haves should help the have-nots. He didn't feel that a suburban parish should have sixteen classrooms when an inner city parish couldn't afford eight. In his view, the archdiocese should come to the assistance of a new parish. He explained it this way: "When we start a new parish - we do one or two a year - the cardinal gives the parish the property. Then we build what we think the place and the location needs. That would be a rectory and a multipurpose building for a church. Half of the multipurpose building might provide four classrooms, but it could also be used for Sunday Masses. What it usually costs is $2 million and the archdiocese gives the parish up to $1 million. That is the only way the people can handle it. Five percent on $2 million is a large portion of your collection for interest.[13]

Hawkes was sixty-six years old and in poor health by the time Manning retired as archbishop in 1985. On July 17, Hawkes submitted his resignation as attorney of fact for the seven archdiocesan corporations, as treasurer of Don Bosco Technical School and Vicar General for Finance.[14] Manning's successor, Archbishop Roger Mahony, accepted the resignation publicly, on September 6. John Dart wrote in the Los Angeles *Times* that "over his long tenure, Hawkes has succeeded in building the Los Angeles archdiocese into one of the wealthiest in the nation.[15] During September, Hawkes travelled to Rome for the archiepiscopal ordination of his friend, Msgr. Justin Rigali. There he was given special recognition by Pope John Paul II who served as Rigali's principal consecrator. Enroute home, Msgr. Hawkes took ill and he died of a stroke on September 22nd.

Kristina Horton told readers of the Los Angeles *Herald-Examiner* that Hawkes was "a near legendary figure in the archdiocese, known as a hard-headed, realistic business manager both respected and feared for his influence over two successive cardinals."[16] A staff reporter for the Los Angeles *Times* told how Hawkes had directed a massive program of growth and his shrewd business acumen was credited with eliminating the debt incurred in earlier years. "Today, the archdiocese's wealth is an estimated $1 billion, including one of the nation's largest parochial school systems and twenty-three hospitals.[17]

In his official statement, Archbishop Mahony said that "virtually every parish, our high schools and grammar schools, our health care facilities and our social services and charitable facilities have been touched by his concern and effort. Msgr. Hawkes labored day and night that the kingdom of God might be deeply rooted here in Southern California."[18]

An editorial in the Los Angeles *Herald-Examiner* noted that:

> If most Angelenos had been asked to name the city's most powerful people, they probably would not have included Benjamin Hawkes on their lists. Other movers and shakers hereabouts knew better, however. Monsignor Hawkes, who died last weekend at sixty-six, was, until recently, the financial manager of L.A.'s Catholic archdiocese. As such, he controlled assets estimated at up to $1 billion with an iron hand and steely will.
>
> Indeed, Hawkes' detractors fumed about the impersonality with which certain financial decisions were made during his tenure, including last year's controversial decision to close Cathedral High School in Chinatown and sell the property to developers. But even those who criticized Hawkes conceded that he was a brilliant and progressive budgetmeister. Among other things, he instituted centralized banking practices that enabled the archdiocese to receive money from wealthy parishes, then make loans to parishes that serve the poor.
>
> Monsignor Hawkes was significant not just for his actions but for the period in L.A. church history that coincided with his time in office. Historically, the Catholic Church in this country has been largely an immigrant church, serving waves of Irish, Polish, Italian and other newcomers who, after impoverished beginnings, finally reached middle-class status only in the last few decades. For them, prosperity brought new demands for the churches and schools that they and their children required. This demand fit neatly with Hawkes' skill at trading properties and directing building programs.
>
> The twist is that, in L.A., the arrival of countless Hispanics has made the Church once again an immigrant institution that must perforce turn away from buildings and back to people. It thus may not have been coincidental that the newly installed archbishop, Roger Mahony, recently accepted Hawkes' resignation. The monsignor's special skills, after all, may not have gibed so closely with a changing Church. Still, Benjamin Hawkes served his Church and his

> community with a loyalty and efficiency that earned – and deserved – respect and admiration.[19]

The author of a letter to the Los Angeles *Times* said that the true measure of a person was not the derogatory, mean-spirited comments of a few "anonymous churchmen" but the spontaneous remarks of ordinary people. "Why not," she suggested "seek answers from those he helped - the members of the intercity parishes, the schools, the elderly, religious men and women and countless others touched by his generosity."[20]

Though the monsignor and his accomplishments have been generally ignored in subsequent years, a small cadre of a hundred or so co-workers, collaborators and friends gather each year for a Mass offered on the anniversary of his demise.

Notes to the Text

1. AALA, Timothy Manning - Decree, Los Angeles, January 26, 1970.
2. *The Tidings*, December 12, 1975. Hawkes was not consulted about the appointment and was genuinely irritated by it. He would have preferred to refuse it.
3. AALA, Benjamin G. Hawkes. Address given at the Catholic Press Council, October 30, 1975.
4. Loyola Marymount University ALUMNEWS (1980), p. 19.
5. Los Angeles *Times*, October 18, 1982.
6. *Viz.*, Russell Chandler and Robert Welkos.
7. *The Tidings*, July 16, 1982.
8. *Ibid.*, July 23, 1982.
9. Los Angeles *Times*, October 18, 1982.
10. *National Catholic Reporter*, October 29, 1982.
11. Los Angeles *Times*, October 23, 1982.
12. AALA, William J. Byron, S.J., to Benjamin G. Hawkes, Washington, D.C., December 23, 1983.
13. (San Francisco, 1989), p. 168.
14. AALA, Benjamin G. Hawkes to Roger Mahony, Los Angeles, July 17, 1985.
15. Los Angeles *Times*, September 6, 1985.
16. Los Angeles *Herald-Examiner*, September 23, 1985.
17. Los Angeles *Times*, September 23, 1985.
18. *Ibid.*
19. Los Angeles *Herald-Examiner*, September 24, 1985.
20. Los Angeles *Times*, October 10, 1985.

21. *Friends, Advisors and Collaborators*

Timothy Manning played his cards close to the chest. To all except his closest collaborators, he was a model of diplomatic evasiveness, sharing only those plans, thoughts and projects which directly concerned the moment. Even with his official archdiocesan consulters, whose role he redefined and whose membership he expanded, Manning often operated on a dual track disclosing certain facts and reserving others. To put it bluntly, there was a serious communication gap at the highest levels of the archdiocese during his incumbency. When this was brought to his attention on several occasions, the cardinal would smile, acknowledge the problem and then do nothing about it. He simply preferred to do business that way. And, in the end, his track record matched and even surpassed most of his "more open" confreres in the American hierarchy.

MSGR. JAMES HOURIHAN - CONFIDANT

In one of his writings, John Steven McGroarty, the Poet Laureate for the State of California, spoke of a confidant as "one who writes the faults of his brothers in the sand for the winds to obscure and obliterate and who engraves their virtues on the tablets of love and memory.[1] Timothy Cardinal Manning had only one acquaintance who fit into that category.

James Hourihan was born in Dunmanway, County Cork, Ireland, on January 4, 1907. Ordained a priest from All Hallows in Dublin, June 20, 1931, he served as assistant priest in the Diocese of Los Angeles-San Diego at Pasadena, Boyle Heights and East Los Angeles. In 1946, Hourihan was named founding pastor of Saint Luke's parish in Temple City. Nine years later, he returned to Pasadena as pastor of Saint Andrew's to succeed Joseph T. McGucken who was moving on to the bishopric of Sacramento. He remained there for the next forty-one years. Made a monsignor in 1962, he retired twenty years later. His book on *The History of Saint Andrew's Parish*, issued during the parochial centenary in 1986, was highly acclaimed.

Hourihan knew Timothy Manning initially in Ireland and their unique relationship lasted for over sixty years. The longest and closest of Manning's friends, he saw and visited with him at least weekly. He boasted that "we never discuss anything that touches the official scene. He needs an occasional respite from all of that and I make sure he gets it at my house." Hourihan travelled with Manning every year, both to Ireland and on his missionary journeys.

When the monsignor retired from the active ministry, the cardinal wrote him a letter which said: "You have not labored for the notice or esteem of superiors or parishioners, yet you have richly deserved recognition from both sources. So much of yourself has been indentured in that service. God alone knows the totality of your giving and He reserves to Himself the totality of its reward."[2] He succumbed at Nazareth House on July 8, 1997.

FRIENDS

Like many of the world's prominent people, Timothy Manning had only a handful of acquaintances who would qualify as close friends but have them he did. E.E.Y. Hales was once quoted as saying that "the making of friends is the best token we have of a person's success in life." There were three priests who fit neatly into the *innermost* circle and they were younger men with whom he could laugh, reminisce and play cards. Each in his own way knew where to draw the line and none ventured across it.

Leland Boyer spent the greatest portion of his priestly life in the Confraternity of Christian Doctrine before becoming pastor of Saint Bede's parish in LaCanada. Boyer's family beach house served as a perfect "hideout" for the cardinal, especially on those occasions when he was "unavailable to the press." Lawrence Donnelly, a canon lawyer and longtime pastor of Saint Michael's parish in downtown Los Angeles, served as Manning's master of ceremonies for most of the bishop's early years. A perfect diplomat, he had an uncanny ability of anticipating episcopal appointments at the national level. He was a low-key, quiet and knowledgeable raconteur who engaged in fascinating conversations. Finally, there was John Reilly, referred to by his clerical peers as the "court jester." An accomplished mimic, he could recall and act out an event as well or better than any professional comedian. An educator, principal, seminary rector and pastor, John was an adept card player who never failed to make the cardinal laugh, something not always easy, given Manning's melancholic temperament. Interestingly, Manning kept his closest friends at arms-length when it came to influencing policy. Nor did he show them any special partiality. Msgr. Donnelly served as pastor of one of the poorest parishes in the archdiocese.

ADVISORS AND COLLABORATORS

Manning was open to suggestions and, in the case of the Priests' Senate, he actively sought their participation in the decision-making process. While, in the cardinal's case, "listening" may have been elevated to the status of virtue, the final decision was always his and he never avoided taking responsibility for unpopular decisions.

ALPHONSE ANTCZAK

Someone observed that if the editorship of *The Tidings* "were an elective post, Alphonse Antczak would easily have won the position when it became vacant in 1973."[3] Born in 1922, the young Antczak was brought to Los Angeles in 1931, settling in San Antonio de Padua parish in Boyle Heights. His pastor was Msgr. Leroy Callahan who did heroic work for Archbishop Cantwell in the growing Mexican parishes of the east-side. After graduation from Loyola High School, Al enrolled as an English major at Loyola University. There he became a protege of the legendary Father Vincent Lloyd-Russell. Al joined the staff of *The Loyolan* and served twice as editor of that college newspaper, before and after World War II.

Antczak joined *The Tidings* staff in 1947. During the ensuing forty-two years, he witnessed and wrote about myriads of topics touching upon the Archdiocese of Los Angeles, including the five great western migrations - European displaced persons (late 1940s), easterners (1950s), Cuban refugees (1959), Asian boat people (mid 1970s) and the Central Americans (1980s). He moved among these new people as friend, advocate and chronicler.

In August of 1973, Al became the fifteenth editor of *The Tidings*. During the next sixteen years, he continued and expanded the policies of California's oldest Catholic newspaper. During the Antczak years, *The Tidings* operated in the black and continued to help subsidize such projects as the construction of the Education Building, the Catholic Charities headquarters and Santa Marta Hospital. Substantial annual grants were also distributed to numerous inner-city parishes during the tenure of the post World War II editors. *The Tidings* also won awards for reporting, editorials and layout. Among those citations, none pleased the editor more than the one given for the paper's editorial support of farm workers at Rancho Sespe in Ventura County. During four archbishops, Alphonse Antczak was a primary witness and faithful chronicler for the life of the Church in Southern California. He verbalized his role as that of reporting the works of God's people fulfilling their spiritual destiny.

He was for his generation what Matthew, Mark, Luke and John were for theirs. In scriptural terminology, he was an evangelist *par excellence*, an embodiment of the conciliar notion of ecclesial service in California's southland. The cardinal never worried about any aspect of *The Tidings* with Antczak at the wheel. He trusted him implicitly and often boasted that the editor had a sixth sense for what was appropriate in a Catholic newspaper.

MSGR. ROBERT E. BRENNAN

As a friend, Msgr. Robert E. Brennan (1908-1986) was on the "inactive" list. During their days together in Rome and in the years immediately after, the two were quite close, but that relationship cooled as Brennan became increasingly cranky and difficult, especially in his role as a pastor.

Brennan had been educated in music and liturgical activity in the Eternal City. He was, in those days, an *avant-gard* promotor of liturgical modernization. Then abruptly and without explanation, he reversed directions and retreated into the vociferous role of outspoken critic, opponent and even obstructionist of any and all kinds of post-conciliar changes. After retiring as archdiocesan Director of Music, Brennan served as pastor of Our Lady of Guadalupe (Santa Barbara), Our Lady of the Holy Rosary (Sun Valley), Saint Gregory (Los Angeles) and Saint Elizabeth (Altadena).

In retirement, Brennan lived at Queen of Angels Seminary in Mission Hills, next door to San Fernando Mission and the Archival Center. Almost weekly, after the cardinal finished his work in the archives, he would stop to greet Brennan. But he often remarked that the "Brennan of earlier days" never resurfaced, much to the cardinal's disappointment.

FRITZ BURNS

Early in his life, Fritz Burns (1899-1979) shrewdly concluded that California would be the nation's focal point for the rest of the twentieth century. After World War I, he settled in Los Angeles and began work in the development of sale of real estate. One of Mr. Burn's earliest

Msgr. John A. Rawden
Chancellor

Msgr. Gary Bauler
Vocations

Msgr. John Barry
Religious Education

Msgr. John Cremins
Chant

Cardinal bestows appointment as Gentleman-in-Waiting to Sir Daniel Donohue.

Msgr. Peter Healy
Diaconate Program

Msgr. Paul Dotson
Cemeteries

projects was centered in the San Fernando Valley. He visited the Old Mission and thereafter became supportive of programs to restore the "fountainhead of Christianity" to its original dimensions. His interest in what later became Panorama City was clearly an outgrowth of his love for the seventeenth of California's missionary outposts.

The Burns imprint was felt in many areas of the state, as well as in Hawaii, where industrial parks and residential communities began to appear in the years after World War II. Burns served as president, director and general partner in numerous land and investment companies, including Fritz Burns and Associates. He also found time to organize and serve as president for the National Association of Home Builders.

Burns always gave much of the credit for his success to his wife, the former Gladys Guadalupe Carson, a descendant of Juan Jose Dominguez, who had come to Alta California with Gaspar de Portola in 1769. Gladys, active in a multitude of charitable endeavors, was awarded the *Pro Ecclesia et Pontifice* medal by Pope John XXIII in 1960. Burns and his wife took a leadership and supportive role on behalf of Saint Anne's Maternity Hospital, contributing to the hospital's delivery room. Wherever there was some charitable need – there was Fritz Burns! He was a longtime director for the Saint Vincent de Paul Society and the Archbishop's Fund for Charity. And he was intimately associated with the outreach programs sponsored by the Knights of the Sovereign Military Order of Malta.

Mr. Burns died at his home in Hancock Park on February 19, 1979. At his funeral obsequies, held at Saint Basil's Church, Cardinal Manning said that "Fritz Burns was a unique blessing given by God to Southern California. His charitable programs touched the lives of countless people and he asked nothing in return." The benefactions of Fritz Burns have and are reaching far beyond his simple grave through the foundation which he established while still alive.

MSGR. CLEMENT CONNOLLY

During all of Manning's tenure as Archbishop of Los Angeles, the office of priest secretary was occupied by Msgr. Clement Connolly, an Irish-born priest ordained for service in the Archdiocese of Los Angeles at Saint Patrick, Thurles, Ireland on June 14, 1964.

The late Msgr. John J. Devlin, who served as secretary for Bishop John J. Cantwell from 1922 to 1929, used to say that the position of secretary "consisted primarily in carrying the bishop's bags, driving his car and training the altar servers for ceremonies." While there were obviously other facets of the position unmentioned by Devlin, none surpassed that of "controlling access." (Devlin once boasted that the high-point of his life occurred on the day that he kept the famed Irish patriot, Eamon de Valera, waiting in the reception room for half an hour before ushering him into Cantwell's office).

Given Manning's open door policy with priests and curial staff, it was difficult for Connolly to control access, but he tried valiantly, much to the distress of outsiders having legitimate reasons for wanting to see Manning. In that sense, he was overly-protective. Yet, for the most part, Connolly served Manning well, especially in the final years when the cardinal's health began deteriorating and he dreaded being alone.

Connolly was also a positive influence when Manning drifted into those melancholic moods so characteristic of some Irish. The two liked to sing and often did so publicly. And, daily, they recited morning and evening prayer together, practices the cardinal highly esteemed. On his deathbed, the cardinal penned a homily for deliverance at Connolly's silver priestly jubilee in which he quoted Shakespeare that "a friend should bear a friend's infirmities and Clement did mine."[4]

SIR DANIEL J. DONOHUE

Daniel Joseph Donohue, a native of Jersey City, studied philosophy along with the other disciplines associated with the ministry of Father Paul Watson at the Catholic University of America. Through his father, a prominent pediatrician and specialist in internal medicine, Daniel knew Francis Cardinal Spellman and other members of the American hierarchy, including J. Francis A. McIntyre, then the Coadjutor Archbishop of New York. He studied briefly for the priestly ministry and, later, for the brotherhood of Saint John of God. Subsequently he worked for United States Steel Corporation in their newly-formed psychological screening program.

Described by the Los Angeles *Times* in 1982 as "one of the most influential and honored Catholic laymen in the nation,"[5] Daniel exchanged marital vows with Bernardine Murphy in the presence of James Francis Cardinal McIntyre on January 16, 1954. After the unexpected death of his wife, Daniel continued her many charitable works as President of the Dan Murphy Foundation. He was, at one time, the only layman on the board of directors for the National Shrine of the Immaculate Conception and also was a trustee for the Catholic University of America.

In late 1974, at the behest of Timothy Cardinal Manning, Daniel was named a Gentleman-in-Waiting to His Holiness, Pope Paul VI, thus becoming one of only two Americans holding that title.[6] Throughout

Manning's tenure as Archbishop of Los Angeles, Sir Daniel Donohue was easily the most generous contributor to the charities of the Holy See and the local Church.

BISHOP WILLIAM R. JOHNSON

During his years as rector of Saint Vibiana's Cathedral, Msgr. William R. Johnson (1918-1986) and the cardinal became friends and, in 1970, it was Manning who recommended him for the bishopric and, later, for the newly-established episcopal seat at Orange. Ordained in 1944 by Archbishop John J. Cantwell, Johnson served in several pastoral positions before becoming director of Catholic Charities in 1956. From 1962 to 1968, he was pastor of Holy Name parish and he occupied a similar post at American Martyrs in Manhattan Beach, 1968-1971. Johnson was appointed a papal chamberlain by Pope John XXIII in 1960 and a domestic prelate by Pope Paul VI in 1966.

Johnson played an active part in the refurbishment of Saint Vibiana's Cathedral in the mid 1970s and it was he who commissioned the modernistic mural placed in the sanctuary for the cathedral's centennial. Generally, it was scorned by priests and laity alike, but it remained in place for the rest of the years that Saint Vibiana's served as the archdiocesan mother church. Manning had great respect for Johnson's easy-going but dogged determination. At Johnson's funeral, in 1986, he portrayed the Bishop of Orange as "a man of many parts. He had a mind quick to understand and when that mind was made up, it was reinforced by an unbending will. Friends he cherished to his heart with hoops of steel. His protocol, generosity and hospitality were legendary. He had a soft heart and compassion and emotion flowed from it."[7]

SISTER MIRIAM JOSEPH LARKIN

Long before bishops began naming women to policy-making roles in curial offices, Cardinal Manning decided to appoint one to the most unlikely position of all for a woman, that of directing the Liturgy Commission. His rationale was simple enough - she knew more about the liturgical norms and practices of Vatican Council II than any priest then on the local scene.

Sister Miriam Joseph Larkin, a member of the Saint Joseph of Carondolet Religious Community since 1946, had been a music professor at Mount Saint Mary's College. She was uniquely qualified for her position. During her dozen years, the seemingly endless list of directives issued by the commission became the norm for many other areas of the country. Cardinal Manning remarked several times that the ease with which the Church in Los Angeles adjusted to the spirit of the council was due, in great measure, to the careful catechesis that emanated from the Liturgical Commission.

Miriam Joseph spent many of her years at the Chancery Office putting out ecclesial brushfires by soothing priests and laity who were either upset about new changes or irritated by changes that never came. When no one could satisfy an irate caller, the complainer was diverted to extension 59 where Sister smothered the caller with patience and kindness. On many occasions, she intervened for those who got in trouble of one kind or other and, more often than not, the offender never knew that Miriam Joseph had come to his defense. She was one of the few who had the temerity to confront the Vicar General on delicate issues. He would invariably tell her it was none of her business, order her out of the office and then quietly agree to whatever it was that she wanted. He once referred to her as "Little Miss Fix-it" and, in fact, that was a pretty good description.

During those years, Miriam Joseph was the central conduit by which information flowed from one department or agency to another at the Chancery. She was the first to practice "shuttle diplomacy" and, not infrequently, she was the last recourse at court for those who needed, wanted or deserved special attention. Cardinal Manning could never say "no" to her and, much to his annoyance, she knew all the nooks and crannies where he used to hide out.

ARCHBISHOP JOSEPH T. MCGUCKEN

Manning's friendship with Archbishop Joseph T. McGucken (1902-1983) stretched back to the early 1930s. A native of Los Angeles, McGucken was ordained in 1928 in the seminary chapel adjacent to Rome's Basilica of Saint John Lateran. It was McGucken who consecrated Manning to the bishopric in 1946 and their friendship perdured even after McGucken left Los Angeles to serve in Monterey-Fresno, Sacramento and San Francisco.

When Manning was named to the cardinalate in 1973, the then Archbishop of San Francisco accompanied him to Rome and later to Ballingeary and Gougane Barra in Ireland. McGucken's maternal grandfather came from Castleisland in County Kerry and he loved everything about his ancestral homeland, its people, its history, its humor.

During the years that there was a McGucken in San Francisco and a Manning in Los Angeles, the two prelates talked by phone each day and

Msgr. John P. Languille
Catholic Charities

Sister Miriam Joseph Larkin
Liturgical Commission

Msgr. John Mihan
Elementary Schools

Msgr. August Moretti
Matrimonial Tribunal

Msgr. Timothy O'Connell
Family Life Bureau

Msgr. Laurence O'Leary
Propagation of the Faith

Msgr. Jeremiah Murphy
Colleges and High Schools

Msgr. Royale M. Vadakin
Ecumenism

seldom did either act independently on issues of mutual concern. The two were proteges of the legendary John J. Cantwell and they prolonged that pioneer's influence in California another forty-two years after his death in 1947. In his homily for McGucken, the cardinal said "he was foremost and eminently a churchman. He had no other vocation, no other diversion, no other ambition except the Church.[8]

THE PICZEK SISTERS

In Cardinal Manning's opinion, Isabel and Edith Piczek were among "the most outstanding ecclesial artists of contemporary times."[9] From their modest and unobtrusive studios in the Echo Park district of Los Angeles, the Hungarian-born sisters produced some of the finest murals, mosaics and stained glass in America.

Shortly after the Communists took over their homeland, the sisters escaped to Vienna. Later, they literally painted their way across war-torn Europe, finally arriving in Rome at the outset of the 1950 Holy Year. In the Eternal City, Isabel and Edith won the celebrated Galleria di Roma prize and were commissioned to create a 377 square foot fresco mural at the Pontifical Biblical Institute, an unheard of distinction for women. At the invitation of the Canadian hierarchy, the sisters set up studios in Hamilton and Toronto. Then, in 1955, they came to the United States where their first commission was a 2,880 foot mural for the cathedral at Reno.

Since 1958, the Piczeks have lived and worked in Los Angeles at their Construction Art Center. Cardinal Manning was responsible for having their artistic masterpieces adorn churches, convents and cemeteries throughout the archdiocese. Locally, the Piczek art can be seen at Saint Phillip's Church (Pasadena), Saint Mary Magdalen (Camarillo), Saint Victor (West Hollywood), Saint Bridget of Sweden (Van Nuys), Saint Catherine Laboure (Torrance) and Our Lady of the Assumption (San Buenaventura). Their talents have a decided ecumenical attraction too. The Air Force Chapel at Nellis Air Base, Messiah Baptist Church and B'nai David Synagogue in Los Angeles are perhaps the three finest examples of their outreach, award-winning art.

The unassuming sisters see their vocation as a "cultural and religious mission." They feel compelled to be "always moving forward," concerned as they are that the old ways will disappear or trap those who insist on a piety not in keeping with the times. Believing that much of modern art has a de-humanizing effect, the Piczek sisters portray the destiny of humankind in forms of glass, paint and tile, while acknowledging that the "real artwork" is implanted in the soul of the observer.

MSGR. JOHN A. RAWDEN

Unquestionably, one of the unsung heroes of the Manning regime was Msgr. John A. Rawden who occupied the position of chancellor for the entire fifteen years. Born July 31, 1927 in Ohio, Rawden was ordained on April 27, 1955. He served in several pastoral assignments prior to being named secretary to James Francis Cardinal McIntyre and director of archdiocesan insurance.

In the ecclesial structure of the local church during the years immediately after Vatican Council II, the chancellor was entrusted with keeping the records and files for the curia, along with whatever else might be assigned to his position by the local ordinary. In Los Angeles, the chancellor was primarily charged with looking after clerical personnel. The enormity of that task can best be appreciated by comparing statistics of those times with contemporary figures. In 1974, for example, there were 594 diocesan priests (plus another 171 serving here from other dioceses), as compared to a fewer number in modern times. Now it takes five full-time priests, a personnel board and a staff of seven people to perform pretty much the same functions that Rawden and his secretary did two decades ago.

Harkening back thirty years when he served as chancellor, the cardinal made many other demands of Rawden who, for most of his tenure also served as administrator and later pastor of Immaculate Conception, a huge downtown parish of mostly Hispanic peoples. With Manning's retirement, Rawden moved to Santa Barbara where he became a hospital chaplain. His memoirs would indeed be revealing if ever he decided to write them.

MSGR. ROYALE M. VADAKIN

"Quiet, unobtrusive and exceedingly effective" are words readily associated with Msgr. Royale Vadakin who figured prominently in the operations of the Archdiocese of Los Angeles during the Manning years. A native of Michigan, born March 27, 1938, Royale Vadakin was ordained priest by James Francis Cardinal McIntyre on April 30, 1964.

In 1971, he was named Director of the Office of Ecumenical and Inter-Religious Affairs and during his years in that position, the Archdiocese of Los Angeles emerged as the foremost practitioner of ecumenical activity in the country. Vadakin also served as President of the Priests' Senate and RECOPS (the Regional Conference of Priests' Senates). Actively involved in the formation of the diaconate program in Los

Angeles, he was named chair of the Commission on Peace and Justice and chaplain for the Catholic Labor Institute.

He was appointed Rector of Saint Vibiana's Cathedral in 1984 and later served as regent for Loyola Marymount University and trustee for Mount Saint Mary's College. Manning frequently utilized Vadakin's organizational ability on task forces and search committees. Because of his uneasiness in dealing with civil officials, Manning often asked Vadakin to represent him in that arena.

BISHOP JOHN J. WARD

The role of auxiliary bishop is that of being a "silent partner" and no one epitomized that position longer or with more dignity than John J. Ward. Born September 28, 1920, John Ward was the last of the priests ordained by Archbishop John J. Cantwell. No priest has ever filled more positions in Los Angeles than he - assistant pastor, seminary procurator, curial secretary, canonical judge, pastor, chancellor, vicar general and auxiliary bishop.

Manning once said that Bishop Ward was the most treasured inheritance from the McIntyre regime. He was destined to carry the shepherd's staff along *El Camino Real* for more years than any of the state's auxiliary bishops and longer than all but a handful of its residential bishops.

In addition to his work at the Chancery Office, Ward confirmed in all the 319 parishes then comprising the four county Archdiocese of Los Angeles. At various times, he was also director of the Campaign for Human Development, regent for the Saint Vincent de Paul Society, moderator of the Liturgical Commission, director of the Cardinal McIntyre Fund for Charity and busy pastor.

He was for many years the official "stand in" when Manning was unable to fulfill an engagement. As attorney of fact, he routinely signed literally thousands of checks and other official documents. One-time secretary of the archdiocesan tribunal, Ward was a canonical expert who kept abreast of the legal and canonical changes affecting the local scene. He served as vicar for Religious during the tumultuous years of the 1960s. Through all of his years of service, Bishop Ward never lost his love and attraction for his native city. Once, when there was speculation that Ward was being considered for the newly created archbishopric of Oklahoma City, he defused the rumor by saying that "I would rather be an altar boy in Los Angeles than an archbishop anywhere else." And he meant it!

Notes to the Text

1. *Past Eighty* (Los Angeles, 1943), no. pagination.
2. Quoted from James Hourihan, *The History of Saint Andrew's Parish* (Pasadena, 1986), p. 104.
3. Francis J. Weber, *A Centennial History of The Tidings* (Mission Hills, 1995), p. 103.
4. In one of his last oral interviews, the cardinal admitted that he had experienced three major disappointments in his life, all of them in areas beyond his immediate control. The first dealt with his cousin, Father James Cronin, a priest of the Archdiocese of San Francisco, who had wandered from the ministry. Manning kept in touch with him over the years but was unable to effect his return to the clerical life. Cronin was killed crossing a street in Newport Beach on August 14, 1975. Secondly, was the problem of the Immaculate Heart Sisters which Manning valiantly but unsuccessfully tried to resolve. While he did manage to reinstate the vows of Mother Eucharia Harney on her deathbed, he was frustrated in attempts to bring about a wider reconciliation among the Sisters, many of whom he had known for over half a century. Finally, the cardinal was disappointed that he "couldn't get a favorite candidate made a bishop," something which he attributed to his not being native-born. In a surprisingly candid observation, he said that "Rome owed me that favor - they did it for Cantwell," an obvious reference to his own appointment. What Manning overlooked was that times and procedures had changed markedly since 1946. See AALA Memorandum - Timothy Cardinal Manning, Los Angeles, July 8, 1983.
5. Los Angeles *Times*, October 18, 1982.
6. *The Tidings*, November 15, 1974.
7. Quoted in Francis J. Weber (comp.), *Times of Tension. Moments of Grace* (Mission Hills, 1990), p. 416.
8. *The Tidings*, November 4, 1983.
9. Francis J. Weber, *Vignettes of California Catholicism* (Mission Hills, 1988), p. 57.

22. *Archdiocesan Chronicle*

Judging from all extant statistics, between 1946 and 1985 Timothy Manning as auxiliary bishop, Bishop of Fresno, Coadjutor and Archbishop of Los Angeles conferred the Sacrament of Confirmation on more persons than any other prelate in United States Catholic annals, an estimated 650,000 people. And he never tired of that duty which he felt was paramount to his role as chief shepherd.

In 1970, for example, he and his two auxiliaries confirmed 37,000 children alone. The archbishop disclosed that fact in a press conference where questions centered around the means taken to prepare and protect youngsters from those powerful elements in the community that prey on youth. Manning declared that through anointing with chrism and the imposition of hands, children were strengthened with grace and made soldiers of Christ. He recalled that the gifts of the Holy Spirit were imparted at confirmation and they were wisdom, understanding, counsel, fortitude, knowledge, piety and fear of the Lord. He also mentioned the fruits of the Holy Spirit, charity, joy, peace, patience, benightedness, goodness, longanimity, mildness, faith, modesty, continence and chastity, all of which were important spiritual boosts for Catholics growing into adulthood.[1]

Even before he became a cardinal, Manning was frequently asked to preach at important events, none of which exceeded in significance the dedication of Saint Mary's Cathedral in San Francisco on May 5, 1971. He was at his best, word-wise, noting that "In the land of Our Lord we are told that the mountains of Tabor and snow-capped Hermon looked down with envy on lowly Sion because the glory of the Lord had rested upon it. So too, in fancy, we see far-off Mount Diablo and Mount Tamalpais, Twin Peaks and all the hills that form a corona around this lovely city look with envy on this beautiful thing, this white-winged thing, *La Paloma,* which has taken rest in the glory of God upon this Cathedral hill."

> We search our minds for ways that might somehow capture the significance of this shining moment. We turn our

> eyes to the most beautiful thing that this age of technology has produced. It is the climax of our age. In steel and concrete, the products and symbols of our time, the bridge across the Golden Gate raises its mighty head above the sky-line. Its immense tower, with ribs of steel and flesh of concrete, seems to us like another Adam at the dawn of creation. It is beautiful, majestic, poised – yet somehow incomplete – waiting for its completing. This cathedral building is like another Eve drawn from the side of Adam, steel of its steel, bone of its bone, flesh of its flesh. It is raised up as complementary to the bridge, the sacred and the secular. This Eve shall be the mother of all the churches, the mother of all the living in this city and archdiocese.
>
> Again, just as the bridge crosses over the void to the ulterior shore and allows people to cross from one place to another and just as its towers are shrouded in the cloud, so also this building is somehow a bridge, a bridge that crosses the void that separates us from the other shore which is that of heaven, across which persons may commerce in traffic to reach the ulterior shore. The cloud which surrounds it is the holy cloud that represents the presence of God here among His people. That, over there, is a location; this here is a presence.[2]

Occasionally, Manning would express himself on"areas of concern" that he felt needed clarification. Early in 1974, for example, he cited several matters, including interfaith couples without a firm religious commitment. He called for more attention to parochial educational programs to provide in-depth understanding of what married life entails:

> Our people and their life styles are being affected by the changing values of society regarding marriage and the family and the divorce rate among Catholics is climbing steadily.[3]

After several years of study and with the careful management of available finances, Manning was able to announce a retirement plan for lay employees in October, 1977.[4] This pension plan was designed to be supplemental to Social Security benefits. Each full-time employee hired prior to his or her sixty-first birthday would be eligible for coverage upon attaining twenty-five years of service. The initial enrollment was 2,808 and, by the end of the second year, the number had expanded 3,817. This program was funded by the archdiocese at a cost of $6,000,000.

The existing Blue Cross program was broadened and, by the end of 1982, total claims paid, plus the management fee, amounted to $2,559,000. Early in 1977, allowances were increased and, in 1982, benefits included payment for home and office visits, something that was unavailable in many contemporary business plans.[5]

Through the seventies the cardinal engaged in much travel in the service of the Church, apart from journeys to the missions. He conducted a mission for U.S. military chaplains in Berchtesgaden, Germany. He flew to Hickam Field, Hawaii, to conduct memorial services for Vietnam war dead. He travelled by jet, small planes, jeeps, Marine helicopter, whose call name, incidentally, was "Angel One." There were also journeys of healing to the sick, the elderly, the imprisoned.[6]

In 1980 Manning and Bishop Thaddeus Shubsda made a pilgrimage to Poland, during which the cardinal kept a diary. He described the country in great detail, noting that "Warsaw has been rebuilt, its old town meticulously restored. The ancient churches, buildings, monuments and squares are perfectly reconstructed from reproductions of the originals." Most of all, he was impressed by the spiritual aura of Poland:

> There is something about the Poles that transcends their history and their culture, or rather, that is the very texture of their culture and history. It is their faith. The faith is vibrant, reasoned, practiced. Vocations to religious life are superabundant. Priests teach catechism as much as thirty hours a week to children of all ages. The hierarchy is a model of post-conciliar collegiality and fulfillment.
>
> You will know a tree by its fruit. This is the formula given to us by the Lord. Poland has bred men and women of great historical and artistic dimension: Chopin and Paderewski in the musical field; Joseph Conrad, the writer; Copernicus, the father of modern astronomy; and the great Madam Marie Curie, the discoverer of radium.

To Manning, Karol Wojtyla was the "greatest name that will live on in the history of Poland."

> Time stands aside while he straddles the world as a champion of human dignity and human rights; a custodian and proclaimer of the Gospel of Christ over against the counterfeits; an incomparable leader of the Church he shepherds,

> and a tender child of his heavenly mother to whom he dedicates everything that he is and does – *Totus Tuus*.[7]

Manning believed in accountability and he never failed to make public those accomplishments which served for the betterment of the archdiocese. In 1982, he noted that since his arrival; ten parishes had been established and property for another had been acquired. During more recent times, it had become necessary to set aside a minimum of two million dollars for the establishment of a new parish, a figure that included the property, a multipurpose building and a rectory. Generally, the multipurpose building accommodated four classrooms for school or confraternity use. The cardinal explained that it was only through a program of "sharing" that growth was possible. Parishes with surplus funds were encouraged to place their excess monies on deposit at the chancery where they drew a modest interest. Those funds were then loaned to needy parishes at a rate cheaper than any bank would charge. He noted that in 1982, nine of the ten churches constructed were without debt.[8]

The appearance of P.J. Kenedy's *The Official Catholic Directory* in 1983 was heralded with great acclaim because the Archdiocese of Los Angeles had replaced Chicago as the largest see in the nation. Los Angeles listed 2.37 million Catholics, 4,157 more than the Windy City. The Los Angeles archdiocese showed an increase of 66,440 over 1982 figures, while Chicago reported a decrease of 8,295. The statistics confirm the prediction made some fifteen years earlier by James Francis Cardinal McIntyre that Los Angeles would become a world center with an orientation to the Pacific. They also gave substance to the observation by Manning that Los Angeles was a new Ellis Island, a multi-cultural archdiocese, the nation's largest.[9]

Manning customarily issued letters to the faithful on a regular basis. For example in 1977, he observed that the season of Lent had once more arrived. Times were bothered with disputes about doctrine and standards for moral conduct. Some healing elements were needed for peace of mind. He proposed that Lent should provide such a time for this holy searching. "The Church had a three-fold exercise for this observance:"

> The first was prayer. Ample opportunities are given us for liturgical prayer. Let us use those. Let us relish the New Rite of Penance. Beyond that, however, there is great need for prayer of contemplation. Let us absent ourselves from the noises of the day for a period of quiet to meditate and pray according to the Gospel of Jesus. Peace comes flowing from it.

> Mortification is the second. Our bodies have five senses; sight, touch, taste, smell and hearing. They can be like wayward, undisciplined children. At the moment of death we will have to surrender them. Mortification, as the word implies, has a resonance of death. Let our Lent, then, be a striving to obtain mastery of these senses. Doing so, we become like athletes for Christ and fitted instruments for the work He wants us to do.
>
> In third place, there is "almsgiving." In olden days when beggars lined the streets, the necessity for alms was constantly before the eye. Not so now. We cling to our possessions for very life. Let us release our hold and endow the poor. But there is an almsgiving of love also. Release that too. Let it flow over the unwanted, the disabled, the mentally handicapped, the illegal alien, the shut-in, and the countless others who are our brothers and sisters in Christ.[10]

In one of his Christmas letters, the cardinal noted that "the inspired Word of God gives us the beautiful narrative of the birth and infancy of Jesus. This is done so that our lives will be touched and enriched by this design of the Almighty. Jesus is the image of the invisible God. Our response to Him must be a total submission of mind and heart in faith and love."

> Each year we are given a liturgical celebration to bring these truths again and again before our minds. Each year we renew the response of our faith and love. We go over to Bethlehem to see these wonders that have come to pass.
>
> We pray that Our Lady of Angels, the fair Mother of the Lord, will manifest Him to us. In the warmth of family and friends may we taste His peace. It is only in that spirit that we can wish each one of the People of God a happy Christmas.[11]

Speaking at Easter sunrise services in the Hollywood Bowl, Manning said that "we are congregated within the shoulders of this majestic Bowl. Coming from the pluralistic origins of race, religion, geography and social status, we somehow, within the embrace of this conclave, fashion ourselves into a unity. It is a oneness beyond the powers of a rock festival to create a deeper beauty than a symphony under the stars."

> The sense and cause of our togetherness is triple in its concept: First, we are remotely aware that we spring from a

The cardinal's door was always open, especially to priests.

Press conference at the Chancery Office.

Clare Berger, the cardinal's long-time secretary is shown with Sharon Valenzuela, his house-keeper.

Ethel Bossert worked at the chancery for well over sixty years.

Sam Coney greets the cardinal and Mary Sinclair who had come to Los Angeles with Bishop John J. Cantwell in 1917.

> common stock – that we share a common destiny. The wide dimensions of humanity give a common denomination to our inmost realities.
>
> Secondly, we share the same bewildering awe at the great mystery of life that lies beyond all human explanation. The unsolved riddles of human existence compel us to reach out and touch the grasping hand of brother and sister like tentacles testing for reality.
>
> Thirdly, there is the essential inadequacy of the answers found in this changing world. We tend to stake our cause on values supplied to us in the cresting of our consumer society. The heart is yet unsatisfied. We have turned to sex as a source of recreation and content. Without the sharing of marital covenant, sex becomes no more than a mountain torrent after unseasonable rains sweeping rampages in its hurry to the sea. Money, ambition, glamour, public favor – all of these we have pursued and yet the empty void remains.[12]

APPEALS

Like most priests, Manning never savored the role of mendicant. Yet he probably raised more funds for various charitable purposes during the years of his incumbency than most of his contemporary ecclesiastics in and out the Catholic Church.

In 1970, he appealed on behalf of the Archbishop's Fund for Charity, which would thereafter be known as the Cardinal McIntyre Fund for Charity. He recalled that the fund served a unique purpose, making itself available to those charities that had slipped through the cracks. Manning asked the archdiocesan newspaper to remind its readers that the fund was a response to the needs of certain institutions and agencies which were facing hardship because of inadequate financing, ones who received either no help or inadequate help from the United Way or other sources. Among these programs and needs were emergency relief to families, social services in distressed neighborhoods, maternity care, institutions for the aged; services for the blind, hard of hearing, mentally retarded and physically handicapped, child, health and youth services, and adoption agencies.[13]

Another of Manning's favorite appeals was the Thanksgiving Clothing Collection sponsored annually by the Catholic Relief Service for the destitute in Africa, Asia and Latin America. He noted that:

> The impoverished people in some seventy countries served by the Catholic Relief Services, like the poor of Peru, are poorer this year. Used clothing that Americans can share or spare becomes precious beyond words to millions around the world in dire need. Not only can it provide protection against the cold of winter or torrential seasonal rains or blazing tropical sun, but it can often safeguard the very young against crippling or deadly diseases, aid impoverished men and women to find work or to continue working, enable children to attend school without shame.[14]

The Campaign for Human Development, with which American bishops had begun to break "the hellish circle of poverty" did not appeal to many people, mostly because of careless procedures in allocating its funds. Nevertheless, Manning endorsed the appeal each year. In his letter for 1972, the cardinal noted that:

> By reason of the generosity of our people, an unprecedented sixteen million dollars was collected for this campaign during the past two years. Almost $500,000 of that sum came from our own Archdiocese of Los Angeles. We do not need to stress to you the value of those many sacrificial gifts which added up to such a sum, for you know that Christ reckons what we do in His name as being done for Him – "Whatsoever you do for the least of my brothers, that you do unto me."
>
> The Campaign for Human Development, however, is not just another collection of money. It is, above all, an appeal to open our minds and hearts to the suffering Christ who manifests Himself to us in the person of those who are alone, deprived, despairing for whatever reason. The need today, as ever, is not just to share what we have, but to share what we are. Our presence, our participation in our society, our love for one another should create an environment in which people can grow, develop, and become all that the image of God which is in them calls them to be. That is why we call this a Campaign for Human Development, and that it why the collection is duly the first step on a journey that requires the investment of our "self" in others every day of the year.[15]

In addition to his yearly articles for *The Tidings* during Lent, Manning used that season to seek support for the Catholic Relief Overseas Fund.

> For twenty-six years American Catholics have generously responded to the appeal of their bishops. As a result, Catholic Relief Services is the overseas aid and development agency of the American Catholics. Throughout the tragic events in India and Pakistan, Catholic Relief Services has provided the basic necessities of life to all the suffering. Over $12-million in aid has been channeled through this organization for relief to the refugees and other victims of this conflict. Rehabilitation and reconstruction for the victims, as they return to their homeland, will further challenge the agency's resources. In addition, Catholic Relief Services continues its ongoing programs of social welfare and community development in more than seventy countries throughout Africa, Asia and Latin America, assisting each year over twenty-seven million impoverished men, women and children of all races and religions.[16]

In late 1973, Manning inaugurated the first in a series of appeals for funds with which to sustain the archdiocese in its task of looking after the needs of the local Church.

> We are concerned for the future. Our first duty and desire is to sustain the work begun by Cardinal McIntyre. Each year we strive to keep our schools open, to subsidize inner-city parishes, to help the poor and underprivileged, and to maintain the mounting administration costs of the archdiocese. Last year the parishes subsidized the grade schools with 7.5 million dollars. The high schools required 1.7 million dollars above the tuition receipts; the inner-city parishes, special works and religious communities received 1.4 million dollars. This does not include the amount allowed by the more affluent parishes during the past year for the relief of the indebted parishes, totaling 2.1 million dollars.
>
> For all these reasons we are advised and urged once more to appeal to our people for sustenance more than the weekly parish contribution. We are in fact asking for ten percent of the ordinary income of each parish for two years to provide a fund toward the alleviation of our needs. This would be computed as twenty percent of the income for the year 1972.

> It is not too much to ask. This amount could readily be reached, for example, if each person added an extra ten percent to his weekly contribution over the two-year period. In this way our people will identify with all of the needs of the archdiocese.[17]

The re-organization of the Saint Vincent de Paul Society in 1974 prompted an appeal from Manning to support the stores and workshops operated by the society throughout the archdiocese. Especially did he want to further the "greatest sources of income to the society," which was salvage and paper pick-up at the parochial level. "Bundle Sundays" were begun and on those days people were exhorted to gather any and all items that might be used or sold for the benefit of the poor. The response was surprisingly positive and ever-so-gradually the society bounced back into a thriving agency of the Church.[18]

PRO-LIFE

It was always a mystery to Timothy Manning and many others how the Pro-Choice lobby was able to masquerade its position on abortion as a "womens" issue rather than the "life" issue it surely was and remains. Realizing that the matter would not go away, the cardinal decided to become a spokesman for Pro-Life in all its forms.

Near the end of his predecessor's regime, the Right to Life League of Southern California was formed as a non-profit corporation. Its purpose was "to plan, develop and disseminate a comprehensive educational program in the following areas: the generation of human life and reproductive physiology; moral, medical and legal ramifications of abortion, infanticide, sterilization, artificial insemination and anovulation, euthanasia, eugenic selection and engineering and what constitutes the end of human life."[19]

Manning felt that the league was far better equipped and positioned than the Catholic Church to fight abortion and its related errors. For that reason, he unequivocally supported the league in all its activities. He was especially pleased that so many non-Catholic churches and agencies lent their support. By 1972, well over 5,000 league members were annually expending 12,212 man-hours as volunteers. The Right to Life League was geographically well positioned, with a voice in most of the communities in Southern California. A twenty-four hour lifeline was established in six areas and volunteers were answering an average of 278 calls monthly from young people needing counseling about abortion.

Mayor Tom Bradley and cardinal.

Mayor Sam Yorty meets cardinal.

General Douglas MacArthur greets Manning.

The cardinal with Governor Edmund G. Brown.

A sixty-seven page booklet, *Love for Life From Beginning to End*, was distributed to all students in the archdiocesan school system. Therein young people were able to learn about the moral issues so vital to their spiritual growth. Reprints of pertinent articles from *The Tidings* were prominently featured in the booklet, as was the "Declaration on Abortion" issued on November 18, 1970 by the National Conference of Catholic Bishops.

In addition to his support of the Right to Life League, Manning issued his own periodical statements which made clear his and the Catholic Church's views on the subject. For example, he told a representative from the Copley Press that "Thomas Jefferson said of slavery: 'I tremble for my country when I remember that God is just and that His justice will not sleep forever.' What will it be when the millions of voices of the unborn dead cry to their Creator for vengeance?"[20]

Declaring that "no legislation of man can amend or change God's unchangeable command" the archbishop issued a proclamation concerning abortion in mid-1970.

> Our life is a sacred gift entrusted to us by God. Its beginning and its ending are reserved to Him. The commandment, "Thou shalt not kill," is the unchangeable law of God, from Sinai through Judeo-Christian transmission until this hour. No legislation of man can amend or change it.
>
> Deeply integrated into the sanctities cherished in our country is this same high value set on life and liberty. Our dedication is legendary to the defense of the weak and underprivileged, the most acute of which is verified in the voiceless, defenseless infant in the womb. From the moment of pregnancy, motherhood and life are at issue and at stake. Theories about animation and hominization do not alter the gravity nor the consequences. Our traditions, too, set a high priority on freedom of conscience. We proclaimed it to the nations at Nuremberg when we condemned those who failed to follow their consciences when ordered to destroy human life. We recognize it in the objectors to war, and we may not forfeit it in the issues of our domestic way of life.
>
> Loudly and clearly our voices must guard the religious convictions of every doctor, nurse, social worker, employee of any medical or social welfare agency, in their stand in the defense of the rights of the unborn; their consciences must not be forced into violation; they must not be pressured to

> assist in abortion practices, nor may they advise, counsel or pressure welfare recipients toward the procurement of abortion. All our moral force is pledged to their defense. Hospitals sponsored by men and women of religious principles have the obligation to set and enforce those high moral standards involved in the total care of the patient.
>
> In the name of God, author of all life, we summon all people to resist this terrible evil and unspeakable crime. All the violence, madness and malice of our times are summed up in abortion. We tremble for our country, as we pray that the justice of God will not fall on us.[21]

When bodies of twelve unborn infants were found in a rubbish dump on January 13, 1971, Manning immediately petitioned the Los Angeles County coroner for permission to provide proper burial for them "as human beings in sacred ground."[22] An editorial in the local archdiocesan paper reiterated that "we Catholics believe and there are many others who share this belief, that God infuses a human soul into the human embryo at the moment of conception. At that mysterious moment when the ovum is fertilized, the hand of the Creator is with joined hands of those with whom He has shared His creative power, and a human being comes into existence."[23]

Asked about the feasibility of pursuing anti-abortion litigation, Manning responded that "It is certainly my definite understanding that to date the courts have sought to side-step the issue of the rights of the unborn and have sought to decide cases involving abortion on other grounds, such as the ambiguity and uncertainty of particular statutes and the mother's right to privacy." After outlining the actions taken in California with respect to abortion litigation, Manning referred the query to the Right to Life League which, he said, was "an organization formed in this archdiocese for the purpose of opposing liberalization of abortion laws and educating the general public on the rights of the unborn child."[24]

In March of 1972, Manning wrote to President Richard Nixon to protest the conclusions of the Commission on Population Growth and the American Future, saying that "to follow the philosophy argued in this report will only compound the disaster that awaits us in our tampering with human life."[25] On another occasion, he said "A kiss of love, brought to its ultimate conclusion, is in reality a new-born child. Each child is a love child. To intercept that process of life, to terminate it, is in reality to murder love. We destroy and ravish the earth with war, and the earth answers with spring. We cannot circumvent God's plan for

President Ronald Reagan greets Cardinal Manning.

President Gerald Ford meets American cardinals.

Chief of Police Ed Davis gives plaque to cardinal.

Legendary Supervisor Kenneth Hahn invests cardinal with medallion.

love. There will always be a spring. The Right to Life League is the harbinger of that spring of life and love."[26]

When the United States Supreme Court handed down its decision legalizing abortion, Manning hastened to issue a blistering statement:

> This new slaughter of the innocents . . . out-Herods Herod in its cold and immoral disregard for the sanctity of human life. It was difficult to understand the legal reasoning that led the Supreme Court to ban capital punishment in most states as "cruel and unusual," then this week to decree the death penalty for innocent, unborn children. Respect for life in the United States has been exposed to erosion from all sides. No one of us can be sure that his own life will be safeguarded by law if his continued existence is deemed to be inconvenient to his peers.[27]

A year after the Supreme Court decision, Manning told his priests that "the only practical way to provide for legal protection of this life is to amend the Constitution of the United States. This would clearly establish that the unborn child is a person in the eyes of the law. Our state and federal legislators should be alerted by letters to the need for public hearings on this issue. Several bills have been proposed, but so far none has been submitted to official hearings. Until public hearings are held it is best not to endorse a particular proposal. When that happens the national office of our Catholic Conference will make appropriate interventions so as to secure the best possible wording for the amendment."[28]

Several months later, the cardinal was among those testifying at a hearing before the United States Senate as to why a constitutional amendment to protect the lives of the unborn was necessary.

> I wish to touch briefly on certain objectionable aspects of the Supreme Court's abortion decisions as well as on the appropriate position of the law with regard to human rights. No responsible American wishes to suggest disrespect for the Supreme Court of the United States. But honest disagreement is not disrespect. Recognition of the crucial role played by the Supreme Court in our system of government should not blind us to the fact that the court can err, as our history indicates. In this case we believe it has done so, and its error is a national tragedy.

It is important to make this point because Supreme Court decisions tend to be invested with an aura which places them almost beyond criticism. When the Supreme Court speaks, it is presumed to be the authentic interpreter of the constitution. But its interpretation can be mistaken. In the case of the abortion decisions the court created constitutional doctrine out of opinions which appear arbitrary at best.

Mr. Justice White spoke to this point in his dissent from the majority. "I find nothing in the language or history of the constitution to support the court's judgment. The court simply fashions and announces a new constitutional right . . . with scarcely any reason or authority for its action . . ." The fact is, nevertheless, that the court has spoken and its novel doctrine of virtual abortion on request will stand until concerned Americans avail themselves of the means of redress which the constitution itself provides. I refer of course to a constitutional amendment.

An amendment is necessary first of all to protect the lives of the unborn children who can be killed – indeed, are being killed at this very moment – in the wake of the Supreme Court's decisions. But it is also needed to restore integrity to the law itself, to make the American legal system once more the guarantor and protector of all human rights and the human rights of all.

Human rights stand always in need of vindication and protection. One of the distinguishing characteristics of a civilized society, and a particular concern of the Church, is the special care required to provide protection for those of its members who are least able to protect themselves. Conversely, it is a sign of sickness in a society when it becomes callous to the rights of the defenseless and deaf to the pleas of the weak.

I hesitate to say that the United States as a whole has arrived at such a condition. Yet the stark fact is that the unborn are being destroyed in our country at an unprecedented rate, and the destruction goes on because there is not adequate protection in the law. No one who cherishes this nation's historic commitment to human rights can contemplate this situation with complacency. An amendment

Cardinals Mindszenty and Manning.

Mother Teresa and cardinal.

President Richard Nixon welcomes Cardial McIntyre and Archbishop Manning to the Western White House at San Clemente.

> to protect the unborn is needed now in order that these words may continue to express the reality of American belief and practice.[29]

In January of 1976, Cardinal Manning wrote a pastoral letter in which he asked "protection for the unborn."

> Almost two thousand years ago, Jesus' last words in Saint Mark's Gospel gave to evangelization which the Lord entrusted to His Apostles a limitless universality: "Go out to the whole world; proclaim the Good News to all creation." In the course of twenty centuries, generations of Christians have periodically faced various obstacles to this universal mission. There has been the often humanly insurmountable resistance of the people being addressed. Despite such adversities the Church constantly renews her deepest inspiration, that which comes to her directly from the Lord. On December 8,1975, the Lord's vicar on earth, Pope Paul VI, as he was about to terminate the Holy Year and standing at the threshold of the last quarter of the twentieth century, called all of us to be evangelizers in the modern world as Christ was the evangelizer.
>
> The American bishops, successors to the twelve apostles, the evangelizers of this day, have repeatedly reminded us that human life is a precious gift from God; that each person who receives this gift has responsibilities toward God, toward self and toward others; and that society, through its laws and social institutions, must protect and sustain human life at every stage of its existence. The Church has a duty to speak in behalf of human life and to encourage a just social order and a system of justice that protects, basic human rights, especially the right to life. Governments must also protect human rights. Laws that permit the arbitrary destruction of human life – before as well as after birth – are unjust and immoral.
>
> There is widespread disrespect for the sanctity of human life in our nation today. It is evidenced in many ways, and especially in the destruction through abortion of more than one million unborn children each year. Disrespect for the sanctity of life is also evident in current efforts to persuade people that euthanasia is acceptable. Responding to such abuses of the sanctity of life, the bishops of the United States

> adopted a Pastoral Plan for Pro-Life activities at their annual meeting last November. This plan seeks to activate all the resources of the Church in order to check the trend toward permissive abortion. It calls on all the Church's agencies, institutions and people to take part in a comprehensive effort of education, moral and pastoral guidance, and social action which will restore respect for human life and establish a system of justice in which the basic right to life is protected at every stage and in every circumstance.
>
> We urge Catholics to move out into the society and invite their neighbors, colleagues and friends to take part in this most important effort.[30]

Early in May of 1980, Manning once again expressed publicly and unequivocally his "full measure of support for the Pro-Life movement," noting that "the devastating assault on life at its very beginning is all too familiar to us. With good reason, therefore we express our concern and our conviction."[31]

It was during Manning's time that the annual processions were inaugurated along Sunset Boulevard in Hollywood in reparation for the sins of abortion. The rosary was recited enroute and Mass was celebrated at Blessed Sacrament Church by the archbishop or one of his auxiliaries. Several thousand people responded yearly to this public manifestation of respect for life. Throughout his tenure, Manning remained outspoken and up-front in all the Pro-Life efforts. But here, "as always all our efforts will begin, be carried on, and concluded with prayer. It is with prayer that we gear ourselves for this unique challenge which demands of us all faith, courage, patience and determination. God grant our nation this victory for the dignity and sanctity of the human person."[32]

ETHNIC DIVERSITY

Even in the early 1970s, the Archdiocese of Los Angeles was fast becoming the most diverse Catholic population of any jurisdiction in the United States, maybe in the whole world. Timothy Manning was attuned to these changes, as perhaps few others were. One of his favorite quotations and one which he used often when speaking to newcomers was first uttered by Bishop John J. Cantwell when he addressed the National Association for the Advancement of Colored People in 1921: "Neither your fathers nor yourselves, nor the people whom I represent, have been strangers to intolerance. You and I know full well, to our sorrow be it said, what comes from an intolerant bigotry."[33]

Manning established the practice of having an annual Migrant's Day Mass at Saint Vibiana's Cathedral and he rarely missed being there himself. In 1979, he exhorted those present to "pass on to your children your faith and the fine things of your culture." Addressing them as "My fellow immigrants," he said that "the church was home and haven for all peoples and generations." Noting that there were eighty languages then being spoken in the archdiocese, he pointed out that "all cultures have different traits and talents and each enriches the nation that receives it. Jesus willed to experience every part of the human story," the cardinal said. "He had no shelter at birth. He moved with his parents to a land whose customs and language they did not know and lived there in a ghetto. Jesus is sanctifying the whole experience of exile and migration." In this nation, materialistic and overly-scientific, the cardinal called on immigrants to show the joy of faith, a dimension of life that money cannot buy.[34]

On another occasion, Manning declared that no one is an illegal alien in the Church. He told a congregation of a thousand people, comprised of sixteen nationalities that "from every point of the compass we come together to create one family. Each one of us has equal rights." He related how recently he had been with the Holy Father in Vancouver, British Columbia:

> We had a small private dinner together. He was asking about Los Angeles. I told him that we have eighty-three different languages spoken here and also that there are a large number of undocumented people here. In a beautiful gesture he raised his finger and said: "Undocumented in the state, yes, but not in the Church." There is no such thing as an undocumented person. There is no illegal alien in the Church. Here, we are together. We have a common father, successor to Peter. We go to him and he tells us what in this time and place we must do to give witness to the fact that we are the family of God. With great joy we can tell the large community of Los Angeles that even though we come from every nation under the sun, here in this house we are one family, under one common father, and our mother is the Church.[35]

In 1978, Manning created a vicariate for the Multilingual Apostolate and appointed Father Felix S. Diomartich episcopal vicar for that ministry. Over the ensuing months, directories were issued containing location of Masses celebrated in different languages, along with a list of priests conversant in various lingual strains for the Sacrament of Reconciliation. Diomartich assured those who felt that this ministry was divisive that "all immigration is destined to be absorbed into the American mainstream.[36]

When President Ronald Reagan and the members of the United States Congress formally approved the designation of Martin Luther King's birthday, January 12, as a national holiday in 1984, Manning used that occasion to issue a pastoral letter on racism in which he called on "all of our two million plus Roman Catholics to reflect on the need for racial harmony." He invited each of the parochial communities in the archdiocese "to pray for the courage to live the principle of human dignity, for we are many people living as one people of faith." Noting that Southern California had been "enriched with a variety of ethnic groups that are like-blood transfusions into our culture," he noted with pleasure that "our schools, institutions and parishes have become more aware of and responsive to the needs of what is now a world community."

> Yet there remains a grave responsibility which rests on us to be advocates of racial harmony. We must uproot and isolate all negative feelings and banish from us all fears of change, all paternalism, all stereotypes and scapegoating. Racial harmony is an imperative. The racial question in all its ramifications, is ultimately a moral/ethical one. The fullness of Christian life cannot exist where racial hatred resides.[37]

Manning had a special place in his list of priorities for the Knights and Ladies of Saint Peter Claver, a fraternal organization founded primarily for the Afro-American Catholic community. He once told members attending a national convention that they should be "stand-ins for Christ."

> Stars in Hollywood have stand-ins who resemble them and stand in their stead while lights and cameras are adjusted. When St. Paul writes of "putting on Christ," he means that we should be stand-ins for Christ "so that our bearing, our language, our actions will show that Christ is walking again among us."[38]

Manning's love and affection for Mexican-Americans stretched back to his earliest days in California. When asked about that, he replied that "when I came to Menlo Park, I was so busy explaining my own heritage that I never even thought about poking fun at others who were also alien to American culture." In a feature story by a local newspaper, shortly after Manning became Archbishop of Los Angeles, a writer said that Manning had "turned his attention to the problems of the poor, particularly Mexican-Americans who account for more than one-half of the archdiocese's 1.7 million parishioners." He established an inter-parochial council composed of twenty parishes in the east side *barrio* of Los Angeles and its first project was a voter registration drive financed with $5,000 from the Campaign for Human Development. "The Church has also established a center to deal with Chicano immigration problems, and expanded its bilingual adult education courses.[39]

Speaking at the first *Encuentro Hispano de Pastoral* in 1973, the cardinal said that "the time is ripe for opening the door, the beginning of a great enrichment." Speaking to some 350 delegates, Manning said:

> We in this country have reached a state of spiritual impoverishment for the things in which we had put our trust have deceived us. We are coming to realize that it is religious faith alone that we can trust and rely on. And that faith has been mysteriously and magnificently preserved in the people of Hispanic culture. This event, this *encuentro,* cannot be evaluated solely in terms of the conclusions that may come from it. This event is the releasing of a potency of faith that is inherent in that culture.[40]

Manning's Spanish was probably better than many of his priests. He never hesitated to offer Mass and even preach in Spanish, though he preferred to have someone more fluent than he deliver the homilies at Masses. He made it a point to learn the background of every group to which he ministered. Often he knew more about the Mexican-American heritage than did his listeners. He once told John Dart that "All Latinos, because of their Roman Catholic heritage, belong to the (Catholic) Church," even if they no longer go to the parish for baptism, weddings and other rites. And yet Manning maintained in the same interview that Protestants, to his knowledge, are not trying to rob Latinos of their Catholicism — despite evidence of increasingly active Protestant missions and evangelizing among the "unchurched" Spanish-speaking in Southern California. "There is good-will proselytizing going on to provide religious services, but it's not done out of malice toward the Catholic Church."

Pressed on whether good-will proselytizing of non-churchgoers militated against Catholic claims on all Latinos, Manning responded that he didn't especially like the situation. "I'm endeavoring to give them the full benefit of doubt," he said, "I don't want to be in the position of accusing Protestants of any malice." On the susceptibility of Latinos to proselytizing, Manning observed: "I think it's probably easier to be Protestant than it is Catholic." He said he was thinking particularly of Catholic teachings on divorce, remarriage, abortion and birth control.[41]

Manning enjoyed getting out of his "Ivory Tower" as often as he could. In October of 1970, he received bread and salt, symbols of Slavonic hospitality at Loyola High School from a group of Czechs celebrating the Feast of Saint Wenceslaus. He praised them as "good people who have come to the United States, not to clamor for rights, but to seek a chance to live in freedom." He compared them to the Irish, who, he said, also came to the United States "to breathe free air."

> The Irish know what it is to be hanged for the wearing of the green and the love of the faith, and I can sympathize with the Czechoslovakian people who also have come here to start new lives. We have not come empty-handed. We have enriched this culture, weaving a bright and resplendent garment. I belong here with you, sharing the same faith and same sacrifices.[42]

The archbishop was always anxious to endorse appeals for the Lithuanian people. In January of 1971, he signed a petition and issued a formal statement protesting Soviet treatment of three Lithuanians, one of whom had been forcibly removed from a U.S. Coast Guard Cutter. In a public statement, Archbishop Manning lamented "the forced abduction of a Lithuanian seaman from the protection of our own Coast Guard, with whom he had sought asylum, and the cruel and inhuman sentences passed by the Soviet Union upon a young Lithuanian and his wife who dared to strive for freedom." The archbishop said that "these incidents point up in dark colors one of the great tragedies of our times, namely, the enslavement and repression of a proud nation who had lived peacefully on the shores of the Baltic from time immemorial."[43]

Manning was particularly vociferous in favor of the Salvadorans and attempts to deport them. He asked Secretary of State George Shultz to grant the refugees extended voluntary departure status, thus allowing

Henry Edward, the first of the Cardinals Manning.

Cardinal celebrated Mass outdoors in the city's plaza for the bicentennial of el Pueblo de Nuestra Señora de los Angeles in 1981.

them to remain until conditions subsided in their homeland. In part, his letter said:

> In recent times because of strife in their countries, extended voluntary departure status has been granted to, among others, Ugandans, Ethiopians, Poles and Lebanese. Objective evidence exists of the high level of indiscriminate political terror and violence in El Salvador and of the particular liability of repatriated persons to persecution and death. These facts have been recognized by the United States High Commission on Refugee Affairs. It has designated all Salvadorans outside their country as political refugees.
>
> The Catholic Bishops of the United States have also taken cognizance of the facts of the situation. Motivated by a Christian concern for the human rights and welfare of the Salvadoran refugees, the bishops have, since 1981, asked that Salvadoran refugees be granted extended voluntary departure status. It is true that a nation must safeguard its borders. It is also true that these refugees are present among us in numbers greater than in any other American city. To recognize and ameliorate their plight is but to assert traditional American concern for God-given human rights, foremost of which is the right to life.
>
> Therefore, I ask that Salvadoran refugees in the United States be granted extended voluntary departure status, so they may have a safe haven until the end of the civil war in El Salvador enables them to return to safe and peaceful conditions.[44]

When a Korean airliner was shot down by a Soviet fighter plane in September of 1983, Manning sent telegrams to the Korean consul and to the Korean community in seven parishes of the archdiocese:

> On behalf of the Catholic community of Los Angeles which is enriched by so many Korean members, we wish to extend our sympathies to the nation and its people so sadly afflicted with tragedy. May the merciful Father of all give us consolation, forgiveness and peace.
>
> The Archdiocese of Los Angeles shares in the sorrow of the Korean community in the recent tragedy. Our prayers are promised for the consolation and peace of this worthy people and for God's mercy on us all.[45]

The cardinal presided at a Mass offered at Our Lady, Queen of Martyrs parish in Boyle Heights early in 1985 when the Apostolic Exarch of Armenian Catholics paid a visitation to his people in Los Angeles. Manning expressed his "profound respect and reverence for the primacy and beauty of this rite which adorns the Catholic Church. I would beg you who are inheritors of this rite to preserve it, to assist at it, to live it, and to assure that your children do not lose what you have inherited."[46]

The people of Lebanon were also recipients of Manning's concern. He joined his prayers to those of Pope John Paul II, saying that "we are constant in our deep desire for a resolution that will be respectful and just for all religious persuasions in this country beset by violence. We cherish those among us whose origin and inheritance is Lebanese. The great traditions of the United States in humanitarian and peace keeping missions urge us to support and encourage our own government in its best efforts to accommodate that peace and justice for which we all hope and pray.[47]

On several occasions, Manning offered endorsement and encouragement for the Federation of Cuban Catholic Youth, or the *Comunidades Cristianas Federadas* which, he said, was "a source of great joy." He was "edified by their dedication to the lay apostolate" and described the members as "authentic apostles while you remain close to the priests who share your ideals."[48] The cardinal also encouraged support of those acting as sponsors for Cuban refugees which were coming to the archdiocese in great numbers.[49]

In an interview given when Manning was "two-thirds through a peaceful tenure as archbishop," he noted that the archdiocese has resettled more Southeast Asian immigrants and refugees than any other Catholic diocese in addition to responding to the influx of Mexicans into urban areas. And hoping to build support for family life and against the evils of pornography and abortion, many Catholics had striven to influence the entertainment industry in various ways.[50]

In 1980, Manning praised the Filipino community for its "sustaining love for the Blessed Mother" which he felt was "a source of great hope to the Church in Los Angeles." He rejoiced that they had "not allowed such a great tradition of prayer to diminish in these days."[51] In another letter, Manning "observed with gratitude the growth of the number of Filipino people coming to our shores. They are faithful loyal members of the Body of Christ. In their love for the Church they speak the Gospel message with eloquence."[52]

By the time of his retirement, Manning could point to multilingual churches or centers serving the Chinese, Croatian, Czech, Filipino, German, Hungarian, Italian, Japanese, Korean, Lithuanian, Polish, Portuguese and Vietnamese peoples, along with seven Eastern Rites, Nativity of the Blessed Virgin (Ukrainian-Byzantine), Our Lady of Mount Lebanon (Maronite), Our Lady Queen of Martyrs (Armenian), Saint Andrew (Russian-Byzantine), Saint Anne (Melkite-Byzantine) and the Cathedral of Saint Mary (Byzantine-Ruthenian).

DISARMAMENT

In a venture into the disarmament controversy, Cardinal Manning observed in 1980 that "our culture is in a dance of death and men are squandering life as if we had passed the time of no return. The process of the dehumanizing is in proportion to its technological growth. We are fast approaching the pig-level of the Prodigal Son." Manning pointed out that there were then, in the hands of the superpowers, "weapons of war that included 50,000 nuclear bombs, 200 of which, were they detonated, would destroy all the largest cities of the world in an hour. One Trident submarine could deliver 192 nuclear explosions from a range of 4,000 miles. Every MX missile could carry ten hydrogen bombs, each of the bombs twenty-three times more powerful than the one used on Hiroshima. "But more! The radiation from these explosions would contaminate the food-producing lands, damage the ozone layer of the atmosphere, and cause dangerous genetic mutations. It is too terrible to think about; Jesus said that men would wither away with fear."

Manning felt that "disarmament is the indisputable answer." Yet a necessary condition for disarmament "is the elimination of the causes of violence. Violence is a reaction to conditions of injustice and repression. In the end it only generates more violence." The cardinal said that the "balance of error" that is implied in the arms race must somehow be replaced by the "balance of trust." There is a need for a higher awareness, the supremacy of the moral order. Then only will the demons of hatred and injustice be excised. Manning reminded people that "the beginning of wisdom is surely the fear of the Lord, not the fear of the bomb." We have more to fear from God than from our enemies.

> The justice of God will not sleep forever. Surely the example of our first president kneeling in the snow at the barriers of crisis should urge us too, to do the same in the winter of our distress.
>
> Maybe if we have a conversion of life, a return to our Father's house and love, will His anger be turned away from us and the city of man be spared. If not, then the terrible fires

> will be loosed upon the earth, the mountains will fall upon us and the powers of heaven will be shaken. But the end may not be yet. From the cinders of our burnt-out world God can still raise children unto Abraham. Then, from its ashes, will rise a new heaven and a new earth.[53]

Two years later, Manning called on people to recall the words of Pope John Paul II about disarmament. The pontiff had observed that "the only choice that is morally and humanly valid is represented by the reduction of nuclear armaments." Manning said that it was all there: "the certain horror, the solitary humane and moral choice, reduction of such weapons, their ultimate elimination, bilateral agreements and effective controls." The cardinal took cognizance that "here in California some people are proposing and pursuing an initiative to the voters for a bilateral nuclear weapons freeze." This was intended to be "an appeal to the United States and the Soviet Union to agree to the halt of testing, production and deployment of weapons." For many he said, "this may be a praiseworthy means of giving expression to their convictions on this awesome matter." Read closely, Manning was endorsing the initiative, though he didn't personally think it would have any long-term effect.

On the fortieth anniversary of the atomic bomb devastation at Nagasaki, which was especially destructive to Catholic neighborhoods, Manning exchanged greetings with his cardinalatial counterpart at Nagasaki, Joseph Satowaki. In remarks at a Mass offered at Saint Francis Xavier church, Manning described the faith community of Nagasaki as being "destined to be a victim for the cause of peace." The city's Catholic cathedral was among the landmarks destroyed in the bombing on August 9, 1945, three days after the attack on Hiroshima. Manning spoke of those who share "that hunger inside of us for peace and justice" and asked that they join in invoking Our Blessed Lady and Saint Francis Xavier "in this one cry, this lonesome longing for peace, peace, peace." More than 200,000 people were killed by the twin bombings. Another 140,000 were injured and died within ten years from radiation-induced diseases.

In his written message to Cardinal Satowaki, Manning cited the "unspeakable tragedy" of the bombings of Hiroshima and Nagasaki. He said he sought "to join with you in thought and prayer: To recall the memory of those who lost their lives or bore the cross of years of radiation-caused disease and suffering; to speak aloud the truth that forty years ago the unthinkable became an historical fact and that the aftershock continues not only in scarred and wounded bodies but in the minds and hearts of all people; to bring to mind the words of our Holy Father Pope Paul II that to remember the past is to commit oneself to the future; and to unite with you in deep and fervent prayer for reconciliation among all peoples and nations and for the peace that places our trust in God – whose strength infinitely surpasses our own – and not in weapons."[54]

Notes to the Text

1. *The Tidings*, June 5, 1970
2. Francis J. Weber (comp.), *Days of Change. Years of Challenge* (Los Angeles, 1987), p. 155.
3. *The Tidings*, January 25, 1974.
4. *Ibid.*, September 23, 1977.
5. *Ibid.*, August 13, 1982.
6. *Ibid.*, January 18, 1980.
7. *Ibid.*, August 15, 1980.
8. *Ibid.*, August 20, 1982.
9. *Ibid.*, August 5, 1983.
10. *Ibid.*, February 18, 1977.
11. *Ibid.*, December 23, 1977.
12. *Ibid.*, March 31, 1978.
13. *Ibid.*, December 16, 1970.
14. AALA, Timothy Cardinal Manning to Clergy, Los Angeles, November 4, 1970.
15. AALA, Timothy Cardinal Manning to Clergy, Los Angeles, November 9, 1972.
16. AALA, Timothy Cardinal Manning to Clergy, Los Angeles, March 10, 1972.
17. AALA, Timothy Cardinal Manning to Faithful, Los Angeles, October 10, 1973.
18. AALA, Timothy Cardinal Manning to Clergy, Los Angeles, September 5, 1974.
19. AALA, "Articles of Incorporation of the Right to Life League of Southern California," Los Angeles, April 5, 1971.
20. AALA, Timothy Manning - statement, Los Angeles, May 1, 1970.
21. *The Tidings*, July 10, 1970.
22. *Ibid.*, January 22, 1971.

23. *Ibid.*
24. AALA, Timothy Manning to Joseph E. Berberich, Los Angeles, January 26, 1972.
25. AALA, Timothy Manning to Richard M. Nixon, Los Angeles, March 27, 1972.
26. AALA, Timothy Manning - statement, Los Angeles, December 11, 1972.
27. Los Angeles *Times*, January 26, 1973.
28. AALA, Timothy Cardinal Manning to Clergy, Los Angeles, January 21, 1974.
29. *The Tidings*, March 15, 1974.
30. *Ibid.*, January 7, 1976.
31. AALA, Timothy Cardinal Manning to Clergy, Los Angeles, May 12, 1980.
32. Francis J. Weber (comp.), *Days of Change. Years of Challenge*, p. 192.
33. Francis J. Weber, *John Joseph Cantwell. His Excellency of Los Angeles* (Los Angeles, 1971), p. 123.
34. *The Tidings*, December 21, 1979.
35. *Ibid.*, January 18, 1985.
36. AALA, Felix Diomartich to Timothy Cardinal Manning, Los Angeles, March 1, 1978.
37. AALA, Timothy Cardinal Manning to Clergy, Los Angeles, January 6, 1984.
38. *The Tidings*, August 10, 1979.
39. Los Angeles *Herald-Examiner,* January 29, 1972.
40. *The Monitor*, August 30, 1973.
41. Los Angeles *Times*, February 2, 1980.
42. *The Tidings*, October 2, 1970.
43. *Ibid.*, January 29, 1971.
44. *Ibid.*, November 25, 1983.
45. *Ibid.*, September 9, 1983.
46. *Ibid.*, February 8, 1985.
47. *Ibid.*, Mary 31, 1985.

48. AALA, Timothy Cardinal Manning to Jose Mercado, Los Angeles, November 30, 1979.
49. AALA, Timothy Cardinal Manning to Clergy, Los Angeles, May 14, 1980.
50. Los Angeles *Times*, February 8, 1979.
51. AALA, Timothy Cardinal Manning to Rosary Groups, Los Angeles, September 5, 1980.
52. AALA, Timothy Cardinal Manning to Henry Hernando, Los Angeles, September 23, 1981.
53. Los Angeles *Times*, April 6, 1980.
54. *The Tidings*, August 9, 1985.

23. Historical Interests

History, its preparation, necessity and relevance was uppermost in Timothy Cardinal Manning's list of priorities. He regarded history as a prolongation of the Gospel story into modern times and, for that reason, he was ever anxious to be a part of that noble progression of human events.

FRAY JUNÍPERO SERRA

In the fall of 1928, a young Irish seminarian put aside the love of parents, comforts of home and the pride of life to follow Christ along California's *El Camino Real*. Without knowing it, Timothy Manning was repeating a similar scene that occurred, almost two centuries earlier, when the youthful Fray Junípero Serra traded the familiar haunts of his boyhood for the uncertainties of a far-away apostolate in the New World. In the personages of those two islandic pioneers, the *Presidente* from Mallorca and the cardinal from Ireland, the Church was born, reared and brought to term along the Pacific Slope. Though Junípero Serra and Timothy Manning differed in generation, heritage and language, they shared a determination of projecting the priestly ideals of service to a needy people in a distant land.

Shortly after his consecration as a bishop, Manning prepared a series of reflections about Fray Junípero Serra which he delivered during Lent of 1947. He later sent a copy of the manuscript to Saint Anthony's Guild Press in Paterson, New Jersey. So pleased was the Franciscan publishing house that they offered to issue Manning's "reflections on the apostolate of Junípero Serra" in pamphlet form under the title *The Grey Ox*. The pamphlet filled a long-felt need for an accurate, easily readable and accessible treatise on a man whose popularity was growing in and out of California.

In 1984, as part of observances for the two hundredth anniversary of the friar's death, the Serra Bicentennial Commission proposed that the pamphlet be revised and updated for re-issuance. With a generous grant from Daniel Donohue and the Dan Murphy Foundation, 40,000 copies of Manning's classic treatise were reprinted. When notices appeared offering the forty-eight page brochure *gratis* to those sending a stamped, self-addressed envelope to the Borromeo Guild, over 3,500 requests were received and processed. Manning's carefully prepared work had weathered the passage of thirty seven years remarkably well.

Manning's devotion to Serra and his missionary foundations along California's *El Camino Real* became an oft-repeated feature of his sermons and addresses. Many times he extolled the Mallorcan friar as the personification of the missionary ideal, a role model for young people wishing to serve God and their fellow men and women. The cardinal proposed that the California Catholic Conference take an active part in celebrations marking Serra's anniversary in 1984. On August 28, he went to Carmel for a Mass beginning the bicentennial year:

> This missionary established the first nine of the California missions. He stood almost alone and prevailed when everyone else was ready to give up and return to Mexico, and he has given us a splendid example of missionary zeal and self-sacrifice. It is our fond hope that he will soon be declared Venerable which is the first step toward beatification and canonization.[1]

A year later, for the closing of the bicentennial year, Manning returned to Carmel where, once again, he spoke about Serra in glowing terms.

> Serra left Mallorca. He left behind him the community that he loved so much, the school where he taught, the students ever so dear to him, his books and his profession of teaching. He sailed to Malaga and from there to Cadiz before starting the long ninety-day journey to the new world.
>
> While in Cadiz he wrote a letter to the pastor of his home parish asking him to go to his parents and communicate to them his decision. How necessary it was for him to leave everything – even them, to cut clean all human attachments so that he might be a worthy instrument of the Gospel. That idea of leaving everything is beautifully expressed in that very tender and touching letter for his parents.
>
> But something else remains. Here we would like to borrow the sentiment of Abraham Lincoln at Gettysburg when he

> said that: "It is for us the living to be dedicated here to the unfinished work which they have thus far so nobly advanced – that from these honored dead" – Serra, Lasuen, Crespi, Palou and their compatriots buried up and down the coast – "that from these honored dead we take increased devotion to that cause for which they gave the last full measure of devotion." They are not sealed up in a historic museum. There's a vibrant animation in the Church because of the faith which they brought and it remains for the Church today in all of the dioceses of California to ensure that that particular purpose is pursued.

In his masterful homily, Manning responded to why it had taken two hundred years before the Church had declared Serra "venerable."

> We must say, at this time also, that a large thrust of the awakening of interest in the cause of Junípero Serra was done by non-Catholic historians and authors who somehow caught the genius of the man's life, caught the flame of his dedication and put it into song and story and play. The official investigation of his cause began. It took five years to do so and amounted to 10,000 pages of material before it could be submitted to Rome for the final decision of the Holy See which would indeed declare him worthy of being called Venerable.
>
> We rest his cause there. The work is done. There remains now for the people of the Church to engage in that incessant prayer that is needed that God would answer our petitions and give us the precise and conclusive miracle that will be required to have him declared beatified and finally canonized. All of this will come in God's good time. We have no doubt about this because the record of his sanctity is assured.[2]

And, when Pope John Paul II stood atop the steps of Saint Peter's Basilica, on September 25, 1988, to declare Serra "Blessed," Timothy Cardinal Manning, by then the retired Archbishop of Los Angeles, was seated among other dignitaries from Spain, Mexico and the United States who had come to the Eternal City in homage to the "apostle of California." Perhaps, as he left that noble assemblage, Manning noticed an inscription etched deeply onto the marble of a papal tomb which proclaims that "the faith of the Church is anchored in its history."[3]

EUSEBIO KINO

Manning's interest in California's history was not restricted to Fray Junípero Serra. In November of 1982, the cardinal made a pilgrimage to Magdalena, Sonora, to venerate the mortal remains of Eusebio Kino, the great Jesuit priest, missionary, explorer, astronomer and geographer. He wrote a long and charming essay about that experience in which he outlined Kino's life and accomplishments in the southwest and Baja California:

> A man of great historical significance he surely was. An explorer and cartographer truly. You can sense his excitement when he held a gift of blue abalone shells in his hand. They had been given to him by an Indian from the west. Kino knew that these shells were indigenous to the Pacific Ocean side of Baja California. He had seen them fifteen years before. Now he knew that these shells had come by land from the ocean side of Baja and he had the first hint of an explanation that Baja California was not an island but a peninsula of the vast North American continent. His conclusion would be pivotal for the Mexican exploration by land routes of Alta California and the security of the land from the Russian invasions from the north.
>
> He was a genuine missionary spreading the faith in the Jesuit, as distinct from the Franciscan mission system, making it blossom in the desert wilderness, wedding it to the native language and culture and anchoring it in mission compounds. But none of this is understandable without the deeper understanding of the inner motives that ceaselessly drove him and sustained him in that superhuman task. It was the same spirit that led Xavier to India and the East, drove the Jesuit martyrs of North America to their glorious deaths; the spirit that sent Peter Claver to the slave-markets of Cartagena, that sent Ricci to China, Edmund Campion to an English gallows and hundreds of others to memorable martyrdoms.
>
> It is the incarnation of the spiritual exercises of Saint Ignatius that gave them the vision of Christ as King, under whose standard they desire and accept the poverty, reproaches and humility of the incarnate majesty and whose lives were expended in totality "for the greater glory of God."[4]

CALIFORNIA MISSIONS

Manning visited all twenty-one of the California missions, many of them often. His main regret, while serving as Bishop of Fresno, was that there were no missions in that diocese. When the church at San Fernando Mission was ruined by the earthquake of February 9, 1971, Manning prodded his Vicar General for funds with which to restore the historic house-of-worship. Vibrant faith links past, present and future at Mission Hills, the cardinal said in his homily at the Mass dedicating the new facsimile church. "This is a day of great rejoicing and pride in the faith we have inherited and which we pass on to those who will come after us," he said. "No public aid of any kind was used in the reconstruction," he said. "This was done through funds husbanded through the generosity of the people of the archdiocese." The mission, said the cardinal, compares to Jacob's ladder, linking heaven to earth. Stones alone are not the Church, but people.

> All men have a place in forming the Church and by discipline and sacrifice and a life of prayer we are fitted into the place God has for us. Christ Himself is the temple of the faith of our fathers, a faith the early Franciscans brought to this place up a dusty trail."[5]

Two years later, as part of the observances for the nation's bicentennial, Manning journeyed to San Buenaventura Mission to solemnly consecrate the 194 year old church.[6] Incidentally, it was the first time in the United States that the new liturgical formula for that ceremonial was used. In his remarks, the cardinal observed that "a temple or church is the sign of the eternal presence of God among His people. That concept, alive even in primitive religions, designated a resting place for God, a haven where He could meet His people." He further noted that this historical edifice remained "a sign of that divine presence and a reminder that we ourselves are temples of the loving God."[7]

ARCHDIOCESAN HISTORY

Early in 1961, Manning was asked to write a capsulized history of the Archdiocese of Los Angeles for the *New Catholic Encyclopedia*. With his characteristic thoroughness, the then Auxiliary Bishop of Los Angeles compiled a sixteen page manuscript which traced the ecclesial story from 1781 onwards. Given the limited sources available at the time, the essay was remarkably accurate and comprehensive. The completed opus eventually appeared in Volume VIII when the encyclopedia was finally published in 1966.

Since November of 1962, when the archival program for the Archdiocese of Los Angeles was launched, Manning was a consistent and enthusiastic supporter of efforts to gather, organize and utilize the documents, journals, books and other memorabilia relating to the history of the Catholic Church in Southern California. Few were the days he didn't drop into the archives for a chat or to offer some constructive advice. He encouraged the beginning of the "California's Catholic Heritage" column in *The Tidings*, a weekly essay that appeared for over thirty-two years.

In 1966, he provided the preface for *Readings in California Catholic History* in which he said, "we are provided with an inspiration for the present day, a connecting link with the past and raw material for a definitive history at a later time."

> We are still in the apostolic age of the Church in California. The era which spreads from *El Camino Real* to our present freeway-network is but the relation of five minutes to the hour. Our future is hitched to water. As the water distribution is adequately solved, then California shall stride as a giant into its future. We must take care that our history be not written in water, but in indelible characters.[8]

Late in 1979, Manning approved the concept of relocating the archdiocesan archives to a site in Mission Hills. He made a formal request for a grant to the Dan Murphy Foundation and, on February 5, 1981, the first of twenty-three truckloads of historical materials arrived from the Chancery Office, thus launching the Archival Center on its tenure of service, the first independent archival facility erected under diocesan auspices in the United States.

On September 13, the cardinal came to Mission Hills for dedicatory ceremonies. Speaking at the Mass he said:

> The whole thrust of history, of archives, of salvation is the making evident of God's plan. As we gather at this historic moment to celebrate the Eucharist and to dedicate an archives building, we must be conscious of that statement and try to find the meaning for what we do.
>
> We could probably say that in the whole history of free humankind there is a common thread. It has a twofold

Cardinal preaches homily at San Fernando Mission prior to blessing new Archival Center facility in 1981.

New Shrine of Saint Vibiana.

> aspect: fidelity to God and alienation from Him. One can summarize all salvation history in that term. God covenants with His people, they pledge fidelity; then, deceived and decoyed by the values of the world, they recede from that covenant.
>
> History is the recording of that sequence of events. In the measure to which there is alienation from God and fidelity to Him, there will be a corresponding fidelity and alienation in the brotherhood of humankind. We are drawn to divinity with our brothers and sisters, but history shows that alienation, hostility and war follow upon division. The whole of human history, from the time of Christ up to this very moment, reflects that kind of alienation.
>
> Now history is the memory of a people and today we are exposing the memory of a faith community. We have seen its highs and its lows, its evil and its good. We realize that we have a duty toward those who will come after us. What we do today is history; it's an inheritance. Just as a wealthy person may give children his accumulated wealth, so we of this generation must leave to those who come after us an accounting of the richness with which God has endowed us; a record of the path we have trod.
>
> We are really a part of these archives. It's a place where our precious memories will be stored. But there is something more important, there is another house, my Father's mansion. And that's really where I belong. In my Father's house there are many mansions and there is only one thing I ask – it is that I may dwell in that house all the days of my life.[9]

After Mass, a procession moved from the crowded mission church through the archways to the Archival Center, a two-story, 5,198 square foot mission style building. There, Manning offered this prayer:

> Almighty God, we raise our hearts and minds to You in thanksgiving for the providential solicitude which made this Archival Center a reality. In gratitude to Our Lady of the Angels, the heavenly patroness for this portion of Your vineyard, we pledge to carry out Your designs and to fulfill Your mandate. In recognition that all good things have their origin in You, we ask Your continued blessings over this building, its contents and all who will labor within its walls. May this Archival Center, erected as a token of our attachment to the

> Christian heritage, become and remain a reminder of Your presence among our people. Amen.[10]

On the following day. Manning addressed a letter to the clergy about the new facility at Mission Hills:

> We now have a new Archival Center located at San Fernando Mission. We believe that it is the finest of its kind in the United States. This was planned and built to preserve the rich documentary heritage of the Church in the southland. Part of the facility is established with a specially designed vault with humidity control. We believe this would be the fitting and secure repository for old mission registers.
>
> This letter is an invitation to you to use this facility for the mission registers under your care. The archivist would be glad to hear from you. It would be part of his commitment to provide you with copy-flo prints of these pages which would be needed for marriage, baptismal and funeral information at the local level. Very often such prints are easier to read than the originals. Any other valuable documents you might have could, likewise, be entrusted to the care of this Center.[11]

Cardinal Manning liked to recall that his knowledge of the Archdiocese of Los Angeles stretched back well over a century. When he was ordained in 1934, he purposely cultivated the friendship of the clerical elders, some of whom had been working along *El Camino Real* for over fifty years and all of whom liked to share their experiences with the younger clergy. To that collective memory bank, Manning added another fifty-five years of his own in the ministry of souls in Southern California.

After his retirement, every Friday the cardinal would drive from his home in South Pasadena to Mission Hills where he would spend the bulk of the day at whatever task needed attention in the Archival Center. The archivist liked to brag that it was the only archival facility in the world with a cardinal on staff. For many months, he laboriously read through several hundred files of priests who had served briefly or sporadically in Los Angeles and about whom there was little if any information. He recalled practically every one of them and was able to fill in dates and appointments heretofore known only to the recording angel. Another task to which he eagerly involved himself was that of recording how the various parishes got their saintly names. Though this was originally intended to be an"in-house" project, it proved to be so popular that two lengthy articles on the subject were prepared for *The Tidings*.[12]

The publications of the cardinal's homilies, addresses and talks was not one he initially endorsed or even approved. At first, he adamantly refused to discuss the possibility of such a book and, even after listening to the reasons why such a volume was desirable, he registered unmistakable reservations. However, after taking up his task at the Archival Center, Manning ever-so-gradually began taking an interest in the project, becoming almost enthusiastic as the months unfolded. Each week he would read through his voluminous writings on file, selecting a cross section that warranted a more lasting format. It was decided that, except for identifying the occasion of each entry and indicating its source, it would be best to avoid editing or otherwise commenting on the selections. Each entry would stand on its own merit.

The first volume, *Days of Change. Years of Challenge* was published by the Borromeo Guild in 1987. In his Preface to that 353 page book, Archbishop Justin Rigali, President of the Pontifical Ecclesiastical Academy, said:

> The collection is the expression of the heart of a man as seen from seminary days to full maturity and beyond. It is the manifestation of the passion of his youth. In a sampling, it is the revelation of that inner power which has made him what he is and which has endeared him to succeeding generations of Catholic people in Los Angeles, throughout Southern California and indeed throughout the Church.
>
> From what is now an elegant written record there emerges the profile of a man of God: Timothy Manning. Before all else he is a priest and bishop of the Church of God. As such, by definition he is a minister of God's holy word.
>
> As one who has known and loved him for many years and who for several decades has been conscious of the special impact of his ministry, I now suggest that the secret of his success is found in the fascination inherent in the word of God. These simple reflections of the cardinal are the application of God's word to many circumstances of pastoral ministry and human life. What gives these writings instant credibility is that the word of God is first lived by the man himself, then proclaimed, communicated and applied by him as a minister of the Church.[13]

The second volume, for which Manning approved the selections but was too ill to proofread, brought to 311 the number of entries. Published under the title *Times of Tension. Moments of Grace*,[14] that 446 page tome was prefaced by Archbishop Pio Laghi, the Apostolic Pro-Nuncio to the United States.

> In my four decades of service to the Church as a papal diplomat, I have traveled widely and have been blessed with the opportunity to meet and know countless bishops. Some of these men have been great scholars or intellectuals; some, zealous and dedicated missionaries; some, very skilled as organizers and administrators. All of them have been successors of the apostles and teachers of the faith.
>
> In a very real sense, Cardinal Timothy Manning possessed these qualities to an eminent degree. Whoever takes the time to read and reflect on the talks compiled in this volume will quickly note that the heart, mind and soul of a very dedicated pastor is revealed therein. Cardinal Manning's ministry as priest, bishop and cardinal spanned more than half a century and was carried out at the very center of the nation's entertainment industry. While the cardinal himself would never presume to be classified as an entertainer, in so many ways his words, which were always marked by sincerity, solid scholarship and wit, were most appealing and served to draw men and women closer to God through the spiritual enrichment they provided.
>
> Less than two months ago, the cardinal's earthly conversation with and about God came to an end. What could not be halted by the cardinal's death, however, was the enormous impact that his life had on the many people, Catholics and non-Catholics alike, who knew him personally or whose lives were touched in some way by this devoted pastor of souls.

The overwhelmingly positive reaction to the earlier two volumes motivated a third and final one encompassing a collection of Manning's invocations, blessings and dedications which appeared in 1990 under the title *Hours of Consecration. Minutes of Prayer*. Therein were seventy-three entries spanning the years 1959 through 1988. This last volume was, perhaps, the favorite of the trilogy.

Though he loved his Irish homeland and everything about it, Timothy Manning was a committed missionary whose first allegiance, the mo-

Prayer card bearing reproduction of a ceramic tile placed on an outside wall of Saint Vibiana's Cathedral for the golden priestly jubillee of Timothy Cardinal Manning. The plaque was made by Isabel and Edith Piczek.

Cathedral before renovation.

Cathedral after renovation.

ment after ordination, was California. Often, as he spoke his way along *El Camino Real*, he would be heard to repeat the aspiration of his spiritual mentor, Fray Junípero Serra: "In California is my life and, there, God willing, I hope to die."[15] God heard and granted that prayer.

SAINT VIBIANA'S CATHEDRAL

One of the old-time parishioners of Saint Vibiana's Cathedral, among the last to visit the venerable building before its closure in 1996, insists that she saw the ghost of Cardinal Manning, motionless but sad, standing in the gutted sanctuary of the historic house-of-worship. Surely Timothy Manning had a long and cherished relationship with Saint Vibiana's. There he was ordained a priest (1934), consecrated a bishop (1946), celebrated his silver priestly jubilee (1959), observed his golden sacerdotal anniversary (1984) and was buried (1989). It was a fifty-five year relationship, longer perhaps than with any other priest or lay person since it had opened in 1876.

Of his own choice, the newly installed Timothy Manning chose to live at the Cathedral rectory when he became metropolitan archbishop in 1970. In response to a reporter who asked why he was living there and not "at a private home," Manning responded "Saint Vibiana's is on skid row, it's the cathedral church and, I think it's more appropriate for me to be associated with the cathedral. And it brings me down among the people. Come down and see it sometime."[16]

A few years later, Manning pointed out that "the cathedral church is geographic to this civic center, so also she has a moral commitment to its activities. She too is a servant to the citizenry. The pursuit of justice, the enforcement of law, the defense of freedom, the autonomy of religious exercise, the concern for the aged, the guidance and education of the young, the rights of the emigrant - all of these, and more, are her concern too and she must be a vigilant mother."[17]

On yet another occasion, Manning rejoiced "in our association with Saint Vibiana's Cathedral, the head and mother of all the churches of the city and the archdiocese. It is our hope that more and more of our Catholic organizations will see fit to schedule their periodic celebrations around its altar. Individuals, too, should come and see the church and its surroundings. In that way will we become conscious of one another as brothers and sisters, and of our need to serve one another in love."[18]

In one of his essays about Los Angeles, the cardinal said that:

> Down our way, life on 5th Street is like a dry river-bed from which human dignity has been drained away. There are no lower levels. Our skidrow expression for 5th Street is "on the nickel."
>
> Recently a movie was made with that title. A poster advertising the movie showed a broken wine bottle on a sidewalk with a green sprig stuck into it. The poster bore the legend "You can find love in the most unusual places."
>
> Something beautiful born of love is happening in the strangest places of inner city. A whole new population is entering the derelict streets east of Main. Children's voices are heard in the air again. Love meets them there.
>
> The Mother Church of the archdiocese is a beacon of hope for them. The Brothers of Charity, St. Vincent's Center, the House of Hospitality, the Franciscan concerns flowing out of St. Joseph's and the Downtown Women's Center – all of these are stirrings of love that are like a leaven to the surrounding community.[19]

The *Ordo Missae* exhorts Catholics to "see the cathedral church and their own church as signs of the spiritual Church which their Christian vocation commissions them to build and expand." In obedience to the spirit motivating that directive, Manning wanted to have the cathedral refurbished as part of the archdiocesan celebration for the bicentennial year of American Independence. Four years prior to the event, Manning began preparations by writing to a few prominent Catholics in the archdiocese, pointing out that "since 1876, it has stood watch over the changing city, pointing heaven-ward in constant reminder of our eternal values." He further noted that:

> Time and the elements have gravely effected the structure, and it will be necessary for us to face extensive repairs. Because of its historic position in the Los Angeles skyline and Los Angeles history, it is imperative for us to preserve it. Our proposal is to reinforce the entire existing structure to meet the present-day code requirements. It will also be necessary to demolish and rebuild in exact duplication the tower which will house the ancient bells.

Manning went on to observe that "because of the civic and religious responsibilities which all of us share, I am making bold to appeal to you in the hope that we might find a sympathetic hearing. We have many problems to solve toward this end. The cause is beyond our resources. We venture to rest some of our hopes on contact with a few dedicated foundations. We hope that this will find favor with yours." After asking for a specified amount or pledge, the cardinal hoped "that together we might ensure this precious relic for another century and another generation of citizens of the City of Our Lady of the Angels."[20]

When the cathedral was re-opened on May 1, 1976, Cardinal Manning asked that the dedication booklet reprint an essay by his confrere in the College of Cardinals, John Wright:

> Why celebrate the anniversary of the dedication of a cathedral? For that matter, why a cathedral? The question is not factitious. It is, in fact, widely asked – together with such questions as Why Life? Why Art? Why Beethoven? Why Kindness? Why bother?
>
> Persons who put aside beauty, even majesty, in the worship of God, on the pretense that thus they may pray more spiritually, forget that God is a Maker of all things, visible as well as invisible; that man is a creature composed of body and soul; that the person, including the believing person, is a psychosomatic unity; that God is the Lord of our bodies as well as of our souls; that He is to be worshipped in public as well as in secret. The Creator of this world is the Father of our Lord Jesus Christ; there are not two Gods, one of matter, one of spirit; one of Law, and one of the Gospel of Love. There is one God, and He is Lord of all we are and all we have; and therefore, all we do must be stamped with His seal and signature.[21]

MANNING'S ANNIVERSARIES

Manning observed his silver episcopal anniversary on October 16, 1971 at Saint Vibiana's. The cathedral was filled on that occasion principally by archdiocesan priests. Presiding was James Francis Cardinal McIntyre. Others at the event included Archbishop Joseph T. McGucken, his consecrator and Archbishop Thomas A. Connolly and Bishop James E. Walsh, the two co-consecrators. Bishop Walsh, former superior general of Maryknoll had only been released in 1971 after twelve years in a Chinese communist jail. Manning spoke of Walsh coming back "like Lazarus from the dead." In his homily, Manning reflected on how much had happened in the previous twenty-five years.

> The world has been turned upside down, and things that were nailed down have come loose. Bishop Walsh had never known there was a Vatican Council until the day he was released from prison, and yet that council is like a continental divide in the history of the Church. From it flows forward that future which God has planned for his beloved people.

Archbishop Manning said most of the Church's troubles will have subsided "once we have stabilized the priesthood, once we have put it in clear perspective." That perspective, he said, cannot be achieved until it is seen in relationship with the bishop, because the bishop and priest are united as one. The priest, he said, must be a collaborator with the bishop, must make the bishop present to his people and must love the bishop. "We must grow in love together, with Paul our pope and Timothy, our bishop. He also called for affirming the validity of the visible structured Church:

> It is besieged, it has become the object of scrutiny and criticism. It has been put in opposition to the charismatic Church. But we must realize that even though this human structure and institution, composed as it is by God's will, of human fallible beings, has yet been guaranteed perpetuity and the spirit of Christ is incarnated in that institution. It is that simple.
>
> And while the Spirit breathes where it will, while there is manifestly all over Christendom the stirring and the activity of the Spirit, we must acknowledge the reality of this institution. We must subscribe to this wonderful teaching authority, not within the strict limits only of what may be infallible, but that the heart and mind be sensitive and docile to the general, universal teaching of pope and bishops. Before God Almighty we profess our faith today in that Church. It is for that we live, and for which, God willing, we would die.
>
> This is our profession of faith in this our hour of grace. The future remains in God's hands and we ask Him in the words of Newman that He might "support us all the day long until the shadows lengthen and the evening comes and the fever of life is over and our work is done.[22]

Following the Mass, a luncheon for the bishops and priests was held at the minor seminary. There, the Priests' Senate presented the archbishop with a formal resolution which read:

> His twenty-five years as bishop have been full and fruitful in the service of God and the people of God. Our hearts are with him – and our prayers – as we bespeak for him the continued light and counsel and strength of the Holy Spirit in the years which lie before him.[23]

Manning combined the celebration of his fortieth sacerdotal anniversary with the conferral of papal honors on eighteen outstanding men and women of the archdiocese. He noted in his homily that "these have been selected especially to underscore this particular truth, taken as they are from the whole spectrum of our community life, engaged as they are in the various contacts with the world for the preservation of life, for the lawful conduct of order in our civil society, for the whole area of recreation which must be sanctified, for the education of our young, for the restoration of what someone recently called an ethical compass to all business dealings that make up the six days of the week that give us contact with the world. In all these selected members will be our indication of the underlying commitment which we must make: that once we have been sanctified by the bread of the Lord, then we have the obligation to go out and to mingle in various forms of business and life and culture and politics, and through the integrity of our very lives be a leaven in that segment of society touched, sanctified and redeemed by our presence."[24]

At his own insistence, Manning's golden priestly anniversary was "low key." He combined the observance with the ordination of priests for the archdiocese at Saint Vibiana's Cathedral on June 16, 1984. In the only allusion to his jubilee, Manning quoted the prophet that "young man shall see visions, and old men shall dream dreams. These young men will step up from here into an unknown future to spend themselves for the service of God and neighbor. And, who knows, perhaps in the year 2034, some of them will come limping back to celebrate their golden jubilees here."[25]

The Holy Father sent a lengthy feliciation, noting that "by means of the priesthood you were uniquely united to Christ whose image you supply, and therefore, you have been transfigured, becoming another Christ:"

Consequently, the magnificent description of St. Gregory of Nyssa may be totally applied to you, "You, then, while you were one among many, suddenly you were required to be the teacher, the ruler, the sanctifier and the steward of the mysteries."

Your rank and role in the Church were wonderfully increased in 1946 when by consecration as a bishop you became a successor of the apostles, a participant in their dignity and a sharer in their prerogatives. In virtue of that you were not only empowered to proclaim, in your own name, the holy word of God and to preside over God's people and to direct authoritatively those entrusted to you, but, moreover, fortified with the power of the Holy Spirit, you created new bishops and priests for the Church. There is no one who cannot see that great honor you have brought upon yourself and what progress to the Church.[26]

AMERICAN BICENTENNIAL

The celebration of the American bicentennial was observed widely in California, especially in Los Angeles. On September 28, 1975, Cardinal Manning celebrated Mass outdoors in the historic old Plaza to inaugurate the festivities. He and the other concelebrants moved in procession from the Church of Our Lady of the Angels, the city's first church, across Main Street into the plaza.

Catholics of Los Angeles were encouraged to attend the forthcoming Eucharistic Congress at Philadelphia. Manning said that "whether one goes in person to the event or not, each must somehow share in the Congress, faith and spirit." He encouraged that "special efforts be made to win back those who have discontinued the practice of regular attendance at Mass." And he especially invited young Catholics to offer hours of public service to their fellows "as their gift" for the bicentennial.[27]

In July of 1976, Manning issued a lengthy "tribute to America on her birthday" in which he quoted James Cardinal Gibbon's observation that "if I had the privilege of modifying the Constitution of the United States, I would not expunge or alter a single paragraph, a single line, or a single word of that important instrument. The Constitution is admirably adapted to the growth and expansion of the Catholic religion, and the Catholic religion is admirably adapted to the genius of the Constitution. They fit together like two links in the same chain."

Cardinal Manning at ceremonies consecrating the historic church at San Buenaventura Mission.

Cardinal arrives at Santa Cruz Island for Mass at La Capilla de Santa Cruz de Rosario.

"In a humble spirit and a contrite heart may we find favor with Thee, O Lord; and may the sacrifice we this day offer up be well pleasing to Thee, Our Lord and God."

✠ TIMOTHY MANNING

1934 — June Sixteenth — 1959

Manning asserted with pride that "the political community is founded on human nature and, therefore, belongs to an order established by God himself. The words of Lincoln are inspired: 'This nation, under God, shall have a new birth of freedom.' It is from God and under God, because individuals and families of themselves cannot achieve a truly human life. They need a wider community to pursue the 'common good.' The political community exists for no other individual or partisan purposes. Its sole justification is to promote the 'common good,' which is the total of those conditions which enable individuals, families and organizations, to achieve fulfillment."

He voiced concern that so few Americans, Catholics included, participated in the electoral process because of distrust, apathy or indifference. "As citizens we are all called to become informed, active and responsible participants in the political process." Two years earlier, only 36% of those eligible voted in the national congressional elections. Manning concluded his tribute by invoking a prayer composed by Thomas Jefferson:

> Almighty God, Who has given us this good land for our heritage: we humbly beseech Thee that we may always prove ourselves a people mindful of Thy favor and glad to do Thy will. Bless our land with honorable industry, sound learning and pure manners. Save us from violence, discord, and confusion, from pride and arrogance, and from every evil way. Defend our liberties, and fashion into one united people the multitude brought hither out of many kindreds and tongues.
>
> Endow with the spirit of wisdom those to whom in Thy Name we entrust the authority of government, that there may be justice and peace at home, and that through obedience to Thy law, we may show forth Thy praise among the nations on earth. In time of prosperity, fill our hearts with thankfulness, and, in the day of trouble, suffer not our trust in Thee to fail; all of which we ask through Jesus Christ our Lord. Amen.[28]

LOS ANGELES BICENTENNIAL

As early as 1946, the then Auxiliary Bishop Timothy Manning said that "Los Angeles is growing at a tremendous rate and in a few years will probably be the largest city in the world."[29] Indeed the city dedicated to *Nuestra Señora de los Angeles* would be a metropolis of legendary limits. It was within the context of the archdiocese that sprung from the *pueblo* that Timothy Manning made the following observations, on March 19, 1948: This wonder-cry "is yet the progeny of the new age, still seeking to find its ultimate strength, awkward in its growth, yet inching its way upward to tower above its contemporaries in the American family of towns.

> Over the hills and into the adjacent valleys it spills like something poured out, waiting to assume its permanent form, to congeal and settle. It knows only the restless Pacific and the rock-rimmed desert for its boundaries.
>
> Much of its fame is founded on intangible things: the green and gold of its citrus orchards, outlined against the snow of its hills; the languid climate slowing the pace of mind and body, and enriching our language with the lovely word *mañana*; the latent wealth of the black and liquid gold in the earth below us; the dubious brilliance of our stellar system over the holy wood; the spurious sowings of a thousand creeds in a wheat field, waiting for the harvester; the unpredictable instability of the earth beneath, reminding us that we have not a lasting city; the ceaseless ebb and flow of the great heart of humanity that is contained within our streets.
>
> Our roots are altogether Catholic. We are Catholic by conquest and the blood of the *conquistadores* flows in our veins. The little Plaza Church is hidden under the shadows of the great municipal buildings, but hidden only as a pearl of great price. Its origin is coeval with the *Pueblo*, they bear a common name, they share a common patronage. It was a place of worship (1781) five years before the first Catholic structure was erected in the City or State of New York.[30]

Because of the long and close association of the Catholic Church with the *El Pueblo de Nuestra Señora de los Angeles*, Manning considered it appropriate to take an active part in the city's bicentennial. Four days of public events opened early in September. The principal observance was a Mass in the kiosk of the old plaza which was celebrated by the cardinal himself. Manning's homily on that occasion touched a number of bases. He pointed out that:

> There are eighty-three languages spoken in our city. If you wished today you could hear Mass in Spanish in the Plaza

> church across the street. You could go up ten minutes from here and hear Mass in Italian and in Cantonese. Up on the hill in Croatian. Down the street in Japanese. In English at the Cathedral. Above and beyond in Tagalog, Korean, any one of twenty languages – our Mass and our faith are articulated today. By our birth we are a people of God, this people under the patronage of Our Lady of Angels.
>
> While there will be a great deal of political rhetoric and other kinds of accolades spread over us during the twelve month celebration, it is very important for us to realize that we are called to a rededication, that this centennial year must be for us of the Church a time of renewal whereby we can bring all the peoples of our city to an awareness not only for our origins but of our dependence on God.

While not wanting to sound "abrasive and severe," he used the occasion to point out that there was an enemy corroding the very foundation of our culture:

> Do you realize that here two blocks away is the largest prison in the world? Right here. "L.A. is the place." Do you realize that over there in that building is a morgue that has housed victims of 1,500 murders since the first of the year? five last night, three out here on Burlington Street, at our doorstep.
>
> Do you realize that at any given moment there are a thousand runaway boys and girls on the streets of Hollywood? Do you realize that we have men lying on the sidewalks of Main Street. Human garbage with no one to care or pick them up? Do you realize that we have marginal people coming to us from all lands looking for something of the good life – and this is what they find?
>
> We have an enormous enemy that's eating us out. There is need for this rededication, going back to our origins, affirming again the moral code that binds us together. You have to measure the strength with which we can match against the enemy.

Never one to mention a problem without offering solution, the cardinal issued a call for action:

> In our midst we have to build this solid tower. And what is that tower? It's the family. It's the Christian family that is the

> basis, the bedrock of all our perseverance, of all our faith, of all our patriotism. We have to come back and define the ways and the means whereby we will remain together instead of making pilgrimage to that courthouse over there where innumerable divorces are dished out by the day – or to the hospitals and clinics that are aborting babies and throwing them into garbage cans.
>
> That's no family on which to build a culture or a civilization. We have to go back on our knees and create within the Christian home that little Church where we profess and make real the larger Church, where there is that loving service of one to another. There in that domestic Church is that indoctrination of faith and citizenship and patriotism and there too is the propagation of the good news of God.[31]

A year later, on the very day of the bicentennial, the cardinal blessed his personal gift to the city, a mosaic reproduction of a 14th century mural depiction of the Annunciation to Mary. The seven by ten foot mosaic panel, fashioned by the talented artist, Isabel Piczek, was affixed above the front entrance to the Church of Our Lady of the Angels. Manning recalled that the original had been painted by Italian artist Ilario da Viterbo in 1393 on the sanctuary wall of the little Portiuncula chapel of Santa Maria degli Angeli in Assisi.[32]

The last of the major anniversaries of which Manning was a participant occurred in 1986, the fiftieth anniversary of the Archdiocese of Los Angeles. The cardinal spoke offhandedly to a Leadership Celebration about the establishment of the archdiocese in 1936 by Pope Pius XI.

> For forty-seven of the fifty years of the existence of the archdiocese, I have been associated with its administration – as secretary, chancellor, vicar general, auxiliary bishop, coadjutor archbishop and archbishop.

Manning bragged he had been intimately familiar with the history of the archdiocese almost since its establishment. "My recollections are that the priorities that have surfaced in this year of convocation are an outgrowth of the priorities that motivated Archbishop Cantwell and Cardinal McIntyre in their administrations."

> First of all was the need for vocations, the building of our seminaries in Camarillo, the relocation of our junior semi-

nary in San Fernando and the insistence that it remain as a seminary against much of the popular pressure of the time. There was the immense thrust of Cardinal McIntyre to build schools, and more than that, his historic efforts to lift the inequitable tax on our schools. Single handed he went up and down this state until he had the assurance that the vote would be favorable.

There was the founding of parishes on the east side and the guarantee that each parish would have a school. Tribute must be paid to the wonderful parish priests who built what is here today, the parishes, the schools, paid for them and even for the security of the future. But above all, that which surfaces so beautifully in the convocation is the spiritual care of our people. Because the Lord says to us what he said to Martha, "You're busy about many things, you're concerned about too many things," there's only one thing necessary: That is the knowledge and the service of God Our Lord as we see Him, especially in our brothers and sisters. That's the prime thrust of all these administrations.

In these hurried moments, it is impossible to concentrate an overview of the fifty years except to beg of you as you take this leap forward to look back. You cannot drive a car safely forward without a rear view mirror. That must be a part of our journey, that we look back as Moses in the Canticle says, "Remember the things that are past. Ask your fathers and they will tell you." So from the vantage point of fifty years, we implore a benediction upon all of you under the wonderful leadership of your archbishop to take this journey into the future knowing that we who have come through the long shadows of years send out a benediction.[33]

Notes to the Text

1. *The Tidings*, July 13, 1984.
2. *Ibid.*, September 6, 1985.
3. Francis J. Weber, *Catholic California* (Mission Hills, 1992) p. 206.
4. *The Tidings*, November 19, 1982.
5. *Ibid.*, November 8, 1974.
6. *Ibid.*, December 17, 1976.
7. Francis J. Weber, *A History of San Buenaventura Mission* (Santa Barbara, 1977) p. 123.
8. Francis J. Weber, *Readings in California Catholic History* (Los Angeles, 1967) p. ix.
9. Francis J. Weber, *Dedication Ceremonies for the Archival Center, Archdiocese of Los Angeles* (Mission Hills, 1981), Pp. 11-14.
10. *The Tidings*, September 18, 1981.
11. AALA, Timothy Cardinal Manning to Clergy, Los Angeles (September 14, 1981).
12. See Francis J. Weber's *Golden State Catholicism* (Mission Hills, 1970) Pp. 202-205.
13. Francis J. Weber (comp.), *Days of Change. Years of Challenge* (Mission Hills, 1987) p. vi-viii.
14. Francis J. Weber (comp.), *Times of Tension. Moments of Grace* (Los Angeles, 1990) p. iv.
15. Francis J. Weber, *A Bicentennial Compendium of Maynard J. Geiger's The Life and Times of Fray Junípero Serra* (Los Angeles, 1985) p. 104.
16. *The Loyolist* 46 (May 11, 1973), 6.
17. *The Tidings*, January 14, 1977.
18. Francis J. Weber (comp.), *Times of Tension. Moments of Grace*, p. 326.
19. *Ibid.*, February 6, 1981.

20. AALA, Timothy Cardinal Manning to Prospective Donors, Los Angeles, October 25, 1972.
21. Boston *Pilot*, April 25, 1975.
22. *The Tidings*, October 22, 1971.
23. *Ibid.*, October 22, 1971.
24. *Ibid.*, June 21, 1974.
25. *Ibid.*, June 22, 1984.
26. AALA, John Paul II to Timothy Cardinal Manning, Rome, June 3, 1984.
27. AALA, Timothy Cardinal Manning to Clergy, Los Angeles, June 29, 1976.
28. *The Tidings*, July 2, 1976.
29. AALA, Timothy Manning to Mother Immaculata, Los Angeles, April 15, 1946.
30. Quoted in Francis J. Weber, *California Catholicism. A Holy Year Tribute* (Los Angeles, 1975), Pp. 24-25.
31. *The Tidings*, September 12, 1980.
32. *Ibid.*, September 4, 1981.
33. *Ibid.*, December 5, 1986.

24. Miscellaneous Statements and Interviews

Not unlike many people in the public arena, Cardinal Manning distrusted the press and felt that, more often than not, reporters put a hostile spin on their accounts of happenings, both in and outside the Church. For that reason, he gave relatively few interviews. Two noteworthy exceptions occurred over the years, one in 1979 and the other in 1984. In accord with our attempt to allow the cardinal to speak for himself both of those interviews are here reproduced without any annotations.

1979

Question: Should it be the role of the Catholic Church to speak out on social injustice?

Manning: It is part of the Church's destiny to help improve the world. The Church has a duty to speak out on social matters, especially where injustice is involved, so that man's dignity, destiny and rights are adequately enunciated.

Q: Does the Church have a tendency to shy away from getting involved in issues like terrorism and revolutionary upheaval?

A: The Church is primarily a peacemaker. Armed revolution and violence are alien to the mission of the Church. Her duty is to enunciate the principle of morality. Violence does not serve such an end.

Q: Is there an ongoing rebellion within the Church, and will this make for a stronger and wiser Church?

A: The Church is the extension of the mission of Christ. Demands from human nature, extraordinary commitments of discipline, fidelity and loyalty are unpleasantly falling into human nature, so there always will be a segment in all of us resisting that demand. Yet that discipline is necessary. Call that rebellion if you will, it is there. Of course, it makes for a wiser and stronger Church.

Q: The larger family has long been accepted as a norm in the Catholic marriage. What is the Church's attitude on this today?

A: I question the manner in which the inquiry is formulated. I think that large families have been identified to a great extent with the Catholic Church, but to state that it is the law or the desire of the Church (is something) I dispute. The families were large to a great extent because of the innate trust of divine providence. There is today a greater preoccupation with material things. The enjoyment of a better life inclines the family to limit the number within the family. The Church does not determine or dictate the size of a family.

Q: Has the Church been shaken by the stand taken by the women in Italy pertaining to birth control and abortion?

A: I can't speak for the Church as a whole, but as a representative of the Church and as a lover of Italy, knowing the intense love that the Italian parent has for a child, it's horrifying to think that this could happen.

Q: Considering the turbulence of the times, is God dead?

A: The moment you remove God from the human condition, you have taken away all of the props of man's morality. You have a freeway to all of his lesser, lower desires which end up in turbulence. To the extent that God is removed from society, yes, it happens. When you eliminate God and religion, which is the expression of God, it could be said that God is dead.

Q: What are the major problems facing the parochial schools today?

A: The major problem is survival, due to the tremendous cost of retaining these schools. The cost has to be carried by our people, not by tuition, which is totally inadequate. Last year alone in Los Angeles we had to come up with $7 million to cover the cost.

Q: Do you have conflicts with the government?

A: We have a constant encounter with the government, for there is the possibility of the government always wanting to interfere with our schools. There is an isolation of the private schools from any government support even though these are American children exercising their right to higher education. But because the public schools seem to be the established schools in the country, everything else must suffer.

Q: Should taxpayers support private schools?

A: We're not asking for support. We're saying a child has the right to support and parents should determine how that should be used. That's the basis of our claim and of our assertion about discrimination against the American child. I think it is a grave injustice to the child to exclude him from that support. We are all taxpayers and our money is being used by public schools. Why shouldn't the child who goes to private school be supported also?

Q: Is busing a way to give children a better education?

A: We will have to wait for time to determine that question. I support busing for it is the law of the land. I have been on the committee to encourage our people to abide by the law.

Q: Do you see the Church breaking away from the celibacy doctrine? Will priests and nuns be allowed to marry?

A: There is no time that this will come about. There will never be permission for priests to marry.

Q: Why are young people leaving the more-established churches today?

A: The two great hungers in young people today are for community and for a sense of belonging. In accepting the Church, they have to accept the whole Christ of discipleship within the Church, and this is not easy. We all want the easy way, but to follow Christ we must follow the cross. That's asking a lot. And our sense of community is larger than they want. The largeness of our Church causes one to lose the feeling of intimacy

Q: Have the large religions lost their personal touch due to their extended size?

A: Yes, there is truth in that. There is always the danger of becoming too impersonal. The answer is to create smaller communities and to draw them, from time to time, into the larger community that is happening today.

Q: Does the Church find it difficult to break away from its older traditions, and to accept a more moderate role?

A: The Church may not deviate from the objective moral law of which she is the custodian. No matter where it hurts, no matter how much she loses, she cannot deviate. Take, for example, sexual morality, which is the raw nerve today and the cause of many problems. The Church is rigid and stable. Take it or leave it, she cannot deviate. Even though the great tendency today is to the soft and easy way, the Church does not do that.

Q: When the Berrigans burned their draft cards at Catonsville, they made the statement, referring to Vietnam, "Our Church has remained silent on this unholy war." Were they correct?

A: Well, they were correct to the extent that whenever you have a gripe you need a scapegoat, and the Catholic Church is a very handy scapegoat. The Berrigans and all their kind are quick to throw mud at the Church.

Q: Weren't the Berrigans a cleansing movement within the Church for arousing emotions against an unholy war?

A: No, for they didn't allow for the quiet alternatives which the Church engages in for human distress. The work of the Church is in its diplomatic expertise to solve the difficulties, not in the flamboyant card-burning and marches. I don't say the Church is perfect in its attitudes, but it cannot be faulted.

Q: Why are so many people being drawn into cults?

A: I think it is an easier way. We're all running away from the hard way, and if we find something that takes less discipline, we buy that.

Q: With the investigation into the Armstrong Church of God, do you see the time that government will investigate more churches?

A: I'm very concerned about that. I hope that those who have a good overview of the situation will be able to analyze for us and find out how valid or justified the state is in this matter. It is a very sensitive area. I do hope that the correct people who will evaluate all of this will give us clear principles on this matter, for they are needed.

Q: Do you see a danger to separation of Church and state in such investigations?

A: On principle, I'm against the investigations. It's a dangerous trend. But I am open to wiser judgement, and to see where the principles are that I have stated. We can draw our conclusions from there.

Q: How do you see the Catholic Church's role in the turbulent years ahead?

A: I see the Catholic Church more and more becoming the only answer to man's needs, whether he likes it or not. The Church may lose many by its demands. But where else can people go to get sure and positive answers except the Catholic Church?[1]

1984

PSA: Your work here in the Los Angeles archdiocese has certainly put you in touch with the refugees from numerous wars in Central America. Many Catholic priests and nuns working with the poor in these countries have endorsed a "theology of liberation." The pope recently criticized this drift. Can you tell us why?

Manning: Actually, there are many "theologies of liberation." What the Church is insisting on is the initial liberation from sin. All these other evils are the consequences of sin. Now, in the Third World, the idea has been growing that liberation from social evils cannot be effectively obtained except in terms of revolution and violence. And that puts them somewhat in the lap of Marxism. Because Marxism is fundamentally a belief that the whole interpretation of history is an economic one: the rise and fall of economic cultures; the fight between the haves and the have-nots. Marxism asserts that the only way to overcome social evil is through the violent overthrow of systems of the haves. We cannot subscribe to that. That's the main concern of the Church – that such Marxist overtones should not be found in our pursuit of liberation. It in no way diminishes the concern of the Church for the people of Latin America. She is committed to the cause of the poor – to their welfare, and to the alleviation of the subhuman conditions in which many live.

PSA: Were you surprised by the statement from the Vatican (on liberation theology) ?

Manning: Oh, no. It's a very fine statement. It's an excellent statement. Easy to read, easy to understand, very compassionate and much needed. I think it was timely, and it's informative and instructive.

PSA: What will be the effect?

Manning: Well, at least it clarifies the issue. And the Church apparently intends to follow it with a more elaborate doctrine – instruction on the care of the poor. This is just the opening statement.

PSA: The priests and nuns who work in these Central American countries so often do become activists because of the sheer nature of the oppression.

Manning: Yes. It's an experience of desperation for them.. You see the inhumanity firsthand. That's why I say that they have so much compassion, understanding and identity with the poor. Their best witness is living at the level of the poor whom they serve, which is what they do. But they must not preach any kind of violence, any violent overthrow of any system.

PSA: The problems in Latin America, among other factors, have caused the number of Hispanics in the U.S. to rise rapidly. Are they, in your opinion, a problem for this country, or are they enriching our culture?

Manning: Oh, I think the Hispanics are bringing with them a kind of blood transfusion into our culture. One of the things I find fascinating is the way they are repopulating a country that is trying to decimate itself through abortion. You have these millions of abortions going on, and at the same time you have people who absolutely love their families and their children. In the areas where the Hispanics are congregating their children are all over the place. And I think that's God's answer; that's the America of tomorrow.

PSA: During the current campaign, the separation of Church and state has emerged as a central issue. The Reverend Jerry Falwell and other fundamentalists assert that politics and religion are inseparable, while others see great danger in mixing the two. What are your thoughts on this? Can Americans ask that political leaders be "moral" without having them favor the teachings of one religion over another?

Manning: In their personal lives, we're not the judges. The Church is a watchdog in all matters of legislation and reserves the right to speak out if there is some issue that it considers a moral one. But that's not imposing the Church's position on the polity.

PSA: The pope has decreed that the Catholic Church will not get politically involved, and has ordered priests and nuns to abandon any political office they may hold. Yet, didn't the pope himself strike some sort of political deal with the leaders of the Polish regime that had the effect of dampening dissent against the government?

Manning: No. You used the expression "the Church getting politically involved." I disagree with that. The Church certainly gets morally involved, but not politically.

PSA: What is the distinction?

Manning: The big distinction is that if there is a situation in which human dignity or human destiny is threatened or diminished, the

Church has a command to pronounce on that particular issue so that her responsibility for preserving human life and dignity is assured. The intervention of the American [Catholic] hierarchy in nuclear matters is not a political intervention. It is simply the teaching Church giving an overview of modern weaponry and the hazards of war. Someone has to say that. That's not a political statement. That's a moral judgment. The Church certainly has to live with existing governments in all the countries of the world. She is in fact a society herself, and has systems of concordance and agreements with existing governments whereby there are mutual understandings that will allow the Church a certain stroke of activity and freedom, even though she has to make certain concessions for that purpose. That's not being political.

PSA: Does this accommodation by the Church include supporting certain political leaders and not others?

Manning: The Church is very, very careful that there is no positing of her influence with one candidate or another. And you get individual people who throw their weight behind candidates. But the Church as such doesn't do that.

PSA: The fundamentalists espouse many of the same beliefs that the Catholic Church does. For example, opposition to abortion, pornography and so forth. What about prayer in the public schools? Does the Catholic Church favor that as well?

Manning: Well, the Church hasn't pursued it, hasn't made any political thrust.

PSA: Is that because you have your own Catholic schools?

Manning: Yes. This would not become a major issue for the Church to pursue. If it comes, fine. If it doesn't, okay.

PSA: Since the fundamentalists are also talking about moral concerns, do you welcome their new power?

Manning: Well, first I would like to have a clear notion of who a "fundamentalist" is and what "fundamental" teaching is – I don't. My concern would be rather the influence that any religious group would have on a given individual in the administration of the country. I think that the position of the Church, our Church, is that we enjoy magnificent freedom in our nation; we have full liberty to exercise our faith and express our convictions. We will always be assertive in areas that involve human dignity and human life, but we do not get involved in the actual process of government or try to influence individual incumbents. If that is the political life of the United States, I would have to be very cautious about it.

PSA: Do you think we've gone too far in putting politicians under the microscope?

The cardinal enjoyed queries from youngsters which he always felt were friendly and sincere.

This press conference at the Archdiocesan Educational Building was held to answer queries about the death of Pope John Paul I.

Manning: Yes, I think it's probably debatable whether such severe scrutiny is desirable. Of course, it's the press's right to scrutinize and demand accountability. But that does not diminish the responsibility we have to recognize that all authority ultimately comes from God. The human vessel in which it is contained deserves our respect. But correspondingly, living in glass houses is good for us – it makes us aware of the integrity of the lives we have to lead.

PSA: The Catholic Church still opposes all forms of birth control and allowing women to become priests, while Protestant churches have accepted these things. Is the Catholic Church keeping pace with the times, and does it want to?

Manning: The Church is a custodian of and committed to the Law of God, the natural law of God. No matter how progressive, or how compromising, other churches might be with modern situations, the Catholic Church says unequivocally that every sexual act in marriage must be open to the possibility of conception. Anything that interferes with that has to be harmful. So keeping up with the times is a misnomer. The stability of marriage, the absence of violence, the overcoming of pornography – all of these things are interrelated. They're signs of the times, and they're not getting better.

PSA: What about women priests?

Manning: The Church is a spouse which is symbolized by the male priest serving the Church. The Lord did not give any indications of other than the male priest. So the Church will not change that. Other churches that have ventured into that; we'll see how they're going to do.

PSA: Have the voices advocating greater liberalization within the Catholic Church fallen silent, or are they still there?

Manning: Oh, they're still there. But I think that they're diminishing because they haven't gotten anywhere. They may have a following among people who determine for themselves whether or not they're going to control life, the possibility of conception. But then, of course, there is always a freedom among qualified people to research and find out the basis for the position of the Church. That's valid study and that will go on. The Church will always call on theologians to underpin what she teaches.

PSA: There was a Catholic fundamentalist movement for a while. Has that gone away?

Manning: Well, again, we have to distinguish. The word "fundamental" is becoming a catchword for so many things. Basically, you and I and all of us, no matter who we are, are called to a conversion any time in our lives. It's a process all through our lives of getting disengaged from the attachments that drag us down. We have an orientation to God and to another destiny other than the horizontal destiny which we have here on earth. So there is a constant ambushing of people spiritually to alert them, to bring them to an awareness of this. And call them what you will, "born again," "renewed" or whatever, we have many movements in the Church that are doing that. They're very healthy, as long as they're under the management and control of the teaching Church. But if they go off by themselves, then they're in trouble.

PSA: You've lived in a century which has seen a great deal of turmoil and bloodshed. With your historical perspective, would you say that the people of the United States are healthier spiritually now than we've ever been?

Manning: I don't think so. I don't like to say it, but violence is part of our culture; pornography is the daily diet. The breakup of homes through divorce, the secularization of all institutions – that is depriving people of a dimension of their lives. They must find this dimension privately, or in their churches – but they're not going to church. And they're not finding that added dimension.

PSA: So are we spiritually healthy?

Manning: I think there is a remnant that is much healthier. There is a corps of wonderful people, and I'm speaking particularly of young people, people of great idealism and integrity, who are striving for something other than material reward. Things are presented to us as being the essence of life today – that's what we hear from advertising and TV. So there is a remnant that is healthy, but by and large, I'd say that the culture itself is sick.

PSA: How does the Church, how does the person reading this interview, who might be without a spiritual life, go about getting that? Is the answer to join that Catholic Church?

Manning: No, I don't say that. I think people should return to the roots of their own religion – for example, a Jewish person – there's a whole wealth of totally magnificent religious resources there. The psalms, the Old Testament, the Law. And all the other religious bodies have in their foundations and in their origins great enthusiasms, great ideals. Go back to those.

PSA: The Catholic Church is not a proselytizing religion. It doesn't go out and try to bring people in. Why is that?

Manning: Because, as the Vatican Council said, we have to respect the need for freedom of conscience. I can't hold a club over your head and say, "Look, you become a Catholic or else!" You've been gifted with a freedom to determine for yourself. I can present you with reasons, with what I think, but it's your decision.

PSA: The number of people without any religion at all is going up, is it not?

Manning: Yes.

PSA: So it would almost seem that the desperation of these times would demand that the Catholic Church seek out new members.

Manning: The hunger is there. We're finding many, many people are coming to us for an investigation. And we now have a whole new approach. Previously, an individual might begin a course of instruction. Now it takes a couple of years of processed initiation into the practices of the Church, involving not just the individual, but a sustaining group in the parishes and so forth.

PSA: So often in the modern era, the products of science and scientific revelations about the nature of the universe seem to pit the scientist against Church teachings. In a society such as ours, where so many people are without religion, has the scientist replaced the theologian in the sense that he suggests that science can actively cure man's problems, while the theologian seems to suggest that we be more passive?

Manning: That question, of course, is perennial. It's as old as science and the Church. I think that if you approach it from the fact that all of creation is God's creation, then all the laws that are gradually being discovered by scientists are simply revelations of the total magnificence of creation. Now, what other people will do with scientific discoveries is another thing. Take the discovery of the atom – the atom is the revelation of the magnificent force that God put in creation. But someone who decides to drop an atom bomb on a city? That's a perversion of science – not a conflict between science and religion. The scientist has his own scope. The theologians in the Church are going to watch what he does. And if the theologian finds that the use of a scientific discovery is basically detrimental to human life, then the Church must advise against its use.

PSA: You have participated in two papal elections. Could you give us an idea of what something like that is like?

Manning: It's very, very impressive. Of course, much of it is under an oath of secrecy, but what may be revealed is the nature of our voting. There are no nominations, no candidates. The 110 of us cardinals eligible to vote are brought into the Sistine Chapel and given a blank slip of paper. When your turn comes you write the name on that piece of paper of the person you think is most fitted to become pope. He doesn't have to be a cardinal, it could be anybody. And then one by one you step out into the center of the chapel and call on God to witness that this is the person that you think should be pope.

Then, when the ballots have been received, they are brought down to the center of the chapel and counted by three cardinals. To be elected you have to have two-thirds [of the votes] plus one. So then the man who is presiding goes in front of the stall where this cardinal is seated and asks him if he is willing to accept the election. When he says yes, then he is the pope.[2]

MISCELLANEOUS STATEMENTS

Whether it was conferring the sacraments, presiding at graduations, assisting at testimonials, attending meetings or making pastoral visitations, Cardinal Manning's evening commitments, after a full day at the Chancery Office, were an endless procession of appearances that rarely left time for a quiet interlude with his close friend, Msgr. James Hourihan. He carried with him at all times a small accordion-like schedule for several months in advance, a practice that allowed him to plan and adapt his homilies, talks and statements to the needs of the particular congregation or audience to whom he ministered The phenomenal range of his interests and concerns is evident from a cursory glance at the hundreds of topics he spoke and wrote about over the years.

CONSCIENTIOUS OBJECTORS

Just prior to Christmas, 1970, when thoughts are directed to the Prince of Peace and hearts seek the advent of justice, freedom, order and peace, Manning spoke out on a thorny issue of the time, conscientious objection.

> While we long for peace we are faced with the reality of war. One of the terrible components of war is the fact that the risk of injury, capture, imprisonment, the burden of killing and being killed falls heavily on the young men of our nation. The Church cannot fail to honor those who respond to their country's call, who sacrifice their freedom and pledge their lives for a just cause: "There is no greater love than this; to lay down one's life for one's friends."
>
> We believe that it is timely, however, to offer a word of pastoral counsel in relation to those who, on the grounds of conscience, object to bearing arms. Some young men, reviewing war as it is waged in our day, feel compelled in

> conscience to adopt a position of non-violence "provided this can be done without injury to the rights and duties of others or to the community itself." By the word "conscience" we mean, not a decision based on emotion or sentiment, but a judgment painstakingly arrived at through a rational and searching consideration of objective facts.

He reminded people that Vatican Council II had urged that laws make humane provision for such young men provided that they agree to serve the community in some other way. He felt it was also important to observe that "the laws and court decisions of our country make such provisions."

> True conscientious objection, by the fact that it is based on the dictates of conscience, is morally defensible. The true conscientious objector loves his country no less than his brother-in-arms, and is prepared to serve it no less willingly. While he rejects the violence of war, he is ready to serve in a non-combatant or civilian capacity. Catholics, then, may be among those who are conscientious objectors because of religious convictions.

The archbishop said that it was not "easy for an individual to stand against prevailing tradition and opinion on this issue." Yet such persons "deserve the understanding and acceptance of their parents, their priests and their community."[3]

One of the more venerable outreach programs of the archdiocese was the Catholic Labor School which, over many years had "profited many and helped to identify the Church with the social issues of our time." Early in 1971, Manning said that he "would like to encourage this movement." He earnestly asked "the priests to give publicity to the present school program and to give every encouragement to the working people of their parishes to participate in this course designed for their advantage."[4]

PRISONERS

Remembering back to his youth, when members of his own family and many of his friends were imprisoned or in hiding from hostile British soldiers, Manning always exhibited great empathy for prisoners. Customarily, his first Mass on Christmas would be offered in the Los Angeles

County Jail where, in 1973, there were 3,500 prisoners. On New Year's Day, he would visit and offer Mass for women inmates at the Sibyl Brand Institute. A decade later, he noted that "in our county of Los Angeles we have the distinction of having the largest jail population in the free world. At any given time there are 21,000 adults and juveniles in prison." From this, he said, "it can be gathered that a great pastoral responsibility lies here. This applies not only to those incarcerated but especially so to the victims of crime and violence in our midst." He was pleased that the Saint Vincent de Paul Society and the Office of Religious Education sponsored the apostolate to the detained.

> A group of religious sisters and prison chaplains dedicate themselves to this cause. We ask particularly for the charity of prayers for this portion of our shepherding. Competent volunteers are sought to help. A beatitude awaits those who serve.[5]

In his Lenten pastoral for the Year of Reconciliation and Renewal, Manning told how the Lord began His public mission with a fast of forty days, proclaiming through the land - "Reform your lives! The kingdom of heaven is at hand." The cardinal felt compelled to issue that same urgent call to repentance.

> Penance is a gift which comes to us from the free hand of God. We must ask Him for it. It is not something we can acquire on our own. It implies a turning away from sin and a conversion to God. We shall not turn from sin unless we are convinced of its evil. God grant that we may see it so. The fear of God must once more enter into our being. We must strive for an awesome awareness of His presence and of His hatred of sin. We must shake off our own complacent self-righteousness.
>
> The traditional practices of penance are vigils, fasting and almsgiving. Somehow these touch us at our most sensitive spots. They strike at our human self-conceit, at our disordered fleshly drives, and at our greed for material goods, which the world holds out to us as the only goal of all our earthly striving.[6]

In a guest editorial for a local newspaper, Manning said that "signs of the times point to a transformation of our American culture. Once we subscribed to the proposition that America was powerful because it was

Cardinal Manning dreaded formal press conferences which he felt were often purposely antagonistic.

Cardinal Manning faces reporters on September 4, 1978 at Los Angeles International Airport.

good, that it was good because people worked hard, that production was the proof of virtue. All of this has passed through the Watergate of our history, and is no more." The cardinal worried that "we have degenerated into pandemic venereal disease, pornographic stimulation and gutter vulgarity. Violence in the streets, reproduced on our television screens for our evening diversion, cries out for justice but penetrates not through our conditioned eyes." As for the cure, he suggested a new generation would bring hope and joy again through the human family. There would be a new scale of values that antiquates all the material dimensions that were the measurements of his time:

> Is there a constant in our way of life, a norm by which we can live in hope that all is not lost? Yes. We believe that it is conscience. "Man's dignity demands that he act according to a knowing and free choice." Such a choice does not result from blind internal impulse nor from mere external pressure. In the depth of his conscience, man detects a law that he does not impose on himself, but which holds him to obedience. Always summoning him to love good and avoid evil, the voice of conscience can, when necessary, speak to his heart more specifically: Do this, shun that. The responsible person must weigh the facts before acting. He may not act in accordance with his whims and wishes. For man has in his heart a law written by God. To obey it is the very dignity of man; according to it he will be judged.[7]

That Manning's observations about life were not the musings of an ivory tower theologian came to the surface in a press conference at the Claretian Center where he was hosting a Catholic-Jewish dialogue. A reporter asked the cardinal about his views on gun control. He responded that he felt "very strongly about it. I have seen with my own eyes, on my own corner, a man shot to death."[8] The incident had occurred about two years earlier. Manning was standing on the corner of Second and Main Streets with his secretary about 9 p.m. A car slowed and a shot rang out and a man staggered out and fell at the cardinal's feet. The automobile sped off. After the man was anointed, he was taken to a local hospital where Manning visited him. Unhappily, he died a few days later. Manning had also been present at the Chancery Office in 1967, when Father John Thom was shot by a middle-aged woman who was later committed to Patton State Hospital.

MEDIA

The media were blamed for much of the failure to communicate positive moral values to the younger generation. At a luncheon of the Los Angeles chapter, Religious Public Relations Council, the cardinal said that "violence is in the news and at our doorstep." He said that "the communications media must take a lot of the blame. The TV is an extra person in everybody's room. Violence and genital sex are accepted forms of entertainment. Many good things are happening, but they don't make the news," he observed. "People are hungry for the Scriptures and we need to foster the word of God." Manning said the Church must act as "custodian" for cultural values without which the culture cannot survive. "We need to bring people away from secular values," he added. The cardinal urged "increased dialogue between secular media personnel and the religious community." Such would "help promote positive moral values." In particular he encouraged newspapers to refuse to accept advertisements for X-rated motion pictures.[9]

At the 28th annual Mass for Catholics in the Motion Picture Industry, Manning once again deplored the preoccupation with violence and sex as an entertainment venue. He exhorted his listeners to bring light into darkness and by their actions to "edify and build up the people of God."

> By His grace God is infusing into us a sense of instrumentality so that by our own contribution, however little, by placing ourselves totally in the hands of God, we can become instruments that can change gradually that element of darkness and bring it into the light.
>
> God willing, the avenging hand of God will be held back so that it will not fall on us like it fell on Ephesus and places in the Roman world that Paul wrote to and that came crumbling down and are now but a memory because of alienation from all of morality and God.[10]

R.C.I.A.

The Restored Rite of Christian Initiation, commonly referred to as R.C.I.A., was initially resisted by many priests and certain others who were quite satisfied with their "convert classes" of earlier years. Manning understood how some might feel intimidated by the new movement which he called "one of the glories arising in the aftermath of the

Second Vatican Council." In a letter to the priests, the cardinal explained how the R.C.I.A. "looks deep into the past and revives many of the beautiful initiation rites of the early Church. It looks forward to a new enrichment of this pivotal event when one enters into membership in the Catholic Church." He said that the traditional convert methodology was "yielding to a revised structured preparation for full membership." While measuring his words carefully and graciously, Manning made it clear that the R.C.I.A. movement was one he endorsed and encouraged.[11]

IMMIGRATION

In 1984, Manning wrote a letter to the Speaker of the United States House of Representatives, Thomas O. O'Neill, in which he expressed his "very deep concern" about pending immigration legislation.

> Our thoughts on the subject of immigration legislation are rooted in two fundamental principles revolving around our right to provide for ourselves and our families. The first principle we allude to is the right of nations to regulate migration across their borders. The second principle is the concept recently enunciated by Pope John Paul II in his encyclical On Human Work, *i.e.*, that human persons have a right to emigrate from one country to another to seek employment. The latter of these two principles encapsulates for us the thesis that we have a fundamental right to acquire the things of this earth in order to sustain our livelihood and to enhance our physical and spiritual well being.

The cardinal said borders were never meant to be a means of "frustrating our pursuit of freedom and happiness" nor to be a net "to unjustly snag those who truly merit an opportunity to seek livelihood within the host country. Manning said no law should create a worse evil than that it seeks to correct. "If a law were to foster discrimination, violations of personal liberties and the forced separation of families as a result of the law's enforcement, such a law must come under serious question."

After spelling out the six principles already enunciated by the administrative board of the National Conference of Catholic Bishops, Manning said that:

In the long run, the pressures and problems of immigration, legal or illegal, must be dealt with at their source. If workers in other countries could obtain employment at just wages in their homelands, there would be far less pressure on them to emigrate. If American workers could be assured of employment at just wages, they would have less reason to fear competition from immigrants. The establishment of just international economic order, which would provide adequate employment for all, has long been a goal of Catholic teaching and action.[12]

TAX EXEMPTION

Though he envisioned his role of shepherdhood as predominantly spiritual, Manning was aware of needs at the administrative level, one of which was the necessity of protecting the Church's exempt status under the Internal Revenue Code. In 1984, he reminded the priests that if "a religious or charitable corporation participates in a political campaign it not only looses tax exemption on all of its properties, but its parishioners are denied the right to take a deduction for their contributions." He presented some guidelines which had to be observed:

Endorsements: There may be no endorsements of political candidates. You may not encourage votes for or against any candidate via a sermon, parish bulletin or sample ballot. This includes indirect statements, *e.g.*, labeling a candidate as pro- abortion.

Financial and Other Support: Financial or any type of campaign support may not be provided to any candidate, party or organization opposing a particular candidate or party, *e.g.*, volunteers, facilities. Also, we may not establish or support a political action committee.

Partisan Literature: Campaign literature cannot be distributed on our property. However, we cannot control access to public property, *e.g.*, the street outside the church.

Voter Education: It is the opinion of our attorneys that permitting the distribution of newsletters or pamphlets that include candidates' statements or voting records, or the results of candidate polls or questionnaires on Church or school property constitutes participation or intervention in a political campaign by the church or school and that therefore parishes should be cautioned not to permit the use of their property or facilities in the distribution of such material.

On the other hand, all parishioners have the right to engage in political activities as do all citizens. This right includes the right to speak for or against candidates, distribute rating sheets concerning their voting records and philosophical and political beliefs and otherwise to be equal participants in a democratic society. This includes the right to distribute on public streets and public property hand bills, rating sheets and other papers as long as local laws are complied with and as long as these activities do not take place on church and school property. Parishioners should be understanding of the need for the Church to protect the tax advantages which it and its parishioners enjoy under existing laws and be willing to comply with the rules that the government properly sets disqualifying Church and charitable organizations from conducting or participating in political matters.[13]

PORNOGRAPHY

One of the "epidemics" that Manning often referred to was pornography, which "devastates the personal and the social well being of contemporary" life. He felt that it was "imperative that we be alerted to it and take measures of healing and protection." Pornography traffic was everywhere available. "It uses every means of social communications. We find it in paperbacks, magazines, tabloids, films, video cassettes, subscription television, video games, coin-operated machines, erotic telephone messages" and elsewhere. A $7 billion dollar industry, it was often mob-controlled.

In all this calamity we must have a Christian duty and response. We must first of all engage in the formation of a Christian conscience about this. The consenting indulgence in any of the means by which pornography is propagated is an occasion of sin, of grave sin, and must be dealt with as such. Complicity, participation, assistance and use of such unclean material is incompatible with our Christian vocation and witness. Such material is intrinsically evil and obscene. Adults must assume a more responsible role in supervising the reading material and visual preoccupations available to

> young people. Never may such tempting or alluring material be allowed in the home or taken for granted as part of an adult and mature life-style.
>
> Existing laws must be enforced. Public assertiveness and confrontation must sound the alarm. The president must be commended for his efforts against pornography but must be urged to require U.S. attorneys to enforce anti-pornographic laws. Moreover, there may be no compromising with the clear teaching of the Church on sexual ethics and the principles of *Humanae Vitae* must remain irreformable. All in all, the time has come for action so that this insidious epidemic may have antidotes in our Catholic way of life, a casting out of the unclean spirit whose name is legion, to save a generation on the brink of utter degradation. So doing, God will be glorified by a generation, chaste and God-fearing.[14]

Although he was not an avid sports enthusiast, the cardinal liked an occasional football or basketball game. In his earlier years, he played golf several times a month. Once he called sports an "education in courage." At the first annual Tidings All Catholic Southern California Football Teams awards presentation, he said:

> Sports are not simply an exercise for the muscles, but a school for moral values and for education in courage. Sports can run the risk of degrading men if they are not based on and supported by the human virtues of loyalty, generosity and respect for the rules of the game.[15]

In his capacity as President of the California Catholic Conference, Cardinal Manning testified before the State Senate Industrial Relations Committee about changes in the Agricultural Labor Relations Act in 1984.

> There have been repeated efforts over the years to weaken or dilute the basic strengths of the ALRA. We have repeatedly urged the legislature to resist efforts to make changes in the basic law. We continue to be convinced that agricultural labor peace is best served by adhering to the original legislation agreed to by all parties through extensive consultation and negotiation.
>
> With respect to Section 1160.3 of the labor code, we oppose any efforts to eliminate the "make-whole" provision of

the act. Given the particular vulnerability of the state's farm workers to unfair labor practices on the part of either employers or labor organizations, we are of the opinion that the maximum protection should remain fixed in the law. Both agricultural employers and labor organizations need appropriate incentives to deal with their agricultural employees with fairness, justice and within the full protection of the ALRA.[16]

Notes to the Text

1. Los Angeles Herald *Examiner*, February 20, 1979.
2. *PSA Magazine*, III (November, 1984) 93-105.
3. *The Tidings*, December 18, 1970.
4. AALA, Timothy Manning to Clergy, Los Angeles, February 2, 1971.
5. The Tidings, December 31, 1982.
6. AALA, Timothy Manning to Faithful, Los Angeles, March 2, 1973.
7. Los Angeles *Times*, July 15, 1974.
8. *The Tidings*, November 7, 1975.
9. Los Angeles *Times*, May 30, 1974.
10. *The Tidings*, March 10, 1978.
11. AALA, Timothy Cardinal Manning to Clergy, Los Angeles, February 8, 1982.
12. Quoted in *The Tidings*, April 27, 1984.
13. AALA, Timothy Cardinal Manning, Los Angeles, March 27, 1984.
14. *The Tidings*, September 7, 1984.
15. *Ibid.*, December 28, 1984.
16. *Ibid.*, May 11, 1984.

25. *Final Years*

Cardinal Manning anticipated his "golden years" with the usual anxiety that older people have, but never with regrets. By the time he approached the age for retirement mandated by Vatican Council II, he had come to terms with a notion that would have been unthinkable when he first became a priest and bishop. His was the second generation of bishops to consider stepping aside, and he did it with customary grace and poise.

ARCHBISHOP MAHONY'S APPOINTMENT

While clerical prognosticators spend long hours discussing episcopal appointments, few of their learned predictions or fanciful conjectures ever materialize. Roman officials have their own elaborate and mostly secret process for making such decisions and, as often as not, they short circuit their own system, much to the distress of observers. Especially has that been the case during the pontificate of John Paul II who seemingly delights in violating all the traditional precedents. In the early 1980s, discussions as to who would succeed Timothy Cardinal Manning as archbishop became a cottage industry in Los Angeles, with even staff writers for national and local newspapers expressing their "learned" views.

In a lengthy article for *California Magazine*, Greg Critser predicted that criteria for the appointee would focus on "leadership qualities, a track record in social justice and the ability to strategize with large, diverse populations." He did not consider Bishop Juan Arzube "among those seriously considered" because he was "politically inept." More plausible, he conjectured, was Auxiliary Bishop William J. Levada who had strong political connections in Rome and who was "socially progressive but doctrinally orthodox." The author acknowledged that among the Los Angeles clergy "the name most often mentioned as the ideal candidate is that of Stockton Bishop Roger Mahony."[1]

In May of the following year, Kerry Webster wrote a series of articles on "The Power and the Glory-Catholicism in L.A." for a local Los Angeles-based newspaper. Noting that "the selection of an archbishop of the Roman Catholic Church is a process rooted in secrecy, centuries-old tradition and labyrinthine Vatican policies," he said "there is no public campaigning, no open lobbying. Even the leading candidates themselves never are entirely certain they are being considered."

"Inevitably," the writer continued, "names emerge. Of the half dozen mentioned as likely successors to Cardinal Timothy Manning as Archbishop of Los Angeles, three in particular are thought to be contenders." The first of Webster's candidates was Bishop Roger Mahony, "a youngish, charismatic leader who has spoken out forcefully on social issues such as nuclear war and the right of farm workers." Another was Thaddeus Shubsda, Bishop of Monterey, "a strong traditional authority figure who has combined doctrinal conservatism with a warm personal style." The third was Auxiliary Bishop William Levada, "said to be a brilliant scholar with experience in the influential Roman Curia." Others mentioned included Archbishop Patrick Flores (San Antonio), Archbishop Robert Sanchez (Santa Fe), Bishop Rene Gracia (Corpus Christi) and Bishop Ricardo Ramirez (Las Cruces). Then the writer openly admitted that "there is no way to tell which names actually are on the list being perused by Pope John Paul II."[2]

Even the historian, with all the advantages of hindsight, must issue a disclaimer at this juncture, simply because no one, not even the appointee, will know the whole scenario on the appointment until the Vatican Archives for the 1980s are opened to researchers and that isn't likely to happen in the near future. There were, of course, a number of viable candidates, not a few of whom openly expressed their willingness to carry the metropolitan cross in Southern California. One eastern archbishop told Vicar General Msgr. Benjamin Hawkes to "pack your bags if I get the nod." Another told a clerical friend that he "would live longer in Los Angeles with its mild climate and less boisterous surroundings." Both considered themselves likely candidates.

The "process" for discerning candidates took about three months and probably was the most exhaustive of any during the ten years that Archbishop Pio Laghi served as Apostolic Delegate and Pro Nuncio to the United States. There were three principal candidates: Bishop William J. Levada, Bishop Roger M. Mahony and Msgr. Justin F. Rigali, with Archbishops Theodore E. McCarrick (Newark), John R. Quinn (San Francisco) and Robert F. Sanchez (Santa Fe) as runners-up.

It was determined early on by Roman officials that beyond being native-born, the ideal candidate should have (1) personal piety, (2) loyalty to the Church's magisterium, (3) theological astuteness, (4) administrative experience, (5) pastoral proclivity, (6) lingual facility, (7) diplomatic smoothness, (8) social awareness, (9) political credentials, (10) leadership ability, (11) episcopal seniority and (12) a proven track record. Only one of the candidates measured up to all twelve of the requisites and his name was Roger Michael Mahony. All other things being equal which, in this case they were, Archbishop Pio Laghi passed along Mahony's name to the Sacred Congregation of Bishops who, in turn presented the candidate to Pope John Paul II. On July 16, 1985, the Holy Father named Mahony to the archbishopric of Los Angeles.

In his book on the power structure of the American Catholic Church, Thomas J. Reese said that "there is some suspicion that Cardinal Timothy Manning of Los Angeles supported the candidacy of Roger Mahony as his successor."[3] Even today, if the priests of the Archdiocese of Los Angeles were asked their view as to whether Mahony was Cardinal Manning's choice as his successor, most would probably answer in the affirmative. The evidence at hand, however, does not validate that commonly held view.

In August of 1981, in a lengthy oral interview, Manning was asked "what kind of person should be named Archbishop of Los Angeles in 1984?" His response was: "One who speaks fluent Spanish, is pastoral minded, a good administrator (if Msgr. Hawkes is not around), and one whose image before the public is good." When further pushed as to whether he would "lobby to see such a person named," Manning said "not unless I was asked. The archdiocese may need a person totally different than I. It would be wrong for me to interject myself in that process." Responding to another query about episcopal appointments in general, Manning responded that he "would not initiate a suggestion. For example, I would not propose a particular person for a given place . . . I wouldn't feel comfortable interjecting my viewpoint."[4] Several years after Mahony's appointment to Los Angeles, this portion of the oral interview was read back to Manning and, at that time, he stood by his earlier statements. Hence, it is reasonable to conclude, from evidence presently at hand, that Mahony was not the cardinal's hand-picked successor, except insofar as he failed to exercise a veto.

Whatever his personal views may have been, Manning reacted quickly and positively to the appointment. He wrote the clergy that "it has seemed good to the Holy Spirit and to the successor of St. Peter, Pope John Paul II, to select Roger Mahony, Bishop of Stockton, as the fourth Archbishop of Los Angeles in California. This appointment is good news of great joy for me and for all our people.[5] In the next day's issue of *The Tidings*, Manning issued a formal statement:

The cardinal and Bob Newhart.

Bob and Dolores Hope welcome Cardinal.

Cardinal offers Mass in Jail.

Manning greets inmates after Mass.

> The Archdiocese of Los Angeles, which covers the three counties of Los Angeles, Ventura and Santa Barbara, rejoices today in the nomination by Our Holy Father, Pope John Paul II, of Bishop Roger Mahony, as its next archbishop. The preeminence of this jurisdiction, the largest in the United States, is ripe for new leadership. It has cause to have its voice heard in all of the issues facing the Church today. The areas of orthodoxy of beliefs; the sure guidance needed in the complexities of today's moral conduct and values; the social problems that surface so relentlessly in our community; the vast immigration and ethnic issues to which the Church must attend – all these are to be a part of the shepherding.
>
> Then there is the inner life of the Catholic community – its call to holiness, to evangelization, to renewal of life. The service of the community is the province of priests and religious. These too will look to a new archbishop for leadership and for modeling. It is the obvious judgment of the Holy See that Bishop Mahony has all those qualities. That decision is surely ratified by all who know him. For me personally it is a joy. For the greater glory of God, I welcome him as my successor.[6]

The formal letter from Bernardin Cardinal Gantin confirming Manning's resignation and the appointment of his successor was released a few days later:

> On the occasion of the announcement of your resignation from the Metropolitan See of Los Angeles, the Holy Father has directed me to convey to you his deep and abiding appreciation of the invaluable service that you have given to the People of God in Los Angeles these past fifteen years as well as for the sentiments of sincerest love and esteem expressed in your letter of October 15, 1984. His Holiness gives thanks to Almighty God for the noteworthy example of steadfastness, fidelity and profound commitment which you have manifested throughout these years.
>
> Pope John Paul II is well aware of the challenges and difficulties that you have had to face in such a large and complex See as Los Angeles, but he also knows with what strong faith in the Lord and with what zeal for the Church you have striven to meet them and to lead the archdiocese to an

> ever greater knowledge of the Gospel. Further, the Holy Father is cognizant of the love you have shown to the poor, immigrants and refugees, but above all, for the love and personal concern you have demonstrated towards your priests; they have responded with equal admiration and respect.
>
> His Holiness prays that you will continue to find great happiness and satisfaction in the days ahead through the awareness of the admirable work that has been done by the Lord through your priestly ministry of over fifty years and an episcopal ministry of almost thirty-nine years. Furthermore, the Holy Father is confident that you will experience much joy and peace not only in the privilege that has been yours as a successor of the apostles but also in the consciousness of your ongoing unity with the Church in Los Angeles through the bond of priestly prayer and love. With fraternal affection and fervent prayers, the Holy Father imparts his Apostolic Blessing to you, to your fine successor, Archbishop Mahony, and to the entire ecclesial community of Southern California.[7]

It was at that time that Manning issued a "benediction" to the clergy and faithful of the archdiocese:

> Scripture says that there is an appointed time for everything under the sun. There is a time to be born and a time to die. To resign from high office is in respect of an appointed time. It is to die a little. It is the master's call to the ploughman at day's decline, to come in from the fields. For half a century of years my calling has been to serve God's honor and His people's needs. Now it is done. There remains but the articulation of my gratitude.
>
> May my thanks be a benediction on all those who have sustained me in this holy task by their skills, their example and their prayers. Those were the intimates of my household; the members of the official family; the contemporaries in the summer of my youth and in the autumn of my aging; the vast nameless number of those who have prayed for me, in season and out, in desolation and consolation. Their names are written in my heart and in the Book of Life.
>
> Coupled with thanksgiving must be an appeal for mercy, God's mercy, and yours, my friends, my people. Through

Cardinal's chapel at his home in South Pasadena.

Holy Father welcomed by Cardinal Manning and Archbishop Mahony in September, 1987.

Cardinal Manning's last public appearance at the Hollywood Bowl.

> human frailty there has been many a hurt, known and unknown. For these, I ask forgiveness and a remembrance only of my remorse and my regrets. An uncertain measure of years remains. In these, the field-hand has duties to do in the master's kitchen and at the master's table. These tasks are lowly ones, off-stage and apart from the spotlight's glow, yet they are metaphors of love. It is a time for the reflection that we are but unprofitable servants and have done only what we were supposed to do.
>
> And so we exit and we say farewell. We make our own the words of Cassius to Brutus at Philippi: "Forever and forever, farewell! If we do meet again, we'll smile indeed; If not, it's true this parting was well made."[8]

RETIREMENT

Cardinal Manning first disclosed his thoughts about retirement in an interview with John Dart in 1983. He had been impressed with the apparent ease and grace with which his predecessor faced and overcame that challenge fifteen years earlier. He told Dart that he would "follow the now-customary practice of offering his resignation some months before my actual (seventy-fifth) birthday" even though he was in excellent health. Describing the prostate surgery that he had undergone a few months earlier, the "wiry cardinal" said that it had been very successful and that he had no after-effects whatsoever. Upon retirement, Manning revealed that "he would expect to be active helping in parish work," just as Cardinal McIntyre, then well over eighty years old, did when Manning succeeded him in January, 1970." Described by Dart as "a conservative on many matters," Manning was portrayed as seeing changes as invigorating for the Catholic Church. "New leaders, new styles. It's good."[9]

A while later, another interviewer spoke to Manning about his plans for the future. Alluding to Immaculate Conception Parish across the street, the cardinal said "I began in that church fifty years ago and this is as far as I've traveled," he said laughing. "Not very far, is it?" The reporter responded that in terms of distance it hadn't been far, "but within the hierarchy of the Roman Catholic Church, he has come a great way." By this time Manning had submitted his formal letter of retirement to Pope John Paul II. "Just when the Pope will choose to act on Manning's letter is a matter of great speculation within Roman Catholic circles. There also is great speculation over who will be the Irish-born Manning's successor." Manning says he will play no part in the debate.

> It's left to the Pope to determine when and how that will be processed. I'm just biding my time until I'm told when that will be effected. I am not concerned. I'll just go on doing what I'm doing until I have definitive information.

When asked what he considered to be the most noteworthy achievement of his tenure as archbishop, Manning replied, with a smile, "I've survived." And after his retirement from the post is accepted, he added, he planned on remaining in the Los Angeles area "doing priestly work."[10]

A few months later, the Los Angeles County Board of Supervisors voted unanimously to award Cardinal Manning the county's highest recognition, the Distinguished Service Medal.

> Cardinal Manning has provided outstanding religious leadership to people of all faiths in Los Angeles County. He has worked to bring people together with mutual respect and understanding. Cardinal Manning is respected across America and throughout the world and the citizens of Los Angeles County are grateful and proud to have him represent our community. He is richly deserving of this honor.[11]

The cardinal entered his retirement with the satisfaction of having fulfilled his official mandate to the Church in Southern California. There were no regrets, only a willingness to adapt to this final challenge of a long and productive life. He opted to take up residence in a bungalow next to Holy Family church in South Pasadena, a parish which he had earlier entrusted to his priest secretary. He established a routine which remained fairly consistent for the rest of his life, offering daily Mass in the small chapel of his new home, accepting offers to give retreats and days of recollection and motoring daily to his smaller quarters at the Borromeo Guild, across the street from the Chancery Office.

He adamantly refused the offer of his successor for an office in the chancery itself, nor would he accept offers to appear at any function in the archdiocese that did not emanate directly from Archbishop Mahony. He maintained a cordial relationship with Mahony, offering advice only when asked. On Fridays he would drive out to the Archival Center in Mission Hills and spend most of the day working at whatever task he was given. Afterwards, he would often go next door and offer Mass for

Cardinal visited the U.S.S. Midway on June 6, 1975.

Manning was flown to the U.S.S. Enterprise off the coast of California in 1987.

Cardinal Manning poses with his successor, Archbishop Roger Mahony.

the *Cursillistas*. All day Saturday, he would visit hospitals, rest homes and residences of ailing and retired priests. In his frequent encounters with priests and lay people, Manning was always careful to avoid any remarks that might be misinterpreted.

A reporter for the Altadena *Weekly* interviewed Manning early in 1986, just a few days after he had been formally welcomed to South Pasadena. He asked the cardinal about "the small red book peeking out of his breast pocket," thinking it might be a Bible or a catechism "or something holy." Instead, he was told that it was a "daily reminder" a calendar of secular activity in which "he records his appointments just like you or me. Cardinal Manning believes in another world on earth with a full schedule, trying to ease the anguish of entangled hearts.'"[12]

In March of 1986, Manning received a personal letter from the Holy Father:

> After your resignation from the See of Los Angeles and after the appointment of your successor, Archbishop Roger Mahony, you very kindly expressed to me again your sentiments of communion in the Lord. On my part I wish to assure you of my enduring gratitude for your faithful partnership in the Gospel. I know that during these past months you have generously continued to serve the people of Los Angeles as priest and bishop, in close union with the new pastor of the flock. I am sure that in all your activities you have found great peace and strength through the intercession of Mary, the Mother of the High Priest.[13]

Manning was re-visited by reporter Ira Rifkin of the Los Angeles *Daily News* who wrote that the cardinal "still spends time around the collection of buildings west of downtown that serves as headquarters of the Roman Catholic Archdiocese of Los Angeles. No longer, however, is his office on the second floor of the chancery building on West 9th Street, the nerve center of the local churches. These days, he answers his mail and sorts through a lifetime collection of personal files in a one-room, unmarked office tucked behind the Borromeo Guild bookstore. The reporter said that "with the pressure of the job behind him, he is more relaxed, more approachable. He is quick to smile and willing to speak personally to a degree he rarely did publicly while in office." He noted that "for Manning, a basically shy man, retirement happily has meant no longer being required to dutifully attend civil and social circuit dinners."

Asked whether he had any reluctance to stepping down, the cardinal smiled and said: "I never wanted to be anything else but a priest. As a general statement I have no misgivings. I did the best I could with the lights I had at the time," As to future plans, he responded that "I'll be seventy-seven before the year's out and at that age there is no claim to be made on any extended time." Further he remarked that "I can't help but reflect on my own mortality," he said. "It's a certainty for everyone, but as you grow older you become involved in a state of wonder over what it will be like and how it will happen. It's a wholesome reflection, I believe. Not morbid."[14]

The first year of his retirement was the busiest. He travelled to Africa, Asia, New Guinea and the Pacific to visit and encourage Lay Mission Helpers. Then he went to South America to visit the priests of the Cork missions in Peru. He travelled to Wyoming, Washington, Savannah, Charleston and Phoenix to conduct retreats or to preach at major events including a visit to the nuclear aircraft carrier *USS Enterprise* at sea off the coast of California. And daily there was a holy hour in his private chapel or wherever he happened to be. Asked about his retirement, Manning told a journalist for the *Catholic Sun*: "Retirement is the wrong word, I call it recycling."[15]

Notes to the Text

1. "Signalling the Pope," *California Magazine* (May, 1984), 140. The entire article also appeared in the *National Catholic Reporter*.
2. Los Angeles *Herald-Examiner*, May 30, 1985.
3. *Archbishop* (San Francisco, 1989), p. 47.
4. AALA, Biographical Interview with Timothy Cardinal Manning, Los Angeles, August 24, 1981.
5. AALA, Timothy Cardinal Manning to Clergy, Los Angeles, July 18, 1985.
6. *The Tidings*, July 19, 1985.
7. *Ibid.*, August 2, 1985.
8. *Ibid.*
9. Los Angeles *Times,* November 16, 1983.
10. Los Angeles *Daily News*, February 10, 1985.
11. *The Tidings*, May 3, 1985.
12. February 13-19, 1986.
13. *The Tidings*, April 11, 1986.
14. Los Angeles *Daily News*, July 13, 1986.
15. Quoted in *The Tidings*, October 10, 1986.

26. Final Illness, Death and Burial

In November of 1988, the cardinal began experiencing a nagging back pain which responded to none of the traditional medical treatments. As the weeks rolled on, the pain intensified but he kept to his schedule with the explanation that resting at home didn't seem to alleviate the discomfort. In March, he journeyed to Idaho for the episcopal ordination of Tod Brown as Bishop of Boise.

One day he collapsed in his downtown office, but quickly regained his composure. He was adamant that his illness not interfere with the duties of others. On May 18, the announcement was made that Manning had cancer which had begun in the lungs and then spread to the spinal regions. A report in the local newspaper said that "the wiry, soft-spoken prelate" had received a letter from Pope John Paul II in which the pontiff said that "having heard of your present illness, I wish to assure you of my spiritual and affectionate union at this time."[1] An archdiocesan spokesman said that Manning "has had at least sixteen radiation treatments" at the Kenneth Norris Jr. Cancer Center, University of Southern California.[2]

On the same day, Manning released a statement saying that:

> I am aware of the gathering anxiety among those I have served and loved for over a half a century. Meanwhile, I am under the expert care of physicians who encourage the continuation of my ministry according to my abilities. I leave everything in the hands of the good Lord. May His all-holy will be done. In the prayers of the faithful I ask only in the words of Cardinal Newman for "a safe lodging, a quiet rest and peace at the last." May the Lord in His kindness reward all those who pray for me, in His mercy wipe away my sins and in His love call me home.[3]

In his final appearance, the cardinal spoke at Mary's Hour which was held at the Hollywood Bowl on May 21. In one of his most moving addresses, delivered in obvious pain, Manning ended his public career as he had begun it, under the mantle of Our Lady. After explaining why Mary was presented as "mother" at the foot of the cross, he said that "each member of the Church, each one baptized, has to walk behind the Lord on that journey to the cross believing, loving, hoping, trusting in His all holy wisdom, His all holy providence, holding our hands in hers and crying out to her from the depth of our being: Holy Mary, Mother of God, pray for us sinners now, and at the hour of our death. Amen."[4]

At the end of that month, Manning asked that a message of gratitude be placed in the pages of The *Tidings*:

> Since the fact of my serious illness has become public knowledge, countless messages have reached me. These have come from long-time friends, from former parishioners of Saint Gregory's and Saint Brendan's, and from the community of faith which has adopted me as its own in Holy Family, South Pasadena, from school children, from seminarians, religious and brother priests.
>
> Many people whom I do not personally know, both Catholic and non-Catholic, have comforted me with their words. Each communication contains pledges of Masses, prayers and other sacrifices. It will be obvious that an individual response to each letter is beyond my capacities. I trust in the added understanding of those who wrote that the heart's gratitude will endure despite the lack of sacramental expression of it in correspondence.[5]

Throughout his life, Manning had a very positive and healthy attitude towards death which he once defined as the "final art of living." A decade earlier he had written about the final moments in these words:

> What matters then is not the size of the estate and its beneficiaries, not the wording of the obituary in the next day's papers, nor the prestige of the funeral arrangements, nor the testimonies of widespread friends. Only one thing counts. When the Lord reaches into our very being, as Christ did to the prophetic fig tree at the entrance to Jerusalem, will He find the fruit of holiness for which He looks and for which alone we were made?[6]

Manning's last homily, delivered by his physician, Dr. Brian Henderson, was prepared for the silver jubilee of his priest-secretary. After enumerating the "times of emotional stress, problems without solutions, angry protests beneath our windows, agonizing disappointments and family distresses" that formed the sinew of their relationship, the cardinal concluded by saying that "we await in joyful hope for the coming of the Lord."[7]

Sixteen days after entering the hospital, Timothy Cardinal Manning returned his noble soul to the Lord at 2:15 p.m. on June 23, 1989. His cause of death was listed as a "cerebrovascular accident, due to marantic endocarditis, due to adenocarcimona of the lung."[8] On the very day of Manning's demise, Archbishop Roger Mahony sent a letter to Pope John Paul II outlining the cardinal's last earthly moments. He pointed out that "the cardinal loved Your Holiness fervently, faithfully and obediently every moment of his life. He so appreciated all of the personal marks of friendship which you showed over the years of your pontificate."[9]

The nation's premier newspaper told its readers that "Timothy Cardinal Manning, who brought social conscience and theological conservatism to the more than 2.5 million Roman Catholics he served for fifteen years as Archbishop of Los Angeles, died of cancer" yesterday in Los Angeles.[10] The local press reported in a similar vein that "Timothy Cardinal Manning, a mild-mannered Roman Catholic prelate who led the Los Angeles archdiocese through a fifteen year period that saw it grow into the nation's most populous and ethnically diverse" has passed from this life to the next.[11]

Messages of condolence poured into the Los Angeles chancery from all parts of the nation and from many countries. President George Bush was among the first to "send our heartfelt sympathy to the clergy and laity of" the archdiocese. He told Archbishop Mahony that Manning had "served God and His fellow man with devotion and humility. I know he will be greatly missed."[12] Governor George Deukmejian assured Mahony and the archdiocese that "those we hold most dear never truly leave us and memories of Cardinal Manning will always be touched by his lifetime of devotion and service to God and his fellow man."[13] Mayor Tom Bradley observed that the "people of Los Angeles have lost a champion for all that is right and decent."[14]

Archbishop Pio Laghi, Apostolic Pro-Nuncio to the United States, wrote that "Cardinal Manning will be remembered as one of the great American churchmen of this century, and I wish to acknowledge the significant contribution that he has made to the life of the Church in the United States." From Archbishop John Quinn of San Francisco came words of gratitude for one "whom we all loved and revered and who played such an important role for so long among the bishops of California especially." And, from faraway Ireland, Bishop Dermot O'Sullivan of

Kerry thanked God for all Manning had given to the Church of Los Angeles, in the United States and beyond.[15]

In one of his comments, Archbishop Roger Mahony recalled that the cardinal's baptismal certificate indicated that he was baptized the very day he was born. His first breath of life on this earth was hurriedly sealed with the life of Christ in baptism, and his last breath was consecrated with the sacraments and prayers of the Church. Between those two precious moments span seventy-nine years of unique personal holiness, devotion to Jesus Christ and His Church, and fidelity to eight successors of Peter.[16]

Newspaper editorials included one from the Los Angeles *Times* which saluted "the gentle cardinal."

> Cardinal Timothy Manning guided the Archdiocese of Los Angeles during fifteen of its most tumultuous years of growth. His style of leadership was as gentle as his manner, but on important matters he knew where his Church should go and guided it with quiet precision. He made certain, for example, that the archdiocese made room for and made welcome hundreds of thousands of Latino immigrants, a pastoral obligation largely overlooked before he assumed leadership in 1970. He created a forum that gave the parishes of East Los Angeles their voice in affairs of the archdiocese and established a department in the Catholic Welfare Bureau to help eligible immigrants gain citizenship.
>
> Manning was not a dynamic leader, but he was a superb listener and his calm approach essential to seeing his diocese through years of expansion that six years ago led it past Chicago in Catholic population. Because of his quiet demeanor, Manning's description of the nuclear arms race in the early 1980s as a "dance of death" surprised many Southern Californians. It need not have. It was quite consistent with the gentle nature of Manning, who died of cancer Friday at age seventy-nine.[17]

The other major local newspaper said that "because of Cardinal Manning, the Catholics in Los Angeles were spared the growing pains suffered by many in other parts of the country."[18]

Gerard Sherry, a veteran Catholic journalist credited Manning with being "a scholarly, low-key prelate whose main contribution to the Church was his ability to reconcile."

To my venerable and dear Brother
Cardinal Timothy Manning

Having learned of your present illness I wish to assure you of my spiritual and affectionate union at this time. I pray that the Risen Lord who gives us strength in all our trials will grant you the graces and blessings needed to sustain you. May Our Lady, Queen of Angels, watch over you with her loving care.

As a token of my fraternal esteem I willingly impart my Apostolic Blessing.

From the Vatican, April 25, 1989

Joannes Paulus PP. II

Cardinal's last visit to Saint Vibiana's Cathedral.

Joan Cronin (sister), Breda Lucey (niece) and Finbarr Lucey (grand-nephew) of Cardinal Manning at funeral.

> The soft-spoken Timothy Manning really had no interest in power or influence, except insofar as it furthered his pastoral ministry to the Catholic people of the Los Angeles area. He seldom issued statements on public issues, but when he did, he was always brief, to the point and in defense of moral values. He once told me that churchmen should rise above political issues and preach the Gospel of Christ in season and out of season, "even if it is a contradiction of the times." Cardinal Manning was a very holy man, with a deep personal spirituality, manifested in his dealings with individuals and institutions.[19]

Hundreds of priests and laity sent messages. One came from Father Hugh J. Nolan, a prominent ecclesial historian, who felt that the "outstanding feature of his episcopate was his role as a concerned peacemaker for all situations. A somewhat shy, diffident man who lived in really Christ-like poverty and humility, he was an exceptionally patient listener. Authoritarian rule ran contrary to his nature. For the years of his rule his temperament and these virtues suited perfectly Los Angeles, one of the most polyglot archdioceses in the world."[20]

One of the most touching tributes came from Alphonse Antczak, editor of *The Tidings*, who had worked alongside the cardinal for over three decades:

> Timothy Manning was a man who became a priest to work for the salvation of souls. As a priest, a pastor, a bishop, a cardinal he directed his life and work unerringly and undeviatingly toward that goal. He taught and exemplified the purpose of life: to know, love and serve God. That may not seem sophisticated these days. Some years ago he briefly greeted a convention of theologians here at the Century Plaza. "We welcome you to the city of Our Lady. We ask in your deliberations you not confuse us in the faith we learned at our mother's knee." The cardinal was simple, profound, humble, holy.
>
> There was a word the cardinal used frequently in his writing and in his preaching. It is a verb and it perfectly describes his style and his relationship to his people. The verb is to "companion." He companioned his people. He companioned us. Christ companioned his disciples in their fishing boat, in the Galilean countryside, in their daily lives.

> The cardinal had a presence that was mild, calm, peaceful and powerful. One word describes his personality and presence: priestliness. Never ponderous, never prominent, lighthearted but never trivial, it was possible to perceive that his was a life that daily kept in view the horizon of eternity, that unswervingly followed a Gospel compass heading.[21]

Four separate funeral services, all held at Saint Vibiana's Cathedral and all of them open to the public were scheduled for the deceased cardinal. Evening Prayer and Reception of his remains took place on June 27. The following day there was a Eucharistic Liturgy in the morning and Rosary and Vigil service that evening. Finally, the Mass of Christian Burial was offered on Thursday, with more than a hundred cardinals,[22] archbishops and bishops, together with several hundred clergy and religious in attendance. Many parishes also held Masses for the cardinal, including Holy Family in South Pasadena where the cardinal had lived during the final years of his life.

At the Mass of Christian Burial, Archbishop Mahony gave a lengthy homily which he prefaced by observing that the historical details of Manning's life and ministry throughout Southern and Central California were adequately chronicled in a special commemorative booklet available to those in attendance. Among other pertinent observations on how Holy Scripture influenced in the cardinal's life, the archbishop said:

> The full sense of what it means to fall to the earth and die resonated in the cardinal's life: that often being alone and cold, experiencing darkness and uncertainty, and tasting rejection and defeat, would together bring forth much fruitfulness both in one's life, and in one's participation in the salvation of the world as Jesus' disciples.
>
> But this inner dying was not some fatalistic fantasy nor some fleeting venture. Rather, it became the means to draw closer to Jesus and to share in the Lord's own fruitful ministry: "where I am, there also will my servant be."
>
> He not only lived out this continual dying to self – he actually welcomed it as he patterned his own life after that of the Lord. His deepening association with the spirituality of Saint Ignatius of Loyola intensified this commitment, and one of his favorite, constant refrains was that of Ignatius: "Take Lord, and receive all my liberty, my memory, my understanding and my entire will, all that I have and possess."

Archbishop Roger Mahony delivers homily for cardinal's final liturgy.

Members of Holy Family Parish held all night vigil for Cardinal Manning in their parochial church.

Funeral obsequies were attended by five cardinals, a host of bishops and hundreds of priests.

View from choirloft of Saint Vibiana's Cathedral.

He concluded with this exhortation:

> May flights of angels companion you, Cardinal Manning, as your soul comes before the God whom you so loved; May *Nuestra Señora de Los Angeles*, present you to her Son whom you followed without hesitation. "To know Him and love Him, to live in His presence each day is genuine holiness, for the kingdom and the power and the glory are His, now and forever!"[23]

Pope John Paul II sent Archbishop Justin Rigali, a priest of the Archdiocese of Los Angeles residing in Rome, to be his personal representative at the funeral. Rigali read a personal message from the Holy Father:

> At this moment, I wish to reiterate my sentiments of loving solidarity with the whole Church in Los Angeles. I express my personal gratitude for Cardinal Manning's generous partnership in the Gospel over many years, and for his fidelity to me and my predecessors in the See of Peter, and above all for his fidelity to Jesus Christ and his Church.
>
> The Cardinal's death, sanctified by patient suffering offered up in union with Christ crucified, becomes today for the Church in Los Angeles, and beyond, a splendid legacy of faith and love. It evokes all the values of his priestly life, and, in particular, the great object of all apostolic preaching, which is the resurrection of Jesus Christ, the Son of God and Savior of the world.
>
> On this feast of the Holy Apostles Peter and Paul, I invoke eternal peace and joy for Cardinal Manning in their company, and I entrust his soul to Our Lady of the Angels. In the love of the Risen Lord, I send my Apostolic Blessing to the family of Cardinal Manning and to all who mourn his death in Christian hope.[24]

Following services at the Cathedral, a funeral cortege bore the remains of the cardinal to Calvary Cemetery in East Los Angeles. He chose not to be entombed in the episcopal vault of the mausoleum, but in a plot surrounded by scores of priests with whom he had ministered for fifty-five years. As his body was borne up a small knoll in the priests' plot, there began a soft, spontaneous singing of the refrain of a tender Spanish hymn: "*Al cielo, al cielo, al cielo* – to heaven, to heaven, to

Statue of Christ marks Cardinal Manning's grave at Calvary Cemetery in East Los Angeles.

SECRETARIA S. COLLEGII

In Nativitate Domini 1989

Eminentissime Domine et Frater,

Coelesti perfusa laetitia redeunt iam natalicia festa et mihi pergratum est, nomine quoque Em.morum Patrum Cardinalium in Urbe commorantium, vota tibi facere verbis quibus Sancta Mater Ecclesia nos hisce diebus laetitia afficit: **"Gaudeamus gaudio magno quia veniet nobis Salvator".**

Et merito quidem nobis et omnibus hominibus bonae voluntatis est ratio in Domino gaudendi, si mente recogitemus quot quantaque bona humano generi Redemptor noster, e Virgine Maria natus, attulerit atque quot quantaque in dies adhuc misericorditer, nobis testibus, largiri non desinat.

Igitur, dum proxima sollemnitas multorum beneficiorum memoriam revocat et nos ad gratias pie referendas impellit ac simul urget nos Regnum amoris, iustitiae et pacis in Betlehem inceptum toto orbe terrarum magis magisque ad verum perducere, sit Nativitas Domini Eminentiae Tuae fons lucis, consolationis et gaudii. Sit quoque novus albescens annus, Deipara Virgine Maria intercedente, fructuosus in sacro ministerio quod in servitio Ecclesiae impendere nobis incumbit.

Vota haec dum Tecum, Eminentissime Domine, pro debito fraternitatis et in vinculo caritatis peramanter communico, precibus tuis meipsum commendo et maneo

in Domino semper addictissimus

+ Agnellus Card. Rossi

Collegii Cardinalium Decanus

Even Roman officials occasionally make mistakes. This letter from the Cardinal Dean was written to Manning six months after his demise!

heaven." After Archbishop Roger Mahony concluded the prayers at the grave, people lingered and gathered about the cardinal's wooden coffin, touching it, kissing it. Soon it was covered with home grown flowers from the backyards of the east side streets the cardinal had walked many times on the feast of Our Lady of Guadalupe.

On July 23, Archbishop Mahony celebrated a "Month's Mind Mass" in memory of the cardinal. In the homily for that occasion, Mahony characterized his predecessor as "a person whose unbounded love and enthusiasm for Christ permeated his ministry as a priest, bishop and cardinal archbishop."

> He was able to see God's providence at work in every person, each parish community, and in every joy and every sorrow . . . and his love for all those entrusted to his care was so evident in the various groups for whom he extended himself to the fullest measure – parish families, his brother priests, women religious, Catholic and religious education, various ethnic communities and the missions.[25]

During his seventy-nine years Manning accumulated many treasures for the next life, but little of this world's goods. When his will was probated, there was only $9,000 in his account, all of which he left to the five parishes to which he had been most intimately associated during his ministry.[26]

Notes to the Text

1. AALA, John Paul II to Timothy Cardinal Manning, Rome, April 24, 1989.
2. Los Angeles *Times*, May 19, 1989.
3. *The Tidings*, May 19, 1989.
4. Francis J. Weber (comp.), *Times of Tension. Moments of Grace* (Los Angeles, 1990), p. 441.
5. *The Tidings*, June 2, 1989.
6. *Ibid.*, October 31, 1980.
7. *Ibid.*, June 16, 1989.
8. AALA, Certificate of Death of Timothy Manning, Los Angeles, June 27, 1989.
9. AALA, Roger Mahony to John Paul II, Los Angeles, June 23, 1989.
10. New York *Times*, June 24, 1989.
11. Los Angeles *Times*, June 24, 1989.
12. George Bush to Roger Mahony, Washington, D.C., June 30, 1989.
13. Quoted in *The Tidings*, July 7, 1989.
14. AALA, Tom Bradley to Roger Mahony, Los Angeles, June 24, 1989.
15. Quoted in *The Tidings*, July 7, 1989.
16. *The Tidings*, June 30, 1989.
17. Los Angeles *Times*, June 24, 1989.
18. Los Angeles *Daily News*, July 1, 1989.
19. *Our Sunday Visitor*, July 9, 1989.
20. Unidentified newspaper clipping, "Letter to the editor," n.d.
21. *The Tidings*, June 30, 1989.
22. *Vg.* John Kroll (Philadelphia), Joseph Bernardin (Chicago), John O'Connor (New York), James Hickey (Washington) and Edmond Szoka (Detroit).
23. *The Tidings*, July 7, 1989.

24. *Ibid.*
25. AALA, Press Release, Los Angeles, July 12, 1989.
26. AALA, Thomas Workman to Stephen Blaire, Los Angeles, August 16, 1989.

27. *Epilogue*

Unlike many of his contemporary clerics in high places, Manning's path to the archbishopric had nothing whatsoever to do with his own aspirations. Prior to 1967, his name wasn't even considered for that position. But, in God's providence, he outlived whatever restrictions were attached to his episcopal appointment and he ultimately outperformed most others who might have had a greater claim to the position.

This book has outlined the very substantial contributions made by Timothy Manning to those whose lives he touched during the fifty-five years of his sacerdotal ministry. What it says about the "person" of Timothy Manning is not quite so obvious. He was a very private, almost shy man who effectively hid himself behind his public role as priest, bishop, archbishop and cardinal.

It does nothing to diminish Manning's stature to agree with the general perception that he "was not a *dynamic* leader."[1] In Manning's case, he compensated for that deficiency by allowing others to act in his stead. He began his role as archbishop by openly defying conventional wisdom and opting to leave in place the organizational structure and staffing of his predecessor who had a genius for reducing, if not almost eliminating the bureaucracy typical in the post Vatican Council II era. Manning's concept of leadership was akin to that played by the conductor of a symphony. "He need not be himself skilled in a particular instrument, but he can be the unifying force for bringing out harmony." He felt that "team action rises above one's personal likes and dislikes."[2]

The key to understanding Manning's leadership abilities is to make a clear distinction between leading and administering; he excelled in the first and delegated the latter. In an open message written at the time of the cardinal's death, a chum from seminary days at Menlo Park agreed that Manning "was not a great administrator. He left the grave responsibilities of managing the varied affairs of a sprawling archdiocese to associates, clerical and lay he trusted, supported, appreciated. But the desk was not where he could do his best for God and God's people." Rather, "the hallmark of the cardinal's priesthood was his love and commitment to his people. He was forever in their midst, blessing, honoring, remembering, dedicating, encouraging."[3] That theme was echoed by others. A writer for a local newspaper, after extolling the cardinal for his accomplishments, admitted that "he disliked administration, according to those who knew him, and willingly delegated most of the day-to-day operation of the archdiocese to chancery aids."[4]

Yet, Manning was clearly God's man for the time, a wholly different kind of leader from his predecessor. He was "a theologian, a man familiar with the dynamics of history, a man of sensitivity chastened by but not hardened by suffering."

> He understood the personal crises of young men who were caught in the broken continuum of history, the disillusionment and anxiety of the grand old priests who built the churches and gave themselves totally to the confessional, to baptizing, to confirming, to offering the Holy Mass, only to see so many of the Church's externals fall to fragments around them. He was sensitive to the instinctively existentialist thrust of the young ones who suspected "the unexamined principle," the "arbitrary use of authority," the "traditionalist" syndrome. He equally empathized with the older ones who were sick of the dialogue and inaction of those who had, like so many of their antecedents, never learned to appreciate the essential ambiguity of things.[5]

The pitfalls associated with that elusive charism known as "leadership" were well expressed by a befuddled college professor who admitted he was never quite sure whether his students were following him or chasing him. The paramount quality associated with leadership and its obvious master-key is intelligence, which can harmonize the trinitarian concept of facts, ability to reason and intuition. Beyond a competence based on training and the gradual accumulation of experience and skill, the leader's mind needs enough resiliency to weigh, logically and objectively, all the alternatives before arriving at ultimate conclusions. To emotional balance, tested self-discipline and a strong sense of personal morality, must be added a fair, honest, frank, kindly, straight-forward and firm integrity. Keeping in mind the distinction between leading and administering. Timothy Manning emerges with high marks.

The door of Manning's office at 1531 West Ninth Street was always open, especially for members of the curial staff and priests. He once told a reporter that "anybody who asks may see me; you may have to wait, but no one is denied access."[6] And that was no idle comment. "He was a superb listener and his calm approach was essential to seeing his archdiocese through years of expansion."[7] He said that "when you listen to someone, you solve half his problem. I'm not saying that we didn't do that before; I just did more of it."[8]

Though he was occasionally given to periods of melancholic depression, Manning endeavored to be an optimist. In an interview with the cardinal conducted at Rome during preparations for the Holy Year, Wally Burke said that Manning, "a veteran observer of the ebb and flow of faith and morals, has become neither cynical nor pessimistic. Instead he is sensitive, gentle, outgoing and has an optimism laced with Irish good humor and wit. He is optimistic about the role of religion, despite the changing times." He quoted the cardinal as saying:

> I feel that this is one of the greatest moments in the history of the whole Church. I say that because while the Church is making the great transition into the technological age, naturally she is suffering the effects of change which all institutions suffer.[9]

He rarely lost his temper. When something went wrong with a relationship or an unpleasant encounter, Manning would apologize. He classified his own temperament as "passive and phlegmatic" which, he admitted, was "a common trait among the Irish." While denying that his temperament influenced his actions "in any dominant way," he agreed that it did have a bearing on his writings. When queried as to whether he avoided confrontations, Manning responded "whenever I can," observing that "nothing is gained by confrontations."[10] One of the more astute priests of the archdiocese once observed that he had "never seen the cardinal give the impression of being restless. The burdens of his office rest lightly on him." He saw that as "a grace, for a man of sensitivity cannot be cold or casual about decisions that have a deep and lasting effect on other people."[11]

Manning instinctively saw the good in people and only later that which was tainted by the frailty of human nature. Especially was that true with his fellow priests. When the antics of some errant cleric were related to him, he found it difficult to comprehend. On one occasion, after listening to an especially unpleasant incident, he replied: "That's hard to believe. I knew his mother and she was such a lovely lady."

Those who knew him before and after Vatican Council II uniformly testified that he absorbed much of the spirit of the council. The post-conciliar Manning was considerably more flexible in his demeanor with others. Apart from his role as archbishop Manning's more attractive human traits jumped out at people, even reporters. One writer for a prominent local newspaper recognized the cardinal as "a purposely non-controversial prelate who sees his role best characterized as 'servanthood' for Catholics."[12]

A personally spiritual man, Manning did all the things traditionally associated with priesthood and he did them well. He recited his breviary, read Holy Scripture, made his meditation, said the rosary, did spiritual reading, practiced the virtues and made a daily holy hour. In a busy world, he found time for the Lord.

Though not innovative by nature, Manning seized upon suggestions of others and often encouraged proposals, ideas and plans presented by subordinates. His permissive nature served him well because it allowed him to divert attention from himself. Having no identity crisis, he was not threatened by the accomplishments of others, but was perfectly content when the credit for this or that project went to others. Manning often remarked that "there is always plenty of credit to spread around." He was fond of a quote from Alexander Pope that reflected that philosophy: "Be not the first by whom the new is tried; nor yet the last to set the old aside."

By choice, Manning lived simply. A news account told how the cardinal lived "in a three-room apartment at the priests' house on Second and Main in the skid row area. His lifestyle, like his living quarters, was a model of Christian simplicity and a witnessing to Gospel values which his clergy and people admire and appreciate."[13]

However one cuts the cake, Timothy Manning emerges as a truly remarkable figure on the national and local ecclesial scene of the American Catholic Church.

Notes to the Text

1. Los Angeles *Times*, June 24, 1989.
2. AALA, Biographical Interview with Timothy Cardinal Manning, Mission Hills, August 24, 1981.
3. AALA, John Connolly to Parishioners, Oakland, July 9, 1989.
4. Los Angeles *Herald Examiner*, May 27, 1985.
5. John V. Sheridan, "Los Angeles - An Example of Charity and Collegiality," *Aquila* (Waterford, 1974), p. 25.
6. Gary Diedrichs, "A Day in the Life . . . Timothy Manning, Cardinal," Los Angeles *Magazine* (May, 1981), 12.
7. Los Angeles *Times*, June 24, 1989.
8. *Ibid.*, February 2, 1979.
9. *Twin Circle*, December 21, 1973.
10. AALA, Biographical Interview, August 24, 1981.
11. John V. Sheridan, *op cit*, p. 25.
12. John Dart in the Los Angeles *Times*, February 2, 1980.
13. Pasadena *Star News*, November 11, 1977.

APPENDIX ONE
Papal Honors

Long before the term and the practice became popular, Timothy Cardinal Manning exercised the virtue of affirmation. No accomplishment, greeting, gift or other expression of service to the Archdiocese of Los Angeles went unnoticed. The greatest quantity of Manning's correspondence on file at the Archival Center are letters of gratitude.

MONSIGNORS

PROTHONOTARY APOSTOLICS

O'FLAHERTY, Rev. Msgr. Raymond
HAWKES, Rev. Msgr. Benjamin G.

PRELATES OF HONOR

ATWILL, Rev. Msgr. William
ACTON, Rev. Msgr. John
BARRY, Rev. Msgr. John
BARRY, Rev. Msgr.William
BIEDERMANN, Rev. Msgr. Arnold
BIRCH, Rev. Msgr. John J.
BRAMBLE, Rev. Msgr. Wm. K.
BROSNAN, Rev. Msgr. John
BULLUM, Rev. Msgr. Peter
CASLIN, Rev. Msgr. Peter C.
COKUS, Rev. Msgr. Joseph
COLEMAN, Rev. Msgr. Francis
CONDON, Rev. Msgr. Michael J.
CONNOLLY, Rev. Msgr. Clement J.
COSGROVE, Rev. Msgr. John V.

COTTER, Rev. Msgr. Richard
CREAN, Rev. Msgr. Timothy J.
CREMINS, Rev. Msgr. John P.
DALY, Rev. Msgr. Dominic
DEADY, Rev. Msgr. John P.
DIOMARTICH, Rev. Msgr. Felix
DOHERTY, Rev. Msgr. John B.
DONNELLY, Rev. Msgr. Lawrence
DUGGAN, Rev. Msgr. Wm. M.
DUVAL, Rev. Msgr. Anthony L.
ENGLISH, Rev. Msgr. Tobias P.
FEEHAN, Rev. Msgr. Joseph
FLACK, Rev. Msgr. John
FOSSELMAN, Rev. Msgr. John A.
FRILOT, Rev. Msgr. Eugene P.
DESSERT, Rev. Msgr. James
GARA, Rev. Msgr. Robert
GLENNON, Rev. Msgr. James
GRILL, Rev. Msgr. Philip
HACKETT, Rev. Msgr. John
HOBAN, Rev. Msgr. Michael
KEARNEY, Rev. Msgr. Joseph V.
KELLY, Rev. Msgr. Matthew
KENNEDY, Rev. Msgr. Christopher
KENNEDY, Rev. Msgr. Thomas
KIEFER, Rev. Msgr. Thomas A.
LANGUILLE, Rev. Msgr. John
LYNCH, Rev. Msgr. James
MARRON, Rev. Msgr. Matthew
MARUM, Rev. Msgr. Kieran
MIHAN, Rev. Msgr. John A.
MORAN, Rev. Msgr. Michael
MORETTI, Rev. Msgr. August
MULCAHY, Rev. Msgr. Donal
MULCAHY, Rev. Msgr. James
MURPHY, Rev. Msgr. Jeremiah
MURRAY, Rev. Msgr. Richard H.
McCABE, Rev. Msgr. Vincent
McGRATH, Rev. Msgr. Andrew
McNAMARA, Rev. Msgr. John
NAVIN, Rev. Msgr. Cyril
O'BRIEN, Rev. Msgr. Kenneth

O'BRIEN, Rev. Msgr. Thomas Lawrence
O'BRIEN, Rev. Msgr. Patrick J.
O'CALLAGHAN, Rev. Msgr. James A.
O'CONNELL, Rev. Msgr. Thomas
O'GORMAN, Rev. Msgr. Augustine
O'LEARY, Rev. Msgr. Lawrence
O'MALLEY, Rev. Msgr. Thomas
O'REILLY, Rev. Msgr. Bernard
O'SULLIVAN, Rev. Msgr. Peter
RAWDEN, Rev. Msgr. John A.
REILLY, Rev. Msgr. John J.
SCHNEIDERS, Rev. Msgr. Joseph
SEDAY, Rev. Msgr. Paul Felix
TORGERSON, Rev. Msgr. Lloyd A.
VADAKIN, Rev. Msgr. Royale M.
WALLACE, Rev. Msgr. Francis
WOOD, Rev. Msgr. Cyril
YOUNG, Rev. Msgr. John M.

CHAPLAIN OF HIS HOLINESS

ALZUGARAY, Rev. Msgr. Joseph
BAULER, Rev. Msgr. Gary P.
COLBERG, Rev. Msgr. James P.
COLLINS, Rev. Msgr. Fachtna P.
CURRY, Rev. Msgr. Thomas J.
DOTSON, Rev. Msgr. Paul T.
GALLAGHER, Rev. Msgr. Patrick J.
GARCIA, Rev. Msgr. Peter
GUTIERREZ, Rev. Msgr. Louis
HEALY, Rev. Msgr. Peter C.
HEFNER, Rev. Msgr. Helmut A.
HERNANDEZ, Rev. Msgr. Alfred
HERRES, Rev. Msgr. Joseph
LEUER, Rev. Msgr. Anthony
LIRETTE, Rev. Msgr. Arthur J.
MATAS, Rev. Msgr. Juan
NAUGHTON, Rev. Msgr. John
NIEDERAUER, Rev. Msgr. George H.
OCHOA, Rev. Msgr. Armando X.
O'CONNELL, Rev. Msgr. Timothy

PARKER, Rev. Msgr. John C.
POLLARD, Rev. Msgr. Joseph
REILLY, Rev. Msgr. Patrick
ROHDE, Rev. Msgr. John W.
STEIN, Rev. Msgr. Robert
WEBER, Rev. Msgr. Francis J.

GENTLEMAN IN WAITING TO HIS HOLINESS

DONOHUE, Sir Daniel	1974

KNIGHTS OF SAINT GREGORY

ALLEGRETTI, Mr. Albert J.	1982
AUTH, Mr. Robert	1974
BALAMASEDA, Mr. Luis	1980
BANNAN, Mr. Charles	1982
BARTOLOTTI, Mr. Gene	1984
BERGIN, Mr. Thomas	1974
BOLGER, Mr. Michael	1982
BRANDLIN, Mr. John J.	1982
BREWSTER, Dr. Stephen	1982
DILLHOEFER, Mr. Edwin	1978
DONOHUE, Rosemary	1982
DOWNEY, Mr. James	1974
DUNN, Mr. Richard	1974
DUNN, Mr. Joseph	1982
GRANT, Jr., Mr. Richard A.	1974
HAGAN, Mr. Peter	1974
HAWLEY, Mr. Philip	1980
HEGENER, Mr. Joseph	1978
HILL, Mr. Edward	1980
JOHANSING, Mr. Walter	1978
JOSEPH, Jr., Mr. Benjamin	1980
KANNE, Jr., Mr. Francis	1974
KELLY, Mr. James	1982
LAWLER, Mr. Oscar	1982
McMENAMIN, Mr. James	1980
NALLY, Mr. Joseph	1982
OLSEN, Mr. Kenneth	1982
O'MALLEY, Mr. Peter	1982

O'MALLEY, Mr. Walter 1974
PEELER, Mr. Joseph 1982
PIKE, Mr. Thomas 1978
STRUB, Mr. Robert 1982
SULLIVAN, Mr. Roger 1982
WAGNER, Mr. Francis 1978
WILSON, Dr. John C. 1982
WOLFE, Mr. Charles 1980
WILLIAMS, Mr. Horace 1974
YOUNG, Dr. F. Roman 1978

PRO ECCLESIA

BARRY, Ms. Marian Hancock 1984
BRENNAN, Mrs. James E. (Virginia McCarthy) 1974
CORDERO, Ms. Ida G. 1974
DELANY, Ms. Marye 1984
DONOHUE, Miss Rosemary 1982
ELSHOFF, Ms. Irene 1981
GOCKE, Mrs. Miriam 1974
HENRY, Mrs. Helen (Nina) 1978
HUGHES, Miss Irene 1980
LIRETTE, Mrs. Mary 1978
LOWRY, Mrs. Ida Frances 1974
PARADISO, Mrs. Margaret 1974
POLITO, Mrs. S. Robert (Rose) 1978
RAMSDEN, Mrs. H.D. (Mary Ann) 1978
RICKS, Miss Dolores Jean 1980
ROBERTO, Mrs. Gertrude 1984
SIBERZ, Mr. Bert 1984
SORENSEN, Mrs. Doris 1974
SPELLMIRE, Miss Verona 1974
THOMAS, Mrs. Vivian 1980
WALSH, Mrs. Henry (Helen) 1978
WALSH, Miss Marie T. 1978
ZINGARELLI, Mrs. Laura 1974

BENEMERENTI

ANTCZAK, Mr. Alphonse 1984
AVILEZ, Mrs. Grace 1984

BARRY, Mrs. Marian Hancock	1983
BELL, Ms. Marion	1984
BERGER, Miss Clare	1984
BOSSERT, Miss Ethel	1984
DELIMA, Ms. Corrine	1984
ESCALANTE, Ms. Josephine	1984
GARCIA, Mr. Jose R.	1974
HERON, Mrs. Katherine	1984
HILL, Mr. Ed	1980
JOHNSON, Mr. Charles	1984
KIRSNIS, Mrs. Elizabeth	1980
LE GRAS, Mr. William	1984
LANGEVIN, Mr. Richard	1984
LOZANO, Ms. Estella	1984
LUCERO, Miss Grace	1984
MARTIN, Mrs. Virginia	1984
MARTINEZ, Ms. Mary	1984
MELLO, Mr. Antone	1984
MESA, Mr. Salvador	1980
METICHECCHIA, Ms. Anna	1984
MINOVICH, Ms. Vivian	1984
MONTEZ, Mr. Raul	1984
NUNIS, Dr. Doyce	1984
ORMONDE, Ms. Betty Lou	1995
PEFFER, Mr. Edward	1984
PIMENTEL, Mrs. Justina	1980
PIMENTEL, Mr. Salvador	1980
RICHARDSON, Mr. Donald L.	1974
RUSZAK, Mr. John	1984
SANCHEZ, Ms. Ramona	1984
SKVICALO, Ms. Ann	1984
TOMICH, Ms. Therese	1984
TOMPKINS, Mr. Paul	1984
TRUXAW, Mr. John	1984
WHALING, Mr. Richard	1984
WALLEY, Ms. Dorothy	1984
YOST, Ms. Helen	1984

APPENDIX TWO

Statistical Growth - Archdiocese of Los Angeles[1]

1970-1985

Year	Total Catholics	Total Priests	Total Parishes	Total Religious Women[2]
1970	1,743,164	1,434	321	3,226
1971	1,791,932	1,404	324	3,168
1972	1,975,500	1,409	324	3,200
1973	1,984,429	1,440	319	3,007
1974	2,099,749	1,447	319	1,959
1975	2,208,989	1,456	319	1,910
1976[3]	1,918,000	1,290	278	1,761
1977	1,950,000	1,273	278	1,658
1978	1,964,000	1,281	278	3,836
1979	2,069,682	1,265	278	2,545
1980	2,231,180	1,278	279	2,487
1981	2,303,560	1,295	281	2,643
1982	2,370,000	1,297	283	2,866
1983	2,374,021	1,295	283	2,642
1984	2,561,602	1,313	283	2,484
1985	2,650,000	1,401	284	2,543

1. Statistics here are taken from *The Official Catholic Directory*, 1971-1986 (P.J. Kenedy & Sons, New York).
2. There appears to be an inconsistency in the census for Sisters in this list.
3. These figures reflect the creation of the Diocese of Orange.

APPENDIX THREE
Archdiocesan Expansion

Agencies, Commissions, Departments, Programs, Boards, Bureaus, and Ministries established during the archiepiscopate of Timothy Cardinal Manning

Priests Senate - 1970
Diaconate Program - 1972
Clerical Placement Board - 1972
Family Life Bureau - 1972
Retirement Plan for Priests - 1972
Episcopal Vicars - 1973
Team Ministry - 1973
Continuing Education for Clergy - 1973
Encuentro Hispano de Pastoral - 1973
Commission on Aging - 1974
Communications Commission - 1974
Charismatic Renewal - 1974
Marriage Encounter - 1974
House of Prayer - 1975
Conciliation and Arbitration Board - 1977
Pastoral Councils - 1977
Retirement Plan for Chancery Employees - 1977
Multilingual Apostolate - 1978
Peace and Justice Commission - 1983
Ad Hoc Womens Task Force - 1985

APPENDIX FOUR
Manning's Credo

(Timothy Cardinal Manning's "belief in Papacy and Pope" is here reproduced from *The Tidings*, March 26, 1976.)

The time has come when I must make a declaration of my faith in papacy and pope. It is urgent and timely. There are two passages in the gospels which confer a marvelous and exceptional power upon Peter and which are, therefore, the basis for my belief about his successors, the popes of Rome.

THE FIRST is on the occasion, near Caesarea Phillippi, when Peter in the name of the twelve, made his profound profession of faith in Jesus as the Christ, the Son of the living God, "and Jesus answered him . . .

"You are a 'rock'; and on this rock I will build my Church, and the jaws of death shall not prevail against it. I will entrust to you the keys of the kingdom of heaven. Whatever you declare bound on earth shall be bound in heaven; whatever you declared loosed on earth shall be loosed in heaven." (Matt. 16:, 18, 19)

THE SECOND reference is the occasion after the resurrection when Jesus appears to His disciples by the lakeshore and, having received a protestation of love from Peter who had denied Him, says to him, "Feed my lambs; feed my sheep." (Jn. 21: 15.17) There are many other texts that show a preference for Peter. He is always named first when "The Twelve" are named. It is from his boat that Jesus teaches. He, once he is repented of his denial, must convert his brethren. Satan has desired to have him but Jesus has prayed for him that his faith fail not.

The quotations we have mentioned, however, form the basis of belief. The first of these is written in Latin and Greek in letters six feet tall upon a gold Mosaic that runs the entire span, high above the arches in the Basilica of Saint Peter in Rome.

THE TEACHING of the Church concerning the Pope is defined as faith in the First Vatican Council and repeated in Vatican II.

"If anyone says that it is not according to the institution of Christ our Lord himself, that is, by divine law, that St. Peter has perpetual successors in the primacy over the whole Church; or if anyone says that the Roman Pontiff is not the successor of St. Peter in the same primacy, let him be anathema. If anyone says that the Roman Pontiff has only the office of inspection or direction, but not the full and supreme power of jurisdiction over the whole Church, not only in matters that pertain to faith and morals, but also in matters that pertain to the discipline and government of the Church throughout the world; or if anyone says that he has only a more important part and not the complete fullness of this supreme power; or if anyone says that this power is not ordinary and immediate over each and every church or over each and every shepherd and faithful member, let him be anathema."

THE PASSAGES of Scripture and the decrees of First Vatican are under close scrutiny by Scripture scholars and by theologians. Such research is valid within the competence of their respective skills. We must respect that. However, it is very upsetting when popularizations of their views are picked up by the less wise and become obstacles to the firmness of their belief. The Church has said:

"The faithful must shun the opinion first, that dogmatic formulas cannot signify in a determinate way, but can offer only changeable approximations to it, which to a certain extent distort or alter it; secondly, that these formulas signify the truth only in the indeterminate way, this truth being like a goal that is constantly being sought by means of such approximations. Those who hold such an opinion do not avoid dogmatic relativism, and they corrupt the concept of the Church's infallibility relative to the truth to be taught or held in a determinate way."

WHAT THIS AMOUNTS to is a "red flag" of caution put up by the Church to shelter my faith. Within it, I assert my unchanging belief in the supreme, full, immediate and universal power of the pope in the care of souls. The Second Vatican Council confirms what was said at the First:

"In this Church of Christ the Roman Pontiff, as the successor of Peter, to whom Christ entrusted the care of His sheep and His lambs, has been granted by God, supreme, full, immediate and universal power in the care of souls. As pastor of all the faithful his mission is to promote the common good of all the Churches. he is therefore endowed with the primacy of ordinary power over all the Churches."

THE FIRST VATICAN Council had intended to define the position of bishops in the Church but the Italian war interfered and the Council had to be terminated. It was the glory of Vatican II to have done so and given us a clear teaching on bishops. This we find in the same Decree, *Christus Dominus.* We quote:

"The bishops also have been designated by the Holy Spirit to take the place of the apostles as pastors of souls and together with the Supreme Pontiff and subject to his authority, they are commissioned to perpetuate the work of Christ, the eternal pastor. (No. 2) Together with their head, the supreme pontiff, and never apart from him, they have supreme and full authority over the universal Church, but their power cannot be exercised without the agreement of the Roman Pontiff."

FROM THESE brief quotations we have a clear basis of faith and understanding of the relationships of bishops and pope. Together with the pope and never without him. To give too much emphasis to one truth without the balance of the other is to distort. Faith keeps the balance.

Since he is the pastor of souls, and of my soul in particular, I for my part have certain responsibilities toward the supreme pontiff. There are three: reverence, obedience and prayer. He is not simply a figure head of a great world-wide organization to receive the adulation of hundreds of thousands in Saint Peter's Square. He is the Vicar of Christ, the "stand in" for Christ and my reverences must be accordingly. My obedience is two-fold, in his disciplinary provisions for my spiritual guidance, and to his teaching in matters of faith and morals. My prayers for him are liturgical in every Mass I attend where his name is mentioned in the Eucharistic prayers; it is also a part of my private prayer life, praying for his intentions each day and for the guidance of the Spirit in all his activity.

THE POPE EXERCISES his responsibilities of guiding the children of the Church either directly or through a series of congregations and offices which are set up and staffed in Rome. Regularly directives are issued from these organizations; they are done so after consultation with the pope, and merit the same respect and responses as do his direct pronouncements.

Perhaps this piece on the papacy has had too many official quotations. Yet they are very necessary because there is so much vague, foggy and superficial reference to the pope today that it is urgently necessary to restate his position in the Church and pledge to him the devotion and obedience due him.

"Father of providence, look with love on Paul our pope, your appointed successor to St. Peter on whom you built your Church. May he be the visible center and foundation of our unity in faith and love. Grant this through Christ our Lord."

APPENDIX FIVE
Homily to Angelenos in 2076

(This "homily to Angelenos in 2076" was preached by Timothy Cardinal Manning as part of the centennial celebrations for Saint Vibiana's Cathedral. It was printed in *The Tidings*, May 7, 1976.)

One hundred years from now others will gather here to celebrate its bicentennial. Who can tell whether some undiscovered weapons of destruction will have left this basin like the ruins of Carthage.

Maybe Los Angeles will be but a titular see for some bishop residing in a man-made island in outer space.

Perhaps the bishop will be the great grandson of a Vietnamese or Korean refugee, and our Irish and Spanish names will be as unfamiliar as theirs are today. God knows.

To those who would be gathering for a possible celebration in the Cathedral 100 years hence, the cardinal has a message from the grave.

We reach out to join with you in professing the same unchanging faith, the faith of our forefathers, and we forefathers to yours.

There will still be a one, holy, Catholic and apostolic Church, grounded on the apostles and ruled by a pope of Rome.

Maybe a great heresy, like Arianism, will have swept across the Church of Christ, teaching, suffering, serving.

To you, from our graves, we send our greetings and our love. The form of this world, like our mortal graves, will pass away. The everlasting only will remain. Pray for us who have gone before you, marked with the sign of faith and who sleep the sleep of peace.

May the country which you serve still be a nation under God, dedicated to the protection of family life, the guarding of liberty and the pursuit of happiness.

And may Our Lady of Angels, *Nuestra Señora de Los Angeles*, continue to look upon and love you all - Your Eminence the Archbishop of Los Angeles, your assistant bishops, clergy and people of God in year of Our Lord 2076.

APPENDIX SIX
Golden Rose of Tepeyac

There was a long and historical precedent for the bestowal of the Golden Rose of Tepeyac upon Timothy Cardinal Manning by the Metropolitan Chapter of the National Shrine of Our Lady of Guadalupe. In the early centuries of the Church, it was the custom for the pope to give a golden rose that he had blessed at Eastertime to one or another of the prominent monarchs or nobles of Europe.

The rose's stem, leaves, buds, and blossoms were fashioned of pure gold, sometimes set with rubies and sapphires, and anointed with balsam and musk. It was a symbolic message from heaven. Originally, the golden rose was an annual gift from the popes to the city prefects of Rome. Its bestowal entailed an elaborate series of ceremonies lasting the better part of a day.

On the fourth Sunday of Lent, known then and now as "Rose Sunday," the Holy Father carried a crimson-dyed golden rose in solemn procession from the Lateran Palace to Santa Croce in Gerusalemme. There he would celebrate Mass and deliver a homily on the rose as a symbol of the spiritual joys attached to the approaching Feast of Easter. The rose's fragrance, he would note, foretold the splendor of the Resurrection.

As the pope returned to the Lateran, he was met by the city's prefect who would accept the golden rose and then carry it inside the church, accompanied by a solemn procession of religious and civil officials. What began as a purely Roman custom of cementing the relationship between the city of Rome and its clergy gradually spread to other locales. After 1309, when the Pope Clement V took the papacy to Avignon, the golden rose was awarded to French and Tuscany personages.

During ensuing centuries, the golden rose evolved from a pastoral Easter greeting into a conscious instrument of international diplomacy. In 1490, Isabelle of Castile received a rose in recognition of her accomplishments against the Moors. In 1521, a rose was sent to King Henry VIII of England, along with a letter bestowing upon him the title "Defender of the Faith." The last male monarch to receive a rose was the Austrian Archduke, Ferdinand, in 1780.

Occasionally, the golden rose is still awarded to female sovereigns - the Grand Duchess of Luxembourg received one in 1956. And recent popes have begun the practice of bestowing golden roses upon notable shrines, such as those of Our Lady of Fatima (1965) and the Virgin of Luyan (1982).

No one who has ever seen *Der Rosenkavalier* will forget that magical moment when the youthful Octavian enters the palace bearing the perfumed symbol of betrothal, the silver rose. To Sophie, for whom it was intended, the rose seemed "like heavenly, not earthly roses; roses from the highest paradise . . . like a message from heaven."

The opera's "Presentation of the Roses" alludes to a custom much older than Richard Strauss and Hugo von Hofmannsthal. And one suspects that the long and engrossing history of this most sumptuous and symbolic of Easter presents, the Golden Rose, is far from finished.

APPENDIX SEVEN
Manning's Episcopal Lineage

1. ***TIMOTHY MANNING***, Titular Bishop of Lesvi and Auxiliary Bishop of Los Angeles. Consecrated 15 October 1946 in Saint Vibiana's Cathedral, Los Angeles, California, by Joseph Thomas McGucken, Titular Bishop of Sanavus and Auxiliary Bishop of Los Angeles, assisted by James Edward Walsh, M.M., Titular Bishop of Sata and Thomas Arthur Connolly, Titular Bishop of Sila and Auxiliary Bishop of San Francisco.

2. ***JOSEPH THOMAS McGUCKEN***, Titular Bishop of Sanavus and Auxiliary Bishop of Los Angeles. Consecrated 19 March 1941 in Saint Vibiana's Cathedral, Los Angeles, California, by John Joseph Cantwell, Archbishop of Los Angeles, assisted by Daniel James Gercke, Bishop of Tucson and Philip George Scher, Bishop of Monterey-Fresno.

3. ***JOHN JOSEPH CANTWELL***, Bishop of Monterey-Los Angeles. Consecrated 5 December 1917 in the Cathedral of Saint Mary, San Francisco, California, by Edward Joseph Hanna, Archbishop of San Francisco, assisted by Thomas Grace, Bishop of Sacramento and Joseph Sarsfield Glass, C.M., Bishop of Salt Lake.

4. ***EDWARD JOSEPH HANNA***, Titular Bishop of Titopolis and Auxiliary Bishop of San Francisco. Consecrated 4 December 1912 in Saint Patrick's Cathedral, Rochester, New York, by Giovanni Vincenzo Bonzano, Titular Archbishop of Melitene, Apostolic Delegate to the United States, assisted by James Edward Quigley, Archbishop of Chicago and Denis Joseph O'Connell, Bishop of Richmond.

5. ***GIOVANNI VINCENZO BONZANZO***, Titular Archbishop of Melitene and Apostolic Delegate to the United States. Consecrated 3 March 1912 in the College de Propoganda Fide, Rome, by Raffaele Cardinal Merry del Val, Secretary of State of His Holiness, assisted by Pietro Berruti, Bishop of Vigevano and Thomas Francis Kennedy, Titular Bishop of Hadrianopolis.

6. ***RAFFAELE MERRY del VAL***, Titular Archbishop of Nicea. Consecrated 6 May 1900 in the Church of Santa Maria in Via Monserrato, Rome, by Mariano Cardinal Rompolla del Tindaro, assisted by Edmond Stonor, Titular Archbishop of Trapezus and Guglielmo Pifferi, O.S.A., Titular Bishop of Perohyreon.

7. ***MARIANO RAMPOLLA DEL TINDARO***, Titular Archbishop of Hereclea in Europa and Apostolic Nuncio to Spain. Consecrated 8 December 1882 in Saint Peter's Basilica, Rome, by Edward Cardinal Howard, assisted by Alessandro Samminiatelli Zabarella, Titular Archbishop of Tyana and Carlo Laurenti, Titular Bishop of Amathus.

8. ***EDWARD HOWARD***, Titular Archbishop of Neocaesarea and Auxiliary Bishop of Frascati. Consecrated June 1982 in Saint Peter's Basilica, Rome, by Carlo Cardinal Sacconi, assisted by Salvatore Nobili Vitelleschi, Titular Archbishop of Seleucia and François Xavier de Merode, Titular Archbishop of Melitene.

9. ***CARLO SACCONI***, Titular Archbishop of Nicea and Apostolic Nuncio in Bavaria. Consecrated 8 June 1851 in the Church of Saints Vincent and Anastasius, Rome, by Giacomo Filippo Cardinal Fransoni, assisted by Giuseppe Valerga, Latin Patriarch of Jerusalem and Rudesindo Salvado, O.S.B., Bishop of Port Victoria, Australia.

10. ***GIACOMO FILIPE FRANSONI***, Titular Archbishop of Nazianzus. Consecrated 8 December 1822, in the Church of the Benedictines (Campo Marzio), Rome, by Pier Francesco Cardinal Galleffi, assisted by Gianfrancesco Falzacappa, Titular Archbishop of Athens and Giuseppe Della Porta Rodiani, Titular Archbishop of Damascus.

11. ***PIER FRANCESCO GALLEFFI***, Cardinal and Titular Archbishop of Damascus. Consecrated 12 September 1819 in the Church of Saints Dominic and Sixtus, Rome, by Alessandro Cardinal Mattei, Bishop

of Ostia e Velletri, assisted by Meraldo Macioti, Titular Bishop of Elusa and Francesco Albertini, Bishop of Terracina, Sezze e Piperno.

12. ***ALESANDRO MATTEI***, Archbishop of Ferrara. Consecrated 23 February 1777 in the Church of Santa Maria Regina Coeli, Rome, by Bernardino Cardinal Giraud, Archbishop emeritus of Ferrara, assisted by Marcantonio Conti, Titular Archbishop of Damascus and Giuseppe Maria Carafa, Bishop of Mileto.

13. ***BERNARDINO GIRAUD***, Titular Archbishop of Damascus. Consecrated 26 April 1767 in a chapel of the Apostolic Palace of the Quirinal, Rome, by His Holiness Pope Clement XIII, assisted by Scipione Borghese, Titular Archbishop of Theodosia and Ignazio Reali, Titular Archbishop of Athens.

14. ***CARLO REZZONICO***, Cardinal Bishop of Padova, the future Pope Clement XIII. Consecrated 19 March 1743 in the Basilica of the Twelve Holy Apostles, Rome, by His Holiness Pope Benedict XIV, assisted by Giuseppe Cardinal Accaramboni, Bishop of Frascati and Antonio Saverio Cardinal Gentili.

15. ***PROSPERO LAMBERTINI***, Titular Archbishop of Theodosia (the future Pope Benedict XIV) Consecrated 16 July 1724 in the Pauline Chapel of the Apostolic Palace of the Quirinal, Rome, by His Holiness Pope Benedict XIII, assisted by Giovanni Francesco Nicolai, O.F.M.Ref., Titular Archbishop of Myra and Nicola Maria Lercari, Titular Archbishop of Nazianzus.

16. ***VINCENZO MARIA ORSINI***, O.P., Cardinal Archbishop of Manfredonia (the future Pope Benedict XIII). Consecrated 3 February 1675 in the Church of Saints Dominic and Sixtus, Rome, by Paluzzo (Paluzzi degli Albertoni) Cardinal Altieri, Prefect of the Sacred Congregation de Propaganda Fide, assisted by Stefano Brancaccio, Archbishop-Bishop of Viterbo e Tuscania and Costanzo Zani, O. S. B., Bishop of Imola.

17. ***PALUZZO (PALUZI degli ALBERTONI) ALTIERI***, Cardinal Bishop of Montefiascone e Corneto. Consecrated 2 May 1666 in the Church of San Silvestro in Capite, Rome, by Ulderico Cardinal

Carpegna, assisted by Stefano Ugolini, Titular Archbishop of Corinth and Giovanni Tommaso Pinelli, Bishop of Albenga.

18. ***ULDERICO CARPEGNA***, Bishop of Gubbio. Consecrated 7 October 1630 in the Pauline Chapel of the Apostolic Palace of the Quirinal, Rome, by Luigi Cardinal Caetani, assisted by Antonio Ricciulli, Bishop emeritus of Belcastro and Vicegerent of Rome, and Benedetto Landi, Bishop of Fossombrone

19. ***LUIGI CAETANI***, Titular Patriarch of Antioch. Consecrated 12 June 1622 in the Basilica of Santa Maria Maggiore, Rome, by Lodovico Cardinal Ludovisi, Archbishop of Bologna, assisted by Galeazzo Sanvitale, Archbishop emeritus of Bari and Vulpiano Volpi, Archbishop emeritus of Chieti.

20. ***LODOVICO LUDOVISI***, Cardinal Archbishop of Bologna. Consecrated 2 May 1621 in the private chapel of his consecrator, near Saint Peter's Basilica, Rome, by Galeazzo Sanvitale, Archbishop emeritus of Bari and Prefect of the Apostolic Palace, assisted by Cosmo de Torres, Titular Archbishop of Hadrianopolis and Ottavio Ridolfi, Bishop of Ariano.

21. ***GALEAZZO SANVITALE***, Archbishop of Bari. Consecrated 4 April 1604 in the chapel of the Apostolic Sacristy, Rome, by Girolamo Cardinal Bernerio, O.P., Bishop of Albano, assisted by Claudio Rangoni, Bishop of Piacenza and Giovanni Ambrogio Caccia, Bishop of Castro di Toscana.

22. ***GIROLAMO BERNERIO***, O.P., Bishop of Ascoli Piceno. Consecrated 7 September 1586 in the Basilica of the Twelve Holy Apostles, Rome, by Giulio Antonio Cardinal Santoro, assisted by Giulio Masetti, Bishop of Reggio Emilia and Ottaviano Paravicini, Bishop of Alessandria.

23. ***GIULIO ANTONIO SANTORO***, Archbishop of Santa Severina. Consecrated 12 March 1566 in the Pauline Chapel of the Vatican Apostolic Palace by Scipione Cardinal Rebiba, Titular Patriarch of Constantinople, assisted by Annibale Caracciolo, Bishop of Isola and Giacomo de'Giacomelli, Bishop emeritus of Belcastro.

24. ***SCIPIONE REBIBA***, Titular Bishop of Amicle and Auxiliary of Chieti. Elected Titular Bishop of Amicle and Auxiliary to Giovanni Pietro Cardinal Carafa, Archbishop of Chieti, 16 March 1541. To date, after extensive research, no record of his consecration has been found.

This episcopal lineage is here traced through the diligent research of Charles N. Bransom, Jr.

APPENDIX EIGHT
Manning's Cardinalatial Crest

THE COAT OF ARMS OF HIS EMINENCE,
TIMOTHY CARDINAL MANNING
THIRD ARCHBISHOP OF LOS ANGELES IN CALIFORNIA

The personal coat of arms of Timothy Cardinal Manning was combined with those of the Archdiocese of Los Angeles, indicating his status as Ordinary and Metropolitan. The arms are described as if one were holding the shield in front of oneself, thus the left side, as we look at the arms from the front, is called dexter (right) and the right side is sinister (left).

Dexter: The arms of the Archdiocese of Los Angeles

> Three sets of golden angels' wings each guarding a golden rose of Our Lady. This signifies the name of the City of Our Lady of the Angels, of the Portiuncula.

Sinister: The arms of the Manning Family

Three golden crescents appear on a red shield with a golden border. Research at Dublin Castle revealed that the Manning family arms date from 1578.

Motto: MAGNIFICAT

When Timothy Manning became a bishop in 1946, he chose the motto *Magnificat* because of his great devotion to Our Lady. It is the first word in the Latin version of Our Lady's Canticle in Saint Luke's Gospel.

External Ornaments:

The double-traversed cross denotes that this is the coat of arms of a metropolitan archbishop.

The flat, red ecclesiastical hat, or galero, with cords and fifteen tassels on each side, signifies that the bearer of the arms is a Prince of the Church. Although Timothy Cardinal Manning was elevated after the use of the galero was suppressed by Pope Paul VI, it remains the heraldic device used to indicate cardinalatial rank.

Index